Emperor
Septimius Severus

For my wife Sini, and children Ari and Nanna, for their patience; and for the Great Masters Uderzo and Goscinny

Emperor Septimius Severus

The Roman Hannibal

Dr. Ilkka Syvänne

Pen & Sword
MILITARY

First published in Great Britain in 2023 by
Pen & Sword Military
An imprint of
Pen & Sword Books Ltd
Yorkshire – Philadelphia

Copyright © Dr. Ilkka Syvänne 2023

ISBN 978 1 39906 665 5

The right of Dr. Ilkka Syvänne to be identified as Author of this work has been asserted by him in accordance with the Copyright, Designs and Patents Act 1988.

A CIP catalogue record for this book is
available from the British Library.

All rights reserved. No part of this book may be reproduced or transmitted in any form or by any means, electronic or mechanical including photocopying, recording or by any information storage and retrieval system, without permission from the Publisher in writing.

Printed in the UK by CPI Group (UK) Ltd, Croydon, CR0 4YY.

Pen & Sword Books Limited incorporates the imprints of Atlas, Archaeology, Aviation, Discovery, Family History, Fiction, History, Maritime, Military, Military Classics, Politics, Select, Transport, True Crime, Air World, Frontline Publishing, Leo Cooper, Remember When, Seaforth Publishing, The Praetorian Press, Wharncliffe Local History, Wharncliffe Transport, Wharncliffe True Crime and White Owl.

For a complete list of Pen & Sword titles please contact

PEN & SWORD BOOKS LIMITED
47 Church Street, Barnsley, South Yorkshire, S70 2AS, England
E-mail: enquiries@pen-and-sword.co.uk
Website: www.pen-and-sword.co.uk

Or

PEN AND SWORD BOOKS
1950 Lawrence Rd, Havertown, PA 19083, USA
E-mail: Uspen-and-sword@casematepublishers.com
Website: www.penandswordbooks.com

Contents

Acknowledgements viii
List of Plates ix
List of Maps and Diagrams xi
Introduction xii
Abbreviations xiii
Maps xiv

Chapter 1   The Background   1
1.1. Roman Society   1
1.2. Governing the Empire   2
1.3. The Armed Forces and the Security Apparatus in ca. AD 193   4
    1.3.1. The Basic Structures   4
    1.3.2. The Land Forces   4
    1.3.3. The Tent Group called the Contubernium   5
    1.3.4. Legions   6
    1.3.5. Auxiliaries, National Numeri and Temporary Allies   19
    1.3.6. The Strategic Reserve: Rome and its Surroundings   20
    1.3.7. The Civilian Police Forces and Militias   24
    1.3.8. Strategy   25
    1.3.9. The Roman Army on a Campaign   26
    1.3.10. The Imperial Navy   50
    1.3.11. Siege Warfare   55
1.4. The Sources   56

Chapter 2   Severus's Career Before 193   58
2.1. African Background   58
2.2. Career   61

Chapter 3   Pertinax, 1 January–28 March 193   66
3.1. The Beginning of the Reign of Pertinax   66
3.2. Pertinax the Old Campaigner   67
3.3. The Assassination of Pertinax   69

Chapter 4   The Year 193: The Power Struggle between Didius Julianus, Niger, Septimius Severus and Albinus   72
4.1. The Empire auctioned off to the highest bidder, Didius Julianus, on 28 March 193   72
4.2. Niger, Septimius Severus and Albinus Enter the Stage in April 193   75

| Chapter 5 | The Civil War Between Septimius Severus and Niger in 193–194 | 89 |

5.1. The Setting of the Stage in 193–194   89
5.2. The New Infantry Phalanx of Septimius Severus (after Modestus 12–14 and Vegetius 3.14–17)   93
5.3. Septimius Severus's Campaign Plans   97
5.4. The Battles of Hellespont and Cyzicus in the Autumn of 193   100
5.5. The Battle of Cius and Nicaea in about December 193   104
5.6. The Severans Exploit their Victory: The Conquest of Asia Minor in 194   106
5.7. The Battle of Issus in the Spring of 194   110
5.8. The Siege of Byzantium 193 – late 195 or early 196   116

| Chapter 6 | The Wars in the East 194–195 (or 194–199?) | 121 |

6.1. The Purge   121
6.2. The First Stage of the War against the Oshroeni, Adiabeni and Arabs in 194   121
6.3. The Jewish and Samaritan Insurgencies in 194–195 or ca. 194–199   124
6.4. The Second Stage of the War against the Oshroeni, Adiabeni and Arabs in 194–195   127
6.5. The Gothic War that never came in about 194/195   128
6.6. The Third Stage of the War against the Oshroeni, Adiabeni and Arabs in 195   128

| Chapter 7 | The War between Septimius Severus and Albinus in 195/196–197 | 132 |

7.1. The Gathering of the Storm in 195–197   132
7.2. The Battles of Tinurtium and Lyon, or the Battle of Tinurtium/Lyon, in February 197   141
7.3. Payback Time: The Purge of the Supporters of Albinus   156

| Chapter 8 | The Armenian, Parthian and Hatran Campaigns in 197–199 | 161 |

8.1. The Preparations   161
8.2. The Narrative Sources for the Parthian Campaign   161
8.3. The Narrative of the Parthian Campaign   166
8.4. The Two Sieges of Hatra in 198 or 198–199   174
8.5. The Reorganization of the Eastern Frontier   182

| Chapter 9 | Egypt and the Red Sea in 199–200 | 185 |

9.1. Visit of Egypt and Severus's Strategic Goals   185

| Chapter 10 | Return to Rome in 200–202 | 189 |

10.1. The Rise of Plautianus   189
10.2. The Danubian Frontier from 197–202   193
10.3. At Rome in 202: the Decennial   194

Chapter 11	**The Return Home: Campaign in Africa in 202–203**	197
11.1.	Preparations and Africa before 202	197
11.2.	The Campaign in the Desert	198
11.3.	The Persecution of Christians	200
Chapter 12	**Conspiracy**	201
12.1.	Back in Italy and Rome, 203–204	201
12.2.	The Plautianus Affair in 204–205	201
Chapter 13	**The Years of Relative Peace in 205–207**	209
13.1.	The Loose Living of Antoninus and Geta in 205–207	209
13.2	The Other Troubles in 205–207	211
Chapter 14	**The Military Education for the sons: the Campaigns of 207–211**	215
14.1.	Britain from 197–207	215
14.2.	The Military Campaigns of Antoninus Caracalla in 207?	218
14.3.	The Preparations for the British Campaign in 207–208	220
14.4.	The expedition felicissima Britannica. Campaign Season 1: The year 209–210	224
14.5.	The 210 Campaign by Antoninus and the Death of Severus at York on 4 February 211	232
14.6.	Caracalla's Campaign in 211 and the End of the British War	236
Chapter 15	**Septimius Severus, 'The Most Glorious of the Emperors'**	240
Appendix 1: Arrian and Roman Battle Tactics		244
Appendix 2: Frontinus and Combat Tactics on Land		281
Notes		283
Select Bibliography		296
Index		300

Acknowledgements

First of all, I would like to thank Pen & Sword Commissioning Editor Phil Sidnell for accepting the proposal for a book which had been waiting on my 'bookshelf' for several years. He also deserves a big thank you for his patience. Special thanks are also due to Production Manager Matt Jones, Copy Editor Tony Walton and the marketing and other staff of Pen & Sword Publishing for their stellar work and for the outstanding support they give to the author. I would also like to thank many of my friends and family for their support and patience. If there are any mistakes left, they are the sole responsibility of the author.

List of Plates

Coins of Pertinax. (Source: Bernoulli)
Coin of Didius Julianus. (Source: Bernoulli)
Coin of Pescennius Niger. (Source: Bernoulli)
Coins of Clodius Albinus. (Source: Bernoulli)
Coins of Septimius Severus. (Source: Bernoulli)
Coins of Julia Domna. (Source: Bernoulli)
Coins of Caracalla. (Source: Bernoulli)
Coins of Geta. (Source: Bernoulli)
Coin of Plautilla. (Source: Bernoulli)
Coin of Macrinus. (Source: Bernoulli)
Coin of Antoninus (Elagabalus/Heliogabalus). (Source: Bernoulli)
Bust of Pertinax (Capitol). (Source: Bernoulli)
Bust of Pertinax (Louvre). (Source: Bernoulli)
Bust of Didius Julianus (Capitol). (Source: Bernoulli)
Bust of Didius Julianus (Vatican). (Source: Bernoulli)
A possible statue of Clodius Albinus (Vatican). (Source: Bernoulli)
A possible statue of Clodius Albinus, profile (Vatican). (Source: Bernoulli)
Bust of Pescennius Niger (Capitol). (Source: Bernoulli)
Bust of either Pertinax or Plautianus, the latter being likelier. (Source: Bernoulli)
Bust (profile) of emperor who is either identified with Septimius Severus or Clodius Albinus. (Source: Bernoulli)
Bust (front) of emperor who is either identified with Septimius Severus or Clodius Albinus. (Source: Bernoulli)
Bust of Septimius Severus. (Source: Bernoulli)
Older version of Septimius Severus (bust in Munich). (Source: Bernoulli)
Bust (front and profile) of either Julia Domna or Plautilla. (Source: Bernoulli)
Bust of Caracalla. (Source: Bernoulli)
Bust (front and profile) of Julia Domna. (Source: Bernoulli)
Bust of Geta. (Source: Bernoulli)
A nineteenth-century photo of a bust of Julia Domna. (Public Domain)
Markouna bust of Julia Domna. (Source: Bernoulli)
A possible bust of Clodius Albinus. (Source: Bernoulli)
Bust of Septimius Severus (Capitol). (Source: Bernoulli)
Septimius Severus and Julia Domna, relief. (Source: Bernoulli)
Septimius Severus, front and profile (Gabii Louvre). (Source: Bernoulli)
Statue of Septimius Severus at the British Museum. (Author's photo)
Bust of Septimius Severus at the British Museum. (Author's photo)

A coin depicting Septimius Severus and Julia Domna at the British Museum. (Author's photo)
A gilded bronze bust of Septimius Severus found at Brescia. (Picture © Giovanni Dall'Orto/Wikipedia)
Bust of Caracalla at the British Museum. (Author's photo)
Young Caracalla. (Public Domain, Wikimedia Commons)
Head of Septimius Severus (Cologne/Köln). (Public Domain, Wikimedia Commons)
Portonaccio sarcophagus depicting a battle between the Romans and Germans ca. AD 180–190. (Public Domain/Wikimedia, user Jastrow)
Legionary Q. Petilius. (Author's drawing after Lindenschmit)
Antoninus Magnus (Caracalla). (Author's drawing)
Trierarches of the Misenum Fleet. (Author's drawing)
A multipurpose horseman. (Author's drawing)
Lanciarius, Legio II Parthica. (Author's drawing)
Foot archer. (Author's drawing)
Praetorian. (Author's drawing)
Legionary horseman. (Author's drawing)
Centurio of *cohors voluntariorum*. (Author's drawing)
Legionary in leather *lorica segmentata*. (Author's drawing)
Legionary in typical period equipment. (Author's drawing)
Various types of *pila*. (Author's drawing)
Legionary gear for use against cavalry. (Author's drawing)
Imperial family: Julia Domna, Septimius Severus, Geta (face defaced) and Caracalla. (Author's copy (repainting) of the Berlin tondo, slightly restored version)
Bust of Roman emperor (probably Pertinax), British Museum. (Author's photo)
Head of Septimius Severus. (© Marie-Lan Nguyen/Wikimedia Commons (user Jastrow) 2009)
Roman auxiliary in light gear. (Author's drawing)
Roman legate. (Author's drawing)
Roman auxiliary in leather armour. (Author's drawing)
Roman auxiliary in mail armour. (Author's drawing)
The aftermath of the Battle of Lugdunum on 19 February 197. (Author's drawing)
Cavalry helmets, British Museum. (Author's photo)
Septimius Severus after a bust. (Author's painting)
Septimius Severus. (Author's painting)
Caracalla after a bust. (Author's painting)
Caracalla with bare chest. (Author's painting)
A bust of Julia Domna (Munich). (Public Domain, Wikimedia Commons, user Bibi Saint-Pol)

List of Maps and Diagrams

Locations of the Legions in 193	xiv
Locations of the Legions in 211	xv
Parthia/Persia	xvi
Enemies and Allies	xvii
North-Western Half of the Roman Empire	xviii
Armenia	xix
Hellespont, Sea of Marmara and Bosporus	xx
Balkans	xxi
Battle of Issus in 193 (strategic map)	xxii
Traditional imperial battle order with the auxiliaries placed in front of the legions	28
Legions and auxiliaries deployed as cohortal *duplex acies* with reserves behind	28
Legions and auxiliaries as four phalanxes/legions (*mere*)	28
Cavalry in Italian drill formation	47
Combined and joint arms formation in the Column of Trajan	48
Cavalry battle formations (medium and small)	49
Arrian's cavalry array in the *Ektaxis kata Alanon*	49
Roman naval deployment	50
Century	93
The Principal Roman Combat Formations according to Modestus in *ca.* 275 (New Style Legions; Old Style Legions; A Mix of Old and New Style Legions)	94
Battles of Cyzicus, Cius and Nicaea in about December 193	105
The Probable Location of the Battle of Issus in 194	115
Siege of Byzantium	117
Septimius Severus's Campaign against the Jews and Samaritans, and the Oshroeni, Adiabeni and Arabs in 194–195	130
The Battle of Lugdunum/Lyon on 19 February 197	152
The Battle of Lugdunum stage 1	153
The Battle of Lugdunum stages 2–3	154
The Neighbourhood of Ctesiphon according to Barrington Atlas	167
Septimius Severus's Parthian War in 197–198	172
The Defences of the City of Hatra during the Parthian Era	177
Septimius Severus's African Campaign in 202 and the advance of the border/frontier in Africa during his reign	199
Britain during the reign of Septimius Severus	222
Roman marching camps in Scotland	225
Campaign in Scotland in 209–210	231
Campaign in Scotland in 210	235
Campaign in Scotland in 211	238

Introduction

This book has been long in the making. It began as a project to understand the development of the Roman Army and its cavalry forces at a time when I wrote my doctoral dissertation in 2002–2003, after which I wrote the core text that contained the reigns from Commodus up to Carus by about 2009–2010. This first manuscript has since then been divided into separate biographies of these emperors, in the process of which the material has been considerably expanded. The text of this book was finished by the end of January 2019, but some illustrations and comments (from recent studies) were added to it at a later date. It is thanks to the encouragement of my wife and children that the book was taken out of the old files and finishing touches added.

Abbreviations

HA *Historia Augusta, Scriptores Historiae Augustae, Augustan History*
HI heavy infantry
LG legion
LI light infantry
PP Praetorian Prefect

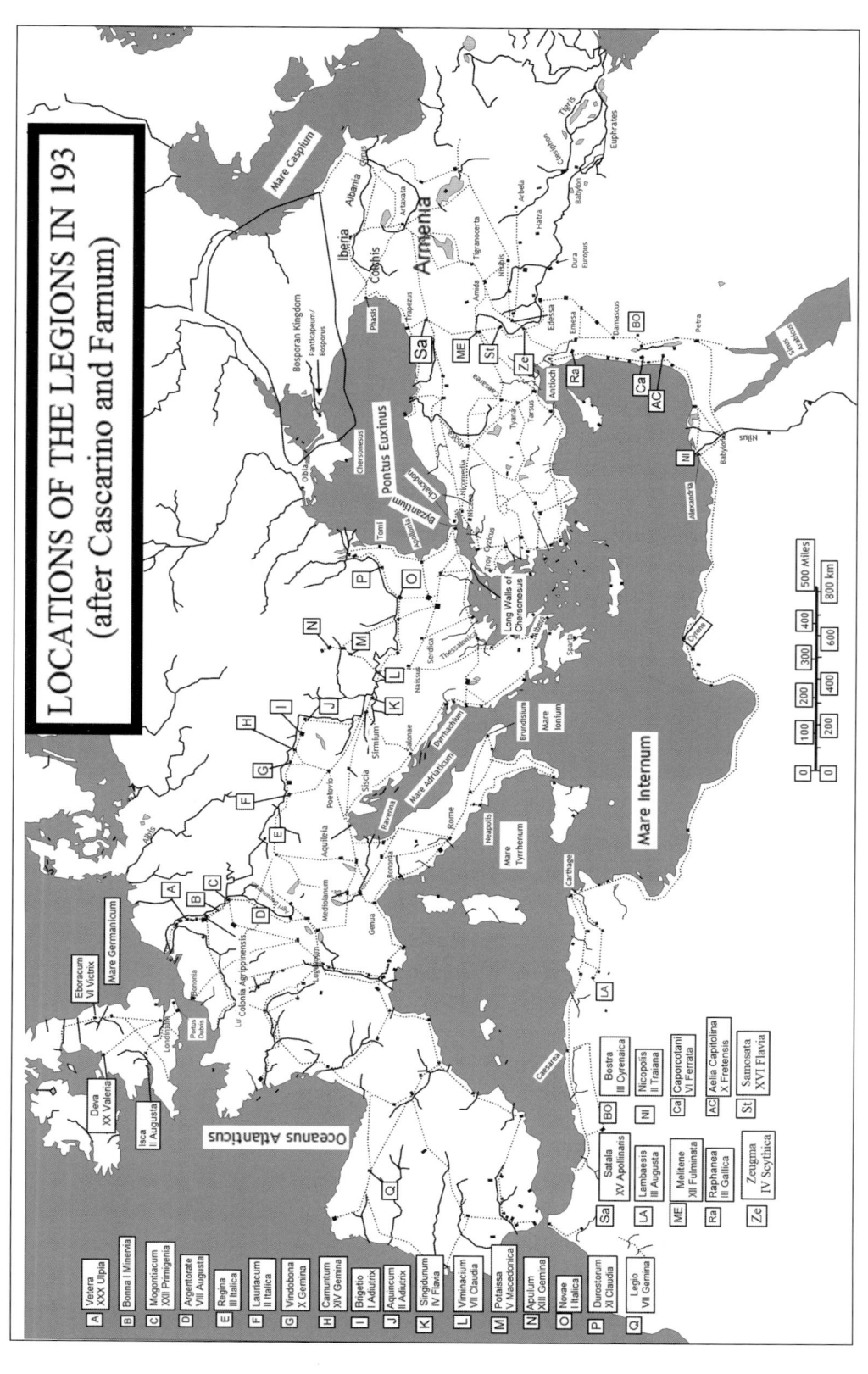

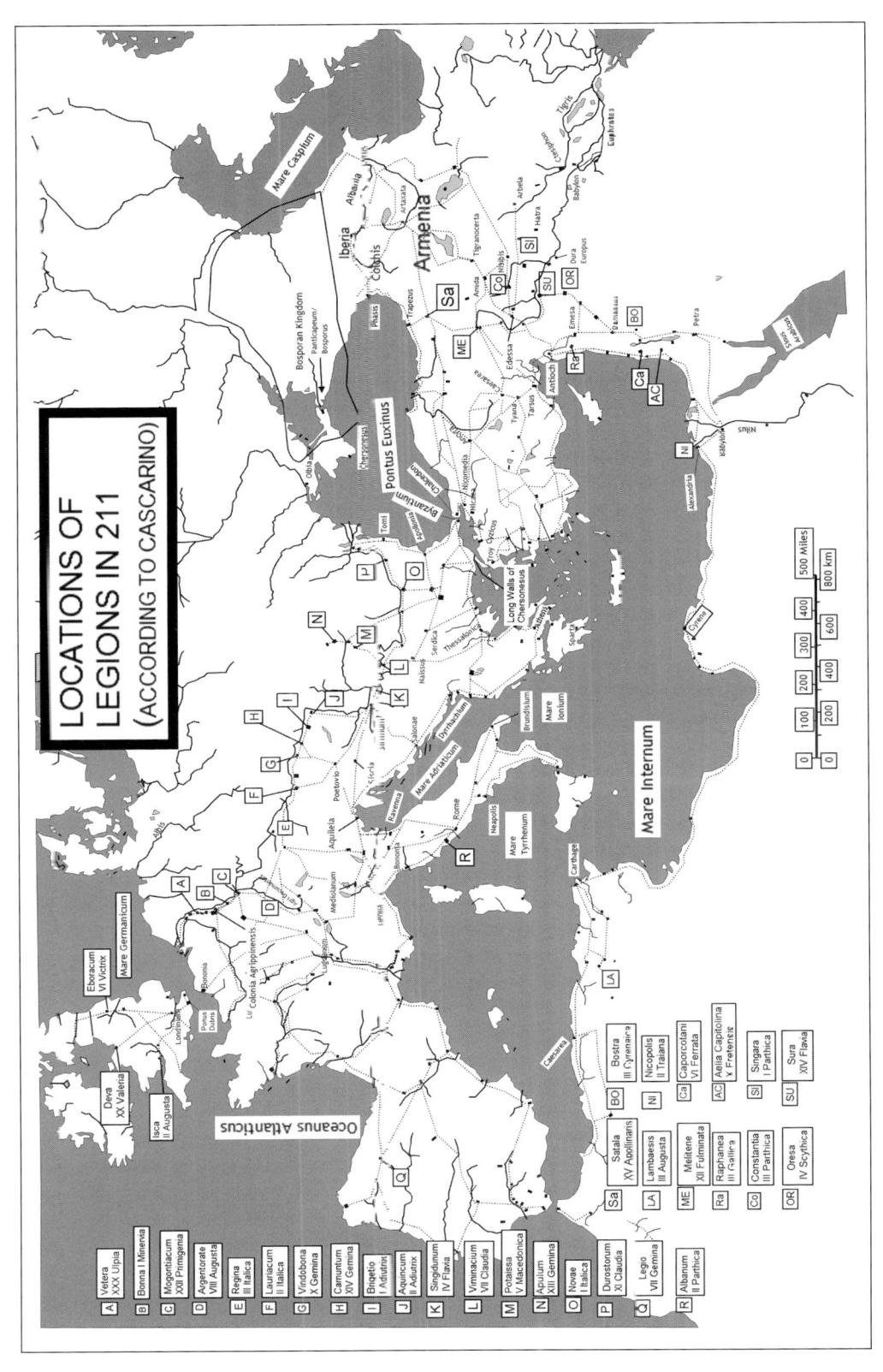

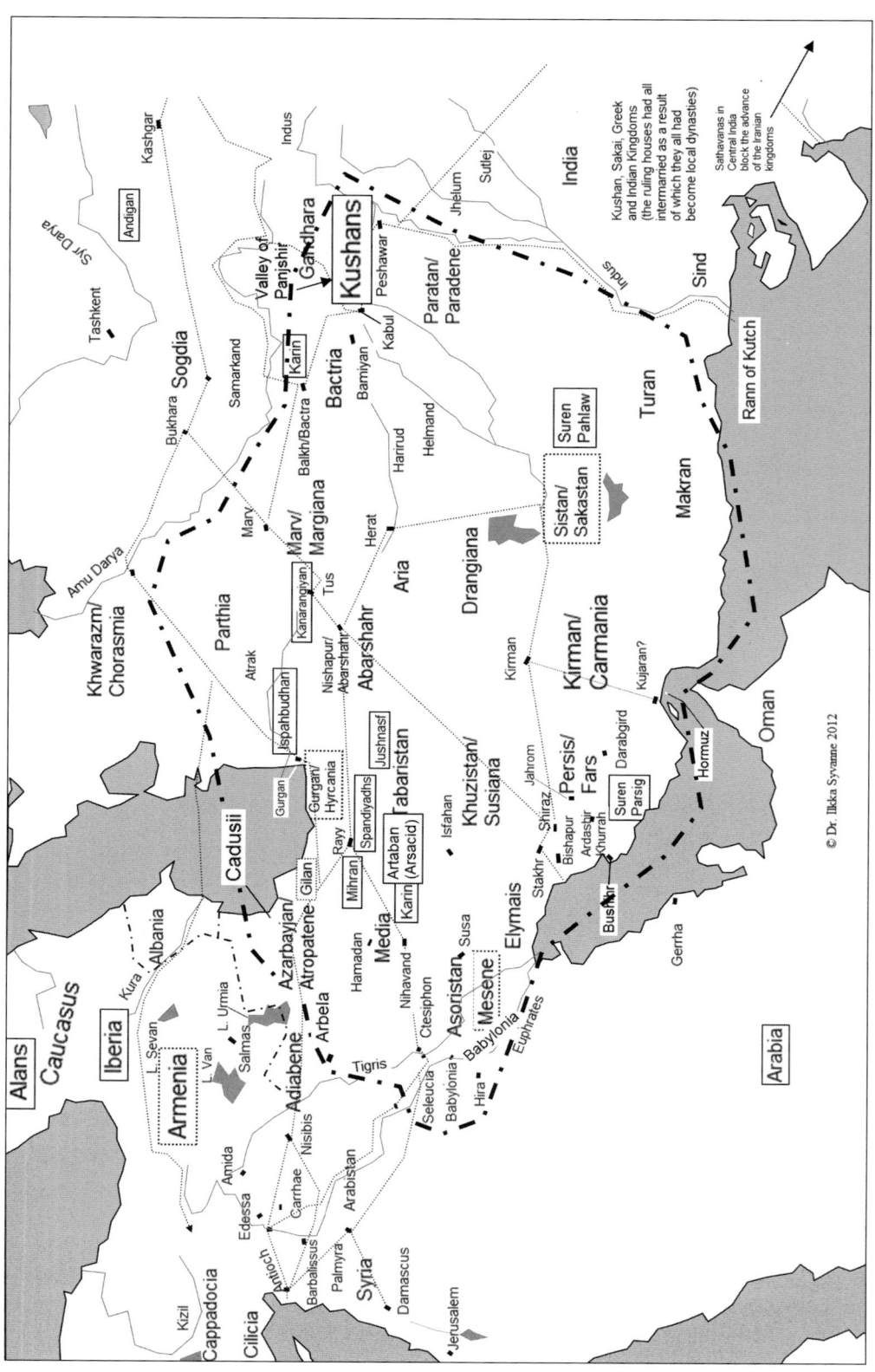

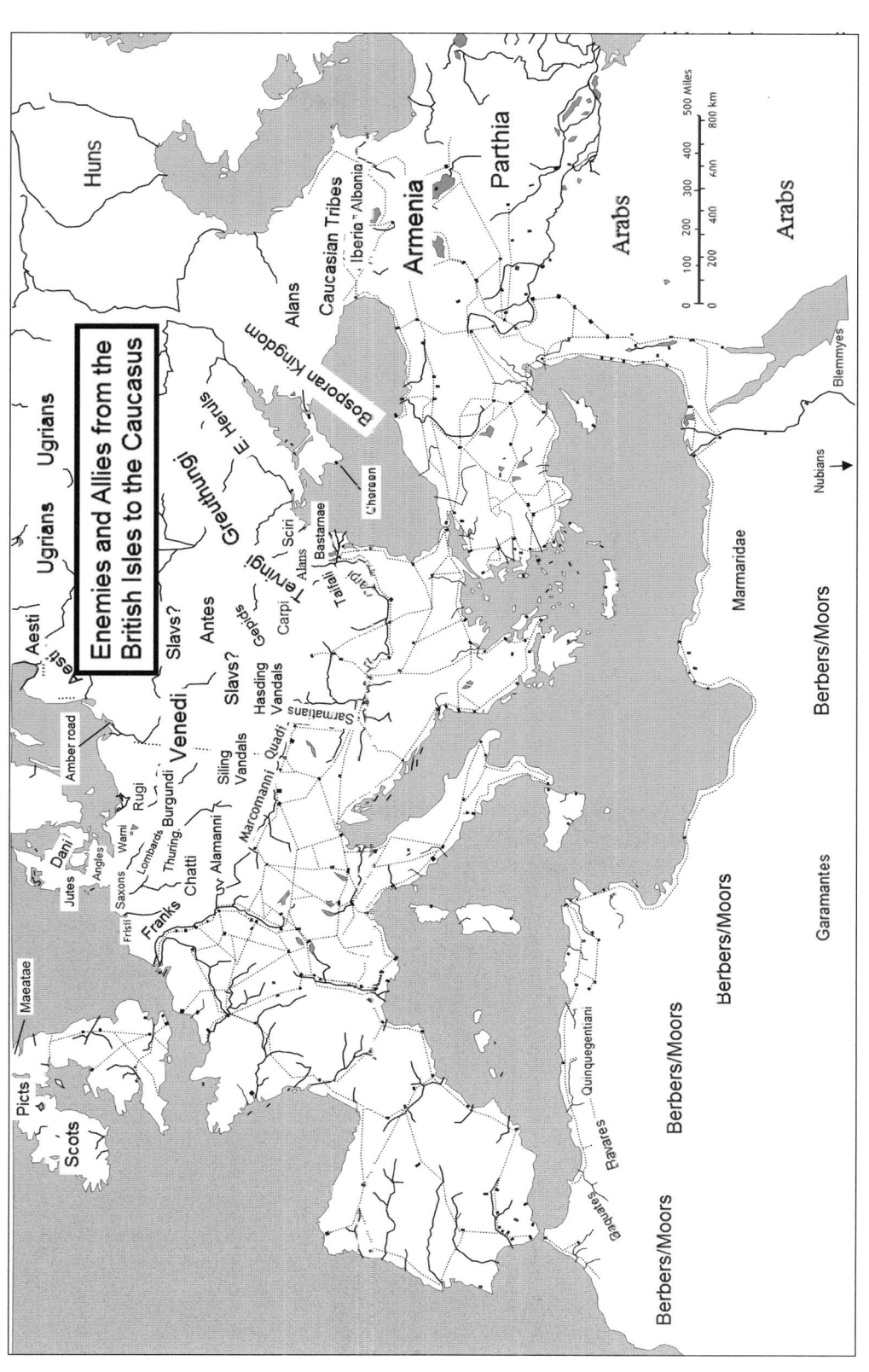

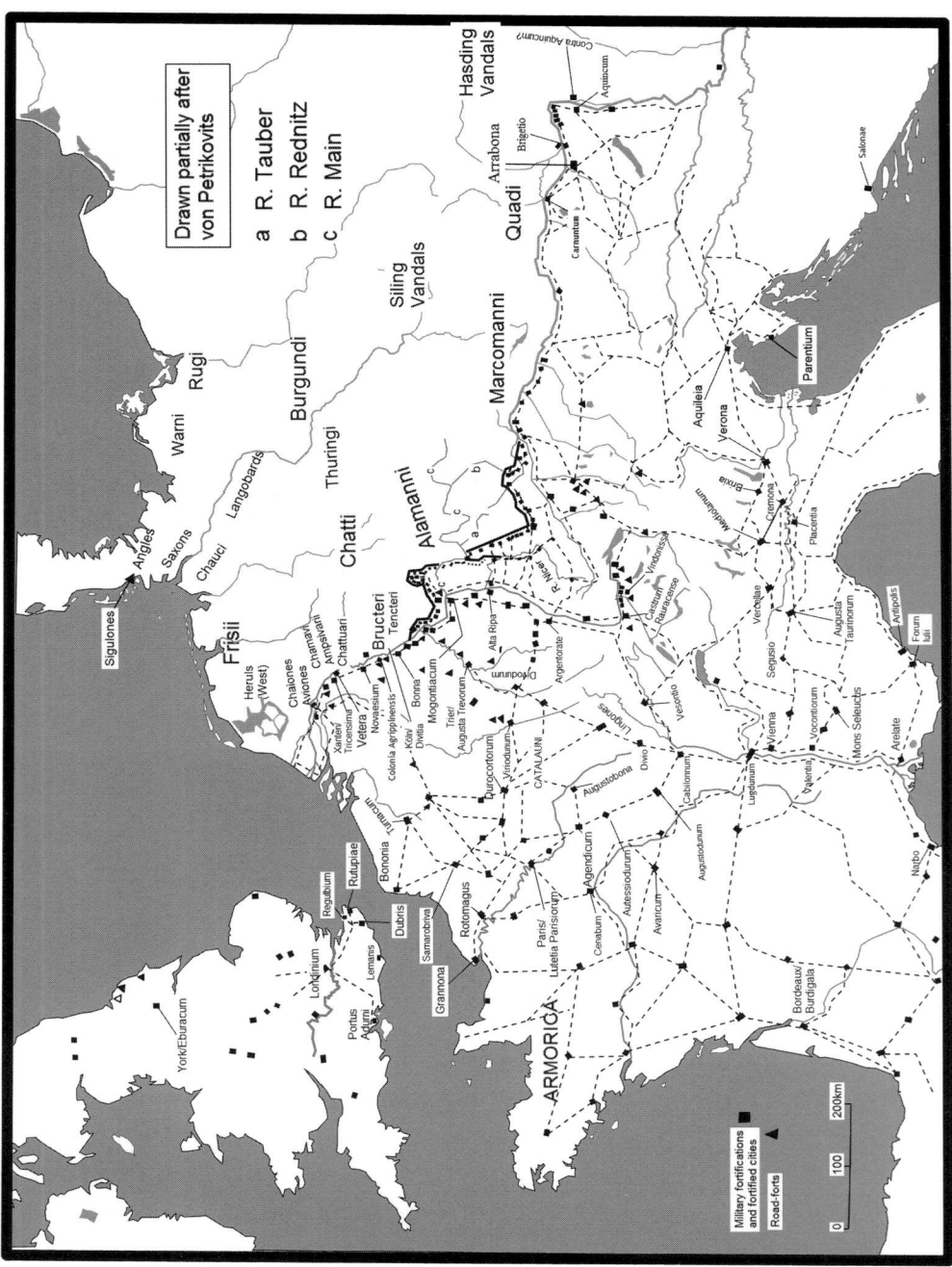

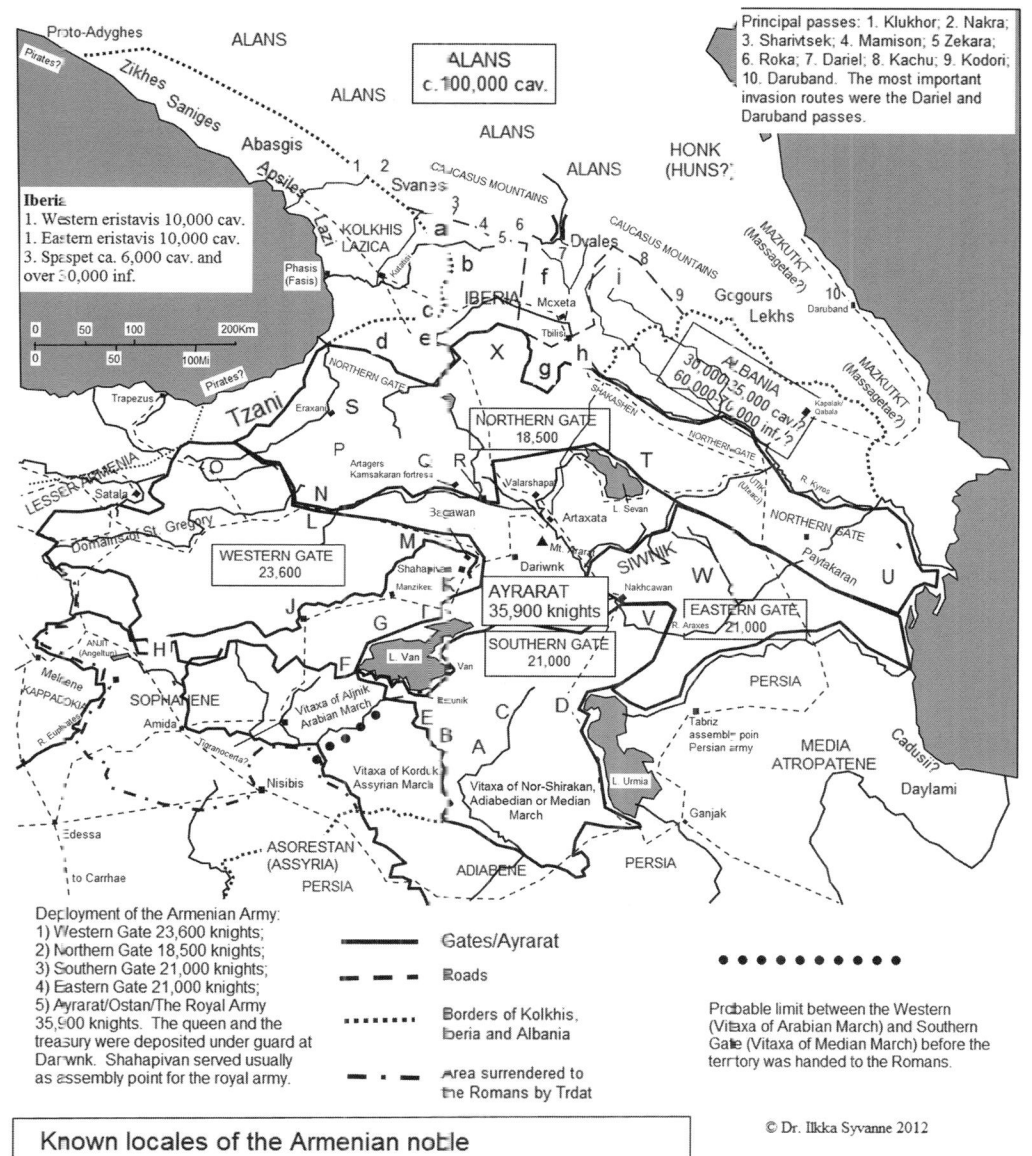

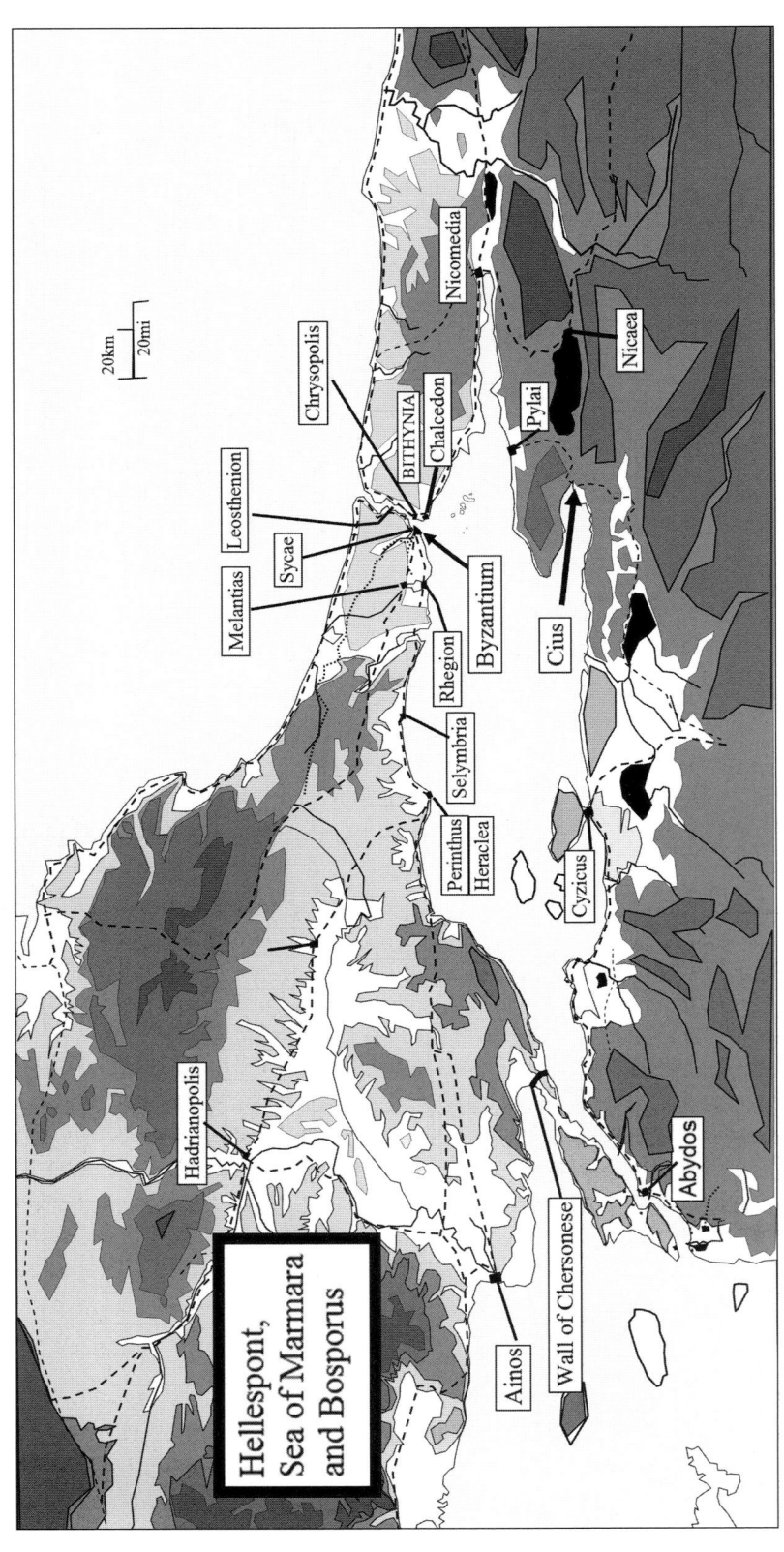

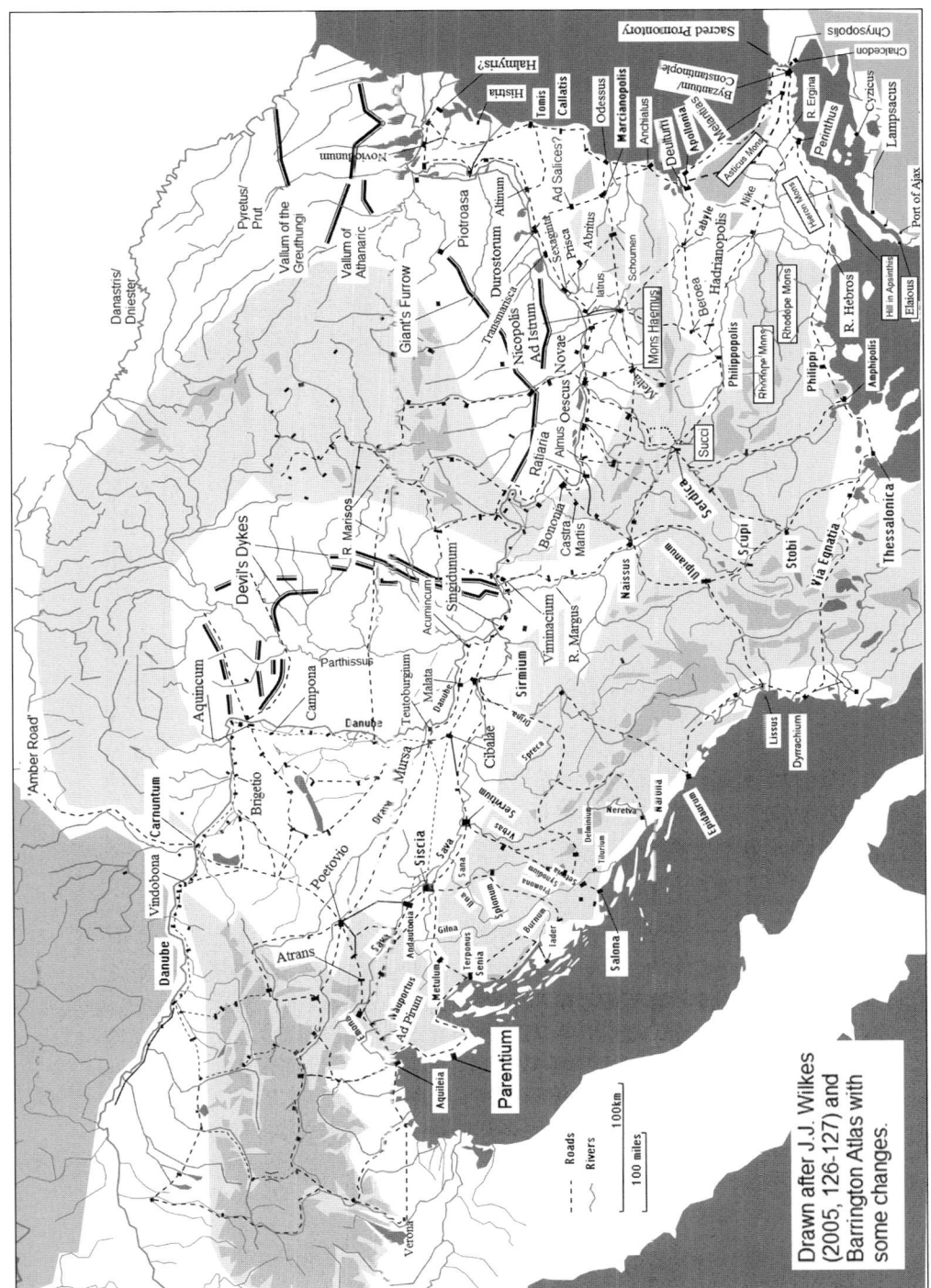

Drawn after J.J. Wilkes (2005, 126-127) and Barrington Atlas with some changes.

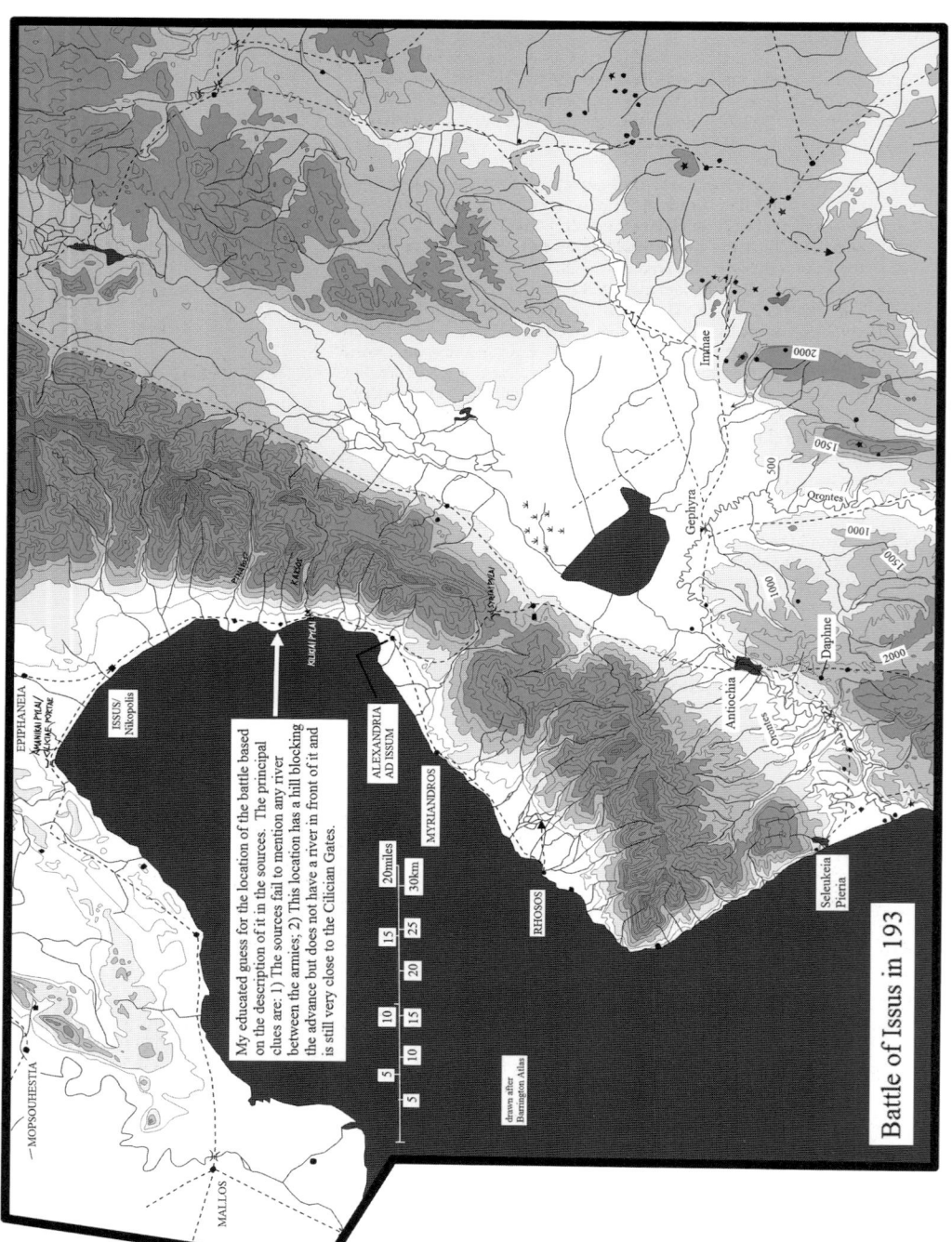

Cavalry *testudo*

Arrian, *Ars Tactica* 36.1: "When the charge of the horsemen is over, the troopers halt next to each other on the left side of the rostra. They turn their horses' heads backwards while placing their shields protectively in front of their own backs and horses. The formation is the same as the infantry shield interlocking (*synaspismos = synaspismos*) called tortoise (*chelone = testudo = foulkon*)."

I interpret this to mean either the slight interlocking of the shields in width so that the troopers pulled the heads of the horses backwards and downwards towards right. The shield would have been placed slightly towards the right to make certain that the horse's head would be covered. In the illustration, which shows the array with two ranks, I have made the educated guess that Arrian's *thureos*-shield meant the standard oval shield with the dimensions of ca. 90 cm in width and 100 cm in height. The actual size could also be different because the the *Sylloge Tacticorum* (ca. 905) which also mentions the cavalry tortoise (*chelonê, synaspismos, syskouton*) has its *kataphraktoi* (39.1 compared with 38.1) carry shields that were ca. 82 cm in width and ca. 105 cm in height. Fortunately the *ST* gives us more details than is provided by Arrian. According to this treatise (ST. 43.6-8) in the tortoise combat array each file of cavalrymen occupied in width ca. 63 cm (horse ca. 45 cm in width plus rider's feet), but fails to specify clearly the depth of each cavalry rank. Fortunately, the *Strategikon* (9.5.) comes to the rescue. According to the *Strategikon*, in the cavalry close order each file had a width of 3 ft. (ca.94cm = ST 43.6-7) and each rank a depth of 8 ft. (ca. 2.5 m). This would mean almost nose to tail array when the average length of the horse is 2.4 m. I would suggest that both the close order and tortoise order were indeed arrayed so that the horses were almost nose to tail as stated by the *Strategikon* for the close order.

In combat this formation would have been used by such cavalry forces that remained immobile to receive the enemy volley of javelins or arrows. It is probable that these would have charged at the enemy immediately after they had received the enemy missile attack. This formation required very highly trained horses, which the Romans clearly had because they also taught their horses how to kneel and recline in conjunction with the infantry *testudo*.

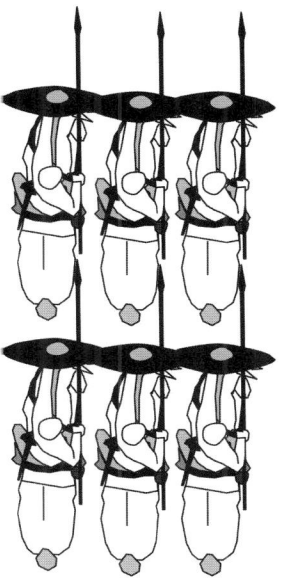

© Dr. Ilkka Syvänne 2022

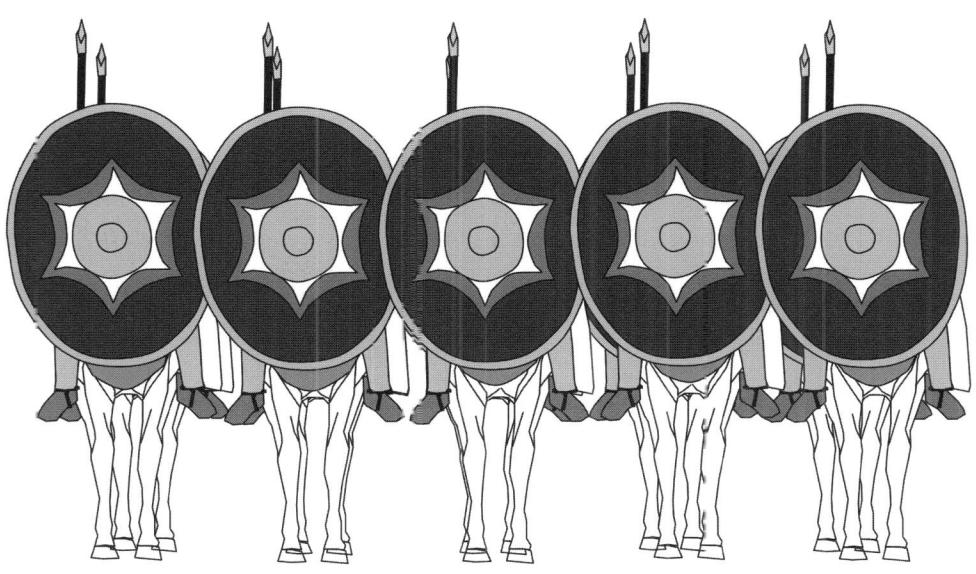

Chapter One

The Background[1]

1.1. Roman Society

The Romans lived in a class society that was divided into judicial and social hierarchies. The judicial hierarchy segregated the populace into freemen, freedmen and slaves. The freemen were further divided into classes according to their judicial status. At the top were the Roman citizens, and below them the foreign freeborn men with varying rights. The legal position of the latter varied greatly according to the treaties that their nations or cities had been granted by the Romans, and also according to their own legal systems. The slaves could buy freedom or be granted it by their masters, and when this happened they became freedmen. The freedmen had no political rights, but their children were considered freemen with full rights.

The official social categories of the Roman citizens in their turn were as follows: the senatorial order, equestrian order and the plebs. The senatorial order was a hereditary order with a minimum property requirement of 1 million sesterces, but which received new members when the emperor wanted to reward his supporters or friends. The highest-ranking military and civilian offices were the privilege of the senatorial class, and as a sign of their position they wore the *toga laticlavius*. For internal secutity reasons, the senators were allowed to travel away from Italy only with the approval of the emperor. The rich senators were a privileged class who were liable to pay only donatives (paid every five years, or when the army campaigned, or to celebrate some important occasion) and very small inheritance taxes. This meant financial problems for the emperor, because the wealthiest citizens – the senators who owned most of the property – contributed only very little to the exchequer.

The equestrian class was a non-hereditary order with a miminum property requirement of 400,000 sesterces. In order to become a member, one had to apply successfully. The equestrians thus consisted of a mix of inherited money and self-made men. There were two reasons for the willingness of the people to apply to join the equestrian order: 1) some of the important positions within the imperial administration and armed forces were reserved for equestrians; 2) the successful equestrians could hope to be enrolled into the senatorial order. The equestrians wore the *toga angusticlavius* as a sign of their rank. The importance of the equestrian order had grown steadily because the emperors considered the members of this heterogeneous order to be generally more loyal and professional than the senators. It was because of this that the emperors had reserved the most important military positions – the two or three Praetorian Prefects – for the members of the equestrian order.

The plebeian order (or plebs) comprised most of the free population, and included both rich and poor. The wealthiest members of the plebs (decurions with citizenship) were allowed to wear the *toga praetexta* to separate them from the middle-class and poor. The rest of the plebs consisted of: 1) the wealthy (businessmen, merchants and bankers etc.); 2) the middle-class plebs (artisans, boutique keepers, merchants, bakers, artists, intellectuals/philosophers etc.); and 3) the poor plebs (peasants, carriers, labourers etc.), who made up the majority.

In practice, the class structure of the society was not as clear as the official divisions would imply, because the emperor and the imperial family – and members of the former imperial families – formed a separate privileged class above the rest. Furthermore, the friends of the emperor – who could include senators, equestrians, freedmen and even trusted slaves and imperial women – often wielded unofficial power thanks to their closeness to the emperor. Furthermore, from the mid-second century onwards, the old judicial and social standings and divisions had become muddled thanks to the appearance of a new form of class division which divided the people into *honestiores* and *humiliores*. The former consisted of the senators, equestrians, veterans and decurions, who all had legal privileges, while the latter comprised everyone else. In addition to this, Hadrian, Antoninus Pius or Marcus Aurelius created honorary ranks with judicial privileges: the Praetorian Prefects obtained the rank of *viri eminentissimi*, the senators the rank of *clarissimus* and the officials of the court the rank of *perfectissimi*. The aim of this policy was to secure their loyalty to the emperor, and it was a very cheap way to do this.

The Roman economy was based on agriculture, but there were also very significant artisan and merchant classes. The tax income from agriculture varied from one year to another, which meant that the emperors could not rely on it. Other sources of income consisted of the produce of the imperial estates and mines, donatives, extraordinary taxes levied when needed, confiscation of the property of the rich with various excuses such as faked charges, and tolls and customs (collected from internal and external trade). Of these, the long-distance trade with Arabia, Africa, India and China was a particularly important source of revenue, and therefore also played an important role in the field of diplomacy and strategy. Most of the taxes went to the upkeep of the armed forces. Some emperors obtained additional funds in emergencies by selling imperial property and/or by receiving loans.

1.2. Governing the Empire

The Roman Empire remained officially a republic, but in practice the emperor was a dictator whose power rested ultimately on his control of the armed forces. The emperor therefore possessed executive, legislative and judiciary powers, controlled Rome's foreign policy and military forces, appointed all civil and military functionaries, proposed and legislated imperial legislation and acted as the Supreme Court. The inherent weaknesses of the system were that the Principate (the rule of the early Roman emperors) lacked an orderly system of succession, and that the emperors could not put any trust in the loyalty of their generals if these were given large military forces. It was also important for the emperors to court the important members of the senatorial and equestrian classes by showing proper respect to tradition because these formed the elite of society.

The imperial central administration consisted of the emperor, his imperial family, the *consilium* (private council) and his household staff, who were all housed on the Palatine

Hill (in the Imperial Palace). The members of the council consisted of those whom the emperor considered competent and loyal. The advisors were called either *amici* (friends), *comites* (companions) or *consiliarii* (counsellors/advisors). The *consilium* advisory body helped the emperor on matters of domestic and foreign policy, on all military matters and in cases requiring legal expertise. The inner circle of trusted friends who accompanied the emperor on his travels and military campaigns were called *comites*. In practice, the emperor's decisions could also be influenced by anyone who had access to him. These included obviously his wife (when he had one), children, relatives, the staff of the imperial bedchamber and others, depending on the situation.

The emperor's household staff can be considered to have been his imperial chancellery, consisting of bureaus/departments/ministries. It was his chancellery/household that executed the wishes of the emperor. The heads of the departments of the household staff (the procurators) were usually equestrians, while the rest of the staff usually consisted of domestics (imperial freedmen and slaves dressed in white clothing). The procurators of the imperial household comprised the following: 1) *a rationibus* (in charge of the imperial accounts, treasury and finances, which included the payments to the troops etc.), assisted by the *magister rei privatae* (in charge of the emperor's personal finances); 2) *a libellis* (in charge of the petitions to the emperor); 3) *ab epistulis* (imperial correspondence), divided into Greek and Latin sections; 4) *a cognitionibus* (hearing of judicial matters); 5) *a studiis* (preparation of files, reports and dossiers for the emperor); 6) *a censibus* (examination of the financial standing of persons seeking to become senators or equestrians); 7) *a commentariis* (archives); and 8) *a memoria* (secretarial services). Besides these departments, the emperor's household included many other functionaries, the most important of which were the *cubicularii* of the imperial bedchamber because they had access to the emperor, empress and their children. The teachers of the children of the imperial family could also obtain very important positions in the Empire through their influence.

The Senate was still officially the legislative body of the Empire which nominated the administrators and the emperor, and voted on treaties with foreign powers and so forth, but in practice its role had already become ceremonial under Octavianus Augustus. The Senate retained official control over Italy and the provinces still under its jurisdiction, but in truth the emperor could intervene in their affairs at his will. In short, the emperor controlled everything so long as he retained control of the armed forces.

The Roman Empire had three geographical administrative areas: 1) Rome; 2) Italy; and 3) the Provinces. The city of Rome was the capital of the Empire, with about 1–2 million inhabitants, and was controlled by the emperor through his representative, the *Praefectus Urbis Romae/Praefectus Urbi* (Urban Prefect of Rome). The city of Rome was fed by Egyptian and North African corn. The city itself was divided into regions controlled by curators. Italy, which ranked second in the hierarchy, was formally under the jurisdiction of the Senate, but in practice the emperor controlled it too through his own representatives, the most important of whom were the representatives of the emperor's Privy Purse. The Italians possessed Roman citizenship. The provinces, the lowest rank in the hierarchy, were divided into imperial and senatorial provinces. The most important imperial provinces were ruled by imperial legates (*legati Augusti pro praetore*) of senatorial rank (ex-consuls or ex-praetors), the only exception being Egypt, which was governed by a *Praefectus* of equestrian rank. The rest of the imperial provinces were governed by procurators of equestrian rank. The emperor decided the length of their stay in office. The senatorial provinces were governed by proconsuls (*proconsulares* chosen from the ranks of ex-consuls or ex-praetors) for a term of one year. The provinces were important because they provided the bulk of the tax income.

At the local level, the administration of territories was performed by the city councils in Italy and the provinces. The cities were further placed into different categories depending on the rights granted by the Romans. The city council controlled the people, taxation, the movement of goods, valuables and money, and the observance of laws. The municipal administration of all the cities of the Empire consisted of three levels: 1) the popular assembly of citizens, which was no longer functioning in the third century; 2) the municipal council or the order of decurions (also called the Senate), which consisted of former magistrates and/or wealthy citizens with the unenviable duty of having to pay taxes when these fell short of the requirement; 3) the magistrates, who had executive powers.

1.3. The Armed Forces and the Security Apparatus in ca. AD 193

1.3.1. The Basic Structures
The security apparatus at the disposal of the emperor in *ca.* AD 193 consisted of units of bodyguards (*Praetoriani, Equites Singulares Augusti, Speculatores*) and spies (*Frumentarii, Peregrini*), special units posted in the city of Rome (*Vigiles, Urbaniciani*), the regular armed forces (legions, *auxilia, numeri*), national *numeri*, the navy (Praetorian and provincial fleets), civilian paramilitary forces and foreign allies.

1.3.2. The Land Forces
Rome's land forces consisted of: 1) the forces posted in or near the capital; 2) regular legions (citizens); 3) regular auxiliary forces (non-citizens and citizens); 4) national *numeri*;[2] 5) veterans called for service; 6) urban and rural paramilitary militias; and 7) the allies.

Most of the regular forces (legions, auxiliaries, *numeri*) were stationed in forts, fortresses and garrisons close to the borders of the Empire to provide a zone of exclusive security for the provinces and the interior. It is possible that these forces were already called by their late Roman name *limitanei* (forces posted close to the *limes* – frontier) because the *HA* (*Pesc.* 7.7; *Alex. Sev.* 58.4) already calls them such under Pescennius Niger and Alexander Severus. The frontier forces, with the walled sections of the frontier and other fortifications, served four strategic purposes: 1) their presence deterred would-be invaders; 2) they could be used to engage the enemy in the border region; 3) they could be used for surprise attacks and as staging posts for major invasions/raids; and 4) they gathered intelligence. Forces posted in the capital (the *Praetoriani, Urbaniciani, Peregrini, Equites Singulares Augusti, Speculatores* and possibly also others), together with the Italian population which could be conscripted into new legions or temporary formations based on the existing paramilitary units, formed the last-ditch reserve for the emperors. However, as we shall see, it was also possible to raise other forces from the provinces when the need arose.

The basic deployment pattern was defensive, but the actual strategy depended on the emperor and situation. Some emperors thought it advisable to strengthen their own position with military glory, while it was also possible that the situation demanded the taking of the offensive, for example to punish a neighbouring tribe or kingdom or to implement the will of the Roman Empire on them. It was possible to assemble a sufficient force for an invasion by drawing detachments from other frontiers and by obtaining allies and raising new units, or an emperor could use diplomacy and other methods to cause trouble for the enemy. The downside of bringing together border units was that this weakened other sectors of the frontier which the neighbours could exploit by invading. The major weaknesses of the Roman system were: 1) it was dangerous to entrust large numbers of soldiers to a competent commander (potential usurper); 2) it lacked adequate reserves. Emperors could also secure the frontiers without having to resort to the overt use of their armed forces, for example through their networks of alliances, with spies or diplomacy and through trade policies

1.3.3. *The Tent Group called the Contubernium*
The basic building block of the legions and auxilia was the *contubernium*, the tent group. The size of the tent was standardized for ten men so that the surveyors could calculate and measure the required size for a marching camp. The size of the tent therefore determined the size of the tent group, both for infantry and cavalry.

In the case of the heavy infantry, the tent group was a file of eight men in combat formation, plus one recruit (*tiro*) and one servant. The man who commanded this unit was called the *decanus* (commander of ten), and he was the man who led the file forward by being the front-rank man. It was also possible to divide this eight-man group into two files of four men, to unite two such groups into a sixteen-man file, or even to have four eight-man groups as a thirty-two-man file. However, the fact that the Romans trained between a quarter and a third of their infantry to fight as archers meant that the heavy infantry file could also include archers, which were usually classed as light infantry. This means, for example, that an eight-man infantry file could in practice include two archers, so that the actual heavy infantry file consisted only of six men, behind whom stood two archers, or that this file was further divided into a file of three heavy-armed men and one archer, as can be found in Josephus (quoted later in this book). However, as noted above, it was also possible to post the heavy-armed fighters according to figures divisible by four, so that the light-armed men were posted behind, in front of or between the files, or on the flanks of the heavy-armed, as deemed necessary by the commander.

In the case of light infantry proper, the *contubernium* consisted of two combat files of four men, plus a recruit and servant. The light infantry in turn could be divided into two-man files, or united to form eight-man or sixteen-man files. In normal circumstances, the recruits and servants were left behind to protect the marching camp or baggage train, but if needed these men could also be used to bolster the number of fighting men.

The composition of the cavalry *contubernium* was determined by the quality and type of the unit. According to the *Strategikon* (1.2), the minimum requirement was that every three to four horsemen would maintain one servant/squire, which means that the minimum number of servants/squires per ten-man tent was two. However, the better units could have as many as five squires for the five cavalrymen per tent, while the officers obviously had even more. It is quite clear that the number of servants/ squires varied according to the quality of the unit and its expected depth in formation.[3] Regardless of this basic structure, it was also possible for the commander to adopt other unit sizes by combining or dividing units, as we shall see, so we should recognize the size of the cavalry tent group as reflecting only the general quality of the unit and the size of the tent.

1.3.4. Legions

The consensus view among historians is that by the end of the first century AD, the regular Roman legion had a paper strength of about 5,120 heavy infantry, plus the recruits, servants, horsemen and specialists. However, it is possible that this is a mistake, and that the actual paper strength of the legion was about 6,000–6,100 footmen and 600–736 cavalry, plus the specialists and supernumeraries, as the figures in Vegetius (see below and the narrative) and John Lydus (*De Magistr.* 1.16) imply. This would in its turn mean that the consensus version would often be the actual combat strength of the legion when it marched in its entirety into battle. It is also possible that the figures in Vegetius, and the organization behind them, were created during the second century as a result of the Marcomannic Wars, but this is merely my speculation. However, the reality was even more complex. In practice there were detachments of both cavalry and legionary infantry (e.g. 1,000–3,000 footmen plus varying numbers of cavalry), entire legions of *ca.* 5,120 or 6,100 footmen with their cavalry, and even oversized legions (new recruits added prior to the campaign). This means that the actual combat formations were adapted to the size of the force, just like Julius Caesar and Pompey adapted their formations at the Battle of Pharsalus in 48 BC.[4]

On the basis of Josephus's text, the consensus view is that the legionary cavalry consisted of 120 or 128 men, but this is a mistake. Josephus referred only to the number of horsemen accompanying each legion in the marching formation, but at the same time he stated that there were other horsemen in front and rear. References in John Lydus and Pseudo-Hyginus (5.30) suggest a probability that the legions were accompanied by three different types of cavalry: 500-man *turmae* of mounted archers, 500-strong *vexillationes* and 600-strong *alae*. The only anomaly is Vegetius, who claims that the legions had varying numbers of horsemen plus supernumeraries. The different manuscripts of Vegetius actually have three different totals: 726, 732 and 736. It is probable that this should be interpreted as follows: the regular component consisted of 726 men (one of the figures), which in turn consisted of twenty-two *turmae* (22 × 32 plus twenty-two decurions), which would then reach the figure of 736 (the last of the numbers) when one adds to it seven centurions and a standard-bearer, trumpeter and cape-bearer. However, in addition to this there would have been a separate tribune or prefect, who would have served as the overall commander of the entire cavalry unit. It is possible that Vegetius's figure represents the size of the cavalry units among Septimius Severus' reformed Parthian legions (see later), or it may indicate the strength of the cavalry component resulting from the reforms of Gallienus, as is usually assumed. It is also possible that it represents the enlarged cavalry component of the last quarter of the third century. My own educated guess is that Vegetius' enlarged cavalry component was adopted by Septimius Severus for his Parthian legions, but this is obviously uncertain.

According to the consensus view, which is largely based on Pseudo-Hyginus, the traditional infantry component of the legion consisted of ten cohorts, of which the first cohort had 800 legionaries (plus 100 recruits and 100 servants) and the rest of the cohorts 480 legionaries (plus recruits and servants). The first cohort consisted of five double-strength centuries of 160 men, and the cohorts numbered two to ten consisted of six centuries (eighty men plus recruits and servants), which were grouped as maniples of 160 men for combat, when the men used their *pila* (javelins). The legion therefore had fifty-nine centuries. In addition to the soldiers making up the *contubernia* (and their recruits and servants), the legions also included artillerymen, medics, doctors, clerks, those in the logistical services, engineers, architects and artisans etc. to support their operations.

Most of the positions of highest command in the armed forces were reserved for the senators, but the equestrians acted as commanders of the Praetorian Guard, the Parthian legions and the legions posted in Egypt. The command hierarchy of a regular legion consisted of the following: 1) one imperial propraetor legate (senatorial rank, in command of the legion, or legions if governor); 2) one laticlavian tribune (senatorial rank, second-in-command, a young nobleman learning his soldiering); 3) one camp prefect (third-in-command, an experienced veteran in charge of the camp); 4) five angusticlavian prefects (equestrian rank, in charge of cohorts etc.); and 5) one *sexmenstris* tribune, possibly in charge of the legionary cavalry. The NCOs of the first cohort, in order of seniority, consisted of the following centurions: the *primus pilus, princeps prior, hastatus prior, princeps posterior* and *hastatus posterior*. The centurions of cohorts two to ten, in order of seniority, were: the *pilus prior, princeps prior, hastatus prior, pilus posterior, princeps posterior* and *hastatus posterior*. The soldiers were also hierarchically ranked.[5] The following diagram of legionary organization is based on my monograph *A Military History of Late Rome 284–361* Volume 1 and Bohec (1994), but includes some changes.

Probable command structure of the regular legion c. AD 90-260
(S) = senatorial office; (E) = equestrian office
– One Legate (S) until the reign of Gallienus, who abolished the office; or Prefect (E) for the Egyptian and Parthian legions (created by Septimius Severus, see later). After Gallienus, the commanders were prefects (E); commander of the legion.
– One Laticlavian tribune (S), changed by Gallienus into *tribunus maior* (E); in charge of one cohort and second-in-command of the legion.
– One *Praefectus Castrorum* (camp, medics, siege equipment etc.). (E)
– One *Praefectus Fabrorum* (workmen, construction etc.). (E)
– Five tribunes (E), each in charge of one cohort of 480 men.
– One *tribunus sexmenstris* (in charge of cavalry?). (E)
– Five centurions of the first cohort (incl. *primus pilus* who could act as *praepositus* for the cohort).
– Fifty-four centurions (called *centenarii* by the end of the third century):
  – Five unattached centurions that could be detailed for variety of purposes; these could be used e.g. as acting *praepositi* (commanders for the cohorts; of 480 men).
  – Nine centurions, each in charge of two centuries (160 men in total).
  – Nine groups of four centurions, each in charge of one century (eighty men).
  – Four cavalry centurions (each with 128 horsemen).

– Sixty-four infantry *decani* one of whom was *optio*/second-in-command to centurion (each *decanus* part of and in charge of their eight-man file/*contubernium*, in addition to which came a *tiro*/recruit and one servant used for the guarding of the camp).
– Sixteen cavalry decurions (each in charge of their thirty-two-horseman *turma*).
– First cohort of 800 men (five centuries of 160 men), plus 100 recruits and 100 servants.
– Second to tenth cohorts, each of 420 footmen (including the *decani* 480), plus sixty recruits and sixty servants per cohort.
– 496 horsemen (with the decurions 512). Vegetius may have been wrong in adding the decurions to the strength of the *turma*, because the Roman cavalry organization was based on the Greek one; however, if Vegetius is correct, and I believe that he is, then these should be added to the total for a total of 512, plus sixteen decurions and about 128 servants/squires.
– At least about 715 artillerymen in charge of the fifty-five *carroballistae* (cart-mounted bolt/arrow shooters) and ten *onagri* (single-armed stone-throwers).
– Ten *speculatores* (formerly scouts, but now couriers, police officers and executioners).
– *Proculcatores* and *exploratores* scouted the roads. It is not known whether these counted as part of the cavalry or were separate from it. In practice, the *mensores* could also act as scouts.
– Unknown numbers of military police with the title of *stator*, and unknown numbers of guard dogs. Inside each camp there was also a police station called a *statio* under a tribune. Some of the soldiers were also used as sentinels (*excubitores*), and there were other specific guards for various things.
– In addition there were unknown numbers of other specialists and bureaucrats, consisting of surveyors, *campidoctor* (Chief Instructor), *haruspex* (read the entrails prepared by *victimarius*), *pullarius*, *actuarii*, *librarii* (*librarius a rationibus* also worked for the state post and could act as a spy), *notarii* (could act as spies on the activities of the commander), *commentariensis* (archivist under head curator), heralds, standard-bearers, *draconarii*, cape-bearers, trumpeters, drummers, engineers, workmen, artisans, hunters, carters and cartwrights, doctors, medics etc.
– The legates/prefects were also guarded by a unit of *singulares* (both infantry and cavalry), which sometimes consisted of detached auxiliaries. (Confusingly, the staff officers in training could also be called *singulares*). These bodyguards were replaced by *protectores* detached by the emperor from his staff, at the latest during the reign of Gallienus as a safety measure against usurpations. It is possible that the actual combat strength of the legion was the *ca.* 6,100 infantry and 732 horsemen mentioned by Vegetius, so the consensus size for the legion would have represented the actual full combat strength and the missing numbers would have formed the *singulares* of the legate/prefect and possibly also those who had been detached for other duties.
– The legion also included beasts of burden (depending on the units, these could be horses, asses, mules, camels or oxen).

In practice, the actual fighting strength of the legions rarely reached their paper strength because of injuries, sickness, wounds, deaths and problems with recruiting, but when the Romans were planning to conduct a military campaign, they usually bolstered the numbers with additional recruits so the units could then actually be above their paper strength. However, we should still remember that the legions rarely marched out in their entirety, even when fighting close to their own base. In most cases the legions would have left behind at least a skeleton force to protect their own camp, and if the legions operated further away it was far more usual for them to dispatch detachments there rather than march the whole legion away from its base. It is possible that the sixth-century author John Lydus describes the organization of such legionary detachments, because none of the other sources give any evidence for such an organization. On the other hand, it is possible that the list proves that the names of the units had changed to reflect the armament carried by the different legionaries, so that only those who carried the heavier panoply were considered to belong to the cohorts. It is clear that his list predates Constantine the Great because it fails to mention the *limitanei* and *comitatenses*, but includes the *praetoriani*. This means that we can use it to shed light on the earlier practices.

According to John Lydus (*De Magistr.* 1.46), the professional Roman army consisted of units (*speirai*) of 300 *aspidoforoi* (shield-bearers)[6] called cohorts; cavalry *alae* (*ilai*) of 600 horsemen; *turmae* of 500 horsemen; *vexillationes* of 500 horsemen; and legions of 6,000 footmen and the same numbers of horsemen. I have speculated that the 6,000 footmen and the same numbers of horsemen refer to the division of these two arms of service into separate forces under Gallienus, but it is clear that in practice the cavalry and infantry had always been separated on the battlefield into their own units and divisions in the same manner. John's referral to cavalry units of 600-man *alae*, 500-man *turmae* and 500-man *vexillationes* is interesting because it suggests that the legions were accompanied by three different types of cavalry components. It would be easy to dismiss these as references to the different types of auxiliary cavalry units accompanying the legion, but Pseudo-Hyginus's text (30; the 1,600 *vexillarii* must be the missing legionary cavalry for the three legions) confirms that we should interpret these as different types of legionary cavalry. Nevertheless, it is still clear that the Romans always attached auxiliary cavalry – and probably also auxiliary infantry – to serve administratively under the legionary commanders, and these were then divided into infantry and cavalry units for combat purposes.[7]

Lydus' referral to the cohorts of 300 *aspidoforoi* is also curious because it does not correspond with any of the known figures for the cohort, but it is consistent with the six-deep formation (fifty files of six ranks = 300) without the light-armed troops who would have made up the seventh and eighth ranks (fifty files of eight ranks = 400). It is consistent with the four-deep formation (seventy-five files of four ranks), but the problem with this is that if the formation was doubled in depth to eight ranks it would have had an extra file of four. Therefore, the six-deep array is more likely. This means that Lydus did not include the light infantry in his cohortal structure, so he followed the same scheme as Josephus in his description of the legion (see later). The resulting unit would therefore have been well short of the 480-man cohorts envisaged by the vast majority of historians, and also of the 555-man cohorts of Vegetius. The regular organization would actually have required that there be 320 shield-bearers (four centuries of eighty men), behind which would have been placed the legion's 160 light-armed men for a total of 480 men, the traditional size for the cohort. It therefore is probable that the 300 *aspidoforoi* should be interpreted as the *pedites singulares* of the legionary commander. It is possible that Lydus has confused the legionary cavalry and the auxiliary forces with each other, but this is less likely on the basis of Pseudo-Hyginus (30), and Lydus' own list of different types of soldiers (see below). Both of these sources make it clear that the 1,600 cavalry are actually three different types of legionary cavalry.

The referral to the 300 *aspidoforoi* is also interesting because we find this figure too in the *Historia Augusta* (Pert. 11.1), which refers to a wedge/globe (*cuneus/globus*) of 300 Praetorians who attacked the Imperial Palace in 193, but the problem with this is that the Epitome of Dio (74.2) claims that only the 200 boldest attacked the palace. One can reconcile these if we assumed that only 200 men out of the 300 made the final attack as a wedge, and in fact the figures of 200 plus 100 are consistent with the numbers of bodyguards in Arrian's *Ektaxis kata Alanon*, in which he had 200 selected bodyguards and 100 *logchoforoi*. Furthermore, if there were twenty-four ranks in the wedge (numbering one, two, three, four, five men and so forth per rank), it had exactly 200 men, a figure which is consistent with the above. The rest of the force – 100 men – would have been deployed behind them. It is quite possible that the wedge in front which was protected by the men behind was one of the forms that a *globus* could take, but it is still clear that this was not the only one because Vegetius (3.17, 19) notes that the *globus* could look like *drungus* (an irregular throng of men, in Greek *drouggos*) and also states that the *globus* meant any independently operating formation that had separated from the main body. Taken together with the other evidence (see the quotes and discussion below), this suggests a very high probability that the Romans employed a separate type of cohort consisting of 300 heavy-armed men alongside their other kinds of cohorts, that was typically deployed six-deep for combat. Regardless, the uncertainty remains.

The list shown below from Lydus' text gives a comprehensive list of various types of troops, but when reading this the reader should keep in mind that the same men could be used for a variety of roles just by changing their equipment. The *ocreati*, *hastati/doryforoi*, *pilarii/akontistai*, *lanciarii* and *verutarii* mean different ranks in the combat formation. The front ranks (depending upon the depth of the formation of ranks one and two, one to four, one to eight, one to three or one to six) would have been equipped either with the *hastae* as *hastati/doryforoi* against cavalry, or with the *pila* as *pilarii/akontistai* against infantry. The first rank of these would have always been equipped with greaves, so it was called the *ocreati*, while the rear ranks of the formation would have always used some sort of javelin, as the various names (*lancea*, *verutus*) imply. The archers, slingers and artillerymen would have been deployed behind the heavy-armed infantry or wherever needed.[8] The list is based on the edition and translation of Bundy (Lydus, pp.69–75) and Syvanne (*A Military History of Late Rome*) with some changes.

Lydus's Legions:

alai apo ch hippeôn	*alae* of 600 horsemen (former auxiliary cavalry)
vexillatiōnes apo f hippeôn	*vexillationes* of 500 horsemen (former legionary cavalry)
tourmai apo f toxotôn hippeôn	*tourmae* of 500 mounted archers
legiōnes, legiones apo hexakischiliôn pezôn	legions of 6,000 infantrymen
tribounoi, dēmarchoi	*tribuni*, tribunes
ordinarioi, taxiarchoi, ordinarii	*ducenarii* and centurions?
signiferai, sēmeioforoi	*signiferi*, standard-bearers (during Vegetius's day called *draconarii*)
optiōnes, optiones	chosen men (centurion's deputies/vicars) or registrars
vēxillarioi, doryforoi	*vexillarii*, spear-bearing men belonging to *vexillationes*, i.e. legionary cavalry
mēnsōres	*mensores*, camp-surveyors
toubikines, salpistai pezōn	*tubicines*, infantry buglers
boukinatōres, salpistai hippeōn	*bucinatores*, cavalry buglers
kornikines, keraulai	*cornicines*, horn-blowers
andabatai, katafraktoi	*andabatae*, cataphract cavalry
mētatōres, chōrometrai	*metatores*, land-surveyors
archytēs kai sagittarioi, toxotai kai beloforoi	*arquites* and *sagittarii*, archers and arrow-bearers
praitōrianoi, stratēgikoi	*praetoriani*, praetorians, general's men
lagchiarioi/lanchiaroi, akontoboloi	*lanciarii*, lance-throwers
dekemprimoi, dekaprōtoi	*decemprimi*, heads of ten, *decani*
benefikialioi, hoi epi therapeia tōn beteranōn tetagmenoi	*beneficiales*, those giving medical aid to the *veterani*/veterans
torkouatoi, streptoforoi, hoi tous maniakas foreuntes	*torquati*, torc-wearers who wear necklaces (rewarded for bravery), and those who wear *manicae* arm-guards
brachiatoi, ē toi armilligeroi, pselioforoi	*brachiati* or *armilligeri*, bracelet-wearers (rewarded for bravery)
armigeroi, hoploforoi	*armigeri* (armour-bearers), arms-bearers (hoplon-bearers)
mounerarioi, leitourgoi	*munerarii*, servants or soldiers (*munifices*) doing fatigues and services
dēputatoi, afōrismenoi	*deputati*, deputies appointed for a specific task

auxiliarioi, hypaspistai — *auxiliarii*, auxiliaries (note the use of *hypaspistai*/shield-bearers for foreign troops, which is suggestive for their later use as a term for *bucellarii*)

kouspatōres, fylakistai — *cuspatores*, gaolers

imaginiferai, eichonoforoi — *imaginiferi, imaginarii*, image-bearers, i.e. bearers of the emperor's image

okreatoi, pezoi sidērōi tas knēmas peripefrakmenoi — *ocreati*, infantry with iron greaves to protect the calves

armatoura prima, hoplomeletē prōtē — *armature prima*, first arms service

armatoura sēmissalia, hoplomeletē meizōn — *armature semissalis*, advanced arms practice

hastatoi, doryforoi — *hastati*, spearmen

tessarioi, hoi ta symbola en tōi kairōi tēs symbolēs tōi plēthei perifēmizontes — *tesserarii*, who announce the watchword to the soldiery at the time of encounter

dracōnarioi, drakontoforoi — *draconarii*, the bearers of the dragon standard

adioutōres, hypoboēthoi — *adiutores*, adjutants

samiarioi, hoi tōn hoplōn stilpnōtai — *semiarii*, the polishers of arms

baginarioi/vaginarioi/thēkopoio — *vaginarii*, scabbard-makers

arkouarioi, toxopoioi — *arcuarii*, bow-makers

pilarioi, akontistai — *pilarii*, javelin throwers

beroutarioi, veroutarioi, diskoboloi — *verutarii*, throwers of *verutum/spiculum* javelin (Veg: shaft 3½ft, iron tip 5in)

founditōres, sfendonētai — *funditores*, slingers

ballistarioi, katapeltistai (katapeltēs de estin eidos helepoleōs, kaleitai de tōi plēthei onagros) — *ballistarii*, catapult-men. A catapult is a kind of city taker/siege engine; it is called by the soldiers/multitude *onager* (wild ass)

binearioi, vinearioi, teichomachoi — *vinearii*, wall-fighters or men who fought with the siege sheds

primoskoutarioi, hyperaspistai, hoi legomenoi protēktōres — *primoscutarii*, shield-bearers who are now called *protectores*

primosagittarioi, toxotai prōtoi — *primosagittarii*, first archers (i.e. mounted bodyguard or commanders of LI?)

klibanarioi, holosidēroi, kēlibana gar hoi Rhōmaioi ta sidēra kalummata kalousin, anti tou kēlamina — *clibanarii*, the horsemen who wear iron armour, for the Romans call iron coverings *celibana*, that is to say *celamina*

flammoularioi, hōn epi tēs akras tou doratos foinika rhakē exērtēnto — *flammularii*, who bear at the end of their spears scarlet banners

expeditoi, euzōnoi, gymnoi, hetoimoi pros machēn	*expediti*, well-girt, lightly clad and mobile, ready for battle (i.e. non-encumbered with baggage train and lightly equipped for ease of movement)
ferentarioi, akrobolistai	*ferentarii*, skirmishers
kirkitōres, hoi peri tous machomenous periiontes kai chorēgountes hopla metō epistamenoi machesthai	*circitores*, who go about the fighters and give them arms
adōratōres, beteranoi, teirōnes	*adoratores*, honourably retired soldiers; *veterani*, those who had grown old while in service; *tirones*, recruits not yet permitted to fight

The legionary equipment[9]

The key to understanding the period's legion is to understand that it varied according to the tactical role of the soldiers, and also varied from one legion to another, and that the legionaries could be used for many different tactical purposes just by changing their equipment. If the legionaries were used to fight pitched battles in the open, they usually wore armour and heavier equipment, while if they were employed in difficult terrain or as light infantry or skirmishers they were equipped appropriately with lighter equipment and could be without any armour.

The legionary could therefore be equipped with: 1) the *lorica segmentata*[10] (segmented plate armour, the usual kind being the Newstead-type); 2) the *lorica squamata* (scale armour); 3) *lorica hamata* (mail armour); 4) rigid and soft leather armour; 5) muscle armour (usually bronze or rigid leather); 6) *thoracomachus* or *subarmalis* (padded coat of linen, leather or felt), which was always used under the armour but could also be used on its own; or 7) no armour. It is also possible that they continued to use the *lorica plumata* (mail with small scales attached), and that composite armour – consisting of segmented armour and mail – had already been introduced. The front-rankers could also wear as additional protection the *manica* (arm-guard, vambrace) to protect the sword-arm and the greave to protect the left lower leg (or greaves for both legs). The *lorica segmentata* was a light specialized type of armour which increased the mobility of the swordsman while providing him with good protection, but it was very costly to manufacture and maintain. It was possibly because of this, and because the general standard of the legionary was falling as a result of their salaries being the same for a long period, that the evidence suggests that it was gradually abandoned in favour of the longer mail and scale armours from the Marcomannic Wars onwards. The trend was that the legionaries used more and more armour, together with more protective helmets and shields, while they also adopted tighter combat formations and melee weapons that had longer reach.

The key evidence for this consists of the general preference for the oval and flatter types of *scuta* shields (sing. *scutum*) over the earlier rectangular cylindrical *scutum*. The latter type was the shield par excellence for the independently operating swordsman who fought like a *murmillo*, just like the *lorica segmentata* was his perfect armour. The rectangular cylindrical *scutum* was ill-suited to the wide interlocking of shields, which meant that the employment of this shield implied their use roughly rim-to-rim in close order, with the further implication that the front-rankers were expected to be able to fight as individual swordsmen after they had thrown their heavy *pila* (sing. *pilum*) javelins. On the basis of the literary evidence and works of art, the Roman shields had three different kinds of grips: 1) the single horizontal handle behind the boss, which was highly usable for punching (on rectangular *scutum*, oval, hexagon and round shields); 2) the old hoplite/cavalry grips/leather straps with grips for hand/wrist and arm that was well-suited to shoving with the shield and for use in the phalanx with spears (oval, round, hexagon and octagon shields); and 3) shields with both styles of grip (hexagon, octagon, oval and round shields). The important point is that the different grips and shields required different fighting styles and unit tactics.

As I noted in my previous book on Caracalla, the change in shields and armour suggests that the general standard of the legionary recruits had probably fallen, because as I have said the salaries had stayed the same for a long time. The commanders did not trust that their legionaries would stay and fight without the psychological and physical support provided by the close formation with interlocked shields. Fighting with the old-style shields and tactics was left to the elite legions or to the specialized *antesignani/lanciarii*. The fact that the legions had become less mobile meant that the importance of skirmishers and the missile arm increased.

The same tendency towards heavier equipment can also be detected in the legionary helmet. The newer types of helmet provided better protection against strikes from above and at the neck, throat and face. The most visible example of this is the adoption of the so-called Imperial Italic H (Niedermörmter) helmet and the adoption of cavalry helmets by infantry (e.g. Niederbieber, Buch, Regensburg, Friedberg, Kalkar-Hönnepel, Dura), but the Romans continued to use other types of helmets (variants of older helmets, segmented, leather etc.). This affected the way that the legionary could fight: the long neckguards and cheek-pieces forcing the men to hold their heads more upright than before, which was well suited to fighting with the *hasta* spear and *spatha* sword.

The principal shafted weapons employed by the Roman legionary consisted of the *pilum* (heavy javelin), *hasta* (spear) and *lancea* (two variants: light javelin and thrusting spear), but other types were also employed. The *pilum* was primarily used as a javelin, with a maximum throwing distance of about 20 metres, but could also be used for thrusting. The *hasta* was mainly used for thrusting, but could also be thrown. The length of the *hasta* is not known with certainty, but in my opinion it had two basic variants: the shorter 2.5-metre version that was primarily used against infantry and the longer 3.74-metre version[11] which was largely used against cavalry. The *hasta* was primarily used by the front-rankers (ranks one to four or one to eight), it being less easy to use for those posted in the rear. For an example of this, see Appendix 1. The standard tactic with all shafted weapons against infantry was that the front rank threw them first and then used their swords, while the second rank supported them with their shafted weapons and those behind them did so with thrown weapons/missiles. The standard tactic against cavalry for the front rank was to use the shafted weapon for thrusting or throwing according to the situation, while the rear-rankers supported them either with spear/javelin thrusts or with thrown weapons/missiles. However, all shafted weapons could be used for thrusting or throwing at any time in combat, no matter what the normal combat doctrine. Light javelins were used by the rear-rankers (ranks four to eight in an eight-man file) and by skirmishers, and their maximum effective range was about 30–40 metres.[12]

The principal bladed weapons weapons used by the Romans were the *spatha* (long sword), *gladius/semi-spatha* (short sword) and *pugio* (dagger). The above-mentioned changes in equipment and tactics had also meant that the *spatha* became the primary bladed weapon by the end of the second century. The *spatha* was primarily used as a cutting weapon, which played a role in the adoption of the oval shield as the principal type of defensive equipment because the rectangular shield was not well suited to the long sword combat technique. The adoption of the *hasta*, *spatha* and flat or slightly curved oval shield meant that the legionaries had acquired the equipment and tactics of the auxiliary forces. The usual assumption among scholars is that the *spatha* – a sword for long cuts and thrusts – was adopted because most of the enemies the Romans faced in the second century fielded large numbers of cavalry. The shorter *gladius/semi-spatha* (also known as a *machaira*) continued in use, but was used primarily in infantry combat. It is probable that at this time such weapons were primarily the so-called ring-pommel swords (48cm long, originally a Sarmatian sword) which were introduced into the Roman Army during the second century. The dagger was only meant to be used as a combat weapon in emergencies at really close quarters.

The likeliest reason for the change of legionary equipment and tactics during what was known as the 'Antonine revolution' in military hardware was that it represented the lessons learnt during the Marcomannic Wars (166–80). It is unlikely to be a coincidence that the equipment the Romans started to use were those used by their enemies, the Germans and Sarmatians. The most obvious of these borrowings were the trousers (German), ring-pommel sword (Sarmatian) and scabbards (Sarmatian) – the Roman auxiliary 'medium infantry' was also equipped like the elite Germanic warriors.

Besides the soldiers of the line, the legionary combat infantry included a number of other specialists, including clubmen, archers, slingers, siege-engineers and artillerymen. The fact that legionaries were trained to perform a great variety of tasks gave the Roman commanders a great deal of flexibility. The Romans trained between a quarter and a third of their legionaries as archers, and all men were able to use slings and throw stones. The archers, slingers and men equipped with light javelins were usually deployed behind the heavy infantry, but they could also be placed between the heavy infantry files, on the flanks of the heavy infantry or even in front. If placed ahead, they usually retreated behind the heavy infantry if they faced enemy infantry, but when they were up against enemy cavalry it is possible that they remained in front as the commander could use them to break up the enemy charge, either with a wedge or an irregular formation. The principal types of bows used were recurved composite bows, wooden bows, crossbows with composite or metal construction (*arcuballista*) and the torsion-powered crossbow (*manuballista*). The slings had two variants: the traditional sling and the staff-sling. The legionary artillerymen used torsion or tension (steel or bronze springs) powered *ballistae*/catapults (dart, spear and stone throwers) and *onagri* of various calibres (stone throwers). Siege engineers specialized in the construction and use of various other kinds of siege engines. The legionaries were also equipped with spades, axes, hatchets, pickaxes and so forth, which they could use in combat if needed.[13]

The fully trained legionary cavalryman was expected to be able to fight as a mounted archer, lancer, javelin-thrower, swordsman, axe-wielder and when called for also as a foot soldier. The Romans thus expected their cavalry to be used as line cavalry, as assault and skirmish troops and even as infantry. The protective equipment of legionary cavalry consisted of armour (whether *lorica segmentata*, mail, scale, muscle cuirass or lamellar) or padded coats of leather/felt/linen – although no armour at all was worn on occasion – as well as shield and helmet. The horses could go without armour or be protected with side coverings and chamfrons (head armour). The offensive equipment of the cavalry consisted of various types of spears/lances (*lancea*, *xuston/xyston*, *hasta*, and Gallic or Sarmatian *contus*), the *spatha* sword, *pugio* dagger, sling, composite bow and crossbow. Of these, the *lancea* and *xyston* were either thrown or used for thrusting (with underarm and overarm techniques), while the *hasta* and *contus* were primarily used for thrusting but could also be thrown if needed. The *spatha* was primarily used for cuts, but could be used as a thrusting weapon when the need arose.

Legionary with a sylindrical rectangular *scutum* and a new type of *lorica segmentata* (Alba Iulia in modern Romania, 3rd century)

Croy-Hill Relief, Antonine Wall (usual estimated date Antonine)

Right: Panoply of a *miles*, end of the 2nd century AD. Drawn after Graham Sumner in D'Amato, 2009, f.117 p.106, but with some changes. Note the hoplite type *aspis* and greaves.

The Background 17

Roman soldiers according to Paul Coussin:
25) 2nd cent. Era of Marcus Aurelius, legionary or Praetorian: Attic-helmet, segmented armour, oval scutum, Iberian sword. After the reliefs in the Column of Aurelius and Arch of Constantine
26) Same era, legionary, segmented armour, rectangular scutum. After the Column of Aurelius.
27) Same era, footman, perhaps Praetorian. Scale armour, small oval shield, peculiar pilum, after the reliefs of Aurelius and Arch of Constantine.
28) Same era, footman, Attic helmet, probably leather or linen armour, small scutum (parma Bruttiana?), Iberian sword. When wearing mail armour, the Column of Aurelius depicts both infantry and cavalry with the same kit.
29-31) 3rd cent. Era of Septimius Severus. Footmen, Attic and Phrygian helmets. segmented armour (29), no armour (30), leather armour (31), scuta rectangular, oval and hexagonal. The sword is often worn on the left. each of the forces carries different types of helmets and shields. After the Arch of Septimius Severus.
- These reconstructions of Coussin show what can be deduced on the basis of the works of art. However, I would suggest that it is probable that the shields were actually often larger than in this reconstruction because the artists depicted these in this way so that the shields would not hide the other details. The same concerns the length of the spears which are likely to have been considerably longer and are shown short only that these would fit the reliefs. The best evidence for the longer length of the spears are: 1) the military manuals state that the spearheads of three ranks reached beyond the front rank (means lengths ca. 2.5-3.74 m); 2) works of art depicting ships have spears that can be called as pikes because the space did not limit the length depicted in the painting. **See also Appendix 1.**

the torsion-powered crossbow was very useful weapon for land and naval battles and for siege warfare.

A funerary relief of a cavalryman, Apulum (Alba Julia), 2nd century AD, probably eques vexillationis of the legio XIII Gemina. Equipment according to D'Amato: a helmet with an eagle metallic crest (Hedderheim type). scale armour, sword, two or more javelins (Josephus BJ 3.96). Drawn after D'Amato/ Sumner.

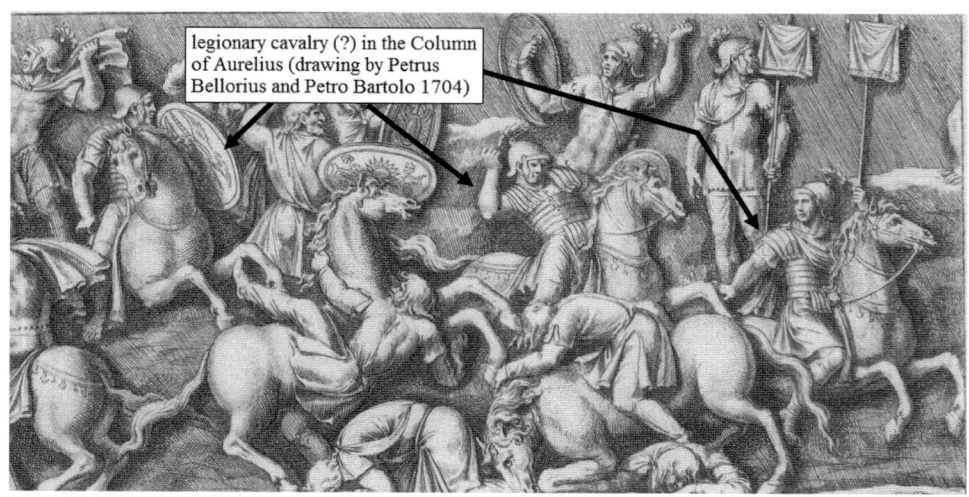

legionary cavalry (?) in the Column of Aurelius (drawing by Petrus Bellorius and Petro Bartolo 1704)

Roman soldiers in the Column of Marcus Aurelius. The relief shows adluctio, the addressing of troops.

Roman soldiers in the Column of Marcus Aurelius

1.3.5. Auxiliaries, National *Numeri* and Temporary Allies

The organization of the regular auxiliaries closely resembled that of the legions and was similarly based on units of *ca.* 500–1,000 men. The original reason for the willingness of the provincials to join the ranks of the auxiliary corps was that it offered a chance to obtain Roman citizenship through distinguished service or after completion of their service. However, by the late second century the Romans were facing serious recruiting problems thanks to the Edict of Antoninus Pius, which stated that the children of auxiliaries did not automatically become citizens, and this when auxiliaries were required to serve for twenty-eight years before being discharged. Another major reason for the reluctance to sign up was that a significant number of auxiliaries were already citizens, which made service in the *auxilia* unpopular. This is possibly why the Romans started to recruit ever increasing numbers of ethnic tribal *numeri* to ensure that they had roughly the same numbers of auxiliaries as before.

The regular auxiliary forces consisted of: 1) the versatile cavalry *alae* (wings) that were equipped for duty as skirmishers and line cavalry as needed; 2) 'medium infantry', typically equipped with a basic helmet, mail or scale or ersatz armour – or with no armour at all – flat shields, *hasta* or *lancea* spears and/or javelins, and long *spatha* sword; 3) mixed cohorts of cavalry and infantry; 4) foot archers; and 5) slingers (slings and staff-slings). Regular auxiliary units also included formations that exploited the native fighting styles of their recruiting grounds: 1) specialist units of javelin-throwers; 2) lightly equipped mounted javeliners such as the Moors; 3) mounted archers recruited mostly from the East; 4) Sarmatian-style *kontoforoi* armed with a Sarmatian *kontos/contus* (a heavy spear used with two hands), sword and bow; and 4) cataphract *alae* (with both man and horse armoured), at least one of which is known to have existed, though it is likely that there were more. Most of the Roman cavalry usually consisted of the auxiliary horsemen.

What follows is based on my earlier books (e.g. *MHLR Vol.1* and *Caracalla*) and on Le Bohec (1994), and reveals the organizational structure of the auxiliary units. However, in practice their size could vary greatly. The prefects belonging to the equestrian class were used as commanders of the auxiliary cavalry *alae*, and also of the *ca.* 500-man *cohors quirgenaria*, but the roughly 1,000-man *milliaria* units were commanded by equestrian tribunes. It is likely that the tribunes were assisted by sub-prefects or their like. Decurions commanded thirty-two-man cavalry *turmae*, the senior decurion being called the *decurion princeps*. Groupings of three *turmae* were put under centurions (also the title of those commanding the auxiliary foot). Just like with the legions, the auxiliary units had a wide variety of support personnel (clerical staff, logistical services etc.).

The national *numeri* were from tribes and client kingdoms and appear to have consisted of both volunteers and those forced into Roman service as a result of a defeat. This was the most flexible type of unit in Roman service. They could be raised and disbanded at a whim, so some units were short-lived while others could be kept in service and enrolled into the permanent military establishment. The *numeri* can therefore be considered mercenaries, which also means that their size (units between 100 and 1,000 men) and composition varied widely. The overall cost of these mercenaries was lower to the exchequer than was the case with the regular forces. The use of these mercenaries gave the Romans an opportunity to exploit the national characteristics of the recruits according to the needs of the moment, and also enabled the Romans to bypass much of their training because they already knew the rudimentaries of fighting. The Romans usually put centurions in charge of the national *numeri*, with the title *praepositi*, but the larger units could also be commanded by men of the equestrian class. The NCOs usually consisted of Romans or Romanized provincials. Naturally, these units also had other support staff like clerks, cooks, workmen etc., who enabled the soldiers to do their duty, which was fighting. The *numeri* could be grouped together with legions or auxiliaries, in which case they were placed under the commander of the legion or auxiliary unit.[14]

The system of dividing units into *seniores* and *iuniores* units probably dates from this era. The best proof of this is the existence of a unit called the *equites itemque pedites iuniores Mauri* for the reign of Caracalla (Handy, 176). These units were formed so that the 'mother unit' – the *seniores* unit – could separate from itself a detachment to form a new *iuniores* unit. This system was probably created either by Commodus, Septimius Severus or Caracalla. Commodus is the likeliest candidate because he had Parthian archers and Moorish javeliners as bodyguards (Handy, 176; Herodian 1.15.2).

In addition to the regular auxiliaries and mercenary *numeri*, the Romans made use of forces drawn from the allied tribes and kingdoms. These were provided on a treaty basis (*foedus* = treaty) and were called either *foederati* or *symmachiarii*.

The following list shows the basic structure of the auxiliaries in Roman service:

Approximate size and organization of auxiliary units:

Unit	Foot	Horse	Centuries	*Turmae*
Cohors Quingenaria Peditata	480		6	
Cohors Quingenaria Equitata	480	128	6	4
Cohors Milliaria Peditata	800		10	
Cohors Milliaria Equitata	800	256	10	8
Ala Quingenaria	512		16	
Ala Milliaria		768 (campaign strength?)	24	
		1,024 (paper strength?)	32	
Numeri (mercenaries)	varied	varied	varied	varied
Foederati (treaty-based allies)	varied	varied	varied	varied

The attached illustrations (opposite) show some of the different types of auxiliary units and *numeri*, but are by no means comprehensive because the auxiliaries possessed all the many types of troops in Roman service. See also the Plates section.

1.3.6. The Strategic Reserve: Rome and its Surroundings[15]

In 193 there were ten Praetorian cohorts, each with about 500 men and an unknown number of cavalry. The principal uses for the Praetorians were to act as bodyguards for the emperor and as his elite forces on campaign, but the Praetorians were often given special missions such as spying, assassination or police work. Service in the Praetorian Guard was a privilege reserved for the Italians. They were usually commanded by between one and three prefects, one of whom was usually a legal expert tasked with advising the emperor on legal matters.

The Background 21

auxiliary archers in Marcus Aurelius's Column (Sarmatians?)

Tombstone of the mounted archer Maris of the *ala Parto et Araborum*

Note the use of the shower archer technique with three arrows on the left hand and the use of the servant behind to replenish the arrows!

Antonine tombstone of the *lancearius* Ulpius Tertius (drawn after Bishop & Coulston)

A tombstone depicting an auxiliary footman from the IV Dalmatian Cohort. Source: Duruy.

A tombstone depict auxiliary horseman. Source: Duruy.

There were also 300 cavalry *Speculatores* who were housed in the same barracks as the Praetorians. Their commander was called a *Trecenarius* (a centurion in charge of 300) and his lieutenant was a *Princeps Castrorum*. It is believed that the *Speculatores* may have been personal lifeguards of the emperor, just like the later and earlier 300 *Excubitores*. The *Speculatores* were also required to perform special assignments, just like the Praetorians. An additional unit was the *Numerus* of *Statores Augusti*, which were

The emperor Marcus Aurelius surrounded by his bodyguards (probably *Speculatores*) in the Column of Marcus Aurelius

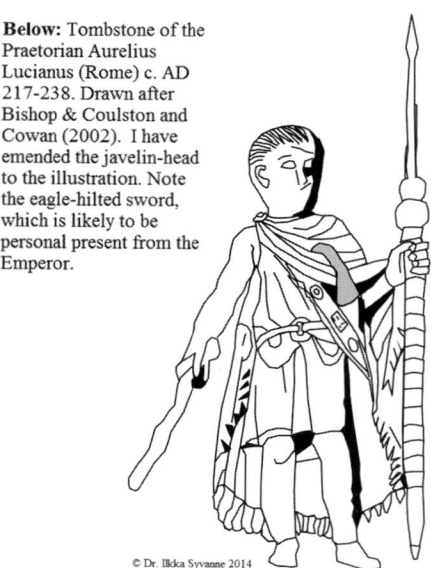

Below: Tombstone of the Praetorian Aurelius Lucianus (Rome) c. AD 217-238. Drawn after Bishop & Coulston and Cowan (2002). I have emended the javelin-head to the illustration. Note the eagle-hilted sword, which is likely to be personal present from the Emperor.

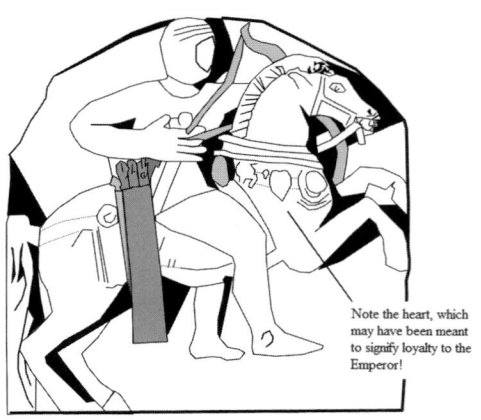

Note the heart, which may have been meant to signify loyalty to the Emperor!

FLAVIVS PROCLVS/EQ[ues] SING[ularis] AVG[usti] DOMO/ [pi]LODELPIA AN[norum] XX/STIP[endiorum] ... H[eres] F[aciendum] C[uravit] at Mainz. Adapted from K.R. Dixon's drawing who dates the tombstone to the 1st century AD, but this is probably a mistake and the tombstone should be dated to the 2nd century AD. The artist may have mistakenly drawn the bowstring on both sides of the horse's neck, but it is also possible that the double string actually belongs to the bridle. Note the separate quivers for javelins and arrows! I have emended to the drawing with dotted lines portions that can be guessed to have existed, and I have highlighted important details (horned saddle, arrow quiver, javelin quiver, bow, bowstring, arrow) with grey color.

used as military police. Trajan had created a unit called the *Equites Singulares Augusti* out of his unit of bodyguards when he became emperor. These consisted of cavalry drawn from the barbarian tribes (mainly Germans), numbering some 1,000 horsemen who were commanded by two tribunes, *Decurion Principes*, aided by sixty-four decurions. These men could also be used as personal bodyguards of the emperor and were housed in the so-called New Camp, their overall commander being the Praetorian Prefect. The *Equites Singulares Augusti* was an independent unit that the emperor could use against the Praetorians. It is also likely that the staff of the Imperial Stables (*stratores*/equerries and grooms, the *Stablesiani*, under the *Tribunus Stabuli*) were considered part and parcel of the cavalry bodyguards of the emperor. For further details of these forces, see my biography of Caracalla.

Ever since the days of Augustus, the emperors had also used a unit called the *Evocati Augusti*, which consisted of veteran praetorians who had been called back to service as bodyguards and special operatives used for spying and assassinations. According to Dio (55.24.8), the *Evocati* were a separate corps which carried batons like centurions, which makes it likely that these were usually the centurions mentioned in the sources that committed many atrocities in the name of the emperor.[16]

The capital also housed a number of other garrisons. These included the special operations units/spies known as the *Peregrini* and *Frumentarii*, which were housed separately at the barracks on the Caelian Hill. The *Peregrini* were commanded by a *Princeps*, a *Subprinceps* and centurions, but nothing else is known with certainty, largely because they were secret police employed by the emperor. It is probable, however, that the *Peregrini* (meaning foreigners) were used as spies mainly in foreign countries, while the *Frumentarii* spied on the natives of Rome. The *Frumentarii* were originally in charge of bread supplies, but by this time their primary uses were as imperial couriers and for special missions tasked with spying and assassinations, among other duties. The *Frumentarii* served under the *Princeps* of the *Peregrini*. Other important units in the city included the Urban Cohorts (*Cohortes Urbanae/ Urbaniciani*), the *Vigiles* and detachments

Above: a tombstone of Evocatus. Date 3rd cent.
Source: Montfaucon

from the two Praetorian fleets (at Misenum and Ravenna). The Urban Cohorts consisted of three cohorts, each with about 500 men. Their commander was the Urban Prefect (*Praefectus Urbi*), who belonged to the senatorial class. They served for twenty years, and service in the unit was the privilege of the Italians. They guarded and policed the city, but were also detached for other duties, including participation in military campaigns. The attached drawing of the tombstone of Nigrinus demonstrates the military functions of the *Urbaniciani*. In addition, the *Urbaniciani* could be used as undercover operatives, just like the other special units posted in the capital. The *Vigiles* consisted of seven cohorts of 1,000 men each, acting as both firemen and policemen, using the sword only in extreme emergencies. Their commander was the Prefect of the *Vigiles*. The *Urbaniciani* appear to have been housed in the same barracks as the *Praetoriani*, but the *Vigiles* were stationed separately throughout the city, as was only natural for firefighters and policemen.[17]

In addition to these units, the city of Rome always possessed various forces of which we know next to nothing, including some sort of staff college that consisted of staff officers drawn from the ranks of the *primipilares*. It is possible that this unit was one of the unknown bodyguard units that the sources refer to at about this time. These mysterious units included the *Scholae* and the *Candidati* (dressed in white) drawn out of the sixth and seventh *scholae*, and also the *Ostensionales* (Paraders = later *Armaturae?*), *Protectores* and *Aulici/Corporis in Aula*. It is possible that these were created under Commodus, who certainly used foreign units of bodyguards (Parthians and Moors), but they could have been formed by Septimius Severus. For more discussion of these alternatives, see my biography of Caracalla.

The units posted in Rome obviously wore the same type of equipment as other forces, but as they were elite units their equipment would have been both better looking and probably also of higher quality. It is probable that the Praetorians and other bodyguards wore the Attic-style helmets or other fancier types of helmets to separate them from the regular troops. The *Urbaniciani*, as a better-paid elite unit, also appear to have worn more fancy equipment, but the *Vigiles* did not. If the Moors and Parthians, who served among the bodyguards of Commodus, were retained as units belonging either to the *Aulici* and/or the *Equites Singulares Augusti*, it is probable that they used their native equipment.

The Italian populace formed the last reserve for all emperors., as the Italian communities – just like the other cities of the Roman Empire – still trained their youth to serve in the citizen militias, which could be used to form legions whenever needed. It was largely due to this that after the murder of Commodus in 193, various contenders for power were able to raise such large numbers of soldiers as they did. Indeed, the Italian youth and older men formed a formidable opposition for any professional army, which is well demonstrated by that fact that the Italians defeated Maximinus Thrax's elite army in 238.

1.3.7. The Civilian Police Forces and Militias[18]

The regular policing of the cities and countryside was the responsibility of the civilian police forces and militias (paramilitary forces of civilian levies), which kept the public order, tracked down criminals, collected taxes, prevented banditry, barbarian raids and piracy, controlled the movement of people and goods, and protected the towns and cities. It was only when these measures were insufficient that the Romans had to use professional military forces for the upkeep of order, as was the case in Judaea and Samaria, where local resistance to the occupiers was so heavy. Egypt was another problem spot, but here it sufficed to have more civilian police forces and militias than any other province of the Empire.

The civilians, however, did not perform their duties unsupervised, the Romans establishing administrative posts called *stationes* in most of their provinces in the late second century. The soldiers called *milites stationarii* (sing. *stationarus*) posted at the *stationes* were commanded by the *beneficiarii consularis*, and the *beneficiarii* were commanded by the *speculatores* who had been detached to serve among the staff of the governor or in the legions. The principal duties of the *beneficiarii* were to control traffic and collect customs, taxes and *annona* (grain provisions for the army), but they could also be used for police work and surveillance duties, the latter of which could include persecution of the Christians. Emperors also used their corps of *frumentarii* for similar police duties, just like the veterans (*evocati*) who had been recalled to service.

The funerary monument of Markos Aurelios Diodoros (Marcus Aurelius Diodorus) from Hierapolis in Phrygia shows the police forces of Asia Minor and their equipment. The equipment of a policeman/ranger consisted of a leather banded *lorica*, a thick *subarmalis* underneath, spears, club and a *fustis* (?). From other sources we know that they could also use swords and shields. Some of the men were mounted while others served on foot. The dogs were used to track down bandits and criminals. The leather banded *lorica* resembles closely the leather *lorica segmentata* worn by the soldier included in the Plates sector and it is likely that we are here dealing with the same type of equipment. Jyrki Halme has suggested to me that this type of armour had been copied from the chariot drivers. This sounds correct. Drawn after D'Amato.

1.3.8. Strategy

If one uses the terminology used by Luttwak in his seminal study of Roman grand strategy, one can call the Roman Empire a hegemonic empire which controlled its core territories directly and its outlaying territories indirectly.[19] The Romans controlled their client states and tribes through a combination of bribery, diplomacy and threat of military action, or with actual military action when necessary. The legions were spread along the borders, so the basic deployment pattern was defensive (see the maps at the beginning of this book). However, this system was not static, the Romans taking the offensive when there were emperors who sought to increase their prestige among the armed forces and populace, or when there was a need to launch a pre-emptive strike. The problem with this system was that the professional army was so small that there were no reserves besides the levies that could be raised from the cities and towns. This meant that whenever the emperor collected forces for an invasion or whenever the enemy attacked in strength, the Romans had to collect troops from other sectors of the frontier which were thereby weakened, which could result in an enemy invasion of such weakened areas. At this point in history, this was not a major problem because the Empire still possessed reserves of well-motivated citizen levies in the form of militias.

However, the primary functions of the military were the upkeep of internal security and the protection of the emperor against usurpation. It was because of this that the emperors spied on their populace, senators and officers, and that the emperors were hesitant to give any general the command of large forces which they could use for the usurpation of power. This was problematic when there were two or more powerful foreign enemies threatening the Roman borders simultaneously. There is no doubt that this was a major strategic weakness, but it is clear that the usurpers were always a greater threat to the emperors than foreign enemies.

The second major problem with the Roman system was the slowness of the strategic mobility of their armies, which depended on the speed of horses, feet, oxen and ships. The only way to limit this problem was to have timely information of the plans of potential enemies across the border, which the Romans did indeed attempt to obtain through their spy networks and alliances. The sources for intelligence gathering across the border consisted of operations conducted by regular forces, including naval units. They had special scouting units for this purpose, but could also obtain intelligence in the course of their regular duties, for example from travellers and merchants. In addition to this, Rome had units that specialized in intelligence gathering. These consisted of the *Peregrini*, who appear to have conducted intelligence gathering in foreign lands, and the *Frumentarii*, who conducted internal security missions. All of the bodyguard units were also used for intelligence gathering, while the emperors used informers and members of the religious establishment for internal security purposes. The latter exposed all such persons who had asked representatives of the emperor the wrong types of questions about the future of the emperor or their own future.

1.3.9. *The Roman Army on a Campaign*
The following long passage from Josephus's *Jewish Wars* is the best summary of Roman military methods that I know of, so I think it worthwhile to quote him at length:

> 'Another task remained. He [Josephus] understood that the Romans owed their invisible strength above all to discipline and military training; if he despaired of providing similar instruction, to be acquired only by long use, he observed that their discipline was due to the number of their officers, and he therefore divided his [Jewish] army on Roman lines and increased the number of his company commanders [*taxiarchoi* = tribunes or officers in general?]. He instituted various ranks of soldiers and set over them decurions [*dekadarchoi* = *dekarchoi* = leaders of ten men, i.e. a *decarchos/decurion* was a leader of a file] and centurions [*hekatontarchai* = leaders of 100 men], above whom were tribunes [*chiliarchoi* = leaders of 1,000 men or in this case probably commanders of cohorts], and over

these generals [*hegemontes* = *duces/legates*] in command of more extensive divisions [*tagmata* = legions]. He taught them the transmission of signals, the trumpet-calls for the charge [*proklêsis*] and retreat [*anaklêsis*], attacks by the wings ["*prosbolas te keratôn*" = the wings advanced forward while the centre remained behind] and enveloping manoeuvres ["*periagôgas*" > sing. *periagôgê* = turning/wheeling; i.e. the outflanking wing(s) were turned/wheeled to attack the enemy's exposed flanks], how relief should be sent by the victorious portion to those who were hard pressed and aid extended to any in distress [manoeuvre described by Josephus here is the quarter wheel/*epistrofê* with outflanking by victorious sections; i.e. the victorious sections wheeled and attacked the enemy on the flank to assist those units that had not met with success or which had been forced to retreat]. He expounded all that conduces to fortitude of soul or bodily endurance; but above all he trained them for war by continually dwelling upon the good order maintained by the Romans and telling them that they would have to fight against men who by their vigour and intrepidity had become masters of well-nigh the whole world.' (Josephus, English tr. by Thackeray, 1926, vol. 2, 545ff., with additions in square brackets)

The above summary shows that in the opinion of Josephus, the principal combat tactics of the Romans consisted of two different versions of double outflanking conducted by the wings: the sending of the wings forward (*epikampios emprosthia*; Vegetius's fourth and fifth formations) and the outflanking with a longer line, both of which were then wheeled towards the centre (*hyperfalaggesis*, *hyperkerasis*). However, this gives us only a partial description of the many different tactical variations that the Roman Army was able to perform. The two tactical variants that Josephus trained his Jewish forces to perform were just those that he thought he could get his untrained men to carry out in the short time that he had for their training. We can add to these the tactic of seeking to crush the enemy's centre with a deep formation, wedge or *globus* (an independently operating unit), as well as surprise attacks and ambushes. In addition, Josephus's description shows nicely how the individual units (centuries, maniples, cohorts etc.) were expected to be able to operate independently of each other while also providing support for one another. The expectation remained the same throughout the existence of Roman Empire.

We know from other sources that the Roman infantry combat formations consisted of two basic variants: the cohortal arrays which could have one to four lines of cohorts, and the phalangial formations. The cohortal formations had two additional basic variants: heavy armed auxiliaries in front with legions behind (location of the light infantry varied); legions and auxiliaries deployed side by side so that cohorts were divided into two lines and the light infantry were placed where needed. The final deathblow to the earlier use of the auxiliaries in front came when Caracalla granted citizenship to all freeborn men. The only real difference between the phalangial and cohortal arrays was that in the latter system the reserves consisted of separate units, while in the former the reserve second line (when used) usually consisted of one half of each file in the array. The light infantry was always posted where thought most useful. When the baggage train accompanied the army, the Romans usually placed it behind the battle formation, but it was more typical for it to be left in a fortified camp or city. The *carroballistae* and other artillery pieces could also be used to support the combat line, as can be seen in the Column of Trajan.

28 Emperor Septimius Severus

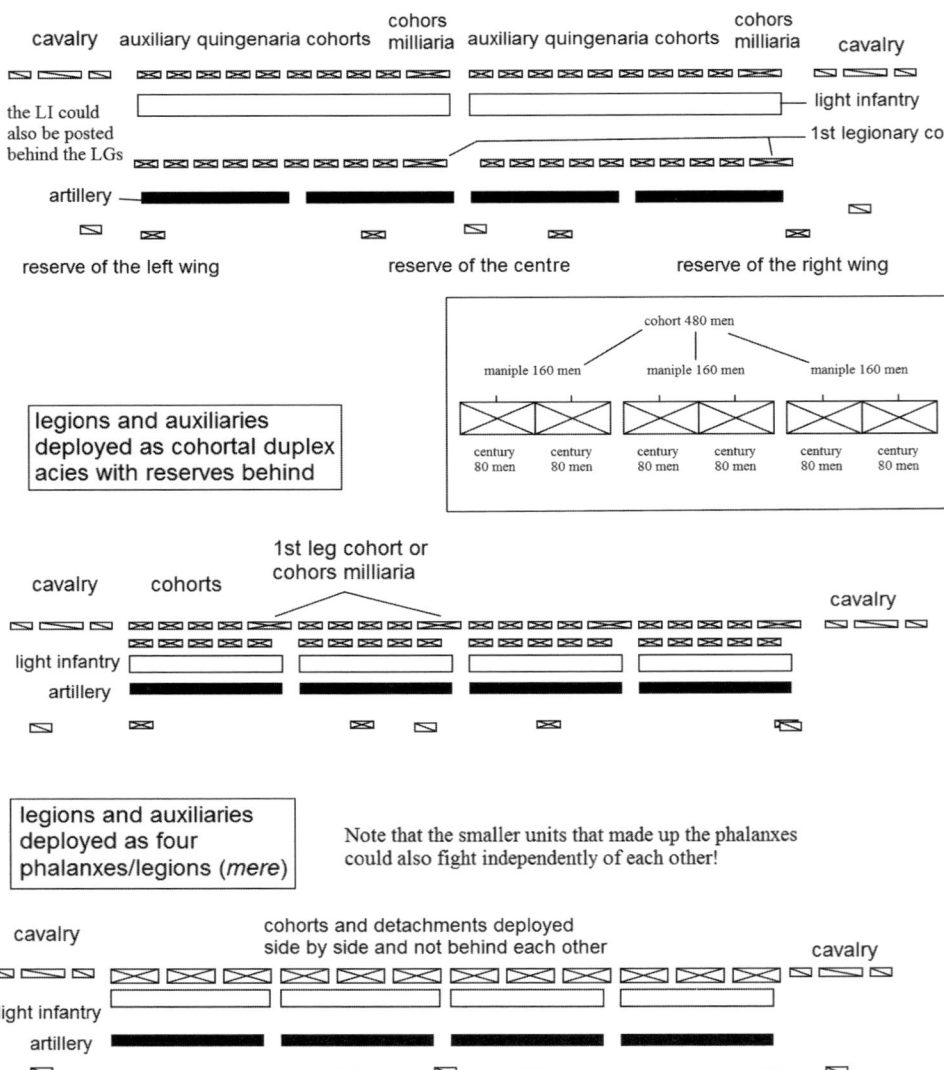

The above-mentioned basic combat formations could be altered if the commander so wished. These grand tactical variants consisted of: 1) the *epikampios opisthia* (rearward-angled half-square used to protect the flanks); 2) the *epikampios emprosthia* (forward-angled half-square used to crush the enemy's wings), with its variant which was to send the wings forward while keeping the rest behind, possibly with the light-infantry posted in front to protect the advancing wings with missiles; 3) the sending of one wing forward while holding back the rest; 4) a long lateral phalanx usually with reserves, which was used to outflank the enemy either with the *hyperkerasis* (outflanking on one flank) or the *hyperfalaggesis/hyperfalangesis* (double outflanking); 5) an oblique attack to the left or right to outflank that wing (used when the Romans had fewer men); 6) a crescent to outflank the enemy on both flanks; 7) a convex array used to break the enemy's centre; and 8) the hollow square or oblong, both of which were used as safe marching arrays, defensive arrays and as offensive arrays in situations where it was feared that the enemy could outflank the Romans.[20] (See Appendices.)

The quotes from Josephus (see above and below) do not include any complete discussion of the unit formations and manoeuvres used by the Roman infantry. However, the narrative sources and other sources such as Arrian (with Aelian and Asclepiodotus), Modestus, Vegetius, Urbicius, the *Peri Strategikes/Strategias* and the *Strategikon* give us enough detail to understand that the Roman infantry was trained to make their formations deeper or shallower (heavy infantry typically of four, eight, sixteen or thirty-two ranks), to wheel and turn their formations, to turn as individuals, change facing, countermarch and to vary the density of their array. These manoeuvres enabled them to use a lateral phalanx to outflank the enemy or prevent them from doing so, a column[21] or wedge to break the enemy formation, a hollow wedge as a counter-measure against an enemy wedge, and possibly also a hollow rhombus (possibly also known as a *globus*) if *caput porcinum* meant the same as the Viking *svinfylking* and had been adopted in the second century as a response to the Marcomannic Wars. However, this is not certain, and I have offered other explanations in earlier books such as *Caracalla* and *Britain in the Age of Arthur*. The wedge array appears to have included at least two different variants: the tactical one in which larger units united their sides to form a wedge, and the small unit version which is described in the context of the murder of Pertinax (see Chapter 3.3), and which in the example mentioned had 200 men advancing in front of the remaining 100 men. The wedge could also be posted in front of the formation to break up charging cavalry. When the wedge advanced in front of the battle array, it was called the *globus*. The sending of light-armed troops and/or club/mace-bearers in front of the battle line, either as a wedge or in open/irregular formation, had the same intention. The Romans also used the so-called saw array, in which units advanced back and forth to disorder the enemy array (= *peplegmene*?), and the independently operating *globus* formation (a group/unit of infantry or cavalry that operated independently), and could form a double front and circle (*amfistomos falagx* and *orbis*) to face enemies behind or around them, an improved version in which the rear half of the double front marched to the rear to form a second phalanx, with empty space between the two. In addition to this, there was a manoeuvre called the *antistomos difalaggia*, which meant that the Roman units opened up an avenue for an enemy cavalry wedge, chariots or elephants to pass through, so that the enemy then faced phalanxes on both of their flanks. (See Appendices.)

The basic infantry unit orders were: 1) open order which was used during marching; 2) close order (*pyknosis* in Greek military theory) in which the men placed their shields circa rim-to-rim and were also tightly arrayed in depth; 3) irregular order, called *drouggos/drungus* (throng); and 4) three variants of the tortoise (*testudo/chelone/foulkon/fulcum/synaspismos*) array.[22] The Romans preferred to use the *hasta* or *logche* spears when they faced cavalry and the heavy *pilum* or other type of javelin when they opposed infantry because the former had a longer reach when used for thrusting. However, both types of shafted weapons could be used for thrusts and throwing against both types of enemy when necessary.

The accompanying images show legionaries using the close order in attack. The men were deployed in ranks and files, but since the cohesion of the formation would have suffered in the course of advancing I have shown the files in the accompanying drawing not as straight lines. It was because of this that some commanders preferred to wait for the enemy to advance, but this was always done at the cost of some of their fighting spirit, as was observed by Julius Caesar.

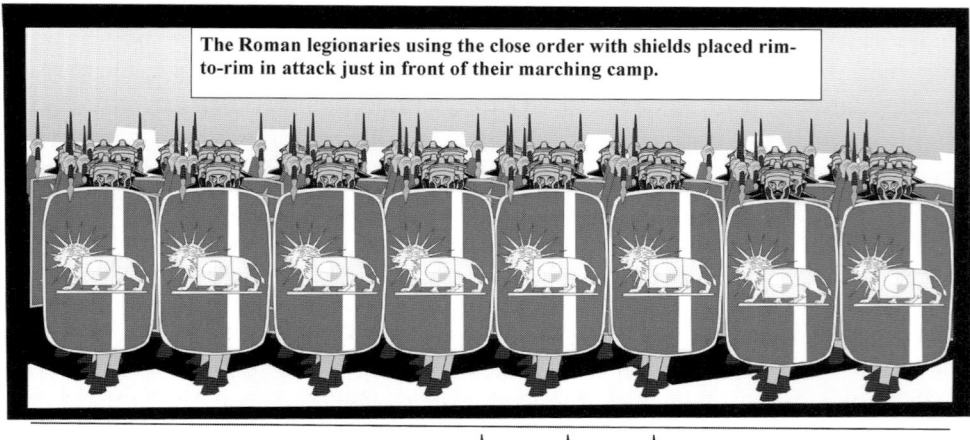

The Roman legionaries using the close order with shields placed rim-to-rim in attack just in front of their marching camp.

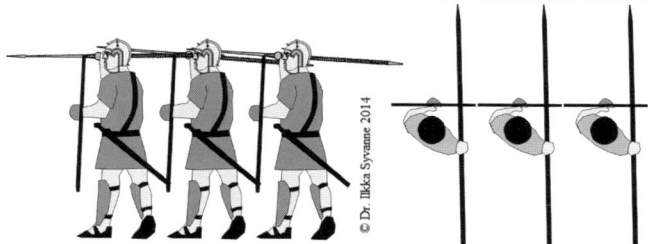

Close order (shields rim-to-rim) used in combat when the men were fully armoured. This array (men armed with either javelins or spears) could be used against both infantry and cavalry (in this case some of the men would probably have used the underarm grip) even if it was more typical to use this order against footmen. This unit order could also be used by men using the curved rectangular shield.

There were several variants of the tortoise formation.[23] The standard *foulkon/testudo* was meant for use against infantry, in which the shields were placed rim-to-boss both in width and depth; the troops could also kneel when necessary to receive missiles, but it was expected that the men would rise to their feet when the enemy came close enough. Its use is exemplified in the following passage from Dio:

'One day when they [Mark Antony's men when they were retreating away from Parthia in 36 BC] fell into an ambush and were struck with fast-flying arrows, they suddenly made by joining their shields ["*synaspisantes*"] the *testudo* [*chelonê* = tortoise], and rested their left knees on the ground. The barbarians had never seen anything of the kind before and thought that they had fallen from their wounds and needed only one finishing blow; so they threw aside their bows, leaped from their horses, and drawing their *Akinakes/*daggers came close to put an end to them. At this the Romans rose to their feet, spread out the phalanx at a word [this implies that the shields were interlocked in width before this], and each one attacked the man nearest and facing him; thus they cut down great numbers since they were contending armed against an unprotected foe, men prepared against men off their guard, heavy infantry against archers, Romans against barbarians. All the survivors immediately retired and no one followed them for the future. This *testudo* and the way in which it is formed deserve a word of explanation. The baggage animals [*skeuoforoi*], the light-armed troops [*psiloi*], and the cavalry [*hippoi*] are marshalled in the centre of the army [*strateuma*]. Those infantrymen who use the long oblong, hollow, cylindrical shields are drawn up around the edges, making a rectangular figure [*plinthion*]; and, facing outward and holding their arms ready for combat [I have here followed Cary's more accurate translation for the 'ta hoopla' instead of Forster's 'with spear-points projecting'. Dio makes it clear below that only shields were visible to the enemy] they enclose the rest. The other infantrymen, who have flat shields, form a compact body in the centre and raise their shields above themselves and above all the rest, so that nothing but shields can be seen in every part of the phalanx alike and all the men by the density of formation are under shelter from missiles. It is so marvellously strong that men can walk upon it, and whenever they get into a hollow, narrow passage, even horses and vehicles can be driven over it. Such is the method of this arrangement, and this shows why it has received the title of *testudo* [*chelonê* = tortoise] – with reference to its strength and to the excellent shelter it affords. They use it in two ways: either they approach some fort to assault it, often even enabling men to scale the very walls, or where sometimes they are surrounded by archers they all bend together – even the horses being taught to kneel and recline [the Roman cavalry horses were clearly superbly trained for various tasks] – and thereby cause the foe to think that they are exhausted; then, when the others draw near, they suddenly rise, to the latter's great alarm. [It is probable that the kneeling of the footmen in the outer edges of the hollow square was also meant to make it easier for the archers, slingers, staff-slingers and operators of *carroballistae* to shoot over their heads straight at the approaching enemy. The kneeling of the horses would have enabled their riders and others to form a sloping tortoise such as is described by Arrian in his *Ektaxis kata Alanon*, for which see Appendix 1, and the *Strategikon* in 12A7, for which see Syvänne, 2004.] (Dio 49.29–30, tr. by Forster 249ff, with comments and changes)

The above account suggests that the Romans also employed a combat formation in which the different ranks in the formation used different shields, with only the men posted at the edges of the formation using cylindrical shields while the rest in the middle used flat shields. The term *synaspismos* and the spreading of the formations for attack suggest that the array was also compacted in width, with shields placed roughly rim-to-boss. It should be noted, however, that the cylindrical shields were not well suited for this, so it is possible that Dio means only the depth of the formation. I would suggest that in normal circumstances when the front-rankers had cylindrical shields, these were often arrayed only rim-to-rim in width, even in the *testudo* formation. Whatever the case, the use of concave round shields by hoplites demonstrates that the cylindrical shape of the shield did not prevent the use of the tight rim-to-boss formation. Furthermore, extant works of art prove that the Romans did not always use separate shields for different ranks, as the attached illustrations well show. However, when this was the case, it is clear that the men on the edges – who were usually those posted in the front rank – were expected to fight like the gladiators known as *murmillones*. The typical shield for a *murmillo* was the cylindrical rectangular *scutum*, but they could also use cylindrical oval shields. Therefore, it is clear that the Romans expected that the front-rankers could fight as individuals. This is not surprising, because the front-rank men were expected to be the best fighters of their units. This means that under normal circumstances, the front-rankers either used their spears/javelins for thrusting or they threw their spears/javelins and then used their swords. Several sources also indicate that the Romans used the tortoise formation more aggressively in attacking. In this case, the array was definitely also contracted in width so

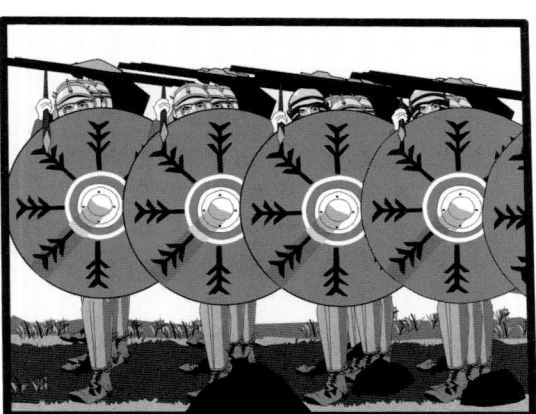

The offensive version of the *testudo* was used primarily against infantry. The flat round or oval shields were better suited for this (shown in these images), but the rectangular cylindrical shields were also used in particular at the outer edges of the *testudo*. If there was a need to receive a missile attack or cavalry, or just to rest, the entire formation could also kneel as described by Dio.

The spears were meant to be used against cavalry and the javelins against infantry. It was possible to change these during the approach because the rear rankers usually had javelins even when the front rankers had spears.

The positioning of the shields in the shield roof appears to have varied. Sometimes the rear rankers rested their shields on top of the shields in front as depicted here and at other times placed these below those. See page 87. The way how the shields were interlocked in width also varied.

Above: Advancing *testudo* from the front when the men used round flat shields. The shields were interlocked in width either by placing the left side of the shield rim-to-boss with the shield on the left or vice versa. It was also possible to use other types of shields so that for example the edges had rectangular cylindrical shields (as depicted below) and the inner ranks flat oval or round shields
Below: Reconstruction of the Roman *testudo* in Lipsius.

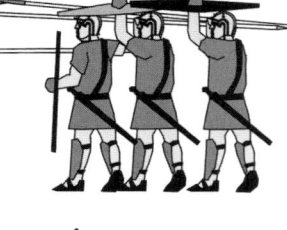

that all shields were interlocked rim-to-boss in both width and depth. A flat shield was obviously better suited to this.[24]

The second major variant of the tortoise was the *foulkon/chelone*, which was meant to receive a cavalry charge. This array is described by both Arrian and the *Strategikon*. The front-rank man and ranks two to three interlocked their shields in depth, while the fourth-ranker held his shield above his head and above the shield of the man in front of him. In the *Strategikon*, the front-ranker kneeled, the second-ranker crouched slightly above him and the third-ranker stood almost upright, the fighter in the fourth rank being perfectly upright. The first and second ranks rested their spears against the ground and pointed them towards the enemy, whereas the third and fourth rank held their spears like javelins and threw them when needed. Arrian does not specify how the three front ranks interlocked their shields, only stating that the front-rank man held the spear underarm and the next three ranks like a javelin. This method could have been used either with the front rank kneeling or by men staying erect. If the men were armed with actual javelins (i.e. *pila* or *lanceae*), the spearheads of the fourth rank would not protrude significantly out of the front. It was therefore better to employ the longer *hastae* when facing cavalry. The ranks behind them provided support with missiles. The width of this formation (with shields almost rim-to-rim) was not the same as in the other tortoise arrays because the shields were interlocked only in depth to allow the soldiers to point their spears towards the enemy between and above the shields.

The third variant was the siege *testudo*, the aim being to enable soldiers to climb a defensive obstacle such as a wall. In this version, the man closest to the wall stood upright, the second rank stooped a little, the third and fourth increased the stoop and the rear rank kneeled, so the formation resembled a slope. However, as the reliefs in the columns of Trajan and Marcus Aurelius show, it was also possible to use the *testudo* with the soldiers not stooping, although in my opinion these represent the approach stage rather than the final stage next to the wall. The attached illustrations show two reconstructions of the siege *testudo* by Lipsius. See also page 87.

The fact that Roman infantry and dismounted cavalry used various different types of shields during this era means that the commanders always had to take into account the type of shields that their soldiers carried. Therefore they were not at liberty to order their men to assume any infantry order or formation that could be found in the Roman drill manuals.

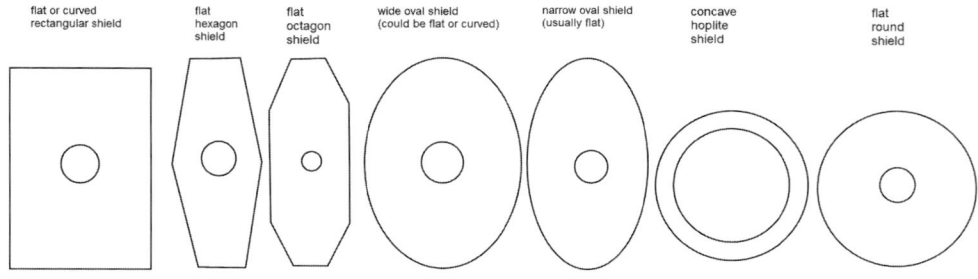

Josephus's following summary of the Roman military shows that when the Roman Army followed its own military doctrines to the letter, it rarely lost:

'One cannot but admire the forethought shown in this particular by the Romans, in making their servant class useful to them not only for the administration of ordinary life but also for war. If one goes on to study the organization of their army as a whole, it will be seen that this vast empire of theirs has come to them as the price of valour, and not as a gift of fortune.

'For their nation does not wait for the outbreak of war to give men their first lesson in arms; they do not sit with folded hands in peacetime only to put them in motion in the hour of need. On the contrary, as though they had been born with weapons in hand, they never have a truce from training, never wait for emergencies to arise. Moreover, their peace manoeuvres are no less strenuous than veritable warfare; each soldier daily throws all his energy into his drill, as though he were in action. Hence that perfect ease with which they sustain the shock of battle: no confusion breaks their customary formation, no panic paralyses, no fatigue exhaust them [Josephus's own account of the Jewish Wars testifies that these are exaggerations]; and as their opponents cannot match these qualities, victory is the invariable and certain consequence. Indeed, it would not be wrong to describe their manoeuvres as bloodless combats and their combats as sanguinary manoeuvres.

'The Romans never lay themselves open to a surprise attack; for, whatever hostile territory they may invade, they engage in no battle until they have fortified their camp. This camp is not erected at random or unevenly; they do not all work at once or in disorderly parties; if the ground is uneven, it is first levelled; a site for the camp is then measured out in the form of a square. For this purpose the army is accompanied by a multitude of workmen and of tools for building.

'The interior of the camp is divided into rows of tents. The exterior circuit presents the appearance of a wall and is furnished with towers at regular intervals; and on the spaces between the towers are placed "quick-firers" [*oxybelê* = dart-shooters], catapults [*katapeltai*], "stone-throwers" [*lithobolot*] and every variety of artillery engines [*organa*], all ready for use. In this surrounding wall are set four gates, one for each side, spacious enough for beasts of burden to enter without difficulty and wide enough for sallies of troops in emergencies. The camp is intersected by streets symmetrically laid out; in the middle are the tents of the officers, and precisely in the centre the headquarters [*praetorium*] of the commander-in-chief [*hêgemon*], resembling a small temple. Thus, as it were, an improvised city springs up, with its market-place, its artisan quarter, its seats of judgment, where captains [*lochagoi* = *primi pili*?] and colonels [*taxiarchoi* = prefects or tribunes or officers in general?] adjudicate upon any differences which may arise. The outer wall and all the buildings within are completed quicker than thought, so numerous and skilled are the workmen. In case of need, the camp is further surrounded by a fosse, four cubits deep and of equal breadth.

'Once entrenched, the soldiers take up their quarters in their tents by companies [*kata syntaxeis* = in tent groups each equalling one file], quietly and in good order. All their fatigue duties are performed with the same discipline, the same regard for security; the procuring of wood, food-supplies, and water, as required – each party has its allotted task. The hour for supper and breakfast is not left to individual discretion: all take their meals together [this fact was sometimes exploited by their enemies who attacked at the designated hour or before it so that the Romans would lack the necessary energy for combat]. The hours for sleep, sentinel-duty, and rising, are announced by the sound of the trumpet; nothing is done without word of command [this could be a weakness if the individuals did not use their own initiative when necessary, but in practice the Roman officers and soldiers did often display personal initiative at the right moment]. At daybreak the rank and file [*stratiôtai* = soldiers] report themselves to their respective centurions [*hekatontarchai*], the centurions go to salute the tribunes [*chiliarchoi*], the tribunes with all the officers [*taxiarchoi* = prefects or officers in general?] then wait on the commander-in-chief [*hêgemon* = legate/*dux*], and he gives them, according to custom, the watchword and other orders to be communicated to the lower ranks. The same precision is maintained in the battle-field: the troops wheel smartly round in the requisite direction [*epistrofê* = quarter-turn/wheel as a unit], and, whether advancing to the attack or retreating, all move as a unit at the word of command.

'When camp is to be broken up, the trumpet sounds a first call; at that none remain idle; instantly, at this signal, they strike the tents and make all ready for departure. The trumpets sound a second call to prepare for the march; at once they pile their baggage on the mules and other beasts of burden and stand ready to start, like runners breasting the cord on the race-course. They then set fire to the encampment, both because they can easily construct another (on the spot), and to prevent the enemy from ever making use of it. A third time the trumpets give a similar signal for departure, to hasten the movements of stragglers, whatever the reason for their delay, and to ensure that no-one is out of his place in the ranks. Then the herald, standing on the right of the war-lord [*polemarchos* = prefect of the camp or more likely the commander?], enquires three times in their native tongue whether they are ready for war. Three times they loudly and lustily shout in reply, "We are ready," some even anticipating the question; and, worked up to a kind of martial frenzy, they along with the shout raise their right arms in the air. Then they advance, all marching in silence and in good order, each man keeping his place in the ranks, as if in face of the enemy.

'The infantry are armed with cuirass [*thorax*] and helmet [*kranos*] and carry a sword [*machaira*] on either side: that on the left is far the longer of the two [*xifos* = *gladius*], the dagger [*pugio*] of the right being no longer than a span [*spithame* = 23.12cm]. The picked infantry, forming the general's [*strategos*'s] guard [In Arrian's *Ektaxis* 22.2, the selected guard from the phalanx consisted of 200 footmen. Traditionally, the selected guard was drawn from the auxilia, but the word 'phalanx' in this case implies in no uncertain terms that the men were drawn from the legions. In addition to this he was accompanied by 100 lightly equipped *logchoforoi*. Arrian's text has a lacuna at 23 and it would also be possible to interpret the *amfi* so that there were 100 *logchoforoi* on both sides of him, but Josephus BJ 3.120 makes it clear that the *logchoforoi* were a separate force; see later. This means that the commander had 300 infantry bodyguards, which was the traditional size for the unit of bodyguards.], carry a lance [*logche/lonche* = *hasta* = spear; or (?) *lancea* = javelin or fighting spear, the former being likelier] and round shield [*aspis* = *parma*], the regiments of the line [*falagx* = phalanx] a javelin [*xuston* = *pilum* or shorter *hasta* = throwing heavy javelin/spear] and oblong buckler [*thureos* = *scutum* = long oblong shield]; the equipment of the latter further includes a saw, a basket, a pick and an axe, not to mention a strap, a bill-hook, a chain and three days' rations, so that an infantry man is almost as heavily burdened as a pack-mule.

'The cavalry carry a large sword [*machaira makra* = a long double-edged sword called a *spatha*] on their right side, a long pike [*kontos* = ca. 3.74m-long spear] in the hand, a buckler resting obliquely in the horse's flank, in a quiver slung beside them three or more darts [*akontia* = javelins] with broad points and as long as spears [*doratia*]; their helmets [*krane*] and cuirasses [*thorax*] are the same as those worn by all the infantry. [Arrian, *Techne Taktike* 4.7–8 classifies the Roman cavalry into those who carried a *kontoi* in the manner of Alans and Sarmatians, and the rest who carried a *logche* lance. All were equipped with the long *spatha* sword, *thureos* shield, iron helmet, *peplegmene thorax* (meaning the chain mail armour), small greaves and small axes. However, after the reign of Hadrian they were also all taught the use of the crossbow and composite bow, which is mentioned at 43.1 and 44.1. See Appendix 1. In short, Hadrian added new abilities for the cavalry which are not mentioned by Josephus.] The select cavalry, forming the general's escort [In Arrian's *Ektaxis* 22.3 he was also surrounded by his select cavalry, but he fails to give any size for this. This makes it possible that he had either 200 or 300 cavalry bodyguards. In my opinion the latter is the likelier figure because that was the traditional strength for the unit of bodyguards then and later.], are armed in precisely the same manner as the ordinary troopers. The legion which is to lead the column is always selected by lot.

'Such is the routine of the Roman army on the march and in camp, such are the various arms which they bear In battle nothing is done unadvisedly or left to chance: consideration invariably precedes action, and action conforms to the decision reached. Consequently the Romans rarely err, and if they do make a slip, easily repair their error. They consider, moreover, that a well-concerted plan, even if it ends in failure, is preferable to a happy stroke of fortune, because accidental success is a temptation to improvidence, whereas deliberation, though occasionally followed by misfortunes, teaches the useful lesson how to avoid their recurrence. They further reflect that one who profits by a happy accident can take no credit for it, while disasters which occur contrary to all calculations leave one at least the consolation that no proper precautions were neglected.

'By their military exercises the Romans instil into their soldiers fortitude not only of body but also of soul; fear, too, plays its part in their training. For they have laws which punish with death not merely desertion of the ranks, but even a slight neglect of duty; and their generals are held in even greater awe than the laws. For the high honours with which they reward the brave prevent the offenders whom they punish from regarding themselves as treated cruelly.

This perfect discipline makes the army an ornament of peace-time and in war welds the whole into a single body; so compact are their ranks, so alert their movements in wheeling to right or left, so quick their ears for orders, their eyes for signals, their hands to act upon them. Prompt as they consequently ever are in action, none are slower than they in succumbing to suffering, and never have they been shown in any predicament to be beaten by numbers, by ruse, by difficulties of ground, or even by fortune; for they have more assurance of victory than of fortune. Where counsel thus precedes active operations, where leaders' plan[s] of campaign [are] followed up by so efficient an army, no wonder that the Empire has extended its boundaries in the east to the Euphrates, on the west to the Ocean, on the south to the most fertile tracts of Libya, on the north to the Ister [Danube] and the Rhine. One might say without exaggeration that, great as are their possessions, the people that won them are greater still.

'If I have dwelt at some length on this topic, my intention was not so much to extol the Romans as to console those whom they have vanquished and to deter others who may be tempted to revolt. Perhaps, too, any cultured readers who are unacquainted with the subject may profit by an account of the organization of the Roman army.' (Josephus, English tr. by Thackeray, vol. 2, 597–609, with additions in square brackets)

The Roman Army described here was a military machine that was expected to work like clockwork, according to pre-established rules and precepts. It was also a learning organization, in that if it had made a mistake it learnt from it. This and other sources prove that the Roman way of fighting was based on harsh training, good discipline and equipment, efficient intelligence gathering, efficient logistical systems, the use of fortified marching camps and pre-battle councils of war. Also of note is the use of the 'lightly armed' *logchoforoi* (equipped with the *logche* and *aspis*), bodyguards who were armed like the hoplites or *triarii* of the past, and one may assume like some of the spear-armed auxiliaries of their own day.

Josephus provides further detail of the Roman way of fighting:

'But Vespasian ... now set out from Ptolemais, after drawing up his army from the march in the customary Roman order. The auxiliary light-armed [*psiloi*, "*psilous tôn epikourôn*"] and archers [*toxotai*; note that the archers are separated with the word kai (= and) from the auxiliaries. It is probable that these archers actually consisted at least partially of the legionaries trained as archers; see later. The fact that the vanguard consisted of infantry means that the terrain ahead was considered unsuitable for a cavalry vanguard.] were sent in advance, to repel any sudden incursions of the enemy and to explore suspected woodland suited for the concealment of ambuscades. Next came a contingent [*moira*] of heavy-armed Roman soldiers, infantry and cavalry. They were followed by a detachment composed of ten men from each century, carrying their own kit and the necessary instruments for marking out the camp; after these came the pioneers to straighten out bends on the route, to level the rough places and to cut down obstructing woods, in order to spare the army the fatigues of a toilsome march. Behind these Vespasian posted his personal equipage and that of his lieutenants with a strong mounted escort to protect them. He himself rode behind with the pick of the infantry and cavalry, and his lancers [*logchoforoi*; it is this separation of the picked foot and horse from the spearmen that suggests that the latter should be added to the 200 foot guards for a total of 300 foot guards]. Then came the cavalry units of the legions; for to each legion are attached a hundred and twenty horse [It is this referral that has caused most historians to think that the cavalry component of the legion was merely 120 or 128 horsemen. However, it is quite easy to see that these horsemen are actually those that protected the flanks of the marching formation, and not the entire cavalry strength of the legion. The rest of the legionary cavalry would have been placed where Josephus states that there was cavalry. This explains the only anomaly in the sources regarding the strength of the legionary cavalry. All the other sources state in no uncertain terms that the legions had 500, 600 or 732 horsemen, which I noted for the first time in my presentation in 2011 and after that in many subsequent studies.]. These were followed by the mules carrying the siege towers and the other machines. Then came the legates, the prefects of the cohorts and the tribunes, with an escort of picked troops [note that these higher-ranking officers were also protected by units of their own bodyguards]. Next [were] the ensigns surrounding the eagle which in the Roman army precedes every legion, because it is the king and the bravest of all the birds; it is regarded by them as the symbol of empire, and, whoever may be their adversaries, an omen of victory. These sacred emblems were followed by the trumpeters, and behind them came the solid column, marching six abreast [The 'six abreast' has been taken to mean that the legions would have been organized in groups of three. This is partially true because the legionaries could fight as three deep, like for example Josephus BJ 2.173 and 5.131 show. However, this is slightly misleading because the legionary organization was still based on the *contubernia*. In this case the heavy-armed legionaries marched six abreast because the legionary archers had been posted in front and behind. In the examples of Josephus, the legions were organized for combat so that three men in a half-file were equipped as heavy-armed and the fourth as an archer, like is described in the following quote. However, in situations in which the *contubernia* were below strength, the commander obviously adapted his organization to match the reality, and it was also possible that the depth of the array was three deep in such cases.] A centurion, according to custom, accompanied them to superintend the order of the ranks. Behind the infantry the servants attached to each legion followed in a body, conducting the mules and other beasts of burden which carried the soldiers' kit. At the end of the column came the crowd of mercenaries, and last of all for security a rearguard composed of light and heavy infantry and a considerable body of cavalry.' (Josephus, *Jewish War*, 3.115ff., tr. by Thackeray, 611ff. with some changes)

Josephus continues in the same vein:

'However, Vespasian, hearing that the main body of the Jews was assembled in the plain outside the town, sent thither his son with six hundred picked cavalry. Titus, finding the enemy in prodigious strength, sent word to his father that he required more troops. For his own part, observing that, although most of his cavalry were burning for action without waiting for the arrival of reinforcements, there were others who betrayed secret dismay at this immense number of Jews, he took up a position where he was audible to all and spoke. "Let him remember that the Jews, however dauntless and reckless of life they may be, are yet undisciplined and unskilled in war and deserve to be called a mere rabble, rather than an army. Of our experience and our discipline is there any need to speak? If, alone of all nations, we exercise ourselves in arms in peace-time, it is for this very object, that in war-time we need not contrast our numbers with those of our opponents. What would be the use of this perpetual training, if we must be equal in numbers to an untrained foe before we face them? [i.e. Titus publicly expected that his elite cavalry would be able to defeat the numerically superior foe but in practice still felt it necessary to call for reinforcements before this.] Consider again that you will contend in full armour against men that have scarcely any, that you are cavalry against infantry, that you have generals and they have none; these advantages greatly multiply your effective strength, as the enemy's disadvantages greatly detract from his. Wars are not won by numbers, however efficient the soldiers, but by courage, however few the men: small forces are easily manoeuvred and brought up to each other's support [this refers to the use of second line reserves and also to mutual support of units in line]; whereas unwieldy armies do themselves more injury than they receive from the enemy." ... As Titus had harangued them a supernatural frenzy took possession of his men, and when, before the engagement, Trajan joined them with four hundred cavalry, they chafed as though these partners had come to detract from their own credit for the victory. [The Romans were using a double line: the 600 horsemen of Titus formed the front line and the 400 horsemen of Trajan the second line. Other good examples of the use of cavalry reserves are: Tacitus, *Histories* 3.15–17; Caesar's *Gallic War* 7.13, 8.28. It is actually possible that the Romans could also use a third cavalry line when the cavalry wings of infantry were deployed as a vanguard, because the Romans could employ separate cavalry wings for each of their infantry lines. See e.g. Appian, *Hannibalic War* 7.4.19ff.] Vespasian at the same time sent Antonius Silo with two thousand archers to occupy the hill opposite the town and beat off the enemy on the ramparts; these troops, in accordance with their instructions, prevented any attempts from that quarter to assist the Jewish army outside. Titus now led the charge, spurring his horse against the enemy, [while] behind him, with loud shouts, came his men, deploying across the plain so as to cover the whole of the enemy's front, thereby materially increasing their apparent strength. [This means that the cavalry was deployed in a shallow formation, e.g. three deep and 200 files wide, to increase the width of the line. It is possible that this line was further divided into units of 100, 200 or 300 horsemen. Titus and his entourage, consisting at least of the standard-bearer, trumpeter and cape-bearer, would have added an extra file to the width of the line, presumably in the centre of the formation, and it is also possible that the width would have been increased even further by the other likely supernumeraries such as centurions, trumpeters and standard-bearers so that one can guess that there were in truth about 660 horsemen in the front line. The standard-bearer of Titus would have been on his right, his trumpeter behind him and his cape-bearer behind the standard-bearer, as in the *Strategikon*, so that these made up altogether an extra file when the regulars were behind them. However, the likeliest combat formation for the first line in this case is actually the single-rank formation (this became later the favourite of medieval knights), which was used to trample over the enemy, as instructed in Arrian, *Tactics*, 17.5. The 400 horsemen, possibly with the supernumeraries even up to 450 horsemen, posted in the reserve could have been deployed in like manner or in a deeper array, e.g. five deep, and may even have been divided into two separate reserves on the flanks or even in greater number of units behind the front. Josephus unfortunately fails to tell us how these were arrayed.] The Jews, though dismayed by the impetuosity and good order of this attack, for a while sustained the Roman charges [this means that the Roman cavalry attacked and when the Jewish line held, they threw their *kontoi* and/or javelins from their holsters and turned back and repeated the charge]; but pierced by the lances [likely to be the Gallic *kontoi* that could be thrown or used as a shock weapon] and overthrown by the rush of cavalry they fell and were trampled under foot. [The Roman cavalry was trained to crush infantry formations by trampling over them. The initial charge above weakened the cohesion of the Jewish line with thrown missiles, and it was only when the Romans observed that the enemy line had been disordered and openings had been created that they pressed home their charge and ran over the enemy line. This tactic is described on numerous Roman tombstones. It is this that makes it very likely that Titus arrayed his front line as a single-rank formation.] When the plain on all sides was covered with corpses, they dispersed and fled to the city, as fast as

A tombstone of a Roman horseman trampling an enemy (source: Cagnat).

A tombstone of a Roman auxiliary horseman trampling an enemy (source: Duruy).

each man's legs could carry him. Titus, hotly pursuing, now cut down the laggards in the rear, now made lanes through their bunched masses; here rode ahead of them and charged them in front, there dashed into groups which had fallen foul of each other and trampled them to pieces. For all, in short, he sought to intercept retreat to the walls and to head them off into the plain, until at length, by superior numbers, they succeeded in forcing a way through and flinging themselves into the town.' (Josephus, *Jewish War*, 3.470ff, tr. by Thackeray, 707ff. with some changes and comments)

Josephus also wrote:

'Titus, now anxious to secure a safe passage for the baggage and camp-followers, drew up the flower of his forces facing the northern and western portions of the wall, in lines seven deep: the infantry in front, the cavalry behind, each of these arms in three ranks, the archers forming the seventh line in the middle. [*The legionaries were in this case actually formed up four deep with the three ranks in front being equipped as heavy infantry and the fourth rank as archers. The fourth rank of archers corresponds with the training scheme followed up by the Romans, which was to train between a third and a quarter of the recruits to use bows. The legionaries could be arrayed in this shallow formation because they consisted of picked forces and they also had cavalry behind as reserves.*].' (Josephus, BJ 5.130–1, tr. by Thackeray, 239 with comments)

The above, with my comments, show many important organizational features of the Roman Army. Firstly, it shows that the legionary infantry could be formed three deep. The problem with this is that the military treatises (Pseudo-Hyginus 1; Aelian; Arrian; Vegetius, see narrative; Urbicius, see *MHLR Vol.5*, *Peri Strategias* and *Strategikon*), roughly from the reign of Hadrian onwards, divide the heavy infantry formation into ranks of four (four, eight, sixteen, thirty-two ranks) and the light infantry into ranks of two (two, four, eight, sixteen), with the implication that the standard Roman heavy infantry combat formation during and after Hadrian was always divisible with the figure of four. This does not tally with Josephus's figures or those of the earlier Republican era, and suggests the possibility that Hadrian reformed the Roman legions according to the Greek model. However, I would still suggest that we should interpret the evidence differently. The formations mentioned by Josephus actually conform with the system of having the tent group form the basic file, if we take into account the fact that the Romans trained a quarter to a third of their infantry as archers (Vegetius 1.15). It is clear that Josephus's three-deep legionary formations should be interpreted to mean that their fourth rank of archers had been posted elsewhere, and in the case of the six-deep array this had happened to the seventh and eight ranks of archers. In short, the basic organization in all of the sources is the same, namely the tent group, so that in normal circumstances the Romans would have deployed their heavy-armed men four, eight, sixteen or at most thirty-two ranks deep, and their lightly armed troops separately from this, but when necessary they could also adopt the shallower array of three, six or twelve-rank formations, with the archers posted where needed. The details given of the

Praetorian 300-man unit attacking Pertinax (see Chapter 3.3) also suggest that the Roman infantry could be arrayed with different unit depths and in many different formations. It was also possible to bolster the depth of the array if there was a preponderance of soldiers or to make it shallower when there were too few men.[25]

Josephus's text forms one of the important pieces of evidence for the bodyguards used by the Roman governors and higher-ranking commanders during the campaign. This question has been studied in detail by Speidel (1978, esp. 4–22), who notes that the commanders and officers always drew their units of bodyguards from the units serving under them, so that the legates had legionaries as their bodyguards, but then went on to state that the *singulares* (bodyguards) of the provincial armies were always selected from the auxiliary forces of the province. The preceding should be enough to make it clear that the legionaries could also serve in the bodyguards of the governors and generals (*duces* and legates) in the provinces. However, he is still quite correct that on the basis of the extant evidence the overwhelming majority of the *singulares* were drawn from the auxiliary units. The evidence such as we have suggests that the *singulares* were equipped exactly like the formations that they were drawn from. This means that even the so-called *logchoforoi* are likely to have consisted of the *hasta* and shield-armed auxiliaries. The strength of the *singulares* units appear to have varied according to the needs. The only precise numbers are the above mentioned and the 600 *equites singulares* of Titus and *ca*. 1,000 *equites singulares* of Trajan, whose unit of bodyguards became the *Equites Singulares Augusti* after he became emperor. The provincial *singulares* consisted of both *pedites* and *equites singulares*, but the sources usually mention only the latter, possibly because only the cavalry could accompany the commander when he moved quickly from one place to another.[26]

The above quotes from Josephus and the marching column of Arrian in Appendix 1 show what sort of array the Romans used when there was no threat of enemy attack against the flanks or when they were forced to march in a long column because of the restricted terrain. However, from other sources – including Arrian's *Techne Taktike*[27] – we know that this was not the formation that the Romans typically would have used even in difficult terrain when there existed an imminent threat of enemy attack, unless the situation compelled them to. It was far more typical for the Romans to march as a hollow square or oblong, a rearward-angled half-square or as two, three or four marching columns surrounded by light infantry and/or cavalry, and also to place their baggage train behind their battle-ready forces.

The attached illustration of a marching camp, which I have drawn after the reconstruction of Lenoir (after Pseudo-Hyginus), shows how the Romans arranged their armies safely within such fortifications, as described in the already quoted text of Josephus.

These quotes from Josephus do not include specific reference to the cavalry orders used by the Romans, but fortunately we know these from other sources, the most important of which is the sixth-century *Strategikon*, which preserves older Roman traditions. According to this text, Roman cavalry units employed three unit orders: for marching the open order and for combat either the close order (each file with a width of *ca*. 90–100cm) or the irregular order called the *drouggos* (a throng of horsemen not organized into ranks and files). Arrian adds to this the cavalry *chelone*, which was basically a tight formation in

44 Emperor Septimius Severus

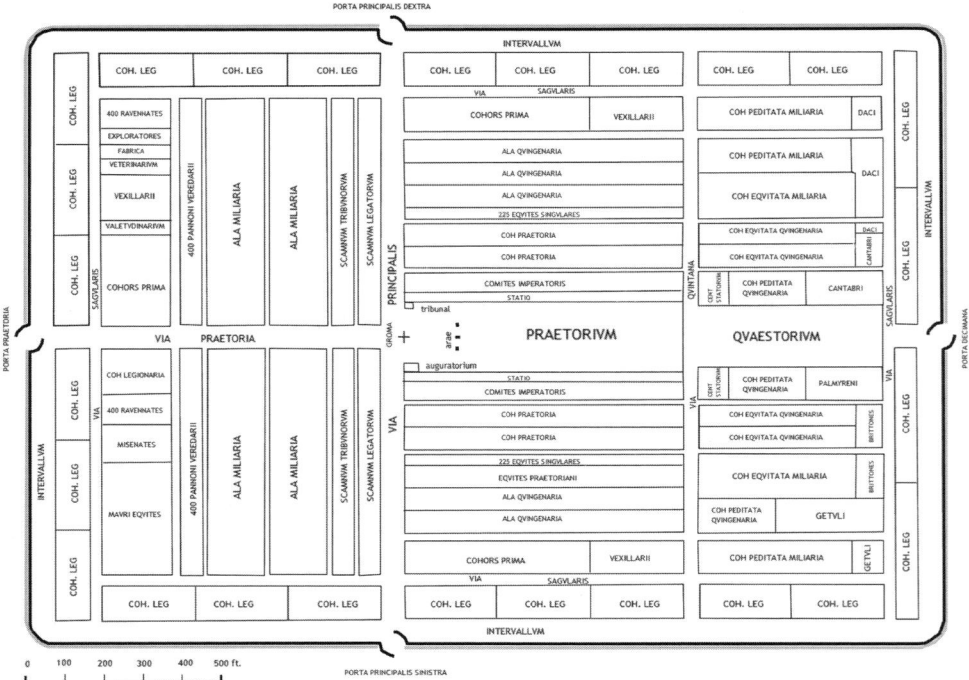

which the stationary horses were posted close to each other, with the heads of the horses turned backwards, while the troopers protected themselves and their horses with shields.

Josephus's text illustrates that it is probable that the three-deep cavalry formation was also used by the Romans. It is also included in the military treatises: Aelian (18.7) and Arrian (*Taktike* 16.12) mention a cavalry array three deep and nine wide for a total of twenty-seven men. This is obviously five men short of the strength of the cavalry *turma* of thirty-two horsemen (possibly with the decurion thirty-three men). This may imply that the Romans used the shallower three-deep array when the *turma* was below strength or that when the decurion decided to do so he posted the surplus men somewhere else. The other cavalry formations used by the Romans were based on multiples of four or five, but these could also be modified according to the situation. Those divided according to the files of four include the rectangular arrays of Aelian (18.5–6), Arrian (16.9) and Asclepiodotus (7.4). Aelian mentioned the array which was eight wide and four deep, which was the same as the thirty-two-horseman *turma*. Asclepiodotus also refers to an array used by the Persians, Sicilians and Greeks which was sixteen files wide and eight ranks deep for a total of 128 horsemen. The fact that this was divisible with the size of a *turma* means that it was also used by the Romans. Aelian (18.6) and Arrian (*Taktike*, 16.11) both refer to the square formation ten wide and five deep, and the latter adds to it the array twenty wide and ten deep. Arrian (16.10–11) considered the square formation with a depth of five or ten the best of the cavalry arrays, because it was the easiest to control and organize, and because in this array the officers fell as a single body against the enemy. The organization which was based on the figures of fives would probably have consisted of three groups of thirty-two plus three decurions and one centurion for a total of 100 men; or six groups of thirty-two (192) plus six decurions and two centurions for a total of 200 men. It is no wonder that this system became the standard method by the time the *Strategikon* was written in the 590s. However, the fact that the *Strategikon* includes so many different depths for the cavalry arrays based on the quality of the unit makes it clear that the Romans always adapted the depth of their formations according to the situation, even after the square and oblong arrays became the standard.

As we have already seen, the Roman cavalry was highly versatile and could be used both for charging in close order and as a skirmishing force in an irregular formation, not to mention the specialist wedge and rhombus formations. The standard tactic against infantry appears to have been either to prepare for the cavalry attack with missiles or to charge against the infantry in the hope that they would lose their morale, and if this did not happen to engage them with missiles, after which the charge was repeated. When the commander judged the situation ripe, the charge was carried on up to the infantry, who were then trampled under the hooves. The usual cavalry tactic against another cavalry force seems to have combined the elements of harassment and charge according to which was chosen by the commander. The fact that such a giant as Maximinus Thrax was recruited into the cavalry and then into the bodyguard of the emperor Septimius Severus suggests that at least some of the Roman cavalry commanders preferred to recruit impressive-looking, tall and heavy men on large horses to give them an edge in the charge and cavalry combat at close quarters.[28]

The principal advantage of heavy and large men and horses in close order was that they often frightened the enemy, who fled before the two forces came into contact, while if the enemy held its ground so that the forces halted in front of each other and then engaged in a melee, the heavier horses and bigger men had a distinct advantage. Large, heavy horses could push over lighter horses, while their riders could hit their foes from above. The downside in the use of heavier horses was that they were more expensive, required more fodder, lacked the stamina for long campaigns and battles, and were less agile and fast than smaller mounts. In short, the principal advantage of the taller cavalrymen and heavier horses used in close order was their impact on enemy morale during the charge itself, but they were much harder to maintain during the campaign. Another advantage of the close order used by heavy troops was that it made it more difficult for any cowards amongst their ranks to shy from contact. This in its turn made it more likely that the unit would make contact with the enemy formation. There were also advantages of the more open order and irregular order in combat, when used in conjunction with the gallop: the sight of the fast-advancing horsemen was frightening, and these orders made the formation more mobile so they could gain the advantage of position. The disadvantages of the open and irregular orders were that they made it easier for the less courageous in the ranks to avoid contact with the enemy, and that it was possible for these units to ride through each other without one side emerging victorious. None of these elements, however, were decisive: the decisive element was the will to win.[29]

The other cavalry formations mentioned by the military theorists and which were definitely used by the Romans were the rhombus (128 men)[30] and the wedge (sixty-four men). The case for the rhomboid (Aelian 19.7–9; Arrian, *Taktike* 17.1–3) and wedge (Aelian 19.1; Arrian, *Taktike* 17.1–3), which were not drawn according to ranks and files, is uncertain because they were not based on the thirty-two-man *turmae*, but I would not entirely preclude the possibility that there were units able to use such arrays. Later sources suggest that the Romans could also use larger variants of the cavalry wedge.[31] According to Arrian (*Taktike* 16.3–5, 7), the wedge was particularly well suited to penetrating enemy formations and for performing wheeling movements, while the rhombus was good for wheeling and in defence. Arrian (*Taktike*, 17.5) also includes the single-line/rank array, which could be used for fast surprise attacks or when the intention was to trample opponents (the favoured tactic of the medieval knights), but its use in battles was not recommended because it lacked depth. Arrian (*Taktike*, 16.1–2) notes that all of the cavalry formations he mentioned (square, oblong, rhombus and wedge) were good when used in the right circumstances, so it is clear that he foresaw the Romans using all of these. The texts of Tacitus[32] suggest that at least the elite Batavians (the precursors of the *Equites Singulares Augusti*) could also form a defensive circle array against other cavalry, while Arrian suggests that the Romans could also employ the hollow cavalry square in like manner.

The Romans trained their cavalry (legionaries, auxiliaries and *numeri*) to be equally adept at scouting, skirmishing and pitched battles.[33] Their principal combat roles were skirmishing, guerrilla warfare, protection of the infantry during marching and battles, outflanking of the enemy in combat and pursuit of the defeated enemy. However, the Romans did occasionally deploy their cavalry separately from infantry. Despite the fact that after the reign of Hadrian the Romans drilled their cavalry to be equally adept at all types of fighting, in practice the cavalry consisted of five basic categories, largely thanks to the fact that they also included specialist units, units drawn from subject nations, mercenaries and allies:

- The Romans continued to use their cavalry in the traditional manner as Romano-Gallic-Spanish cavalry (legionaries and auxiliaries). These were equipped with a shield, helmet, sword and javelin(s) or spear(s). However, after Hadrian these were also trained to use crossbows and bows when needed, and to fight like the Sarmatian and Parthian *kontoforoi* and cataphracts. Their horses were usually unarmoured, but could also have chamfrons and armour for the front and sides. Most of the Roman cavalry belonged to this highly versatile category.
- The mounted archers, primarily consisting of auxiliaries and *numeri* of eastern origins, formed the second category of cavalry.
- The third category was super-heavy cataphracts (man and horse armoured, and rider armed with a spear, shield, sword and possibly a bow).[34]
- The Sarmatian *contarii* (*kontoforoi*/lancers) and Arabic lancers formed the fourth category.
- The Moorish/Berber extra-light cavalry javelineers formed the fifth category.[35]

The extant evidence (e.g. Caesar, Josephus, Tacitus, Arrian and Trajan's Column) suggests that the Romans usually used a second reserve line of horsemen when they deployed their cavalry separately. The same evidence also suggests that these arrays formed the basis for the Late Roman Italian Drill, which is described in the sixth-century *Strategikon*. This had three different variants: 1) a small cavalry army with less than 5,000 men that had

The Background   47

only a single reserve division; 2) a medium-sized cavalry force with 5,000–15,000 men which had two reserve divisions; and 3) a large cavalry army in excess of 12,000–15,000 men which had four reserve divisions.

We do not know when the Romans introduced the different parts of the array depicted below. My own educated guess is that it achieved its final form under Gallienus as a result of the destruction of the cavalry army of Decius at Abrittus in 251, which demonstrated the need for the third line. Consequently, I have not included the third line in the following reconstructions. The attached diagrams, based on my interpretation of the reliefs in Trajan's Column, show the two basic variants used by cavalry: the Italian Drill Formation, in which the cavalry is deployed separately in front, and the African Drill Formation (more accurately the Illyrikian Drill), which probably depicts Roman cavalry in a situation in which it would have started pursuit from the flanks of the Roman infantry. After that I have included the two most likely cavalry formations when the Romans had fewer horsemen, along with the other cavalry arrays used.

The divisions (*mere*) in this system were divided into units of *koursores* (runners/skirmishers) and of *defensores* (defenders). The *koursores* were usually placed on the flanks of the *defensores*, but they could also be placed in the centre. The principal missions of the *koursores* were skirmishing and pursuit in irregular order, while that for the *defensores* was to maintain close order and act as defenders for the runners. The Romans could also use their entire cavalry line for a charge, either in close or irregular order. The standard

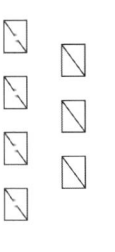

resulting array if the men are interpreted as units

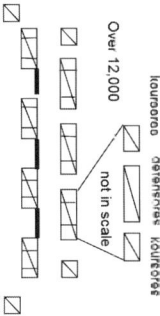

Italian Drill Formation in the Strategikon: 1st Line 3 divisions with the outflankers (right) and flank guard (left); 2nd line 4 divisions with fill-up banda in between and rear guards behind the flanks

However, it is likelier that the actual cavalry array would not have had the third line rear guard at this time because it is probable that these were introduced only after the defeat of Decius at Abrittus in 251. For the reasons behind this conclusion, see Syvänne, Gallienus. The existence of the fill-up *banda* between the second line divisions is also uncertain.

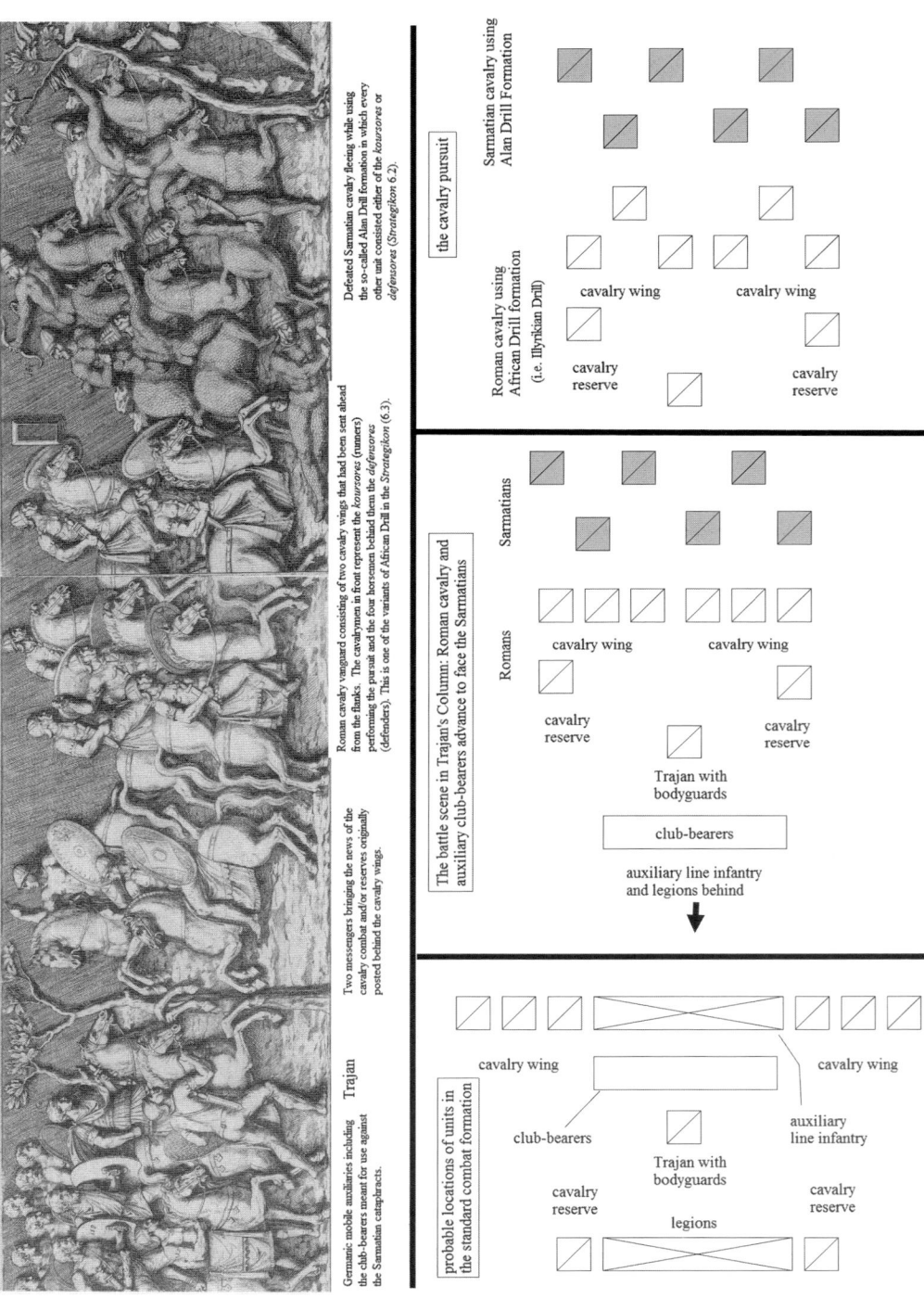

tactics were the double outflanking with numerically superior forces, outflanking with one flank if both sides had equal numbers, and the crushing of the enemy centre by attacking with the central division while the wings were refused in situations where the Romans were outnumbered. When possible, the Romans attempted to improve their chances with separate units of ambushers.

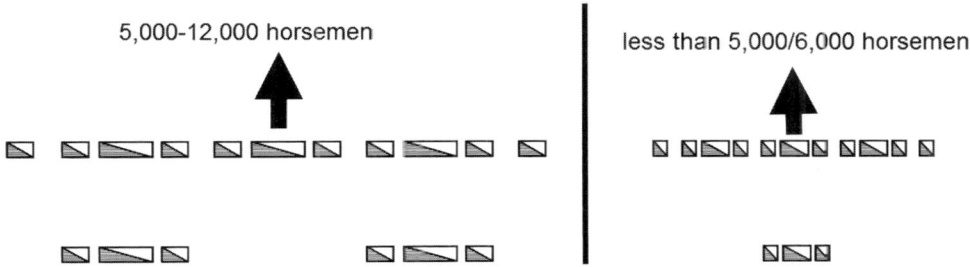

The information in Arrian's *Taktika* and *Ektaxis kata Alanên*, and the deployment pattern of cavalry within hollow infantry squares in later sources (which were based on earlier practices preserved in Aelian's texts), suggest that the Romans also used different types of mounted arrays. Arrian's text includes an alternative formation which had a single line of cavalry usable as mounted archers and lancers in front, with two reserve divisions behind plus the commander's bodyguard cavalry. The deployment pattern of cavalry within hollow infantry squares suggests a possibility that the Romans could also deploy a reserve unit for each of their front-line units (see Appendix 1).

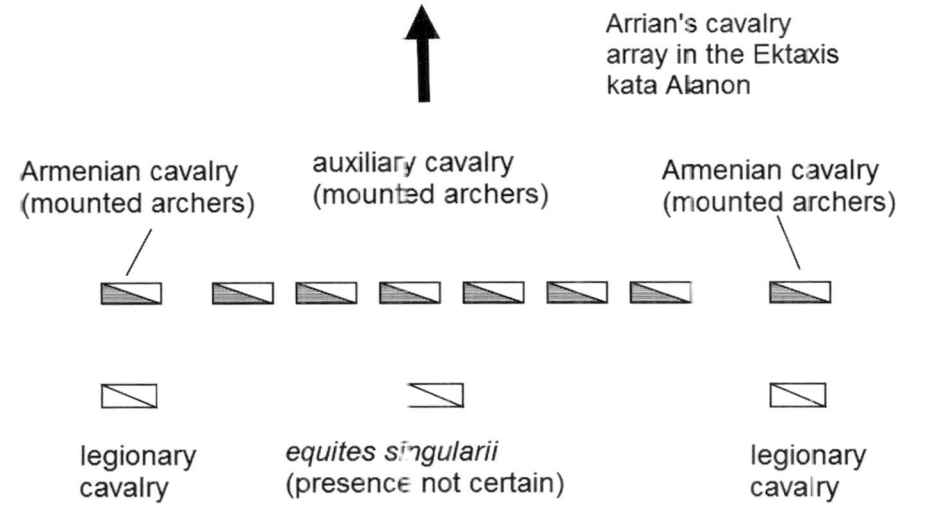

1.3.10. The Imperial Navy[36]

The Imperial Fleet can be broken down into the two Praetorian fleets of Italy and the Provincial fleets posted in the provinces. The Praetorian fleets were the *Classis Praetoriae Misenatium/Misenatis* and *Classis Praetoriae Ravennatum/Ravennatis/Ravennas*, while the Provincial fleets consisted of the *Classis Alexandrina, Classis Syriaca, Classis Nova Libyca, Classis Germanica, Classis Pannonica, Classis Moesica, Classis Britannica, Classis Pontica, Classis Nova Libyca, Classis Africana* and *Classis Mauretanica* (which comprised 13 *liburnae* or biremes).

The attached map shows how these fleets were distributed. The Praetorian fleets served as strategic reserves, while the day-to-day defence and protection of the sea lanes and rivers was left in the hands of the Provincial fleets.

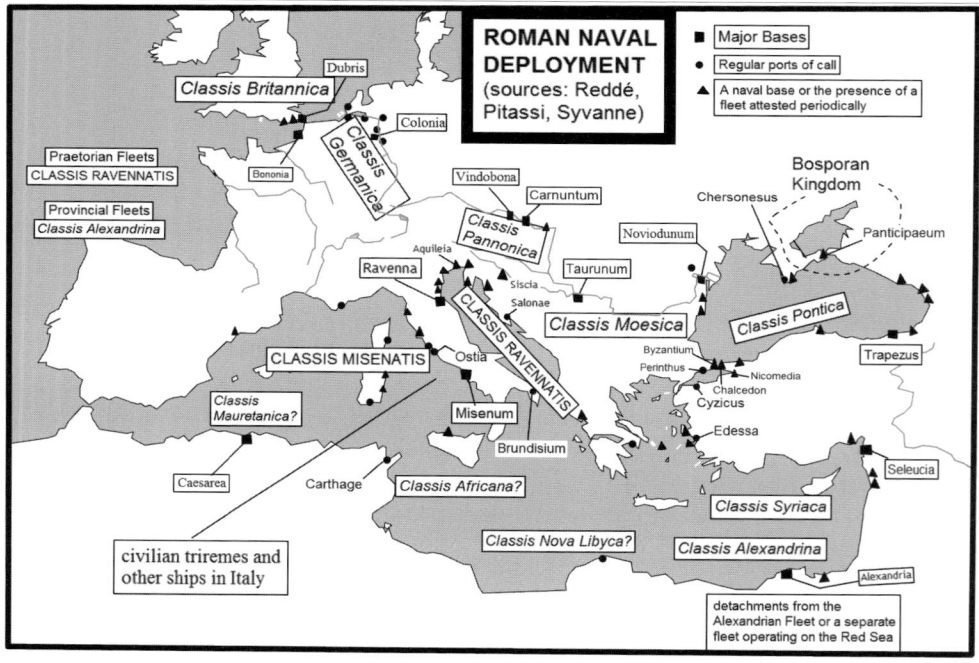

The emperor set up goals for the use of the navy for each particular period, as how the fleets were used depended on the emperor's overall strategy, if indeed he had one. When employed well, the navy could help the emperor achieve his political, economic or military objectives, which could include simultaneously any combination of a trade embargo, diplomacy, establishing alliances, threats of military action, special operations and actual military action.

However, the typical uses for the Roman fleets consisted of five major missions: 1) to control the seas and rivers; 2) to project power ashore with amphibious operations, blockades and active siege operations; 3) to raid enemy coasts and shipping when necessary (meaning the Irish Sea, North Sea, Black Sea, Red Sea, Arabic Sea and Indian Ocean, the Mediterranean by this time being a Roman 'lake', known as *mare Nostrum* or 'our sea');

4) to protect shipments and trade routes; and 5) to protect cities, coastal areas and other frontiers. The navy was also instrumental in the collection of taxes and enabled the Romans to transport men and supplies where needed. In essence, Rome's ability to maintain the Empire was entirely based on its control of the seas. The projection of power from land to sea had two forms: the Romans could capture places that could be used as harbours to deny enemy access to the sea; and the Roman harbours were protected by walls and artillery. Coastal defence consisted of passive/defensive measures (forts, towers, fortified cities and towns, and citizen militia having their ships along the coasts and rivers) and the active/ offensive measures undertaken by the fleets. The citizen militia and their merchant ships were used to prevent smuggling and piracy. Italy and the provinces were also occasionally required to contribute warships (mostly triremes) with crews, meaning that the civilian populace of the coastal cities formed a similar last reserve to the citizen levies on land.[37]

The actual professional staff belonging to the fleets was classed as auxiliary forces. The main recruiting ground for the Misenum fleet lay in the East, and for the Ravenna fleet in the Danubian and Illyrian provinces. The Provincial fleets naturally recruited most of their staff from the provinces. Just like on land, the sailors and marines of the Praetorian fleets were better paid than the rest, receiving the same salaries as the *equites cohortis*, whereas those of the Provincial fleets received the same salaries as the *milites cohortis*.[38] The lowly status of the navy is also visible from the fact that it included freedmen. The length of service for the mariners was twenty-eight years, after which they were rewarded with Roman citizenship. The officers of the navy belonged to the equestrian class, but some of the emperors also appointed freedmen and foreigners as admirals. According to Vegetius (4.31), each of the Praetorian fleets had a single naval legion attached to them. This presumably means that these men were not classed as auxiliaries.

The fleet of Misenum was tasked with protection of the western shores of Italy and was used as a reserve fleet for Gaul, Spain, Mauretania, Africa, Egypt, Sardinia and Sicily. However, in practice the Misenum fleet was used all over the Empire as it was the most powerful fleet in the Mediterranean. The Ravenna fleet was tasked with protection of the Adriatic and was used as a reserve fleet for Epirus, Macedonia, Achaia, Propontus, Pontus, the Orient, Crete and Cyprus. Just like its Misenum counterpart, however, it could also be used elsewhere. The same was true of the Provincial fleets, which could also be used outside their own area, as Septimius Severus's Caledonian campaign demonstrates. The Praetorian fleets also had another duty, which was to post permanent detachments of mariners in the city of Rome to operate the canvas awnings of the Colosseum and to stage mock naval battles with gladiators. They were also required to send detachments of mariners to assist the field armies when needed, as shown by Pseudo-Hyginus's treatise. The Praetorian fleets were usually placed under their own separate prefects, but under Septimius Severus – and presumably also under Caracalla – they were united under a single prefect (see PIR2 Cn. Marcius Rustius Rufinus), with the implication that both fleets were used to support the imperial campaigns.

Historians have been unable to reach a concensus view regarding fleet sizes, but the Misenum fleet has been estimated as having at least of one 'six' (type: *hexeres/sexeres*), one 'five' (type: *penteres/quinquereme*), ten 'fours' (type: *tetreres/tetreris/quadrireme/ quadrieres*), fifty-two triremes and fifteen *liburnae*, with the Ravenna fleet having at least quinqueremes, six *quadriremes*, twenty-three triremes and four *liburnae*. It is probable that these figures are below the actual strengths, because according to Jordanes (*Getica* 29, after Dio), the port of Ravenna could apparently hold 250 ships, although it is of course possible that many of these were transport ships.

The suppression of piracy and transport of personnel and supplies was primarily left to the Provincial fleets, so their ships were typically lighter and more mobile, containing the following vessels: one trireme, which served as a flagship for the commanding prefect; *liburnae*; blue-coloured scouting ships (*scaphae exploratoriae*); plus other smaller vessels and boats. The *liburnae* were further specialized into sea-going and riverine classes, according to the location of the fleet. Later evidence suggests that the river fleets could consist of very large numbers of vessels. For example, the *Classis Moesica* had 225 *naves lusoriae* in 412, which would have required a minimum of 10,000 men to crew the vessels.[39]

The command structure of each Provincial fleet consisted of the following: Fleet Prefect (*praefectus classis*); 2nd-in-command *subpraefectus*; *navarchi*, each in charge of several ships; and *trierarchi* (captains of ships). The ships naturally also had their own junior officers, which comprised at least the following: armourer (*armorum custos*); standard bearers (*signiferi*); trumpeters (*tubicines* and *cornicines*); helmsman (*gubernator*); bow-officer/helmsman's adjutant (*proreta/proretus*); *nauphylax* (supply officer or ship-guard, or both?); man to give timing for the oarsmen (*hortator*); and musician providing the rhythm to oar movements (*symphoniacus*). The larger ships also had two doctors/medics (*medicus, subunctor/strigilarius*), attendants to the sacrifices (*victimarii*) and various other attendants. From the point of view of naval combat, the most important specialists were the pilots (*gubernatores*), rowers (*remiges*), sailors (*nautae*), marines/soldiers (*milites*), specialist elite front-rank fighters (*propugnatores*), artillerymen (*balistarii*) and archers (*sagittarii*), while there were also divers (*urinatores*), craftsmen (*fabri*), sail-trimmers/makers (*velarii*) and rowing masters (*celeustae* or *pausarii*). Each of the fleets also naturally possessed administrative and other support staff.[40]

When required, the fleets, just like the land forces, contributed detachments of ships and marines for a particular campaign. The best such example in the era under examination is the British campaign from 208–211.[41]

Ships

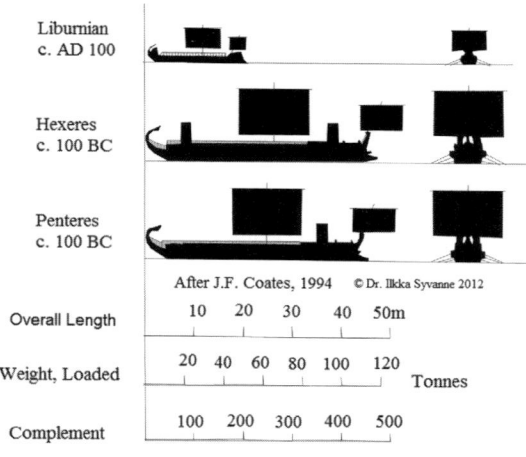

There are no reliable figures for the size of the Roman fleets at any given point in the history of the Principate or Late Rome. My own conservative estimate is that the Roman Navy consisted of at least one 'six', two 'fives', fourteen 'fours', eighty-three triremes, 523 *liburnae* and 1,776 patrol boats.[42] This means that the navy consisted of at least some 75,000–120,000 fighting men and seamen. These figures do not include the huge workforce needed to maintain this navy, nor the civilian forces temporarily raised for individual campaigns.

The Romans used a great variety of specialist ships, boats and rafts for all sorts of needs. Most of the transport ships were provided by civilians. The standard warship of the period was the galley, which came in many sizes and shapes. The workhorse of the Roman Navy was the fast and mobile *liburna*, the precursor of the eastern Roman *dromon*. The *liburna* was ideally suited to chasing pirates and yet large enough to encounter any enemy ship with the expectation that it would prevail. *Liburnae* had two ranks/remes of twenty-five oars on each side for a total of 100 oars. However, the Romans also used larger ships, most of which were delegated to the Praetorian fleets to provide them with a combat superiority over the other fleets. These were the *hexeres/hexeris* (six rowers usually on two or three banks, but could also consist of six banks), quinqueremes (five rowers usually on one to three banks, but could also have five banks), quadriremes (four rowers usually on one or two banks, but could also have four banks) and triremes (usually three rowers on three banks), which were equipped with both *onagri* and *ballistae* artillery, as probably were the *liburnae*. Most of these war galleys were equipped either with rams or hybrid ram/spur-bows, a transitional version of the spur that broke oars of enemy ships and acted as a boarding platform.[43]

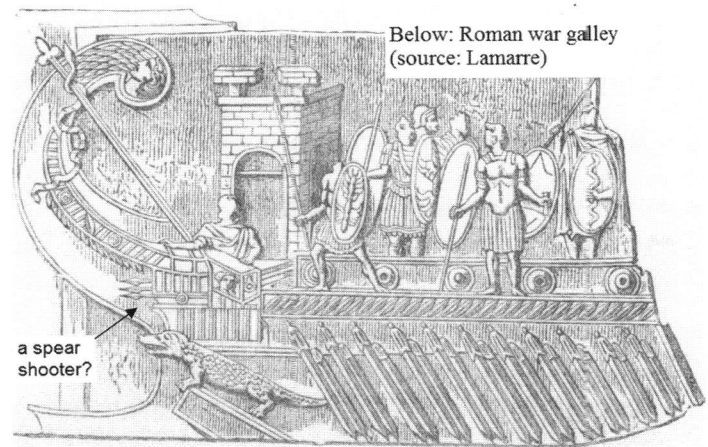

Below: Roman war galley (source: Lamarre)

a spear shooter?

Roman galleys on a painting at Pompeii. Note the long length of the spears. Niccolini.

Naval Tactics[44]

The key to understanding ancient naval warfare is to realize that sailing was usually avoided in winter and in bad weather. This set limits to the time of year when the Romans conducted their military campaigns. However, as always there were exceptions to the rule, the Romans occasionally taking a risk and campaigning during winter or in bad weather. A vital difference between land and naval warfare was that knowledge of winds, tides, locale and signs of weather were far more important at sea.

Nevertheless, naval combat followed the same principles as on land. First of all, it was important to send scouting boats and ships to obtain intelligence. The Romans also preferred to surprise or ambush their enemy, or at least to use superior ships and crews against them. At this time the Romans had naval mastery or supremacy in all the theatres of operation, none of their enemies possessing ships that could fight with Roman war galleys on anything near equal terms. Rome could thus expect to defeat any enemy fleet, even when outnumbered.

There were numerous standard naval battle formations: 1) the crescent formation, with the best ships and men posted on the wings to outflank the enemy; 2) the convex array, with the best ships and men placed in the centre to break through the enemy fleet; 3) a double convex array, for greater security; 4) a line abreast with reserves; 5) a double line abreast, for maximum safety when there were enough ships; and 6) a defensive circle. One of the main traditional naval tactics was the use of the *diekplous* manoeuvre to penetrate the enemy formation, in which one galley rowed forward into the space between two enemy galleys, followed by further galleys with the first shearing the enemy's oars and the second ramming the immobile ship. There was also the *periplous* manoeuvre, in which the galleys on either wing extended their line and outflanked the enemy.[45]

When the Romans used ships equipped with artillery, combat started at a distance of about 300–600 metres with the *ballistae* and bows. *Onagri*, slings and staff-slings joined in the action from about 150 metres. The *ballistae* shot primarily incendiary darts, while the *onagri* shot fire stones and fire-bombs. The Romans started to use their light javelins and darts at a distance of about 40 metres, and then their heavy javelins from 20–30 metres. When they reached close quarters, they either rammed the enemy vessel, sheared its oars, grappled the enemy ship for boarding or remained at a distance and continued to use their missiles.

The fighting force on board consisted of marine soldiers (*milites*), sailors (*nautae*) and oarsmen (*remiges*), but could also include land forces to bolster their numbers. The sailors and oarsmen thus had a double duty, as they were expected to be able to fight as well as man the ship. On the basis of Vegetius's (4.44) account, it is clear that the naval soldiers were usually better protected than average legionaries and auxiliaries. They wore cataphract armour or *lorica* (designating various types of armour, but on the basis of extant works of art this appears to have usually been muscle armour) with helmet and greaves, and had *scutum* shields which were stronger and larger than those employed on land to withstand the enemy's missiles. Their better training and equipment meant the Roman marines could expect to defeat their enemies in hand-to-hand combat.

According to D'Amato (2009b, 13) *miles* of the *legio Adiutrix* in the Arch of Constantine taken from a monument from the time of Marcus Aurelius. This legion was originally raised as a naval legion so that it is possible that its equipment reflected those used by marines also later.

A marine of the Misenum Fleet. He wears a cloak, muscle armour, greaves, HedderheimNiederbieber-helmet, hasta-spear, spatha-sword and a round shield. The shield emblem is based on D'Amato. The image has appeared before in my biography of Caracalla.

1.3.11. Siege Warfare

The Romans had inherited from the Greeks the best siege engines and techniques available, and it was thanks to this that they enjoyed absolute superiority over all their enemies in both defensive and offensive sieges. The fact that the Romans were usually ready to spend any amount of time and effort – regardless of the cost – in the taking of an enemy fort, the best example of which is the siege of Masada in Judaea, made them even more formidable. However, as we shall see, this was not true of every offensive siege.

Siege equipment used by the Romans included artillery (*ballistae*, *onagri*), cranes, siege towers (including the *helepolis*, known as the 'city-taker'), battering rams, siege sheds, pickaxes, drills, sambucas (counter-weight tubes), a flamethrower operated by bellows used against stone walls, mantlets and various kinds of ladders. For illustrations of the siege engines, see the text on the sieges of Hatra in Chapter 8. The artillery could be used to shoot fire-darts, fire-bombs, stones, arrows, darts and spears. Offensive siege techniques included the assault, the undermining of the walls, clearing the enemy from the walls with missiles – for example with artillery pieces mounted on siege towers and/or mounds – and a blockade to starve the enemy. Defensive siege techniques consisted of the use of all the above-mentioned pieces of equipment, along with counter-mining, padding to protect the walls, counter-mounds and towers, and the use of relief armies. Naval forces could also be used for blockades, assaults and providing supplies if the city was located on the coast.[46]

1.4. The Sources

The sources for the reign of Septimius Severus consist of the narrative histories, earlier and later military treatises, legal texts, inscriptions, works of art, archaeological finds, and coins and medallions. All these different types of sources need to be analyzed in such a manner that their limitations are taken into account. In the following comments I concentrate my attention only on the most important narrative sources and leave out comments on the rest. There are plenty of commentaries and analyses of how to examine the other types of material available, so I need not bother with those here. The most important of the narrative sources are Dio, Herodian and the *Historia Augusta*.

Septimius Severus has always been considered one of the greatest Roman emperors, but opinions on the consequences of his reign have varied. Some modern historians have thought that the problems of the third century were the result of his policies regarding the armed forces, but I believe this is definitely a mistake because the problems started only after the murder of Alexander Severus. Even then, one might say that the problems really started only when Gallienus became sole emperor. Modern historians have also followed up the opinion of those pro-senatorial sources who detested Severus's son Caracalla and have accused Severus of having unleashed a monster on the inhabitants of the Roman Empire. This is once again the result of faulty reading of the sources which are hostile towards Caracalla, as I have already demonstrated in my biography of Caracalla. In his own lifetime and after, Caracalla was actually idolized by the vast majority of the population and soldiers of the Roman world, and it was largely thanks to the influence of Dio that his name came to be heard with horror. However, Dio was not only hostile towards Caracalla; he was also antagonistic or at least held negative views about many of the policies of Severus.

Our most important source for the reign of Severus is Cassius Dio, who was one of the advisors of Severus. However, Dio is not an unbiased reporter. He was horrified by the treatment the senators received from Severus, he did not like the emperor's aggressive foreign policy or building programmes, and most importantly did not like that Severus put Caracalla in power. All this has to be kept in mind when analyzing his text.

Herodian was a near contemporary of Severus and therefore in a position to know the gossip of the day. However, there is one major problem, which is that we do not know enough about Herodian to make judgements regarding his ability to obtain information on the inner workings of the Empire. All that we know of Herodian is based on the information he provides of himself in his histories. All we know for certain is that Herodian had very positive view of Severus, often seeming to present the official version of events.

The third major source for Septimius Severus consists of the books of the so-called *Historia Augusta* (also known as the *Scriptores historiae Augustae* or *Augustan Histories*). The consensus view was once that these books were a late fourth-century forgery by a single hand, but the latest research has once again established them to belong to the turn of the fourth century and to have been written by several different people. This source has a relatively positive view of Severus, even if it shares the senatorial view regarding Severus's policies towards the Senate and its view regarding his successor, Caracalla. It is probable that the *Historia Augusta* (Aelius Spartinianus) also influenced later historians like Aurelius Victor to present Septimius Severus in a more favourable light.[47] The authors of the *Historia Augusta* which are of concern to us here (and their subject matter) are as follows, although despite mentioning these here, I also use the traditional *Historia Augusta* (shortened as *HA*) when I refer to these:

Aelius Lampridius: Commodus;
Julius Capitolinus: Pertinax, Clodius Albinus, Opellis Macrinus;
Aelius Spartianus: Didius Julianus, Pescennius Niger, Septimius Severus, Antoninus Caracallus, Antoninus Geta.

Left: Quadrireme (four) with four banks. A bronze coin of Gordian III (Cabinet de France). Source: Duruy.
Right: Trireme with three banks. An ancient painting in the gardens of Farnese. Source: Duruy.

- There were several different ways how the 'sixes', 'fives', 'fours' and triremes were built. The most common versions had: a) one to three banks of oars for the 'six'; b) one to three banks for the 'five'; c) one or two banks for the 'four'; d) and three banks for the trireme. For these variants, see for example the studies of J.S. Morrison (*Greek and Roman Oared Warships*) and M. Pitassi (*Roman Warships*). However, as can be seen from the accompanying illustration of the 'four', there were also other variants in existence.

Chapter 2

Severus's Career Before 193

2.1. African Background

Basically all that we know of the early life of Septimius Severus comes from the pen of Aelius Spartianus, and it is therefore worth quoting him at length:

'Severus … was born in Africa, at the town of Leptis/Lepcis Magna [in Tripolitania]. His father's name was Geta. His ancestors had been Roman knights. His mother was Fulvia Pia. His uncles on his father's side were Aper and Severus who had both been consuls. His grandfather on his father's side was Macer and his grandfather on his mother's side was Fulvius Pius. He was born six days before the Ides of April in the second consulship of Erucius Clarus and first of Severus [modern research puts the date at 11 April 145 or 146]. When he was still but a child, and before he had been drilled in the Latin and Greek literature, in which [he] was later so well-versed, he would not play any other game but one in which bundles of rods and axes were carried before him with boys standing about him while he himself sat down in the seat and play-acted a judge. In his eighteenth year, he delivered a public oration. Afterwards he went to Rome to continue his studies, and with the support of his kinsman Septimius Severus, who had been consul twice, he received from the deified Marcus [Aurelius] the broad stripe [he was made senator]. … His youth was full of fury and wickedness, which were sometimes criminal in nature. He was charged with adultery, but he pleaded his own case and was acquitted by Didius Julianus, the Proconsul of Africa, and his immediate predecessor in proconsulship, his colleague in his consulship, and again preceded him as emperor. He omitted the office of the tribune of soldiers, and became *quaestor* and performed his duties diligently. After the term had ended, he was allotted the province of Baetica and from thence he went into Africa to settle his domestic affairs because his father had passed away. And while he was in Africa, he was assigned to Sardinia instead of Baetica because the Moors had laid waste the latter. Therefore he served as a *quaestor* of Sardinia, and was then appointed as an aide for the proconsul of Africa. [Severus thus bypassed the regular career pattern of serving as a military tribune. He became first *quaestor* at Rome and after he had completed his year, he was nominated as *proquaestor* of the senatorial province of Baetica, but was then transferred to Sardinia. The *quaestorship* gave Severus invaluable experience of logistics.] … While in Africa he consulted an astrologer … he told him of all the things which afterwards came to pass. [This piece of text comes undoubtedly from Severus's own biography. The intention would have been to convince the readers that it had been his destiny from birth to become an emperor. It had been written in the stars. Even if one cannot entirely preclude the possibility that Severus really consulted an astrologer and really believed horoscopes, it is still far more likely that the references to horoscopes and omens from his childhood and youth come only from the pen of Severus himself and his only purpose was to convince the audience that it was his divine right to rule.] By the favour of the Emperor Marcus [Aurelius], he was made a tribune of the people, the duties of which he performed with austerity and vigour. It was at that time that he married Marcia, of whom he says nothing himself in his autobiography. But after he became emperor, he erected statues in her honour. In the 32nd year of his life he was appointed as *praetor* by Marcus [Aurelius] … He was then sent to Spain [Hispania] and there he had a dream [I have left out the details, but this is just another piece of propaganda promising Severus the throne.] . . Even though he was not present in the city, he still gave games. Then he was given the command of the Legio IV Scythica placed near Massilia [all editors and translators of the text suggest that this must be a mistake because this legion was never stationed there but in Syria], and then went to Athens in part to continue his studies and in part to perform sacred rites and in part to see the public buildings and monuments of the city. But because he suffered some wrongs there from the Athenians, he became their enemy, and when he was emperor he took vengeance on them by reducing their privileges. After this he was appointed as legate of the province of Lugdunensis [in Gaul]. And having lost his wife and wishing to take another, he inquired what were the horoscopes of marriageable women, and as he heard that there was a lady in Syria (I mean Julia) whose horoscope predicted that she was to be married to a king [once again likely to be a purposeful story spread by Severus himself], he courted her through friends, and married her, by whom he was soon after made a father. His strictness, honour and self-restraint caused him to be much beloved by the Gauls as [any other] person never was. He was transferred from thence to govern Pannonia and after that he was allotted the proconsular province of Sicily. At Rome he received from his wife a second son. Being in Sicily he was accused of consulting the Chaldeans or astrologers about his imperial future for which he was ordered to be heard before the prefects of the guard, who acquitted him because Commodus was now beginning to be detested and crucified the person who had accused him. [If true, it is possible that underneath all the quite apparent cynicism present in the advertising of his divine destiny, Severus was still a superstitious man However, it is inherently more likely that the accusation was false because the accuser was crucified. In light of this, the accuser had probably sought to act as an informer by bringing forth a false charge so that he could obtain Severus's property as a reward. It is fairly unlikely that the prefects would have dared to let Severus go free in the paranoid atmosphere of Commodus's rule, if there were any grounds for the accusation.] Following this he was appointed as consul for the first time with Apuleius Rufinus by special appointment of Commodus. [This also speaks strongly against the veracity of the previous accusation.] After this he spent an entire year at Rome without employment, and then by the recommendation of Laetus, he was given the command of the army in Germany [this is a mistake and should be Pannonia]. When he came to Germany [Pannonia], Severus distinguished himself in this office in such a manner that increased his already illustrious reputation.' (Aelius Spartianus, *HA Sev*. 1.1ff., tr. by Bernard, p.227ff. with changes, additions, corrections and comments)

Several historians have tried to add flesh to the bones given by Aelius Spartianus, but regardless of this, most of what we know is entirely based on the above. Nevertheless, it is still clear that modern research has brought to light several important points. The first of these is that Severus rose to a position of dominance during a century when ever-larger numbers of Romans of African origins achieved important posts in the Roman administration and military. These men included Septimius Severus's relatives, and it was these and other Africans who opened up the doors for the career path of Septimius himself.[1]

Senatorial career path	L. Septimius Severus	P. Septimius Geta
Vigintivir	?	decemvir
Military service	? (HA: no tribunate)	tribunus of the legio II Augusta (ca. 174/176)
quaestor	quaestor designate for Baetica, transferred to Sardinia in 170/171	quaestor of Crete and Cyrenaica ca. 176/177
quaestorian duties	legate of the proconsul of Africa in 173/4	
aedile or tribune of the plebs	emperor's candidate as tribune of the plebs in 175/6 or 176/7	aedile of frumentum (cerm) in 177/8 and the curator of the city of Ancona
praetor	praetor (ca. 178) without imperial recommendation sent to Hispania Citerior with judicial duties	praetor hastarius, ca. 180
praetorian duties	legate of the legio IV Scythica in Syria (ca. 180/182) 182-185 disgraced propraetorian legate of Lugdunensis, ca. 185/188 proconsul of Sicily in 189/190	legate of I legio Italica ca 181/182 182-185 disgraced proconsul of Sicily ca. 185/186 propraetorian legate of Lusitania ca. 187/188
Consulate	consul suffectus in 190	consul suffectus ca. 191 consul ordinarius in 203
consular duties	propraetorian legate of Pannonia Superior in 191-193	propraetorian legate in Moesia Inferior ca. 192/193 propraetorian legate in Dacia in 195 (before and after)
Sacedoces		fetiales ca. 180

Above: A bust of Marcus Aurelius (Capitol). Source Duruy. Note the forked bear. It is possible that the busts of Severus that have forked beard date from the period after he fictitiously adopted himself into the family of Marcus Aurelius by claiming to be his son so that the busts that do not have the forked beard would belong to the period before that. However, there is also another possible reason for Severus to wear forked beard, which is that Serapis/Sarapis is sometimes depicted with a forked beard and Severus was a devotee of this god.
Below: A bust of Commodus, son of Marcus Aurelius (source Duruy)

The above diagram presents what we know of the careers of both Septimius Severus and his brother Geta, which is based on the diagram of Anne Daguet-Gagey (497).

As the above quoted passage has made clear, L. Septimius Severus was born into a powerful provincial family in the Tripolitanian city of Lepcis/Leptis Magna on 11 April, either in 145 or 146. His father was Geta, who never held any public office. His mother was Fulvia Pia. From the point of view of Roman aristocracy, his father was an obscure provincial, but men of his family had already attained the position of senator. He had mixed ancestry of Roman knights and local Punic nobility, and his native language was Punic. While his sister never learnt to speak Latin well, he learned both Latin and Greek as foreign languages, doing so well. However, he still spoke Latin with a thick African provincial accent, which caused some amusement among the cultured elites. It is usually assumed that Septimius Severus was the younger brother, on the basis that his *cognomen* was not the same as his father's and that his brother Geta died before him so is believed to have been the older brother, but this is not certain. For instance, it is clear that Septimius was appointed as *quaestor* considerably before his brother, which may imply that he was actually the older sibling.

2.2. Career

The first important appointment in Severus's career was as legate of Legio XVI Flavia in about 180/182. This was his first real military command and also provided him with experience of Rome's eastern provinces. According to Aelius Spartianus (*HA Sev.* 9.4), Severus's stay in the East was not entirely happy because when he was administering the area, the people of Antioch laughed at him. Spartianus fails to give the reason, but Severus's thick African accent would be the most likely. This caused resentment in Severus, which he later remembered when he had defeated Niger and his Antiochian supporters. According to the official version, Severus did not yet meet his future wife, Julia Domna, while he was in the East, but I would not preclude this possibility because he certainly visited the area – in my opinion it is quite likely that Severus did meet Julia then and that the two became lovers. The fact that none of the sources mention this is not evidence that it did not take place, because it is difficult to believe that Severus would have read horoscopes of all sorts of ladies from all corners of the Empire in an effort to find a wife when he then was governor of Lugdunensis, as the official version goes, spread by Septimius's claims. It is far likelier that the two met when Severus was in the same area as his future wife.

We do not know whether Severus was sacked from his post at the same time as his superior Pertinax was recalled or whether he administered the area in his absence until the next governor and his future ally, Domitius Dexter, arrived as new governor. What is known is that he fell from favour at the same time as Pertinax, because after his command of the legion ended, he went to Athens to study and see the sights. Septimius was always seeking to improve his education, so that was the natural course of action for him. He spent the next few years without employment until the Prefect of the Guard, Perennis, fell from favour. His fall opened up the career path once again for Severus. Cleander, the *cubicularius* and new favourite of Emperor Commodus, was corrupt to the bone and sold offices to the highest bidder. Pertinax and Severus were by now both back in favour. It can be assumed that the two men offered bribes for their next appointments, even if the sources do not specifically state this. Pertinax was duly made governor of Britain, while Severus was appointed governor of Gallia Lugdunensis in *ca*. 185/188.

As governor of Lugdunensis, Severus did not possess any large military forces – only the 500-strong Urban Cohort of Lugdunum and whatever forces had been detached to serve under him. According to the sources, Severus's first wife, Paccia Marciana, died very soon after his arrival in Gaul. Spartianus claims that he then sought out marriageable ladies with the right horoscope, choosing Julia Domna because she was predicted to marry a king. As I noted above, this sounds like a story concocted up later to prove Severus's right to rule,[2] and I would not preclude the possibility that Severus and Julia Domna had already met in Syria while he was a legate there and that she became his mistress. The reason why I suggest this is that if Bassianus (later given the name Caracalla) was really Julia Domna's son, his promotion to high office well before his brother would be easier to explain if the age difference was greater than in the official version. That official story could have been invented so that Bassianus was not thought to be born out of wedlock. I would not even preclude the possibility that the mother of Bassianus was actually Paccia Marciana, as claimed by Aelius Spartianus (*Caracallus* 10.1), and that she died while giving birth to him, Julia Domna then adopting him as her own son. Aelius Spartianus could have learnt of such a rumour from Marius Maximus, who was one of his sources and close to the Severan family. However, if we assume that Aelius Spartianus has preserved for us the correct version of how Severus asked Julia Domna to marry him, then Severus sent a letter with the help of Syrian merchants to Emesa, as suggested by Birley (pp.75–76), and she arrived in Gaul at the latest in the summer of 187; according to the official dating, Julia became pregnant immediately and Bassianus was born on 4 April 188 at Lugdunum. He was named after the *cognomen* of Julia's father, Bassianus (a good example of the fact that one cannot judge the order of siblings on the basis of *cognomen* alone), but we do not know what was his *praenomen*. In my opinion, it is far more likely that Septimius Severus and Julia Domna met while Severus was in Syria and that the later stories of horoscopes were invented to hide the fact that Severus had a long extramarital affair with Julia while his first wife was still alive, when Severus himself was known for his strict laws against adultery.

The governorship of Lugdunensis ended in 188 and Severus returned to Rome. His name was then drawn from the ballot and he became the governor of Sicily. At this time Julia was once again pregnant, and a second son was born early in 189, named Geta after Severus's father and brother. It was after this, in the spring or early summer of 189, that Severus journeyed to assume his position as governor of Sicily. It was also in 189 that Pertinax was appointed as Prefect of the City. In 190 there were a record total of twenty-five consuls, all of whom had been 'appointed' by Cleander. This may mean that Severus had once again given a bribe to Cleander. Disaster then followed for Severus when some of the most important men in Rome – Pertinax included – plotted to get rid of Cleander, which convinced Commodus to have Cleander killed on 19 April 190. This spelled trouble for Severus, one of those whose career Cleander had promoted. I would suggest that it is in light of this that we should see the accusation that Severus had consulted the seers or astrologers while in Sicily concerning the lifespan of Commodus. I further suggest that the informer had merely attempted to exploit the situation to his own

Severus's Career Before 193 63

Left: A bust of Julia Domna (source: Duruy)
Above: The imperial family: Septimius Severus, Julia Domna, Bassianus/Antoninus (Caracalla) and Geta. (Source: Duruy).

- Two statues of Julia Domna according to Duruy.
- Considering the fact that Septimius Severus erected several statues of his first wife Paccia Marciana, I wonder whether some of the statues or busts that have been identified as Julis Domna would actually represent Severus's first wife. The one on the right could be such because she does not have the same kind of hairdo as is usually used to identify Julia Domna or Plautilla. Although, it is also possible that some of the works of art that have been thought to represent Plautilla could actually represent Paccia.

benefit, but since the powerful men in Rome now included some who considered Severus as their man, it was the accuser who was crucified.

Aelius Spartianus's text makes it clear that the key figure of the last years of Commodus's reign, the Praetorian Prefect Laetus, favoured Septimius Severus. Laetus was also an African, and even the Christian Pope in Rome was from the same area. At this time Africans occupied several key positions in the Empire, and it is therefore not surprising that they promoted the career of Severus. The fact that Laetus supported the advancement of Severus suggests that at some point in the past Severus had managed to form a good working relationship with him. It was thanks to this that Severus – and presumably his brother too – obtained key military commands, Severus being appointed as governor of Pannonia Superior (with three legions) in 191 and Geta governor of Moesia Inferior (two legions) in 192.

We do not know the exact timing for the forming of the plot to kill Commodus by Laetus, the new *cubicularius* Eclectus and Commodus's mistress, Marcia, as the sources offer us two conflicting versions of events. The *Augustan Histories* claim that they hatched the plot together with Pertinax, with the implication that he was involved from the start, but this is contradicted by both Dio and Herodian, both of whom suggest that Pertinax was chosen as emperor only after the plotters had already killed Commodus. Evidence for the latter is tainted by the fact that Septimius Severus claimed to act as the avenger of Pertinax, which would have influenced all accounts which were written under the Severan dynasty. On the basis of the arguments put forth by Birley and Simon Elliott, I find the account of the *Augustan Histories* the more likely version.[3]

If the plot was formed early on, then it is clear that the conspirators probably coordinated their actions with Pertinax (who was subsequently chosen as Commodus's successor) and that they trusted Severus and his brother Geta, the pair being given command of five legions in areas which had easy access to Italy. If these conspirators had worked in the background to dismiss the accusations against Septimius regarding the consulting of the seer, then it is possible to think that Severus, despite his cynical use of predictions, horoscopes and omens to his own benefit, still believed in them. However, considering the cynicism of Severus, I would rather suggest that the accusation was false and that the accuser was primarily crucified because the conspirators wanted to promote their trusted man, Severus, to higher posts. Their backing of the careers of trusted men did not stop at Severus and Geta, as they also placed other Africans (or men who were trusted for some other reason) into key positions. These included the Africans Clodius Albinus, who was made governor of Britain, and Marius Maximus, who was given command of a legion serving under Geta.

If the conspiracy to kill Commodus was an ad hoc reaction to an imminent threat by Laetus, Eclectus and Marcia, then Septimius, Geta, Albinus and others had just been promoted to positions of power by Laetus only because of their personal connections with him. Their command of large numbers of soldiers thus had nothing to do with any long-term plan to assassinate the emperor. It is entirely plausible that Michael Sage is correct when he states that Laetus chose Septimius solely because they shared an African background, and that Septimius's lack of military background meant his appointment was considered a safe choice for an area close to Italy. Unfortunately, due to conflicting evidence in the sources, we just do not know what the truth is.[4]

However, when finally given such an important command, Septimius Severus proved a man up to the job. Spartianus's text suggests that he made the most of his appointment by distinguishing himself as an excellent commander. This proved to be of utmost importance when Commodus and Pertinax were then murdered. Severus was liked by the men who served under him and had also formed good relationships with other key figures in the Balkans and Germany. The appointment of his brother to command the Moesian forces further strengthened his position, but we should still remember that it was Severus who made himself popular with the soldiers when the time came to usurp power.

The plotters were finally ready to put into action their plan to assassinate Commodus on New Year's Day 193. The erratic behaviour of Commodus had by then assumed such proportions that there was deemed to be some urgency to do this. If the plot had been formed early, as suggested by Birley and Elliott, it is also probable that the conspirators had urged the deranged Commodus to continue with his erratic behaviour to blacken his name so that his murder would not appear so heinous. Yet if the plot was an ad hoc reaction to an imminent threat posed by Commodus, a version promoted by Sage, then the conspirators acted because they felt that their lives were in imminent danger. The New Year's Eve celebrations offered the plotters suitable circumstances for the murder, because the guards were thus careless of their duties. Marcia initially tried to poison Commodus, but the emperor vomited out the poison, whereupon the plotters sent the athlete Narcissus to strangle Commodus in his bath. This second attempt was successful.

Chapter 3

Pertinax, 1 January–28 March 193

3.1. The Beginning of the Reign of Pertinax

If the conspiracy to kill Commodus had been planned in advance, as claimed by the *Historia Augusta*, Laetus and Eclectus immediately informed their co-conspirator, Pertinax, that the deed had been accomplished. If, on the other hand, Dio and Herodian are correct, then the conspirators gathered together and discussed what to do next – their lives would have been in immediate danger because the Praetorians and populace had loved Commodus. In the latter version, in order to save themselves, the killers decided to offer the throne to Pertinax, who was initially apprehensive because it was possible that it was a trick to test his loyalty, so he sent his most trusted companion to see the corpse. After receiving confirmation of the fact, Pertinax went to the Praetorian Camp in secret. His sudden arrival initially caused agitation among the rank and file, but Laetus and his henchmen soon calmed them. Pertinax then made a speech in which he stated that Commodus had died a natural death (a necessary lie to calm the Praetorians) and that Laetus and Eclectus had suggested that he should take the power, also promising a donative of 12,000 sesterces to each man who supported him. However, as a result of his mediocre oratorial skills, he made a blunder towards the end of his speech, declaring that with the help of the Praetorians he would set right the current disturbing situation, which sounded like a threat rather than a reassurance. Consequently, the men hesitated, but when Laetus's henchmen finally shouted their acclamation, the rest followed.[1]

Pertinax then went to the House of the Senate, but as it was still dark the doors were closed. Pertinax ordered them to be opened, but the janitor could not be found. Consequently, Pertinax walked to the Temple of Concord and sat there waiting for the necessary arrangements to be made. While he was there, the veteran politician and military commander Claudius Pompeianus – brother-in-law of Commodus – came to meet him. As Birley and Simon Elliott have noted, the fact that Pompeianus had not been anywhere near Rome for ten years suggests that he had at least been forewarned to bring support for his former protégé Pertinax – whom he had taken on as an aide to help restore Pertinax's reputation after he fell from favour under Commodus – at the time of his elevation to power.[2] I would go so far as to suggest that if the conspiracy had been formed well in advance, then Pompeianus had been the brains behind the plot, the *eminence grise*. Pertinax is said to have offered Pompeianus the throne, which the latter refused. This must have been a mere gesture to impress outside observers.

When the Senate doors were opened and all consuls, magistrates and other senators were in attendance, Pertinax announced in a symbolic gesture of humility that the soldiers had chosen him as their emperor but that he was willing to resign due to advanced age and poor health. As expected, the senators acclaimed him unanimously. At the age of

66, Pertinax was now emperor. The senators then spilled out all their suppressed anger towards Commodus, wanting to drag his corpse through the streets with a hook. When Pertinax informed them that the former emperor had already been buried, there was uproar. The senators demanded that the corpse be dug up, his statues overthrown, his name erased from all public and private records and the names of the months that Commodus had changed be restored. Apart from digging up the body, all the rest of their motions appear to have been carried through. After the senators had been given time to vent their anger, Pertinax finally spoke again and expressed thanks to the Senate, in particular to Laetus. The consul Falco then foolishly interrupted him with an accusation that with these words, Pertinax had shown what kind of emperor he would be because behind him stood Laetus and Marcia. Pertinax upbraided him by noting that Falco was a young man who clearly did not understand the necessity of obedience until the right opportunity presented itself. After this, Pertinax was voted the customary titles and powers, and exceptionally also the title *pater patriae* (Father of his Country), which the previous emperors had only accepted after a suitable waiting period. However, he rejected the titles given to his wife and son.[3]

These events reveal the actual standing of Pertinax among the senators and their long-suppressed hatred towards Commodus and all he stood for. They show that Pertinax could put very little trust in their support, as the senators showed no real devotion towards him and were intensely hostile towards the men and women who had put him in power. However, the senators were not the principal threat to Pertinax's position and life.

3.2. Pertinax the Old Campaigner

When Pertinax finally entered the Imperial Palace, the tribune of the Praetorian Guard asked for the watchword. Without thinking, Pertinax answered '*militemus*' (let us be soldiers), which he had always used in all his commands. The already nervous Praetorians became even more so because they knew Pertinax's reputation as a military disciplinarian. On the following day, 2 January, Pertinax gave the same watchword. This was too much for the Praetorians, who had loved Commodus and were not keen to serve under an emperor who was known as a stickler for discipline. They feared the loss of their privileges acquired during the reign of Commodus. Consequently, the next day, when the annual oath of loyalty was to be taken, some of the Praetorians tried to stage a coup. They dragged, much against his will, a senator named Triarius Maternus into the Praetorian camp. Maternus managed to flee naked to the palace, where he told Pertinax what had happened. He was allowed to go unharmed and flee the city. It was only then that Pertinax realized that he had to alleviate the fears of the soldiers, and he ratified without delay all the concessions made by Commodus to the soldiers and veterans.[4] This episode reveals that most of the upper-class senators, including the new emperor, had been quite out of touch with the mood of the soldiers.

The governors were immediately informed of the change of emperor, but some of them initially suspected that it was a trick by Commodus, who had safeguarded his position by keeping as hostage the children of the governors. However, it did not take long for them to find out the truth, and all duly declared their loyalty to the new emperor. Having previously been appointed by Commodus himself, Pertinax kept all of those appointed by

Commodus in their posts. However, there were also vacancies to fill. Pertinax appointed his father-in-law, Sulpicianus, as his successor to the important post of the Prefect of the City. According to Birley, the only other recorded promotion was a favour to Septimius Severus, who had immediately ordered his legions – who stood the closest to Italy in readiness to interfere if necessary – to swear an oath to Pertinax. Birley says the man in question was probably the emperor's cousin Fulvius Plautianus, who had only recently been condemned for certain offences, but who now found himself in favour because he was related to Septimius. Birley has also ingeniously suggested that the likely position into which Plautianus was appointed was that of *praefectus vehiculorum* (Prefect of Vehicles), who was in charge of the imperial post. If a relative of his was placed in such a position, it would go some way to explain Septimius's later ability to react to the changes occurring in Rome with the speed that he did.[5]

Immediately upon receiving the reins of power, Pertinax began a series of reforms. He restored exiles, abolished trials for treason and restored the names of those unjustly executed. He also found the state coffers practically empty at a time when the Empire was in the midst of economic turmoil. The situation was made worse by his donative to the troops and gifts of money to the populace to secure their support. Consequently, the new emperor auctioned off Commodus's luxury possessions, including the imperial carriages, some of which had moving seats, mileometers and clocks, while others were said to be designed for the indulgence of Commodus's vices. Several youths, concubines, buffoons and other extraneous personnel were sold. According to the malevolent gossip of Julius Capitolinus (*HA Pert*. 7.8–9), some of these found their way back to attend to the ageing emperor's pleasures. In order to restore faith in the Roman currency, Pertinax also restored the silver content of the coinage to the standard of Vespasian, which had the unfortunate side-effect of there being even less money available to pay the troops. Pertinax also aimed to improve the economic basis of the Empire by making a number of agricultural reforms. Furthermore, in order to encourage commercial activity he lowered customs tariffs.[6]

These measures were steps in the right direction, but with his characteristic 'skill' to alienate his potential base of support, Pertinax tried to regulate the Senate. Commodus's old favourite Cleander had sold praetorships and had thereby upset the order of seniority, so Pertinax ordered that those who had held deserved praetorships should take precedence over those who had been adlected. Unsurprisingly, this move caused much disaffection among the people affected.[7]

In the field of foreign policy there was an immediate change, to the great satisfaction of Pompeianus and all those whose wishes had been pushed aside at the very beginning of Commodus's reign. Just before his murder, Commodus had handed over a subsidy in gold for a barbarian delegation from beyond the Danube. The new emperor immediately sent men to stop the delegates and demand the money back. In order to impress the barbarians, they were told that the famed general Pertinax was now ruler of Rome, the implication being that there would be a return to the policies of Marcus Aurelius.[8]

One of the responsibilities of a Roman emperor was to secure the corn supply of the capital so that the unruly plebs would stay calm. Pertinax visited Ostia in early March to see in person that everything was in order on that score, it having previously been his responsibility as city prefect. The enemies of Pertinax – or rather their manipulator,

Laetus (see below) – exploited his absence by staging another coup. The Praetorians acclaimed the consul Falco as emperor, but the attempt failed. Although the Senate declared Falco a public enemy, Pertinax pardoned him. Thereafter, once again showing his characteristic knack for saying the wrong thing at the wrong time, Pertinax managed to fire up the anger of the soldiers still further with a speech. In it he vented his feelings against the soldiers' lack of proper gratitude towards him, even though he had given them as much as Marcus Aurelius and Verus at their accession, which was not actually true. Pertinax was already known for his avarice and this only worsened the situation, since there were many Praetorians, soldiers and freedmen present in the *curia* (Senate house) when he spoke who could pass on his words to others.[9]

According to the *Historia Augusta*, Falco had been unaware that he was being declared an emperor by the Praetorians. So it appears possible that Laetus, together with Pertinax, had framed Falco in order to get rid of both him and their other enemies among the Praetorians. Unsurprisingly, Pertinax put his trusted man Laetus in charge of the purge, which was carried out in the name of the emperor. As noted above, Falco was spared, but many of Laetus's and Pertinax's opponents in the Praetorians were tried in show trials and then executed, which obviously further damaged Pertinax's standing among the Praetorians. Laetus's relationship with the emperor then suddenly turned sour, Pertinax apparently angered by the unwise advice given by the Praetorian Prefect. It is not entirely certain what was the cause of the rift between the men, but henceforth Laetus was no longer a supporter of Pertinax.[10]

3.3. The Assassination of Pertinax

On 28 March, Pertinax planned to visit the Athenaeum for a poetry recital but suddenly changed his mind, sending his escort back to the Praetorian camp where the rest of the Guard was staying. Simon Elliott suggests that Pertinax may have sensed that the Praetorians were up to something, which is why he sent them back to the camp. A disturbance then broke out in the camp. It is not known what caused the mutiny, but the two likeliest sources were that it was initially instigated by Laetus's henchmen but they could not control the troops, or alternatively that the Praetorians simply could no longer tolerate any of Pertinax's orders. The former seems to me the more likely. Whatever the cause, the disturbance was reported to Pertinax, who reacted by sending his father-in-law Sulpicianus to the camp to calm down the Praetorians and by summoning a special meeting of the Senate. Once again, Pertinax failed to understand what was afoot, not taking the disturbance seriously enough. As Pertinax was inspecting the Imperial Palace slaves in the portico, some 200 or 300 men with drawn swords marched there to kill him. The palace staff, who hated Pertinax, urged on the Guards. The emperor, informed by his wife of the approach of the Praetorians, sent Laetus to talk some sense into them, but Laetus merely went home in disguise – he did not want to be present when the murder that he had instigated took place. Dio writes that Pertinax could still have saved the day, or at least forced a standoff, by ordering the *vigiles* and *Equites Singularis Augusti* (who were in attendance) to kill the mutineers or by locking himself inside the palace, but instead he tried to overawe them by confronting them in person. At first this seemed to work and the men sheathed their swords, but then a Tungrian named Tausius[11] shouted,

'This sword the soldiers have sent you!' and struck the emperor. The rest followed his example. The only person who came to Pertinax's assistance was Eclectus, who managed to wound two of the attackers before himself being killed. Pertinax's head was cut off and stuck on a spear. He had ruled Rome for just eighty-seven days.[12]

The events described above are also interesting from the point of view of military tactics. Julius Capitolinus (*HA Pert.* 11.1ff.) states that the 300 men were formed in a wedge, but then calls the same array a *globus*. As discussed above, a *globus* should not be taken as a synonym for a wedge in this case, because a *globus* meant any independently operating unit in any formation (Vegetius 3.17, 3.19), which here was the 300-man unit in its entirety. However, there are two problems with this account: it was impossible to form a wedge with 300 men without some of them being left outside the formation, while the *Epitome* of Dio (74.2) claims that only the 200 boldest attacked the palace. These two discrepancies give us an opportunity to reconstruct the actual formation. The wedge could be formed by grouping 200 men together so that each successive rank had one more man until the twenty-fourth rank. However, the *Byzantine Interpolation of Aelian* (Dain ed. L) states that the infantry wedge could not have only a single man at the apex. If the array was formed according to this scheme, then the soldiers formed thirteen ranks and the last rank had twenty-seven men for a total of 195 men. The missing five men could in this case have consisted of supernumeraries, or the 200 men may just be interpreted as an approximation. It is unfortunate that we do not know if there was a difference in how the Romans and Macedonians formed their smaller wedge, such as is depicted here. This means that either around 200 or exactly 200 men out of the 300 formed the wedge, while the rest stayed behind. There are unfortunately two possiblities regarding the remaining 100 men. It is possible that these consisted of archers (a third of the footmen were trained as such) or other types of skirmishers (slingers, javelin throwers), or that they were equipped like the rest. In the former case, the light-armed (these would probably have been archers) would have supported the wedge with missiles by assuming

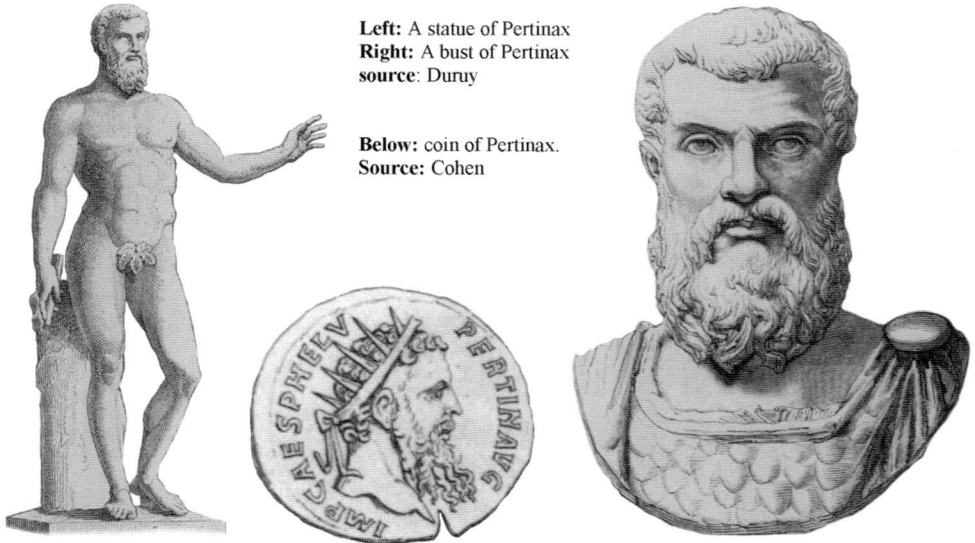

Left: A statue of Pertinax
Right: A bust of Pertinax
source: Duruy

Below: coin of Pertinax.
Source: Cohen

an irregular formation if there was a need. In the latter case, the men would have probably supported the wedge by assuming the close-order combat formation, which in this case would probably have been either four ranks deep and twenty-five files wide, or five ranks deep and twenty files wide, the former being likelier. It is also likely that three centurions accompanied the 300 men, even if this is not mentioned, and directed the action. This instance thus proves that the Romans used two different kinds of wedges: the grand tactical one in which it was formed by large units, and the smaller cohortal one in which there were 200 men with others behind the wedge.

Chapter 4

The Year 193: The Power Struggle between Didius Julianus, Niger, Septimius Severus and Albinus

4.1. The Empire auctioned off to the highest bidder, Didius Julianus, on 28 March 193

When the news of Pertinax's murder reached the ears of the city prefect, Sulpicianus, the father of Pertinax's wife, he at once sought to have himself declared emperor. He was a relative of the emperor, but in this case this fact worked heavily against his candidacy. The Praetorians would not accept anyone likely to seek vengeance, so two tribunes of the Guard went to seek a more suitable emperor. Waiting outside the Senate House, they found Didius Julianus and his son-in-law, Cornelius Repentius, who had come to a meeting called by the late Pertinax. The tribunes pressed Julianus to take the throne, but although he maintained that another man had already been chosen, the tribunes pushed aside his opposition and took him to the Praetorian camp. Sulpicianus's supporters, however, denied them access to the camp.[1]

Above: the Praetorian camp in the city of Rome. Source: Duruy.

The Power Struggle between Didius Julianus, Niger, Septimius Severus and Albinus

Above: A drawing of a relief depicting Praetorians at Louvre. Source: Duruy.
Below: A drawing of a scene in the Arch of Constantine the Great. This has been borrowed from a Trajanic relief, but can be considered to be roughly accurate also for the reigns of Constantine and Septimius Severus. It depicts Praetorian cavalry and infantry (shown by the scorpions in the helmets) in combat against the Dacians. Source: Bellori and Bartoli, 17th century.

Both candidates then began to bid for the throne. This lasted until Julianus climbed a wall from where he shouted that the Guards should not elect as their emperor a man who was likely to take vengeance on them for the murder of Pertinax. He also gave assurances in writing to them that he would restore the good name of Commodus. Sulpicianus answered by raising his offer to 20,000 sesterces per man for their support, but Julianus promised with a loud shout 5,000 more, holding up his fingers to indicate the amount. This won the Praetorians to his side, and the notorious auctioning off of the Empire ended with Julianus invited inside the camp. The soldiers then acclaimed him with the name of Commodus and lifted up their standards, which once again had portraits of Commodus on them.[2]

Julianus organized a meeting of the Senate to confirm him in office. The Praetorians formed up a phalanx, carrying their standards as if they were marching to combat while keeping the new emperor under the protective cover of their shields and spears. They escorted him in this manner first to the Senate and then to the palace. The aim was to cow the senators and populace into obedience through the sight of armed force. The Senate convened in the evening and was presented with a fait accompli. Julianus also informed the Senate that he had appointed two new Praetorian Prefects, which meant the end of Laetus's career. Unsurprisingly, the cowed senators confirmed Julianus in office.[3]

Because of his African connections, Julianus seems to have been confident that the provincial armies would also affirm him in office. However, he was mistaken in this belief, as there were strong forces opposing him who were already preparing the ground for his overthrow. According to Herodian, the key problem was that Julianus did not have the money he had promised to the soldiers, who voiced their dissatisfaction within a day of having nominated Julianus – the populace following their example. Julianus, unable to find enough money from the state coffers thanks to the spendthrift ways of Commodus, subsequently lowered the quality of the coins. The next day, 29 March, the mob was already voicing its hostility towards Julianus when he appeared in public, their shouts becoming ever louder at the Circus Maximus, where they shouted insults at Julianus while extolling the qualities of Pescennius Niger. It is probable that this open support for Niger had been instigated by Pescennius's supporters, friends and clients, who in turn must have been urged on to do so by members of the Praetorian corps who were annoyed by Julianus's failure to honour his promises. Julianus responded by promising the mob money, but this achieved nothing. He then ordered his men to stop the unrest with violence. As a result, the mob occupied the Circus Maximus, where they stayed the

A coin of Didius Julianus.
Source: Cohen

night and the following day. They then called on Pescennius Niger and the Syrian Army to come to their support, the ringleaders of the mob having revealed their true colours. The fact that the mob was allowed to leave unmolested means that many members of the Praetorians were silently supporting them.[4] Niger's henchmen had clearly known what was afoot and had acted swiftly to put forth their candidate for the throne. Niger must have been making preparations to usurp the throne even before the murder of Pertinax for his men to be at such readiness to act in the manner they did. The same seems to have been true of Septimius Severus, who also acted quickly to secure his claim to the throne.

4.2. Niger, Septimius Severus and Albinus Enter the Stage in April 193

When Niger, the governor of Syria, heard of the murder of Pertinax, the auctioning off of the throne and the reaction of the populace and their public support for him, he was elated. The speed with which the populace had reacted to the rise of Julianus means that Niger cannot have had any role in this, but as noted above, it is probable that he had already sent instructions to his supporters in Rome to work for the downfall of Pertinax. On the other hand, if he had not planned to usurp power against Pertinax, then his supporters in Rome had clearly reacted to the rise of Julianus without any instructions, so their actions actually forced Niger's hand. Whatever the truth, Niger reacted to the situation as one would expect, exploiting the pleas for help coming from Rome to gather the support of the Syrian legions and populace. These duly declared him emperor, Niger being well liked as a governor among both the people and the army. He was also amicable by nature and hailed from an illustrious family. When news of his declaration as emperor spread in Europe, Herodian claims that most areas of the Empire voiced their support for Niger. In addition to this, he received envoys from satraps and princes from the lands beyond the Euphrates and Tigris (including Oshroene and Adiabene), who congratulated him and promised their military support if needed. Niger thanked them, but said he did not need their help. An elated Niger believed he had already won, growing careless and spending the following weeks in festivals and spectacles at Antioch when he should have marched immediately to Illyria to secure the loyalty of the armies there, after which he should have marched on Rome.[5]

Septimius Severus would not make any such mistake. After having received the news of Pertinax's demise – quite probably at Carnuntum, the provincial capital of Upper Pannonia – Septimius first secured the support of his three legionary legates and their legions (I Adiutrix, X Gemina and XIV Gemina) for his claim to imperial power. In order to entertain any hopes of success, he also needed the support of the governors of Lower Pannonia (Legio II Adiutrix), Raetia (Legio III Italica) and Noricum (Legio II Italica). Lower Moesia with its two legions (I Italica and XI Claudia) was already secured by the fact that his brother Geta was its governor. Consequently, Septimius Severus first moved to secure the support of C. Valerius Pudens, governor of the neighbouring province of Lower Pannonia. This he seems to have obtained by promises, because Pudens was later rewarded for his support. Septimius seems to have gained the support of the other strategically placed governors as well, and he must also have sent envoys to the governors of Upper Moesia, Dacia and Upper and Lower Germania. Septimius knew that it was

A bust of Severus according to Duruy, but could actually be someone else.

A bust of Severus according to Duruy and Bernoulli. Wikipedia suggests Albinus, but I am inclined to agree with the earlier view.

A Bust of Niger according to Duruy

A bust of Albinus according to Duruy

inevitable that he, Niger and Albinus would fight a war to see who would become emperor after Julianus. He realized that it would be impossible to seduce Niger to become his ally because Niger had already been declared an emperor by the populace in Rome, but he could try to convince Albinus to remain neutral. Consequently, Septimius sent envoys to Albinus, the governor of Britain and commander of three legions and large numbers of auxiliaries, to secure his neutrality. Herodian implies that Severus dispatched envoys to Albinus only after he had reached the city of Rome, but the likelier course of events is that Severus had already sent feelers of alliance to Albinus at the beginning of his revolt; Herodian also notes that Severus read his letter and Albinus's answer to the Senate, and then gave orders for coins of Albinus to be struck and statues erected. There had to be enough time for this exchange of messages between the men for this to happen. According to Herodian, Severus convinced Albinus to accept the position of Caesar (successor) under him, with the excuse that he, Severus, was already an old man suffering from gout and that his sons were still very young. In short, Albinus was neutralized with mere words, promises and gestures. Dio rightly considers Septimius Severus as the shrewdest of the three contenders for the throne. At some point, Septimius also sent envoys to Novius Rufus, governor of Further Spain and legate of VII Gemina, and Naevius Quadratianus, legate of III Augusta in Numidia, to secure their backing, which he obtained in due course. The network of contacts created earlier proved their worth in this crisis. In addition, before acting, Septimius needed to ensure that his sons, who had been held as hostages in Rome, were brought to safety. Birley has suggested that this was done with the help of L. Fabius Cilo. Plautianus may also have played a role.[6]

After Severus had dispatched his envoys, the loyalty of the legions to the contenders for the throne and hence the strategic situation in 193, was as indicated below in a list based on that of Anne Daguet-Gagey (pp.462–64), to which I have added comments inside parentheses. She had based her list on the extant coins and other evidence which demonstrate the loyalty of the legion.

Septimius Severus

Legion	Province	Base
I Adiutrix	Pannonia Superior	Brigetio
I Italica	Moesia Inferior	Novae
I Minervia	Germania Inferior	Bonnae
II Adiutrix	Pannonia Inferior	Aquincum
II Italica	Noricum	Lauriacum
III Cyrenaica	Arabia	Bostra
III Italica	Raetia	Regina Castra
IV Flavia	Moesia Superior	Singidunum
V Macedonica	Dacia	Polaissa
VII Claudia	Moesia Superior	Viminacium
VIII Augusta	Germania Superior	Argentorate
X Gemina	Pannonia Superior	Vindobona
XI Claudia	Moesia Inferior	Durostonum
XIII Gemina	Dacia	Apulum
XIV Gemina	Pannonia Superior	Carnuntum
XXII Primigenia	Germania Superior	Mogontiacum
XXX Ulpia	Germania Inferior	Vetera Castra

Pescennius Niger

II Traiana	Egypt	Nicopolis
III Gallica	Syria	Raphnaea
IV Scythica	Syria	Zeugma (?)
VI Ferrata	Syria-Palestine	Caparcotna (Kfar Otman, Galilee, Israel)
X Fretensis	Syria-Palestine	Aelia Capitolina (Jerusalem)
XVI Flavia	Syria	Samosata

Governor of Cappadocia (on the basis of the route taken by Severus's forces in 193–194, I am of the opinion that these two legions were loyal to Niger)

XII Fulminata	Cappadocia	Melitene
XV Apollinaris	Cappadocia	Satala

Clodius Albinus (neutralized through promises)

II Augusta	Britain	Isca Silurum/Caerleon
VI Victrix	Britain	Eboracum/York
XX Valeria Victrix	Britain	Deva/Chester

L. Naevius Quadratianus (secured by Severus for himself)

III Augusta	Africa Proconsular	Lambaesis

L. Novius Rufus (secured by Severus for himself)

VII Gemina	Spain	Legio/Leon

On 9 April, when Septimius Severus heard that his family had been hidden safely away, he was finally ready to act. According to Dio, Severus had managed to win over to his side everywhere in Europe except Byzantium. He had the military backing he needed and his henchmen at Rome were ready to act as his fifth column inside the territory held by the enemy. The Legio XIV Gemina was summoned to give its support for Septimius and the troops duly saluted him as their emperor. Septimius declared himself as the avenger of Pertinax and added his name to his imperial name Imperator Caesar L. Septimius Severus Pertinax Augustus. One of Septimius's legions, I Adiutrix, had served under Pertinax twenty years before, and the six legions of the two Moesias and Dacia had likewise been commanded by Pertinax previously. It had been a good choice for Laetus and Pertinax to place these legions in the hands of their trusted men.[7]

Meanwhile, Julianus had tried in servile fashion to endear himself with the populace, the Senate and men of any importance. He banqueted, flattered, bribed and promised anything and everything to anyone, but his behaviour was so slavish that nobody trusted him. This was to have serious consequences. Julianus clearly did not make any real preparations to secure the loyalty of the legions in the provinces, which was a major mistake. His behaviour resembled that of Niger and Albinus, who were also very slow to act. In contrast to all these, Severus was a shrewd man of action.[8] The following quote from Herodian shows how Severus first gathered support for himself, then acted with

The Power Struggle between Didius Julianus, Niger, Septimius Severus and Albinus 79

great skill and speed to keep the initiative in his hands, revealing himself as a master of manipulation, stratagems and unconventional warfare:

The whole of Pannonia was commanded by Severus, a Libyan. He was a man of great abilities, good administrator, used to physical toil and suffering, ready to encounter any physical hardship, and quick to make decisions and equally vigorous in their execution ... his encouragement was the remembrance of several dreams ... Severus has published most of these in his autobiography and by his public images ... [It is quite possible that these dreams had indeed encouraged Severus to act on a subconscious level, but it is far likelier that the shrewd Severus had invented these dreams and omens to convince his followers of his own divine destiny. This was one of the standard ways of encouraging the soldiers in the Roman military tradition.[9] Furthermore, the fact that his elder son, Caracalla, went on to act in a similar manner, apparently in a massive deception operation,[10] strongly suggests the probability that Severus was using one of the standard stratagems expected from good commanders. Regardless, even if there are very strong reasons to believe that Severus cynically manipulated his soldiers and the population by publicizing these dreams, one cannot entirely preclude the possibility that he had really seen such and that these had encouraged him to take the course he had, as he himself claimed.] Severus thus raised into high hopes ... resolved to find the inclinations of the army. At first therefore he gained to his party the legionary commanders and prefects [*hegemons*],[11] tribunes [*chiliarchs*] and senior centurions ... to avenge the death of Pertinax, whose virtues still lived in the memory of the soldiers in Illyricum for under his command they had gained several great victories over the Germans during Marcus Aurelius's reign .... Therefore when he told them his motive was only to avenge the blood of Pertinax, they, without the least of reserve contended to declared Severus emperor .... [Severus listed many other reasons as well, including the treacherous behaviour of the Praetorians, but these I have left out to present the main claim. He manipulated his audience with great skill.] Having gained the Pannonians to his side, he dispatched messengers to the neighbouring Illyrian provinces and their governors, whom by great hopes and promises he soon bribed to his party. No man was better qualified at deception and giving assurances of goodwill than Severus. He had no respect for oath and lied and perjured himself if it secured him some advantage. Dissimulation was natural to him and his tongue was always ready to utter things contrary to the sentiments of his mind .... He then convened the soldiers together from all areas and assuming the name of Severus Pertinax ... addressed the soldiers .... [The giving of a speech was one of the standard ways used to gain the support of soldiers for something, which in this case was the usurpation and advance to Rome The speech extolled the soldiers and promised victory with rewards. Severus also noted that he had previously commanded one of the legions serving under Niger, which gave him expert knowledge of the situation.] As soon as Severus had done speaking, the soldiers expressed their zeal for his service with loud acclamations calling him Augustus and Severus. He judging it proper to admit no delay, ordered them to furnish themselves with only bare necessities and make ready for [a] march to Rome, and having distributed proper allowances in money and supplies, he set out on the journey. Every measure was used to accelerate the marching speed of the army. He took the shortest routes, made forced marches, never halting or remaining at any place longer than it was absolutely necessary for the soldiers to rest themselves. He himself bore an equal share of their labours. He slept in a common tent, carried and consumed the same food and drink as the soldiers … by these measures he gained the goodwill of the soldiers. [These were the standard ways in which the Roman commanders gained the goodwill of soldiers and were also subsequently copied by Severus's son, Caracalla. This also had the security function of making it very difficult for assassins to poison Severus's food and drink.] (Herodian 2.9.1ff., tr. by J. Hart (London, 1759), pp.87–94, with changes, corrections and comments)

The passage above demonstrates nicely how Severus manipulated the officers and soldiers with speeches that were designed to gain the support of the soldiers. He claimed to be avenging the wrongs that they and the Roman Empire had suffered, strengthening these claims with mention of divine support – as represented by the dreams he had seen – and promises of victory and rewards. According to Aelius Spartianus, the sum which was paid as a bribe to each soldier was exceptionally large. Severus was from the start aware of the importance of gaining the support of the soldiers with exceptionally large sums of money, while simultaneously cynically criticizing Julianus for his bribery of the Praetorians. Whittaker has noted that it is very possible that Severus only promised this money at this stage and did not yet pay it, so the soldiers expected to be rewarded once they got to Rome itself. Herodian has left out of the above discussion one important detail, which is included in Dio: that Severus surrounded himself with 600 chosen men (*equites singulares* or *pedites et equites singulares*) who protected him day and night. Severus took his personal safety very seriously, and it was largely thanks to this that he was able to survive the assassination attempts that followed.[12]

According to Aelius Spartianus, Julianus did not fear Albinus or Severus, but was wary of Niger, and therefore dispatched a *primus pilus* centurion with orders to kill Niger. This was a natural reaction on his part when the populace had shown its support for Niger, but not his other two rivals. Nevertheless, the attempt on the life of Niger failed miserably because he was well protected by his army. When Julianus then received the unexpected news of the revolt of Septimius Severus, he became troubled and convened a council of advisors to analyze what course of action to take, also gathering the Senate to gain its support. The council of advisors urged Julianus to block the passes of the Julian Alps and presumably also to send assassins against Septimius. Julianus did dispatch assassins, but failed to secure the passes, which was a grave mistake. The Illyrian army was quantitively and qualitatively superior to his own forces, and the defence of the passes would have greatly reduced those disadvantages. Instead, Julianus chose to tackle Severus in Rome, either attempting to convince him to abandon his usurpation or assassinating him. The Senate was used to declare Severus a public enemy, while the soldiers of Severus were given a period of grace after which they would be considered public enemies too if they did not desert him.[13]

At the instigation of Julianus, the Senate dispatched legates of consular rank to the soldiers with orders to convince them to abandon Severus. These legates included the elderly Vespronius Candidus, who had served in Dacia and whom the soldiers detested. His inclusion among the legates was a mistake of huge proportions, Julianus apparently mistakenly believing he possessed some influence over the men as a result of his previous command. At the same time, Julianus sent Valerius Catullinus as Severus's replacement, and the *centurio* Aquilius – a notorious assassin of senators and *duces* (generals) – with orders to kill Severus. In addition to this, Julianus dispatched Tullius Crispinus, the Praetorian Prefect, to take control of the fleet at Ravenna. Julianus also put to death Laetus and Marcia, the murderers of Commodus, fearing that they would side with Severus. Meanwhile, Julianus marched the Preatorians outside the city to train them and build field fortifications against the approaching enemy. The Praetorians, however, had grown lazy under Commodus, and many stopped at the fleshpots of the city and hired substitutes to perform their duties. Julianus also ordered the men of the Misenum fleet to train for combat, but according to Dio these men did not even know the drill. Julianus started to train elephants for fighting too, but these threw off both the combat towers and their drivers.

Severus was initially frightened by the appearance of the envoys sent by the Senate, but managed to bribe the legates to his side so that they actually addressed his soldiers on his behalf and deserted to his side. The fleet at Ravenna also went over to Severus, so Tullius Crispinus duly returned to Rome. Severus then divided his army so that it advanced along numerous routes, helping to facilitate supplies while also spreading terror more widely among the enemy. Septimius also dispatched special operatives disguised as civilians in advance to the city of Rome. His principal henchmen were Peducaeus Plautius Quintillus, son-in-law of Marcus Aurelius, and L. Fabius Cilo. According to Dio, Julianus attempted to kill Severus by sending a succession of assassins, but they all deserted to Severus.[14]

When news of the failure of all his moves was brought to Rome, a desperate Julianus suggested to the Senate that they, the Vestal Virgins and the priests should go out to meet the soldiers of Severus to convince them to switch sides Julianus's position was fast becoming hopeless, and the senator Quintillus – Severus's man, who was also an augur with consular rank – opposed him openly. Quintillus was supported by a number of other senators. An angered Julianus left the Senate building and sent an order to the Praetorians to march from their camp to either force the senators to obey or kill them. The Praetorians refused outright, indicating that Severus's covert operatives had already bribed some of their number. Humiliated, Julianus returned to the Senate with the suggestion that they divide the Empire between him and Severus. The Senate agreed to this, whereupon Julianus sent Tullius Crispinus to inform Severus of his offer to split the Empire.[15] At the same time, Julianus appointed Veturius Macrinus as a third Praetorian Prefect. This was either a conciliatory gesture or was intended to make Macrinus suspect in the eyes of Severus, who had already written to Macrinus to offer him an appointment as Praetorian Prefect. By this time, many special operatives of Severus disguised as civilians had already entered the city of Rome. When their presence became known to the populace, the mob panicked and openly started to support Severus in an act of self-preservation. At this, Julianus lost his wits completely, making human sacrifices of young boys with the help of magi, contrary to the Roman custom. This sign of desperation showed that Julianus was prepared to try anything to hold onto power and life.

When the news of the offer to divide the Empire was publicized, the populace and Severus both suspected that it was just a stratagem and that the real mission of Tullius Crispinus was to assassinate Severus. Consequently, Severus made a declaration that he considered Julianus an enemy, not a colleague, a popular move that was well received by the soldiers. In addition to this, Severus ordered his soldiers to kill Tullius Crispinus on sight, as he had been advised to do by Julius Laetus.[16] Consequently, when Severus's vanguard came across Crispinus, rather than listen to him they killed him and the senatorial decrees were ripped up. At about the same time, the soldiers of Umbria deserted to Severus. When the latest news was brought to Julianus, he appointed Flavius Juvenalis as successor to Crispinus and once again convened the Senate to ask their opinion, being powerless to do anything without their support. However, he still made one last desperate attempt to save the situation without their permission: he sent orders for Lollianus Titianus to arm the gladiators at Capua and asked the elderly and infirm Claudius Pompeianus, who was at his estates at Tarracina, to share the throne with him. Pompeianus refused, on the grounds that he was too old and his eyesight was poor.

In the meantime, Severus had sent secret messages to the military tribunes and centurions, offering them rewards if they persuaded the soldiers to obey him and killed the murderers of Pertinax. The leading figure among these was probably the new Praetorian Prefect, Flavius Juvenalis, who had been appointed by Julianus to replace Tullius Crispinus. Juvenalis was later Severus's nominee and a colleague of Plautianus, but may have been the sole prefect for a while, as implied by the inscription ILS 2428. He was amply rewarded for his treachery. By now Julianus had been deserted by all except Repentius, his son-in-law, and the Praetorian Prefect Genialis.[17] Julianus retreated to the Imperial Palace and begged to be allowed to abdicate in favour of Severus. Even his bodyguards abandoned Julianus. When this became known, the Senate was convened by the consuls, who included Consul Suffectus M. Silius Messala and Severus's supporters. The Senate voted that Julianus should be killed and a delegation be sent to Severus. An assassin was sent to the Palace to fulfil the wishes of the Senate and Severus, Julianus being killed while alone and begging for mercy.

In addition to this, with the help of disloyal messengers, Severus's soldiers and agents intercepted all letters that Niger had dispatched to the city of Rome. This meant that Niger was unable to attempt to influence opinions within the city. Severus also dispatched Plautianus to the city to capture Niger's children. The delegation of 100 senators met Severus at Interamna on the Via Flaminia, about 50 miles (80km) from Rome.[18] After this, Septimius Severus played out one of his trademark stratagems, which was later so well emulated by his son Caracalla. Herodian tells the story:

> 'When Severus was informed of the decision of the senate and the death of Julian, it raised his mind into greater hopes, and he used a stratagem to try to take the killers of Pertinax prisoner. In order to achieve this, he sent private letters to the tribunes [*chiliarchoi*] and centurions [*hekatontarchoi*] containing great promises if they would persuade the soldiers of Rome to obey his orders. In the meantime he sent a public order to the garrison that they were to march out of the camp unarmed [The camp actually contained both the Urban Cohorts and the Praetorians, with the implication that both were ordered out. This fact has not usually been noted.]

as they were accustomed to do when attending the emperor to a sacrifice or festival and take their oaths of allegiance to Severus and at the same time insinuating that they would be enrolled again as his bodyguards in return for this. The soldiers were credulous enough to believe him, especially as they were persuaded by their tribunes; and accordingly left their arms and came out of their camp dressed only in their ceremonial clothing with wreaths of laurels. When they came to the camp of Severus ... Severus ordered them to assemble .... Accordingly, he mounted the rostrum, but as they were gathering about him with loud acclamations. they were all at a given sign taken into custody. For Severus had ordered that while they were still standing and gazing at their new emperor, with their attention distracted, his soldiers should surround them as if they were enemies and without wounding or striking anyone, they should enclose them in a ring of shields and keep them in place by pointing their lances and spears that the fear of being wounded would prevent the few unarmed men from resisting those who had the advantage of arms and numbers. [This suggests that at this time the Roman footmen were trained to fight like hoplites in a phalanx.] When he had thus caught them, as it were in a net of arms and [made] them all prisoners, Severus addressed them ... "You see by this experience how much superior we are in wisdom, strength and number to you. We have taken you with ease and hold you as captives without the least of opposition. Your fate is in my power to do as I please because you stand before me as victims of my power .... You have murdered with your own hands that venerable old man, that beneficient prince, whose life it was your duty as his guards to have defended .... You have insolently sold by auction ... that glorious empire of the Roman people .... Nor had you either courage or honour enough to protect him whom you chose for your master, but have like shameless cowards deserted him. For such ... you deserve to die .... But I shall not imitate the example of your murderous hands by defiling my own with your blood .... I shall nevertheless spare your lives .... I hereby order my soldiers whose prisoners you are [to] strip you of your military rank and uniform and send you away empty-handed. And I here solemnly swear by the gods that if one of you shall ever after be found within a hundred miles from the city of Rome, he will be executed ...." The Illyrian soldiers seized them, took away their daggers, ... and having stripped them of belts, clothes and everything belonging to a soldier sent them off naked. All this they were obliged to take patiently, for what could they do, thus craftily circumvented, naked against armed, few against many? ... Severus had made use of another stratagem. For fearing that after they were stripped and cashiered, they might run back to their camp and take arms again; he dispatched some soldiers, whom he could trust, with secret orders to take the alternate routes and short-cuts, steal into their evacuated camp and seize their arms and by shutting up the gates hinder them from re-entering in case they should attempt it .... After this, Severus marched the rest of his army arrayed in order of battle to the city of Rome. [Dio 75.3 adds that Severus himself changed to civilian attire while his soldiers, both infantry and cavalry, remained fully armed.] As soon as he appeared, he struck terror and astonishment into all the Romans .... The people and the senate, with laurels in their hands, received him as the only man and first emperor that had achieved such enormous successes without bloodshed.'

(Herodian 2.13.1ff., tr. by Hart, pp.98–102, with some changes, corrections and comments)

Dio also recounts the same event:

'Before reaching Rome he [Severus] summoned those remaining Praetorians, surrounded them in a plain ... relieved them of their arms, took away their horses, and expelled them from Rome .... One man, as his horse refused to leave him, but kept following him and neighing, slew both the beast and himself. [This proves nicely that the Praetorian Guard also included cavalry.]' (Dio 75.1, tr. by Foster, p.327, with comments of author)

Septimius Severus's whole campaign against Didius Julianus was a true military masterpiece from start to finish. Severus manipulated the military leadership and soldiers with propaganda, omens and money, and acted as if he was the avenger of the wrongs they and the Roman Empire had suffered. He neutralized Albinus with cheap promises he did not intend to keep, and protected himself with a group of loyal soldiers so that it was impossible to assassinate him. He undermined his enemy's position with skilful

Left: Marcus Aurelius making sacrifices at the temple of Jupiter at Rome. Source: Duruy.
The scene would have been similar when Septimius Severus entered the city of Rome. He always visited the temple of Jupiter first before proceeding anywhere else.

Right: A statue of Albinus according to Visconti.

propaganda and special operations, bribed his enemies to change sides and fooled the Praetorians to surrender without a fight.

Severus set a superb example for his eldest son, Caracalla, to emulate, and indeed Caracalla became Septimius's greatest pupil, but with the significant difference that whereas Septimius was sometimes ready to let his enemies live – as he did in the case of the Praetorian Guard – Caracalla was not. However, at least in this case Septimius's actions were well justified, for if he had killed the Praetorians he would have alienated large numbers of Italians who were related to them or would entertain suspicions that Septimius might pose a threat to their lives too. Severus was able to gain much more goodwill for his cause by abstaining from bloodshed at this stage. The situation would change later, but it would not have been wise to do such a thing when Septimius needed the support of the Senate and the Italian people during his campaign against Niger. Albinus could have exploited this while Severus was away in the East.

However, it is clear that Severus entered the city of Rome as conqueror, making no attempt to hide it. The fact that his army entered the city fully armed made this obvious to everyone. Severus first went to the Capitol to make sacrifices at the Temple of Jupiter, followed by sacrifices at other temples, after which he proceeded to the palace on the Palatine Hill. His soldiers were billeted throughout the city, even in temples and at shrines, seizing whatever supplies they wanted without paying while threatening to destroy the city. This caused both resentment and fear. Next day, Severus, accompanied by soldiers and armed friends (*amici*), entered the Senate. It would be interesting to know who these *amici* mentioned in the *Historia Augusta* were. Were they just Severus's friends who had armed themselves, were they his private bodyguards (later called *Bucellarii*) or were they the bodyguard unit at the time known as the *Aulici* (later known as *Protectores* and then *scholae*)? Severus promised not to kill any senator without the Senate's approval, but as Dio noted, he failed to respect this in practice. Hypocritically, he also promised not to use informers or confiscate senatorial property, which he likewise failed to follow. Regardless, his speech convinced most of the senators, but apparently not all as according to Herodian there were senior senators who knew Severus's true character. These told others in secret that Severus was a master of lies and lying, and ready to use any deception to obtain his goals. While Severus was still inside the Senate, the soldiers outside threatened to mutiny if the Senate did not pay them 10,000 sesterces each (some 2,500 denarii = one year's pay), Augustus's soldiers having received a similar sum when he entered Rome over two centuries before. Severus was unable to calm the men with words and therefore gave them a large donative, but which was still only one-tenth of the demand (1,000 sesterces per man) according to Dio 46.46. It is uncertain whether the soldiers had received the donative that Severus had promised them at the beginning of his campaign. It was possibly because of this that they demanded it now, or maybe this was a new demand resulting from the precedent set by Augustus, as stated by the sources. The latter is, I believe, more likely. In my opinion, it is also possible that Severus merely used his soldiers with the demand so that he could wash his hands of the demand made to the senators. He could now claim that it was not him who demanded that the senators pay the donative but his soldiers – his hands were tied. I would suggest that this is the case. Severus was a crafty fellow who knew how to manipulate those with lesser brains. Unfortunately, it is impossible to know if this was the case because the sources

(Dio 46.46; *HA*, Sev. 7.6–7) represent the incident in such a way that the initiative came from the soldiers and it was only with difficulty that Severus had been able to pacify them. Whatever the truth, it would seem that the soldiers had by now obtained a healthy appetite for money, and they would present similar demands once the army began its next campaign.

Severus next staged a propaganda show in the form of a state funeral and deification for Pertinax, with full pomp, thereby fulfilling Severus's promise to his soldiers and officers. He had revenged the murder of their beloved commander and emperor Pertinax by dismissing the Praetorians, and it was now time to bury Pertinax with due honours. However, despite his promises to the Senate, he eliminated all the friends of Julianus.[19] In addition to this, Severus distributed money to the populace and put on shows to please them, and then reorganized the grain supply for the city in such a manner that there were no further shortages. Severus thus used a stick and carrot approach with the senators and populace. The presence of his soldiers frightened them, while the bribery and promises calmed their minds. He also rewarded his friends by removing their debts and gave his daughters (with sizeable dowries) in marriage to Probus and Aetius.[20]

The decision to sack and exile the entire Praetorian Guard, with the exception of those officers who had deserted to Severus's side, was of pivotal importance because he thereafter changed the composition and organization of the force and the way it was recruited. Prior to this, the Praetorian Guard had been the privilege of those from Italy, Spain, Macedonia and Noricum, but henceforth the membership of the Guard was to be open to all legions of the Empire, becoming a reward for those who had proven themselves in combat. However, thanks to the fact that Severus had access only to his Illyrian army, the new Praetorian Guard came to consist solely of men drawn from its ranks. The resulting vacancies in the Illyrian force were filled by recruiting a levy of Italians. According to Dio (75.2.3ff.), the change of the way in which the Guard was recruited ruined the youth of Italy, who now turned to banditry and gladiatorial fighting instead of service in the Roman Army. This has rightly been considered an exaggeration by many modern historians, largely because at the same time as Severus did this, he enlarged the size of the Urban Cohorts and *Vigiles*, which at this time were composed of Italians. Furthermore, the decisive change in policy had already been taken by Augustus when he decided to employ a professional army instead of a conscript one. One may add to this the fact that Severus was actually promoting service among the Italian youth by conducting a levy of them to fill up the vacancies in the existing legions and also to form the new Parthian legions (see next chapter). While Dio was certainly correct in stating that the dismissal of the Praetorians contributed to banditry in Italy, this resulted from the fact that the professional soldiers who had made up the Guard were now unemployed and knew no other profession than that of arms.[21] This was basically the only mistake that Severus made during this early part of his reign. It would have been wiser to re-enrol the Praetorians back into the other legions where their services could have been put to good use, just like Constantine the Great later did when he disbanded the Guard. Perhaps Constantine had learned from the mistake of Severus.

The new Praetorian Guard, which now consisted of veteran soldiers from the Danube frontier, was completely reorganized. Septimius Severus added a tenth cohort to it and doubled the size of the cohort so that there were now ten milliary Praetorian Cohorts

(*Praetoriani*), each consisting of 1,000 (i.e. 1,024) footmen for a total of 10,000 (10,240) men. Handy suggests there were actually as many as 16,000 Pretorians in Rome, the equivalent of three legions. These were commanded by the Praetorian Prefect, ten tribunes and sixty centurions. The size of the cavalry contingent is not know with certainty, with suggested figures ranging from 100 to 300 horsemen per cohort, or from about a quarter to a third of the size of the infantry force. In other words, the estimates vary from 1,000–3,000 or from 2,500–3,000 horsemen. One of the compromise estimates is that the cavalry consisted of ten *turmae* of cavalry (with 192 horsemen per *turma*) for a total of 1,920. The larger figure of 2,000–3,000 men is likelier on the grounds that the Parthian legions appear to have each had about 732 horsemen, which implies that Severus sought to increase the number of cavalry per legion. Juvenalis was rewarded with the position of Praetorian Prefect and it is possible that he was the sole prefect for a while, but it is still clear that for most of the reign of Severus, the Praetorians were commanded

Left: Siege *testudo* in the Column of Trajan. **Right:** Siege *testudo* in the Colum of Marcus Aurelius. Source: Montfaucon.

Note the difference in the way how the shield roof is formed in these two images. On the left the rear shields are placed on top of the front one (not shown clearly in this drawing) while on the right the rear shields are placed underneath the shields in front. When used in actual field battle the version in which the shields were placed on top of the front ones removed the freedom of using shields individually towards the front so that when one wanted to get out of the *testudo* array it had to start from the front. In other words, if the front ranker died or fell, the man directly behind him had to bring his shield down really fast. When the shields were placed underneath the shields in front of those, the men retained better control over their shields when the enemy appeared in front because it was not "tied" in place by the shield of the man in front of it.

Below: Coin of Septimius Severus advertising his connection with Pertinax and martial qualities. Source: Cohen.

by two prefects, one of whom was a legal expert (depending on the time, there were always between one and three prefects).[22]

When Severus replaced the Praetorians with his Illyrians, he consoled the Italians by tripling the size of the Urban Cohorts, increasing them from 500 to 1,500 men, so there were 4,500 present at Rome, plus the other units posted at strategic locations. It is also possible that he increased the size of the *Vigiles* at the same time, but this is uncertain.

In addition to this, there exists the problem of who were the *Aulici* or *Corporis in aula*, which are mentioned for the reign of Septimius. According to the *Historia Augusta* (Maximini 3.5), Maximinus Thrax served in the personal court bodyguards ('*Corporis in aula*') of Septimius Severus. Other likely names for this bodyguard unit are the *Ostensionales* (= *Armaturae?*), *Aulici*, *Protectores* and *Scholae* which are mentioned variously for the reigns of Caracalla, Alexander Severus, Maximinus, Balbinus, Gordian and Philip the Arab in different sources.[23] The fact that the *Scholae* are mentioned for the first time under Septimius makes it possible that it was organized by him and formed from the chosen 600 men (*equites singulares*) who protected and accompanied Septimius during the campaign. The presence of Maximinus, who was a native of the Balkans, makes this likely. However, one cannot be absolutely certain about this because there were Parthian and Moorish bodyguards in the court of Commodus, which may mean that the *Aulici* had been created by him or even before him.[24]

The fact that Herodian (3.13.4) claims that Severus quadrupled the size of the armed forces in the city of Rome (in addition to which he posted the Legio II Parthica at Albanum) can be taken to imply that the corps of *Aulici* could have consisted of as many as 10,000 men, which is not impossible, if one includes in this figure Commodus's former bodyguard units of Parthians and Moors and the new units recruited by Severus himself.

Chapter 5

The Civil War Between Septimius Severus and Niger in 193–194

5.1. The Setting of the Stage in 193–194

In the meanwhile, in the East, the lazy Niger had been taken completely by surprise by the speed of Septimius Severus's actions and the fact that Severus had already been hailed as emperor by the Senate. Severus now possessed a combined force consisting not only of the Illyrian army but also another land and naval armed force that posed the most serious risk to Niger's eastern possessions. The Praetorian fleets of Misenum and Ravenna gave Septimius Severus control of the seas, and it is possible that the fleets were already united under one prefect at this time. Niger sent letters to the governors of his various provinces with instructions to guard their coastline and ports. In addition, he dispatched letters to the kings of Parthia, Armenia and Hatra urging them to form an alliance with him. The Armenian king replied that he would remain neutral because he lacked adequate forces to defend himself against the victor of the civil war, but the other kings promised help. The ruler of Parthia ordered his satraps to muster their forces, while Barsenius, the king of Hatra, sent Niger archers (*toxotai summachoi*). It is possible that these archers were the unit later referred to as the *meros* (division, unit) of archers by Herodian, which together with the Moors were sent by Niger to crush rebel cities in 194. The rest of Niger's forces consisted of troops drawn from the garrisons of the East and of lower-class youths of the city of Antioch who volunteered to serve. Niger ordered the passes and heights of the Taurus Mountains to be defended with walls and fortifications to form a protective barricade for Syria, after which he dispatched an army to capture the city of Byzantium. The latter move had a double purpose: the capture of Byzantium would give Niger a beachhead in Europe, while it would also make it more difficult for the enemy to cross into Asia if the city was held by Niger's forces. According to Aelius Spartianus, Niger killed many distinguished men and gained control of Thrace, Macedonia and Greece while Severus was still on his way east.[1]

The sources fail to give us any details of how Niger dealt with the threat posed by the Legio III Cyrenaica and its commander, P. Aelius Severianus Maximus. We know that these troops sided with Severus because the legion received the title 'Severiana' for its loyalty and Maximus was reappointed as governor of Arabia by Severus, but unfortunately we do not know for certain when these troops declared their loyalty to Severus. It is possible that this took place only after Niger's defeat at Nicaea (see later).[2] If it took place now, it is not known for sure whether Niger left part or all of the VI Ferrata and X Fretensis legions behind to deal with these when he marched west, or if he took both formations with him in their entirety because he sorely needed professional soldiers. I consider the latter of these options the likeliest because this area was troubled by bandits immediately after the war. It is possible that Niger even armed the local Samaritans and/ or Jews, in the same manner as he did civilian volunteers further north, to fight on his behalf against III Cyrenaica and its auxiliaries.

The form of help given by the ruler of Parthia is difficult to assess because none of the sources specifically refer to the existence of Parthian units in Niger's army. The only possible candidate mentioned in the sources would be the *meros* of archers referred to by Herodian, but this could be explained to be the unit of archers sent by the king of Hatra. What we do know for certain is that Vologaesus IV of Parthia, the King of Kings, could not commit his royal army to support Niger because he faced a revolt, which has been noted by Birley on the basis of Msiha Zkha. It is possible that Vologaesus induced the Oshroeni and Adiabeni to revolt against the Romans.[3] If this is the case, we do not know when the revolt took place because at least initially Vologaesus gave his support to Niger. The probable change of heart could have come as a result of Niger's defeats at Hellespont, Cyzicus and Cius-Nicaea. However, on the basis of Dio's suggestion that the Oshroeni and Adiabeni claimed to have helped Severus by rebelling against Niger, it is also possible that they did this as soon as Niger had transferred his forces to the west and that they did this on their own accord, or that they and Vologaesus had planned to betray Niger from the start. It is impossible to be absolutely certain on this matter.[4]

However, it is very likely that Hamza (a native of Isfahan, died *ca*. 960) has preserved a muddled account of this same incident. According to Hamza, when Balash b. Khusraw (i.e. Vologaesus) was informed that the Romans intended to invade Persia, he wrote to the petty kings (the satraps of Roman sources) asking for their help. These minor monarchs sent both men and money, which were placed under the king of Hatra. The king of Hatra then made a surprise attack against the camp where the Romans were assembling, killed their king, plundered their camp and then returned to Iraq, where he gave Balash a fifth of the accumulated loot. Hamza has misplaced this event to take place simultaneously with the founding of Constantinople (probably a confusion resulting from the simultaneous siege of Byzantium by Severus), but the only time period that would fit this description that I know of is that under examination here.[5]

If Hamza's information refers to the events that unfolded in 193–194, then it is clear that there were Parthian forces (provided by their petty kings) present among those that the king of Hatra sent to Niger, and which the king of Hatra then used against the Romans once he had betrayed Niger. However, it is still possible that Vologaesus was able to deny direct responsibility if the minor kings in question did not consist of the Parthians 'proper'. Regardless, it is still clear that Severus and Romans would see this as direct aggression. The surprise assault against the Romans in their encampment must refer to some attack made against either Niger's forces or against one of Severus's generals who was sent against the Hatrans in 194 (see later). Considering the need to renew the attack in 195, it is possible that Severus's general was less than successful on the first occasion, but in light of the fact that the king of Hatra sued for peace in 194, this is still less likely than an attack against some commander of Niger. This is the alternative for which we actually have evidence. The Oshroeni, Adiabeni and Hatrans defeated Niger's forces and pillaged and occupied Roman-held territory in about 194.

After having secured Rome, the next thing in the order of business for Septimius Severus was how to deal with the threat posed by Niger. Almost immediately upon his arrival at Rome, Severus seized the families of Niger, Aemilianus and other governors of the provinces who had been retained as hostages in Rome by Commodus, which gave him leverage over all his enemies. The capture of the family of Niger, however, took a while to carry out because they were hidden. Fulvius Plautianus, a trusted friend of Septimius, was put in charge of finding the adult children. In addition to this, Severus dispatched legions to Africa to secure it against any possible advance by Niger through Egypt and Libya. This secured for the city of Rome adequate supplies of grain while Severus campaigned elsewhere. Severus also sent a legion under Fabius Cilo in advance to secure both Greece and Thrace. Cilo did as asked, securing Greece and then advancing into Thrace, but the conquest of Byzantium by Niger made these efforts futile and Niger inflicted a serious defeat on this force near to Perinthus, although the Severans managed to hold on to the city itself. As a result of this and the killing of many important men by Niger, Severus had both he and Aemilianus declared as public enemies by the Senate.[6]

While in Rome, Severus made preparations for the war against Niger, but could not leave the city before he had secured it against Albinus. This was aided by the raising of new soldiers in Italy. According to Herodian, the youth from the cities of Italy were enrolled into the levy and any forces that were still left in Illyricum were ordered to march through Thrace to meet Severus while he was en route to the East. Whittaker is undoubtedly correct in stating that the Illyrian troops in question would have been detachments serving under Marius Maximus from Moesia. Additionally, Severus fitted out a naval force of triremes from the Italian cities, into which he placed troops. Whittaker suggests that this force comprised the Praetorian fleets and the merchant ships of the cities, but on the basis of other information it is clear that the triremes also included warships that the Italian cities possessed as a tax requirement.[7]

It is possible or even probable, as suggested by Birley, that Septimius Severus also raised new legions for the campaign, which were later named the I, II and III Parthicae, just as his enemy Niger did in the East from local recruits. Birley says the reason for the naming of these new formations as Parthian legions was that Severus was campaigning to set Rome's eastern affairs in order. However, it is possible that these new Parthian legions were raised later for the actual Parthian campaign. Regardless, I am inclined to accept Birley's suggestion on the grounds that Herodian mentions the recruiting drive in Italy and because one of the known commanders of these legions, Caius Iulius Pacatianus, was appointed as governor of Oshroene in 195. We know on the basis of extant inscription that Pacatianus commanded one of the Parthian legions, which may have been the I Parthica as suggested by Daquet-Gagey.[8]

While the new recruits of these three legions consisted primarily of Italians, as suggested by Herodian's mention of a recruiting drive among them, it is likely that all three legions were also bolstered by men drawn from the Illyrian legions, who would have formed the front ranks and would also have trained the recruits. The levy of Italian youth would also have been used to replace those veterans from the Illyrian legions who had been transferred to serve in the new Praetorian Guard.

The creation of the Parthian legions may also have seen a reform of the way in which the legions were equipped and organized for combat. The reason for this conclusion is that the Parthian legions appear to have been organized in the manner described by Modestus and Vegetius, who both place an equestrian prefect in command of each new legion, while the *lanciarii* (really only a new name for the *antesignani*, who fought in front of the standard as skirmishers) are for the first time attested for the Parthian legions. The creation of the new legions is also described by Dio. The legionary organization in Modestus has been suspected to be a forgery based on Vegetius, but upon closer look it is possible that Modestus's treatise dates from the year 275 and that it is Vegetius who has misunderstood this text. The text of Modestus, with its phalanx of six ranks of fighters – the fifth-rank men using crossbows – makes a lot more sense than Vegetius's version, which has artillery pieces in the fifth rank. In my opinion, it is probable that Severus did indeed introduce these reforms into the Roman Army, so there were two different types of legions in existence after 194.

It was in the nineteenth century that Victor Duruy raised the prospect that Septimius Severus may have introduced new regulations into the Roman Army. However, he did not suggest what I am proposing here. Duruy suggested that Arrius Menander, a member of Severus's council, wrote four books titled *de Re militari*, having been encouraged to do so by Severus. The main reason for this suggestion is that according to Dio, it was common to speak of Severus's regulations for the army. Furthermore, these same regulations were also included in the so-called *Ulpianus Digest* lawbook and later in the *Digest* of the famous legal text *Corpus Iuris Civilis* of Emperor Justinian.[9] The *Digest* includes general rules and regulations for the soldiers, but I would suggest that Menander's military treatise included not only these but also instructions on how to organize the legions and conduct military campaigns, and that these later found their way into the texts of Modestus and Vegetius. I would further suggest that Menander was the ultimate source for both authors, but that both modified its contents.

Most sources shower praise on Septimius Severus for his great interest in learning and his extensive knowledge of philosophy, even if Dio (and some other sources) include a number of qualifications to that claim, presumably because he (Dio) was not ready to accept that Severus surpassed his own learning, just as he would not admit this in the case of Caracalla.[10] It is for this reason that I would suggest that Severus was intimately involved in the entire process of creating the new Parthian legions, from their organization and equipment to their new combat tactics that increased the importance of the missile component (the *pilum* and *lancea* were now the principal shafted weapons of the legion, not the *hasta*, and there were also additional archers) while thinning the depth of the heavy infantry combat formation. Severus was known as a reformer, and the reintroduction of the javelin as the infantry's principal shafted weapon seems to have been one of his changes. It is uncertain whether he got the idea from the legions serving in Pannonia or whether he came up with these ideas himself as a result of his learning, it being possible that the Pannonian legions had adapted to the local circumstances before he was appointed as their commander.

There is still one major problem with the reconstruction of this new tactical system, namely that the tent group (*contubernium*, *decanus*) traditionally consisted of eight heavy-armed fighting men who usually fought as a single file in combat, plus one green recruit and one servant for a total of ten men, whereas in the text of Modestus and Vegetius the file consists of only six men. The likeliest answer to this problem is that two files of four heavy-armed made up one *contubernium* and four files of two lightly-armed fighters made up another *contubernium* (see below).

5.2. The New Infantry Phalanx of Septimius Severus (after Modestus 12–14 and Vegetius 3.14–17)

The new phalanx consisted of six ranks, the first two ranks forming the so-called stone wall (*murus*) consisting of the heavily armed troops (*gravis armatura*). The first rank (*ordo*) were equipped with at least cataphract armour, helmets, *scuta* (*scutum* = large shield), *spathae* (*spatha* = long double-edged sword), *lanceae* (lance/javelin/spear) and *spiculi* (*spiculum* = *pilum*/heavy javelin). The second rank was equipped with cataphract armour and *spiculi* or *lancea*. Vegetius (3.14) states that in the second line were the cataphracted *sagittarii* (archers) and the best men armed with *spiculi* or *lanceae*. The soldiers of the wall were expected to be mature men who were confident and experienced, who stood like a stone wall that neither gave ground nor pursued the enemy, and fought with *pila*. It is probable that the instruction not to pursue was added after the battle of Lugdunum in 197. The third and fourth ranks consisted of light-armed soldiers (*levis armatura/ferentarii*). The third rank comprised mobile young *sagittarii* and good javeliners, which the ancients called *ferentarii*, while the fourth rank was formed out of mobile shield-bearers, young archers and those who were armed with javelins or lead-weighted darts. The third and fourth ranks fought by advancing in front of the battle array to provoke the enemy with javelins and arrows. They were presumably the *antesignani/lanciarii* which now appear to have been attached permanently to the legions as their auxiliaries. If the enemy forced them back, they retreated behind the first and second line, and if the enemy fled, they and the cavalry pursued them. The slingers of the fifth rank could join the third and fourth ranks in the above action. This rank consisted of the *ballistarii/balistarii*[11] (probably users of *manuballista* or *arcuballista*), *funditores* (slingers), *tragularii* (in this case probably users of the *tragula* javelin) and *fustibalatores* (staff-sling users). The fact that these men were not included among the so-called light-armed of ranks three and four means that they were considered to belong to the heavy-armed, which in this case were clearly equipped as missile forces, as their training allowed. The sixth rank was expected to consist of strong shield-bearing soldiers equipped with the full panoply of equipment. This last rank made the formation two-fronted, so it was possible to face enemies from the front and behind simultaneously.

The basic building blocks of the new Parthian legions of Septimius Severus were still the centuries and cohorts, but their strengths had been increased. Vegetius puts the strength of the cohort at 555 men, while Modestus has 560 men (including the centurions). If we divide these figures by five, we get the size of the century, which is 111

century

```
V 1 1 1 1 1 1 1 1 1 1 1 1 1 1 1 1 1 C
  2 2 2 2 2 2 2 2 2 2 2 2 2 2 2 2 2
  3 3 3 3 3 3 3 3 3 3 3 3 3 3 3 3 3
  4 4 4 4 4 4 4 4 4 4 4 4 4 4 4 4 4
  5 5 5 5 5 5 5 5 5 5 5 5 5 5 5 5 5
  6 6 6 6 6 6 6 6 6 6 6 6 6 6 6 6 6
                    O
```

men. These would have been organized so that 108 legionaries were deployed six deep in eighteen files, plus the *optio* (second-in-command), *vexillarius* (standard-bearer with *vexillum*, who could also be called the *signifer*, carrying a *signum*) and *centurio* for a total of 111 men. The accompanying diagram shows one of the possible ways these could be organized for combat, showing the soldiers (numbers 1–6 indicate ranks), *vexillarius* (V), *optio* (O) and *centurio* (C). The size of the century implies that both the heavy-armed and light-armed consisted of legionaries. It is probable that the heavy-armed and light-armed were housed in separate tents.

The cohort in its turn consisted of the above-mentioned centuries for a total 555 men with the NCOs, in addition to which were the *tubicen, cornicen, draconarius, vicarius* (second-in-command to the *tribunus*) and *tribunus* for a total of 560 men (Modestus's figure). My educated guess is that the *bucinatores* were not included in the regular cohortal structure because they were needed only on very special occasions. In addition to the above, there was also the milliary cohort, the first cohort, with 1,110 men plus the supernumeraries. The likely organizational structure of the new legionary cavalry

---

The Principal Roman Combat Formations according to Modestus in ca. 275

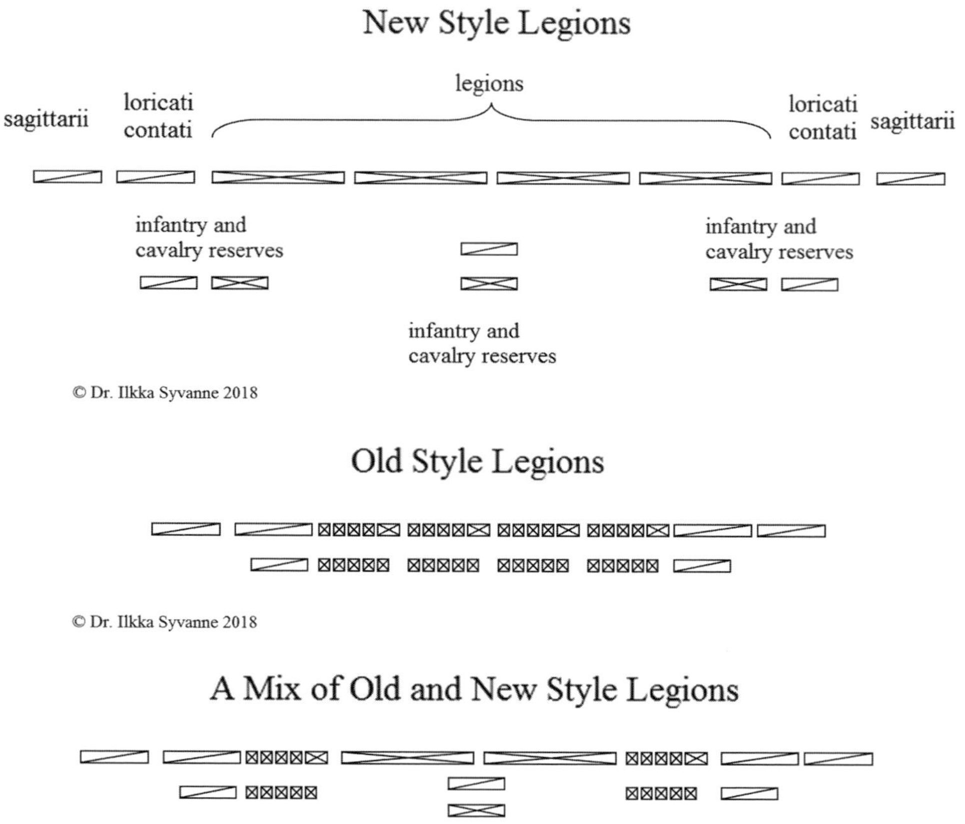

New Style Legions

sagittarii | loricati contati | legions | loricati contati | sagittarii

infantry and cavalry reserves

infantry and cavalry reserves

infantry and cavalry reserves

© Dr. Ilkka Syvanne 2018

Old Style Legions

© Dr. Ilkka Syvanne 2018

A Mix of Old and New Style Legions

was as follows: twenty-two *turmae* of cavalry for a total of 704 horsemen, plus twenty-two decurions, ten musicians, five standard-bearers and five centurions for a total of 746 men. The new legion therefore consisted of nine regular cohorts and one milliary cohort for a grand total of 6,100 footmen plus supernumeraries and 726 horsemen plus supernumeraries. Modestus and Vegetius both foresaw a battle array of four legions deployed side by side, with reserves consisting of infantry and cavalry placed in the middle and on the flanks. The heavy cataphracts were to be placed next to the infantry for its protection, with the medium and light cavalry somewhat wider to outflank the enemy.

One wonders whether it was actually Septimius Severus who created the Legio IV Parthica and not Diocletian in 300, as is usually claimed. The inclusion of this fourth similarly equipped and organized legion would have resulted in the ideal army described by both Modestus and Vegetius. My own tentative guess is that this is a distinct possibility. However, it is at least equally possible – or even likelier – that the IV Parthica was actually formed up under Alexander Severus. It is also possible that as a commander of Illyrian forces, Septimius Severus may already have organized his Illyrian legions in the same manner. At least that would make sense in a situation in which he placed his Illyrian army under Tiberius Claudius Candidus,[1] with the Illyrians used as the core around which new units were formed. The diagrams opposite also include the mixed formation that could result from the inclusion of old-style legions, such as were described by Modestus and Vegetius, side by side with the new type of legions.

Modestus (2.1–2) and Vegetius (1.26) both give us the same description of how the *tirones* (recruits) were to be trained for combat, with the implication that this was also the standard way for the Parthian legions. They were trained to fight in a single line (*simplex acies*), double line (*duplex acies*), hollow square/oblong (*acies quadratum*) and triangle or wedge (*triangulum/cuneus*). The implication is that the standard battle arrays envisaged by Modestus for the third-century Roman armies were the single phalanx, double phalanx and hollow square/oblong formations, while the standard way to break through the enemy line was the infantry wedge. The same would have been true for the second century as well.

Modestus (20) and Vegetius (3.17) both stated that the *dux* was to post chosen infantry and cavalry with extra officers (*vicarii, comites* and *tribuni*) behind the *acies* on the wings and in the centre to act as reserves. In this they follow the standard Roman combat doctrine. However, Vegetius gives a much fuller discussion of the tactical formations and unit tactics, which must also have been part of the training for the new Parthian legions, even if Modestus fails to mention these. The unit tactics in Vegetius include the *cuneus* (wedge) to break through the enemy line and the *forfex* (pincer) which was used to counter this. Both of these arrays were formed by using the reserves posted behind. There was also the *serra* (saw) array, a formation in which units advanced and retreated in a saw-like motion to disorder the enemy. The *globus/drungus* (globe/throng) was an independently operating unit, which could be countered with another *globus*, while the *orbis* was a defensive array in which the men on the edges faced in all directions. The seven different battle formations of Vegetius (3.19–20) consisted of the following: lateral phalanx/rectangle; right oblique, left oblique, forward angled array, forward angled array with light infantry posted in front, right wing sent in advance to outflank while the phalanx was lengthened, and the use of the terrain. It is more than likely that these continued to be used, as the Romans had employed them since the days of the Second Punic War.

The diagram of the ranks, which has been adapted from my earlier works, indicates the probable unit organization of the new Parthian legions. This version is based on the one which is included in Gallienus and shows how these legions would have been organized if they followed the structures present in Modestus and Vegetius. It was also based on the legionary and phalangial standard organization, with the division of the units into groups of four ranks of men so that eight men plus two extra men (recruit and servant) made up a tent group (*contubernium*) commanded by a *decanus* (the comparable phalangial organization in number of men was: 4, 8, 16, 32, 64, 128, 256, 512, 1,024, 2,048, 4,096, 8,191, 16,384). The only possible difference is that Severus's Parthian legions appear to have posted some of their recruits (the young soldiers of the fifth rank) in the combat array proper, rather than being left behind in the camp or among the baggage train as they usually were.

The Ancient Legion of Vegetius (*Epit.* 2.6ff.) and Modestus, with additional comments in brackets

- one *praefectus legionis* formerly *legatus*; commander of the legion.
- one *tribunus maior*; appointed by the emperor, in charge of one cohort (probably the 1st; second-in-command of the legion).
- one *Praefectus Castrorum* (camp, medics, siege equipment etc.).
- one *Praefectus Fabrorum* (workmen, construction etc.).
- *tribuni minores* from the ranks (six tribunes (?) put in charge of the cohorts and cavalry alongside the *praepositi*).
- five centurions of the 1st Cohort (Vegetius's list differs from the other known lists of officers and is also 100 men short of the 1,100 men he gives for the 1st Cohort).
  primus pilus, in charge of four centuries/400 men (this probably means that there were 440 men, which consisted of four centuries each with 110 men).
  primus hastatus, 'now called *ducenarius*' in charge of two centuries/200 men (probably 220 men).
  princeps, one-and-a-half centuries/150 men (probably 165 men).
  secundus hastatus, one-and-a-half centuries/150 men (probably 165 men).
  triarius prior, 100 men (probably 110 men).
- five centurions for the cavalry.
- forty-five centurions of the 2nd–10th Cohorts each in charge of 110 men, 'now' called *centenarii*.
- 1st Cohort: 1,105 footmen (this probably means that there were 720 heavy infantry deployed four deep and 360 light infantry deployed two deep + ten *optiones*, ten standard-bearers and five centurions).
  132 horsemen (128 horsemen and four decurions; in addition to which came one centurion, two musicians and one standard-bearer; when trained to do so, the 128 horsemen could form up a rhombus so that at each apex stood one decurion).
- 2nd–10th Cohorts: nine units of 555 footmen (this probably means that there were 360 heavy infantry deployed four deep and 180 light infantry deployed two deep, plus five optiones, five standard-bearers and five centurions).

- Nine units of sixty-six horsemen (sixty-four horsemen and two decurions; the sixty-four horsemen; the sixty-four men could be formed either as a wedge or two rank-and-file oblongs).
- artillerymen (fifty-five *carroballistae*, each with eleven men and ten *onagri* per legion), 'squires', servants and various kinds of standard-bearers and musicians and other specialists like clerks, medics, wood-workers, masons, carpenters, blacksmiths, painters, siege-equipment builders, armourers etc. (*aquiliferi, imaginarii/imaginiferi, signiferi/draconarii, tesserarii, optiones, metatores, librarii, tubicines, cornicines, buccinatores, mensores, lignarios, structores, ferrarios, carpentarios, pictores* etc.).
- My above hypothesis regarding the organization behind Vegetius's figures suggests that a possible overall fighting strength of Vegetius's legion may have been: 4,400 heavy infantry; 1,100 light infantry; 726 cavalry; at least 660 artillerymen with fifty-five *carroballistae* and ten *onagri*; at least 550 recruits left to defend the marching camp, together with the servants and workmen. The extra men on top of the older paper strengths may actually represent the recruits not normally included in armed strengths, but one cannot be entirely sure of that. It is possible that the recruits also accompanied the legion to combat, Dio's reference to 550 men suggesting this. The obvious problem with Vegetius's information and my reconstruction based on it is that we have practically no evidence to corroborate it, but at least if one presents it in this manner it does make sense and is therefore plausible. Vegetius notes that the legion could also include several milliary cohorts, which probably refers to the Praetorians, which had milliary cohorts after Septimius's reign, or it may refer to the practice of Vegetius's own day to group together different units to form 'temporary legions' that were later called *mere* (sing. *meros*/division) by the Eastern Romans.

Tombstone of Flavius Trypho, tesserarius, *legio II Parthica*, Apamea, (ca. AD 215-218 according to Cowan)

Lucius Septimius Viator, *lanciarius* of Legio II Parthica

5.3. Septimius Severus's Campaign Plans

Severus's plan for the campaign against Niger appears to have consisted of a three-pronged attack: 1) an advance guard consisting of the forces garrisoned in the Moesias, which advanced under *dux exercitus Mysiaci* (=Moesiaci) Marius Maximus[13] against the city of Byzantium; 2) the main land forces under Septimius Severus, which consisted of the Pannonian/Illyrian army and the reinforcements and detachments drawn by Severus from other sources, which advanced on land via Aquileia to the Balkans to join forces with Maximus; 3) a combined force consisting of the Praetorian fleets, civilian triremes and merchant ships, which transported an army to the Hellespont. It is possible that a significant number of men from the army that had accompanied Severus to Rome were now embarked on these ships because it is very likely that they served under Tiberius Claudius Candidus, who held the title *dux exercitus Illyrici expeditione Asiana*. However, it is equally likely that Candidus accompanied Severus and was only dispatched to Asia after Severus had already reached the coast of the Propontis (Sea of Marmara, between the Black Sea and the Aegean). It is also quite possible or even probable that the Praetorian fleets were now united under a single prefect; we know that Cnaeus Marcius Rustius Rufinus served in this capacity at some point under Severus, but it is not certain whether he held that title in 193–194.[14]

Severus needed money to bribe his supporters and finance his campaigns: the soldiers needed their donatives, salaries, equipment and supplies. Anne Daguet-Cagey, who has analyzed the situation facing Severus in some detail, has noted that the state coffers were empty after the reign of Commodus, and that it is improbable that Severus could obtain enough money from the confiscation of property from Niger's supporters. Confiscations of the property of the supporters of Julianus did not change the situation. Under normal circumstances, the emperor could order the rich and the cities in the conflict zones to pay extraordinary taxes, but this option was not yet available to Severus because he was a usurper who could not alienate the mighty and powerful and the inhabitants of the provinces when he still needed to fight against Niger and Albinus. This left him with just one option, which was the devaluation of money by lowering the silver content. The official exchange rate was as follows:

1 aureus (gold coin) = 25 denarii = 100 sesterces = 200 dupondii = 400 as
1 denarius (silver coin) = 4 sesterces = 8 dupontii = 16 as

Septimius Severus was not the first emperor to do this. Nero had lowered the silver content to 93 per cent, Trajan had lowered it to 89 per cent and Commodus had devalued the content twice so that it was only 20 per cent in 190. Pertinax had improved the quality, but Severus did not hesitate to order a further devaluation when the situation demanded it. Despite claiming to be the successor of Pertinax, he lowered the silver content of the denarius to 50 per cent. Daquet-Gagey notes that Severus's monetary reform, which he did in two stages at the beginning of 194 and the summer of 195, signified a turning point in the history of the Roman denarius. Thereafter, the silver content would be lowered by a succession of emperors to finance their policies. This was a wise policy move, as by doing so Severus was able to finance his wars and keep his soldiers happy while not angering the rich and mighty too much. Furthermore, Severus did not debase the gold coins. The soldiers received their donatives in gold and Severus increased the number of donatives. This means that in practice, Severus raised the soldiers' salaries in two different ways. The policy of lowering the silver standard of coins was also followed by Niger to finance his clash with Severus. Both emperors desperately needed money to finance their ambitions.[15]

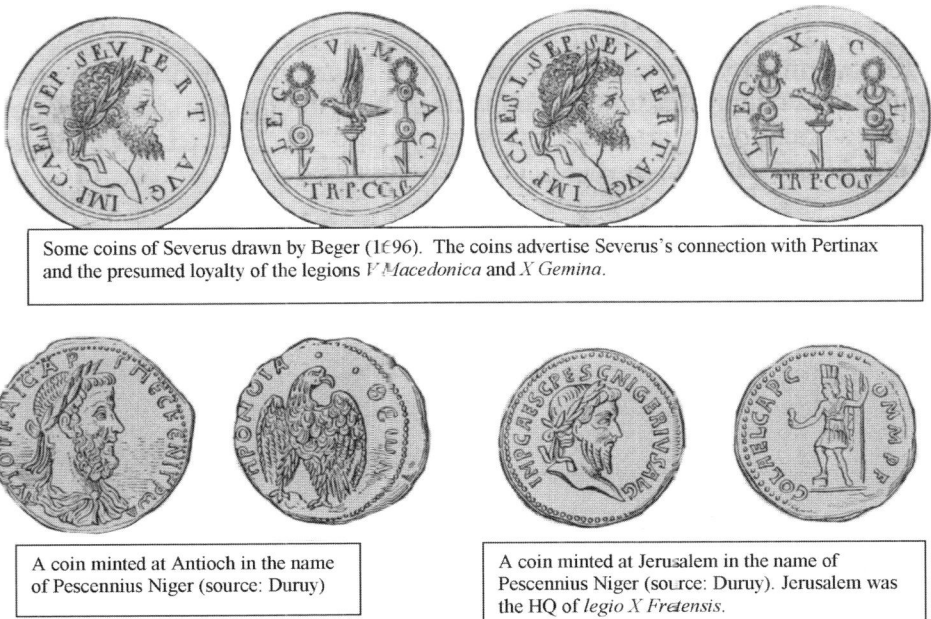

Some coins of Severus drawn by Beger (1696). The coins advertise Severus's connection with Pertinax and the presumed loyalty of the legions *V Macedonica* and *X Gemina*.

A coin minted at Antioch in the name of Pescennius Niger (source: Duruy)

A coin minted at Jerusalem in the name of Pescennius Niger (source: Duruy). Jerusalem was the HQ of *legio X Fretensis*.

Coins of Niger claiming that he was invincible and eternal ruler. Source Duruy

Severus set out from the city of Rome within thirty days of his arrival. Having nominated Domitius Dexter as *praefectus urbi* to secure the capital, he left Rome by the Via Flaminia. He also left ex-centurion Aquilius Felix in control of three important bureaus in Rome: public works, imperial property (*patrimonium*) and the private property of the Antonine family (*ratio privata*). Such control gave his henchmen the ability to bribe their supporters so that they could retain their loyalty in the absence of Severus from the city. Severus also nominated new men for the Senate to make its composition more favourable to his party. However, Severus's campaign ran into trouble soon after leaving Rome, his army mutinying at Saxa Rubra just north of the city. The reason for the revolt was the location chosen for the camp. The *Historia Augusta* fails to explain how Severus pacified the soldiers, but Birley is surely correct in suggesting that it was possibly with a distribution of new coins struck in the legions' honour. The man in charge of the war chest (*arca expeditionalis*) and supplies of the city expedition (*expeditio urbica*) was Rossius Vitulus, which suggests, as stated by Birley, that Severus continued to bribe his men with money. I would suggest that the soldiers simply wanted to be bribed with a new donative because they had now begun a new campaign.[16]

At some point during his eastward march, Septimius met his brother Geta. Aelius Spartianus (*HA Sev.* 8.10) fails to state where, but Birley's suggestion that the meeting took place soon after Severus reached Naissus is probably as close to the truth as we can get. Spartianus says that Severus merely ordered Geta to continue to rule the province which he had been assigned, even though Geta had other hopes. We do not know what these hopes were, but we do know that he desired something more grand, the likely source for this being Geta's subordinate Marius Maximus, who was used as a source by Spartianus. It was either then or before that Marius Maximus was dispatched with the Moesian legions against the city of Byzantium, while Severus followed in his tracks. Severus brought with him the children of Niger as hostages. When Marius Maximus put the city of Byzantium under siege, Niger suggested that he and Severus divide the Empire, but Severus reacted to this with scorn. Severus, for his part, promised to pardon Niger if he went into exile, but he steadfastly refused to pardon Aemilianus.[17] On the basis of the latter, it is possible that this exchange of messages took place after Severus's admirals had already defeated Aemilianus at the Hellespont.

5.4. The Battles of Hellespont and Cyzicus in the Autumn of 193

The sequence of events leading to the decisive Battle of Cius and Nicaea in the autumn of 193 is confusing, largely due to the fact that the sources fail to describe the campaign in detail. I have included below quotes of the relevant sections from the sources to give readers a sense of this problem and explain why I have adopted the interpretation I have:

> 'Niger also sent an army to seize Byzantium, the greatest and most prosperous city of all Thrace, exceedingly populous and wealthy. For being a maritime port situated on the narrowest straits of the Propontis it raises considerable revenue from its duties and fishery …. Niger … hoped by being a master of Byzantium he might cut off the passage of the enemy over these straits from Europe into Asia. The city was fortified with high and strong walls, built with Milesian stones so exactly squared and closely cemented that the joints were not visible but the whole wall looked like one continuous stone …. Severus advanced with all possible speed with his army …. When he received the news that Byzantium had been occupied, as he knew it to be a strong fortress, he ordered his army to cross to Cyzicus …. Aemilianus … being informed of the movement of Severus's army towards Cyzicus also marched there at the head of those he had levied locally and reinforcements sent by Niger. [Note the levying of locals. It is because of this that we should accept the larger figures given by the sources. The Roman armies of the civil war did not consist only of regulars.] When the two armies met, several sharp and bloody battles were fought in those parts which ended in favour of Severus's army. Niger's soldiers were repulsed with great slaughter and this defeat dampened the spirits of the eastern forces and animated those of the Illyrians. Some report that Aemilian betrayed his charge …. Some claim that he was jealous of Niger …. Others assert that he was prevailed upon by the entreaties of his sons, who had written to him, beseeching him to have regard to their safety [Severus was using them as hostages].
> … After this signal defeat at Cyzicus, Niger's forces were dispersed … some fled

to the foothills of Armenia [I take this to mean that there were men drawn from the legions of Cappadocia in this force], others to Galatia and Asia striving to cross the Taurus Mountains .... Severus's army marched through the territory of Cyzicus into the adjacent province of Bithynia. The news of his victory caused an outbreak of discord and factional politics in the cities of all the eastern provinces .... In Bithynia then the inhabitants of Nicomedia ... revolted to Severus and sent ambassadors to him that they were ready to receive his army .... The people of Nicaea, on the one hand, out of enmity to the Nicomedians, declared for Niger, and received his forces as well as those who fled thither from Cyzicus as well as the garrison that Niger sent for Bithynia.' (Herodian 3.1.5–2.9, tr. by J. Hart, London, 1759, pp.109–12, with changes, corrections and comments)

'Aemilianus therefore being beaten soon after at the Hellespont by the *duces* of Severus [this is clearly the first battle between the forces, which is also clearly a naval battle], fled first to Cyzicus [on the basis of Herodian, there were also land battles near Cyzicus], and then to another city, in which he was killed. The troops of Niger were also routed by the same *duces* [this refers to the Battle of Cius and Nicaea]. When Severus received the news of this, he sent letters to the Senate as though the work was done. He next fought in person with Niger [this is a mistake because Severus used generals to defeat Niger], and killed him near the city of Cyzicus [this is another mistake because it was Aemilianus who was killed there], and ordered his head to be paraded on a *pilum*. Niger's children, whom he had hitherto received with the same kindness as his own, and their mother, he exiled. [The following passage makes it clear that Niger's children and wife were exiled only after Niger had been killed near Antioch and not after the Battle of Cyzicus. The wife, children and Niger's entire family were later killed after news of the revolt of Albinus arrived. For this, see *HA Pes. Nig.* 6.1. *Sev.* 10.1.] Immediately he gave the Senate by letter an account of his victory; with the exception of one man he killed no senators who had sided with Niger. He was angry with the city of Antioch because they had both mocked his administration of things in the east and had furnished Niger with supplies, so he deprived them of many of their privileges. (Aelius Spartianus, *HA Sev.* 8.15ff., tr. by Bernard, p.238, with changes, corrections and comments)

'Now Severus made a campaign against Niger. The latter was an Italian, one of the knights, remarkable for nothing either very good or very bad. .. He had as lieutenant general [*hypostrategos*] together with others Aemilianus, who by remaining neutral ... [because] he was a relative of Albinus. [Herodian 3.2.3 includes two other alternatives for the lacklustre performance of Aemilianus. According to some sources, Aemilianus betrayed Niger because he was jealous of his rise, while other sources claimed that Aemilianus betrayed Niger because Severus was using his children as hostages.] Niger was not a man of great intellect .. [and] at this time he was more elated than ever ... that he showed how much he liked those who called him the new Alexander .... When the war broke out Niger had gone to Byzantium and from that point conducted a campaign against Perinthus. He was disturbed, however, by unfavourable omens ... for these reasons he retired to Byzantium. [The actual reason appears to have been the imminent arrival of Severus's fleet and the Moesian army under Maximus, followed by reinforcements under Septimius Severus himself. The omens were just an excuse that Niger would have used to convince his soldiers to abandon the campaign so that he did not need to tell them the actual reason, which was the threat posed to their lines of supply. Niger also continued his flight to Asia.]

'Now Aemilianus while engaged in conflict with some of the generals of Severus near Cyzicus was defeated by them and slain. [*HA Sev.* 8.16 and Herod. 3.1–2 proves that Aemilianus commanded a combined force consisting of a fleet – presumably the Classis Pontica stationed at Cyzicus, which was probably strengthened by a detachment drawn from the Classis Syriaca – and locally raised forces that had been reinforced by Niger's regulars. Aemilianus was first defeated in a naval battle at the Hellespont, after which he was again defeated on land by the forces that had been disembarked. The destruction of Aemilianus's forces, together with his death, threatened Niger's lines of communication.]' (Dio 75.6.1–4, tr. by H.B. Foster, pp.332–33, with some changes, corrections and comments)

We are now in a position to reconstruct the sequence of the beginning of the campaign. The sources quoted above have proved that Severus acted with alacrity whereas Niger's actions were lazy. Severus secured Africa and the Balkans up to Perinthus before Niger was able to do anything, following this up with a fast advance against his foe, who was forced to retreat to Byzantium and assume a defensive position. Niger held Byzantium and Aemilianus, with his combined force, the Hellespont. It is clear that Niger lacked adequate forces to oppose his numerically superior enemy. The Moesian army under Marius Maximus alone would have consisted of a minimum of four legions and *auxilia*, and when we add to this the defeated and therefore depleted legion under Cilo it is clear that even this was enough to force Niger to take the defensive. If we leave the auxiliaries and possible new levies from the calculation, the combined force of Maximus and Cilo would have consisted of five understrength legions, while Niger had at most only four legions at his immediate disposal; it is probable that Niger would have given at least three legions – the Cappadocian ones and one of the Syrian legions[18] – to Aemilianus. It is thus unsurprising that the arrival of Marius Maximus and the Moesian army enclosed Niger inside Byzantium. The siege was to last for three years and is discussed in detail later in this chapter.

We do not know any details of the naval battle at the Hellespont, but may make some educated guesses on the basis of the composition of the forces and locale. Niger's fleet would have consisted mostly of the ships of the *Classes Pontica* and *Syriaca*. The main striking force of these fleets consisted of the galleys of the *liburna* class, so only the flagship would have been a trireme (*trieres*). In addition to this, they had scouting ships and other vessels, but their role in naval combat was always secondary to the bigger vessels. It can be assumed that their numbers would have been bolstered with local civilian ships that the coastal cities were required to possess as part of their tax requirements. One may therefore estimate that the fleet under Aemilianus had perhaps about thirty triremes (the two flagships plus some larger civilian ships) and 100 *liburnae* or their equivalents. One modern calculation gives the Praetorian fleets that now served under Severus the following strength: one 'six', three 'fives', sixteen 'fours', seventy-five triremes and nineteen *liburnae*. These would have been boosted by ships provided by the Italian coastal cities and probably also by the Greek coastal cities, so the Severan fleet may have had at least 150 triremes and eighty *liburnae* or their equivalents. The posting of the fleet at the straits suggests that Niger's fleet was outnumbered, so the Severan fleet was probably even stronger than my conservative figures.

On the basis of the locale and outcome, we know that the Severan admirals (i.e. *duces* and prefects) knew their mettle and did not send too many triremes, fours, fives and sixes into the Dardanelles Strait at the same time, as did Licinius's admiral, Abantus, at the Battle of Hellespont in 324. In that battle, Abantus deployed 200 triremes while Constantine the Great's admirals, under the official command of his son Crispus, used only eighty galleys with thirty or fifty oars against them, the latter's smaller number and better manoeuvrability allowing them to sink a very large number of the tightly packed triremes in the confined space.[19] On the basis of this, it is likely that Severus's admirals or his supreme prefect of the fleets chose to send only smaller vessels into the strait, or if they used the Praetorian fleets to deploy only perhaps about 100 triremes, fours, fives and sixes. It is also probable that the victory was achieved in frontal combat, the strait not allowing the outflanking of the enemy line. On the basis of the fact that the elite of Severus's ships consisted of the two Praetorian fleets, it is probable that his admiral used their larger ships despite the locale because in frontal naval combat with limited scope for manoeuvre the advantage usually lay with larger vessels so long as the galleys maintained their proper distance. Firstly, the larger vessels held the advantage in the number of artillery pieces. They were also superior as regards ramming and collisions, and had the height advantage in boarding actions, which combined with the more numerous crews spelled disaster for the enemy if they could not use several ships against a larger vessel simultaneously. The latter facts suggest the likelihood that the Severan fleet was well ordered and drilled so the enemy was unable to find space to slip between them but was rather forced to fight on Severus's terms in frontal combat. So while we do not possess any details of the Battle of Hellespont in the autumn of 193, it is still very likely that the Severan victory was not the result of using smaller vessels but mainly because the Praetorian fleets possessed larger ships than the enemy and had crews and marines that were up to the task. Regardless of how it was achieved, the naval victory gave the Severans the ability to sail into the Propontis and threaten the route of retreat for Niger's forces posted at Byzantium.

The next stage of the campaign is more difficult to construct. Herodian stated that Severus ordered his army to cross into Cyzicus because he realized that the taking of Byzantium would be difficult. The problem with this is that we do not know what army Herodian meant. Did he mean the combined naval and land forces which had just defeated Niger's navy at the Hellespont, or Cilo at Perinthus, or some of the men belonging to the Moesian army, or the reinforcements that he had brought with him to the scene of operations? My own educated guess is that Herodian meant the forces that Severus had himself brought, and that these were now placed under Candidus, while the Severan fleet sailed to Perinthus where these men were embarked on ships and the expeditionary force sailed to Cyzicus. The reason for the placing of Candidus in charge of the army was that

Severus lacked at this stage of his career the experience of leading large armies in combat. On the basis of subsequent events, Candidus appears to have been the commander-in-chief of the force sent to Asia Minor, with the title *dux exercitus Illyrici expeditione Asiana*. The choice of Candidus was an apt one for the situation, because he had been '*legatus pro pr. provinciae Asiae*' and '*logista civitatis splendidissiame Nicomedensium*'.[20] In other words, Candidus knew the area and its people intimately. Herodian also notes that when Aemilianus was informed of this, he also marched to Cyzicus at the head of locally levied forces and reinforcements sent by Niger. On the basis of this, it would seem probable that Aemilianus had retreated past Cyzicus on the road to Byzantium, and that Niger would have then dispatched reinforcements to him with orders to march to Cyzicus while he himself continued his partial evacuation of Byzantium.

It is not surprising that when the two armies met close to Cyzicus, the battle went in favour of Severus's army. The Illyrian army drawn from the Pannonias would have had four legions and the Praetorian fleets would have had at least two more, so the Severans would have had six understrength legions plus auxiliary forces, while Aemilianus would have had at most two or three legions along with locally raised forces. When Niger heard of the defeat, he crossed the strait and marched towards the enemy. He had no other choice because the Severan forces were threatening his line of communication. The destruction of Niger's force and death of Aemilianus at Cyzicus caused the desertion of Nicomedia and many other cities to the Severans. The desertion of Nicomedia is not surprising in light of the fact that Candidus undoubtedly had many friends there. Nicaea, however, remained loyal to Niger's cause, so it offered a place of refuge to those soldiers of Niger who did not continue their flight to Armenia or the Taurus mountains. It was there that Niger joined the remnants of his army and prepared to continue the conflict. In response to this, the Severans appear to have disembarked their force at Cius.

5.5. The Battle of Cius and Nicaea in about December 193

When the two armies had assembled at Cius and Nicaea, the Severans took the initiative and gained the advantage of position over the enemy by making the first move. Herodian and Dio recorded subsequent events:

> 'The two cities were like armed camps and bases from which they issued out against each other, and after a sharp and fierce fight the Severans gained a victory. The survivors of Niger's party fled to the passes of the Taurus, where they guarded the passes. Niger, having left what garrisons he thought sufficient for the defence of the barriers, hurried to Antioch to raise recruits and money.' (Herodian 3.2.10, tr. by J. Hart, London, 1759, pp.112–13, with changes, corrections and comments)

> 'After this, between the narrows of Nicaea/Nikaia and Cius/Kios [this suggests that the battle took place in the pass just east of Lake Ascania/Askania], they had a great battle of various forms. Some battled in close formation on the plains ['*adv. Sustadon*' means standing close together, fighting at close quarters, the equivalent of the Latin '*comminus*'. On the basis of the location, this probably refers solely to the infantry, and that if there was any cavalry present it was either dismounted or

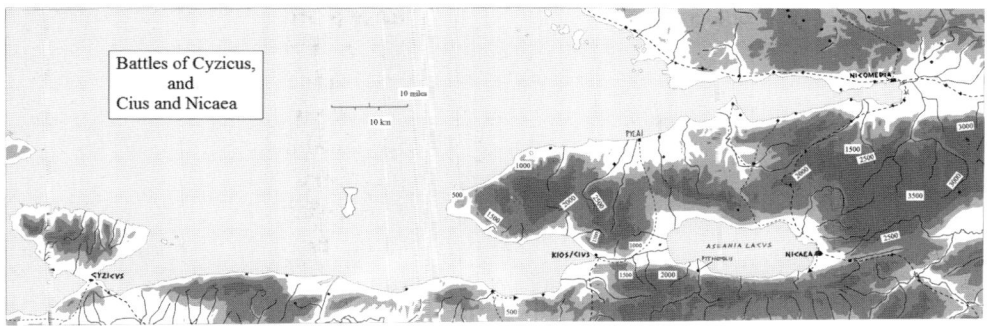

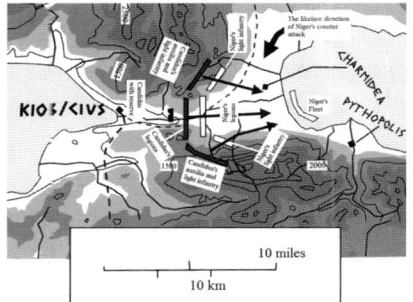

Battles of Cyzicus and Cius and Nicaea in about December 193

1) The Severans land in or near Cyzicus and defeat and kill Aemilianus. Nicomedia deserts to Severus.
2) The defeated forces retreat via Cius to Nicaea while Niger arrives with reinforcements from Byzantium.
3) The Severans pursue the retreating forces of Niger and array for combat in the pass east of Cius under Candidus. The Severans occupy the heights which enables them to force the troops of Niger into retreat. The fleet of Niger helps them to balance the situation.
4) Niger arrives with reserves and forces the Severans into retreat.
5) Candidus regroups the men, makes a counter attack and defeats the forces of Niger which flee to Nicaea.

was posted somewhere in the rear. What is certain is that their numbers would have been relatively small because the army had been shipped here.]; others occupied the hill-crests and hurled stones and javelins at their opponents from the higher ground; still others got into boats and discharged their bows at the enemy from the lake [Ascania]. At first the followers of Severus, under the direction of Candidus, were victorious; for they found their advantage in the higher ground from which they fought. But the moment Niger himself appeared a pursuit in turn was instituted by Niger's men and victory was on their side. [The fact that the followers of Severus were able to seize the heights east of Lake Ascania first suggests a likelihood that the Severans attacked immediately after Niger had reached the city of Nicaea, so Niger was forced to dispatch men eastwards immediately. The fighting in boats belongs to that phase of the fight in which the Severans had forced Niger's troops away from the pass to the lake shore, presumably in such a manner that the Severans made a breakthrough on their flanks. The account leaves open how and from which direction Niger appeared with his reserves. It is possible that he brought reserves in boats and that these landed in the rear of his men, or that he brought cavalry from the north (where Charmidea is located) and attacked the Severans on the flank, or that he brought reinforcements by using the southern route (via Pythopolis). In my opinion the likeliest alternatives are the flank attack from the north and the use of boats.] Then Candidus caught hold of the standard bearers and turned them to face the enemy, upbraiding the soldiers for their flight; at this his followers were ashamed, turned back, and once more conquered those opposed to them. [It is very likely that Candidus had reserve forces, the 'commander's reserve', which helped him to turn the tide.] Indeed, they would have destroyed them utterly, had not the city been near and the night a dark one.' (Dio 75.6.4ff., tr. by H.B. Foster, pp.333–34, with some changes, corrections and comments)

On the basis of these accounts, it is clear that the Severans had begun their march from Cius immediately once they knew that Niger was close to the city of Nicaea, so they were able to occupy the high ground in the pass before Niger's forces could reach the scene. In other words, Niger was once again too slow, which enabled his enemies to take the initiative. When Niger's forces then got to the position opposite the Severans, the latter were able to take advantage of the terrain and force their opponents to retreat, some of them fleeing to the boats to continue their fight from there while the rest withdrew along the shores of Lake Ascania. Niger with his reserves checked the flight of his forces around the lake and regrouped them for a new fight, forcing the Severans to retreat in their turn. Candidus reacted to this setback like good commanders of antiquity were expected to do: he took hold of the standard bearers and forced them around to face the enemy, upon which the men regrouped and sent Niger's troops fleeing back to the safety of Nicaea. Niger's men appear to have continued their flight during the night because we do not hear of any siege of Nicaea taking place the following morning.

A bust of Pescennius Niger (Capitol) according to Duruy.

A bust of Septimius Severus (Vatican) according to Duruy.

5.6. The Severans Exploit their Victory: The Conquest of Asia Minor in 194

As noted above, Niger did not attempt to hold on to Asia Minor, but fled directly to the Cilician Pass (also known as the Cilician Gates), which he garrisoned before continuing his flight to Antioch to raise money and a new army. The rest of his forces, however, had already fled to Roman Armenia after Aemilianus's defeat. These men are likely to have consisted of soldiers from the XII Fulminata and XV Apollinaris legions and auxiliary forces from those parts. If both legions fled to their home bases, then XII Fulminata would have regrouped at Melitene and XV Apollinaris at Satala. Unfortunately, there is no detailed narrative of what happened next. All that we have is the text of Herodian:

'Then Severus' army conquered Bithynia and Galatia and poured into Cappadocia. There they settled down to besiege the fortification. This proved a very arduous task. The ruggedness of the narrow route made the task difficult. The besieged fought valiantly from the top of the fortifications and threw down huge stones on the heads of the assailants so that a few men were able to keep a large force at bay. For the pass was exceedingly narrow and covered on one side by a high mountain and on the other by a steep precipice which had rapid torrents of water pouring down from the mountains. And Niger had used these terrain features when he fortified the place to prevent the passage of Severus' army. While these affairs were thus carried on in Cappadocia, new seditions were blown up from the old cause of mutal enmity in Syria by Laodicea, which hated Antioch, and in Phoenicia by Tyre, which despised Berytus. When these cities heard that Niger had been put to flight, they … declared publicly for Severus. When Niger, who was then at Antioch, was informed … he was highly enraged. He … detached a strong corps consisting of Moorish javelinmen ['*Maurousius te akontistas*'] and a division of archers ['*meros toxotôn*'. The exact technical meaning of '*meros*' at this time is not known. Furthermore, it is very unlikely that Herodian would have used the word in its technical sense. In general, '*meros*' means a division/unit, but by the sixth century it had become to mean roughly a legion-size unit of 5,000–7,000 men consisting of either infantry or cavalry. Considering the situation, I would suggest that we are indeed dealing here with a large division because Niger needed to subdue two sizeable cities and fast. My own educated guess is that he dispatched at least 5,000–6,000 Moors and 5,000–6,000 mounted archers against the cities. The use of cavalry enabled Niger to subdue both cities before they had a chance to organize themselves. However, at the same time I would suggest that it is probable that by doing so Niger had sent away most of his cavalry forces, so he was subsequently forced to rely solely on his infantry at the Battle of Issus.] with orders to attack the two cities, put all they met to the sword, plunder the houses and lay the cities in ashes. The Moors (as they are by nature a savage bloodthirsty race of men despising death and dangers) fell upon the Laodiceans unawares, and without the least remorse butchered all the inhabitants and razed the city. From thence they proceeded to Tyre where they pillaged and slaughtered after which they burned the city to the ground. [The subsequent account of Dio makes it clear that the Adiabeni, Oshroeni and Arabs had also revolted against the Romans, which tied up Niger's resources elsewhere when he would have sorely needed these against Severus.] While these events were taking place in Syria and while Niger was levying all the force he could collect, Severus' army continued their siege of the mountain fortifications. His soldiers were now completely demoralized … and the defenders imagined themselves secure … then all of a sudden a violent storm of rain and snow fell in the night (for through all Cappadocia and especially in the Taurus the winters are very severe). As a result large quantities of water rushed down the mountain stream like a torrent against the fortifications which obstructed its flow until the manmade structure proved inferior against the forces of nature. The load of water pressed against the wall, loosened its cement and sapped its foundation because it had been built in a hurry .... When the besieged observed this, they feared that they might be surrounded by the enemy now that they had been deprived of their defence. Consequently, they deserted their posts and fled. This cheered the spirits of Severus' soldiers because they now thought that the divine providence was guiding them. Perceiving that the enemy had fled, they easily crossed the Taurus Mountains and penetrated into Cilicia.' (Herodian 3.3.1ff., tr. by Hart, pp.113–15, with changes, corrections and comments)

Candidus and the Severan forces under him, including some Pannonian units, completed the victory by pursuing the defeated forces of Niger both on land and sea so that they 'liberated' the provinces of Asia and Bithynia. Septimius Severus appointed Claudius Xenophon as procurator of Asia to govern the newly 'liberated' province. Soon after this, however, there arrived a new commander-in-chief for these forces called Cornelius Anullinus, who had been a proconsul of Africa at the time Septimius gained the throne. Birley is likely to be correct in his speculation that Anullinus was an old and trusted friend of Severus, who had summoned him immediately to become a commander-in-chief of the Pannonian/Illyrian armies in Thrace which had now advanced into Asia Minor. News of the defeat of Niger's forces resulted not only in the desertion of much of Asia Minor and many cities elsewhere, but most importantly caused the defection of Egypt by 13 February 194, followed by the desertion of Arabia from Niger (if it did not take place earlier),[21] as we shall see from the text of Dio which is quoted later. The defeat of Niger at Cius and Nicaea also caused the Parthians to change their view of the situation, subsequently inciting the Oshroeni, Adiabeni and Arabs to revolt against Rome.

Birley notes that the above victories caused the army to acclaim Severus as *imperator*, allowing him to add *Imp. II* and *Imp. III* to his titles, while from the beginning of 194 he also added *pater patriae* to his titles. The mint at Rome advertised his success by striking new coins which celebrated his victories. It was also then that the ancestral gods of Lepcis Magna – Hercules and Father Liber – made their first appearance on Roman coins. These and many other coins, including those minted by Albinus, celebrated the province of Africa for two reasons. Firstly, they celebrated the importance of African corn for the city of Rome, while secondly, they quite purposefully celebrated the African origins of both the Augustus and Caesar, presumably as guarantors of this supply and security of the Empire. The aim was to keep the populace, the senators and Albinus happy with this propaganda.[22]

The above sequence of events suggests that Severus's troops proceeded first against the forces that had fled to Satala and Melitene, after which they moved to the Cilician Gates held by the forces of Niger. We do not know where Septimius Severus was at the time. He may have stayed at Perinthus until late spring to observe the progress of the siege of Byzantium, but he was definitely in the theatre of operations by the summer. By then it would have been apparent that the conquest of the city of Byzantium would take a very long time. Herodian fails to tell us how Severus's generals dealt with the

Top Left: a gorge at the Taurus Mountains (source: Duruy).

Middle right: coin of Septimius Severus with the name Pertinax included. (source: Beger 1696).

Below: The Cilician Gates according to Schlumberger.

It is easy to see why it was very difficult for the forces of Severus to get through the Cilician Gates or any other gorge in the Taurus Range when it was fortified and garrisoned.

remnants of Niger's forces in Armenia. My best educated guess is that these were allowed to surrender because Herodian does not mention any fighting between the soldiers – the only place where he mentions this is before the Cilician Gates. Severus's men were extremely lucky in that the wall was broken by torrents of water caused by rainfall and snow in the Taurus Mountains. The pass itself was extremely narrow. According to Whittaker's estimation (Herodian 270–71), the pass was really a gorge that was 100 yards long and 50ft wide, with steep hills rising above it to a height of 500ft and a tributary of the River Cydnus flowing through it so that the marchable road was only a few feet wide. The timing of the siege and its ending are contested, with Whittaker (Herodian 272–73) noting the different interpretations. Some claim that the siege ended either in the winter or the spring of 194, but Whittaker himself thinks that Herodian implied that the snowfall was unexpected so it would have taken place in the early autumn. In the context of the Battle of Issus, Whittaker (Herodian 274–75) elaborates this further by noting that some historians favour early 194 while others propose late 194. In Whittaker's opinion, the apparent *terminus ante quem* for the Issus campaign would be November 194, but at the same time he notes that the evidence for early 194 is better but by no means conclusive. I am inclined to agree, so I would date the snowfall to the spring of 194, after which followed the Battle of Issus.

It is another unanswerable question why the Severans chose to stay in front of the fortifications at the Cilician Gates and did not attempt to bypass it, for example by advancing through Armenia or along the coast. Perhaps the best answer is that the Severans chose not to sail because the siege of Byzantium tied up naval resources and because sailing was always a hazardous undertaking during winter, while the winter with its snows also made the crossing of the Armenian highlands difficult.

5.7. The Battle of Issus in the Spring of 194

When the defences at the Cilician Gates burst open, the Severan army was free to march south to engage the forces of Niger. The two armies met at Issus, close to the place where Alexander the Great and Darius III fought in 333 BC. To my knowledge, no one has ever tried to reconstruct this battle, despite the fact that the sources offer enough details for this to be done. An analysis of the following sources – once again Herodian and Dio – demonstrates that we can indeed place the battle on the map:

> Niger, being informed of what had happened, assembled a large army consisting of raw and inexperienced men with which he marched to meet the enemy. For a great multitude of recruits, including almost all of the youth of Antioch, had volunteered into his service. The enthusiasm of the recruits helped Niger, but they were far inferior to the Illyrian forces in experience and valour. [This clearly suggests that Severus's army was the same as had previously defeated Niger's forces at Cyzicus and Cius-Nicaea, so it would have consisted of the core of the four Illyrian legions which would probably have been strengthened by detachments drawn from other forces.] The two armies met near what they call the Bay of Issus, in a large plain, enclosed all around with hills, except from the part next to the sea, where it extends in a long and spacious shore as if the nature had formed this spot for an amphitheatre where contending powers might exhibit the tragic scenes of war. Here, they say, Darius fought his greatest and last battle with Alexander in which he was defeated and captured .... [An incorrect statement because Alexander defeated Darius again at Gaugamela, after which he pursued the Persian king in vain because he was killed by his followers. However, Alexander captured the relatives of Darius here. Niger undoubtedly chose this site because he liked to promote himself as Alexander the Great, who had also advanced from the south against the Persians advancing from the

The Civil War Between Septimius Severus and Niger in 193–194

The location of the battle of Issus between Darius III and Alexander the Great according to Duruy.
It is quite probable that this drawing actually shows the view from the spot just behind the location where Niger had placed his left wing. Note that the view to the right is blocked by mountains. This enabled the Severans to post their cavalry in hiding in a situation in which a storm hindered the view even further. For further details, see the text and accompanying map.

north. In the portion of the text not included here, Herodian presents the situation falsely as if it was the forces of Severus when they advanced from the north that were like those of Alexander the Great.] The trophy and monuments of that victory remain to this day. There is a city called Alexandria built on one of the heights .... The two armies pitched their camps opposite each other in the evening and stayed up all night in anxious wait. At the rising of the sun both advanced, each leader encouraging ... his soldiers. They fell on each other with great fury as this was to be the last decisive battle .... The fight lasted for a long time ... and such numbers were killed and wounded on both sides that the streams of rivers which ran through the plains carried more blood than water down into the sea. [Dio's text makes it clear that there were no rivers between the armies, which means that the reference to rivers should either be taken figuratively or that it refers to rivers further south through which the pursuit was conducted.] At last the eastern nations were again routed and the Illyrians drove great numbers of them ... into the sea. The rest fleeing towards the hills were pursued by the conquerors who cut them to pieces together with spectators from the surrounding farms and towns who had flocked there to view the battle from a [supposedly] safe spot. Niger, riding a fast steed, fled with a few followers to Antioch where he found the remainder of the people deserting the place …. He immediately left Antioch and hid himself in a little obscure suburb of Antioch. He was found, captured and beheaded by the pursuing enemy cavalry …. Severus, after Niger was dead, punished all Niger's partisans regardless of whether they had joined his cause voluntarily or involuntarily. But hearing that the fugitive soldiers had passed the Tigris and had gone over to the barbarians because they feared him, he [Severus] published a general amnesty. But he was unable to get them all back, which was the reason why the barbarians after this became more formidable enemies to the Romans in close quarters fighting. Before they knew only how to shoot arrows from their horses and they wore only a part of the panoply of martial equipment and therefore lacked the confidence to come to the close quarters with spears and swords in hand because they wore only light loose garments. [This claim is untrue because the Parthians definitely possessed fully armoured *contus*-bearers who fought at close quarters; it was probably meant to suggest that it was because of Severus's actions that Caracalla and Macrinus later faced the Parthians in close-quarters fighting.] But now a great number of the Romans, many of whom were good craftsmen, fleeing there taught the barbarians not only how to use the arms but also how to manufacture them. [It is probable that this is at least partially true, and that these Roman fugitives taught the Iranians how to form legions armed with swords and rectangular shields; as I have already noted in 2004, these would be the men that Ammianus Marcellinus would later call by the name "*murmillones*". The reason for this conclusion is that the *murmillones* gladiators were armed precisely with this type of equipment, namely rectangular shields and *gladii* swords. Obviously the Iranian *murmillones* would also have worn the *lorica segmentata* type of armour and used *pila* javelins, unlike the gladiators.]' (Herodian 3.4.1–9., tr. by Hart, pp.115–18, with changes, corrections, and comments inside parentheses)

'The next event was a tremendous battle at Issus near the so-called Gates. In this contest Valerianus [L. Valerius Valerianus] and Anullinus [P. Cornelius Anullinus][23] commanded the army of Severus, whereas Niger was with his own ranks and marshalled them for war. This pass, the Cilician Gates, is so named on account of its narrowness. On the one side rise precipitous mountains, and on the other sheer cliffs descend to the sea. [This was not the famous Cilician Gates through which the Severan army had already passed, but a lesser gate close to the city of Alexander ad Issum (see the map of the campaign). None of the sources make any mention of the fleets. On the basis of this, I make the educated guess that the Severan fleet was engaged in the siege of Byzantium, while Niger had lost most of his Syrian fleet at the Battle of Hellespont.] So Niger had here made a camp on a strong hill, and he put in front the *hoplitai* [hoplites, the full panoply bearers, which usually meant the large-shield bearers who were usually armed with spears], next the *akontistai* [javelin-throwers] and *lithoboloi* [stone-throwers], and behind all the *toxotai* [archers]. His purpose was that the foremost might thrust back such as assailed them in hand-to-hand conflict, while the others from a distance might be able to bring their force into play over the heads of the others. His flanks were protected respectively on the right and left by the cliffs on the side of the sea and by the impenetrable forest on the other side. This is the way in which he arrayed his army, and he stationed the beasts of burden in the rear so that none of them would be able to flee in case they should wish it. [This suggests that Niger used the standard combat formation, with the heavy-armed troops placed in front, behind which were the light-armed and behind all the baggage train with reserves, servants and drivers to protect the rear. On the basis of the situation and description of the infantry phalanx, it is probable that Niger's phalanx consisted of four or eight ranks of spear-armed 'hoplites' placed in front, behind which were javelin throwers so that there were sixteen ranks in total in the phalanx (determined by the width of the location). The 'stone-throwers' and archers were then placed behind the phalanx proper. Niger's forces had very advantageous higher positions overlooking that of the enemy. We find this very same basic formation in Arrian's *Extaxis kata Alanon* (see Appendix 1). The posting of the spear-armed in front had the advantage of providing Niger's forces with the double ability of facing cavalry and infantry because the spears could also be thrown when need be. The location and combat formation enabled Niger to negate his disadvantages: 1) Niger had sent most of his cavalry to crush the revolts of the cities and also of the Adiabeni, Oshroeni and Arabs so that the Severan cavalry outnumbered his own; 2) most of his men consisted of green recruits.[24]] Anullinus after making all this out placed in advance the heavier part of his force [literally those who carried the round *aspis* shield, but this should probably be taken to mean the shield-bearers in general] and behind it his entire light-armed contingent to the end that the latter through discharging their weapons from a distance might still keep the enemy in check while the men in front would advance up the slope and keep them safe. The cavalry he sent with Valerianus, bidding him, so as he could, go around the forest and unexpectedly fall upon the troops of Niger from the rear. [The fact that Niger's forces were posted on a hill means that had visibility been normal, they would have been able to see this move quite clearly. Since the following events make it clear that this was not the case, it is clear that the storm that came out of the blue began in the morning, hiding this move, or that Anullinus gave this order to Valerianus only after the storm had begun so that it could be hidden from the enemy's view.] When they came to close quarters, the soldiers of Severus placed some of their shields in front of them and held some above their heads, making a *testudo* [tortoise array], and in this formation they approached the enemy [this was the standard way to protect soldiers against missiles during the attack or defence]. So the battle was a drawn one for a long time, but eventually Niger's men decidedly gained the advantage both by their numbers and by the topography of the country. They would have been completely victorious had not clouds gathered out of a clear sky and a wind arisen from a perfect calm, while there were crashes of thunder and sharp flashes of lightning and violent rain beat in their faces. This did not trouble Severus's troops because it was behind them, but threw Niger's men into great confusion since it came right against them. [In my opinion, Birley (p.117) has needlessly suspected this and other weather miracles which took place at this time as literary inventions, with Septimius Severus soon after this proclaiming himself as the son of Marcus Aurelius. The weather miracles of Marcus Aurelius, however, with his troops being aided by lightning and a sudden rainstorm during the Quadic Wars, are not an exact match with these. Furthermore, the northerly wind at the Battle of Issus would fit the weather pattern described previously in the context of the Cilician Gates. In this locality, cold fronts with snow and rain usually come from the north.] Most important of all, the opportune character of this occurrence infused courage in the one side, which believed it was aided by heaven, and fear in the other, which felt that the supernatural was warring against them; thus it made the former strong even beyond its own strength and terrified the latter in spite of real power. Just as they were fleeing Valerianus came in sight. Seeing him, they turned about, and after that, as Anullinus beat them back, retreated once more. [This combination of fleeing infantry with the cavalry then appearing in the rear of the pursuers makes it very likely that the retreat of the Severan infantry was a feigned retreat so that Valerianus's cavalry could get behind Niger's infantry.] Then they wandered about, running this way and that way, to see where they could break through. It turned out that this was the greatest slaughter to take place during the war in question. Two myriads of Niger's followers perished utterly .... [Valerianus's cavalry could trample fugitives under their hooves and kill at will when Niger's units of footmen lost their cohesion.] Directly Antioch had been captured (not long after) Niger fled from it, making the Euphrates his objective at this point, for he intended to seek refuge among the barbarians. His pursuers, however, overtook him; he was taken and had his head struck off. This head Severus sent to Byzantium and caused to be reared on a cross/pole that the sight of it might incline the Byzantines to his cause. [This did not work.] The next move of Severus was to mete out justice to those who had belonged to Niger's party. Of the cities and individuals he chastised some and rewarded others. He executed no Roman senator, but deprived most of them of their property and confined them on islands. [Severus needed to keep the senators happy because he still needed to face Albinus and his supporters.] He was merciless in his search for money. [Severus needed money to bribe his soldiers and supporters.] Among other measures he exacted four times the amount that any individuals or peoples had given to Niger, whether they had done so voluntarily or under compulsion. He himself doubtless perceived the injustice of it, but as he required great sums, he paid no attention to the common talk.' (Dio 75.7.1ff, tr. by H.B. Foster, pp.334–37, with some changes, corrections, and comments inside parentheses)

So when Niger learnt that the enemy had burst through from the Cilician Gates, he marched to Issus, which offered him an opportunity to post his forces in such a manner that the enemy would not be able to outflank him with superior cavalry. The heights negated the advantages that the enemy's veteran forces had on a level plain. The chosen location also enabled him to present himself as Alexander the Great, which could be used to bolster the morale of the men. However, Anullinus, the overall commander put in charge by Septimius Severus, was not a novice. An analysis of the sources quoted above shows that he was able to manoeuvre his forces in such a manner that he overcame the disadvantages of the terrain. Anullinus exploited the weather both in his attack and feigned flight. The overconfident enemy swallowed his bait and pursued Anullinus's infantry so far that the Severan cavalry was able to attack them from behind. This sealed their fate

The Civil War Between Septimius Severus and Niger in 193–194

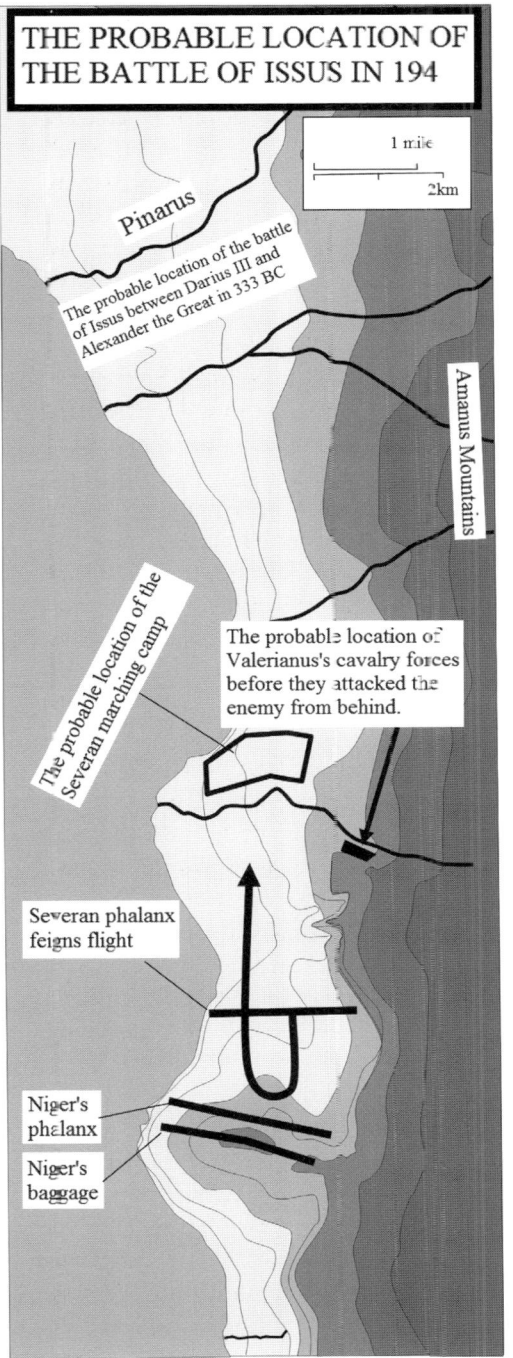

Reconstruction of the Battle of Issus in the spring 194

1) The unexpected clearing of the Cilician Gates opened up the route to the Bay of Issus for the Illyrian Army under Anullinus, which he exploited immediately.

2) Niger advanced with his force to the defensive position along the route taken by the enemy. His forces consisted of hastily collected and trained men. Niger sought to present himself as new Alexander the Great fighting against the barbarians advancing from the north. He had numerical advantage but the Severans had qualitative advantage. Furthermore, it is probable that most of Niger's cavalry was absent so that the Severans had a numerical advantage in cavalry.

3) The description of the location suggests that the battle was fought on a hill that blocked the route from the north, but which did not have a river in front of it. This precludes the Cilician Gates located at the Bay of Issus, because it has a river in it. Dio also makes it clear that it was not fought there but near it. This together with the fact that the Severan army would have consisted of four legions plus probable remnants of one legion for a maximum of 25,000 legionaries plus auxiliary forces makes the location shown on the map as the likeliest one. It has just enough width for this, if the Severans were deployed eight deep with light-infantry behind. This would also mean that Niger, who had numerical advantage, would have deployed his heavy infantry phalanx sixteen deep for extra weight in a situation in which his inexperienced men would have needed this to bolster their morale.

4) It is probable that Niger had deployed his army in such a manner that it was impossible for Valerianus's cavalry to go around the forest located on the mountain so that it became necessary for Anullinus to order his men to feign flight so that Niger's inexperienced men would attack downhill to such a spot where Valerianus's cavalry could attack its rear. The storm mentioned by Dio must have hidden visibility from the hill occupied by Niger's men so that the movement of Valerianus's cavalry was not detected. The other alternative is that Anullinus dispatched Valerianus across the mountains further north to make a long circuit of the enemy lines, but this does not fit the description in the sources. The likeliest location for Valerianus's cavalry prior to their attack is shown on the map. This location would have hidden them from sight.

5) Dio's text makes it clear that the decisive point in the battle was the arrival of Valerianus's cavalry, which makes the above educated guess more than likely. When the cavalry then attacked Niger's forces from behind, these tried to make their way through by whatever route, but so that most of them were forced against the sea and butchered while others made their way towards the mountains with the same result. The death to 1 for the defeated was 20,000 killed. In addition to this the Severans mistakenly butchered a number of civilian spectators who had come to see the event.

6) Niger fled on horseback to Antioch and then attempted to flee to the Parthians but was found out by the pursuing cavalry and beheaded. Severus's ploy to parade Niger's head before the defenders of Byzantium failed to make them surrender.

7) The victory over Niger enabled Severus to launch a campaign against the supporters of Niger so that he could collect money to bribe his soldiers, supporters and possible turncoats among the supporters of Albinus.

and 20,000 of Niger's followers, together with some bystanders, were massacred, largely by the pursuing cavalry. The attached map of the battle shows the probable locations of the forces and the manoeuvre the Severans used. Niger fled to Antioch, and when the enemy reached the city, he attempted to flee to the Euphrates but was caught and killed. This, however, was not the end of the war, as Severus still had to deal with those who had supported Niger.

5.8. The Siege of Byzantium 193 – late 195 or early 196

Dio is an excellent source for the lengthy siege of Byzantium:

'The Byzantines performed many remarkable deeds both during the life and after the death of Niger. This city is favourably located .... The town sits on high ground extending into the sea. The latter, rushing down from the Pontus with the speed of a mountain torrent assails the headland and in part is diverted to the right, forming there the bay and harbours. But the greater part of the water passes on with great energy past the city itself toward the Propontis. Moreover, the place had walls that were very strong. Their face was constructed [of] thick squared stones, fastened together by bronze plates, and the inner side of it had been strengthened with mounts and buildings so that the whole seemed to be one thick wall [this means that it was practically impervious to battering rams] and the top of it formed a circuit betraying no flaws and easy to guard. Many large towers occupied an exposed position outside it, with windows set close together on every side so that those assaulting the fortification in a circle ... they were sure to command both sides of any attacking party. Of the entire circuit the part on land side reached a great height so as to repel any who came that way: the portion next to the sea was lower. There, the rocks on which it had been reared and the dangerous character of the Bosporus were effective allies. The harbours within the wall had both been closed with chains and their breakwaters carried towers projecting far out on each side, making approach impossible for the enemy .... The engines, besides, the whole length of the wall, were of the most varied description. In one place they threw rocks and wooden beams upon parties approaching [these were to be used against those who had advanced close to the wall and were the heavy artillery pieces] and in another they discharge stones and missiles and spears against such as stood at a distance [these were the light artillery pieces]. Hence over a considerable extent of territory no one could draw near them without danger. Still others had hooks, which they would let down suddenly and shortly draw up ships and machines. [These had clearly been copied from Archimedes and formed the last line of defensive machines close to the wall. The standard way to interpret this would be to say that it is incorrect because of this, but I see no reason to doubt the veracity of the statement. It would be really nice to know how Archimedes and now Priscus built these machines.] Priscus, a fellow citizen of mine [i.e. he came from Nicaea like Dio], had designed most of them, and this fact both caused him to incur the death penalty and saved his life. For Severus, on learning his proficiency, prevented his being executed. Subsequently he employed him on various missions,

The Civil War Between Septimius Severus and Niger in 193–194   117

among others at the siege of Hatra, and his contrivances were the only ones not burned by the barbarians. The Byzantines had also prepared 500 ships consisting mostly of the monoremes but some with two banks ['*dikrota*'] all equipped with beaks. A few of them were provided with rudders at both ends, stern and prow, and had a double quota of pilots and sailors in order that they might both attack and retire without turning around .... Many, therefore, were the exploits and sufferings of the Byzantines, since for the entire space of three years they were besieged by the armaments of practically the whole world. [This and another comment of Dio creates a problem of dating; see later]

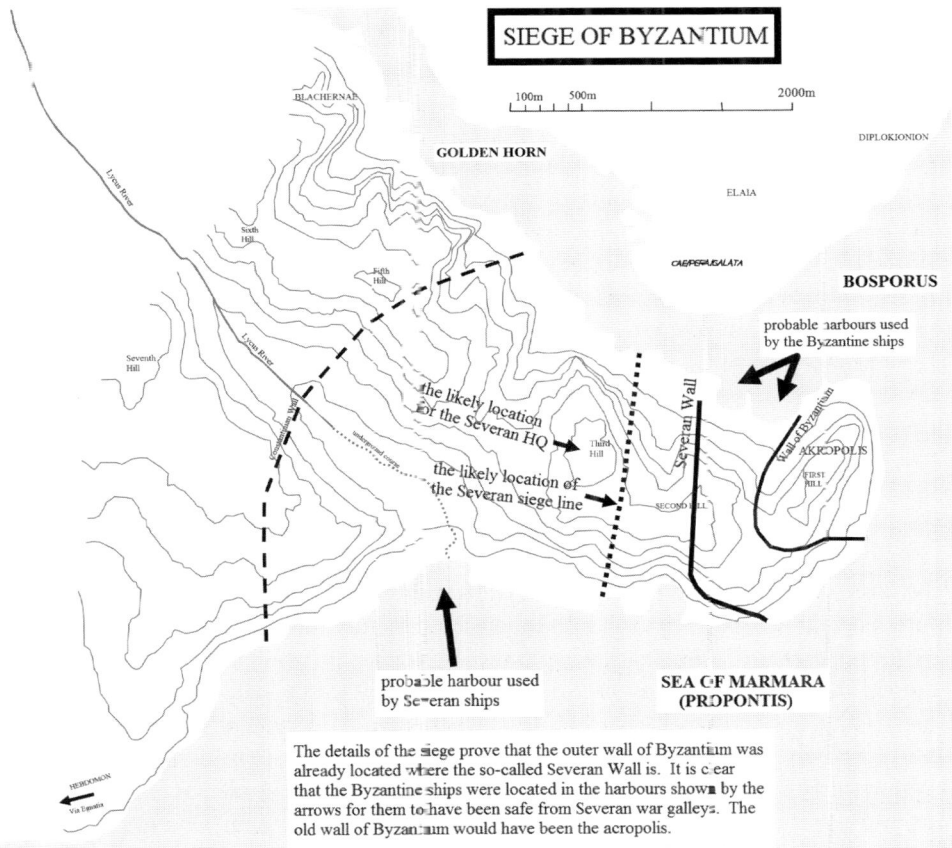

The details of the siege prove that the outer wall of Byzantium was already located where the so-called Severan Wall is. It is clear that the Byzantine ships were located in the harbours shown by the arrows for them to have been safe from Severan war galleys. The old wall of Byzantium would have been the acropolis.

A few of their experiences will be mentioned that seem almost marvellous. They captured, by making an opportune attack, some ships that sailed by and captured also some of the triremes that were in their opponents' roadstead [the vast majority of the triremes would have belonged to the Praetorian fleets]. This they did by having divers cut their anchors under water, after which they drove nails into the ship's bottom and with cords attached thereto and running from friendly territory they would draw the vessel towards them. Hence one might see the ships approaching shore by themselves, with no oarsman nor wind to urge them forwards. There were cases in which merchants purposely allowed themselves to be captured by the Byzantines, though pretending unwillingness, and after selling their wares for a huge price made their escape by sea. [This is undoubtedly the reason why the Byzantines were able to withstand the siege for three years. The lure of easy money was clearly too much for some merchants. However, the fact that this became known would have led the besiegers to take a firmer stance, as undoubtedly happened.]' (Dio 75.10.1ff., tr. by Foster, pp.338–41, with changes, corrections and comments)[25]

The above discussion reveals nicely how well prepared the Byzantines were for the siege and why the Severan forces failed to capture the city easily. Dio implies with his description of the defensive siege equipment that the Severan forces had attempted to approach the walls both from the land and sea side and been able to bring their siege machines and ships right next to the walls, despite the very heavy toll it took in casualties under the heavy barrage of artillery designed by Priscus, because he refers to the Archimedean machines which the defenders then used to draw up both ships and machines. This and the anger at the architect could result only from the use of assault tactics. Even if Dio fails to state the obvious, it is clear that the approach to the wall would have been done under sheds and coverings on the land side while the Severan artillery, archers and slingers provided covering fire. The reference to the land and buildings inside the walls also suggests that the Severans had managed to bring their battering rams against the wall, with poor results, the above-mentioned Archimedean machines putting a stop to this. After this, the Severans apparently settled on starving the defenders, which initially failed because the greedy merchants brought supplies for the defenders. The fact that this was known means that the Severans found it out and put a stop to it. The morale of the defenders was very high, not even the parading of the head of Niger changing that. Regardless, in the end, the blockade did what it was meant to do, as indicated by Dio:

'When all the supplies in the town had been exhausted and the people had been set fairly in a strait with regard to both their situation and the expectations that might be founded upon it, at first, although beset by great difficulties (because they were cut off from all outside resources), they nevertheless continued to resist; and to make ships they used lumber taken from the houses and braided ropes of the hair of their women. [Instructions for the use of women's hair in *ballistae* can be found in a large number of narrative histories and works of stratagems.] Whenever any troops assaulted the wall, they would hurl upon them stones from the theatres, bronze horses [this city was already famous for these], and whole statues of bronze. When even their normal food supply began to fail them, they proceeded to soak and eat hides. Then these, too, were used up, and the majority, having waited for rough water and a squall so that no one might man a ship to oppose them, sailed out with the determination either to perish or to secure provisions. They assailed the countryside without warning and plundered every quarter indiscriminately. [This suggests that the people of the countryside did not expect that the besieged would be able to get out, so there were no guards.] Those left behind committed a monstrous deed; for when they grew very faint, they … devoured one another. This was the condition of the men in the city. The rest loaded their ships with more than these could bear, [and] set sail after waiting this time also for a great storm. They did not succeed, however, in making any use of it. The Romans, noticing that their vessels were over heavy and depressed almost to the water's edge, put out against them. They assailed the craft, which were scattered about as wind and current/waves chose to dispose them, and really engaged in nothing like a naval battle but crushed the enemy's ships mercilessly, striking many with their boat-hooks, ripping many open with their beaks, and actually capsizing some by their mere onset. The victims in the ships were unable to do anything, however much they might have wished it; and when they attempted to flee in any direction either they would be sunk by force of the wind, which encountered them with the utmost violence, or else they would be overtaken by the enemy and destroyed. The inhabitants of Byzantium, as they watched this, ... when they saw their friends perishing all together ... thereafter they mourned .... The entire number of wrecks proved so great that some drifted upon the islands and the Asiatic coast, and the defeat became known by these relics before it was reported. The next day the Byzantines had the horror increased even above what it had been. For, when the surf had subsided, the whole sea in the vicinity of Byzantium was covered with corpses and wrecks with blood, and many of the remains were cast up on shore, with the result that the catastrophe, now seen in its details, appeared even worse than the reality. The Byzantines straightaway, though against their will, surrendered their city. The Romans executed all the soldiers and magistrates but spared the rest except the pugilist who had greatly aided the Byzantines and injured the Romans. [Note how an expert martial artist could be of great use in combat thanks to his unarmed fighting skills.] He perished also, for in order to make the soldiers angry enough to kill him he immediately punched one with his fist and with a leap gave another a violent kick. [For some unknown reason, the martial artist in question sought to be killed. The kick suggests that he was an expert pankrationist.] Severus was so pleased at the capture of Byzantium that to his soldiers in Mesopotamia (where he was at this time) he said unreservedly "We have taken Byzantium too!" [This creates the problem of dating; see later.] He deprived the city of its independence and of its civil rank, made it tributary, confiscating the property of the citizens. He granted the town and its territory to the Perinthians, and the latter ... committed innumerable outrages .... [With] his demolition of the walls of the city ... he abolished a strong Roman outpost and base of operations against the barbarians from the Pontus and Asia. I was one that viewed the walls after they had fallen, and a person would have judged that they had been taken by some other people than the Romans. [*Note how Dio constantly notes the difference between the Romans and Byzantines. At this time, before the granting of citizenship to all freeborn by Caracalla in 212, the vast majority of the population of the Roman Empire were not considered Romans, and neither did they see themselves as such. Caracalla's action was thus one of the most momentous moments in history, making the inhabitants of the Roman Empire Romans.*]' (Dio 75.12.3ff, tr. by Foster, pp.341–43, with changes, corrections and comments)

The above text shows how the city of Byzantium was finally taken thanks to the blockade and the fact that the Severan fleet was able to put a stranglehold on the city. This was to be the principal reason for the surrender of the city to foreign enemies, whether the name of the city was Byzantium or Constantinople. The city was basically impregnable so long as it possessed a navy that could protect its routes of supply. In this case, the Byzantine fleet, despite being 500 strong, was not powerful enough to resist the much larger ships of the Roman Praetorian fleets, even less so when these were overladen with cargo of foodstuffs so that the smaller ships could not exploit their greater mobility to avoid contact with the warships.

From the viewpoint of military history, the most important point in Dio's account of the siege is the mention of the fact that the Roman forces lacked the sophisticated siege engineering skills of the architect, engineer and philosopher Priscus, and that when his skills became known to the emperor he eagerly sought his services. This means that even if the great skills of Archimedes had been preserved among the learned architects, philosophers and engineers, they were not known to the Roman siege engineers. This also proves that very large naval forces could be put to sea by coastal cities when they chose to do so, the implication being that we should put far greater trust in the sometimes huge numbers of ships that the ancient sources give us. However, it appears that in such cases the vast majority of the ships were small monoremes, which were no match for larger triremes in a regular naval battle. It was because of this that the Severan forces were able to starve out the city. To put it simply, it was thanks to the larger ships of the Praetorian fleets that Severus won at the Hellespont and then at Byzantium, and that he was able to defeat Niger at sea so that he could land his troops in Asia Minor.

Chapter 6

The Wars in the East 194–195 (or 194–199?)

6.1. The Purge

Septimius Severus appears to have arrived in the East very soon after the defeat of Niger, so was in a position to secure the region for himself. He did not only face the remnants of the forces of Niger and his supporters, but also the ongoing wars with the Oshroeni, Adiabeni and Arabs. True to his character, Severus launched a purge of Niger's supporters, a necessary course of action in the circumstances. Severus divided the Province of Syria as a safety measure into two, Syria Coele and Syria Phoenice, so that no governor in the region would thereafter possess such a concentration of forces as Niger had. He rewarded those persons, cities and military units in the region who had supported him, while he punished those who had backed Niger. As noted above, the Legio III Cyrenaica was given the title 'Severiana' and its commander, governor P. Aelius Severianus Maximus, was reappointed as governor. The punishment of the wealthy individuals who had supported Niger enabled Severus to reward his supporters handsomely.[1]

6.2. The First Stage of the War against the Oshroeni, Adiabeni and Arabs in 194

It did not take long for Severus to see that it would be necessary for him to launch a military campaign against the Oshroeni, Adiabeni and Arabs. This would provide him with victories over barbarians, would give his men booty and would show him as protector of Roman interests in the region. Dio's opinion was that the only reason for Severus's campaign against them was a desire for glory, which is taking the evidence a bit too far because it is clear that it was also necessary to punish them if Severus wanted to retain the Roman position in the region. Herodian also mentions the troubles in the East after the death of Niger, but only by stating that Severus wanted to attack the king of the Atreni (Hatra) and advance into Parthia to punish them because they had supported Niger in the civil war. On the basis of Dio's text, this is only partially true, as both had initially supported Niger but had then abandoned him at the moment of his first trouble.

As enemies the Oshroeni, Adiabeni and Hatrans were typical of the region. The principal influence on their military practices had been the Parthian and Armenian cavalry. The cavalries of all the tribes were fashioned on the Parthian model, possessing cataphracted multipurpose horsemen who could use bows at long distance and spears and swords at close range. In addition to this, they possessed lighter cavalry consisting of mounted archers and lancers on unarmoured horses, and also Bedouin-style cavalry that could ride camels to the battlefield and then fight on horseback or from atop of their camels, or dismount from their camels to fight as infantry. In the field of cavalry warfare, their forces were roughly equal to those possessed by the Romans, but their infantry was almost completely worthless in the open against Roman foot soldiers. All these nations possessed infantry that was meant to fight in close-quarters phalanxes with spears, javelins and swords, with tactics borrowed from the Greeks and Romans, but the vast majority of the infantry appears to have consisted of archers and slingers. The fighting quality of the foot archers was superb, but that of their close-quarters infantry was poor, being able to fight effectively against the Romans only from atop some wall or mountain fastness. It was only when these infantry forces had great numerical advantage over the Romans that they could expect to prevail. Indeed, it was thanks to this that they were able to besiege the Romans at Nisibis prior to the arrival of Severus, the local Roman forces being simply too small to challenge them in the open. The details of the wars fought against the Romans by the Oshroeni, Adiabeni and Hatrans also prove that they all possessed some expertise in siege warfare so could hope to keep the Romans at bay. The siege equipment that these nations used seems to have been borrowed from the Greeks.

The sparse information that we have of the war against the rebels comes from the pen of Dio, and is quoted here to allow an analysis of the problematic parts of it in greater detail:

> 'During the progress of this siege [of Byzantium] Severus out of a desire for fame had made a campaign against the barbarians – the Oshroeni, the Adiabeni, and the Arabians. The Oshroeni and Adiabeni having revolted were besieging Nisibis: defeated by Severus they sent an embassy to him after the death of Niger, not to beg for clemency ... but to demand reciprocal favours, pretending to have brought about the outcome for his benefit. It was for his sake, they said, that they had destroyed the soldiers who had belonged to Niger's party. Indeed, they sent a few gifts to him and promised to restore the captives and whatever spoils were left. However, they were not willing either to abandon the walled towns they had captured or to accept the imposition of tributes, but they desired those in existence to be lifted from their country. [The most notable point about this account is that the Adiabeni, whose core territories lay to the east of the Tigris in Adiabene, were tributaries of Rome and hence their client kingdom.] It was this that led to the war just mentioned.' (Dio 75/76.1.1ff. {Xiphilinus, Cary ed., 194ff.}, tr. by Foster, p.347, with comment)[2]

The problematic bit in the above is the claim that Severus had defeated the Oshroeni and Adiabeni while they were besieging Nisibis. One could interpret this that Severus had taken a northerly route to Melitene while his Illyrian army was paralyzed in front of the Cilician Gates and that he had inflicted a defeat on the rebels who had crossed the Euphrates, or that the defeat referred to some other raid or invasion by them, or that it meant the rebels had failed to take the city of Nisibis through siege and that it had been one of the cities that had declared their support for Severus (just like the cities of Laodicea and Tyre) – hence Severus had defeated the besiegers. In my opinion, the third option is the likeliest.

Dio continues:

'When he [Severus] had crossed the Euphrates [Dio fails to mention any march against the capital of Oshroene, the city of Edessa, but considering the fact that it lay on the route to Nisibis, this is a distinct possibility. In such a case the likeliest route would have been to use either the northern road or the southern road to Edessa. The most direct route from Antioch to Edessa would have been the northern one which led through the city of Zeugma and then across the Euphrates to the city of Apamea and from there to Edessa. If he chose this route, the intention was to strike at the enemy capital immediately. However, if he chose the more southerly route and crossed the Euphrates at Hierapolis, then the intention would have been to avoid the possibility of contested crossing so that he would have been able to approach Edessa from the south. But since Dio fails to mention any march against Edessa, it is possible that Severus actually avoided this in order to be able to relieve the city of Nisibis as fast as possible. In such a case, he would have either used the route that crossed the Euphrates at Hierapolis or one further south in order to surprise the enemy by approaching Nisibis from the south. The last mentioned would have meant the crossing of the Euphrates somewhere close to the city of Sura or Callinicum, then a march through the deserted territory up to Singara and from there north to the city of Nisibis. This last alternative is the likeliest because what Dio describes next is a march through deserts, but is not conclusive because the terrain in the middle of summer heat could also be thought to be destitute of water. Birley's conclusion on page 115 is that Severus advanced via Zeugma to Oshroene, which was then annexed and C. Julius Pacatianus was appointed as its governor. The ruler Abgar, however, was allowed to keep Edessa and the area around it. On 14 April 195, Julia Domna was also honoured with the title *mater castrorum* to endear the troops with her. This is indeed a plausible course for the campaign, but in my opinion this does not rule out the other options because the conquest of Oshroene could have easily taken place after the relief of Nisibis, and in my opinion it did; see below.] and invaded hostile territory, where the country was destitute of water and at this summer season had become especially parched, he came dangerously near losing great numbers of soldiers. Wearied as they were by their marching and the hot sun, the dust-storms that they encountered harassed them greatly, so that they could no longer walk nor yet speak, but only utter the words "Water, water!" When moisture appeared, on account of its strangeness it attracted no more attention than if it had not been found, till Severus called for a cup, and having filled it with water drank it down in full view of all. Upon this some others likewise drank and were invigorated. [Birley p.116 quite correctly draws attention to the fact that as a native of Tripolitania, Severus was familiar with the desert wells and knew that the water was safe to consume, and was therefore prepared to lead by example. Severus had also served in the area.] Soon after Severus entered Nisibis and himself waited there, but dispatched Lateranus and Candidus and Laetus in various directions among the barbarians named. [These would be the Oshroeni, Adiabeni and Arabs. The latter would presumably be the Scenite Arabs/Bedouins, whose ruler would probably have been the king of Hatra.] These upon attaining their goals proceeded to lay waste the land of the barbarians and to capture their cities. [In my opinion, this clearly describes a march through the southerly route and its deserts straight to the city of Nisibis to relieve it. After this, Severus then stayed at Nisibis, from which he dispatched his three generals against the enemies mentioned.] While Severus was greatly priding himself upon this achievement and feeling that he had surpassed all mankind in both understanding and bravery, a most unexpected event took place. One Claudius, a robber, who overran Judaea and Syria and was sought for in consequence with great diligence, came to him one day with horsemen, like some military tribune, and saluted and kissed him. The visitor was not discovered at the time nor was he later arrested. [This account actually makes it probable that Severus made a deal with this Claudius, contrary to the hostile account provided by Dio. And who would this Claudius have been? The likeliest alternative is that he had been a cavalry officer of Niger, quite possibly some local nobleman with his followers, who had then found himself out of work and had begun to plunder until Severus pardoned him.] And the Arabians because none of their neighbours was willing to aid them, sent an embassy a second time to Severus making quite reasonable propositions. Still, they did not obtain what they wanted, inasmuch as they had not come in person. [The Romans always expected that the rulers of their enemies would humble themselves publicly before Rome.]' (Dio 75/76.1.1ff. {Xiphilinus, Cary ed., 194ff.}, tr. by Foster, p.347ff., with changes, corrections and comments)

The first stage of the operations against the Oshroeni, Adiabeni and Arabs (probably of Hatra and their client kingdoms/sheikdoms) clearly consisted of an advance through the desert regions via Singara to Nisibis, to relieve it from the siege. The route chosen and the timing of such a march in desert conditions were clearly meant to surprise the enemy. In other words, Septimius Severus's goal was to achieve a strategic surprise over his enemies, which he did indeed do by advancing from an unexpected direction during the summer. This was a great achievement, because his enemies consisted of local peoples who were very familiar with desert conditions and the routes which the Romans could use. Severus played this precise knowledge against them. The enemy did not expect the Romans to be able to make such a march, and indeed they were not entirely mistaken because as a native of desert regions Septimius Severus was clearly unaware of the fact that his mostly European forces would be in difficulties in such conditions. The likeliest reason for Septimius's ability to surprise his enemies is that he knew the area well because he had been the legate of the Legio IV Scythica at Zeugma. His wife, Julia Domna, would also have possessed considerable influence in the area through her family connections. Furthermore, we should not forget that Septimius's army included many other persons of importance who knew the area well and who could participate in war councils. Whoever was behind the idea of strategic surprise deserves our admiration, and it is very likely that it was Severus himself because all of his operations appear to have relied on the use of surprise and stratagems where possible. As such, he was a Roman Hannibal.

6.3. The Jewish and Samaritan Insurgencies in 194–195 or ca. 194–199

The above material includes one very important piece of evidence when it is combined with information provided by Orosius (7.17), who refers to an attempted revolt by the Jews and Samaritans which was crushed with military force by Septimius Severus just before his war against the Parthians, Arabs and Adiabeni. The dating, however, is problematic because Severus received the rebel Claudius when he had already reached Nisibis, with the implication that the revolt cannot have been crushed prior to the war. The other possibility is that Dio has purposefully left out the actual reason for the visit, which could have been a demonstration of loyalty to Severus after Claudius had already changed sides and crushed the other Jewish rebels. However, if we accept Dio's dating of events, then it is likely that the Jews and Samaritans attempted to exploit the same chaos as the Oshroeni, Adiabeni and Arabs, and that Claudius was one of the rebel commanders whose visit was connected with Severus's designs, in that he bribed Claudius to change sides. As noted above, it is possible that Niger had levied and armed locals to fight against the Legio III Cyrenaica and other forces supporting Severus. It is more than likely that Claudius actually deserted to Severus and was instrumental in the crushing of the revolt, even if Dio implies the exact opposite. However, if we accept Dio's version[3] as correct, then it is clear that Claudius was not found later because he was forced to flee from Judaea to the East when Septimius's troops crushed the revolt. The visiting of Septimius at Nisibis suggests that he had advanced on the double to relieve the city, with the revolt of Judaea and Samaria delegated to the forces left behind for this purpose. The core of such forces would presumably have consisted of the remnants of the Legio VI Ferrata posted at Caparcotna (Kfar Otman, Galilee, Israel) and Legio X Fretensis at Aelia Capitolina (Jerusalem), plus their auxiliary support forces, the regular garrisons in the area. The Legio III Cyrenaica and its support forces may also have been used for this.

The problematic part of the above interpretation concerns the dating of the revolt or revolts, as the various sources offer different dates and details. Dio refers to a visit by the bandit Claudius, while Orosius places the Jewish-Samaritan War to just after the campaign against Niger, which both imply the year 194. However, since Severus received Claudius at Nisibis, presumably in 194 or 195, it would seem probable that the war lasted at least until 195. Jerome (*Chronicon* a.197, Olympiad 244) dates the Jewish and Samaritan war to 197. However, upon closer examination it becomes clear that his dating is the same as that of Orosius, because Jerome says the war against the Oshroeni, Adiabeni and Arabs (mistakenly stating that Severus took the titles Parthicus, Arabicus and Adiabenicus) was immediately followed by the war against Albinus (*Chronicon* a.207, Olympiad 246). Jerome thus places the Jewish-Samaritan War roughly to the years 194/195. Bar Hebraeus (p.55) states that the Jews and Samaritans fought a fierce war against each other during the first year of Severus's reign (i.e. in about 193/194). Michael the Syrian (Michael Syrus, Michael Rabo, 6.7)[4] states the same, but his dating is quite uncertain because he claims that the reign of Severus began in 198. According to the *Historia Augusta* (Sev. 16.6–7), in the immediate aftermath of the second Parthian War in about 198/199, the Senate voted Severus a Jewish triumph (*Iudaicus triumphus*) for his successes in Syria, which Severus gave to his son Antoninus (Caracalla). This implies that there was some fighting in the area in about 197/199. The *Historia Augusta* (Sev. 17.1) adds that Severus granted several kinds of rights for the cities of Palestine and forbade conversion to Judaism and Christianity, suggesting that Severus thanked those communities that had sided with him during the war.

The above leaves open three main alternatives. Firstly, it is possible that there was just one war which was fought in the immediate aftermath of the fall of Niger, lasting roughly from 194 until 195. In this case it is possible that there was at first a general uprising of the Samaritans and Jews and that the latter then defected to Severus, because he and Bassianus (Antoninus/Caracalla) showed tolerance towards Jews (see below). Most of the evidence supports this conclusion, the only real anomaly being the information provided by the *Historia Augusta* which clearly connects the war against the Jews to the year 198/199. This anomaly can be explained in two different ways. It would be easy to claim that this is just another example of false information in the *Historia Augusta*, but we should remember that it is in general more trustworthy for the reign of Severus than the other sources, which means we should not dismiss its evidence too lightly. Therefore the problem persists. Regardless, there still are possible ways to reconcile its evidence with the other sources, which is that the war in question did indeed take place in 194/195 and that Septimius gave the triumph for his son to celebrate later because he himself did not want to celebrate his Parthian triumph after 198 due to his gout.

The second alterative is that it is possible there were two wars, one being fought after the death of Niger and another in about 197/198/199. In this case it is impossible to know for certain which of these was the war between the Jews and Samaritans and which was the general uprising against the Romans, except that it is probable that Claudius defected to Severus's side in about 194/195. Whichever, the latter would have coincided with the Parthian invasion of Roman territory in 197 and Severus's counterattack in 198. Then there is the third alternative, which is that the war had many different phases and lasted from about 194 until 198/199. It is unfortunately impossible to know for certain which of these alternatives is correct, even if it is at least clear that some serious fighting took place in 194–195 because Dio refers to this in the context of Claudius's visit of Nisibis.

It is very likely that in the conflict between the Samaritans and Jews, Severus actually sided with the latter because all extant evidence points in this direction. It is possible that the war started as a general uprising of the Jews and Samaritans against the Romans, or at least against Severus once Niger had been defeated, but if this is the case then at least a very significant part of the Jewish community deserted and/or sided with Severus, if they had not done so from the beginning. The above-mentioned Claudius could be one such Jewish leader with a Roman name. The reason for this conclusion is that both Severus and Antoninus (Caracalla) are presented in extraordinarily good light in the rabbinic tradition. This is also confirmed by the Roman sources. One such example is the law included in the *Digest* which states (tr. by Goodman, p.482): 'The Divine Severus and Antoninus permitted those that follow the Jewish *superstitio* to acquire honours, but also imposed upon them duties such as should not harm their *superstitio*.' The above-mentioned law against conversion to Judaism and Christianity could be thought as such a duty, while the honours can be thought to also include the rights granted for the communities of Palestine. The forbidding of conversion would probably have been meant to ensure that similar troubles as had recently taken place would not happen in the future. The law, however, was not followed up in practice because people continued to become converts of both religions – the *Historia Augusta* even claims that Caracalla detested the laws that forbade conversion.[5] It was thanks to this tolerance that we find the *Mishnah* including the claim that Antoninus (in my opinion undoubtedly Caracalla) converted to Judaism (tr. by Goodman, pp.482–83):

'Antoninus made candelabrum for the synagogue. Rabbi [Judah haNasi] heard about it and said, "Blessed be God, who moved him to make a candelabrum for the synagogue." Rabbi Samuel son of Rabbi Isaac, "Why did Rabbi say, 'Blessed be God'? Should he not say, 'Blessed be Our God'? If he said, 'Blessed be God', it indicates that Antoninus never in fact converted to Judaism. If he said, 'Blessed be our God', it indicated that Antoninus in fact converted to Judaism.'' There are some things that indicate that Antoninus was converted, and there are some things that indicate that Antoninus was not converted.'

It is actually quite clear that Antoninus did not convert, but this extract makes it apparent that he showed great respect towards the Jews and Judaism. This was clearly the policy followed by both father and son, even if it was the latter who showed greater respect. In light of the fact that the Jewish tradition remembers both in such a light, it is clear that Severus had supported the Jews against the Samaritans. Furthermore, why would the triumph have still been named a Jewish tiumph if Severus supported the Jews against the Samaritans? The obvious answer is that the Romans typically used archaic terms from the past for their triumphs, so the only prestigious term available for Severus and Antoninus in this case was the *Iudaicus triumphus*. In fact, Caracalla not only showered the Jews with privileges, but gave them the greatest gift available by making them all Roman citizens in 212. The same policies were later followed by Heliogabalus/Elagabalus and Alexander Severus. So long as the Jews paid their taxes, they were allowed to live their separate lives, and in practice the Jews were ruled by an 'ethnarch' whose Hebrew title was *nasi* (patriarch). The Judah haNasi mentioned in the extract above was promoted by Antoninus; his descendants held this position during the third century, his grandson coming to possess Gothic bodyguards that he used like a mafia boss to enforce his will.[6]

In my opinion, it is even possible that this Judah should be identified with the above-mentioned Claudius. The use of one native local leader to control an unruly populace is a standard means to control occupied territories with a significant insurgency problem, such as was the case in Judaea and Samaria. I would suggest that even if none of the sources specifically mention this, this was indeed the case in 198/199. In other words, I would suggest that Severus put Claudius (or someone else) in charge of putting down the native resistance in 194/195, that this person or his son became the ethnarches/*nasi* of the Jews,[7] and that the war continued until 198/199. That seems the likeliest alternative in light of the evidence. Furthermore, insurgencies in mountainous areas and deserts are rarely put down fast and easily, and such insurgencies typically require the desertion of significant numbers of rebels before the resistance collapses.

6.4. The Second Stage of the War against the Oshroeni, Adiabeni and Arabs in 194–195

When Severus relieved the siege of Nisibis, he was ready to begin a multipronged attack under Lateranus, Candidus and Laetus against his enemies (see the quote above). One of his commanders advanced westwards from Nisibis to Oshroene, which was devastated. A second commander advanced eastwards across the Tigris into Adiabene, which was similarly devastated, while a third commander marched southwards against the Scenite

Arabs and the city of Hatra. The latter operation was clearly the most successful of the three, causing the Arabs to send envoys to ask for peace terms, although the local rulers refused to be humbled before Severus.

The problem with the above information is that we do not know when the campaign took place. The usual assumption is that Severus spent the rest of 194 in the settling of affairs in the East, which involved punishment of the supporters of Niger, and then began the campaign against his other enemies in the spring of 195. This is the conclusion made for example by Birley (115ff.), but in my opinion that is a mistake. The text refers quite clearly to the situation prevailing in the immediate aftermath of Niger's death, stating in no uncertain terms that the march to Nisibis took place in the middle of summer. The only logical date for this is therefore the summer of 194. However, it is possible that the campaigns of the three *duces* lasted from late summer/early autumn 194 until early winter 195.

6.5. The Gothic War that never came in about 194/195

After this, the extant fragments of Dio (76.3.1, Cary ed., p.198) include information of an intended invasion of Roman territory by the 'Scythians', in other words by the Goths. These were holding discussions regarding such a move, when all of a sudden there were thunderbolts and lightning, accompanied by rain, resulting in the deaths of three of their chief men. The Goths saw this as a sign from the gods and abandoned their plans, and in fact appear to have become Roman allies. I do not see any reason to connect this weather miracle or the previous such miracles at the Cilician Gates and Issus with the fictitious adoption of Marcus Aurelius as Severus's father (see later), and that these miracles were invented, as sometimes suggested. We should not assume that cases of bad weather take place only during our own lifetime and that all previous examples are literary inventions. If these events did play any role in the fiction of the Severans becoming members of the Antonine dynasty, it was that in the aftermath of the weather miracles Severus had an even better opportunity to present himself and his family as Antonines. We should not forget that the weather miracle of Marcus Aurelius was entirely different from those of Septimius Severus.[8]

The placing of the planned invasion of Roman territory in the middle of the Mesopotamian campaign suggests that the Goths were planning to do so in the spring of 195. But why should they have been planning such an attack? As the extant text of Dio does not give us the reason, we can only speculate. It is possible that the Goths just wanted to exploit the chaos within the Roman Empire, that Niger had sent them an urgent plea for help or that the Byzantines had appealed for assistance. The first and third options are the likeliest, but the question is ultimately unsolvable unless new evidence surfaces.

6.6. The Third Stage of the War against the Oshroeni, Adiabeni and Arabs in 195

After this, Dio returns to his narrative of the Mesopotamian campaign:

> 'Severus again made three divisions of his army, and giving one to Laetus, one to Anullinus, and one to Probus, sent them against *Archên* … [There is a lacuna

at this point and we do not know what word was meant. Adiabene, Atrene and Arbelitis have all been suggested as emendations. My suggestion is that Dio meant the same territories, Oshroene, Adiabene and the territory of the Secenite Arabs with the city of Hatra, because Severus had not granted peace to these.] and they, invading it in three divisions, subdued it not without trouble. [This means that all three enemy chieftains surrendered in the presence of Severus and their lands became tributary kingdoms of Rome.] Severus bestowed some dignity upon Nisibis and entrusted the city to the care of a knight. [Birley, p. 117, suggests that this man could have been Valerius Valerianus, whose inscription gives him credit for completing the '*felicissima expeditio Mesopotamena*'.] He declared he had won a mighty territory and rendered it a bulwark of Syria. It is shown, on the contrary by the facts themselves that the place is responsible for our constant wars as well as for great expenditures. It yields very little and uses up vast sums. And having extended our borders to include men who are neighbours of the Medes and Parthians rather than ourselves, we are always, one might say, fighting over those peoples. [This view is based on Dio's own very limited understanding of what it meant to be a superpower in antiquity. As I have already shown in my biography of Caracalla, Dio did not really understand warfare or strategy. The possession of Nisibis and other nearby areas did indeed result in them becoming the scenes of much fighting, but it was better to fight there than in Syria. Severus was basically correct in calling these areas a bulwark for Syria.]' Dio 75/76.1.1ff. (Xiphilinus, Cary ed , 194ff.), tr. by Foster, p.348, with changes, corrections and comments)

The above account suggests that in 195 Severus kept his headquarters at Nisibis while his *duces* conducted a three-pronged invasion of the same lands as previously. The troubles mentioned probably refer to the desert conditions, but the fact that the invaded areas submitted to the emperor means that it was still successful enough for Severus to leave the area as a conqueror when he faced an imminent civil war with Albinus. All three of Severus's campaigns conducted in the course of 194–195 were great successes. Oshroene was annexed and C. Julius Pacatianus was appointed as its governor, but Abgar, the king of Oshroene, was allowed to retain the city of Edessa and its immediate surroundings. Aelius Spartianus (*HA Sev.* 9.8–11) also states that the Adiabeni and Parthians were both brought back to their allegiance. However, Aurelius Victor (20.15–16) claims that Severus reduced the Arabs to a provincial status as soon as he attacked them, but did not subject the Adiabeni to tributary status because their terrain was too barren.

In my opinion, the period evidence in the form of Dio should be preferred in this case, namely that the Adiabeni were also subjected to tribute-paying status.[9] These victories enabled Severus to take the titles of *Arabicus* and *Adiabenicus*, for which he later celebrated a triumph, but Spartianus claims that he refused the title of *Parthicus* on the grounds that it would hurt Parthian feelings. Strictly speaking, Spartianus's claim is slightly inaccurate because Severus did use *Parthicus* as part of the titles *Parthicus Arabicus* and *Parthicus Adiabenicus*, but at the same time it is also correct because Severus did not use the title *Parthicus* alone without qualifications until after his Parthian campaign in 198. This means that Severus did indeed agree to conclude a peace settlement with Parthia at this time. The reason for this was that he needed to deal with Albinus before he could

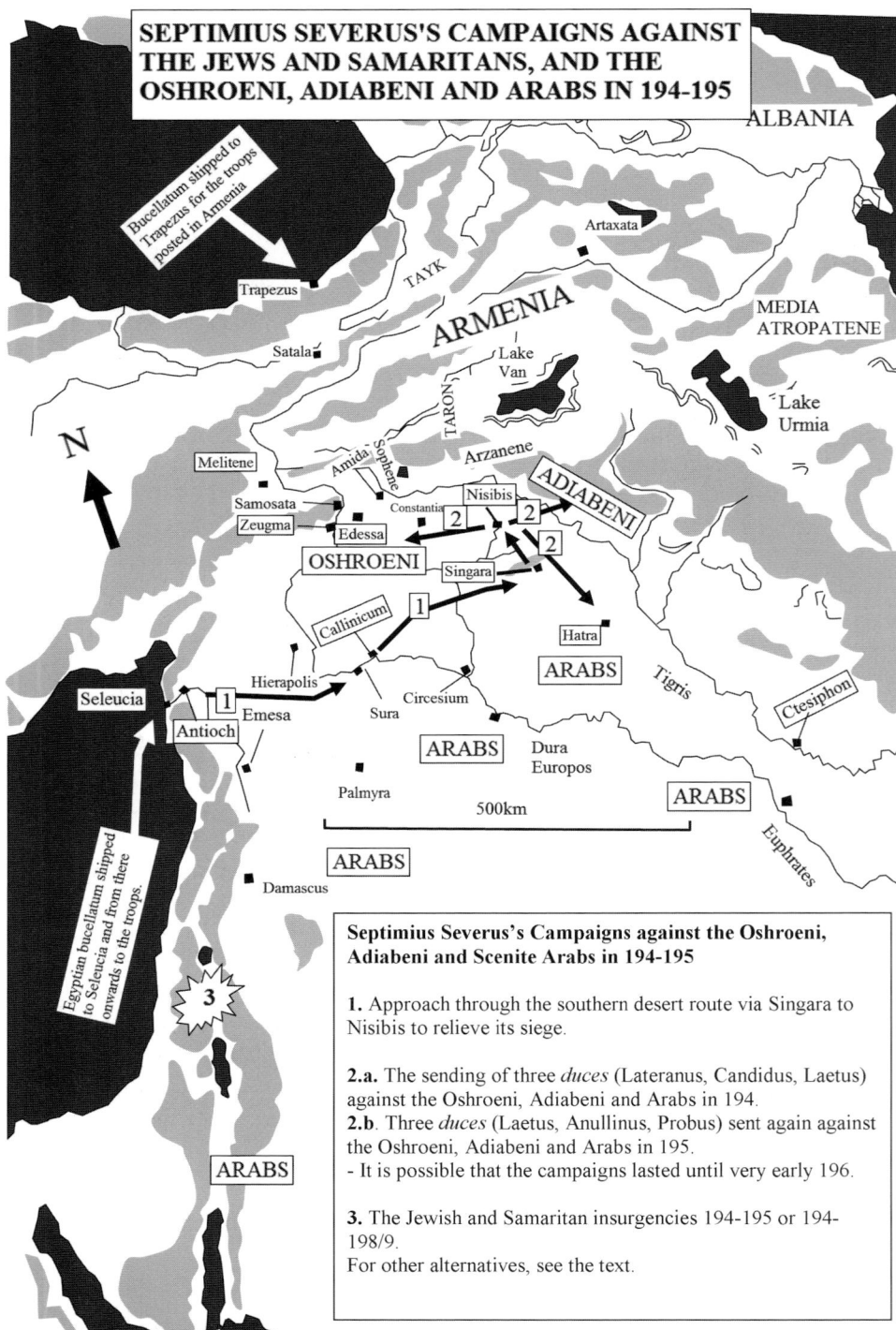

contemplate a major campaign against the Parthians. The Parthians were also fighting a civil war, so the terms suited their needs as well. The annexing of Mesopotamia and the reducing of the Adiabenes and Arabs to the position of client states secured a defensive bulwark for Roman Syria, as stated by Severus himself, in case the Parthians chose not to respect the peace agreement.

Top left and right: Coins of Septimius Severus commemorating his victories over the Parthians, Arabs and Adiabenes. (source: Duruy).
Below left: A coin depicting Julia Domna with the title *mater castrorum* in 195 (source: Beger 1696).
Below right: a coin of Albinus ca. 197 depicting him as Augustus in response to the attempted assassination by Severus's assassins (source: Duruy).

It was thanks to these events that Septimius Severus was able to claim the titles *imperator V*, *VI* and *VII*, presumably all by the end of 195. Severus gave his wife, Julia Domna, the title *mater castrorum* on 14 April 195, which recalled the days of the Antonine dynasty when Marcus Aurelius had given the same title to his wife Faustina. It was also in the same year that Severus adopted himself into the Antonine dynasty by proclaiming himself to be the son of Marcus Aurelius and therefore the brother of Commodus, who was still fondly remembered by the soldiers for his generosity.[10] This was only the first part of his plans to promote his family among the soldiery. He did not yet want to alarm Albinus, his next target of attack. True to his character, he wanted to rid himelf of Albinus through treachery if possible.

Chapter 7

The War between Septimius Severus and Albinus in 195/196–197

7.1. The Gathering of the Storm in 195–197

The exact sequence of events for the period from late 195 until 197 cannot be reconstructed with certainty due to the conflicting evidence in the sources. Whittaker notes the dating problems for the length of the siege of Byzantium, the whereabouts of Septimius and the dating of the naming of Caracalla as Caesar. Dio offers two conflicting dates for the length of the siege of Byzantium, stating that it lasted three years and that Septimius received the news of its fall while still in Mesopotamia. When this is combined with an extant inscription by the Aezani of Asia Minor, this would mean that Septimius stayed in Mesopotamia until the end of 195 and that he also received a delegation of the Aezani in 195, on the basis of titles included in the inscription which would also prove that Caracalla was appointed as Caesar in that year. This would place the event well before Caracalla reached Viminacium, where he is claimed to have been appointed as Caesar by the *Historia Augusta*. Whittaker suggests two likely scenarios: it is possible that Dio made a mistake regarding the place where Septimius was when he heard the news, or that Dio confused it with Septimius's third regal year.[1]

On the basis of the above and other evidence,[2] some (e.g. Birley) think that Bassianus (Caracalla) was already named Marcus Aurelius Antoninus and Caesar in 195, with the implication that it was this that pushed Albinus to lay claim to the position of Augustus in 195 and that he led his legions across the Channel that year. These historians also think that Herodian's version of events is incorrect, so Septimius did not march on the double without any stops from Mesopotamia to Gaul. The best evidence against this are the so-called *Adventus* coins that were struck in the city of Rome at the end of 196, which implies that Septimius must have visited Rome at least briefly and thus marched slowly back west. This is by no means conclusive so it is not surprising that the historians have not reached any consensus regarding the evidence. The titles in the above-mentioned inscription could have been recorded wrongly or later (this is the likeliest alternative), so the event could easily have taken place after 4 April 196, the traditional date for the naming of Caracalla as Caesar. This line of thinking has been adopted, for example, by Barbara Levick. Anne Daquet-Gagey mentions this date for the nomination, but suggests that since the dating is not secure it should be moved a few months earlier. However, none of the historians have questioned the evidence for the visit to the city of Rome in the form of the *Adventus* coins and inscriptions.[3]

I will try to make sense of this. The most important point regarding the traditionally accepted dating of the elevation of Caracalla to the position of Caesar on 4 April 196 is that it is based on his claimed date of birth, which is therefore not secure at all.

A bust of Septimius Severus (Louvre). The forked beard connects him with his new namesake Marcus Aurelius, his newly-found father. Source: Duruy.

A statue of Septimius Severus. Source: Duruy

A bust of Clodius Albinus (Vatican) according to Duruy. Bernoulli considers the identification false.

A bust of Clodius Albinus (Louvre) according to Duruy

Herodian writes the following regarding Severus's opening moves against Albinus:

'Once Niger had been dealt with, the only obstacle that remained in his [Severus's] way was Albinus, who, he heard, began to behave like an emperor [strictly speaking like a king, or *Basileus*, but the meaning is the same] puffed up with the honourable title of Caesar. And, what he most disliked, he was informed that the principal members of the Senate had sent him [Albinus] private letters inviting him to come to Rome while Severus was absent .... For all the nobles preferred to have Albinus as emperor because he had a long line of ancestors of noble origins and had a mild character .... Severus ... declined to attack the man because he did not have plausible excuse ... but resolved to ... attempt to take him out of the way by treachery .... He sent reliable imperial couriers with letters to Albinus, giving them secret orders to deliver the letters publicly but watch for an opportunity to request a private meeting in which case they were to fall upon him and kill him while he was unprotected by guards. He likewise gave them deadly poisons with instructions to tempt some of his cooks or cup-bearers to poison him .... [H]is [Albinus's] friends always suspected Severus's integrity and were continually reminding Albinus to be very cautious against an adversary who was capable of deceiving and every kind of treachery. This estimate they had formed as a result of Severus's actions against Niger's officers whose children he held in custody, as we have mentioned above, and after he had managed to force them to betray their master, he basely murdered both them and their children ... which made Albinus keep a greater number of guards ... and not suffer any of Severus's messengers come into his presence till their swords were taken from them and their clothes had been searched for concealed weapons. When the couriers arrived and had delivered their dispatches in public and desired to meet him in private ... Albinus, suspecting treachery ordered them to be seized and having put them to the torture, ... got a confession of the whole plot. The men were then punished with death, and Albinus began to prepare himself against the enemy who had become exposed .... When Severus was informed of what had happened ... he no longer concealed his hatred of Albinus.' Herodian 3.5.2–6.1, tr. by Hart, pp.118–20, with changes, corrections and comments)

On the basis of Herodian's text (3.6.1ff.), Severus was still in Mesopotamia when this took place, and it was because of this that he began his march westward immediately. If we accept the dating of 195 for the nomination of Caracalla as Caesar, then Septimius began his undercover operations against Albinus immediately after he had finished his wars against the Oshroeni, Adiabeni and Arabs, which also places the beginning of his return trip to have been at the latest in late 195 or very early 196. Whatever the truth, it is clear that before Severus started his march, he needed to secure the goodwill of his soldiers for the new war. He began with a speech in which he gave his justifications for the war: 1) the soldiers had made him the sole Augustus; 2) Albinus was arming himself for war and therefore showed disrespect both to Severus's soldiers and to him; 3) Albinus did not respect the gods, because the gods were on Severus's side; 4) Severus's soldiers had justice on their side because they were only defending themselves against an aggressor; 5) Albinus's forces were a small island army and therefore unable to resist the full might of Severus's army; 6) Severus's army had been reinforced with strong auxiliary forces and included practically the entire Roman Army, so it would have vast numerical advantage; and 7) Severus's men had a sober general while Albinus was known for his life of luxury. Severus ended his speech by extolling the bravery of his soldiers and noting that the enemy had despised the gods by committing perjury against him. The army (undoubtedly with officers and heralds prompting them) responded by declaring Albinus an enemy of the state. Severus sealed his speech with a sizeable donative, after which he gave the order to begin the march west against Albinus. At the same time as Severus secured the loyalty of his army, he also killed Niger's wife, children and entire family as a safety measure to prevent their exploitation by Albinus (*HA Pes. Nig.* 6.1, *Sev.* 10.1).

Severus started his war preparations immediately by dispatching reinforcements to the forces besieging Byzantium while he himself organized the campaign against Albinus. It was absolutely necessary to end the siege of Byzantium as fast as possible so that the besieging forces could be used against Albinus. This was achieved so that Severus received the news of Byzantium's surrender while he was still in Mesopotamia. It is probable that Severus punished the city of Byzantium only when he was already marching against Albinus and had reached the city of Perinthus. In addition to this, he gave large grants of money for the reconstruction of cities that had been devastated by Niger's forces. According to Herodian (3.6.10ff.), Severus did not halt his march because of these measures, but moved his army forward regardless of weather. The soldiers were not allowed any breaks in the march, whether due to heat, cold or public holiday. Severus set an example to his soldiers by marching bare-headed in rain and snow (dates the campaign to the winter) while crossing the mountains. In addition to this, according to Herodian, Severus sent a *strategos* (general, *dux*) with a powerful force to the Alpine passes to guard the routes into Italy. It is usually thought that the man put in charge of this campaign was the first governor of Oshroene, C. Julius Pacatianus, because he afterwards had the title *procurator et praeses Alpium Cottiarum* and was adlected *inter comites* of the *Augusti* (i.e. Septimius and Caracalla, see below). Herodian clearly implies that Septimius did not make any halts during his march but proceeded straight to Gaul, but it is impossible to date the time of the year on the basis of the above because the mention of snow could refer to the conditions prevailing at the beginning, middle or end of the campaign. However, the birthday celebrations of Geta, if true, prove that Herodian is incorrect about Severus not making any halts. We should not take Herodian's text literally because it is clear that Severus could not march his forces in fighting condition without any short halts. It is clear that there were some but at the same time it is also clear that these were kept at a minimum. In fact, it is probable that Severus marched on the double in wintry conditions twice: in early 196 to reach the Balkans fast to secure it and then again in late 196 to early 197 to surprise Albinus.

According to Aelius Spartianus, it was at Viminacium, en route to Gaul, that Septimius named his son Bassianus (Caracalla) as Marcus Aurelius Antoninus and appointed him as Caesar, which he did for four reasons. Firstly, this signalled to Albinus that Septimius no longer considered him as Caesar. Secondly, the soldiers could now expect dynastic continuity with its rewards. The naming of a son as Caesar typically meant the giving of a donative to the soldiers, and I would suggest that this practice was also followed in this case. Thirdly, the name, just like Septimius's own claim to be the brother of Commodus, connected him and his family with the favourite emperors of the past. The upper classes loved Marcus Aurelius, while the soldiers loved Commodus. The fourth reason for the appointment, according to Aelius Spartianus (*HA Sev.* 10.3), was that the move destroyed the hopes that Septimius's brother, Geta, had of becoming his brother's successor. The location of Viminacium means that Septimius probably met his brother there and that Geta had voiced his hopes to Septimius. In light of this, it is probable that Septimius not only appointed his son as Caesar, but also took the precautionary step of removing Geta from his military command at this time. The bribery of soldiers with another donative would probably have been in order.

The traditional dating for the above is 4 April 196, on the grounds that it was Caracalla's official birthday, but it has long been known that the dating is not certain. However, we do also possess other dating evidence for the presence of Septimius in the Balkans roughly at this time, which lends support to the tradition. This comes in the description of how Severus met the future emperor Maximinus Thrax in Jordanes's *Getica* and Julius Capitolinus's *Maximini Duo*. According to both, Septimius was celebrating the birthday of his son Geta (27 May 196) when a man of huge stature named Maximinus asked for permission to wrestle with his soldiers. Septimius allowed him to wrestle first with camp followers, and when Maximinus had bested sixteen of those in succession without taking any rest in between, Septimius ordered him to join the cavalry. On the second or third day, Septimius saw Maximinus not obeying the tribune, and Septimius ordered the tribune to teach military discipline to the barbarian. Maximinus realized that it was the emperor who spoke and came in front of him. Septimius decided to test the man and ordered him to run after his horse. Septimius spurred on his horse to a slow trot, wheeling and circling about until he was weary, and then asked whether Maximinus could still wrestle. Maximinus answered in the affirmative, and Septimius dismounted and ordered his best soldiers to wrestle him. When Maximinus had defeated seven of these in succession, Septimius rewarded him with a gold collar and position in his bodyguards (*Corporis in aula = Aulici = Protectores = Scholae*). Maximinus thereafter became Septimius Severus's personal favourite and was swiftly advanced through the ranks.[4]

My own educated guess, on the basis of these details, is that Septimius probably began his journey from Mesopotamia either very late 195 or early 196 (likelier), so that he reached the Balkans in the spring of 196. This is more likely than the other alternative, according to which he reached the Balkans in 195. Otherwise, Septimius would need to have spent months in the Balkans or at Rome without doing anything in a situation in which his armies had been defeated in Gaul by Albinus's forces.[5]

According to Herodian, when Albinus learnt that Severus was marching rapidly against him, he became frightened because he had made no preparations for this. This contradicts Herodian's previous claim in which he stated that Albinus began to prepare for the usurpation immediately after the failed attempt against his life. We should probably not take Herodian too literally. It is quite possible that Albinus had indeed started making preparations for usurpation but so slowly that Severus's moves caught him unprepared. Herodian continues by saying that Albinus collected his forces, crossed the Channel and sent messages to the governors of neighbouring provinces, ordering them to send money and supplies for his army. Herodian does not mention the sending of

Coins of Pertinax. **Source**: Bernoulli.

Coin of Didius Julianus. **Source**: Bernoulli.

Coin of Pescennius Niger. **Source**: Bernoulli.

Coins of Clodius Albinus. **Source**: Bernoulli.

Coins of Septimius Severus. **Source**: Bernoulli.

Coins of Julia Domna. **Source**: Bernoulli.

Coins of Caracalla. **Source**: Bernoulli.

Coins of Geta. **Source**: Bernoulli.

Coin of Plautilla. **Source**: Bernoulli.

Coin of Macrinus. **Source**: Bernoulli.

Coin of Antoninus (Elagabalus/Heliogabalus). **Source**: Bernoulli.

Bust of Pertinax (Capitol).
Source: Bernoulli.

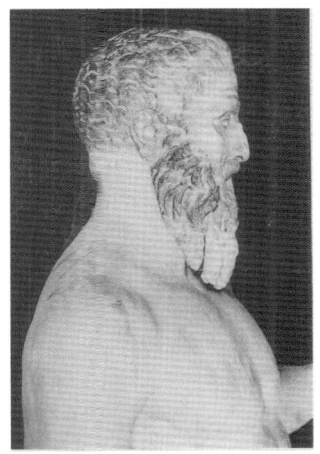

Bust of Pertinax (Louvre).
Source: Bernoulli.

Bust of Didius Julianus
(Capitol). **Source**: Bernoulli.

Bust of Didius Julianus
(Vatican). **Source**: Bernoulli.

Possible statue of Clodius Albinus (Vatican). **Source**: Bernoulli.

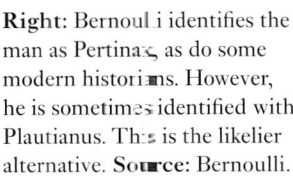

Left: Bust of Pescennius Niger (Capitol). **Source**: Bernoulli.

Right: Bernoulli identifies the man as Pertinax, as do some modern historians. However, he is sometimes identified with Plautianus. This is the likelier alternative. **Source**: Bernoulli.

Bernoulli suggests that this bust may represent Septimius Severus, but today many historians identify the man with Clodius Albinus. It is impossible to be absolutely certain, largely thanks to the fact that some of the coins of Severus and Albinus look so much alike. In my opinion, however, the identification with Septimius Severus is more likely because the beard style and profile are closer to that of the Louvre bust of Severus. **Source:** Bernoulli.

Bust of Septimius Severus. **Source:** Bernoulli.

Older version of Septimius Severus (bust in Munich). **Source:** Bernoulli.

Julia Domna according to Bernoulli, but one could also think that this woman could be Plautilla. **Source:** Bernoulli.

Bust of Caracalla. **Source:** Bernoulli.

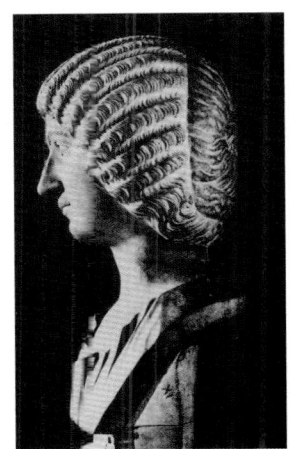

Bust of Julia Domna. **Source:** Bernoulli.

Bust of Geta. **Source:** Bernoulli.

A nineteenth-century photo of a bust of Julia Domna.

Markoura bust of Julia Domna. **Source:** Bernoulli.

According to Duruy a bust of Clodius Albinus, but according to Bernoulli this identification is wrong. **Source:** Bernoulli.

Bust of Septimius Severus (Capitol).
Source: Bernoulli.

Septimius Severus and Julia Domna.
Source: Bernoulli.

Septimius Severus (Gabii Louvre).
Source: Bernoulli.

Septimius Severus, profile (Gabii Louvre).
Source: Bernoulli.

Left: A statue of Septimius Severus at the British Museum.

Top: A bust of Septimius Severus at the British Museum.

Below: A coin depicting Septimius Severus and Julia Domna at the British Museum. (Photos by the author)

A gilded bronze bust of Septimius Severus found at Brescia. (Picture © Giovanni Dall'Orto/Wikipedia)

A bust of Caracalla at the British Museum. (Photo by the author)

Young Caracalla. (Public Domain, Wikimedia Commons)

Head of Septimius Severus (Cologne/Köln). (Public Domain, Wikimedia Commons)

Left: Portonaccio sarcophagus depicting a battle between the Romans and Germans ca. AD 180–190. (Public Domain/Wikimedia, user Jastrow) Note in particular the use of very peculiar types of helmets and the use of leather armour resembling the so-called *lorica segmentata*. It should be noted that a great variety of other types of helmets and shields were also in use at this time.

Legionary Q. Petilius, Bonn (drawn after Lindenschmit): Quintus Petilius, Q(uinti) f(ilius) Ofentina (tribu) Secundus, domo mediolanus, miles leg(ionis) XV primigeniae, an(norum) XXV, stipend(iorum) V, Heres ex t(estamento) f(aciendum) c(uravit). Wears tunica, Mainz-*gladius*, *pugio*-dagger, papyrus roll, *pilum*, *paenula*-cloak/mantel (soldier's *sagum*-cloak with the addition of *cucullus*-hood).

© Dr. Ilkka Syvanne 2016

ANTONINUS MAGNUS (CARACALLA) 211-217

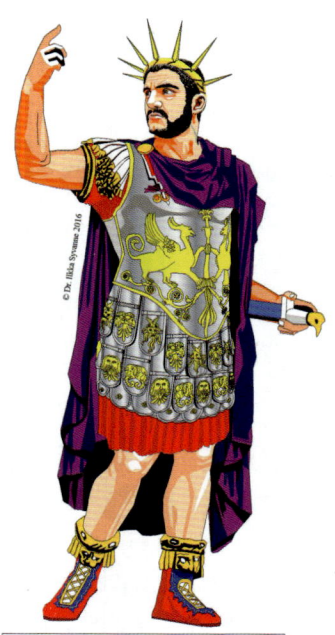

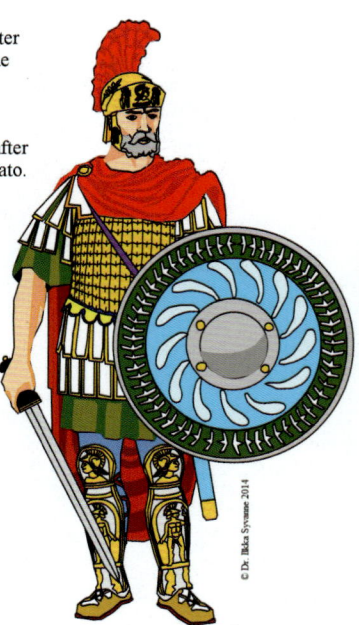

Top left: Antoninus Magnus better known as Caracalla. He wears the Sun-diadem to celebrate Helios.

Top right: *Trierarches* of the Misenum Fleet. Armour drawn after Mattesini and shield after D'Amato.

Source: Syvänne, *Caracalla*.

© Dr. Ilkka Syvanne 2014

Below: a multipurpose horseman described by Arrian. He could belong to either the auxiliary or legionary cavalry.

Source: Syvänne, *Caracalla.*

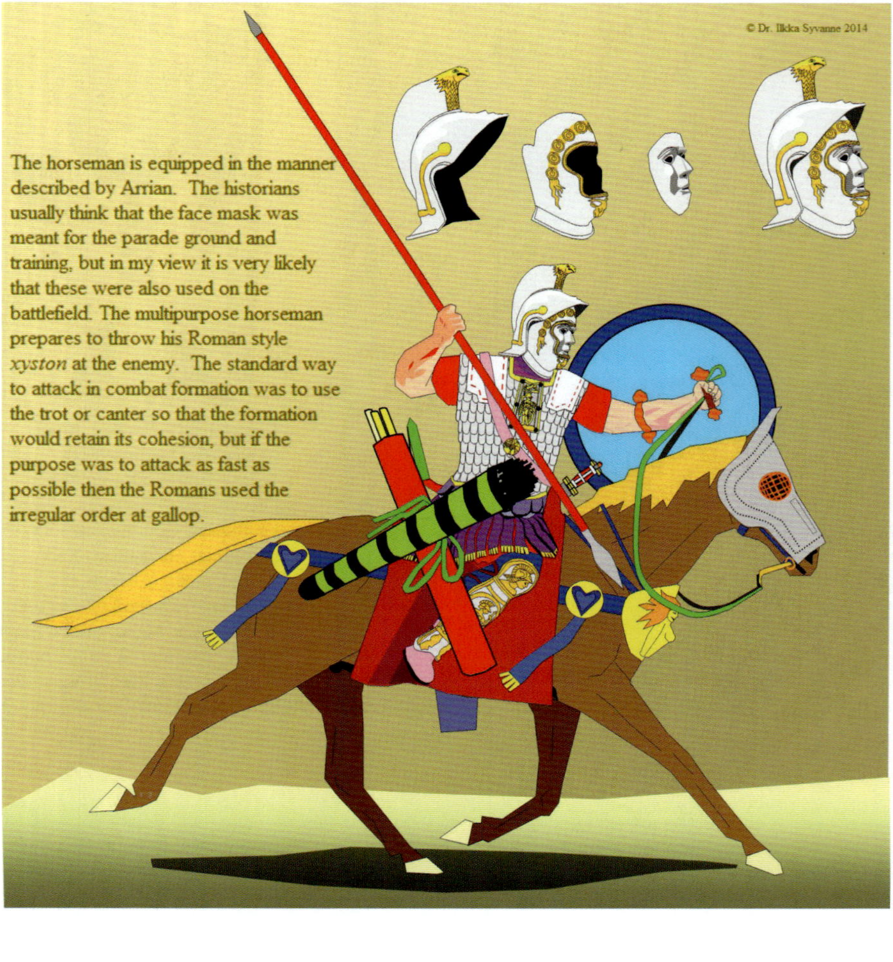
© Dr. Ilkka Syvanne 2014
The horseman is equipped in the manner described by Arrian. The historians usually think that the face mask was meant for the parade ground and training, but in my view it is very likely that these were also used on the battlefield. The multipurpose horseman prepares to throw his Roman style *xyston* at the enemy. The standard way to attack in combat formation was to use the trot or canter so that the formation would retain its cohesion, but if the purpose was to attack as fast as possible then the Romans used the irregular order at gallop.

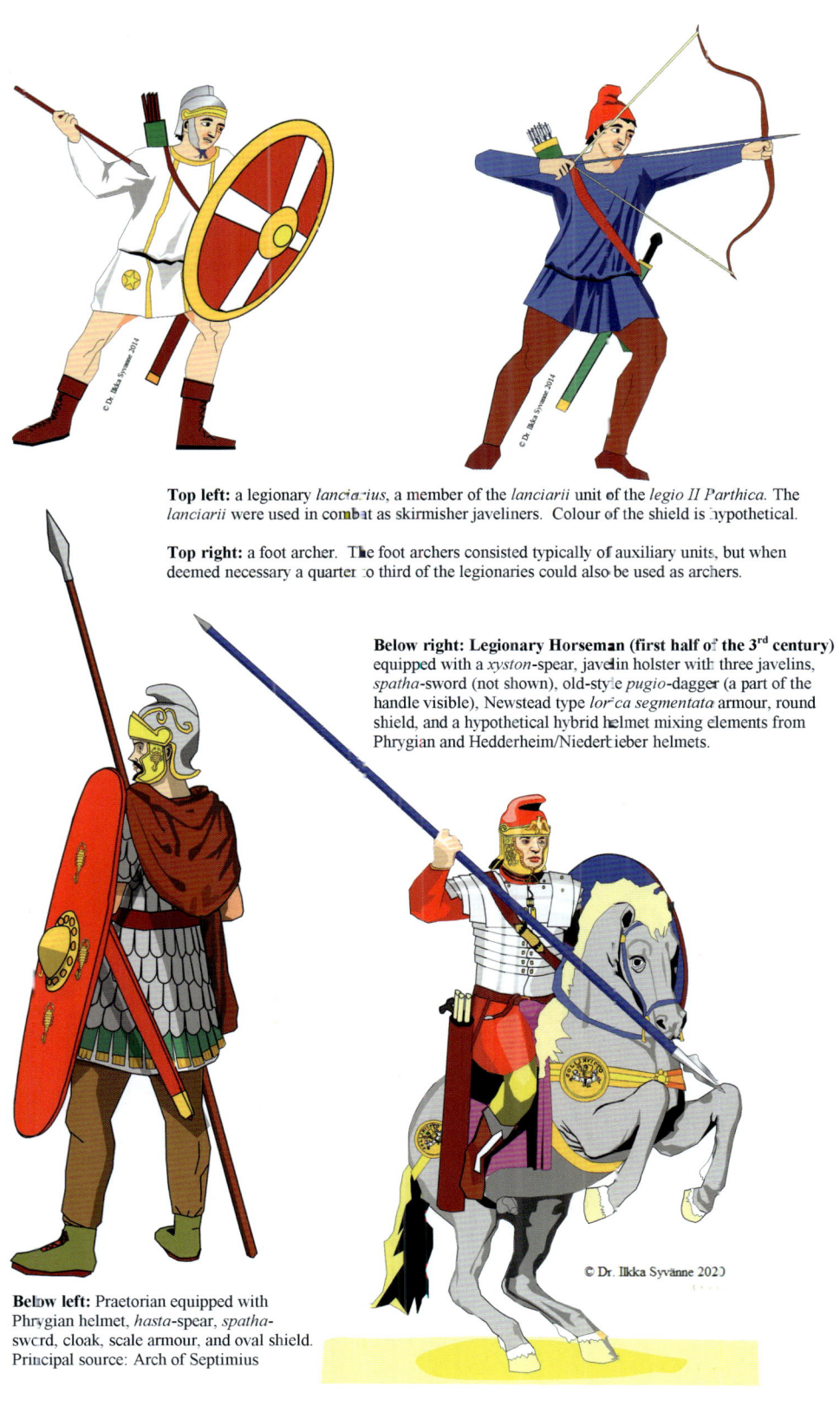

Top left: a legionary *lanciarius*, a member of the *lanciarii* unit of the *legio II Parthica*. The *lanciarii* were used in combat as skirmisher javeliners. Colour of the shield is hypothetical.

Top right: a foot archer. The foot archers consisted typically of auxiliary units, but when deemed necessary a quarter to third of the legionaries could also be used as archers.

Below right: Legionary Horseman (first half of the 3rd century) equipped with a *xyston*-spear, javelin holster with three javelins, *spatha*-sword (not shown), old-style *pugio*-dagger (a part of the handle visible), Newstead type *lorica segmentata* armour, round shield, and a hypothetical hybrid helmet mixing elements from Phrygian and Hedderheim/Niederbieber helmets.

Below left: Praetorian equipped with Phrygian helmet, *hasta*-spear, *spatha*-sword, cloak, scale armour, and oval shield. Principal source: Arch of Septimius

Top left: Centurio of *cohors voluntariorum* in the Portonaccia Sarcophagus. Drawn after D'Amato and original work. He wears a Hellenistic helmet and leather *lorica segmentata*. Drawing has appeared in Syvänne, *Caracalla*.

Top centre: Legionary in leather *lorica segmentata* armour equipped with a medium-sized *hasta*-spear, short *gladius*-sword, rectangular *scutum*-shield and Phrygian helmet. Drawn partially after the Arch of Septimius Severus.

Below right: Legionary (*legio II Parthica*) equipped with the longer version of the *hasta*-spear intended for use against cavalry, long *spatha*-sword, dagger, *manica* arm-guard, Niederbieber-type helmet, scale armour and oval shield.

Below middle: different types of the heavy *pilum*-javelin (pl. *pila*), which was one of the standard types of shafted weapons used by the legionaries.

A legionary in typical period legionary equipment using the Imperial Italic H-helmet, medium-sized *hasta*-spear, long *spatha*-sword (behind the shield), *pugio*-dagger, oval shield and the Newstead *lorica segmentata*. However, other types of helmet, armour, shields and spears were also used.

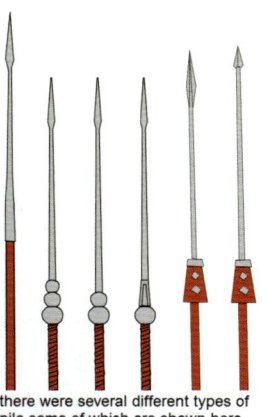

there were several different types of pila some of which are shown here

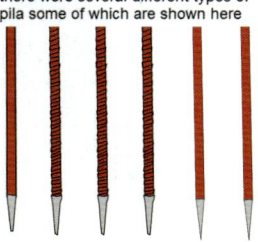

Imperial family: Julia Domna, Septimius Severus, Geta (face defaced) and Caracalla. (Author's copy (repainting) of the Berlin tondo, slightly restored version)

Bust of Roman emperor (probably Pertinax). (British Museum, Author's photo)

Head of Septimius Severus. (Photograph © Marie-Lan Nguyen/ Wikimedia Commons, user Jastrow, 2009)

Top left: auxiliary equipped with Pseudo-Attican helmet, socketed *pilum*-javelin, *spatha*-sword, and oval shield. Principal source: Arch of Septimius Severus.

Top right: a senatorial *legatus* (legate/commander of a legion and other units attached to it).

Below left: auxiliary equipped with Pseudo-Attican helmet, *hasta*-spear, *spatha*-sword, leather armour and oval shield. Principal source: Arch of Septimius Severus.

Below right: praetorian equipped with Pseudo-Attican helmet, *hasta*-spear, *gladius*-sword, cloak, chain mail armour and sexagonal shield. Principal source: Arch of Septimius Severus.

Left: The aftermath of the Battle of Lugdunum on 19 February 197. The horse of Septimius Severus trampling the headless corpse of Albinus on the street of the city of Lugdunum. (Author's drawing; the city scene is homage to the great artists Uderzo and Goscinny)

Above and below: Cavalry helmets, British Museum. (Author's photos)

Top left: Septimius Severus.
Top right: Septimius Severus.
Below left: Caracalla.
Below Right: Caracalla.
(Author's paintings)

Centre: A bust of Julia Domna (Munich). (Public Domain, Wikimedia Commons, user Bibi Saint-Pol)

soldiers or levying of new ones, but it is quite obvious that these were also required. Some of the governors obeyed, while others did not. According to Daquet-Gagey, the provinces of Belgica, Lugdunensis and Aquitania in Gaul and Tarraconensis in Spain, with its governor Lucius Novius Rufus, rallied to his side. Only Tarraconensis had a legion, the VII Gemina, but on the basis of the fact that it was granted the title *pia* (loyal) after the war, it is practically certain that it sided with Severus or at least failed to give any support for Albinus.[6] In addition to this, the governor of Noricum may also have joined the cause of Albinus, but it is uncertain whether he had the support of the Legio II Italica. Aelius Spartianus adds that the legion in Arabia was reported to have joined Albinus, but this was of minor importance for the outcome of the civil war – only a nuisance far to the east. If true, however, its revolt may have helped the Parthians to invade Roman territory in 197, but Bowersock is probably correct in stating that the story is untrue. On the basis that the legion retained its title Severiana, it is more or less certain that it remained loyal to Severus. Bowersock suggests that the key to understanding what happened lies in the wording of the *Historia Augusta*, which states that it was reported. He proposes that the supporters of Albinus spread this piece of disinformation to the troops of Severus in a bid to make their loyalty waver. This is indeed the likeliest answer to the problem and would also explain why there is no evidence for the suppression of the revolt of the Arabian legion.[7]

Crucially, Upper and Lower Germany with their legions remained loyal to Severus. The problematic part in all of this is the dating of the crossing of the Channel. What is certain is that it took place before the December games described by Dio (76.4.1ff., Cary ed., pp.202–04), because Albinus had declared himself Augustus by then, but this condition fits both 195 and 196 and is therefore not conclusive. All three main sources for the reign of Severus refer to the period in which his generals and Albinus fought against each other well before the arrival of the emperor. The subsequent numbers present at the Battle of Lyon/Lugdunum and the above-mentioned reference to the preparations immediately after the failed assassination attempt mean that Albinus's forces did not consist solely of his regular soldiers, but also included local levies and probably tribal allies.[8]

Anthony R. Birley (121ff.) notes that some of the preparatory steps must have taken place before the end of 195 and prior to Septimius's own march west. Severus had sent his men to secure Rome, the rest of Italy and the northern provinces because his hold of the East and Africa were secure. Additionally, Severus had also improved the road network running through Noricum and Raetia into Gaul, so he had started to make preparations for the eventual war with Albinus at the latest in 195. This implies that Septimius had formulated a strategic plan for his war well in advance in case the assassination attempts failed. Birley lists some of the men who Septimius employed on this occasion, stating that Fabius Cilo was dispatched from Bithynia to take over the governorship of Upper Moesia. Birley also suggests that Julia Domna's brother-in-law, Emesene Avitus Alexianus, was now appointed as legate of Legio IV Flavia at Singidunum (Belgrade). The city of Rome was at least partially secured through Septimius's kinsman Fulvius Plautianus, who was appointed as Prefect of the *Vigiles* by early summer 195, while another trusted man, Domitius Dexter, served as City Prefect. After the Mesopotamian campaign ended – or even before it – Severus sent men to assist the besiegers of Byzantium. Candidus marched the Illyrian army back west, while Marius Maximus led his forces to the Danube after the capture of Byzantium. In my opinion, it is possible that Maximus's force was strengthened with the addition of marines from the Praetorian fleets. The Dacian legions (V Macedonica and XIII Gemina) and auxiliaries were formed into the Dacian army, which was placed under Tiberius Claudius Claudianus, a Numidian ex-equestrian officer who had served with Geta as a legionary commander. Since Geta was then still the acting governor of Dacia, it is probable that the change of command took place only when the Dacian forces had been brought to Viminacium. Candidus's force appears to have formed an advance guard for Septimius's army, just like it had during the campaign against Niger, because en route in Noricum the *exercitus Illyricus* was forced to hunt public enemies. As noted above, this implies that there were supporters of Albinus in Noricum who had to be dealt with. Septimius did not forget the securing of the western and north-western approaches to Italy: Caius Iulius Pacatianus was sent to Italy to secure the Alps with the title *procurator et praeses Alpium Cottiarum*, while Titus Cornasidius Sabinus was appointed to guard the *Alpes Graiae et Poeninae*, presumably as his subordinate. Pacatianus had under him one of the new legions, which I presume to be the Legio II Parthica.[9]

On the basis of the above, in my opinion Septimius Severus's campaign plan appears to have consisted of four different elements: the supporters already in place in Gaul (four legions in the Germanias) and Raetia, the vanguards sent in advance from the east and the main army under Septimius. Rossius Vitulus was put in charge of the supplies. Just like previously against Niger, Severus seems to have dispatched two advance forces, the northern of which consisted of Candidus's *exercitus Illyricus*, which was advancing along the Danube to secure the northern route to Gaul while also squashing any local support for Albinus and collecting loyal forces along the way. The southern advance guard comprised the soldiers sent with Pacatianus to Italy to secure the Cottian Alps, with the probable additional mission of securing the southern advances (*Alpes Maritimae*) into Gaul, or alternatively there being some third general who had that duty. However, in light of Herodian's statement that Pacatianus was put in charge of guarding the Alpine passes and route into Italy, it is more than likely that Pacatianus was in charge of the defence of Italy and all forces posted in the north of Italy or the Alps. It is possible that this operation was supported by the Praetorian fleets, which would have been free to redeploy, even if this is not mentioned by any of the sources. The support of these fleets would surely have been necessary if the intention was to operate along the Rhone (*Rhodanus*). The third component of the force would have consisted of the main army under Septimius himself, which appears to have advanced along the northern route. This force included at least the Dacian army, Praetorians, and legions and detachments drawn from the eastern garrisons, and may also have included at least some of the units of the Moesian army because it is probable that Marius Maximus was the source of the *Historia Augusta* for the events that took place at Viminacium. It is quite likely that these forces included the Legio II Parthica, but I would suggest that the legiones I and III Parthica were left in the East so that Severus was able to take with him some of that region's veteran legions. In addition to this, the force included large numbers of foreign allies, as was stated by Septimius in his speech. These would have consisted of Easterners and Goths.

The two contenders for the throne adopted entirely different propaganda in coins to gather supporters. Septimius minted more than 342 different issues of coins during his first years in power. These advertised the distribution of largesse, the games and entertainment, the support of the gods (especially the martial gods) for Severus, the martial prowess of the emperor and the peace that this would bring. The coins that were struck for Antoninus after he had been nominated as emperor stressed the hope for perpetual security that his nomination had brought. After Severus reached Rome, Antoninus received a new title of *princeps iuventutis* to signify his position as heir to the throne. In contrast, even if the coins of Albinus also sought to prove himself as the favourite of the gods, his coins stressed the loyalty of the army and also Albinus's *clementia* (clemency) and *aequitas* (equity, fairness), which made him the favourite contender for many of the senators. Severus no longer felt it necessary to stress the loyalty of the army to him at this time and did not advertise either clemency or fairness. He was a harsh man, as his name implied, and he did not attempt to hide it.[10]

The first battles between the forces of Albinus and Severus's supporters took place when Septimius was still in either Thrace, Moesia or Pannonia, because according to Spartianus the news of these clashes reached Septimius while he was in Pannonia. According to Spartianus, all the initial encounters between the armies ended badly for Severus, with Albinus's *duces* defeating those of Severus. The extant inscriptions confirm this claim. Albinus defeated the governor of Germania Inferior, Virius Lupus (I Minervia at Bonnae and XXX Ulpia at Vetera), but failed to conquer the province. Albinus also got the better of the forces of Germania Superior (VIII Augusta at Argentorate and XXII Primigenia at Mogontiacum), putting under siege the city of Trier, which was defended at least partially by Legio XXII Primigenia under its legate Claudius Gallus.[11] It is uncertain what the role of the VIII Augusta was in these events because it is possible that the Legio XXII Primigenia had marched alone to Trier. When news of these defeats was brought to Severus, he consulted augurs in Pannonia who promised him victory. This reveals that Severus was forced to resort to the use of religion to restore the confidence of his army when his forces had been defeated in a series of battles and the vanguard under Candidus had to fight in Noricum to clear up the route. It is quite possible that the news of these defeats reached Severus when he was in Viminacium and that the nomination of Caracalla as Caesar, with the likely giving of a *donativum* to the soldiers, formed a part of the process of restoring the morale among the soldiers.[12]

This brings up the question why Severus would have wanted to visit the city of Rome, as suggested by the series of *Adventus* coins minted at Rome, dedicatory inscriptions and the large amount of legislation passed in Rome between October and the end of December 196, when his forces in Gaul had just suffered a series of defeats. The obvious answer would be that there were troubles in the city which the narrative sources fail to mention. It is possible that it was because of these that Septimius went in person before the Senate and forced the senators to declare Albinus a public enemy, but it is also possible that this declaration had been made before his arrival at his request. The only reference to such troubles is the making of pro-Albinus shouts by the audience at the games held at Rome in December. The year in question can be either 195 or 196. If it is the former, then it is unlikely that these shouts would have had anything to do with the defeats, while if it is the latter, then the shouts could be connected with these. If the latter is true, then the visit of Rome can be timed on the basis of this. The dedication to 'the deified Nerva, his ancestor' was made by Septimius on 18 September 196, while the events at the games prove he was clearly no longer at Rome in December 196. In such a case, the second of the reasons for the visit to Rome could have been that Severus did not want to waste time when the northern route was still blocked by the operations taking place in Noricum, taking advantage of the opportunity to secure the capital. If Septimius did not visit Rome as Herodian's text implies, then it is clear that the *Adventus* coins and extant inscriptions were meant as a ruse to keep the populace in suspense over when the emperor would come and to mislead Albinus of the emperor's plans so that he would concentrate his forces in Lyon while Septimius was actually advancing north of there. However, the former of these alternatives is likelier and is the consensus view among historians. In short, it is probable that Septimius visited Rome very briefly in the autumn of 196 to make certain that the city was securely held while he fought against Albinus. The sudden burst in legislative activity from 1 October to 29 December suggests that Severus was at Rome during that period, after which he returned to his troops. It is also possible that it was then that Severus appointed his kinsman C. Fulvius Plautianus as *praefectus praetorio* (Praetorian Prefect), because he can be attested to have been such on 1 January 197. In other words, Severus now placed his personal safety in the hands of his relative from Lepcis Magna, who had presumably demonstrated his loyalty prior to this.[13]

Two *adventus* coins of Severus drawn by Beger (1696)

The sources mention two successes for Septimius prior to his own advance to Gaul. The first of these are the adventures of the grammarian/schoolmaster Numerianus, who taught children writing. According to Dio, Numerianus went from Rome to Gaul, pretending to be a Roman senator dispatched by Severus to raise an army for him. Numerianus was able to assemble a small force with which he defeated a number of Albinus's cavalry and performed some other daring deeds. When Severus learnt of these, he believed that Numerianus really was a senator working for him, sending him a message to increase the size of his force. This proves that new forces were recruited and levied by both sides for the civil war. Numerianus did as asked and performed several audacious operations, the most notable of which was the capture of 70 million sesterces that were duly sent to Severus. Numerianus went to meet Severus after the war and told him the truth about his background and actions. Severus rewarded Numerianus in the manner he wished, which was to be allowed to retire to a country place with a small allowance for his daily deeds. These details suggest that Numerianus was operating somewhere in the south of Gaul, because the two men met only after the war had ended. The extraordinary exploits of Numerianus show how chaotic the situation was in the middle of a civil war. Numerianus's capture of 70 million sesterces was a major achievement, and it is possible that Numerianus was able to hold most of the territory south of Lyon for Septimius for the duration of the war.[14]

The second of the successes is mentioned by Spartianus, but he gives too few details to be certain what happened. He merely stated that soon after the initial successes of Albinus, many of his friends (*amici*) deserted him and many of his *duces* were captured and punished. It is impossible to be certain what is meant by this. The desertion could have been of the commanders in Noricum, so that the path was finally cleared for Severus to march his Illyrian, Moesian, Dacian and eastern forces through the northern route. The capture of the *duces* may refer to the same location because it would have been easy to capture them when they had been betrayed. The other alternative is that the desertions and captures relate to events that took place, for example, as a result of Numerianus's actions in Gaul prior to the Battle of Lyon, because Spartianus specifically states in the same context it was after military operations had been conducted with varying success in Gaul that the decisive battle took place at Tinurtium. In my opinion, however, the former is still likelier as that would explain better the visit to Rome and subsequent return to the Balkans to lead the Roman armies via the northern route. The mention of fighting in Gaul with various fortunes can be taken figuratively to mean all the fighting taking place between the forces of Albinus and Severus.[15]

The consensus view among historians is that Severus returned swiftly to Pannonia from Rome, and there is no reason to doubt this. It is also quite likely that Cilo escorted Septimius back to Poetovio, where Cilo assumed the position of governor of Upper Pannonia. Antoninus Caracalla apparently remained there. From here, Severus marched through Pannonia, Noricum and Raetia into Upper Germany, where he would presumably have received reinforcements from the legions and auxiliaries posted in the two Germanies. The exact route taken is not known, but in my opinion it is probable that Severus marched along the road running through Vindonissa to Castrum Rauracense, and from there via Vesontio to Cabillonum. Once he had reached the strategic crossroads at Cabillonum, all Severus had to do was to march south towards the headquarters of Albinus in Lyon, but en route there were still outlying forces and outposts of Albinus that had to be defeated. As the former governor of Lugdunensis, Severus knew the area intimately and was able to plan his campaign in the best possible manner.[16]

7.2. The Battles of Tinurtium and Lyon, or the Battle of Tinurtium/Lyon, in February 197

According to Aelius Spartianus, the decisive battle between the forces of Severus and Albinus took place at Tinurtium (Tournus), while other sources place the battle close to Lyon (Lugdunum). Most modern historians consider the Battle of Tinurtium to be separate from the Battle of Lyon, but there are also some who think that these are one and the same battle. The reason for the latter opinion[17] is that Spartianus states that this was the decisive encounter and his text refers to Septimius being dismounted and describes how Albinus died. The principal reason for the former conclusion is that Tinurtium was so far north of Lyon that the encounter there must have been a separate battle, but this is by no means conclusive as it is possible that the decisive battle could have been named after the locale where Albinus and his defeated forces fled. However, I am still inclined to follow the consensus view here because it explains the reasons for the suspicions held towards Julius Laetus. I therefore begin my account with a quote from Aelius Spartianus in the *Historia Augusta* which gives us the only details of this battle, or rather of a skirmish. I have also included material which clearly refers to the decisive last battle, which I have accepted to have taken place near Lyon.

> 'The *duces* of Severus were at first defeated by those of Clodius Albinus, which caused him to consult the augurs of Pannonia about his fortune, who told him that he should be the conqueror ... his adversary would perish by the side of a water. It was not long after this that several of the friends of Albinus abandoned him, and came and presented themselves before Severus and others of his *duces* were taken prisoners upon whom Severus exacted punishment. After a great many operations had been carried out in Gaul with varying success, Severus achieved his first success against Albinus at the battle of Tinurtium, but he was thrown from his horse and the army believing him to have been killed by a lead-ball ['*plumbeae*', probably either a lead ball thrown from a sling, as usually translated, or a lead-dart called a *plumbata*, five of which were placed behind the shield] was just upon the point of making another emperor. [The latter may possibly be Julius Laetus. This may imply confusion between two battles, but it is likelier that Laetus was really considered for the throne at this time, which was the reason for the later suspicions towards him. After this point, the account describes the events that took place after the actual Battle of Lyon.] It was just then that Severus became angry at the senate when he read its resolutions praising Clodius Celsinus, who was from the city of Hadrumentum and kinsman of Albinus because this seemed like the senate had recognized Albinus by this. He, thinking that he could not find any better revenge, proclaimed the deification of Commodus first among the army and then in a letter to the senate which proclaimed his victory over Albinus. Next, he commanded that the bodies of the senators who were killed in the fight should be mutilated. The body of Albinus being brought to him half-dead, he ordered to be decapitated and carried to Rome with the letters .... He [Albinus] was overcome the eleventh day of the Calends of March [19 February. 197]. At Severus's orders the body of Albinus was exposed before his house [this would presumably be Severus's house in Lugdunum, which he would have bought while he was governor of the province] for the public. Severus rode his horse over the corpse and when the horse shied, he spoke to it and loosed the reins so that the horse could trample the corpse ... he ordered Albinus's body to be thrown into the Rhone together with the bodies of his wife and children .... [According to the *HA Cl.Alb.* 9.3–6, Albinus fled and stabbed himself, or was stabbed by a slave. He was brought to Severus half-alive. Some suggest that he was killed by soldiers who claimed a bounty for this. His head was put on a pike and paraded before the soldiers and then at Rome. Severus

initially pardoned Albinus's wife and children, but then killed them anyway and threw them into the river.] He put to death an infinite number of persons of the party of Albinus and amongst them many leading men and several ladies of quality and all their estates were confiscated .... Many nobles of Spain and Gallia were also put to death ... he gave the soldiers more money than any other emperor ever did and ... he left his sons greater fortune than any other emperor at death. For he had amassed to himself the greatest part of the gold and silver that was in Gallia, Spain and Italy. He was the first that constituted the Office of Procurator of the Private Affairs of the Emperor; or Keeper of the Privy Purse.' (Aelius Spartianus, *HA Sev.* 10.7ff., trans. by Bernard, pp.240–42, with many changes and additions)

This account makes it obvious that Spartianus connected the decisive clash between Severus and Albinus with the Battle of Tinurtium. However, as mentioned above, it is likely that this battle was only a prelude for the Battle of Lyon, forcing the party of Albinus to retreat south and take defensive positions just north of the city of Lyon. It should be kept in mind that it is possible that Spartianus is correct after all and that the flight of Albinus just continued to Lyon. The details provided by Spartianus suggest that the battle was hard fought and that Severus was forced to advance close to the fighting to encourage the men, possibly with the reserves consisting of the Praetorian Guard. He was hit either by a lead slingshot or by a *plumbata* lead-dart. In my opinion the latter is more likely, with Severus having come within less than about 30 metres of the enemy. The account also makes it clear that the presumed death of Severus did not demoralize his men; it is probable that it made them fight with even greater determination. The discussion regarding the choosing of a new emperor proves that the men were not ready to accept Marcus Aurelius Antoninus (Caracalla) as the legitimate successor, but neither were they ready to acclaim Albinus. It is probable that the candidate whom they chose was Julius Laetus, who was later executed because he was accused of having imperial aspirations. If we accept that Albinus was present with all his troops at this battle, it means that he was forced to retreat close to his headquarters, where he arrayed his men for battle once again. However, if Spartianus has confused the battles, then it is possible that Albinus's army was actually commanded by his generals. In my opinion, however, the likeliest alternative is that the Battle of Tinurtium was only a skirmish between the light-armed forces of both sides, with Severus actually leading the vanguard. Whatever the truth, it is now time to quote the two sources which provide the most details regarding the decisive battle between Severus and Albinus. Dio is the most thorough, but Herodian has still preserved details missing from the former and is quoted first:

'As soon as Severus reached Gaul, several long distance skirmishes happened in different places [The term used is '*akrobolismos*', with the implication that light-armed troops skirmished with each other. It is possible that quite a few of the skirmishers of Severus consisted of eastern mounted archers. In my opinion, this refers also to the above-mentioned encounter at Tinurtium. It is unlikely to be a coincidence that Severus was hit by a thrown lead missile.], but the decisive battle occurred at Lugdunum [Lyon], a great and flourishing city from which Albinus sent out his forces to fight the battle while he himself remained within its walls.

[This would imply that Albinus left command in the hands of his subordinates, but this is uncertain on the basis of Dio. I would suggest that Herodian's text is misleading, and that Albinus only sent his men from the city and then followed them.] The action was bloody and obstinate; victory long remained doubtful .... For the Britons are not inferior to the Illyrians in manliness and bloodthirsty courage. [In my opinion this implies that the Illyrian army was posted on Severus's left wing while the regular army of Britain was posted opposite them on Albinus's right wing. Albinus's plan appears to have been to try to decide the outcome of the battle and war with his regulars posted on his right.] In this battle between two such powerful armies the winner was not easily decided. And, as the writers of those times relate (at least such of them as had greater regard to truth than interest) ... that in the part of the battleline where Severus and his own army ['*ho Sevêros kai ho autôi stratos*', meaning presumably the Praetorian Guard] were located, Albinus's army had the advantage. Severus fled and was thrown off his horse, and was obliged to throw off his imperial cloak to conceal his identity. The victorius Britons pursued and started to chant their hymn of victory [implying that the pursuers probably consisted mainly of infantry], rejoicing they had already won, when a fresh army that had not been involved in the battle came up under Laetus, one of Severus's generals; who, as they report, had purposely stayed behind with his army to watch the result of the battle so that his forces would be fresh for the purpose of regaining the empire for himself. As soon as he heard that Severus had fallen, he advanced with his fresh forces. And, indeed, the ensuing events seemed to confirm this report. For afterwards, when Severus had gained the victory, and settled everything according to his wish, he liberally rewarded all his other officers for their good services, but put Laetus to death probably as a result of his intended treason. But not to anticipate my story, Laetus, appearing with his new army, gave Severus's soldiers fresh spirits. Severus was remounted on his horse and dressed in his imperial cloak. Albinus's soldiers, thinking the victory completely gained, had broken their order, and were too overconfidently pursuing the enemy, when all of a sudden this additional body of fresh troops came, and charged them so vigorously that after a short resistance they were broken .... [The cavalry under Laetus trampled the scattered foes under their hooves or used spears, javelins and swords.] Severus's troops pursued them to the city cutting to pieces all they overtook. The contemporary historians vary the number of killed, wounded and prisoners on both sides according to their own purposes. Severus's army plundered and burned the city of Lugdunum, seized Albinus [and], having taken off his head, carried it to Severus. Thus they raised the trophies of two great victories, the one gained over the nations of the east, and this so soon after obtained in the north. Here I cannot but remark that we shall hardly find the achievements of Severus paralleled in history, whether we consider the multitude of the forces [note the numbers also in Dio's text; Herodian quite clearly agrees with his figures: this was a major battle with massive armies], the upheaval among the nations, the number of battles and the distance and speed of his marches. [We are in the dark about the actual number of battles because the sources group most of those that took place in Gaul as skirmishes. However, even with the ones that we know about there were many.] The battles of Caesar against Pompey, and the wars of Augustus against Antony and Pompey's sons, and before that the civil wars at Rome of Sulla and Marius and others, when two Roman armies faced each other were enormous. But this one man destroyed three princes already invested with imperial power. One, ... the occupant of the imperial palace ... through clever trickery. [Note that Herodian appreciated very highly the trickery of Severus in the context of warfare.] To overthrow another ... in the east. ... The third, ... by his bravery ... [Note that Herodian does merit Severus with bravery in his battles against Albinus, so that at least in his opinion Severus's decision to throw away the imperial cloak to hide his identity at this battle was not a sign of any cowardice – perhaps one should think it a wise act of self-preservation.] These are successes hard to match.' Herodian 3.7.2ff., tr. by Hart, p.124ff., with changes, corrections and comments)

Dio's longer account of events is as follows:

'The struggle between Severus and Albinus near Lugdunum is now to be described. At the outset there were a hundred and fifty thousand soldiers on each side. [This was clearly a massive battle, and contrary to modern misplaced scepticism about such numbers there is no reason to doubt their veracity. There is just too much evidence for the use of such numbers throughout the centuries for this not to mention specific reference to the massive size of the forces in several sources. Since it is clear that these totals could not be achieved solely by relying on the regulars, the legions and auxiliary forces. it is clear that both commanders had levied additional troops from the local populations.[18] This means that contrary to common belief, Roman civilians could still be expected to serve in armies as general levies when called to do so. This should come as no surprise because naval forces were augmented in a similar way every time there was a major naval operation. However, just like it was during Republican times previously described in the quote from Herodian, these levies were not enrolled into regular armies, but disbanded when no longer needed. Additionally, it is clear that both commanders augmented their numbers with foreign allies. In the case of Albinus, these would have consisted of the Britons that had retained their tribal traditions and Caledonians. In the case of Septimius Severus, they comprised at least those from the East and the Goths, and may also have included other Germanic tribesmen and Dacians.] Both leaders took part in the war, since it was a race for life and death, though Severus had previously not been present at any important battle. [This implies that Albinus left the walls of Lugdunum and led the army in person. I would suggest that this is the likelier alternative.] Albinus excelled in rank and education, but his adversary was superior in warfare and was a skillful commander. [This means that Dio was ready to admit Severus's superb skills as a commander, even though Severus did resort to the same kind of stratagems as later did his son Caracalla. However, in the case of Caracalla, Dio was unable to hide his hostility and claimed that the same treacherous traits were a sign of cowardice, none of which is true. War is an art of deceit. For further details, see my biography of Caracalla.] It happened that in a former battle Albinus had conquered Lupus, one of the *strategoi* [= *duces* = generals] of Severus, and had destroyed many of the soldiers attending him. [This refers to the above-mentioned defeat of Lupus and the army of Lower Germany.] The present conflict took many shapes and turns. The left wing of Albinus was beaten and sought refuge behind the rampart, whereupon Severus's soldiers in their pursuit burst into the enclosure with them, slaughtered their opponents and plundered their tents. [This implies that there was a separate camp for the left wing of Albinus's army. The right and centre were probably housed inside the city of Lugdunum, because Herodian mentions that Albinus dispatched his men to the battle from there and it was there that the right wing fled. It is quite possible that Albinus's plan was to order his left wing to retreat to their camp so that the Severan right wing and its cavalry would be removed from the battle. None of the sources mention how the Severan right wing conducted its attack, but one can imagine how this was done on the basis of the tactics described in the Introduction and Appendix. The regular Roman cavalry either skirmished with a series of files of javelineers before charging into contact, or they advanced together as units and created openings in the enemy formation with concentrated volleys of javelins, after which they advanced into the openings and broke up the enemy array; the *contarii* units in their turn charged straight at the enemy; and the mounted archers and cataphracts used bows before engaging the enemy. Depending on the armament of the unit, the Severan infantry would either have used the *pilum* and *gladius* tactic or the hoplite charge.] Meantime the soldiers of Albinus arrayed on the right wing, who had trenches hidden in front of them and pits in the earth covered over only on the surface, approached as far as these snares [This is misleading because the soldiers of Albinus had to be far enough from the trenches for the stratagem to work. Firstly, they had to be relatively far away from those when the Severans approached so that none of their missiles would fall into the trenches and expose their existence. Secondly, when the Severans were nearing the trenches the men of Albinus could not approach too close to these for the very same reason.] and hurled javelins from a distance. [These details suggest the use of legionary type infantry for this manoeuvre, with the implication that cavalry was posted behind as a reserve. This would also have been quite natural in a situation in which the fighting was expected to take place on a hill.] Then instead of advancing, they turned back as if frightened with the purpose of drawing their foes into pursuit. This actually took place. Severus's men, nettled by their brief charge and despising them for their retreat after so short an advance, rushed upon them without a thought that the whole intervening space could not be easily traversed. When they reached the trenches they were involved in a fearful catastrophe. The men in the front ranks [*protostatai*] as soon as the surface covering broke through fell into the excavations and those immediately behind stumbled over them, slipped, and likewise fell. [This once again suggests that these consisted of infantry.] The rest crowded back in terror, their retreat being so sudden that they themselves lost their footing, upset those in the rear, and pushed them into a deep ravine. [*faragx* = a mountain cleft, a deep chasm, ravine, gully. This may mean that there was a deep ravine just behind the Severan line and that Albinus had lured the Severans to advance past it. The problem is, what was this ravine? Had it been built by Albinus's men or was it a natural one? And was it just behind the Severans or on their left flank as usually assumed? For example, LeBohec, 2013, p.55ff., maps on plates XII–XVI assumes that it was on the left flank. My own educated guess is that it was a natural one and behind the Severans, with Albinus's army having been deployed along the ridges of the hills just north-west of the city in such a manner that the Severan left flank was allowed to advance to the top of the hill, only to be surprised by the combination of trenches in front and ravine behind. This location fits the description of the battle in Herodian and Dio, and is also just as wide as an army of 150,000 men would have needed when deployed as a phalanx, which means that it is the likeliest location for the battle. It goes without saying that this was a good plan.] Of course there was a terrible slaughter of these soldiers as well as of those who had fallen into the trenches, horses and men perishing in one wild mass. [The subsequent mention of the locale where Laetus was posted with his cavalry, the details of the combat and the location on the hill make it probable that the cavalry on both sides was posted behind their infantry. The inclusion of horses among the perishing in one mass refers only to those who fell into the ravine behind, because Dio specifically refers to the front-rankers and men in an infantry context. However, I would not preclude the possibility or even probability that in some sections of the left flank the pursuit would actually have been done by the book, so the pursuers would have consisted of the light-armed and cavalry, the heavy-armed having opened up their ranks for the pursuers to pass through. However, it is still clear on the basis of the text that the vast majority of the Severan pursuers must have consisted of the heavy-armed footmen posted in front, who charged forward into the trench when the enemy started its retreat, and that the rear-rankers in this formation first pushed the men from behind into the trench pell mell, then later when they fled also pushed the cavalry and light infantry posted behind into the ravine.]. In the midst of this tumult the warriors between the ravine and the trenches were annihilated by showers of missiles and arrows. [Note the effectiveness of Roman missiles.] Severus seeing this came to their assistance with the Praetorians [*doruforoi*], but this step proved of so little benefit that he came near to causing the ruin of the Praetorians and he himself ran some risk through the loss of a horse. [He would have come to the rescue in a situation in which his men were fleeing downhill with the enemy in pursuit, so it is no wonder that this happened. It is possible that Severus actually brought his reserves too fast forward to save the day and that his men were therefore embroiled among the fleeing mass while the enemy was still in formation. In other words, it is possible that he should have waited slightly longer so that his fleeing left-wing soldiers and their pursuers would have become more scattered and disordered and the sudden appearance of his well-ordered Praetorians would have made greater psychological impact on both, especially on the disordered pursuers. However, this is pure speculation on my part.] When he saw all his men in flight, he tore off his riding cloak [the imperial purple cloak], and drawing his sword rushed among the fugitives, hoping either that they would be ashamed and turn back or that he might himself perish with them. [This is likely to be the official version, while Herodian's less heroic one would have been the truth.] Some did stop when they saw him in such an attitude, and turned back. Brought in this way face to face with the men close behind them they cut down not a few of them, thinking them to be followers of Albinus, and routed all their pursuers. [This is quite clearly part of the official propaganda.] At this moment the cavalry under Laetus came up from the side and decided the rest of the issue for them [meaning that Laetus with his cavalry reserves was located on the right wing]. Laetus, so long as the struggle was close, remained inactive, hoping that both parties would be destroyed and that whatever soldiers were left on both sides would give him supreme authority. When, however, he saw Severus's party getting the upper hand, he contributed to the result. [This is likely to be the official propaganda version, in which it was Severus who conquered his enemies through his personal bravery. However, if we assume that Laetus was not attempting to claim the throne, then it is possible to think that Laetus was forced to await and not commit his cavalry to a battle in which the fighting was still taking place close to the hills. With cavalry it was certainly wiser to wait until the fugitives and pursuers had reached the plain, and until the pursuers had lost their order so that his cavalry could overrun them with ease. It is quite possible that this would have been the official version that Laetus gave as his excuse, because from a military point of view this would have made sense. However, this is again only speculation on my part.] So it was that Severus conquered. Roman power had suffered a severe blow, since the numbers that fell on each side were beyond reckoning. [This refers once again to the massive size of the armies. Most of the casualties are likely to have consisted of the recently levied civilians.] Many even of the visitors deplored the disaster, for the entire plain was seen to be covered with the bodies of men and horses. Some of them lay there exhausted by many wounds, others thoroughly mangled, and still others unwounded but buried under heaps. Weapons had been tossed about and blood flowed in streams, even swelling the rivers. Albinus took refuge in a house located near the Rhone, but when he saw all its environs guarded, he slew himself. I am not telling what Severus wrote about it, but what actually took place. [This means the more brutal version in the *HA* is likely to be Severus's official version. It was clearly of greater propaganda value for its brutal humiliation of the usurper and his family. However, it is impossible to know which of the versions is correct because Dio was not among the greatest admirers of Severus.] The emperor after inspecting his body and feasting his eyes upon it to the full while he let his tongue indulge in appropriate utterances, ordered it – all but the head – to be cast out, and he sent the head to Rome to be exposed on a cross/pole ['*anestaurôsen*']. As he showed clearly by this action that he was very far from being an excellent ruler, he alarmed the populace and us even more than before by the commands which he issued. Now that he had vanquished all forces under arms he poured out upon the unarmed all the wrath he had nourished against them during the previous period. [This only shows that Septimius was wise enough to hide his plans as long as it was necessary.] He terrified us most of all by declaring himself the son of Marcus and brother of Commodus; and to Commodus, whom but recently he was wont to abuse, he gave heroic honours, while reading before the senate a speech in which he praised the severity and cruelty of Sulla and Marius and Augustus as rather the safer course, and deprecated the clemency of Pompey and Caesar because it proved their ruin. [Septimius's son, Caracalla, followed the same policy, but this speech takes us further to the future because it would have been delivered at Rome.] (Dio 76.6.1ff. (Xiphilinus, Cary ed., p.206ff.), tr. by Foster, p.353–56, with changes, corrections and comments)

The arrival of Septimius Severus and his forces was not a surprise for Albinus, which enabled him to choose and prepare the battlefield well in advance. His plan appears to have consisted of three main elements, the first of which was to occupy the heights just north of the city of Lugdunum (Lyon). This gave him the advantage of position over his enemy and was just wide enough to accommodate his entire 150,000-strong army. The second part of his plan was to dig trenches in front of his right flank, which were then covered to hide their existence. His plan then was to lure the enemy to attack so that they would pass through a ravine, which would make their retreat difficult, into the pre-prepared trap. The idea was to let the enemy climb the hill and be lured to charge into the trenches and pits. It was this that made me place the site of the battle at the locale depicted in the accompanying map, it being the only one that has ravines long enough to cause the Severans trouble during their flight.[19] It was a sound plan which reflected the relative strengths and weaknesses of the respective armies. Albinus was clearly aware that, despite the parity in numbers, his army was weaker than that of Severus. The only professional forces that Albinus had consisted of those he had brought from Britain. Since it is clear that he had to leave at least some troops behind to man the forts, he cannot have brought his entire force of roughly 50,000 regulars with him. He would in all probability have left at least 10,000 of these behind. However, it is probable that Albinus levied new recruits to replace those that he left behind so that the regular force he led from Britain to Gaul still consisted of about 50,000 men.

Holder has roughly calculated the number of Roman soldiers posted in Britain under Hadrian. The number of units indicated below in the first column are Holder's, while the total numbers of soldiers are my rough estimates based on the known campaign strengths for such units and probable paper strengths:

3 *legiones*	*ca.* 14,400–15,000 infantry and 1,600 cavalry
1 *ala milliaria*	*ca.* 768–1,024 cavalry
10 *alae*	*ca.* 4,800–5,000 cavalry
6 *cohortes milliaria*	*ca.* 4,800–6,000 infantry
39 *cohortes*	*ca.* 18,780–19,500 infantry
Total:	*ca.* 37,980–40,500 infantry and 7,168–7,624 cavalry

The general estimation for the size of the army in Britain for the period after this is over 50,000 men, and it is unlikely that it would have been any less when Albinus usurped power, hence my guess that he took with him about 50,000 regulars, the ranks of which had been filled with new recruits to replace the men left behind. The above figures give us a rough understanding of what were the relative portions of the different types of troops within Albinus's regular forces, but it is unlikely that Albinus could significantly bolster the number of cavalry by levying new men. Therefore, my educated guess is that most of the new levies consisted of infantry. It is probable that most of the new forces were recruited in Britain rather than in Gaul. My estimate is that Albinus would have added about 50,000 footmen and some 5,000 horsemen from the tribal areas under Roman control in Britain, and perhaps about 10,000 tribesmen from outside it (Caledonia and Ireland). It is probable that Albinus took at least 10,000 men from the British fleet to bolster his numbers, so he would not have needed to levy any more than about 24,000 men in Gaul. My educated guess is that the 150,000 men mentioned by Dio consisted of the following elements:

Regular army of Britain with the new levies
40,000 infantry and 10,000 cavalry

Navy
10,000 infantry

Tribal levies in Roman Britain
50,000 infantry and 5,000 cavalry

Tribal levies outside the borders
10,000 infantry and 1,000 cavalry

Levies of Gauls
23,000 infantry and 1,000 cavalry

cohors urbana **at Lugdunum**
ca. 500 men

Total: 133,500 infantry and 17,000 cavalry

Readers should keep in mind that this is nothing more than my best educated guess. The only certainty regarding the composition of Albinus's army is that it had fewer regulars and cavalry than Severus's army, which consisted of most of the legions of the Empire with the addition of Eastern and Gothic cavalry (mostly local settlers like Maximinus Thrax).

The army that Severus led to the decisive battle consisted of the crack forces of the Empire. It included the Praetorian Guard, which now consisted of the Illyrian legionaries, and the Illyrian and Moesian armies which had now become used to winning. Their sizes would have been bolstered with new recruits and levies so that some troops could be left behind in garrisons. It also included detachments drawn from Dacia's two legions, presumably detachments from the Eastern and Germanic legions, and possibly the two legions of Noricum and Raetia in their entirety because both can be attested to have been loyal to Severus. Additionally, Severus undoubtedly had soldiers from the Urban Cohorts, the *Equites Singulares Augusti*, *Aulici*, auxiliary forces and from many other units and new levies. The following list is my best educated guess regarding the composition of the regulars in the army of Severus:

1) **Praetorians**
10,000 infantry and 2,000 cavalry

2) *Equites Singulares*
2,000 cavalry

3) *Aulici*, Urban Cohorts and other units posted at Rome
1,000 cavalry

4) Illyrian/Pannonian army
4 legions, *ca.* 20,000 infantry and 2,100 cavalry
auxiliary forces, *ca.* 10,000 footmen and 4,000 cavalry

5) Moesian army
4 legions, *ca.* 20,000 infantry and 2,100 cavalry
auxiliary forces, *ca.* 10,000 footmen and 4,000 cavalry

6) Dacian army
Detachments from 2 legions plus auxiliaries
ca. 6,000 legionaries and 1,000 cavalry
ca. 3,000 auxiliary footmen and 2,000 cavalry

7) Eastern regulars
Smaller 2,000-man detachments from the 2 legions of Cappadocia and 4 legions of Syria-Palestine with their auxiliaries:
ca. 12,000 legionaries and 3,200 cavalry
ca. 6,000 auxiliary footmen and 6,000 cavalry

8) Forces from Raetia and Noricum
I have here made the educated guess that these units would have been left in their garrisons because there had been trouble in Noricum.

9) Forces from the Germanic provinces
Probably only detachments from the Legio VIII Augusta with its auxiliaries because one of the legions was besieged at Trier and the 2 others had been defeated.
ca. 3,000 legionaries and 500 cavalry
ca. 1,500 auxiliary footmen and 1,000 cavalry

My educated guess for the size of the regular force under Severus at the Battle of Lugdunum would therefore add up to:
101,500 infantry and 30,900 cavalry
to be rounded down to 100,000 infantry and 30,000 cavalry

It is quite possible or even probable that my rundown of the numbers sent by the different garrisons to Severus's army are inaccurate, with some sending more and others less, or that some of the units that I have left out of the figures still sent forces. Nevertheless, the above list of units and numbers should make it clear that the figures given by Dio for the size of the armies were easily attainable in the case of Septimius Severus.

Severus could easily obtain 100,000 regular footmen and 30,000 regular horsemen, so he would have needed no more than about 20,000 additional men to reach the figure of 150,000 given by Dio. This number could have easily been attained with new recruits from Italy, Gaul and the Balkans or with horsemen provided by the Armenians and Goths. This is my best educated guess for the forces available for Severus at the Battle of Lugdunum. His army had a clear advantage in regulars and cavalry, so Severus did not need to use levies to the same extent as Albinus. We know that one of the newly recruited Parthian legions was left to defend the Alpine passes leading to Italy, and I believe that the two (or maybe three) other Parthian legions were left in the East. It is clear that with the exception of the Parthian legions, most of the newly levied men were added to existing units to bolster their numbers, which meant the fighting power of these units was not significantly lowered; the newly recruited men could be posted in the rear ranks in front of the file closers, who kept them in place. It is no wonder that Severus's regular-heavy army was prepared to attack the army of Albinus, even when it had been posted on a hill. It is therefore safe to say that Severus did not show superior tactical abilities in this battle; he just trusted his elite army to win a frontal slugging match against an enemy in a strong defensive position. Two massive armies of 150,000 soldiers were now poised to begin the slaughter, but we should not forget that this was not the entire strength of these armies because the numbers do not include the recruits and servants left behind in the camp (two out ten men) or the other specialists, artisans, engineers and so forth. We should therefore add at least 40,000 men to the totals on each side.

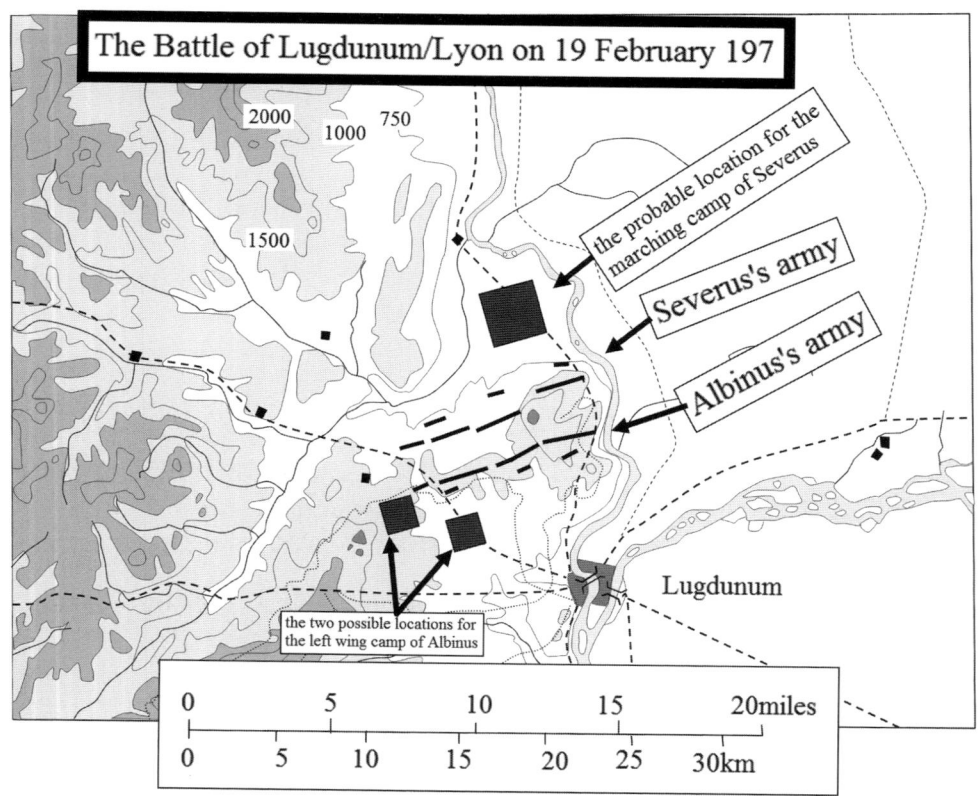

This last and decisive battle assumed truly epic proportions, which were very rarely matched in Roman history. Herodian mentions the civil wars of the Republican era, but even if the totals involved in those wars were greater than on this occasion, the decisive battles were actually fought with smaller armies. The only comparable battle in Roman history took place just over a century later when the armies of Constantine the Great and Licinius faced each other.

As noted above, both sides appear to have posted their infantry in front and most of their cavalry behind as reserves. The actual combat formation probably varied from one unit to another. The case is not so clear for the left flank of Albinus and the right flank of Severus, because even if Laetus was clearly in charge of cavalry reserves on Severus's right, this does not preclude the possibility that there were also cavalry posted to the right of the infantry phalanx because the terrain certainly would have made this necessary. I would suggest that Severus, who had large numbers of cavalry, did indeed place a separate large cavalry wing on his right flank to protect the infantry phalanx and outflank the enemy. Even if it is clear that there were horsemen present, presumably as reserves of the left flank, these were not needed there to the same extent as on the right flank because the left was rested against the river. It is probable that most of the front-line cavalry force posted on the right flank consisted of the Easterners and Goths, because none of the sources specifically mention any role for these in the battle.

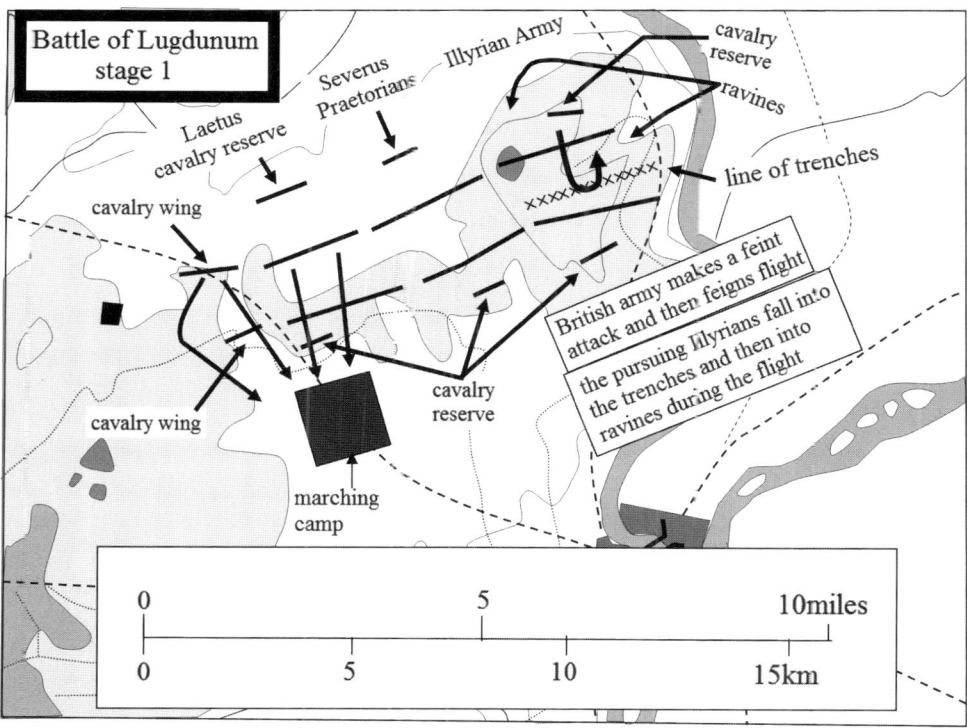

I would similarly suggest that Albinus posted the bulk of his numerically inferior cavalry on his left wing because his right was protected by the river. Even if Albinus deployed all of his cavalry to his left, it is clear that his horsemen were numerically inferior to the cavalry forces of the enemy, and it is therefore not surprising that his left wing collapsed almost immediately at the beginning of the battle. Even if not specifically mentioned by any source, it is obvious that the numerically superior Severan right-wing cavalry immediately outflanked the left flank of Albinus. There remains the question of where Albinus placed his marching camp, which served as a place of refuge for his left wing. He could have positioned it just behind the left wing on level terrain or further to the left on a hill. Despite the fact that the Romans usually placed their marching camps on higher locales, I would suggest that in this case the camp was directly behind Albinus's left wing, because had it been on the hill it would have protected the left wing from outflanking. It is difficult to think that Dio would have failed to state that Albinus rested his left wing against the marching camp and his right wing against the river. In light of the sequence of events, it is also possible that Albinus's plan was from the start to order his left wing to flee to the camp so that the Severan right wing – with its strong cavalry forces – could be lured away from the battlefield. This would have left the decision of the battle in the hands of Albinus's veteran regulars, who were clearly deployed on his right wing. Whatever the truth, it is still clear that the Severan right wing did not exploit its success by attacking Albinus's centre, instead pillaging the enemy camp.

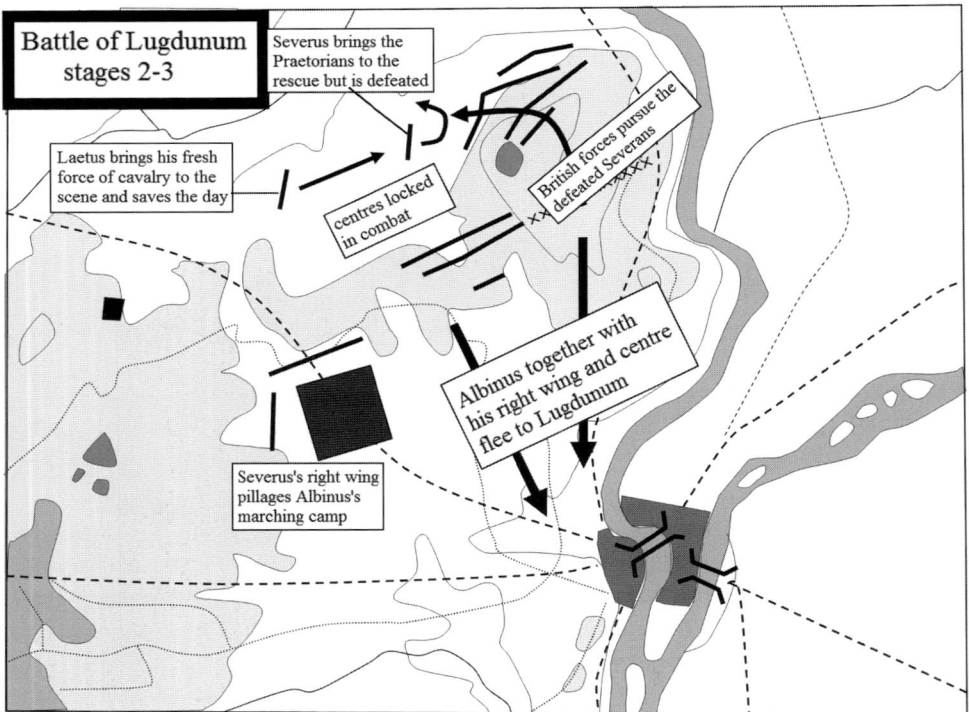

The battle was decided on the left wing of Severus. It was here that Albinus had prepared in advance the hidden trenches and pits. As noted above, I would suggest that Albinus purposefully allowed the Severan left wing to reach the hill so that it would have the ravines behind it. The advance toward the enemy increased the aggressiveness of the Severan force, which in this case worked to the advantage of the defenders. The

British troops then advanced, threw their javelins and feigned flight, which induced the Illyrians to charge forward. If the flight of the left wing of Albinus had taken place before this, the feigned flight of his right wing would obviously have seemed even more believable. It is because of this that I would suggest that Albinus had indeed ordered his left wing, which consisted of the levies, to flee to the marching camp at the beginning of the battle. The Severans foolishly followed and fell into the trenches. On the basis of Dio's description, most of the men who fell into the trenches seem to have consisted of heavy-armed legionaries, but the inclusion of horses among the casualties means that the front-rankers had also opened up their lines for the cavalry reserves to pursue their fleeing foe. It was because of this that we find the instruction for the two front ranks not to pursue in Vegetius. The panicked Severans then fled, with the result that they forced those behind them into the ravines while Albinus's men peppered the disordered and panicked Severans with missiles.

It was then that Severus tried to bring his Praetorian Guard to the rescue. The details of the collapse of his left wing suggest that Severus was with his reserves behind the centre, and that it was because of this that his forces had not become embroiled in the panic. However, when Severus then advanced to the left, the panic also infected his Praetorian Guard and he was himself thrown off his horse. Severus acted swiftly and cast away his imperial cloak so that his enemies would not recognize him. It is possible that he did attempt to rally his men while he was on foot, as stated by Dio, but it is more likely that he did not do so. The British troops started to chant their victory, but this proved premature. Severus's left wing and his Praetorians had been put to flight, but there was still one reserve force left to use on the right flank, which had defeated its opposition. The centres of both armies, meanwhile, were apparently locked in combat.

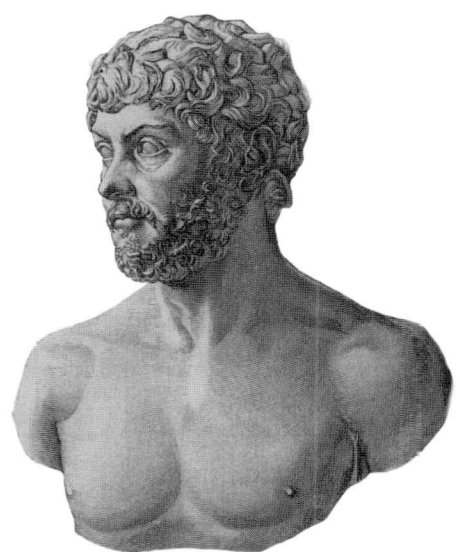

Clodius Albinus according to Duruy. Identification uncertain.

A bust of Septimius Severus. Source: Visconti.

The battle was then decided by Laetus, who was in charge of the right-wing Severan cavalry. The arrival of his fresh horsemen was too much for the scattered British forces to bear. They were scattered and fled in disorder, possibly also being attacked in the left flank. It is possible that Laetus did have imperial aspirations, as he was later accused of, and that he came to the rescue only when Severus had fallen from his horse and was assumed dead. But it is equally possible that he had just waited long enough for the pursuing enemy to scatter so that his cavalry charge would have maximum impact on the enemy. Whatever the truth, the arrival of Laetus undoubtedly decided the day. The troops of Albinus were routed and pursued determinedly by the Severans, the ground being covered with piles of corpses. Albinus attempted to flee through Lugdunum, but when he noted that escape was impossible he either killed or attempted to kill himself. According to the latter version, Albinus was half-dead when soldiers brought him before Severus, who ordered his head to be cut off. Whatever the case, the severed head was placed on a pike/cross and paraded before the troops, and the family of Albinus was killed and then thrown into the river.

The diagrams on pp.152–4 show the main stages of combat during the battle.

7.3. Payback Time: The Purge of the Supporters of Albinus

There then followed a purge of all supporters of Albinus and a reorganization of the territories previously held by the usurper. Lollianus Gentianus was appointed as governor of Lugdunensis, tasked with conducting a census, which was needed in the aftermath of the devastation caused by war, and the *cohors urbana* of Lugdunum was disbanded as a punishment for its support of Albinus. Claudius Candidus was nominated as governor of Tarraconensis and dispatched to Spain, where he had Novius Rufus and other supporters of Albinus executed. The Legio VII Gemina was rewarded with the title *pia* (loyal) for its refusal to support Albinus. Valerius Pudens was nominated as successor of Lupus in Lower Germany, while Marius Maximus was nominated as governor of Belgica. Virius Lupus was rewarded with the position of governor of Britain and dispatched there to punish the Maeatae, a confederation of tribes north of the Antonine Wall who had exploited the absence of Roman forces by pillaging the province. They appear to have been supported by other tribes close to Hadrian's Wall, and also by some Brigantes. Lupus lacked adequate means to restore the situation and was forced to buy peace from the Maeatae when they threatened to bring the Caledonii into northern Britain. In return for this, Lupus received back some of the prisoners that the Maeatae had taken, but the situation was far from satisfactory for Rome. However, the payment of what constituted a tribute or extortion enabled Lupus to begin a much-needed rebuilding programme to repair the damage done. According to Herodian, it was at the same time as Lupus was dispatched to Britain that Severus divided the land into two provinces to ensure that none of the governors of Britain would henceforth have access to more than two legions, but modern research suggests that the division did not take place until after 211. The procurator Claudius Xenophon was also recalled from Asia and dispatched to Africa with the title *procurator ad bona cogenda* to confiscate the property of the condemned supporters of Albinus from his home province.[20] Severus executed so large a number of upper-class men and women in Gaul, Spain and Africa that he had to create new officials to manage the property that had been confiscated. It was thanks to these confiscations that a significant portion of the olive oil production in southern Spain became state property.

Severus did not march straight to Rome after his victory, but went to Germany and from there to Pannonia. In the meantime, he sent threatening messages to the Senate to keep its members guessing what would happen next. The senators knew that the victorious Severus now possessed the entire correspondence of Albinus and thus knew every word that they had sent to the pretender. They had good reason to be fearful, and consequently sent envoys to both Severus in Germany and Antoninus in Pannonia in which they vowed their loyalty to the victor. Severus, however, needed to secure Germania and Pannonia, and he also faced trouble in the East. He thus marched first to Germany and from there to Pannonia before visiting the city of Rome. The Parthians had also attacked Roman territory, and Severus ordered Claudius Gallus, the legate of Legio XXII Primigenia, to collect detachments from all four legions of Germany with their auxiliaries and march at the double to the East. This was a reward for Gallus's stellar performance as defender of the city of Trier (Treves) against the forces of Albinus. In addition to this, as Birley has suggested, it is clear that Severus must have dispatched Julius Laetus to take command of the eastern defences soon after the Battle of Lugdunum, because we later find him in charge of the defence of the city of Nisibis.[21] It is difficult to know whether this was meant as a reward for Laetus's decisive role in the battle or an attempt to get rid of a potentially dangerous competitor by putting him in charge of a city soon to be besieged by the enemy.

The Parthian ruler had defeated the Persians and Medes in battle in Khorasan in 195. The details of the clash suggest that it was fought somewhere close to the Caspian Sea, which means that Vologaesus IV had travelled back to the Parthian heartlands to obtain enough men to oppose the Persians and Medes. Before going there, he had also asked Narses/Narsai/Narseh, the king of Adiabene, to send reinforcements, but Narses had refused, presumably because he had by then become a vassal of Severus. The battle in Khorasan was an epic encounter between two massive eastern cavalry armies. Vologaesus's army consisted of 120,000 horsemen, and his opponents must have had at least the same number of men. When Vologaesus was moving his army to Gurgan and was about to cross a small river, he found that the Persians and Medes had encircled his army, implying that he had carelessly marched into an ambush. The resulting battle began badly for the Parthians and they were forced to flee to nearby hills to regroup. The *Chronicle of Arbela* claims that the Parthians surrendered all of their horses to the Persians, then the Persians surrounded the mountain, and pursued and slaughtered them. This statement is quite clearly misleading because the Parthians would not have been able to counter-attack in the manner that they soon did if this had taken place. The actual meaning is likely that the Parthians abandoned all of their spare horses to the Persians It is probable that at least some of the Persians did stop to loot these mounts and thereby disordered their own ranks even if the *Chronicle* fails to state this, because it was after this that the regrouped Parthians launched a counter-attack. The Parthian assault proved irresistible, attacking downhill against their disordered pursuers, who had also divided their forces by surrounding the mountain. The Parthians pursued the enemy relentlessly as far as the Caspian Sea, into which they threw the corpses of their enemies. The death toll among the Persians and Medes must have been staggering. The Parthians then turned back and attacked the Persians who were on the other side of the mountain. The resulting battle was hard fought, the two opponents fighting for two days with neither side able to gain the advantage. This suggests that the Persians and Medes had brought to the battlefield truly mindboggling numbers of men. On the third day of the engagement, when the Parthians once again arrayed their men for battle they discovered that the Persians and Medes had fled during the night.[22]

While Vologaesus had defeated his enemies, this was clearly not the end of the revolt because he did not attempt to pursue the fugitives, instead turning against his vassals who had recently recognized the Romans as their overlords. We know from Dio and the *Chronicle of Arbela* that he marched against the Adiabeni, Oshroeni and the Romans in the newly conquered areas. The first to taste the anger of Vologaesus, however, were presumably the Medes, whose territory lay on the route to Adiabeni, after which it was the turn of Narses, king of the Adiabeni. Vologaesus's royal army destroyed cities and plundered everything in Adiabene, and Narses was captured and then drowned in the River Zab.[23] These actions must have preoccupied Vologaesus for most of 196 and the beginning of the following year, because Julius Laetus was able to reach the city of Nisibis in 197 before the Parthians put it under siege. News of the invasion of Adiabene would have resulted in the sending of reinforcements and Laetus to the East, presumably in February 197.

It was only after Severus had reorganized the provinces and hastily dispatched reinforcements and his best commander to the East that Severus was able to visit Rome to purge the city of the supporters of Albinus. According to Dio, when he finally entered the Senate he gave a speech that horrified the senators:

> 'Now that he had vanquished all forces under arms he poured upon the unarmed all the wrath he had nourished against them during the previous period. He terrified us most of all by declaring himself the son of Marcus and brother of Commodus; and to Commodus, whom but recently he was wont to abuse, he gave heroic honors. While reading before the senate a speech in which he praised the severity and cruelty of Sulla and Marius and Augustus as rather the safer course, and deprecated the clemency of Pompey and Caesar [saying] it had proved their ruin,[24] [Machiavelli, Prince, tr. by Bull, p.93: 'A new prince… finds it impossible to avoid a reputation for cruelty'] he introduced a defence of Commodus, and inveighed against the senate for dishonouring him unjustly though the majority of their own body lived even worse lives. "For if", said he, "this is abominable, that he with his own hands should have killed beasts, yet at Ostia yesterday or the day before one of your number, an old man that had been consul, indulged publicly in play with a prostitute who imitated a leopard. 'He fought as a gladiator,' do you say? By Jupiter, does none of you fight as gladiator? If not, how is it and for what purpose that some persons have bought his shields and the famous golden helmets?" [The intention was presumably to demonstrate that Severus knew every act that the senators did, and that the senators were not really that different from the hated Commodus and could be accused for the same reasons if Severus so chose to do.] At the conclusion of this reading he released thirty-five prisoners charged with having taken Albinus's side and behaved toward them as if they had incurred

no charge at all. They were among the foremost members of the senate. [This probably means that they were too important to be killed and may actually have also secured their survival by informing Severus of their correspondence with Albinus.] He condemned to death twenty-nine men, one of whom was reckoned Sulpicianus, the father-in-law of Pertinax. [Being a relative of the imperial family was always dangerous.] All pretended to sympathize with Severus but were confuted as often as a sudden piece of news arrived, not being able to conceal the sentiments hidden in their hearts. When off their guard ... through facial expression and habits of behaviour, the feelings of every one of them became manifest. Some also by an excess of affection only betrayed their attitude more. [In a dictatorship like the Roman Empire, it was very dangerous to show any emotions, which could cause the death of the person if the emperor or one of his spies noted such.] Severus endeavoured in the case of those who were receiving vengeance at his hands to employ Erucius Clarus as informer against them .... He promised Clarus to grant him safety and immunity. But when the latter chose rather to die than to make any such revelations, he turned to Julianus and persuaded him to play the part. For his willingness he released him so far as not to kill nor disenfranchise him; but he carefully verified all his statements by tortures. [In other words, the executions did not stop at the twenty-nine senators, but included also others whom Julianus then condemned. This makes it quite possible or even probable that Severus had not obtained the entire corresponderce of Albinus, but that the usurper had managed to destroy at least some of this before his capture.] (Dio 76.7.4–9.6, Forster tr., pp.356–57, with comments)

This account is confirmed by Aelius Spartianus and Herodian. The former includes a long list of senators killed, while the latter adds that Severus rode into the city of Rome at the head of his entire army to make his entrance more awe-inspiring. He was greeted with full honours and pomp, but the prevailing feeling among senators was fear because Severus was known to kill people for any trivial reason. When Severus entered Rome he went first to the Temple of Jupiter on the Capitol Hill, and from there to the Imperial Palace. After this, he distributed vast amounts of money to the people to commemorate his victories. He also rewarded his soldiers, who received the first pay rise for a century, permission to wear a gold ring and the right to live at home with their wives. Severus also improved their diet. Herodian accused Severus of undermining the military discipline and obedience, but this is not true because under Severus's son, Caracalla, the rank-and-file soldiers were the most loyal section of society. In my opinion, improvements to the living conditions of soldiers actually increased the combat efficiency of the army because it lured higher-quality recruits into the armed forces. With the salary unchanged for a century and the forbidding conditions of service, it is clear that at this point the average recruit was not of the same calibre as it had previously been.[25]

It was only after this that Severus entered the Senate, where he gave the previously mentioned speech while showing to the senators some of their secret letters to Albinus. However, there is one very significant difference here between the accounts of Dio and Herodian, as according to the latter Severus destroyed all those who were in a prominent position in the Senate or were wealthy landowners in the provinces on the pretence that they had supported Niger or Albinus, whereas his real reason was to get their riches. The two accounts can be reconciled when one remembers that it was after the execution of the twenty-nine senators that Severus employed Julianus to condemn others. Spartianus notes that Severus put to death many men because they had spoken in jest, had not spoken at all or had said something that could have a double meaning. It was not safe to be rich and powerful under Severus. According to the judgement of Herodian, Severus was the equal of the greatest in bravery, endurance and military skills, but in his greed for money he surpassed all others, being ready to murder people under any excuse to increase his wealth. Severus did not attempt to gain the affection of the senators, but ruled through intimidation, while he still strove to bribe the populace with gladiatorial, theatrical and musical shows and the distribution of money. He also ingratiated himself with the people of the provinces by taking the cost of the postal service out of private hands and giving it to the Privy Purse, while the soldiers were duly bribed with the measures mentioned above. The confiscations of property enabled Severus to distribute the wealth to the people and soldiers simultaneously, while still retaining enough property to finance future projects or campaigns. This is a good example of how it was possible to finance the expenditure of the state by confiscating property from the rich. The Roman rich did not pay their fair share for the upkeep of the armed forces and Empire, so one can consider Severus's actions to have had some social justice behind them. Severus acted like a prototype for Robin Hood, but whereas he took from the rich and gave to the poor (the populace and soldiers), the emperor also enriched himself, his family and friends in the process. This was possible because the rich could hardly flee to any neighbouring state without suffering a very serious lowering of their living standards.[26]

This was also the period when C. Fulvius Plautianus, the kinsman of Severus, began his rise to a position of prominence. He was now given the title *clarissimus vir* (right honourable). We know that he had already been appointed as *praefectus praetorio* before 1 January 197, but he must have thereafter demonstrated his loyalty even more fully for him to become the only man whom Severus trusted.[27] Perhaps he had played an important role in the aftermath of the Battle of Tinurtium when the soldiers had already chosen a new emperor, or during the Battle of Lugdunum. It is quite possible that Plautianus had prevented the public declaration of Laetus in the former case, while in the latter case he could have been the man who protected Severus after he had fallen from his horse. We have no way of knowing for sure what it was that resulted in such blind trust, but from this date onwards Plautianus's position became ever stronger so that he became a new Sejanus (the confidant of Tiberius some 180 years previously).

Severus seems to have stayed at Rome for a few months before embarking on his next military campaign: the punishment of his enemies in the East.

Chapter 8

The Armenian, Parthian and Hatran Campaigns in 197–199

8.1. The Preparations

Severus continued his preparations for the eastern campaign while he was still at Rome by dispatching the bulk of his forces by land in advance. The Legio II Parthica was left in Italy at Alba 13 miles from Rome to ensure the security of the city in his absence. Also left behind to ensure the loyalty of the Senate and people were elements from the enlarged Praetorian Guard, together with the Urban Cohorts and *Vigiles*. These forces were apparently placed under the control of the City Prefect, Anullinus, a close friend of Severus. The strategic province of Upper Pannonia was in the hands of Fabius Cilo, with Dacia probably commanded by Severus's brother Geta. Several other military provinces were placed in the hands of men of African origin or connection to secure the loyalty of these forces while Severus was in the East.[1]

Once the preparations were complete, Severus, Julia Domna, Antoninus, Geta and the rest of the imperial entourage boarded a ship at Brundisium, where the emperor had apparently assembled the Praetorian fleets and transport ships for the remaining forces and their equipment and supplies. The exact route taken to the East is not known, but Birley suggests that Severus landed at some Cilician port, from which he then travelled to Syria by road.[2] In my opinion this seems unlikely, because Severus could have sailed straight to Seleucia, the port of the city of Antioch. His immediate goal appears to have been to relieve the city of Nisibis from its siege by the Parthians, and after that to conduct military campaigns against Armenia, Parthia and Hatra. Dio, Herodian and Spartianus criticize Severus by claiming that the war was fought only because of the emperor's desire for glory rather than due to any necessity, but this allegation is unfounded. Rome was a superpower, and to retain its position of authority it needed to reinstate respect for its military might among its neighbours. Furthermore, even a desire for personal military glory was a worthy goal in itself because it secured the position of Severus among the army and populace. Severus thus had two very good reasons to invade.

8.2. The Narrative Sources for the Parthian Campaign

The following quotes from the original sources contain most of what we know of the campaign against Parthia, but they clearly offer conflicting evidence regarding events. It is for this reason that these sources need to be quoted and evaluated in some detail, beginning with Aelius Spartianus:

'Next, when the rumour of a Parthian war called him away, he erected at his own expense statues of his father, mother, grandfather and first wife …. He remitted the people of Palestine the punishments which he had imposed upon them on Niger's account …. [This would have taken place at some point after Severus's arrival in the East and should be connected with the fighting that took place there.] After having given a gladiatorial show and largesse upon the people, he embarked upon the Parthian war …. As for the Parthian war, it was generally said that Severus fought it only out of his desire for glory rather than for any real necessity. He embarked his army at the port of Brindisi [Brundisium] from whence he … came into Syria and forced the Parthians to retreat. After that he returned back to Syria to make preparations for an offensive war against the Parthians in their own country. In the meanwhile, because of the advice of Plautianus, he hunted the remaining supporters of Niger and even accused many of his own friends of plotting to kill him. Others he slew because they had consulted the astrologers and diviners concerning the date of his death. [This is a prime example of the emperor employing astrologers etc. as informers. Such questions betrayed the disloyalty of the questioner. Severus and Plautianus did not forget the importance of internal security even in the midst of making preparations for an invasion of foreign lands.] He suspected in particular all those who seemed qualified to become emperor because his sons were still very young …. But … Severus denied that it had been done by his order; and particularly Marius Maximus says, he did it in the case of Laetus. [It was important for Severus to get rid of potential usurpers and Laetus was undoubtedly the most threatening of the lot. Clearly nobody believed Severus's claim that he was innocent of the orders to execute the man to whom he owed his life and throne.] His sister making a visit from the town of Lepcis Magna caused the emperor to blush because she could scarcely speak Latin. [This highlights that the Punic language was the native language of Severus.] … Summer being over, because in those parts the winter is the best season for war, he invaded the Kingdom of Parthia, and defeated the king and set himself before Ctesiphon which he captured at about the beginning of the winter season. [The sequence of events in the text suggests that Severus and Vologaesus fought a battle in front of Ctesiphon which ended in defeat for the Parthian, after which he fled and Severus began the siege of Ctesiphon.] But as his soldiers lived on the roots of the plants/ herbs, whereby they had contracted various ills and diseases, and in particular the diarrhoea thanks to the unfamiliar food [the inescapable conclusion is that Severus and his staff had not taken enough food with them for this campaign, which is confirmed by Dio's account], which hindered their marches, he could make no further progress when the Parthian army blocked his way. In spite of this, he still stayed in place and captured the city and put the king to flight killing a great number of the enemy and thereby obtained the title *Parthicus* [the whole title is *Parthicus Maximus*]. [This sequence suggests that Severus defeated Vologaesus near Ctesiphon and then captured the city and defeated Vologaesus again. In other words, the Parthian king had brought a relief army to relieve the siege.] His eldest son Caesar Bassianus Antoninus, thirteen years of age, was upon this occasion proclaimed an Augustus by the army and his younger son Geta was declared at

The Armenian, Parthian and Hatran Campaigns in 197–199   163

the same time as Caesar. [The proclamation by the army would not have been a spontaneous action, but a premeditated one in which the emperor posted his men among the soldiers to start the shouting. I do not agree with Barnett, p.23, that such actions would have been spontaneous. There was always someone who instigated such actions.] Wherefore Severus gave to the army a very large donative, which was in truth the liberty to plunder the city of Ctesiphon .... He then returned as a victor back to Syria. The Senate offered him the honour of a triumph for the Parthian campaign, which he refused because he could not stand upright by reason of the gout .... But he permitted his son to celebrate a triumph in his place because the Senate had decreed a Jewish triumph for him thanks to the successes achieved by Severus in Syria. [This means that some fighting had taken place in this area against rebels.] After this, when Severus reached Antioch, he placed the *toga virilis* upon his elder son and appointed him as a consul together with him ... while still in Syria, the two entered their consulships. [This gives us the date 1 January 202, which is clearly incorrect.] Following this, after he had first raised the soldiers' pay, he began his march towards Alexandria while granting numerous rights to the communities of Palestine. He also forbade conversion to Judaism and Christianity under heavy penalties. [See my discussion of this later.]' (Aelius Spartianus, *HA Severus* 14.4, 14.11, 15.1ff., tr. by Bernard, p.403ff., with corrections, changes, additions and comments)

Herodian's version of the campaign is as follows:

[U]nsatisfied with the honour of victories obtained in civil wars and over Roman armies ... he resolved to attempt some foreign conquest ... accordingly he set out on an expedition to the East against Barsenius, King of the Hatra, using as his excuse the assistance given to Niger ... he also planned to attack Armenia, but was prevented by the King of Armenia who approached him humbly with large sums of money, valuables and hostages promising to become his loyal ally. And after this success in Armenia, he advanced immediately against the Hatrans. Abgar [Augaros = Abgarus] fled to him bringing his children as hostages together with large numbers of archers to serve as auxiliaries ....[3] ['*toxotas te pleistous summachous ēgagen*'. On the basis of this it is impossible to be absolutely certain regarding the meaning of archers. Herodian may have meant both foot and horse archers, or only the former, because the Oshroeni certainly possessed both. For the infantry archers, see the illustration taken from Trajan's Column on page 164. The surrender of Abgar must have taken place already before Severus relieved the city of Nisibis, or immediately after it, the former being my preferred option because it is likely that Severus would have marched through Oshroene.] Severus having passed through all Mesopotamia and Adiabene descended on to Arabia Felix [This is a mistake: Arabia Felix was located in modern day Yemen. The real location is the land of the Scenite Arabs.] ... here he sacked many villages and cities, laid waste the country about; then penetrated the frontiers of the Hatrans, and settled down to besiege Hatra, a city situated on the summit of a high ridge, surrounded by enormous strong walls and garrisoned with a great multitude of expert archers.

Note the order of the forces in this battle scene. Most of the auxiliaries (Germans and regulars, equipped with oval shields) are clearly in front while most of the legionaries (*lorica segmentata*, rectangular cylindrical *scutum*) are behind them, and behind all the rest are the Eastern archers, which are possibly Oshroenians.
Source: Bellori, Bartoli (17th century).

Severus's army invested the place and carried on their operations with the utmost ardour, resolved, if possible, to storm it. Every kind of siege engine was employed against the walls and no kind of siege technique was left untried. The Hatran people bravely defended themselves by sending showers of missiles and stones from the walls on to the army of Severus, which caused significant damage. And throwing down clay vessels filled with little poisonous flying insects, which then fell on Severus's army with the result that the insects crawled unnoticed into the eyes and exposed parts of the body and stung the soldiers and inflicted painful and dangerous wounds .... [These were probably either some sort of mosquito or Vespa Orientalis/Oriental hornet, and prove that the Hatrans were well-versed in the various forms of siege technique.][4] The Romans, unable to bear the thick unwholesome air caused by the excessive heat of the sun, were starting to fall ill and die ... this carried off greater numbers than the hand of the enemy. Afflicted with all these ... Severus was obliged to raise the siege and draw off his forces before they all perished. The army was upset because until then they had been accustomed to winning all their battles. [This describes the end of the first siege. For details, see the analysis of the sieges of Hatra.] But fortune which Severus always had on his side soon comforted them .... For the army being embarked on a large fleet of ships and bound for the Roman bank of the river was swept down a long way to the Parthian bank at a distance of not many days from Ctesiphon. [Herodian has hopelessly confused the different stages of the campaign. On the basis of Dio, we know that Severus first advanced against Ctesiphon with his fleet and only after that against Hatra.] The court of the king of Parthia was located in this city and he resided there quite unconcerned at the quarrels of Severus with the Hatrans because he thought that it was no concern of his. [This claim is just incredible and complete nonsense. The Parthians would have known for weeks that the Roman fleet would be sailing down the river. Furthermore, it had been Vologaesus with his imperial army that had besieged Nisibis so it is hardly believable that he would

The Armenian, Parthian and Hatran Campaigns in 197–199   165

not have expected any punishment.] When Severus's army had been carried to these shores by the rapidity of the current against Severus's wishes, the army was disembarked and began to lay waste the region, seizing the cattle for subsistence and setting fire to every village in its way. After a short march, the army stood in front of Ctesiphon where resided the great King Artabanus. [A mistake because the ruler was Vologaesus.] The Romans caught the barbarians unprepared and were therefore able to slaughter all they met and plunder the whole area of the city carrying away captive the children and women. The king fled with a few of his cavalry, leaving behind the royal treasury, jewels and valuables, which fell into the hands of the Roman soldiers. [Spartianus makes it quite clear that the siege involved some serious fighting before the Parthian king fled, so this is once again false.] Thus Severus was honoured with a victory over the Parthians; which was rather a gift of fortune than the result of good judgment. Having gained success so far exceeding his wildest dreams, he dispatched a report to the Senate and people extolling the greatness of his achievements and ordered that his battles and victories were to be painted and publicly exhibited. [This probably referred to the paintings that were carried before an audience, but it is also possible that it meant the Triumphal Arch of Severus which depicts the scenes of this campaign. The reliefs would have been painted at this time, so it is possible that the paintings meant these. See the attached drawings of these scenes on pp. 171–2, together with the analysis.] The Senate decreed him every kind of honour and gave him the titles alluding to the different nations Severus had conquered. Affairs in the East thus prosperously carried, he hastened towards Rome bringing with him his two sons, now young men. [Another incorrect statement. After the Parthian and Hatran campaigns, Severus marched to Egypt with the intention of invading Ethiopia.]' (Herodian 3.9.1ff., tr. by Hart, p.134ff, with changes, additions, corrections and comments)

Dio writes thus of these events:

'The next thing Severus did was to make a campaign against the Parthians. While he was busied with civil wars, they had been free from molestation and had thus been able by an expedition in full force to capture Mesopotamia. They also came very near reducing Nisibis, and would have done so, had not Laetus, who was besieged there, preserved the place. Though already previously noted as a man of excellence in other political and private and public matters, he derived even greater glory from this exploit. Severus on reaching the aforesaid Nisibis encountered an enormous boar. With its charge it killed a horseman who, trusting to his own strength, attempted to run it down, and it was with difficulty stopped and killed by many soldiers – thirty being the number required to stop it; the beast was then conveyed to Severus. The Parthians did not wait for him but retired homeward. (Their leader was Vologaesus, whose brother was accompanying Severus.) [Note that it was the royal army under the King of Kings that had been besieging Nisibis. The presence of the brother of Vologaesus in the imperial entourage implies a political plan in which Severus intended to replace Vologaesus with his sibling. The outcome of the war proves that this plan did not take into account the patriotism of the Parthian population at this time. Regardless, it is still clear that this man was very useful for the contacts and information that he had of the Parthian Empire.] Hence Severus equipped boats [*ploia*] on the Euphrates and reached him partly by marching, partly by sailing. [The plan resembles the one later adopted by Julian, but with the difference that Severus did not attempt to hide his intentions. Julian tried but failed.][5] The newly constructed vessels were exceedingly manageable and speedy and well constructed, for the forest along the Euphrates and those regions in general afforded the emperor an abundant supply of timber. [It is possible this is the official version, which has left out the troubles in the handling of the boats and ships mentioned by Herodian, but in light of the complete mess that Herodian has made of the campaign, it is very likely that Dio is actually correct here.] Thus he soon had seized Seleucia and Babylon, both of which had been abandoned. [This means that Severus and his army, or at least parts of it, advanced further south to Babylon and did not immediately sail and march to Seleucia and Ctesiphon.] Subsequently he captured Ctesiphon and permitted his soldiers to plunder the whole town [Spartianus calls this a donative], causing a great slaughter of men and taking nearly ten myriads [*ca.* 100,000] captives. However, he did not pursue Vologaesus [this leaves out the battle or battles mentioned by Spartianus] nor did he occupy Ctesiphon, but as if the sole purpose of his campaign had been to plunder it, he thereupon departed. This action was due partly to lack of acquaintance with the country and partly to dearth of provisions. [This confirms the account of Spartianus. This is very strange because Vologaesus's brother was accompanying the Roman army, so Severus should have been aware of the conditions. The only explanation for this horrible oversight is that Severus and his staff miscalculated the situation on the basis of the reports given by Vologaesus's brother. He must have claimed to possess far more support among the populace than he did, so the Romans expected to be welcomed by the citizens of Ctesiphon and thus thought they would not need to carry large amount of supplies. The Parthians clearly did not welcome the traitor, but continued to resist by using guerrilla warfare to deny the Romans access to local provisions.] His return was made by a different route, because the food and fodder found on the previous route had been exhausted. [This proves that the Parthian guerrilla campaign was not as effective as when Julian followed the same route in 363.] Some of his soldiers made their retreat by land along the Tigris, following the stream toward its source, and some on boats. [Note that it was possible to row these upstream.] Next, Severus crossed Mesopotamia and made an attempt on Hatra.' (Dio 76.9.1ff., Cary ed., p.216ff., tr. by Forster, pp.358–59, with changes, corrections and comments)

8.3. The Narrative of the Parthian Campaign

When the above sources are analyzed, it seems probable that when Severus dispatched most of his army in advance on land to the East, at least some of these forces assembled on the border of Armenia while the rest marched to Antioch, where the emperor met them with troops he had brought in the ships. After this, in about June, he marched along the direct route towards the city of Nisibis, which was besieged by the Parthian royal army

The Armenian, Parthian and Hatran Campaigns in 197–199

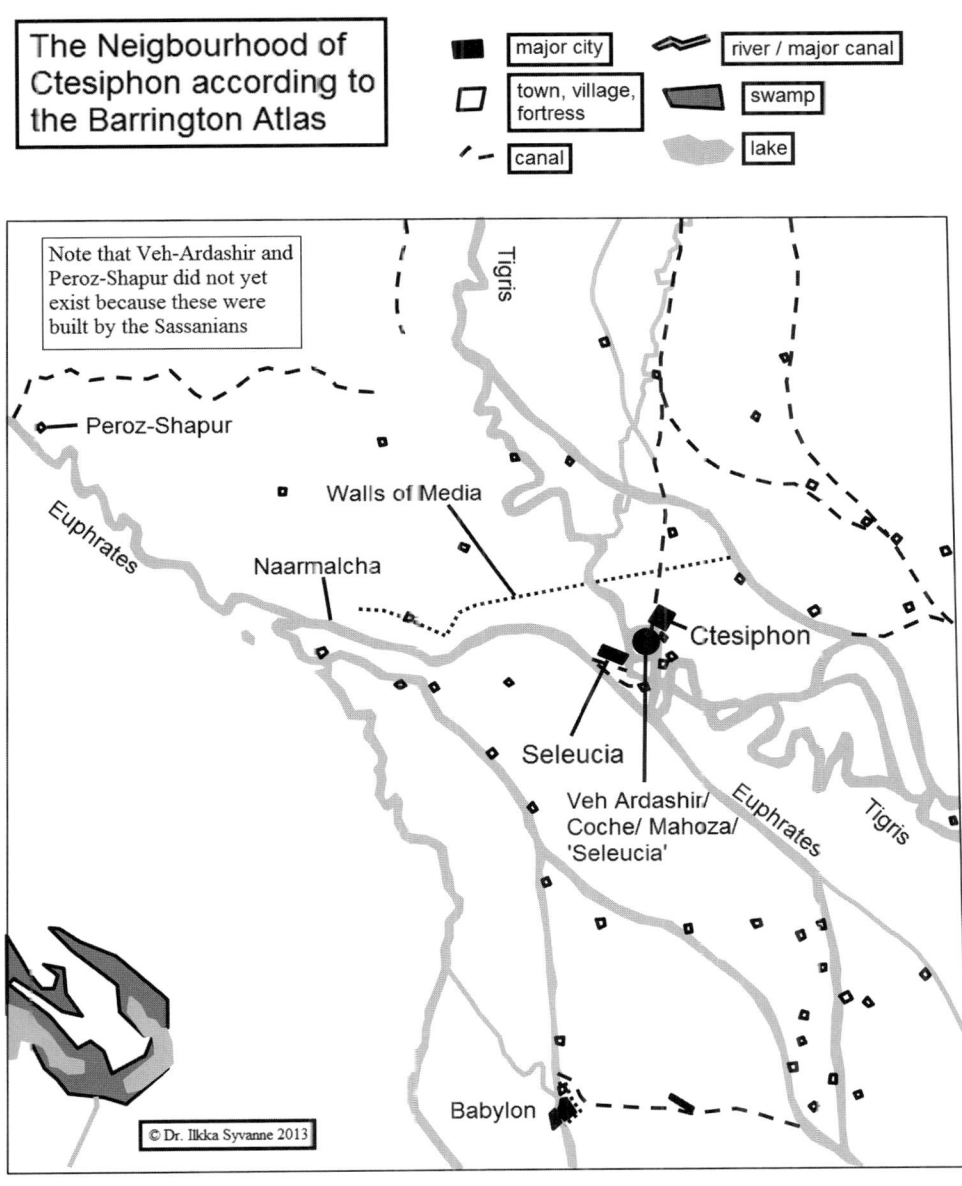

under the King of Kings Vologaesus and ably defended by Laetus. The most direct route to Nisibis went through Osrhoene and Edessa, whose king, Abgar, submitted to Severus and provided him with archers to serve as auxiliaries during the campaign. Vologaesus either abandoned the siege when he heard of the approach of Severus and retired back across the Tigris, or Laetus sallied out of the city and defeated Vologaesus, forcing him to retreat. The main reason for the latter suggestion is that Dio gives Laetus full credit for saving the city. Another reason is that the Arch of Severus depicts a sally with combat between Romans and Parthians outside the walls in the context of the siege. This can have only resulted from a successful surprise attack by the Romans. I would thus suggest that Laetus did indeed achieve a major success before Severus reached the scene. After the city had been relieved, Severus continued his march to Adiabene and gave orders to prepare a fleet on the Euphrates for the forthcoming campaign against Parthia.

Severus's next goal was to deal with Armenia, which had hitherto remained neutral, and return it to client status.[6] Once Nisibis had been relieved it is probable that Severus continued his campaign by marching to Adiabene and from there towards Armenia. The King of Armenia anticipated this by submitting in person. These operations were probably carried out in about June to August.[7] The advance through Adiabene was meant to punish the locals for their failure to respect the terms of their surrender in 195; they were the clients of Rome, not of Parthia. None of the sources mention what happened, but it is likely that the Adiabenes surrendered, just like they had in 195.

Severus returned back to Syria where he then continued his purge of assumed supporters of Niger and other suspects while waiting for the fleet to be built and assembled. Once the preparations were finished, Severus joined his forces. It is probable that the assembly point for the fleet and army was Hierapolis just like it was later for Julian and East Romans.[8] Just like Julian later did, Severus then advanced along the Euphrates, his main army marching on the left bank while the fleet sailed down the river. The sources do not give us the marching formation, but it is clear that it was the hollow square or oblong which was always used when the enemy could threaten the Romans from all sides, as could the Parthians with their massive cavalry forces. The invasion began probably in September or early October 197.

The sources do not give us any size for the Roman army, but it is unlikely to have been any smaller than it was against Albinus, as Severus had marched most of this army to Rome to impress the Senate and populace, and even if he had then detached troops to Britain, Spain and elsewhere, he could bolster his numbers from those already posted in the East and from new allied forces. Severus thus probably had about 100,000 infantry and marines and some 50,000 cavalry, plus a large number of non-combatants.

The *Chronicle of Arbela 6* gives Vologaesus IV (or V) 120,000 soldiers when he fought and defeated the Persian and Mede rebels, suggesting that was the largest number of men available to him. However, considering the likely amount of casualties suffered during the civil war and in the siege of Nisibis, one may surmise that he could no longer put this many men into the field. My educated guess is that he now had about 100,000 men at his disposal. Most of these would have been cavalry. The royal army, which was bolstered with feudal elite cavalry, consisted of about 50,000 cataphracts, which usually fought by using the rhomboid unit formation (each of 128 men), deployed as a crescent, with a reserve led by the King of Kings placed behind. The rest of the army would have comprised the forces provided by the client states and tribes and by autonomous cities. Their troops were primarily light cavalry (mounted archers and javelineers), heavy infantry (spearmen with shields) and light infantry (archers and slingers), the latter of which were used for the defence of cities and forts because their combat value against Roman infantry was very poor. The principal problem for Vologaesus was that his main striking force, the cataphracts, could not cope with the Roman combined arms approach. The Roman infantry was just too disciplined to be broken by the archery and spears of the cataphracts.[9] Vologaesus was well aware of this, which had resulted in him not attempting to face Severus before the city of Nisibis. However, Severus now forced his hand by advancing against his capital.

The Parthians did not attempt to defend Babylon or Seleucia. Indeed, it is possible that the walls of these cities were no longer defensible. Babylon was already in ruins when Trajan visited it some eighty years previously, and Seleucia had been in ruins since Cassius had levelled it in 165. The terrain makes it likely that Severus either continued his journey straight to Babylon merely for sightseeing purposes, or that he divided his forces so that part of it advanced to Babylon while the main army continued its journey to the Tigris, Seleucia and Ctesiphon. The fact that Dio does not mention any battle before the city of Ctesiphon has led several historians, for example Birley (p.130), to conclude that Vologaesus fled without making any serious attempt to defend the city.[10] In my opinion this is a mistake, and historians should put more trust in the *Historia Augusta*. It is very

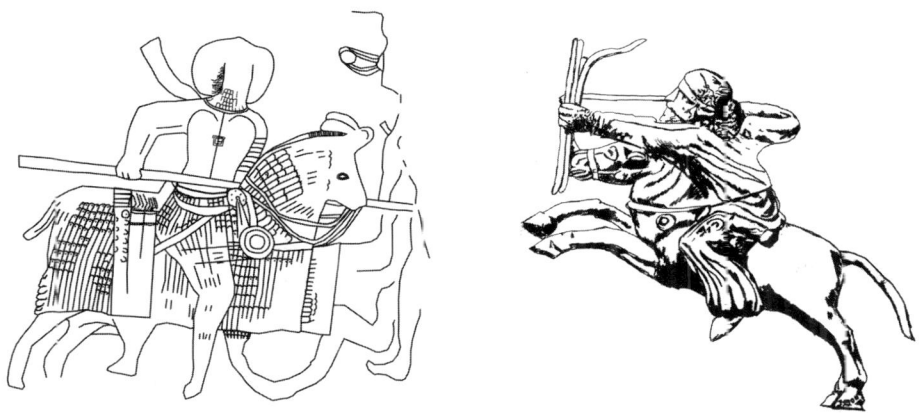

These four images depict the type of forces that Severus would have faced when he fought field battles against the Parthians. Above left is a relief depicting a king of Elymais ca. AD 150. Above right is another image depicting Parthian horseman. This image depicts a lightly-equipped mounted archer which were typically recruited from the subject, client and allied tribes, but could also consist of Parthians proper if these were either poor or did not wear the entire panoply. Below are two graffiti found from Dura Europos (before ca. 250), which depict cataphracts wearing typical Parthian equipment. Of particular importance is that the mounted archers could also be fully armoured, which appears to have been the case with the Royal Parthian Army consisting of the elite cavalries provided by the feudal lords serving under the King of Kings. The images are drawn after those of von Gall and Simon James.

170 Emperor Septimius Severus

1) Laetus sallies out of the city of Nisibis; 2) Laetus's forces inflict a crushing defeat on Vologaesus and his Parthian army; 3) Parthians fleeing; 4) Adluctio (address, speech to the troops); 5) City of Nisibis possibly with Laetus at the gate.

1) Severus advances against Edessa; 2) Abgar surrenders; 3) Armenian King surrenders; 4) Adluctio; 5) Council in Roman camp; 6) Council outside the camp.

The Armenian, Parthian and Hatran Campaigns in 197–199

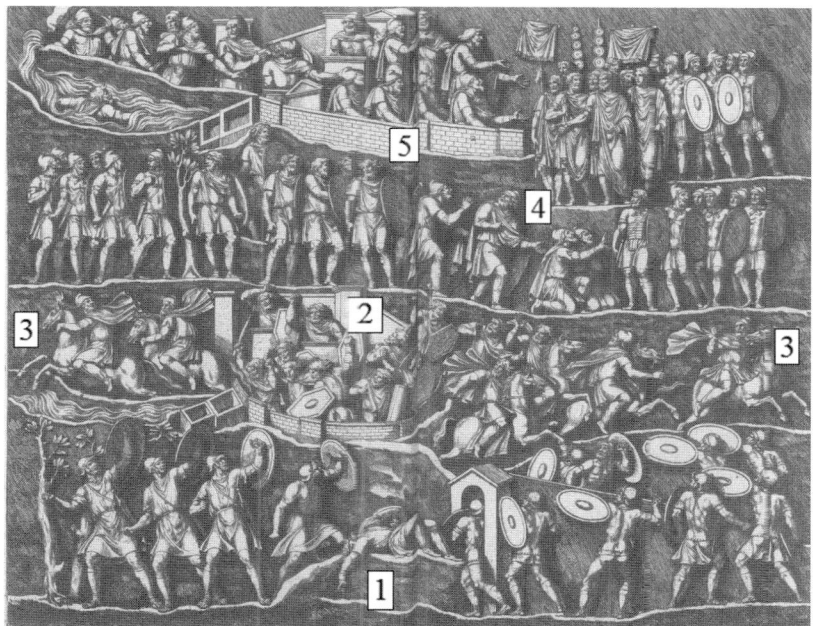

1) The Romans cross the Tigris and fight a battle against the Royal Parthian Army; 2) The city of Ctesiphon; 3) The defeated Royal Army and Vologaesus flees; 4) The inhabitants of Ctesiphon beg for mercy and surrender; 5) The city of Ctesiphon.

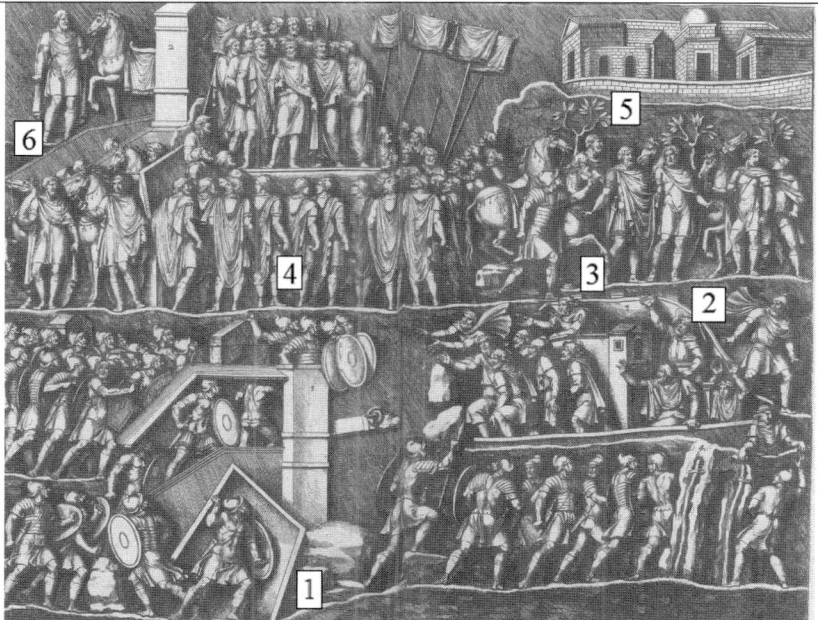

The context of this panel is not certain and the following represents just my educated guess: 1-2) The Romans besiege a city, which may be a city in Adiabene, or some city in Parthia, but the city of Hatra is by far the likeliest. E.g. Sheldon (2010, 170) seems to think so. The last of these is likeliest because the panel does not show surrender even if the defenders clearly beg for help from the heavens. Furthermore, the battering ram is protected by a building which could not be burned like the wooden sheds in the previous panels. In my opinion, this should be seen to represent a siege engine built by Priscus, which could not be burned. The soldiers underneath the city may mean an attempt to build a tunnel; 3) This scene depicts Severus possibly with his sons and officers; 4) Adluctio; 5) Palace or city; 6) Severus's horse?

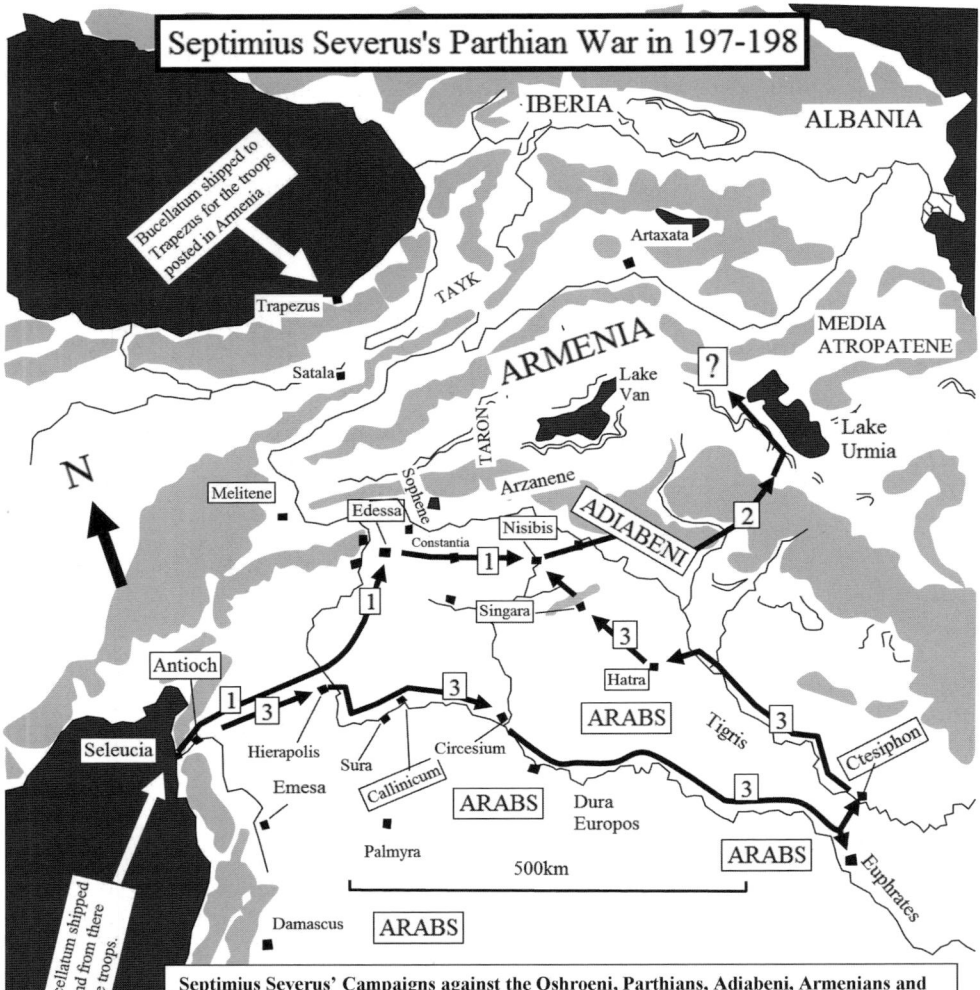

Septimius Severus' Campaigns against the Oshroeni, Parthians, Adiabeni, Armenians and then again against the Parthians 197-198

1) A march past Edessa (King of Oshroene submits) to Nisibis to relieve its siege by the Parthians. I have made the educated guess that Severus approached Edessa from the south so that he would not have faced a contested river crossing. It is probable that Laetus sallied out of Nisibis and inflicted a defeat on the retreating Parthians. It is not known if this happened well before the arrival of Severus's army or when it was already near.

2) A march from Nisibis through Adiabene towards Armenia. I have assumed that Severus used the principal road going through Adiabene to the Lake Urmiah. The King of Armenia came to meet Severus and submitted in person before the Armenian campaign began. It is not known how far Severus had advanced when this took place and it is not known if Severus threatened the Armenians with another army from the direction of Satala. Similarly it is not known which route Severus used to return back to Syria. It is possible that he returned via the same route that he had taken or that he marched through some sections of Armenia to secure it more firmly.

3) A combined force (land and naval forces) attack against the Parthian capital along the Euphrates and then retreat back along the Tigris. The probable concentration point for the Roman armed forces was the city of Hierapolis. The route which the Romans took against the city of Hatra is not known. It is also possible that they would have first marched to Nisibis and only from there south.

The Armenian, Parthian and Hatran Campaigns in 197–199   173

unlikely that Vologaesus would have abandoned his capital without any fight. On the contrary, I believe that he deployed his royal army – with the support of the militia – in front of Ctesiphon, just like the Persians did in 363 when Julian invaded. The result was the same, the Romans defeating the Parthian cavalry and forcing it to flee. It was after this that the Romans besieged the city. On the basis of the *Augustan Histories*, it is possible that Vologaesus attempted to relieve the city once more, but was again defeated. However, even if one cannot entirely preclude the existence of a second major battle, the evidence for it

Captives brought before a victorious general (after a sarcophagus at Rome) according to Duruy. In the 18th century, Montfaucon associated the same scene with the surrender of the Parthians to Severus. However, Duruy is likely to be correct. The identification is uncertain, but the scene in itself does depict the way in which the enemies were forced to beg for peace from the victorious Roman commanders and is therefore broadly speaking representative of similar scenes taking place under Severus.

According to Duruy, Marcus Aurelius receives in this relief the surrender of Parthians. The scenes of surrender shown in the Arch of Severus look quite similar.

Severus celebrated his victories with coins most of which specifically named the victory over the Parthians, but in addition to this his coins now called him the bringer of peace. Source: Duruy

Above a coin of Vologaesus IV (or V). Source: Duruy

is very uncertain. The fact that Vologaesus had failed to pursue the defeated Persians after the battle in Khorasan meant that Persia was still in revolt, which in turn meant that he could not now go there for reinforcements, instead having to go all the way back to Gurgan. There was thus simply no time to attempt the relief of the city after his defeat in the field. Furthermore, it is possible that Vologaesus sought first a place of refuge in Ctesiphon, and fled only after it became apparent that the Romans would capture the city. The Romans did indeed take the city before the winter was over, so the siege cannot have been a long one. Unfortunately, we do not know if Severus was able to use the brother of Vologaesus to obtain the surrender of the city. What is certain is that the populace failed to support the brother of Vologaesus in any significant manner, the Romans being forced to retreat north along the Tigris because they lacked adequate supplies to stay in the area. The Romans had been forced to consume local supplies along their route of march, and were forced to do so again during their retreat. Nevertheless, on the basis that they were still able to briefly besiege the city of Hatra after their Parthian campaign was over, it is clear that they had not committed any disastrous strategic mistake. Furthermore, the Romans clearly had enough supplies to last for the entire campaign, not to mention the fact that they could also feed up to 100,000 captives (which formed part of the booty given to the soldiers) whom they took north. One may speculate that the real reason for Severus's retreat was the need to take the prisoners and other booty back to Roman territory so that the soldiers would remain loyal to their emperor. Indeed, Severus knew that he must keep his soldiers happy.

The defeat of Vologaesus IV and the capture of Ctesiphon enabled Septimius Severus to take the title *Parthicus Maximus* on 28 January 198. Birley (p.130) notes that this was the exact centenary of Trajan's accession, which suggests that the assumption of the title was premeditated. Severus wanted to associate himself with the *optimus princeps*, and the capture of Ctesiphon gave him the opportunity to do so. This in turn means that the city of Ctesiphon was definitely captured before that date, possibly in December 197 because the *HA* dates the fall of Ctesiphon to the beginning of the winter.

8.4. The Two Sieges of Hatra in 198 or 198–199

Dio provides us with the best account of the siege of Hatra. Indeed, without him we would not even know that there were two sieges of Hatra:

> 'Next, Severus crossed Mesopotamia and made an attempt on Hatra, which was not far off, but accomplished nothing. [In my opinion it is probable that he did that while retreating along the Tigris so that his route of retreat passed by the city of Hatra, but it is of course possible that Severus first retreated to Nisibis and advanced from there against Hatra, even if the former is inherently more likely.] In fact, even the engines were burned, many soldiers perished, and vast numbers were wounded. Therefore Severus retired from the place and shifted his quarters. While he was at war, he also put to death two distinguished men. The first was Julius Crispus, a tribune of the Praetorians. The cause of his execution was that, indignant at the damage done by the war, he had casually uttered a verse of the poet Maro, in which one of the soldiers fighting on the side of Turnus against Aeneas bewails his lot and says: "To enable Turnus to marry Lavinia we are meanwhile

perishing, without heed being paid to us." Severus made Valerius, the soldier who had accused him, tribune in his place. [This is an example of informers at work. Informers were encouraged to expose persons with hostile opinions in return for rewards. This obviously encouraged false accusations, as the sources so often state, and ensured that people were constantly frightened about their own utterances. It was extremely dangerous to speak one's mind in a dictatorship.] The other whom he killed was Laetus, and the reason was that Laetus was proud and was beloved by the soldiers. They often said they would not march, unless Laetus would lead them. The responsibility for this murder, for which he had no clear reason save jealousy, he fastened upon the soldiers, making it appear that they had ventured upon the act contrary to his will.' (Dio 76.10.1, Cary ed., p.218ff., tr. by Forster, p.359ff., with changes, corrections and comments)[11]

The texts of Spartianus, Herodian and Dio make it clear that the Roman army had suffered a significant amount of hardship in the course of its Parthian campaign due to illness, which was then exacerbated by the casualties suffered in the course of the first siege of Hatra, which clearly did not go well. Herodian refers to only one siege of Hatra (quoted already above), but on the basis of Dio we know that there were two, the second one being described in the quoted passage later in this chapter. The fact that Herodian's details cannot be reconciled with the information provided by Dio regarding the second siege means that Herodian is describing the first siege.

The combined accounts make it clear that Severus marched against Hatra when he was retreating from Ctesiphon. This means that it is probable that he marched there straight from the Tigris, rather than visiting Roman territory first. As stated by Herodian, Severus invested the city and used every kind of siege engine and siege technique. He thus would have employed *ballistae*, catapults, *onagri* (probably), battering rams, borers, drills, sickles, siege sheds, undermining, mounds, fire bombs, ladders and possibly also *sambucae* and siege towers. For examples of these, see the scenes of the Arch of Severus on pp. 170–1 and the drawings below.

The evidence provided by both Dio and Herodian make it clear that the Hatrans protected their city well. The accounts also reveal that the defenders possessed similar siege experts as the Romans and the Palmyrenes in the next century. Just as later did the Palmyrenes,[12] the Hatrans had particularly powerful long-range defences in the form of archers and artillery, Herodian stating that they defended themselves bravely with heavy showers of missiles and stones which caused significant damage to the Romans. Herodian's account also proves that the Hatrans had at least one trick that may have been borrowed from earlier stratagems: the shooting of poisonous flying insects at the Romans placed inside clay vessels, which caused significant hardship to the besiegers. Dio's text says that the Hatrans managed to burn the Roman siege engines, which means the defenders also employed incendiary weapons, most likely arrows and fire bombs. According to Herodian, the final straw that convinced Severus to withdraw was that the heat and unwholesome air caused many Romans to fall ill and die, with a greater number of soldiers being killed by heat or illness than by the enemy. Herodian notes that the army was upset when Severus gave the order to withdraw, because until then they had always been victorious. Dio refers to these same hardships in a roundabout way by

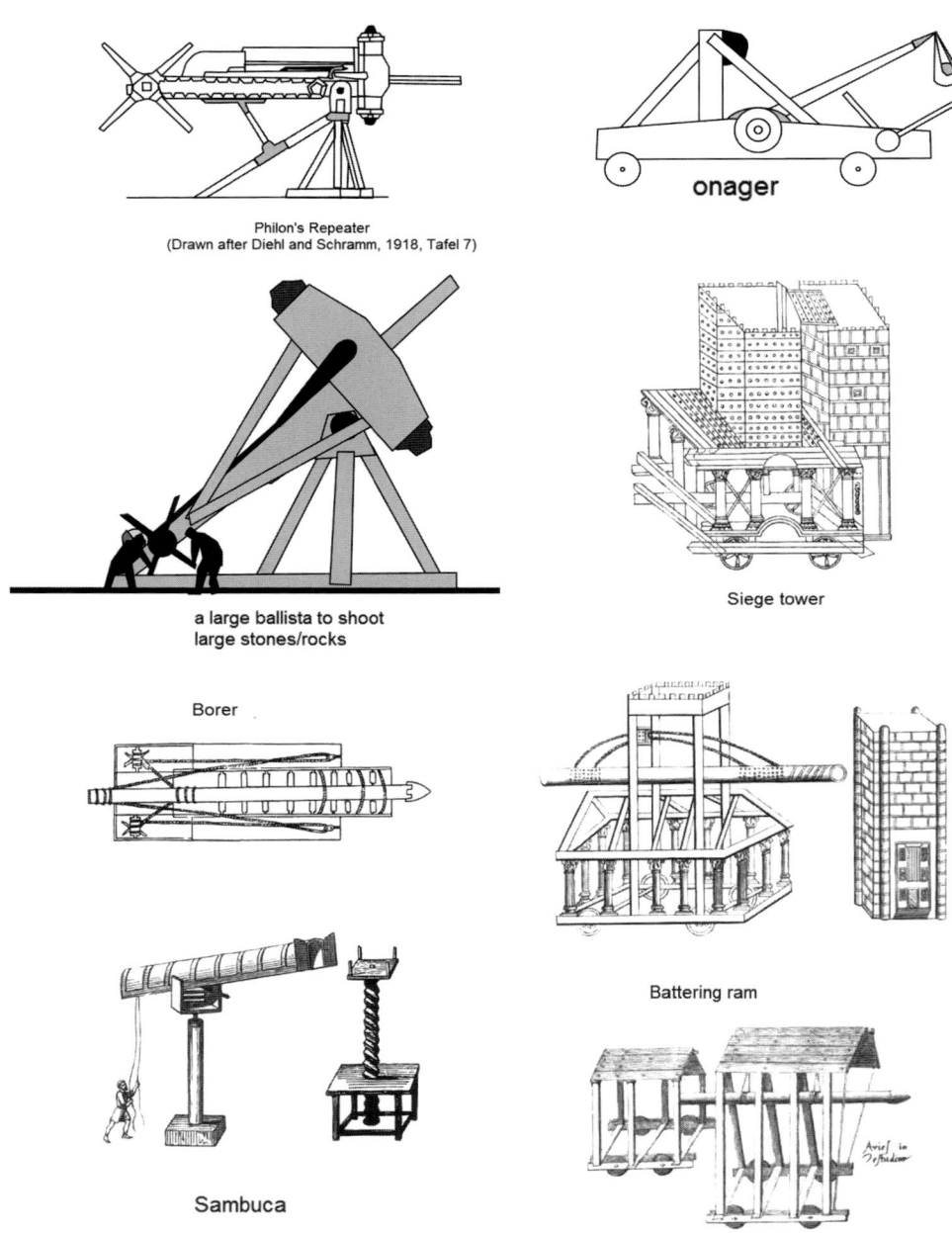

Philon's Repeater
(Drawn after Diehl and Schramm, 1918, Tafel 7)

onager

a large ballista to shoot large stones/rocks

Siege tower

Borer

Battering ram

Sambuca

pointing out the complaint of the Praetorian tribune and the killing of him and Laetus. The soldiers were clearly so dissatisfied with the situation that Severus felt it necessary to eliminate Laetus because he was too popular with them, thanks to his great military achievements. Laetus was thus made a scapegoat for the defeat. The killing of Laetus removed a possible unifying figurehead from any rebellious troops, who now lacked a suitable candidate to replace Severus. His murder without good cause, however, was so

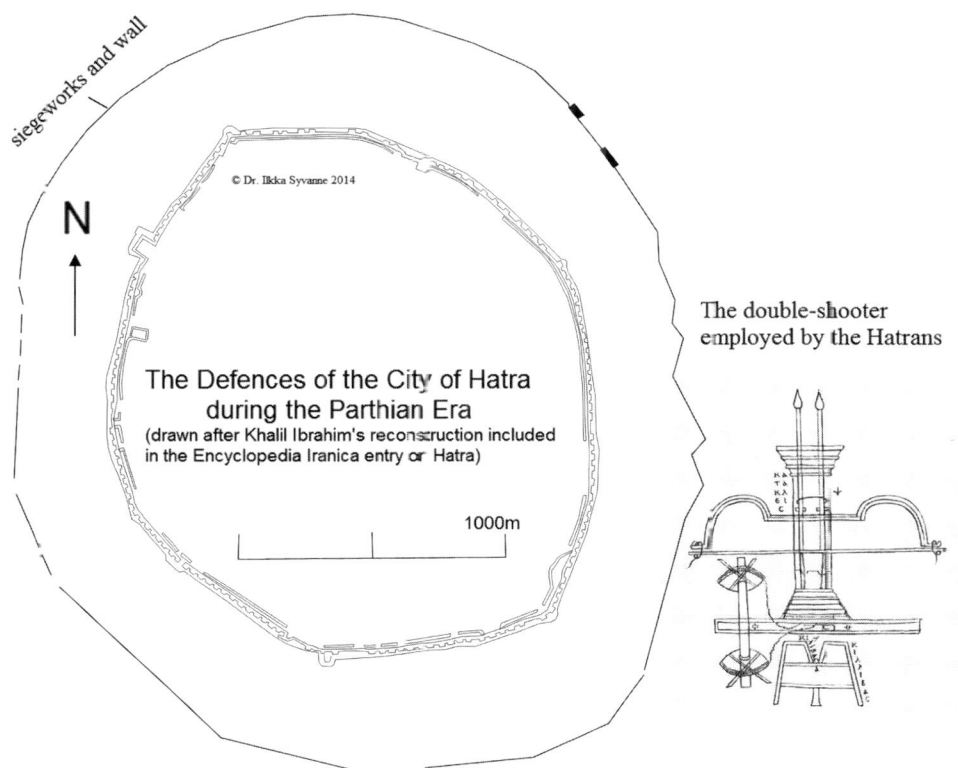

The visible lines of siege works probably date from the Sassanian era when the Sassanians conducted three sieges of Hatra. After the last one of those, the city was taken and destroyed. However, it is entirely probable that the Sassanian siege lines would have been built on the same place as Severus's siege lines because the place of such lines was determined by the length of the archery and artillery fire.

callous that even Severus felt it necessary to claim innocence and frame the soldiers who actually killed Laetus as the culprits Both these men, Laetus and Crispus, were killed while the siege still continued or immediately after it.

Birley (p.131) suggests that the initiative for the murder of Laetus may have come from Plautianus. This is quite plausible because Plautianus was at this time strengthening his position by killing off rivals, with a significant number of Severus's close associates now losing their lives. The most illustrious of these was Claudius Candidus, who was killed either now or a little later. The open dissatisfaction of the soldiers at the orders of Severus undoubtedly made him ready to listen to the advice given by Plautianus, his trusted relative and Praetorian Prefect.

According to Herodian (3.6), there were two versions of why Severus trusted Plautianus. The first version stated that Plautianus came from humble circumstances and that he had been at one time exiled because of accusations of sedition and other crimes. He was a Libyan, like Severus, and some claimed that he was also a relative of the emperor. The second and less flattering version was that in his youth Plautianus had been a boy-lover of Severus, and it was because of this that Severus had promoted him.

Severus had also enriched Plautianus by giving him the property of the condemned and making him the second most important man in the Empire. But Plautianus misused his position and committed so many crimes that, according to Herodian, he made himself one of the most feared prefects of all time. It is impossible to know which of the versions is correct. It is possible that Severus just promoted a fellow Libyan and relative to a position of importance because he trusted the man due to his background, but it could also be that it was because of their earlier sexual relationship. However, it would have been quite easy to jump to such a conclusion because Severus clearly trusted Plautianus blindly. Such a story would have received further support from the fact that Plautianus was known to be bisexual (Dio 76.15.7, Cary ed., p.232). The problem with this claim is that there is no further support for it. None of the other sources repeat the claim that Severus was bisexual, and it was one of the standard tricks in antiquity to accuse one's enemy of being homosexual.[13] Regardless, one cannot entirely preclude the possibility that he would have experimented with his sexuality in his youth. What is certain is that Plautianus was a man whom Severus should not have trusted.

According to Dio (see quote below), after Severus had retreated from Hatra, he immediately began preparations for another siege of the city, considering it a disgrace that Hatra had been able to resist him. We do not know how long these preparations lasted and when the next attempt was made, which brings up the problem that I have already discussed in the context of the events of 194–195. Did Severus conduct a military campaign in person against the Samaritan and Jewish rebels? If he did, there are two possible dates for this: 1) after the first siege of Hatra but before the second; 2) or after the second siege of Hatra. This would date the campaign either to late 198 or to 199. Birley (p.133) suggests the summer or winter of 198 for the second siege of Hatra, which is possible, but in my opinion we cannot entirely preclude 199 if Severus conducted a campaign against the Samaritan and Jewish rebels in 198.

In light of our current knowledge, it is impossible to satisfactorily answer the above question regarding the Samaritan and Jewish rebels. However, one can make a good case for Severus conducting a campaign against the rebels in 198 or 199, because Spartianus (*HA Sev.* 16.7) specifically notes that the *Iudaicus triumphus* was granted by the Senate to Severus for his military successes in Syria.[14] As noted earlier, it is possible that there were two separate revolts in this area, in 194–195 and then again in about 197–198/199 (the rebels taking advantage of the Parthian War), or that there was just one continuous revolt from 194 until about 198/199. The last alternative is probably the likeliest in light of the fact that insurgencies are rarely crushed quickly, except when one side has overwhelming military superiority that is used ruthlessly (meaning the terrorizing of the populace). This would have been the case when Severus was in a position to bring the entire Roman military might bear on the rebels. Nevertheless, it is likely that at least some of the Jews deserted to Severus's side because they later had such fond memories of both Severus and his son Caracalla. As noted, the likely deserters would be the followers of Claudius (is he Judah haNasi?) or someone else, whose descendants then became the 'ethnarchs' of Jews. It is unlikely to be coincidence that the descendants of Judah haNasi had Gothic bodyguards to ensure that their will was followed. It is quite probable that it was Severus who was the first to grant these to the ethnarchs/*nasi* of the Jews.

The Armenian, Parthian and Hatran Campaigns in 197–199   179

Why would Severus have fought such a war either in 198 or 199? The obvious answer is that the crushing of an endemic revolt gave the emperor the chance to redeem his relationship with his soldiers in the aftermath of the less-than-glorious siege or sieges of Hatra. Therefore, the likeliest alternative for the war against the Jews and Samaritans is that it took place only after the second siege of Hatra. Severus needed a military victory, and he exploited this one by giving his elder son, Antoninus, the triumph that the Senate had awarded him. This was a very good opportunity to endear the soldiers and populace with his chosen heir. The wars against the Parthians, Hatrans and Samaritan and Jewish rebels also enabled Severus to give Antoninus his first taste of conflict, which was to become his principal occupation as emperor.

Once the preparations for the second siege of Hatra were finished, Dio recorded that Severus advanced to correct the only blotch on his otherwise illustrious career:

'After laying in a large store of food and preparing many engines he [Severus] in person again led an attack upon Hatra. He deemed it a disgrace, now that other points had been subdued, that this one alone, occupying a central position [Hatra was located in a strategic position in the middle of caravan routes. It was because of this that both the Parthians and Romans sought to control it.], should continue to resist. And he lost a large amount of money and all his engines except those of Priscus, as I stated earlier [The panel in the Arch of Severus which probably depicts the siege has a building to protect the battering ram, which may be taken to depict the engines built under Priscus's instructions.], besides many soldiers. Numbers were annihilated in foraging expeditions, as the barbarian cavalry (I mean that of the Arabians) kept everywhere assailing them with precision and violence. [*The Bedouin cavalry were expert at this type of desert warfare.*]

'... The archery of the Hatrans, too, was effective over a very long range. Some missiles they hurled from the engines, striking even many of Severus's bodyguards [*hypaspistai*], for they discharged two missiles in one and the same shot [This proves that the Hatrans and their engineers had access to artillery manuals such as that of Biton. The illustration on page 177 of a double-shooter is taken from this treatise.] and there were also many hands and many arrows to inflict injury. They did their assailants the utmost damage, however, when the latter approached the wall, and in an even greater degree after they had broken down a little of it. Then they threw at them among other things the bituminous naphtha of which I wrote above [Dio 74.11] and set fire to the engines and all the soldiers that were struck with it. Severus observed proceedings from a lofty tribunal. A portion of the outer circuit had fallen in one place and all the soldiers were eager to force their way inside the remainder, when Severus checked them from doing so by giving orders that the signal for retreat be sounded clearly on all sides. The fame of the place was great, since it contained enormous offerings to the Sun God and vast stores of valuables [The looting of this was obviously the principal purpose of the siege because Severus was always greedy for gold.]; and he expected that the Arabians would voluntarily come to terms in order to avoid being forcibly captured and

180 Emperor Septimius Severus

Hatra, Graffito of a hunter from Beit Ma'nu room no.46 drawn after Roberta Venco Ricciardi. This mounted hunter is representative of the period Hatran mounted archers who made life difficult for the Roman besiegers through their guerrilla warfare. The drawing of the Palmyrene nobles below is similarly representative of the Bedouin forces that the desert cities in this area employed.

enslaved. When, after letting one day elapse, no one made any formal proposition to him, he commanded the soldiers again to assault the wall, though it had been built up in the night. The Europeans who had the power to accomplish something were so angry that not one of them would any longer obey him [This was basically a mutiny, but Severus had obviously brought it on himself by foolishly preventing the attack on the previous day. This was a terrible military mistake such as his son, Caracalla, never made.], and some others, Syrians, compelled to go to the assault in their stead, were miserably destroyed. [It is notable that under Severus the European soldiers were better at besieging, while by the early fourth century it was the Easterners. For this, see my *MHLR* vol.1. The principal difference between these two eras was that by the fourth century, the European soldiers were recruited mainly from the less civilized non-urban areas, where these skills were not needed.] Thus Heaven, that rescued the city, caused Severus to recall the soldiers that could have entered it, and in turn when he later wished to take it caused the soldiers to prevent him from doing so. The situation placed Severus in such a dilemma that

The Armenian, Parthian and Hatran Campaigns in 197–199

A procession of Palmyran nobles about AD 100-150
Note the bow-cases and quivers attached to the rear of the saddles as well as the ends of the spears between the legs (shown with the darker colour). This group was clearly equally well adapted for long and short range combat. The equipment is clearly copied from the Parthians. This is how the Arab/Bedouin armies (when lightly-equipped) would have looked when they came out of the desert to assail the settlements of the sedentary peoples. The wealthier Arab and Bedouin tribes could also bring armour with them (placed in saddle bags carried by the camels) so that they could then put on their armour when needed.

when someone of his followers promised him that, if he would give him only five hundred and fifty of the Europeans [This figure is the principal evidence for the introduction of the unit structure visible in Modestus and Vegetius.], he would get possession of the city without any risk for the rest, the emperor said within hearing of all: "And where can I get so many soldiers?" (referring to the disobedience of the soldiers). Having prosecuted the siege for twenty days he next came to Palestine. [*It is possible or even probable that it was then that Severus crushed the Jewish revolt in an effort to restore the morale of the army.*]' (Dio 76.10.1, Cary ed., p.218ff., tr. by Forster, p.359ff., with changes, corrections and comments)

Dio's text makes it clear that the Hatrans were experts in siege warfare, having retained techniques of the Hellenistic East in their area. In addition to this, they benefited from two other cultural advantages: they possessed vast numbers of mounted archers in their Bedouin cavalry and many more expert archers to protect the walls. The notable thing about their siege skills is that they surpassed the Parthians in this, the latter having been singularly unable to protect their capital, Ctesiphon, which was even bigger than Hatra. However, this time Severus had arrived better prepared than he had been during the first siege. Although his army suffered grievously, they still brought down the outer wall. Severus's elite European troops were ready to charge into the resulting opening, but it was then that Severus made the worst military mistake of his life. When he observed the situation from his elevated position in the tribunal, he ordered the sounding of the retreat, believing that the enemy would surrender when they understood that their situation was hopeless. In my opinion, Septimius's principal aim was to retain the city as a viable commercial city and bulwark against the Parthians rather than to destroy it. However, Riccardo Bertolazzi has suggested another possible reason for calling off the attack. In his opinion, it is possible that it was because of a request by Julia Domna that her husband halted the assault to protect the Temple of the Sun-God and her friends inside the city. Bertolazzi also suggests that the souring of the relationship between Julia Domna and Plautianus resulted from the actions that the latter took in Syria when purging the alleged supporters of Niger, who undoubtedly included friends or associates of Julia Domna and her family. Both of these suggestions are quite plausible, and I believe that both played a role in the hostility that these two held against each other. Bertolazzi is also likely to be correct that the events at Hatra gave Plautianus ammunition for his claims that Julia Domna had formed a conspiracy against her husband, which is alluded to in the text of Aurelius Victor.

Whatever the reason, Septimius made a serious mistake when he called off the attack, as the Hatrans hastily rebuilt their defences rather than asking for terms. When Severus then ordered his European forces to resume the attack, they refused. This suggests that the cost in lives and wounded was of such magnitude that the soldiers were not willing to forgive the mistake made by Severus, and thus mutinied. Consequently, Severus was forced to send his Syrians in to attack, and they were beaten back. As under Severus the Europeans were the experts in siege warfare, not those from the East (as they would later be in the fourth century), the mutiny of the Europeans left the emperor with no choice but to order the retreat on the twentieth day of the siege.

Birley (p.133) proposes that, despite what Dio says, it is still possible that Severus achieved his aim at Hatra, because the Ninth Cohort of Moors was stationed there a few decades later (from 238–240). This is possible, but in my opinion it is more probable that the posting of this unit to support the Hatrans against the Parthians took place under Caracalla, who is recorded to have achieved a military success against the Arabs.[15]

Aelius Spartianus's text (*HA Sev.* 16.9–17.1) states that the humiliating failure at Hatra forced Severus to resort to the bribing of his soldiers with yet another pay raise. As noted above, references to fighting in Syria and the *Iudaicus triumphus* given to Antoninus probably took place after the second siege of Hatra for the dual purpose of crushing the revolt in Judaea and Palestine and to restore the shaken morale of the European soldiers with a military success. It is unfortunate that we do not know this for certain. Nevertheless, it is still clear that Severus thought that the soldiers were now ready for another military campaign in harsh desert conditions, because his next objective was to march to Egypt and from there to move against the Ethiopians of Aksum.

8.5. The Reorganization of the Eastern Frontier

After withdrawing from Hatra, Septimius Severus marched to Syria and from there to Palestine and Judaea where he then defeated the rebels and earned the triumph. From there he continued his journey to Arabia with the intention of going to Egypt and then even further south all the way to Ethiopia (Aksum/Axum). En route he gave privileges to a number of cities in Palestine. He rewarded those cities that had remained loyal during the Jewish and Samaritan uprisings. He also visited the city of Jerusalem (Aelia

Capitolina)[16] and was voted a triumph for his Parthian war, which he declined to accept because he was unable to stand straight on a chariot because of gout. As noted previously, the Senate had also voted Severus a Jewish triumph for his successes achieved in Syria, which Severus gave to his son Antoninus.[17]

Left: Septimius Severus and his sons Antoninus and Geta crowned with victory. Source: Duruy.
Below: coin of Severus minted in the Greek speaking east. Source: Beger 1696.

The annexation of Mesopotamia, the area between the Euphrates and Tigris, led to further reorganization in the East. Strategically, the most important of these was the enlarging of the province of Arabia at the expense of Syria, with the dangerous area of Leja now placed under one governor and the posting of garrisons and guard posts deeper into the desert for the protection of Roman trade routes. These desert outposts included those at Azraq oasis and Dura Europos, but garrisons are attested about a decade later at Anatha, some 80 miles (130km) further downstream, and slighty further at Kifrin. The emperor also appears to have built or reinforced a chain of forts to control the Wadi Sirhan, the 300-mile-long depression running from Basie (Qasr al Azraq in Jordania) to Dumata (Jawf in Saudi Arabia). As Birley notes, Severus knew the desert better than any other emperor in Roman history. Hailing from Tripolitania, Severus was uniquely qualified to deal with the problems of the desert frontiers. His expert knowledge of desert conditions meant that he knew the importance of having outposts deep in the desert to protect the cultivated core areas, project Roman power into the desert and control the trade routes and oases. He thus pushed the Roman frontier deeper into the desert in both Arabia and North Africa. Severus also knew the importance of commercial hubs in desert trade, so he gave privileges to the city of Palmyra (e.g. it became a Roman *colonia*), which can be detected from the great number of families with the *gentilicium* (the hereditary name for the people of the Roman Empire) of Septimius. Some of the Palmyran forces were now also enrolled into the regular Roman Army, with the cohors

XX Palmyrenorum stationed at Dura Europus. The most famous of those who received the Roman *gentilicium* was Septimius Odaenathus, who was made a senator in the early years of the third century. Severus also reinforced the defences in Arabia by posting there Goths that he had brought with him. The first evidence for this comes from an inscription commemorating the commander of *Gothi gentiles* dated 208, but it is clear that these Goths would already have been posted there after the completion of the Parthian War when the defences of the region were reorganized.[18] I would also tentatively suggest that it was at the same time that the leader of the Jews (probably Jonah/Claudius) was given Goth soldiers to serve as his personal bodyguard against his fellow Jews.

Chapter 9

Egypt and the Red Sea in 199–200

9.1. Visit of Egypt and Severus's Strategic Goals

When Severus had reorganized the defences of Arabia to his satisfaction, he continued his journey to Egypt. Even if the sources fail to give us any real analysis for this visit to Egypt, there were clearly several reasons for it. Firstly, Egypt had supported Niger, so it was important to secure it with a personal visit. Secondly, Severus was a man of great curiosity and intellect, and now that he could finally visit Egypt as a tourist he wanted to do so – as a senator he had been forbidden to do that because no senators were allowed into Egypt. However, the main reason for the visit was obviously because Severus intended to conduct a military campaign as far as Ethiopia to secure trade routes running through the Red Sea and Indian Ocean to India and Africa. The aim was to thereby bypass Parthia in such trade.[1] In short, Severus's strategic aim was to hurt Parthia. That there was a need to do this suggests that the Ethiopians at this time were following a trade policy that was detrimental to Roman interests. They may have been instigated to do this through Parthian diplomacy and bribes. The reorganization of the frontiers and defences in Arabia can also be connected to the projected campaign in Ethiopia and the Red Sea theatre because the chain of fortifications along the Wadi Sirhan protected the Roman trade route to the Persian Gulf and Red Sea. Severus was indeed a descendant of Punic traders.

Dio tells us the following about these moves by Severus:

'[H]e next came to Palestine and sacrificed to the spirit of Pompey [actually Pelusium in Egypt] and into (Upper) Egypt. He sailed along the Nile and viewed the whole country, with some small exceptions. For instance, he was unable to pass the frontier of Ethiopia on account of pestilence. [The likely reason for the march to Ethiopia would have been to secure the trade routes passing through it, which brought merchandise and gold from Africa and silk and other produce from India. The principal aim was to bypass Parthian merchants. A visit of Ethiopia with an armed force can only have been connected with strategic aims.] And he made a search of everything, including what was very carefully hidden, for he was the sort of man to leave nothing, human or divine, uninvestigated. [Severus was clearly a very wise man whose appetite for learning was bottomless It is no wonder that he instilled in his son Caracalla an interest in learning.] Following this tendency he drew from practically all their hiding places all the books that he could find containing any secret, and he closed the monument of Alexander, to [the] end that no one should either behold his body any more or read what was written in these books. [It is possible that Severus did all this because of superstitious beliefs, but it is even likelier that he wanted to project such an image to the outside world so that outsiders would stand in awe before his knowledge of secret lore. For the probable use of similar tricks by his son Caracalla, see my biography of him.]' (Dio 76.13.1ff., Cary ed., p.361ff., tr. by Forster, p.362ff., with changes, corrections and comments)

Serapis on a bronze coin of Severus minted at Ptolemais. Note the forked beard, which Severus had copied. Source: Duruy.

Severus as Pharaoh and his queen Julia, Latopolis
Drawn after J.G. Milne

The first stop in Egypt was the tomb of Pompey at Pelusium, which had been built by Hadrian. Birley notes that Libyans typically showed reverence for the dead, but that it is also possible Severus had personal reasons for the visit because the murderer of Pompey had been Lucius Septimius. Marcus Aurelius, whose son Severus now claimed to be, was a descendant of Pompey. As Birley states succinctly: 'This act at Pompey's tomb was loaded with overtones.' The imperial family and their entourage entered the city of Alexandria amid festivities which were marred by only one thing. At the gates of Alexandria were the words 'The City of the Lord Niger', but the Alexandrians managed to save the situation by stating that Severus was the master of Niger. Severus granted to Alexandria and other cities of Egypt the right to have city councils, a right which until then had been denied to them. While in Alexandria he visited the tomb of Alexander, which was then closed, presumably because Severus wanted to discourage others from emulating him – after all, Niger had done so, and any comparison between Severus and Alexander could make the former look the lesser of the two. Severus also donated baths, a gymnasiusm and a temple of Cybele for the city. However, the emperor seems to have drawn most joy from his visit of the temple of Serapis/Sarapis (Serapeum). This was particularly famous because its statue of Serapis hovered in the air thanks to expertly placed magnets. It was rightly considered to be one of the wonders of the ancient world. Severus apparently commemorated his visit with coins, or at least his coins minted at Ptolemais have the face of Serapis on the reverse (see the above illustration). However, it was soon time to continue the march south, Severus's intention being to reach as far as Ethiopia. According to Malalas, when Severus was about to leave the city he had a man called Thermos arrested. Thermos was one of the highest-ranking dignitaries of the city, very popular among the citizens of the city and a friend of Niger. It was too dangerous to leave behind such a man. It is probable that the man behind the arrest was Plautianus and the security apparatus he controlled.[2]

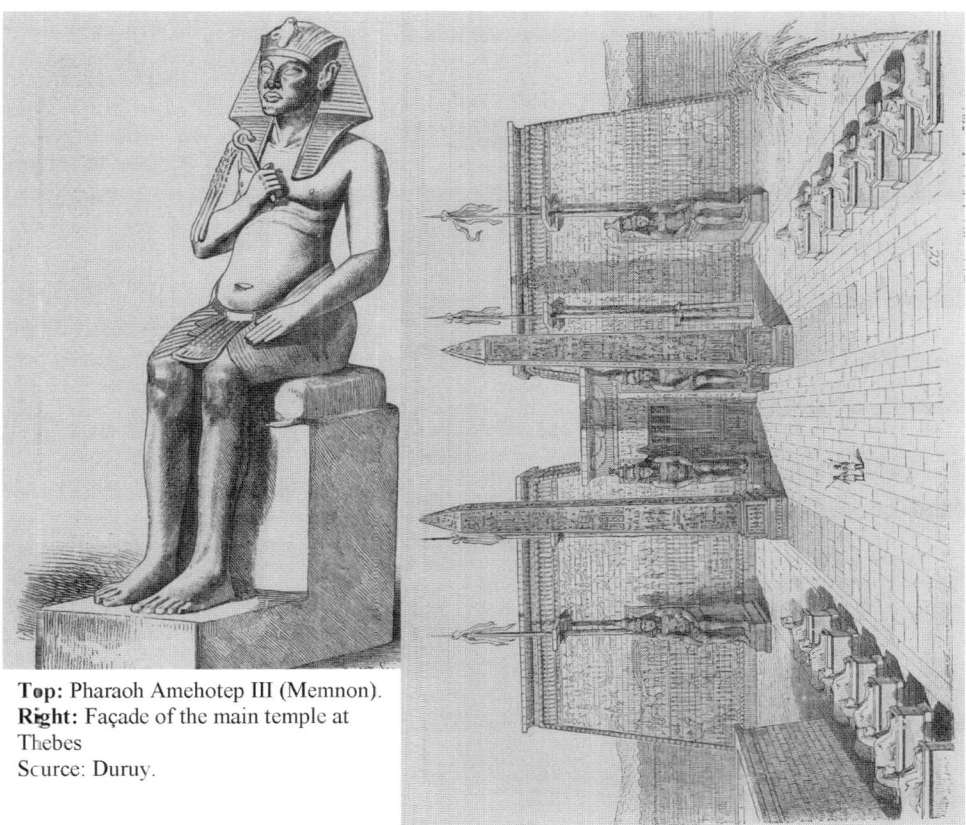

Top: Pharaoh Amehotep III (Memnon).
Right: Façade of the main temple at Thebes
Source: Duruy.

The next stop in Severus's itinerary was Memphis, where he saw the pyramids and the Sphinx. The latter had been renovated by the new Praetorian Prefect, Saturninus, for the visit of Severus. Long-time Praetorian Prefect Flavius Juvenalis (193–199/200) had stepped down to make room for Saturninus, who had prior to this served as Prefect of Egypt. The idea was clearly to put a specialist of Egypt in charge of security during the emperor's visit.[3] From there the journey continued southwards, Severus making stops at the great Labyrinth on Lake Moeris, the city of Thebes – where he saw the colossal 'singing' statue of Memnon (Amenhotep III) – and Philae (Aswan), to carry out sacrifices at the great temple of Isis in late May 200 (see the illustrations above and below). The temple of Isis at Philae was a place of great importance, serving as a holy site for the people south of the Roman border. This gave the Romans the ability to put pressure on these people via their religion. When Severus and his army reached the frontier of Ethiopia, however, he was forced to turn back because of pestilence. The campaign was abandoned and Severus returned north.[4] Severus clearly did not think the campaign to be of critical importance. Furthermore, it was wise to avoid contact with those who carried disease so as not to allow it to reach the Roman Empire.

Restored temple of Isis at Philae (source: Duruy)

A medallion of Severus with Antoninus and Plautilla on the reverse. Source: Cohen.

Chapter 10

Return to Rome in 200–202

10.1. The Rise of Plautianus

In the course of Severus's stay in Egypt and during his march back to Europe, the standing of Plautianus reached heights that had not been seen since the days of Perennis under Commodus or Sejanus under Tiberius. What is remarkable is that Plautianus achieved this with the full acceptance of Severus. He had clearly managed to make himself indispensable in the eyes of the emperor. Plautianus was even able to undermine the position of Severus's wife, Julia Domna, with innuendos of infidelity. In light of the evidence, there are very good reasons to suspect that Plautianus was actually correct with his claims.[1] Dio clearly implies just this, while Aurelius Victor and Aelius Spartianus state in no uncertain terms that Julia Domna's behaviour was scandalous. Severus, however, loved Julia so much that he forgave her infidelities and claims that she had been plotting against him, and it was this that diminished the emperor's otherwise outstanding reputation. It is uncertain whether suggestions of Julia's unfaithfulness referred to sexual liaisons with other full-grown men or to her notorious incestuous relationship with her son or stepson, Antoninus (Caracalla). According to the Latin sources, Julia exposed her private parts to Antoninus, who duly had sex with her and later took her as his wife. The kinder version has it that she was actually his stepmother rather than biological mother. The evidence hints that this is quite possible, but it is also possible that such a story was invented as a cover for their incest. If Antoninus was Julia's biological son and the infidelity meant a sexual relationship between them, then Antoninus would have been about 14 or 15 years of age at the time it happened. If, however, his biological mother was Paccia, then he was of course older. It is also possible that Julia had sex with other men too, because hostile innuendo stated that Caracalla was the son of a gladiator. However, since Plautianus was able to convince Severus that it was now time for Antoninus to marry Plautianus's daughter, Plautilla, there is every reason to believe that the infidelity at this time concerned Julia and Antoninus, and that Antoninus had to be hastily married so he would no longer be near her. It is of course possible that Plautianus's claims were just innuendo to convince Severus that he should marry Antoninus to his daughter, but in light of the overwhelming evidence to the contrary, this is unlikely. I am inclined to accept it as proven that Julia committed incest (either as biological mother or stepmother) with Antoninus. As far as I know, I am the only modern historian who has accepted the ancient evidence as likely to be true. What we are dealing with here is actually a modern prudish tendency not to accept the likely outlandish truth. The case for incest is far more likely than the case against it, being supported by all the sources, while the case against is based solely on a moralistic interpretation of this evidence.[2] It was thanks to his ability to bring to light matters such as this that Plautianus became practically a second emperor in place of the Augustus, Antoninus. This was a very bad mistake for the emperor to make because Plautianus was a treacherous monster, as highlighted by Dio:

> 'Plautianus, who enjoyed a special favour of Severus and had the authority of prefect, besides possessing the fullest and greatest influence on earth, had put to death many men of renown and his own peers. ... After killing Aemilius Saturninus [his co-prefect] he took away all the most important prerogatives belonging to the minor officers of the Praetorians [undoubtedly using the words of Julius Crispus and other tribunes as his justification if he was required to explain his behaviour to Severus], his subordinates, in order that none of them might be so elated by his position of eminence as to lie in wait for the prefecture of the bodyguards. Already it was his wish not to be the only but a perpetual prefect. He wanted everything, asked everything from everybody, and got everything. He left no province and no city unplundered, but sacked and gathered everything from all sides. All sent a great deal more to him than Severus. [He was the man to be bribed because he had the ear of Severus.] Finally he sent centurions and stole tiger-striped horses sacred to the Sun God from the island in the Red Sea .... [Birley, p. 137, is surely right to suggest that these were zebras.] At home he castrated one hundred nobly born Roman citizens, though none of us knew of [this] until he was dead. From this fact one may comprehend the extent alike of his lawlessness and of his authority. He castrated not merely boys or youths, but grown men, some of whom had wives; his object was that Plautilla his daughter (whom Antoninus afterwards married) should be waited upon entirely by eunuchs (and also have them to give her instruction in music and other branches of art). So we beheld the same persons eunuchs and men, fathers and impotent, gelded and bearded. In view of this one might not improperly declare that Plautianus had power beyond all men, over even emperors [Severus and Antoninus] themselves. For one thing, his portrait statues were not only far more numerous but also larger than theirs, and this not simply outside cities but in Rome itself, and they were at this time raised not merely by individuals but by no less a body than the senate itself. All the soldiers and the senators took oaths by his Fortune and all publicly offered prayer for his preservation. <u>The person principally responsible for this state of affairs was Severus himself. He yielded to Plautianus in all matters to such a degree that the latter occupied the position of emperor and he himself that of prefect. In short, the man knew absolutely everything that Severus said and did, but not a person was acquainted with any of Plautianus's secrets.</u> [This was a very dangerous state of affairs for the emperor.] The emperor made advances to his daughter on behalf of his own son, passing by many other maidens of high rank. He appointed him consul [for the year 203, so the appointment took place in 202 during the return trip to Rome] and virtually showed an anxiety to have him for [his] successor in the imperial office. [This is very likely to be hostile innuendo because at this stage Severus clearly planned Antoninus to succeed him.] Indeed, once he did say in a letter: "I love the man so much that I pray to die before he does." ... At temporary stopping-places he endured seeing him located in superior quarters and enjoying better and more abundant food than he. Hence in Nicaea

(my native country) when he once wanted mullet, large specimens of which are found in the lake, he sent to Plautianus to get it. [This was during the return trip to Rome in the hometown of Dio, so he was in a position to know.] So if he thought at all of doing aught to diminish this man's power, its force was made useless by his other contrary actions .... On one occasion Severus went to visit him, when he had fallen sick at Tyana [This is before the entourage reached Nicaea. Tyana was the birthplace of the wonder-maker Apollonius of Tyana, who lived under Domitian and performed similar miracles as Jesus Christ, according to the pagan lore. This was a location which both Severus and Julia wanted to visit.], and the soldiers attached to Plautianus would not allow the visitor's escort to enter with him. [This was unheard of, and it was a mistake for Severus to allow this because it diminished his own authority in the eyes of all.] Moreover, the person who arranged cases to be pleaded before Severus was once ordered by the latter in a moment of leisure to bring forward some case of other, whereupon the fellow refused, saying: "I cannot do this, unless Plautianus bid me." [This was another mistake for Severus to allow to happen.] So greatly did Plautianus have the mastery in every way over the emperor that he frequently treated Julia Augusta in an outrageous way – for he detested her cordially – and was always abusing her violently to Severus, and conducted investigations against her as well as tortures of noble women. This is the infidelity and conspiracy case referred to above, which may indeed have had basis in truth because Julia apparently had an incestuous relationship with Caracalla, all the sources referring to this or implying it in one form or another.] For this reason she began to study philosophy and passed her days in the company of learned men. As for Plautianus, he proved himself the most licentious of men, for he would go to banquets and vomit meantime [a form of bulimia], inasmuch as the mass of foods and wine he swallowed made it impossible for him to digest anything. And whereas he made use of lads and girls in perfectly notorious fashion, he would not permit his wife to see or be seen by any person whomsoever, not even by Severus or Julia .... At this period there took place also a gymnastic contest .... And in this contest Alamanni [this word is corrupt and emended by Forster] women fought most ferociously, with the result that jokes were made about other ladies, who were very distinguished. Therefore, from this time on every woman, no matter what her origin, was prohibited from fighting in the arena. [Even though Plautianus acted like he did, the general mood during the reign of Severus was conservative, so this prohibition is not surprising.]' (Dio 76.14.1ff., Cary ed., p.361ff., tr. by Forster, p.362ff., with changes, corrections, comments and underlining)

In short, Severus made a very serious mistake when he decided to trust Plautianus with his personal security. Plautianus was the man who held the strings of power because he had the ear of the emperor, and the emperor heard only such things that Plautianus wanted him to hear.

The following is list of Praetorian Prefects under Severus, based on the list of Daguet-Gagey (p.346) with some changes (e g. Rufinus added from Syvänne, Caracalla/PIR).

A possible bust of Plautianus. The source Duruy identified this man with Pertinax, but I am inclined to agree with the view that he is Plautianus. A photo of this actual bust is included in the plates.

A bust of Plautianus. Just like Duruy, the source of these two drawings, Visconti, identified this man with Pertinax, but I am inclined to agree with the view that he is Plautianus.

Praetorian Prefects under Severus

Name	Term
Flavius Juvenalis	193–199/200
Q. Aemilius Saturninus	200
C. Fulvius Plautianus	197–Jan. 205
Aemilius Papinianus	205–211
Q. Maecius Laetus	205–211/215?
Valerius Patruinus	?–212.
Marcius Rustius Rufinus	Praetorian Prefect in command of the Praetorian Fleets (Misenum and Ravenna) under Severus and Antoninus

En route to Europe there was an important incident which adds one more person to the list of ancient statesmen and commanders whom Severus idolized and used as his models. According to a later source, while Severus was in Bithynia, he visited Libyssa, the place where Hannibal had killed himself. He honoured his Libyan countryman with a white marble tomb. This wily Libyan of Punic origin obviously appreciated very highly the military skills of his fellow countryman. Just like Severus, Hannibal was known for his treacherous military practices. Notably, his son Antoninus was also an avid admirer of Hannibal. It is clear that Severus had instilled into his son this admiration of Hannibal and his treacherous ways. Caracalla was also known to be an admirer of Alexander the Great, Sulla and Tiberius. While Tiberius and Alexander the Great are not listed among those whom Severus admired, it is possible that he did so because his son was an avid admirer of them. The key point is that both father and son admired statesmen and commanders who were treacherous and cruel, even if they were at the same time experts in the fields of strategy and tactics. It is no wonder that the son of the treacherous and cruel Severus was even more treacherous and cruel than his father.[3]

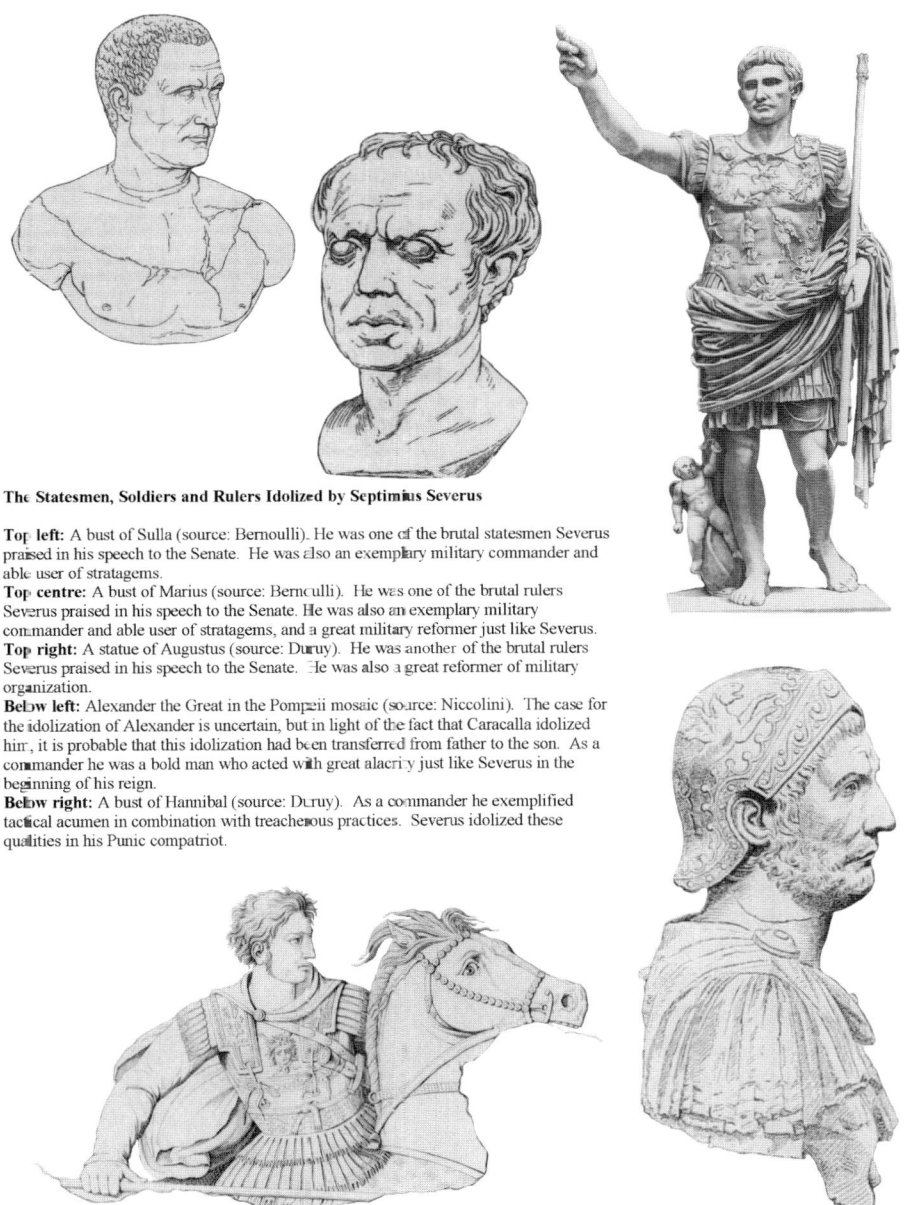

The Statesmen, Soldiers and Rulers Idolized by Septimius Severus

Top left: A bust of Sulla (source: Bernoulli). He was one of the brutal statesmen Severus praised in his speech to the Senate. He was also an exemplary military commander and able user of stratagems.
Top centre: A bust of Marius (source: Bernoulli). He was one of the brutal rulers Severus praised in his speech to the Senate. He was also an exemplary military commander and able user of stratagems, and a great military reformer just like Severus.
Top right: A statue of Augustus (source: Duruy). He was another of the brutal rulers Severus praised in his speech to the Senate. He was also a great reformer of military organization.
Below left: Alexander the Great in the Pompeii mosaic (source: Niccolini). The case for the idolization of Alexander is uncertain, but in light of the fact that Caracalla idolized him, it is probable that this idolization had been transferred from father to the son. As a commander he was a bold man who acted with great alacrity just like Severus in the beginning of his reign.
Below right: A bust of Hannibal (source: Duruy). As a commander he exemplified tactical acumen in combination with treacherous practices. Severus idolized these qualities in his Punic compatriot.

10.2. The Danubian Frontier from 197–202

When Severus and his entourage crossed into Europe, they found a frontier in need of refortification and rebuilding. The removal of forces from the Danube frontier and Dacia to fight wars throughout the Empire appears to have resulted in endemic small-scale raiding of Roman territory along the Danube frontier. This made it necessary to conduct road and other repairs along the entire length of the frontier, although the extant sources record no major invasions of Pannonia or Moesia.⁴ This was merely the result of luck. As already noted, the only reason the intended Gothic invasion never materialized was because their chieftains were killed by lightning. However, the situation in Dacia seems to have been different. Gonzáles (p.97) notes that on the basis of an inscription (*CIL* III 14.485a, *Inscriptiones Latinae Selectae* 9.179), we know that the barbarians launched an invasion of Dacia Malvensis or Dacia Inferior in 200 or 201. He speculates that the invaders were Sarmatian Roxolani, which is quite possible. The other possible candidates would include the Carpi (free Dacians), Sciri (pure Germans), Bastarnae, Vandals and Goths – or indeed all of them, but I would still think that the case for the Goths is the weakest because they served with Severus at this time. Another possibility is that the Goths did indeed invade because some of their kind had not been returned home but had been retained as bodyguards of the Jewish ethnarch. The invasion caused serious damage, and the destruction of at least one military base (restored in 201) is recorded. The response appears to have been to unite the three Dacian provinces as *Tres Daciae*, which was placed under the unified command of Lucius Octavius Iulianus. The unification of the Roman forces stabilized the situation, with the process of the rebuilding of defences starting in 201. In other words, it is possible that Severus oversaw all of these measures when he was passing through the provinces.

Birley suggests that Severus probably visited Upper and Lower Moesia, and possibly also Dacia, at this time, followed by the two Pannonian provinces. In light of the above, this is quite probable. The defences and roads in the Balkans needed repairs. Birley also suggests that Severus could have been at Carnuntum on 9 April 202 to celebrate the *dies imperii* (the anniversary of him becoming emperor), after which he would have followed the stages of his 193 march to Rome nine years before, but notes that this is pure speculation – but it is very good speculation. Birley further suggests that many of the new governors in the Balkans for the year 202 may have arrived with Severus, including L. Aurelius Gallus for Lower Moesia, and Q. Anicius Faustus for Upper Moesia. Faustus had just completed a long term as commander of the Legio III Augusta, during the course of which he had extended the frontiers of the province of Africa deeper into the desert. Birley also suggests a possibility that Severus could have extended Roman dominions north of the Danube at this time, from the River Aluta to the *limes* Transalutanus (a distance of about 25 miles or 40km), even if there is no concrete evidence for this. Such an expansion is indeed possible, because we do not know of all the minor changes in the border that took place.⁵

10.3. At Rome in 202: the Decennial

The emperor's return to the capital was celebrated in grand style. To mark his tenth anniversary in power in 202, Severus granted a grain dole to the populace, while to the soldiers of the bodyguard (presumably the Praetorians) he gave ten gold pieces each. According to Dio, no emperor before him had given so much largesse to the population at once (it amounted to 200 million sesterces). Then the imperial wedding of Antoninus with Fulvia Plautilla, the daughter of Fulvius Plautianus, was celebrated. Plautianus gave a massive dowry, which according to Dio would have sufficed for fifty women of royal rank. This did nothing to endear Antoninus to Plautilla, whom he detested from the bottom of his heart, just like he hated her father Plautianus.⁶

In my opinion, it is quite probable that this was all connected to the treatment of his mother Julia Domna, and it is possible that this feeling had been intensified with the first feelings of incestuous love that Antoninus had towards his mother/stepmother. According to the official or semi-official reckoning, Antoninus was just 14 or 15 years old, but rumour had it that if he was the son of Paccia he was somewhat older. The shortness of Antoninus would have made the official version credible even if he was the biological son of Paccia.

Top left: A bust of Plautilla according to Duruy, but others identify her with Julia Domna.
Top right: A coin of Plautilla (source: Duruy).
Centre right: A cameo of Plautilla (source: Duruy).
Below left: A bust of young Antoninus Caracalla. Source: Duruy.
Below right: A bust of Plautilla. Source: Piranesi.
The marriage of Antoninus and Plautilla was not happy.

There then followed the emperor's decennial celebrations, together with celebrations of his victorious return. The animals killed during these events included sixty bears given by Plautianus, an elephant and 'a corocotta from India' (Birley suggests a hyena). The organizers had built a boat in the amphitheatre able to receive and discharge 400 beasts at once. Altogether, some 700 beasts were reserved for slaughter in the amphitheatre: bears, lions and lionesses, panthers, ostriches, wild asses, bison and other exotic animals. They were divided into groups of 100 for each of the seven days. Birley suggests that the use of 700 animals was influenced by the supposed magic of numbers, Septimius's name deriving from *septimus* (seven).[7]

Left: Coin depicting Septimius Severus's return to Rome (Adventusaugg).
Right: Bronze coin depicting Julia Domna as mother of the Senate, Mother of the Fatherland.
Source: Duruy

A coin of Severus.

The reverse side shows a ship bringing animals presumably for the games.

Source: Cohen

A coin of Severus probably struck in celebration of the granting of the rights of *ius Italicum* for the city of Carthage.

Source: Cohen.

Chapter 11

The Return Home: Campaign in Africa in 202–203[1]

11.1. Preparations and Africa before 202

We know that Severus did not stay for long at Rome, continuing almost immediately to Africa. Exact details of his visit to Africa are not known because there are very few references to it in the sources and extant inscriptions. Certain educated guesses can be made, however, and in doing so I follow Birley. Firstly, on the basis of the inscriptions, it is probable that Severus travelled with his entire extended family, including Julia Domna and his sons Antoninus and Geta, along with Plautilla and Plautianus. Additionally, it is probable that Severus's brother, Geta, and the various cousins Septimii and Fulvii accompanied him. They were to visit their native land in triumph. It is also clear that some military forces accompanied the imperial family, because the plan was to also conduct a military campaign. These included at least the Praetorians and probably the other units of bodyguards.

It is likely that the entourage sailed from Portus/Ostia to Carthage, which was given *ius Italicum* (essentially becoming part of the Italian mainland), a great honour that carried with it freedom from provincial taxation, although Carthage already had that status. At the same time, Severus separated several places from Carthage's territory by granting them the status of *municipium*, thereby being incorporated into the Roman state. The same policy was carried out at Utica, which also received *ius Italicum* but is likely to have lost territory at the same time. Severus also visited the legionary base of Legio III Augusta at Lambaesis and may have inspected the new frontier posts built over the course of five years by the legate Anicius Faustus, who had pushed the border of the Empire further south at the orders of Severus. The troops that had participated in the construction of these forts included a detachment from the Syrian Legio III Gallica, which had been transferred to North Africa after the defeat of Niger. The idea was clearly to post specialists in desert conditions to this area as punishment for taking part in the revolt. The Legio III Augusta replaced these men by sending a detachment to Syria, which then took part in the Parthian campaign. The frontiers were pushed significantly further south between 198 and 202. There is evidence for some sort of military trouble caused by the Moors in Mauritania during this time, which is unsurprising considering the Roman expansion southwards. The principal evidence for this is the unification of the two Mauretanias under a single commander and a victory monument at Bou Hellou 55 miles (90km) east of the capital of Mauretania Tingitana. However, there is no definite proof for the pushing of frontiers southwards in Tingitana, whereas there is for the province of Mauretania Caesarensis.

11.2. The Campaign in the Desert

The route from Mauretania to Lepcis Magna would have been followed up the coastal route, and when Septimius Severus reached his home city of Lepcis he granted it *ius Italicum*, which he had already made for Tyre, the mother city of Lepcis. Severus showered his home city with money: it was improved with engineering projects and new buildings, and numerous works of art were added. Severus followed this with active operations that were meant to secure his native lands from attacks. A screen of defences between Tripolitania and Fazzan had already been built in the form of desert forts, but more was needed. According to Aurelius Victor (20.19) and Aelius Spartianus (*HA Sev.* 18.3), Severus did not only visit his native land and home town, but also conducted a military campaign in the area. These sources state that Severus defeated and drove warlike tribes far away from Tripolis and his birthplace Lepcis Magna, thereby freeing them from the fear of attack. There is no direct evidence for the personal participation of Severus further south of Gholaia, where he founded baths in 202, but I would suggest that it is more than likely he did advance in person up to Garamantes because he was prepared to go far to the north in Caledonia a few years later, even when his physical condition had deteriorated considerably.

The Garamantes and Moors were famous for their javelin-armed light cavalry, but also employed vast numbers of light infantry with spears and shields and bow-armed infantry and cavalry. Their cavalry typically used camels for transport and then mounted their horses

Markouna (Africa) bust of Septimius Severus. Source: Bernoulli

Septimius Severus. Source: Piranesi

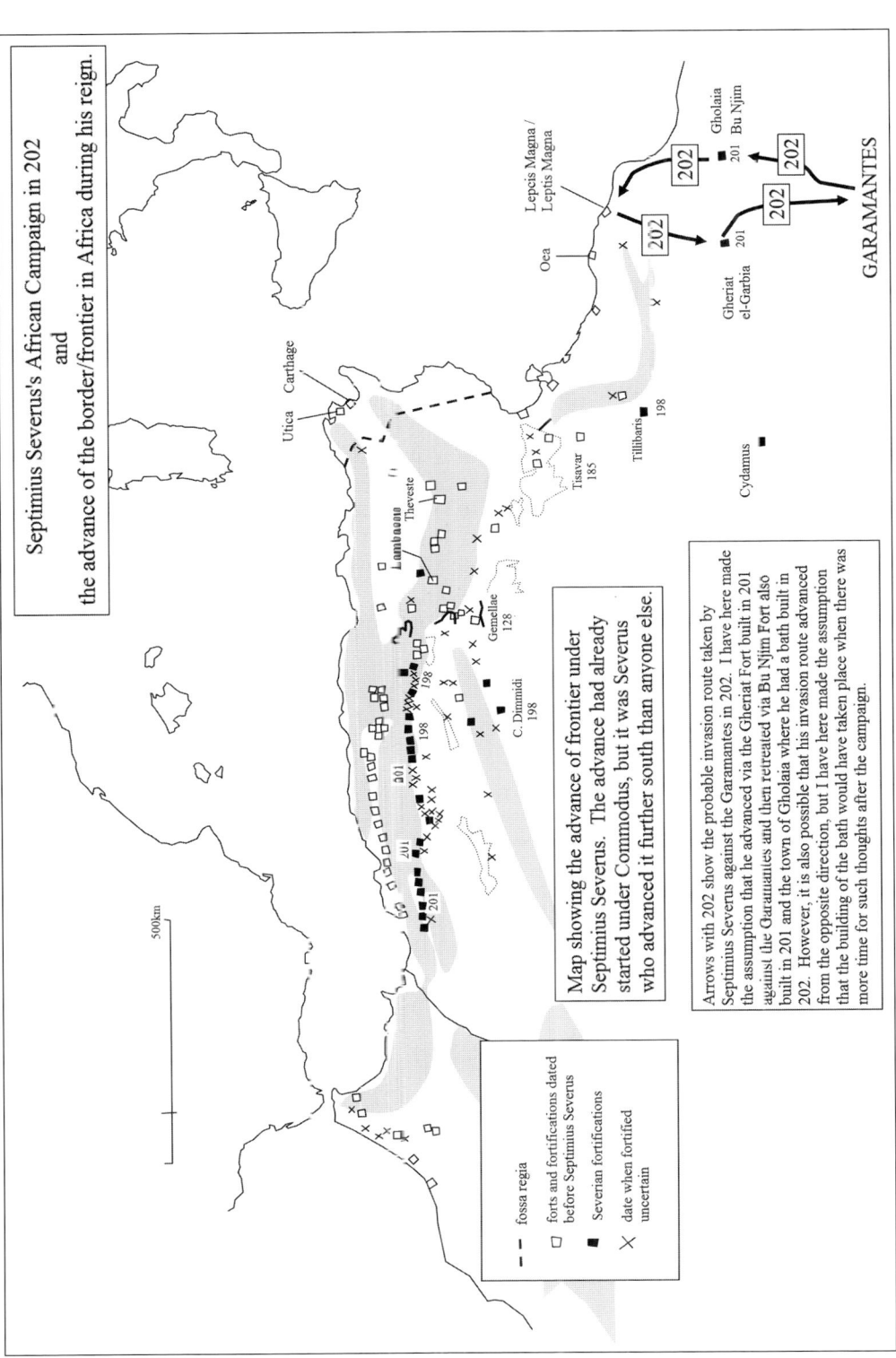

for combat. When the footmen and their families accompanied the Moors and Garamantes, they employed fortified camps consisting of animals tied together to form a barrier. Contrary to what Arrian states (see Appendix 1) about the Cyrenaicans, the Garamantes may have continued to use war chariots alongside their other forces, extant works of art supporting this conclusion. The Moors and Garamantes concentrated more on banditry, brigandage and raiding against Roman lands than on regular warfare and thus usually required only policing from Roman forces. However, when several tribes united they could require the attention of larger numbers of Roman troops, which appears to have been the case when Severus visited the area. As lightly equipped irregulars, the Moors and Garamantes could not oppose the better-organized, trained and equipped professional Roman forces, which possessed all arms of service, from light to heavy types. The campaign lasted at least until the spring of 203 and Rome presumably achieved a significant military success because no further fighting is recorded in this region until mid-third century. It is probable that the campaign was also directed against other tribes besides the Garamantes, several of which are referred to by the sources, including the Nasamones and Ethiopians (not the Ethiopians of East Africa, but their namesakes in the west). It is quite possible that Severus had been making plans for such a campaign while he was in Egypt with the idea of protecting the whole of Roman North Africa from tribes further south. Mattingly (p.83) notes that contemporary Zliten mosaics show the exposure of Libyan tribesmen to wild beasts in the arena at Lepcis Magna, which must have been as a result of Severus's campaign. The emperor was a cruel man set on improving the safety of his native lands, and the most effective way to do this was to conduct a military campaign in the harshest possible manner. The citizens of Lepcis were undoubtedly proud of their regal son and cheered their emperor when prisoners were brought to be eaten by wild animals in celebratory games.

11.3. The Persecution of Christians

According to some Christian sources (including Bar Hebraeus, Jerome and Eusebius), it was in about 202 that Severus launched a persecution of Christians. On 7 March 203, the fourteenth birthday of Geta, the victims of this persecution included Vibia Perpetua at Carthage at a time when the Hittite storm-god of Commagene was worshipped. In my opinion it is possible that Geta was behind the persecution because his name later pops up again in another case of probable Christian persecution, this time in Roman Britain. Perpetua was sentenced to death by the acting governor for being a Christian. However, according to Tertullian, Septimius Severus had followed a different policy, actually protecting high-ranking Christians from the fury of the mob. Tertullian also notes that Severus had a therapist named Torpacion or Proculus, who was a Christian and therefore presumably the person who influenced Severus to act in this way. Birley is suspicious of the whole account, instead suggesting that there was no policy change introduced by Severus but rather that the persecution of the Christians was a continuation of an existing strategy. It is difficult to know which the case is, but on the basis of the extant evidence I consider it probable that the persecution intensified under Severus from the 202 onwards.[2] However, as noted above, it is possible that it was Geta and his friends who were behind it, because by this time he had started to compete with Antoninus in everything, and his brother would become known as the man who ended the persecution of Christians and whom the Jews called a fellow Jew.

Chapter 12

Conspiracy

12.1. Back in Italy and Rome, 203–204

Severus and his family returned to the city of Rome in 203, after which they spent the following years in Italy. It was during this time that Julia Maesa (Julia Domna's sister) and the other Severan women claimed that Antoninus (Caracalla) slept with Maesa's daughters, Julia Mamaea and Julia Soaemias, and that they bore Caracalla two sons who came to be known as Elagabalus/Heliogabalus and Alexander Severus. These events have divided historians both in the past and today, but I belong to the group that believes it is very likely that Antoninus did indeed sleep with both of his cousins and it is thus possible that the two future emperors were his biological sons, or at least Elagabalus. Antoninus preferred to sleep with his cousins and other women rather than with his wife Plautilla, whom he detested. The hatred between Antoninus and Julia Domna on the one side, and Plautianus and Plautilla on the other, was to have dire consequences soon enough.[1]

12.2. The Plautianus Affair in 204–205

Dio and Herodian both preserve a slightly different version of how the relationship between Plautianus and Severus soured, and it is worthwhile relating both in detail because Dio's account, included below, in particular betrays severe hostility towards both Severus and Antoninus:

> 'On one occasion a good many images of Plautianus were made (what happened is worth relating) and Severus, being displeased at their number, melted down some of them. As a consequence a rumour penetrated the cities to the effect that the prefect had been overthrown and had perished. [The melting of the statues made it look like the prefect had fallen from favour.] So some of them demolished his images – an act for which they were afterwards punished. Among these was the governor of Sardinia, Racius Constans, a very famous man …. The orator who accused Constans had made this statement in addition to others: "Sooner may the sky collapse than Plautianus suffer any harm at the hands of Severus, and with greater cause might any one believe even that report, were any story of the sort circulated." Now, though the orator made this declaration, and though moreover Severus himself volubly affirmed it to us, who were helping him try the case, and stated "it is impossible for Plautianus to come to any harm at my hands," still, this very Plautianus did not live the year out, but was slain and all his images destroyed. [This dates the event either to 204 or January 205.].' (Dio 76.1621ff., Cary ed., p.361ff., tr. by Forster, pp.366–67, with changes, corrections, comments and underlining)

Julia Soaemias as Venus (Vatican). Source: Duruy.

Julia Mamaea as Venus. Source: Duruy.

Elagabalus/Heliogabalus (Capitol). Source: Duruy.

Alexander Severus (Vatican). Source: Duruy.

Birley (p.154) connects the rift in the relationship between Severus and Plautianus with their stay in Lepcis in 203, so it would have been the erecting of statues by Plautianus there that caused it. Aelius Spartianus (*HA Sev.* 14.5–7) confirms that the rift between the two men resulted from the fact that Plautianus had erected his own statue among the members of the imperial family, but he does not state where and when this took place. Severus overthrew Plautianus's statues, but was afterwards reconciled with him. The situation could not last, however, because Plautianus behaved so arrogantly that it angered Severus's brother, wife and sons. Herodian and Dio describe the events as follows, beginning with the former:

> 'Antoninus was very averse to the match [between him and Plautilla]. … He refused to eat or sleep with her. In short he hated the old man and abhorred the girl, and threatened to kill her and her father when he would become the sole emperor. This the young woman told her father and complained how she was hated by her husband. … Plautianus considered Severus as a man continually afflicted by sickness and knew that Antoninus was a fierce daring youth; and being terrified at this threat, resolved to forestall him. Besides his fear he had other powerful incentives to make him aspire the imperial dignity. He was immensely rich … he went outside in a very magnificent dress …. It was his custom to have companions run before him clearing the way …. Severus being informed of his arrogant behaviour [this presumably refers to the incident in which his brother Geta warned him of Plautianus on his deathbed in 204] was so highly disgusted at the superlative pride of the man that he curtailed his authority, and often endeavoured by persuasion to bring him to moderation. But Plautianus was too haughty to bear reproof, and therefore resolved to attempt a treason for the empire in the following manner. There was one Saturninus, a tribune [*chiliarchos*] under him …. Plautianus judged him most faithful to his interest …. Accordingly, he sent for him one evening … [saying] "You have in your power to enter alone the chambers where they [Severus and Antoninus] sleep because it is your turn to relieve the night-guard tonight … enter the apartments and kill them both …." [Whittaker in his footnotes in Herodian p.332ff. notes the various modern theories regarding this incident. Hohl considered Herodian's account a fabrication based on the murder of Caius, but Whittaker quite correctly questioned how Dio would have known that Antoninus had fabricated the plot. He suggests the alternative that neither Plautianus nor Caracalla were behind the plot, but that the palace guards and freedmen had plotted the downfall of Plautianus, and that the inspiration behind it was Julia Domna, who hated the prefect. Papinian/Papinianus, the replacement of Plautianus, was a favourite of Julia Domna. In my opinion, however, it is probable that there was indeed a plot because Plautianus knew that Caracalla would kill him immediately after assuming power, as Herodian claims.] The tribune was shocked … but had the presence of mind enough … he was a person far from stupid for he was a Syrian by race … [It is this that presumably raised doubts that Saturninus could have actually acted on behalf of Antoninus and Julia Domna.] [H]e pretended to hear him with a great deal of pleasure … but he asked Plautianus to give him the assassination order in writing …. [This is actually the standard method used in modern armies when a

soldier thinks that an order might be illegal and therefore asks for it in writing to secure his own safety afterwards.] Plautianus blinded by resentment and ambition was weak enough to give the note, telling him to send messengers once he had killed both so that he might appear in the Palace before anyone knew he had seized the power .... But well knowing how difficult, if not impossible, it was to kill two princes lying in different apartments, he stood at Severus' door .... "I approach you ... Plautianus, who treasonably aspires the imperial power, has commanded me to murder you and your son ... and this note is my testimonial ...." Though this information was made with tears, Severus at first could not believe it .... And as he knew that his son hated both Plautianus and his daughter he suspected this might be some trick of the youth .... Having therefore called his son before him, he reproved him for contriving a thing of this kind .... Antoninus at first only swore his innocence .... But the tribune, seeing in what a dangerous situation he stood ... said to Severus ... "Allow me to go out of the room and send one of my friends, whom I can trust, to tell Plautianus that the business has been done ...." Plautianus believed the message .... He put on his *thorax*-breastplate to guard his person, which he concealed under his clothes, and then mounted his chariot and hurried away to the court with only a few attendants .... When he came to the Palace, the Guards who knew nothing of what was transacting gave him ready admittance; and the tribune, meeting him at the entrance, artfully saluted him emperor; and taking him by the hand according to the usual custom conducted him to the imperial apartment .... But Severus had some young men from his personal bodyguards [the *Aulici*?] posted in the room ready to seize him as soon as he came in. Plautianus having entered the door to his great mortification saw what he least expected [with] both the emperors standing alive. He was seized by the Guards, and being in utmost surprise and terror he pleaded and prayed, denying the whole affair, and saying that it was an artifice of his enemies .... Severus, moved at what Plautianus alleged, began to relent and was inclining to think him innocent, until his clothing was torn aside [presumably Antoninus did this] and there was found his shining breastplate. Antoninus, as he was a passionate youth and naturally violently hostile to the man, seeing the breastplate, said to the man: "But answer me to these two things: Do you come to the emperors in the evening without invitation? And what does this breastplate mean? Whoever comes in armour to eat or spend the evening with friends?" And as soon as he had said this, he ordered the tribune and the rest who were present to draw their swords and kill the traitor. The soldiers obeyed the prince without any hesitation and killed him and then cast his corpse into the street .... After his death Severus divided the government of the Camps between two prefects [Q. Maecius Laetus and Aemilianus Papinianus/Papinian].' Herodian, 3.10.8ff., tr. by Hart, p.141ff., with comments and changes)

In contrast to Herodian, Dio (77.2.1ff.) claims that there was no plot and that it had been invented by Antoninus:

'In very truth Plautianus had grown great and more than great, so that even the populace at the hippodrome exclaimed: "Why do you tremble? Why are you pale?

You possess more than the three." They did not say this to his face, of course, but differently. [Such shouts in the hippodrome were undoubtedly stage managed by someone who opposed Plautianus, the likeliest candidate being Antoninus.] And by "three" they indicated Severus and his sons, Antoninus and Geta. Plautianus' pallor and his trembling were in fact due to the life he lived, the hopes that he hoped, and the fears he feared. Still, for a time most of this eluded Severus' individual notice, or else he knew it but pretended the opposite. When, however, his brother on his deathbed revealed to him the whole attitude of Plautianus, – for Geta hated the prefect and now no longer feared him, – the emperor set up a bronze statue of his brother in the Forum and no longer held his minister in equal honor; indeed, the latter was stripped of most of his power. Hence Plautianus became violently enraged [It is easy to see that this could lead to the plot against Severus, which Dio claims did not exist.], and whereas he had formerly hated Antoninus for slighting his daughter, he was now especially indignant, feeling that his son-in-law was responsible for his present disgrace, and began to behave more harshly towards him. For these reasons Antoninus became both disgusted with his wife (who was a most shameless creature), and offended at her father himself, because the latter kept meddling in all his undertakings and rebuking him for everything he did. Conceiving a desire to be rid of the man in some way or other, he accordingly had Euodus, his nurse, persuade a certain centurion [*hekatontarchês*], Saturninus, and two others of similar rank to bring him word that Plautianus had ordered some ten centurions, to whose numbers they belonged, to kill both Severus and Antoninus; and they read a certain writing which they pretended to have received bearing upon this matter. This was done as a surprise at the observances held in the palace in honour of the heroes, at a time when the spectacle had ceased and dinner was about to be served. That fact was largely instrumental in showing the story to be a fabrication. Plautianus would never have dared to impose such a bidding upon ten centurions at once, certainly not in Rome, certainly not in the palace, certainly not on that day, nor at that hour; much less would he have written it. Nevertheless, Severus believed the information trustworthy because he had the night before seen in a dream Albinus alive and plotting against him. In haste, therefore, he summoned Plautianus, as if upon some other business. The latter hurried so … that the mules that were carrying him fell in the palace yard. And when he sought to enter, the porters in charge of the bolts admitted him alone inside and would permit no one to enter with him, just as he had done in the case of Severus at Tyana. He grew a little suspicious at this and became terrified; as he had, however, no pretext for withdrawing, he went in. Severus conversed with him very mildly … "For what reason have you wished to kill us?" He gave him opportunity to speak and prepared to listen to his defence. In the midst of the accused's denial and surprise at what was said, Antoninus rushed up, took away his sword, and struck him with his fist. He was ready to put an end to Plautianus with his own hand after the latter said, "You have forestalled me in killing." Being prevented by his father, Antoninus ordered one of his attendants to slay Plautianus. Somebody plucked out a few hairs from his chin and carried them to Julia and Plautilla (who were together) before they had heard a word of the affair, and said: "Behold your Plautianus!" This speech aroused grief in one and joy in the other .... [T]he man ... was slain by his son-in-law and thrown from the top of the palace into some street. Later, at the order of Severus, he was taken up and buried. Severus next called a meeting of the senate in the senate-house. He uttered no accusation against Plautianus, but himself deplored the weakness of human nature, which was not able to endure excessive honours, and blamed himself that he had so honoured and loved the man. Those, however, who had informed him of the victim's plot he bade tell us everything .... Many were brought into danger by the Plautianus episode and some actually lost their lives [i.e. the known friends and supporters of Plautianus].' (Dio, 77.2.1ff., tr. by Forster, p.372ff., with comments and changes including one sentence from Cary's tr. on p.247)

The two accounts are clearly entirely different, but the key point here is that Dio was intensely hostile towards Caracalla and only slightly less so against Severus, and it is this that has coloured his account. Dio, however, did his job so poorly that he preserved everywhere information that contradicted his own version. In this case it is the words that Dio puts into the mouth of Plautianus that betray Plautianus's intention to murder Severus and Antoninus. In addition to this, Dio quite clearly indicates the ambitions of Plautianus, his hatred of Antoninus and also the anger of Plautianus when his powers had been curtailed by Severus. All of these are motives for murder, just like would have been the reason in Herodian. It is clear that even if one cannot rule out that the superbly clever Antoninus showed his outstanding plotting skills early in life, that Julia Domna instigated the plot or even that Severus himself was behind it, it is still more likely that Plautianus did indeed attempt to kill his benefactors.[2] The downfall of Plautianus obviously meant a purge of all his close friends or supporters. Some of them were killed or exiled, but others were more fortunate, including one of Plautianus's clients, the lowly born (future Emperor) Macrinus. He was spared when Cilo, the Urban Prefect, appealed for his life. Severus subsequently made Macrinus his *Procurator rei Privatae* (Procurator of the Emperor's Private Property, the office of which was created by Severus). Antoninus tried to have his wife Plautilla killed, but Severus imitated Augustus – who had exiled Mark Antony's children – banishing both Plautilla and her brother Plautius, either to the island of Lipara (according to Dio) or to Sicily (Herodian). Antoninus, however, did not forgive, having both killed once he assumed power.[3]

There is no better description of this affair than the analysis made by the political and military savant Machiavelli in his *Discourses* (3.35.40–42, tr. by Atkinson and Sices, pp.272–273):

'I say that all conspiracies found in histories are made by men who are noble or very close to the prince. Because others cannot conspire, unless they are completely mad, since weak men and those not close to the prince lack all the hopes and opportunities that carrying out a conspiracy requires ... those who have conspired were all noble men or the prince's intimates; many of them conspired, impelled as much by too many favours as by too many abuses: as were Perennis against Commodus, Plautianus against Severus, Sejanus against Tiberius. All of them

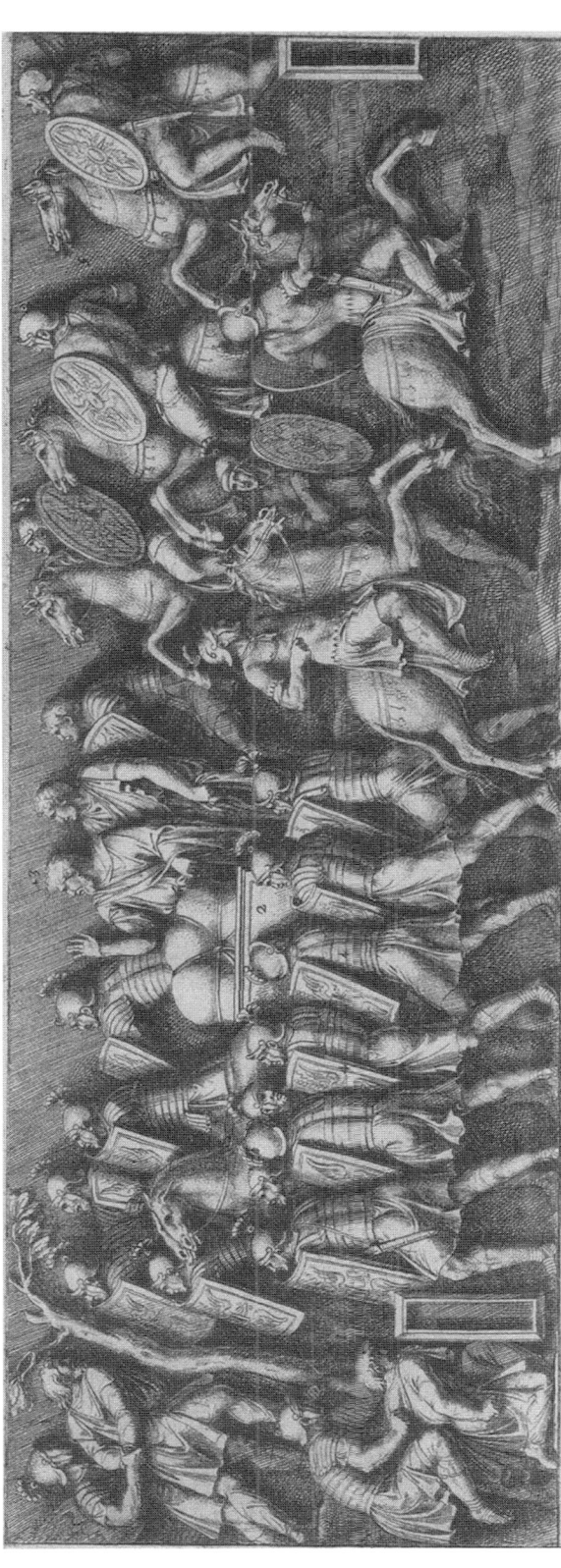

Note the rearward angled half-square formation (*epikampios opisthia*) used for marching in this 17th century drawing of the Column of Marcus Aurelius. This is the same array that was used by Julius Caesar when he advanced to the battle of Sabis, but with the difference that (see my article on the battle of Sabis/Sambre available online at academia.edu) that this array does not have the rear portion behind the cavalry that, when brought forwards, would have made the array a complete hollow square/oblong. It is possible that such a formation followed up behind the cavalry shown here, but it is also possible that the probable auxiliary footman between the horsemen should be interpreted as the rear of the hollow oblong, because after all the front of this array has similarly only one man between the wings.

had such riches, honour, and rank conferred on them by their emperors that they lacked only imperial status to complete the power, and since they were unwilling to do without this they were moved to conspire against the princes. And their conspiracies all had the outcome that their ingratitude deserved.'

Severus did not repeat his mistake of appointing only a single Praetorian Prefect, the successors of Plautianus being Q. Maecius Laetus and Aemilius Papinianus, both of whom served in this post until the end of Severus's life. These men proved loyal to their emperor.

Chapter 13

The Years of Relative Peace in 205–207[1]

13.1. The Loose Living of Antoninus and Geta in 205–207

We know next to nothing about the events that took place between 205 and 208. All that we have are the very few details given by Dio and Herodian, extant inscriptions referring to troubles and propaganda preserved in the imperial coinage. These refer to general unrest, banditry, the mundane ruling of the Empire and loose living by the brothers Antoninus and Geta.

The extant sources state in no uncertain terms that the killing of Plautianus released the worst in both Antoninus and Geta, who outraged women and abused boys, embezzled money and made gladiators and charioteers their companions. Even though Antoninus slept with other women as well, he appears to have had unnatural love towards his female relatives as discussed above, so it is possible that he continued to do so during this period. On top of this the brothers could not agree on anything, competing with each other and supporting opposing charioteer factions, the white, red, blue and green teams. Caracalla appears to have favoured the blues and Geta the greens. Severus did not like what he saw. The last straw for the father was an incident in which both brothers were racing chariots against each other, which resulted in Antoninus falling from his two-wheeled chariot and breaking his leg. One wonders whether this was really an accident? According to Dio, Severus did not neglect his duties as a result of the accident, and indeed was praised for this. He was clearly a dutiful ruler and father. Another reason why the brothers sought the company of charioteers and gladiators was that it enabled them to gather around them ruffians and rogues whom they could then employ against each other. These hooligans and professional duellists could be used to great effect in urban fighting and possibly also in the future fight for the throne.[2]

Severus attempted to reconcile the brothers, dividing his time between the imperial property on the outskirts of Rome and the coast of Campania, where he performed his judicial and administrative work. The emperor wanted to keep his sons away from the corrupting, luxurious and decadent lifestyle of the capital by giving them a taste of clean living. Their enthusiasm for gladiator shows and chariot racing was not considered appropriate for prospective emperors by conservative-thinking senators like Dio, and also by implication by Severus himself. According to Herodian, Severus attempted to reconcile his sons by telling them old tales which demonstrated how quarrels between royal brothers resulted in disaster. He also showed them Rome's treasuries and temples full of money that could be used to keep the soldiers happy, and told them that this would allow them to defeat any external enemies. Herodian states that Severus had quadrupled the number of troops in Rome and stationed a strong garrison (the Legio II Parthica) just outside the city at Albanum to eradicate any outside threat to the imperial family, and had told his sons all this would be in vain if they fought against each other in a civil war. The statement regarding the quadrupling of troops at Rome has in my opinion been needlessly suspected because none of the commentators have taken into account the *Aulici*, *Scholarii* and *Protectores* which are attested for the reign of Septimius Severus. If these corps were as large as the Praetorian corps after its doubling by Severus, it is quite feasible that Herodian's statement is correct. Severus repeated his warning about internecine fighting over and again to his sons, but to no avail because the young men were bursting with energy and as emperors (the Augustus and Caesar) they were in a position to actually cause a civil war. Meanwhile, power-hungry flatterers catered to their lowest desires and encouraged them to act against each other. Severus punished some of these sycophants when he saw them acting in this way, but this was not enough to alter the course of events. The two young men just had too much money, power and free time in their hands.

As noted above, none of these familial problems or his failing health prevented Severus from performing his duties as emperor. Dio, quoted first, and Aelius Spartianus have preserved us a description of the daily routine of Severus:

> 'The following is the style of life that Severus led in time of peace. He was sure to be doing something before dawn, while it was still night, and after this he would go to walk, telling and hearing of the interests of the empire. Then he held court, and separately (unless there were some great festival); and indeed, he did this very well. Those on trial were allowed plenty of water [Dio means water-clock time] and he granted us, his advisers full liberty to speak. He continued to preside until noon. After that he went riding as much as he could. Next he took some kind of gymnastic exercise and a bath. He then consumed a not meagre lunch, either by himself or with his children. Next, as a rule, he enjoyed a nap. Later he rose, attended the remaining duties of administration, and while walking about occupied himself with discussions of both Greek and Latin. Then, toward evening, he would bathe again and dine with his attendants. [This account proves that Severus was very dutiful as emperor. If he ate only twice in the course of day, as stated here, that would have left him exhausted for much of the day. However, I would suggest that Dio has just left out the breakfast and snacks because it would be very strange if Severus would have eaten less often than his soldiers on a campaign.][3] Very seldom did he have any outsider to dinner and only on days when it was quite unavoidable did he arrange expensive banquets .... [H]e showed himself so active that even expiring he gasped: "Come, give it to us, if we have anything to do!"'[4] (Dio 77.17.1ff, tr. by Forster, pp.389–90, with comments and changes)

Aelius Spartianus, meanwhile, tells us:

> 'His [Severus's] clothing was of the plainest; indeed, even his tunic had scarcely any purple on it, while he covered his shoulders with a shaggy cloak. [Severus's aim was to please the rank-and-file with this unassuming appearance. His son Caracalla imitated him for the very same purpose.] He was very sparing in his diet, and was fond of his native beans, [this would have worsened his gout if he suffered from

it. It is possible that he had several different simultaneous medical conditions, of which gout was only one, because gout would not fit the description of the wasting disease that killed him in the end, while it would fit the description of pain when walking.] liked wine at times, and often went without meat. [The avoidance of meat could be connected with gout, but it did not help if he still ate beans.] In person he was large and handsome. [This is likely to be based on his statues and paintings, because Dio calls him short.] His beard was long; his hair was grey and curly, his face was such as to inspire respect. His voice was clear, but retained an African accent even to his old age. After his death he was much beloved, for then all envy of his power or fear of his cruelty had vanished.' Aelius Spartianus, *HA Sev.* 19.7–10, tr. by Magie, p.419, with comments)

One of the most important peacetime duties of the emperor was to make decisions regarding legal cases which were brought to his attention. As a former lawyer, Severus was particularly interested in this aspect of being emperor, as the above quote from Dio reveals. Severus was a conservative man who reformed many of the legal practices to follow his conservative views. He was the first emperor who legislated against abortion. He also issued edicts that protected minors, and others that protected the money that women brought into a marriage from their husbands. Similarly, he eased the severity of punishments for children who suffered as a result of the sins of their fathers. The enforcement of the *Lex Iulia Maiestatis* was also eased. However, in the fields of adultery and public morals, Severus increased the severity of punishments in the name of public morale. This resulted in such large numbers of accused, amounting to thousands, that Severus stopped pressing these cases – there were simply not enough prosecutors for them. It is unfortunately impossible to date the sequence of these laws because Justinian's *Corpus Iuris Civilis* does not contain the locations and dates for them. It is possible in some cases to date a law to the period when both Severus and Antoninus were Augusti, but I have nevertheless not attempted to pinpoint them in time and place, as did the secondary sources mentioned here.[5] What is clear is that Severus attempted to legislate such laws that he considered just and good for the maintenance of public morals, and to emulate the similarly conservative policies of Augustus.

13.2. The Other Troubles in 205–207

The behaviour of Antoninus and Geta were not the only troubles that Severus faced while he was in Italy. Dio has preserved for us a list of conspiracies, while the extant inscriptions and coins suggest that the provinces faced a number of other problems. Dio notes that the execution of Marcus Peducaeus Plautius Quintillus, the last of the remaining sons-in-law of Marcus Aurelius, brought Severus infamy, as did the killing of a number of other senators accused of having conspired against him. We do not know the truth of the matter, but it is clear that accusations were levelled against these men and they were duly executed. Whittaker has suggested that the killing of Quintillus was part of the neutralization of the old Antonine dynasty, as was the marriage of Cornificia to L. Didius Marinus and Vibia Sabina to L. Aurelius Agaclytus, son of a freedman of L. Verus. Both of these men were equestrians and therefore unlikely to cause trouble.

None of the people at the time, Caracalla included, thought that an equestrian could rise to power, as did later happen when Macrinus usurped the throne after having Caracalla murdered.[6]

The case of Popilius Pedo Apronianus is more straightforward and a good example of the workings of the Roman system of informers that was tapped by emperors to expose potential threats. Soothsayers, astrologers, servants, slaves or any other informers revealed to the imperial security organs any use of magic, or the wrong kinds of questions being asked, such as when the emperor would die or whether someone would become emperor. In the case of Apronianus, it was reported that his nurse had dreamed that Apronianus would become emperor and that he had used magic in an attempt to fulfil this dream. Apronianus was duly condemned *in absentia* because he was serving as governor of Asia. The evidence against him had been confirmed under torture, as Roman law allowed. What worried the senators when these testimonies were read out was that one of the men declared that he had seen a certain bald-headed senator spying in at the wrong time and seeing something he should not have. This caused all those who were bald or balding to fear for their life. The senators started looking at each other and to murmur, and some of them – including Dio – also touched their heads to feel if they had enough hair to escape punishment. Their worries soon ended when the speaker read more of the statement, which said that the bald-headed senator had worn a purple-bordered toga. All now knew that the man was Baebius Marcellinus, who duly rose and asked the accuser to recognize him, which the informer did once he had been brought to the Senate. It is clear that the speaker had intentionally paused the statement of the informer for his own amusement to cause angst among the senators. When Marcellinus had been identified, he was led out to be killed, being allowed to say goodbye to his four children before being beheaded. Dio claims that the beheading was done without Severus's knowledge, but it is likely that he approved it because nobody was punished for this act. This incident, just like the previous case against Quintillus, suggests that there were senators who thought it possible to form a plot to overthrow Severus. While Dio criticized the above, he considered the punishment of Pollenius Sabennus as just. Sabennus, who had previously served as governor of the Norici, had treated them unjustly and was delivered to them for punishment. However, his life was saved thanks to the intervention of his uncle, A. Pollenius Auspex.[7]

The most serious of the troubles mentioned by Dio was the case of Bulla Victor the bandit, but as we shall see, we possess only fragments of Dio's text. However, the Bulla incident was very serious indeed and humiliating for Severus, and it is thus worthwhile to quote Dio:[8]

> 'It was at this period that one Bulla, an Italian, established a robber band of about 600 men and for two years [206–207?] continued to plunder Italy under the very noses of the emperors and of so great bodies of soldiers. Pursuit was instituted by numerous person, and Severus emulously followed his trail, but the fellow was never really seen when seen, never found when found, never apprehended when caught. This was due to his great bribes and his cleverness. He got wind of everybody that was setting out from Rome and everybody that was putting into port at Brundisium, learning who and how many they were, and what and how much they had with them. [Bulla clearly had an outstanding network of spies and

The Years of Relative Peace in 205–207   213

informers placed at strategic locales.] His general method was to take a part of what they had and then let them go at once. Artisans, however, he detained for a time and after making use of their skill dismissed them with something extra as a present. [He was clearly a Robin Hood of his day.] Once two of his robbers had been captured and were to be given to beasts, whereupon the chief paid a visit to the keeper of the prison, pretending that he was the governor of his native place and needed some such men, and in this way he secured and saved them. Again, he approached the centurion who was charged with abolishing brigandage and in disguise accused his own self: he further promised, if the centurion would accompany him, to deliver the robber to him. So pretending that he was leading him to Felix (this was another name of the chief), he brought him to a covered defile, suitable for ambuscade, and easily seized him. Later he assumed the garb of a magistrate, ascended the tribunal, and having called the centurion caused his head to be shaved, and said: "Take this message to your masters: 'Feed your slaves, if you want to make an end of brigandage.'" Bulla had, indeed, a very great number of Caesarians [imperial freedmen], some who had been poorly paid and some who had gone absolutely without pay. [This explains the high quality of intelligence available to Bulla and also proves that Severus was too stingy with his payments to servants, even if he paid his soldiers well enough.] Severus, informed of these events one at a time, was moved to anger to think that while having other men win victory in warfare in Britain, he himself in Italy had proved no match for a robber. At last he dispatched a tribune from his bodyguard with many horsemen [*kai telos chiliarchon ek tôn sômatofulakôn sun hippeusi pollois esteile*; this proves nicely how the bodyguards were used for special missions including the policing of the countryside] and threatened him with terrible punishments if he should not bring the culprit alive. Then this commander ascertained that the chief was maintaining relations of intimacy with the wife of another, and through the agency of her husband persuaded her on promise of immunity to cooperate with them. As a result the elusive leader was arrested while asleep in a cave. Papinianus, the Praetorian Prefect, asked him: "For what reason did you become a robber?" The other rejoined: "For what reason are you a prefect?" And thereafter by solemn proclamation he was given to beasts. His robber band broke up, for the entire strength of 600 lay in him.' (Dio 77.10.1ff, tr. by Forster, p.381ff., with changes and comments)

This account does lend some credence to Dio's claim that the cashiering of the Praetorian Guard in 193 and the fact that it no longer consisted solely of Italians, Spaniards, Macedonians and Noricans resulted in banditry, even if Dio nowhere states that Bulla Victor or his followers were former members of the Praetorian Guard or desired to become such. It is easy to connect the above with his earlier statement (75.2.5–6) that the opening up of the Guard to others caused the Italian youth to turn to brigandage and gladiatorial fighting. The unemployed Praetorians knew only how to fight, and they now had only two avenues open to them which gave them a chance to practise their trade: brigandage and fighting as gladiators. It is therefore clear that Bulla and most of his bandits consisted of former Praetorians and other restless Italian youths, strengthened by imperial freedmen dissatisfied with their salaries. The great success that they enjoyed proves that they were indeed very good at what they were doing. However, it is probable that Bulla had practised his trade longer than the two years mentioned here by Dio. He would probably have started as a common highway robber, and as his fame and wealth increased, more and more other bandits and volunteers (probably consisting mostly of his former comrades) joined his band so that it eventually came to consist of the above-mentioned 600 men.

It is quite probable that if Antoninus drew any conclusions from the Bulla case, it was that it would have been wiser to kill all the Praetorians when they surrendered to his father in 193. It is also easy to see that he could have drawn a similar conclusion from the experiences of Julius Caesar during the years 49–45 BC, when he faced the same Pompeians again and again. It is possible that Severus also came to the same conclusion because he idolized Augustus, who was not merciful to his enemies. However, there is still a distinct difference between the father and son. Severus was prepared to show a level of mercy on some occasions, while this was very rare for Antoninus Caracalla.

Peaceful life in Italy was not enjoyable for Severus. His generals were acquiring military glory while he had to contend with the mundane matters of daily governance of the Empire. He feared that his soldiers were growing lazy, just as were his sons. He wanted to give his sons a healthy dose of military life and a military education, and keep his soldiers in training. It is quite possible that he felt his own end was nearing, meaning there was an urgent need to teach his sons the art of soldiering and generalship. It is also possible that he wanted to die as a soldier in the middle of a campaign.

Coin depicting the imperial family:
Septimius Severus, Caracalla, Julia Domna and Geta
Source: Cohen.

Chapter 14

The Military Education for the sons: the Campaigns of 207–211[1]

14.1. Britain from 197–207

Severus found a suitable excuse for war soon enough when the governor of Britain sent him urgent pleas either to send reinforcements or come in person to the province. The island had been a trouble spot ever since Albinus had withdrawn most Roman forces from the island in 196 to fight against Severus. Modern research has established that Severus dispatched Virius Lupus with an army to Britain immediately after his victory at the Battle of Lyon in 197. However, Severus had given Lupus

Septimius Severus and Caracalla. Source: Duruy.

too few men to accomplish the task of pacifying the island, meaning, as we have seen, that Lupus had to pay a bribe to the Maeatae to secure peace. Yet even this had stabilized the situation only temporarily. At some unknown time, possibly between 203 and 205, the Maeatae formed an alliance with the other major tribal confederation of north-east Scotland, the Caledonians, and the war resumed. In the context of the year 207, Dio (77.10.6) notes that Severus was angry at the thought that others were winning wars in Britain in his name while he had been humbled by a mere robber, Bulla, in Italy. This refers to the Romans having achieved several successes against the tribal alliance between 205 and 207, which made Severus yearn for more personal military achievements. Modern archaeology has proven that the Romans repaired or rebuilt barracks and forts along Hadrian's Wall in 206 under Valerius Pudens, then in 207 under L. Alfenus Senecio. This has caused most historians to think that Severus's strategy at this point was to abandon the territory north of Hadrian's Wall and repair and refortify the wall. He had followed the same policy in Raetia. However, neither of these wall-building projects worked as planned, because in both cases military action was still needed both during Septimius's lifetime and afterwards. The first of these fortifications to collapse was Hadrian's Wall in 207 when the Brigantes, who lived just south of it, revolted and joined their northern brethren. The likeliest reason for the revolt is that the Romans would have used Brigantes as forced labour for the rebuilding of the wall, but the British tradition also implies that the persecution of Christians played a role. Governor Alfenus Senecio had no alternative than to send a plea for help.[2]

The revolt of the Brigantes is confirmed by two altars set up to celebrate a Roman victory over them. However, the situation was still grave because the rebels appear to have been able to besiege the city of Eboracum (York). The two altars prove correct Severus's complaint that other persons rather than him or his sons were winning wars in Britain.[3]

These events are confirmed by the later British/English tradition (Nennius 22–23; Bede, *Chronicle* AM 4163, *Ecclesiastical History* 5; Geoffrey of Monmouth, 4.19–5.2), so it is worthwhile examining sections from these sources, starting with Nennius:

> 'After the birth of Christ, one hundred and sixty-seven years, King Lucius, with all the chiefs of the British people, received baptism, in consequence of a legation sent by the Roman Emperors and Pope Euaristus. Severus was the third emperor who crossed the sea to Britain, where, to protect the provinces recovered from barbaric incursions, he ordered a wall and a rampart to be made between the Britons, the Scots, and the Picts [these should be the Britons, Maetae and Caledonians], extending across the island from sea to sea, in length one hundred and thirty-three miles; and it is called in the British language, Guual. Moreover, he ordered it to be made between the Britons, and the Picts and Scots; for the Scots from the west [at this time the Scots lived in Ireland], and the Picts [these would be the Maetae and Caledonians, because the Picts either arrived at this time as stated by Geoffrey or lived along the western coast of modern Scotland] from the north, unanimously made war against the Britons; but were at peace among themselves. Not long afterwards Severus died in Britain.' (Nennius 22–23, tr. by Giles, 1841, with changes and comments)

From Bede we have the following:

> 'In the year of our Lord's incarnation 156, Marcus Antoninus Verus .... In their time, whilst Eleutherus, a holy man, presided over the Roman church, Lucius, king of the Britons, sent a letter to him, entreating, that by his command he might be made a Christian .... In the year of our Lord 189, Severus, an African, born at Leptis, in the province of Tripolis, received the imperial purple .... Having been victorious in all the grievous civil wars which happened in his time, he was drawn into Britain by the revolt of almost all the confederate tribes; and, after many great and dangerous battles, he thought it fit to divide that part of the island, which he had recovered from the other unconquered nations, not with a wall, as some imagine, but with a rampart. For a wall is made of stones, but a rampart, with which camps are fortified to repel the assaults of enemies, is made of sods, cut out of the earth, and raised above the ground all round like a wall, having in front of it the ditch whence the sods were taken, and strong stakes of wood fixed upon its top. Thus Severus drew a great ditch and strong rampart, fortified with several towers, from sea to sea [this is the Antonine Wall and this rebuilding project would have taken place in 208]; and was afterwards taken sick and died at York, leaving two sons, Bassianus and Geta; of whom Geta died, adjudged a public enemy; but Bassianus, having taken the surname Antoninus, obtained the empire.' (Bede, *Ecclesiastical History*, tr. by Giles, 1845, p.10ff., with changes and comments)

And Geoffrey of Monmouth adds:

The Military Education for the sons: the Campaigns of 207–211   217

'Coillus had but one son, named Lucius, who obtaining the crown after his father's decease, imitated all his acts of goodness ... for which purpose he sent letters to pope Eleutherius, desiring to be instructed by him in the Christian religion .... He [Lucius] had no issue to succeed him, so that after his decease there arose a dissension among the Britons, and the Roman power was much weakened. When this news was brought to Rome, the senate dispatched Severus, with two legions, to reduce the country to subjection. As soon as he was arrived, he came to a battle with the Britons, part of whom he obliged to submit to him, and the other part which he could not subdue he endeavoured to distress in several cruel engagements, and forced them to fly beyond Deira [this usually means the area just south of Hadrian's Wall, but in this case could actually mean the area north of it] into Albania. [Albania/Albany usually means the area north of Hadrian's Wall, but in this case may actually mean the area north of the Antonine Wall. In truth, after the defeat of Albinus in 197, Severus dispatched the legate Virius Lupus as a governor with two legions to the area of Hadrian's Wall with the mission to subdue the tribesmen who were in revolt.] Notwithstanding which they opposed him with all their might under the conduct of Fulgenius/Sulgenius [In light of the civil war it is probable that his enemy allied himself with the Romans, but one cannot preclude the possibility that he was the victor of the civil war], and often made great slaughter both of their own countrymen and of the Romans [in the area between the walls of Hadrian and Antoninus]. For Fulgenius/Sulgenius brought to his assistance all the people of the islands that he could find [the Hebrides, Orkneys, Faroe and possibly also Ireland. Notably, according to Bede 3, the Orkneys belonged to the Roman Empire], and so frequently gained the victory. The emperor [this would be Severus], not being able to resist the irruptions which he made commanded a wall to be built between Deira and Albania, to hinder his excursions upon them; they accordingly made one at the common charge from sea to sea [This would be the Antonine Wall and not Hadrian's Wall as usually assumed see above.], which for a long time hindered the approach of the enemy. But Fulgenius/Sulgenius, when he was unable to make any longer resistance, made a voyage into Scythia, to desire the assistance of the Picts towards his restoration. [This Scythia might have been located in Scandinavia, Denmark, Finland or on the southern shores of the Baltic Sea.] And when he got together all the forces of that country, he returned with a great fleet into Britain and besieged York. Upon this news being spread through the country, the greatest part of the Britons deserted Severus and went over to Fulgenius/Sulgenius. [This probably means the massive revolt of the various tribes in 207 which led to the urgent plea for help to Severus. The Brigantes formed the core of the tribes that revolted, and it is quite possible that they would have been eager to join the cause of the Christian Fulgenius/Sulgenius when Septimius Severus was persecuting Christians. It is unlikely to be a coincidence that it is in this precise area where Geta subsequently launched his persecution of Christians.] However this did not make Severus [the governor] desist from his enterprise: but calling together the Romans, and the rest of the Britons that adhered to him, he marched to the siege, and fought with Fulgenius/Sulgenius; but the engagement proving very sharp, he was killed with many of his followers; Fulgenius/Sulgenius also was mortally wounded. [The death of the Roman governor and the rebel leader could explain why the situation was stabilized by the time Severus arrived in 208, and is therefore quite possibly true.] Afterwards Severus was buried at York, which city was taken by his legions. He left two sons, Bassianus and Geta, whereof Geta had a Roman for his mother, but Bassianus [Caracalla] a Briton. [After this, Geoffrey's account confuses the events taking place under Caracalla with those of the late third century and are therefore left out.] (Geoffrey of Monmouth 4.19.1ff, Giles tr., 1848, p.154ff., with comments and changes)

The British/English tradition is thus largely in agreement with what we know from the period Roman sources and the extant inscriptions. However, it adds some important pieces of information missing from the others. It is, for instance, quite possible that the Brigantes had converted to Christianity under their king, Lucius, and that the persecution of Christians that Severus launched in about 202 contributed to their willingness to revolt. Geoffrey of Monmouth also claims that Fulgenius/Sulgenius brought Picts from Scythia to his assistance before 207. In light of the fact that the Picts suddenly make an appearance in this region after the British campaign of Severus from 208–211, it is entirely possible that Geoffrey is indeed correct. The British tradition also has an explanation why the situation had stabilized by the time Severus arrived on the island.

14.2. The Military Campaigns of Antoninus Caracalla in 207?

On the basis of numismatics and extant inscriptions, a number of historians – including Reed, Bender and Birley – have suggested that Antoninus conducted a military campaign in 207. Coins minted in 207 show Antoninus either with Mars or Virtus (both demonstrated military prowess). The fact that these coins depict captives and a river-god is even more important. Another piece of evidence which has been used to support a Germanic campaign in 207 is that the Arval Brothers[4] give Caracalla the titles of *victor felicissimus* and *Germanicus maximus* on 20 May 213, and a Papyrus (dated 29 August 212 – 29 August 213) states the same. However, this is not conclusive because Caracalla could have obtained these titles as a result of his operations in 212. The historians are divided over where this campaign took place. Reed suggests Britain, Bender prefers Raetia and Birley the Middle Danube, all of which are plausible. However, the Middle Danube is the most likely candidate because the governor of Pannonia Superior, Egnatius Victor, and the legate of the V legion, Claudius Piso, made a joint dedication at Arrabona in which they referred to the victory of the emperors and of the Legio I Adiutrix Antoniniana.[5] The title 'Antoniniana' is clearly an early example of Antoninus's eagerness to advertise the loyalty of the units serving under him.

The British tradition can be used to support the alternative that the young Antoninus was sent to Britain in the company of some experienced general when the Roman governor was killed, and that he returned to Rome later in the same year. Furthermore, one cannot entirely preclude the possibility that Severus had sent Caracalla to Raetia to supervise the strengthening of the Raetian *limes* in 207, while the governor of Britain performed similar functions along Hadrian's Wall. The river-god in the coin would obviously be the Main, and the captives those Alamanni who had opposed the strengthening of the *limes*.

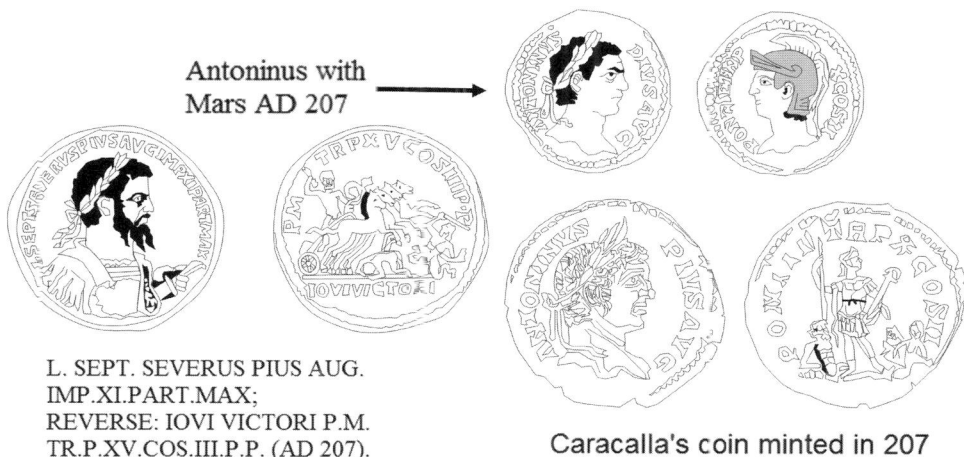

L. SEPT. SEVERUS PIUS AUG. IMP.XI.PART.MAX; REVERSE: IOVI VICTORI P.M. TR.P.XV.COS.III.P.P. (AD 207). Drawn after Cohen.

Antoninus with Mars AD 207

Caracalla's coin minted in 207 with a river god and prisoners

A campaign across the border could have been a necessity in the first place to secure the safety of the work crews. I would suggest an additional alternative: because Raetia is not far away from Arrabona, it is quite possible that Antoninus oversaw the strengthening of the entire Danube line from Raetia up to Pannonia. There are very strong reasons to suspect that the strengthening of the defences in Raetia and Britain were part of a single grand strategy in which Severus planned to build a secure base of operations for further advance into the *Barbaricum* (the area beyond the *limes*). The best evidence for this is that Severus did it in Britain, then his son Antoninus Caracalla did the same in Raetia and the rest of the Danube frontier once he became emperor. It is possible that the operations conducted by Antoninus at the beginning of his reign had actually been planned by his father. In Britain, preparations for advance to the north are also in evidence on the ground. The extant inscriptions prove that one of Septimius's governors (the name is not preserved) built new granaries at Banna (Birdoswald), Cilurnum (Chesters), Vercovicium (Housesteads), Coria (Corbridge) and Arbeia (South Shields). The last of these was actually a massive supply depot which could hold enough corn for 40,000 men for three months, but this was only one part of the projected invasion force which consisted of far more than this number of men. The improvement of several roads in Gaul during the years 202–207/209 were part of this same plan.[6]

As I have noted in my biography of Caracalla, there are problems with the claims that Antoninus campaigned in 207: the dating of the coins is not absolutely secure, the images on coins could be just imperial propaganda without any basis in truth, and the emperors could have appropriated for themselves the successes achieved by their generals. However, when all of the above evidence is taken together, especially the existence of a legion with the title *Antoniniana*, it is very likely that Caracalla conducted some sort of military campaign along the Danube in 207, presumably also strengthening the defences. My suggestion is that since the distances between Raetia and Pannonia are not that great, it is probable that Caracalla operated in both areas, because it is precisely in this area that we see Caracalla during 213 and 214. It is more than likely that Caracalla was implementing the last plans of his father when he did this.

The problems with his sons, the plotters, Bulla, and the problems along the Danube and in Britain were not the only troubles that Septimius Severus faced at this time. Inscriptions at Ephesus in Asia and Sicca Veneria in Africa Proconsularis mention the existence of insidious plots in these regions in 207–208, which were crushed. When this is combined with the coins of Severus (a female figure of Africa with an elephant which has a lion on its feet) from 207, some historians have come to the conclusion that Severus must have crushed the insidious plots in Africa in person. However, there is no firm evidence for this. As if this was not enough, there was also a revolt in Gaul. This is again proven by an extant inscription, which states the *dux*[7] Julius Septimius Castinus (also *legatus* of the Legio I Minervia) crushed defectors and rebels in Gaul with the help of detachments drawn from all four legions of the two Germanias (I Minervia, XXX Ulpia, XXII Primigenia and VIII Augusta). This earned Severus his twelfth imperial salutation.[8] As I stated in my biography of Caracalla, this should probably be connected with the statement that Severus worried that the soldiers were becoming enervated with the long period of peace. It is probable that the rebels consisted of soldiers who had been delegated to the road construction projects in Gaul already mentioned, and that the local Gauls joined them because they did not like paying extra taxes or being corvéed as road construction crews for the forthcoming war in Britain and along the Rhine and Danube frontiers. This, however, is just my own educated guess.

14.3. The Preparations for the British Campaign in 207–208

Planning for the campaign in Britain started immediately after Severus received the urgent plea for help in 207, but it took until the following year for them to be completed. As noted by Birley, at this stage of the planning process Severus consulted all those with specialist knowledge of Britain and the enemy. Once preparations were completed in 208, Severus and Antoninus left the city of Rome and arrived in Britain to prepare the invasion of Scotland (Caledonia) in 209. What is uncertain, however, is whether the rest of the imperial family accompanied them, because Herodian implies (3.14.9) that Geta was summoned to Britain only after the preparations for war had been done. Whatever the truth regarding the sequence in which the imperial family travelled to Britain, it was now time for them to attempt to acquire some military glory.[9]

Preparations had been on a massive scale because Severus aimed to conquer the entire island, which meant the building of the above-mentioned granaries to support sizeable forces in the field. According to Birley, it is probable that Severus also relocated the Tigris bargemen to Arbeia at this time and that it was because of this the town received its name. The bargemen were extremely useful for the shipping of supplies from Arbeia to Coria. The expeditionary army was first marched to Gesoriacum/Bononia (Boulogne) and then shipped to Dubris (Dover), where Severus held an assembly of the troops. We do not know when the local forces were added to their strength but it is probable that this took place somewhere close to Hadrian's Wall. The likely marching route from Hadrian's Wall to Cramond was along the road that ran from Eboracum via Coria and Newstead.[10]

The emperors, Severus and Caracalla, were accompanied by their *comites* and administrations, which provided advice to both during the campaign. The emperors and the rest of the imperial family, once they joined the *Augusti*, would also have been accompanied by a very significant portion of the central administration. We know the names of two administrators: Castor the *cubicularius*, who acted as *a memoria* for Severus, and Euodus. In addition to this, the emperors brought with them their bodyguard units and their commanders, but the sources name only one of the commanders, the Praetorian Prefect Papinianus. Thanks to extant inscriptions we know that some unknown man (the name is missing from the inscription) was appointed as commander of the provincial fleets of Britain, Germania, Pannonia and Moesia (*Classes Britannica, Germanica, Pannonica* and *Moesica*), and that another man was placed in charge of the granaries at Coria. This proves the massive scale of the campaign. Severus had ordered the provincial fleets from Germania, Pannonia and Moesia to send detachments for the campaign. Even if we do not possess similar inscriptions to prove the presence of the Praetorian fleets, it is clear that these would also have dispatched ships for the campaign.[11]

The internal logic of imperial campaigns, the extant inscriptions and the remains of Roman marching camps enable us to make some rough estimates regarding the size of the imperial army. It is clear that the emperors would have been accompanied by the Legio II Parthica (*ca.* 5,000 foot and 500 horse), most of the Praetoriani (*ca.* 8,000 foot, 1,500 horse), *Equites Singulares Augusti* (*ca.* 2,000 cavalry), possibly the *Aulici* (conservative estimate *ca.* 2,000 cavalry), one cohort of the *Urbaniciani* (*ca.* 1,500 foot) and detachments from the *Peregrini, Frumentarii* and *Speculatores* (*ca.* 300 cavalry). These would have added up to *ca.* 14,500 infantry and 6,300 horsemen. It is also probable that they would have drawn detachments from the European legions. If we estimate that each legion contributed about 2,000 foot and 200 horse, and the auxiliaries from the same area contributed *ca.* 1,000 infantry and 600 cavalry, this would add up to (for sixteen legions and their auxiliaries) 48,000 infantry and 12,800 cavalry. However, there exists a very strong possibility that Severus also raised new legions to occupy Caledonia, because this was the standard practice when new territories were annexed to the Empire; we should not forget that Severus had already done the very same thing with his Parthian legions. It is quite possible too that he raised new additional *numeri* among the Moors, because these feature so strongly in future wars. It is also quite obvious that local forces contributed detachments for the campaign or marched in their entirety to the north. I have here estimated that the two legions in Wales contributed *ca.* 6,000 foot and 600 cavalry for the expeditionary army, while the legion posted in Eboracum marched north in its entirety (*ca.* 5,000 infantry and 500 cavalry) because it was located in the combat zone. It is also safe to assume that at least half of the auxiliaries (11,500 foot and 5,000 cavalry) would have joined the expedition. When all of these figures are added together, my own estimation for the size of the land-based expeditionary army is some 85,000 infantry and 25,200 cavalry, but it is probable that this is an underestimation. Furthermore, this figure does not include the naval crews numbering in the tens of thousands, the support forces or the possible newly raised legions meant to occupy Caledonia. In other words, I consider the lower estimates such as have been made by Daquet-Gagey (p.424, 30,000–50,000 fighting men) and Simon Elliott (pp.65, 147, 162–63, a 50,000-man land army plus 7,000 men for the British Fleet) to be on the low side.

The sources provide too few details to make it possible to reconstruct the campaign in detail, which has caused many historians to resort to the use of archaeological evidence. The principal problem with the analysis of the archaeological evidence is that the record

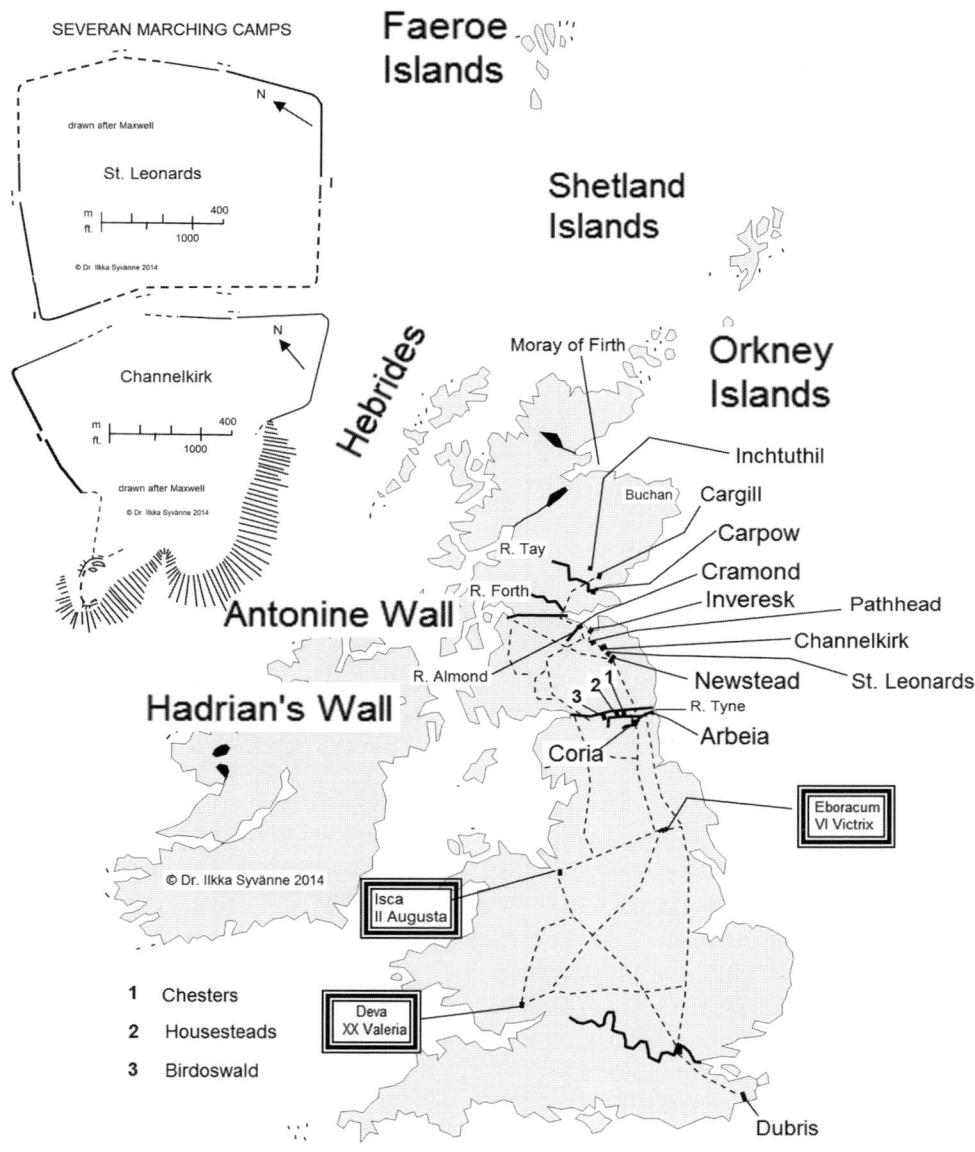

is incomplete, while most of the marching camps (well over 200 camps detected) do not include anything concrete to date them securely. This has led those who rely solely on the archaeological record to make a number of educated guesses which are actually at odds with the evidence provided by the narrative sources. I have noted these other reconstructions with their inherent problems in my biography of Caracalla, and it is because of this that I present only my own reconstruction of events in Britain.[12]

If we use the archaeological record for the estimation of the size of Severus' main field army, we have to base it on the known sizes of the extant large marching camps in the area between Hadrian's Wall and Cramond and the Antonine Wall. The camps in question are located at Newstead, St Leonards, Channelkirk and Pathhead, and their average size is about 165 acres (67 hectares). The next problem is that modern researchers have not found any consensus for the number of men such camps would have held. The typical range of estimates vary from 350 men per acre all the way up to 480 men per acre, which means that these camps could have housed armies of between 57,750 and 79,200 fighting men. However, we should not make the mistake of assuming that these camps would have housed the entire force taken to the campaign, because in addition to this there would have been the non-combatants and the naval forces. It is also very likely that another Roman force would have advanced along the other western Roman road leading from Hadrian's Wall to the Antonine Wall so that the Romans would have reoccupied the entire area between the walls. My own educated guess is that the detachments from Wales and the British auxiliaries (*ca*. 20,000 foot and 6,000 horse) advanced along the western road and the rest of the forces, comprising the main army (60,000 foot and 20,000 horse), took the eastern road to Cramond and the Antonine Wall, while the fleet sailed northwards along the coast. It is also clear that detachments would have been left to garrison important locales to secure the logistical network.[13]

The arrival of the emperors and the massive military preparations frightened the Britons. They duly sued for peace, but Severus dismissed their emissaries. Later events suggest that Caracalla would probably have promised them peace but would then have attacked them anyway, as probably would have younger Severus on the basis of what he did in 193, but this time Severus was seeking two things: military glory and the schooling of his sons, or at least Caracalla, in military life. In the absence of narrative detail, modern historians have once again used coins as evidence of what took place next. One of Septimius Severus's coins dated to 208 depicts a stone bridge over a river. This has been used to suggest that he had a stone bridge built over either the Forth or the Tay in 208, that he built the stone bridge over the Ouse at Eboracum (York) or that this bridge was built somewhere else. It is impossible to achieve any certainty regarding this, but if Severus did build a stone bridge in Britain it was certainly built in 208 in the friendly portion of the island, or at least with one end on the friendly side of the river. The other coin which has been used is one of Antoninus dated either to 208 or 209, depicting a bridge built of ships (a pontoon bridge) over a river. Once again this has led to suggestions that it represents a bridge built over the Forth or the Tay, or that it depicts all of the bridges built during the course of the 209 campaign. In my opinion, the latter suggestion is probably the likeliest alternative because the Romans certainly built many such bridges during that year.[14]

The attached illustrations from the Columns of Trajan and Marcus Aurelius, and on a coin of Septimius Severus, show the two different types of bridges used by the Romans around the second and early third centuries.

Severus spent the rest of 208 in the making of preparations for the offensive north of the Antonine Wall. This initial stage of the campaign appears to have consisted of the securing of the area up to the Antonine Wall, which was clearly rebuilt because the British tradition refers to the restoration of a turf wall by Severus. They also built a permanent forward base at Cramond to serve the operational needs further north. The fleet would have been anchored at the safe harbourage provided by the mouth of the River Almond near Cramond. It is possible that it was during this phase that Severus had the

Septimius and the stone bridge (source Cohen)

stone bridge built over the River Forth. The city of York served as the base of operations for this and subsequent stages of the campaign, and once the preparations for the war were finished, Severus left his son Geta there in charge of the administration. In practice he was guided by advisors and probably also by his mother, Julia Domna. However, it is possible that she joined her husband because there is a referral in Dio (77.16.5) to a discussion between a Caledonian woman (the wife of Argentocoxus Caledonian) and Julia Domna, but this is not conclusive because such a discussion could easily have taken place in York. It is entirely possible that this woman was a hostage or that her husband had become a Roman auxiliary.[15]

14.4. The expedition felicissima Britannica. Campaign Season 1: The year 209–210

The best way to approach this war is to present the evidence given by the narrative sources (Dio, Herodian and the *HA*) and the archaeological evidence. I will first present the archaeological evidence, which I will then put into context with the evidence provided by the written sources.

The Military Education for the sons: the Campaigns of 207–211   225

The accompanying map (drawn after Maxwell and Hanson) shows the marching camps that archaeologists consider date from the Severan period, together with camps which are thought to date from the Flavian period. The archaeologists usually interpret the evidence as that Severus divided his army into two divisions in 209, one led by him and the other by his son Antoninus, but the narrative sources prove this to be false so I have not included any variants of this version in the following discussion.[16] It is clear that the two emperors campaigned together during the first campaigning season. Military logic also backs this up. During the first campaign season, the intention was to force the enemy to fight a decisive battle, and the aim was to make certain that the Romans possessed numerical superiority if this happened.

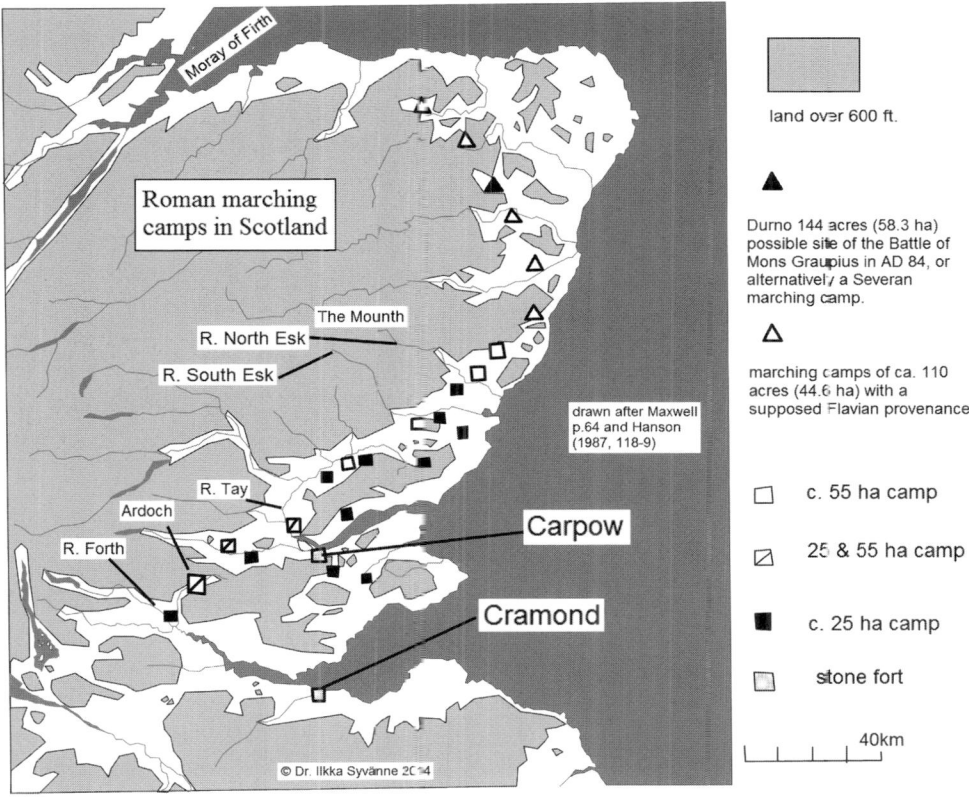

It is now time to turn to the evidence provided by the narrative sources for the first campaign, starting with what Herodian informs us:

'[Severus] received letters from the Governor of Britain relating that the barbarians there were in a state of insurrection, overrunning the country, driving off booty, and laying everything waste; so that for the defence of the island there was need either of greater force, or of the presence of the emperor himself. Severus heard this with pleasure, by nature a lover of glory, and anxious, after his victories in the east and north and his consequent titles, to obtain a trophy from the Britons: moreover, willing to withdraw his sons from Rome, that they might grow up in the discipline and sobriety of a military life, far removed from the blandishments and luxury prevalent in Rome, he ordered an expedition against Britain, although now old and labouring under an arthritic affection; but as to his mind, he was vigorous beyond any youth. For the most part he performed the march carried in a litter, nor did he ever continue long in one place. Having completed the journey with his sons, and crossed over the sea more quickly than could be described or expected, he advanced against the Britons, and having drawn together his soldiers from all sides, and concentrated a vast force, he prepared for war.

'The Britons, much struck with the sudden arrival of the emperor, and learning that such a mighty force was collected against them, sent ambassadors, sued for peace, and were willing to excuse their past transgressions. But Severus, purposefully seeking delay that he might not again return to Rome without his object, and, moreover, desirous to obtain from Britain a victory and a title, sent away their ambassadors without effecting their purpose, and prepared all things for the contest. He more especially endeavoured to render the marshy places stable by means of causeways, that his soldiers, treading with safety, might easily pass them, and, having firm footing, fight to advantage. For many parts of the British country, being constantly flooded by the tides of the ocean, become marshy. In these the natives are accustomed to swim and traverse about being immersed as high as their waists: for going naked as to the greater part of their bodies, they contemn the mud. Indeed they know not the use of clothing, but encircle their loins and necks with iron; deeming this an ornament and an evidence of opulence, in like manner as other barbarians esteem gold. But they puncture their bodies with pictured forms of every sort of animals; on which account they wear no clothing, lest they should hide the figures on their body. They are a most warlike and sanguinary race, carrying only a small shield and a spear, and a sword girded to their naked bodies. Of a breastplate or a helmet they know not the use, esteeming them an impediment to their progress through the marshes; from the vapours and exhalation of which the atmosphere in that country always appears dense.

'Against such things, therefore, Severus prepared whatever could be serviceable to the Roman army, but hurtful and detrimental to the designs of the barbarians. And when everything appeared to him sufficiently arranged for the war, Severus summoned Geta, the younger son, and left him in that part of the island which was subjugated to the Romans, for the purpose of administering justice and directing other civil matters of the government, giving him as assessors the more aged of his friends; and taking Antoninus with himself, he led the way against the barbarians. [This is the first campaign conducted by the united forces of Severus and Antoninus.] His army having passed beyond the rivers and fortresses which defended the Roman territory, there were frequent attacks and skirmishes and retreats on the side of the barbarians. To these, indeed, flight was an easy matter, and they lay hidden in the thickets and marshes through their local knowledge, all which things being adverse to the Romans, served to protract the war.' (Herodian 3.14.1ff., tr. by Giles, pp.157–58, with changes and comments)

The Military Education for the sons: the Campaigns of 207–211

Dio's version of events is as follows:

'Severus, seeing that his children were departing from their accustomed modes of life and that his legions were becoming enervated by idleness, set out on a campaign against Britain, though he knew that he should not return. He knew this chiefly from the stars under which he had been born, for he had them painted upon ceilings of the two halls in the palace where he was wont to hold court. Thus they were visible to all, save the portion which "regarded-the-hour" when he first saw the light (i.e. his horoscope). This he had not engraved in the same way in both the rooms. [How did Dio know this if he had not seen both? I would suggest that there is a very strong possibility that Septimius Severus had purposefully made his horoscope visible and emulated Augustus (Dio 56.23). His aim would have been to lure his potential enemies to consult the astrologers for the expected length of Severus's life, which these would report to him so that the persons could then be executed for treason – after all, the consulting of the horoscope was a clear evidence of hostile intent. This was a very clever ploy on Severus's part, which he had copied from Augustus, and his son Caracalla followed up his example (see my biography of him).] He knew it also by the report of the seers …. Unless Dio's own writing device, this is likely to be yet another example of Severus's ploys towards his superstitious subjects. The former, however, is more likely because Dio follows this with a standard description of an omen foretelling the death. Regardless, it still seems likely that Severus knew that death was approaching.] He took with him very great sums of money. There are two principal races of the Britons – the Caledonians and the Maeatae. The titles of the rest have all been reduced to these two. The Maeatae live near the cross wall which cuts the island in two [the Antonine Wall] and the Caledonians are behind them. Both inhabit wild and waterless mountains, desolate and swampy plains, holding no walls, nor cities, nor tilled fields, but living by pasturage and hunting and a few fruit trees. The fish, which are inexhaustible and past computing for multitude, they do not taste. They dwell naked and shoeless, possess their women in common, and rear in common all the offspring. Their form of government is mostly democratic and they are very fond of plundering.

'They go into battle on chariots with small, swift horses. There are also infantry, very quick at running and very firm in standing their ground. Their weapons are shield and a short spear, with a bronze apple attached to the end of the ground-spike, so that when the instrument is shaken it may clash and inspire the enemy with terror. They have also daggers. They can endure hunger and cold and any kind of wretchedness. They plunge into the swamps and exist there for many days with only their heads above water, and in the forests they support themselves upon bark and roots and in all cases they have ready a kind of food of which a piece the size of a bean [Simon Elliott (2018), p.133, notes on the basis of conclusions of Dr Brian Moffat this is likely to be the heath pea Lathyrus linifolius.] when eaten prevents them from being either hungry or thirsty. Of such nature is the island of Britain, and such are the inhabitants that the enemy's country has …. So Severus, desiring to subjugate the whole of it, invaded Caledonia. While traversing the territory he had untold trouble in cutting down the forests, reducing the levels of heights, filling up the swamps, and bridging the rivers. He fought no battle and beheld no adversary in battle array. The enemy purposely put sheep and cattle in front of them for the soldiers to seize, in order that the latter might be deceived for a longer time and wear themselves out. The Romans received great damage from the streams and were made objects of attack when they were scattered. Afterward, being unable to walk, they were slain by their own friends to avoid capture, so that nearly as many as 50,000 died. [This is definitely untrue. It is quite clear that Severus cannot have lost that many men and still forced the enemy to surrender. However, it is also possible that this is a mistake made by the epitomizer and should be interpreted as the number of barbarians killed.]

'But the emperor did not desist till he had approached the extremity of the island. Here he observed very accurately how slight degree the sun declined below the horizon and the length of days and nights both summer and winter. [This shows Severus's interest in learning and also that his forces went at least up to the Moray Firth, as suggested by Birley.] Thus having been conveyed practically the whole of the hostile region – for he was really conveyed in a covered litter most of the way on account of his weakness – he returned to friendly territory, first forcing the Britons to come to terms on condition that he should abandon a good part of their territory.

'Antoninus also disturbed him and involved him in vain worry by his intemperate life, by his evident intention to murder his brother if the chance should present itself, and finally by plotting against his own father. Once he leaped suddenly out of his quarters, shouting and bawling and feigning to have been wronged by Castor. This man was the best of the Caesarians attending upon Severus, had been trusted in his opinions, and had been assigned the duties of chamberlain. Certain soldiers with whom previous arrangements had been made hereupon gathered and joined [the] outcry; but they were checked in short order, as Severus himself appeared on the scene and punished the more unruly among them. [This is likely to present the instance during the 209–210 campaign when Antoninus learnt of the appointment of Geta as Augustus, presumably at the suggestion of Castor.]

'On another occasion both were riding to meet the Caledonians for the purpose of receiving them and holding a conference about a truce, and Antoninus undertook to kill his father outright with his own hand. [These events took place during the first campaign in 209–210 when father and son were campaigning together.] They were going along on their horses, for Severus, although his feet were rather shrunken by an ailment, [This actually suggests a wasting disease of feet muscles or nerve damage rather than gout or arthritis, as usually suggested by modern researchers, or that Severus had several simultaneous health problems of which the gout or arthritis formed only a part. In my opinion, the latter is likelier.] nevertheless was on horseback himself and the rest of the army was following: the enemy's force, too, was likewise a spectator. At this juncture, in the midst of the silence and order, [This is the standard way the Romans always approached the enemy. It was psychologically threatening and enabled the soldiers to hear the commands.] Antoninus reined up his horse and drew his sword, apparently intending to strike his father in the back. Seeing this, the other horsemen in the

The Military Education for the sons: the Campaigns of 207–211   229

detachment raised a cry of alarm, which scared the son, so that he did nothing further. [Even if one cannot entirely rule out the possibility that Antoninus was angry over the appointment of Geta as Augustus,[17] I would suggest that it is likelier that Antoninus was actually about to give an order for the Roman forces to attack the enemy, as he was in the habit of doing when sole emperor. It is even possible that Severus had ordered Antoninus to do this so that he would not be held responsible for the resulting butchery, but that his soldiers made this impossible.] Severus turned at their shout and saw the sword: however, he uttered not a syllable but ascended the tribunal, finished what he had to do, and returned to the general's tent. Then he called his son and Papinian and Castor, ordered a sword to be placed within easy reach, and upbraided the youth for having dared to do such a thing at all and especially for having been on the point of committing so great a crime in the presence of all the allies and the enemy. Finally he said: "Now if you desire to slay me and have done, put an end to me here. You are strong I am an old man and prostrate. If you have no objection to this, but shrink from becoming my actual murderer, there stands by your side Papinianus the prefect, whom you may order to put me out of the way. He will certainly do anything that you command, since you are an emperor." Though he spoke in this fashion, he still did the plotter no harm, in spite of the fact that he had often blamed Marcus for not ending the life of Commodus and that he had himself often threatened his son with this treatment. Such words, however, were invariably spoken in a fit of anger: on this occasion he allowed his love of offspring to get the better of his love of country; [All of this is likely to be lies of Dio, who was intensely hostile towards Caracalla.] yet in doing so he simply betrayed his other child, for he well knew what would happen.' (Dio 77.11.1ff., tr. by Forster, p.383ff., with comments and changes)

Finally, we have the version as told by Aelius Spartianus:

'On one occasion when he [Severus] so suffered from gout as to delay a campaign, his soldiers in their dismay conferred on his son, who was with him at the time [i.e. it was 209–210], the title of Augustus. Severus, however, had himself lifted up and carried to the tribunal, summoned all the tribunes, centurions, *duces* [generals in charge of detachments] and cohorts responsible for this occurrence, and after commanding his son, who had received the name Augustus, to stand up, gave orders that all the authors of this deed save only his son, should be punished. When they threw themselves before the tribunal and begged for pardon, Severus touched his head with his hand and said, "Now at last you know that the head does the ruling, and not the feet." [If Aelius Spartianus has reported this incident correctly, it is likely that it took place under the following conditions. Severus was himself forced to stay inactive inside his tent thanks to his ailing health, while his son, Antoninus, conducted some very successful military operation against the natives, with the result that when he returned to the camp the soldiers hailed him alone as Augustus. This would have naturally angered Severus when he heard the shouts inside his tent, with the above result. The incident also proves that the ailing health of Severus probably hampered operations during his last campaign.] And even after fortune had led him step by step through the pursuits of study and of warfare even to the throne, he used to say: "Everything have I been, and nothing have I gained."' (Aelius Spartianus, *HA Sev.* 18.9–11, tr. by Magie, with slight changes and comments)

The sources do not mention any sea battles between the Romans and Britons, but even with the seagoing liburnae it would have been an easy task for the Romans to sink the types of ships/boats (small clinkers and curraghs) employed by the Britons at this time. It is possible that some small scale action took place if the Romans managed to surprise the Britons before they could flee.

Seagoing Liburna
length 42m; each side 50 oars in two ranks/remes for a total of 100 oars.
Crew: 1 captain, 3 officers, 6 sailors, 24 marines, 50 upper rank rowers; 50 lower rank rowers; total 134.

Skuldelev 5, c. 1050, 26 men, 17.4 x 2.6 x 1.1m

© Dr. Ilkka Syvanne 2014

(source for the *liburna*: Pitassi)

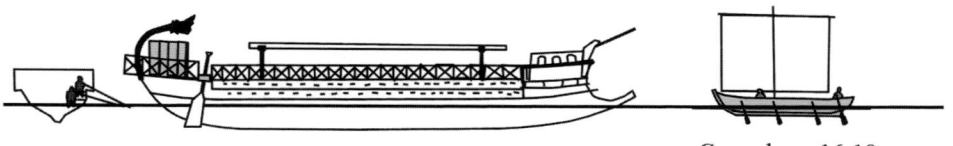

Curragh ca. 16-18 men

On the basis of Dio and Herodian, it is clear that the British fighting tactics had remained largely the same since the first century AD.[18] However, there is one major difference, which is that instead of attempting to fight pitched battles against the invaders, the Britons had learned their lesson and concentrated on fighting guerrilla warfare against the invaders. Regardless, it is still clear on the basis of these descriptions that the Britons could fight effectively at close quarters when they decided to so. It was just that they now did that only in small-scale encounters with Roman foraging or raiding parties, rather than with the main army. This was the clever thing to do. The main army was too large a bite for them. The sources are silent about any naval encounters, so it is possible that the Romans did not face any problems along the coasts or rivers, which is not surprising in light of their massive naval superiority. However, I would not preclude the possibility that the Romans could have encountered some barbarian boats or ships by surprise, and if they did, then it is quite easy to see that the combat would have ended in victory for the fast Roman *liburnae* because, even if these ships were small by Roman standards, they were still huge behemoths by barbarian standards (see the accompanying illustrations). Indeed, Roman ship designs were vastly superior to anything that they faced anywhere.[19]

The main reason for the use of archaeology to trace the route taken by the Romans is that Dio did not give any detailed information regarding this route. It is this that has led to the false conclusion that I referred to above. What Dio's text, and those of others, make

The Military Education for the sons: the Campaigns of 207–211

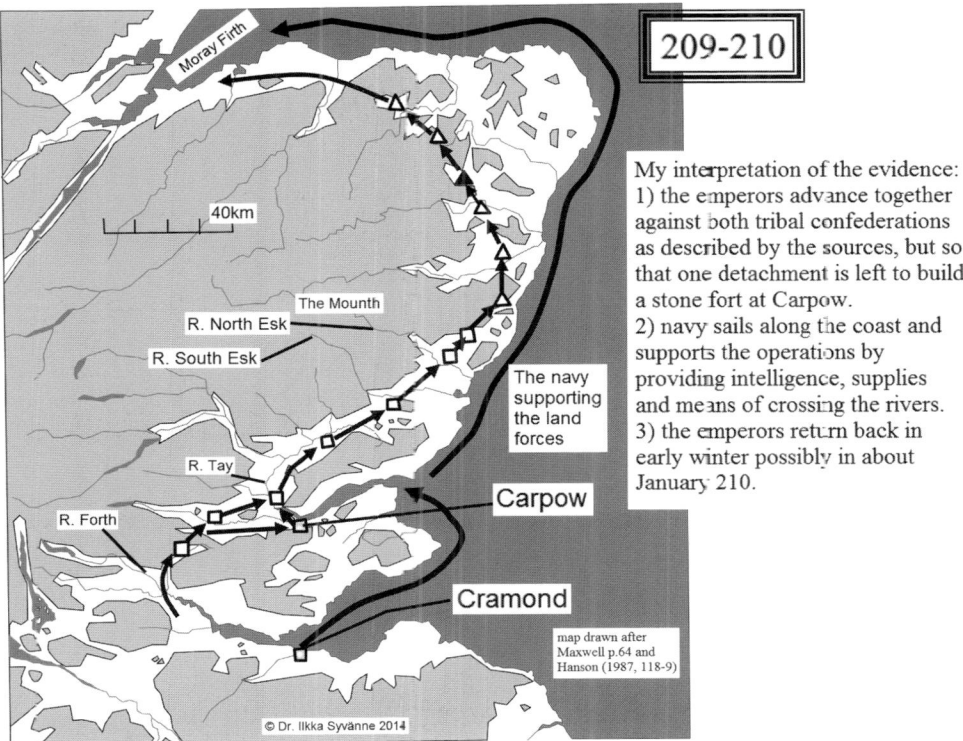

abundantly clear is that the emperors travelled together during the first campaign and that Severus reached the extremity of the island. The attached map shows the likely marching route and the most probable route taken by the fleet in 209. The guerrilla tactics used by the natives failed because the Romans were not dependent on local supplies but brought their own in ships and wagons. This enabled the Romans to outlast the barbarians in a contest of wills. The Romans caused much more damage to the enemy than they did to the Romans, for the livestock and fields provided the livelihood for the natives, which the Romans pillaged and torched. Roman tactics against the guerrilla raids were simple but effective. They first built a safe base camp from which they sent detachments to pillage the surrounding area, after which they moved forward to repeat the same until the enemy submitted.[20]

The sources state that the reason for the appointment of Geta as Augustus, which as I have noted probably took place during the campaign of 209–210, is that Severus wanted to safeguard his younger son against the likely aggression of Antoninus. It is quite possible that this was indeed the reason, but it is also possible that he simply wanted to emulate Antoninus Pius – as claimed by Aelius Spartianus – who left Marcus Aurelius and Lucius Verus as his successors. As we shall see, whatever Severus's intentions were, these failed. In my biography of Caracalla I have also speculated that Antoninus and Julia Domna may have renewed their affair during this campaign – what is practically certain is that the affair was renewed very soon after the death of Severus – with the result that when this news was brought to Severus, perhaps by Castor, Geta was nominated as Augustus, which in its turn would have led to the quite public outcry in front of Severus's tent described above. Unfortunately, it is impossible to be certain on these matters because the sources are so sparing with their details. Whatever the truth, it is clear that Antoninus was angered by it and the brothers were not reconciled by this move.[21]

There is only one possible piece of evidence for the activities of Geta and the imperial administration left behind at York, if we accept Birley's (2000, pp.179–80) suggestion that the martyrdom of St Alban should be dated to this time rather than during the reign of Diocletian. This is obviously very uncertain because all sources date it to the reign of Diocletian, even if the actual circumstances better fit the year 209 than the time period claimed. The reason for this is that the impious Caesar in charge ended the persecution of Christians in the name of the *Augusti* because it only increased the numbers of Christians. This is a very odd claim to have happened under Caesar Constantius I, who would not have been called impious in the first place and who never began any persecution which he would have then stopped, hence Birley's suggestion. The other point is that Birley's claim actually receives support from the British tradition, which connects the war with the persecution of Christians. If Geta did put a stop to the persecution of Christians in Britain, it was certainly a very wise move – the problem with it is the fact that the sources credit his brother Antoninus with this policy. However, the problem can be solved with the supposition that Geta ended the persecution in Britain when it became clear that is was counterproductive, while Caracalla ended it everywhere else.[22]

14.5. The 210 Campaign by Antoninus and the Death of Severus at York on 4 February 211

The peace agreement conducted with the northern barbarians led to the misperception that the war would now be over. However, it was during this period that Severus sought to organize the newly conquered territories while also making certain that the defences were in good shape. The quote below from Aelius Spartianus gives one such instance, showing the ever-dutiful Severus inspecting reconstruction work at the western end of Hadrian's Wall. This took place after his return from the north, but clearly before the next campaign, which was led by his son Antoninus alone.

> 'On another occasion, when he was returning to his nearest quarters from an inspection of the wall at Luguvallum [Carlisle, just south of the western end of Hadrian's Wall] in Britain, at a time when he not only proved victorious but had concluded a perpetual peace, [after the 209–210 campaign, presumably either in the winter or spring of 210] just as he was wondering what omen would present itself, an Ethiopian soldier, ["*Aethiops quidam e numero militari*", meaning presumably a soldier belonging to the *numeri*.] who was famous among buffoons and always a notable jester, met him with a garland of cypress-boughs [this refers to Pluto, god of the underworld, as noted by S. Elliott (2018), p.168] … when Severus in rage ordered that the man be removed from his sight, troubled as he was by the man's ominous colour and the ominous nature of the garland, the Ethiopian by way of jest cried, it is said, "You have been all things, you have conquered all things, now

O conqueror, be a god.'" (Aelius Spartianus, *HA Sev.* 22.4–5, tr. by Magie, p.425, with changes and comments)

The peace achieved as a result of the first campaign proved temporary. The Maeatae revolted very soon after the emperors left, although the sources do not give us a reason. Consequently, we are forced to speculate. It is possible that the terms had been just too harsh for them and that they revolted for this reason. Birley (p.186) has suggested that one possible reason for the revolt could be the upsetting realization that the Romans were there to stay, the most important demonstration of which would have been the building of the stone fortress at Carpow, in particular as the tribal centre of the Maeatae was located only a mile away – at least the later Pictish capital, Abernathy, was and it is very likely that it was built on top of the old tribal centre. The following passages from Dio and Herodian show that this time Severus adopted a policy of extermination as a form of punishment, and that the campaign was conducted by Antoninus Caracalla alone because Severus was too ill to participate. Dio writes:

> 'Upon another revolt of the inhabitants of the island he summoned the soldiers and bade them invade the rebels' country, killing whomsoever they should encounter .... [This campaign was led by Antoninus in person, as Herodian's account shows. This would also have been the campaign in which the Roman army was spread out to devastate as wide an area as possible, which the archaeologists have mistaken to be the first campaign. Severus's order to exterminate the Maeatae actually resulted in the spreading of the revolt because the Caledonians feared that they would be the next object of attack.] When this had been done and the Caledonians had joined the revolt of the Maeatae, he proceeded with preparations to make war upon them in person. While he was thus engaged his sickness carried him off on the fourth of February. Antoninus, it is said, contributed something to the result. [It is possible that this is meant to blacken Caracalla's fame, but Anne Daguet-Gagey has suggested an attractive alternative, namely that this would have actually been an act of mercy on Antoninus's part so we should see the killing as euthanasia. This is a plausible suggestion, but we will probably never know for certain what happened.] Before he closed his eyes he is reputed to have spoken these words to his children ... "Be harmonious, enrich the soldiers, scorn everybody else." After this his body arrayed in military garb was placed upon a funeral pyre, and as a mark of honour the soldiers and his children ran about it. Those present who had any military gifts threw them upon it and the sons applied the fire. Later his bones were put in a jar of purple stone, conveyed to Rome, and deposited in the tomb of the Antonines. It is said that Severus sent for the jar a little before his death and after feeling it over remarked: "Thou shall hold a man that the world could not hold." ... After this Antoninus secured the entire power. Nominally he ruled with his brother, but in reality alone and at once. [This proves that Antoninus had performed admirably during the 210 campaign, because it is very difficult to see how the soldiers would have been behind him otherwise.]' Dio 77.15.1–78.1, tr. by Forster, p.387ff., with comments and changes)

Herodian's version of these events is as follows:

> 'Severus, being now old and infirm, was seized with a lingering illness that rendered him quite incapable of outdoor life. This obliged him to commit the command of the campaign to Antoninus, but he was not interested in the war against the barbarians. [This is the second campaign which took place in 210.] Instead he tried to canvass the soldiers' support for him and cause them to see him as their monarch while perpetually slandering his brother. He considered it a troublesome nuisance that it took so long for his long suffering father to die as a result of his drawn-out illness and therefore tried to persuade his father's doctors and servants to speed up the death with some deed while they tended his father. At last Severus wasted away but [was] really broken by grief after having acquired greater glory in war than any of the emperors before him. None of the emperors could boast of so many victories won both in civil wars against his rivals and in foreign expeditions against the barbarians. He reigned eighteen years and was succeeded by his sons to whom he left more treasure than any father ever bequeathed before and a military power so formidable that nothing could resist it. [The full state coffers and superbly drilled army that was used to winning all wars was Severus's greatest gift to his sons. It was this military machine that Caracalla led to greater military accomplishments on foreign soil than any of his predecessors, his father included.]' (Herodian 3.15.1ff., tr. by Hart, pp.155–56, with changes and comments)

As I have noted in my biography of Caracalla, the nature of the mission, which was to kill everyone the Romans met, suggests that it was now that the Roman army adopted the use of at least two or possibly three separate divisions to fulfil the wishes of the emperor (see accompanying map). The terror tactic, however, was a failure as it merely incited the Caledonians to revolt. Even if the sources fail to mention why the Caledonians joined their brethren in rising up, it seems very likely that they feared they would be the next target of this butchery. There might also be another reason for this, which is that they were exploiting a power vacuum that would have been created if Severus had left garrisons in Caledonian territory that were now withdrawn to march south and crush the revolt. The presence of Roman garrisons in Caledonia is implied by the terms of the peace, which included the handing over of lands to the Romans.[23]

Both Dio and Herodian try to blacken Caracalla's skills as commander and his motives by claiming that his only goal was to canvass support for himself. This allegation is easily proved false, however, because the best way to canvass support from the soldiers was to prove himself an effective general that was able to freely distribute booty to his troops and officers. It is therefore clear that Antoninus Caracalla performed his duties as a general very effectively, inflicting horrible damage on the enemy – a veritable extermination of the people, as was required by his father's command. Regardless of this, it is still clear that Antoninus's principal goal was to gain the military's support for himself because he knew that his father was in very poor health. In this he seems to have been successful because he was the de facto ruler immediately after the death of his father.[24]

The revolt of Caledonia appears to have caused Antoninus to change the Roman strategy so that he stopped roughly at the border between the Maeatae and Caledonians,

The Military Education for the sons: the Campaigns of 207–211

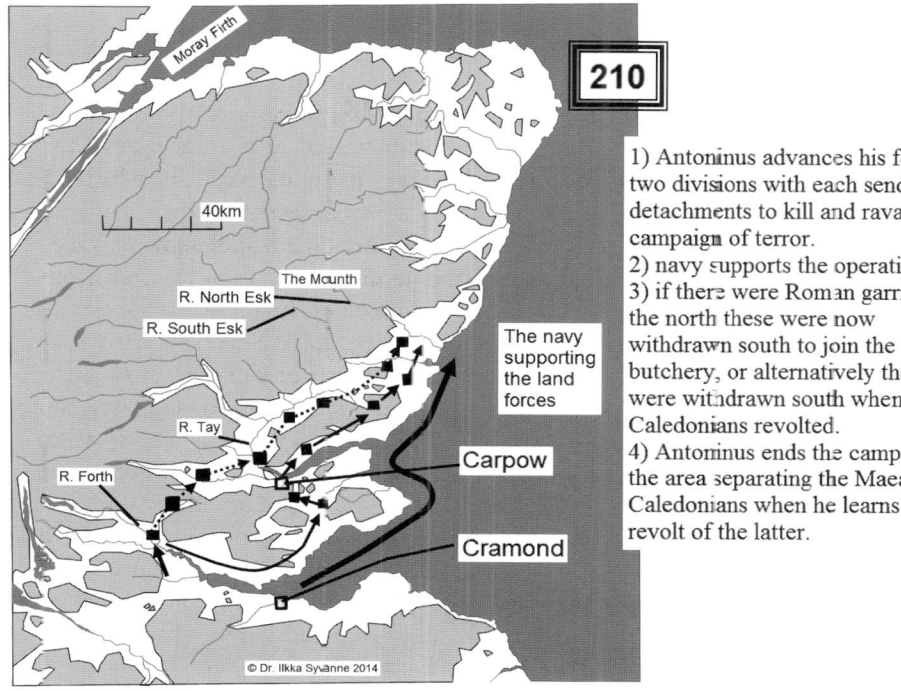

1) Antoninus advances his forces in two divisions with each sending detachments to kill and ravage in a campaign of terror.
2) navy supports the operation.
3) if there were Roman garrisons in the north these were now withdrawn south to join the butchery, or alternatively these were withdrawn south when the Caledonians revolted.
4) Antoninus ends the campaign in the area separating the Maeatae and Caledonians when he learns of the revolt of the latter.

after which he withdrew because he now faced far larger numbers of hostile forces around him than had been foreseen. When the news of this was brought to Severus, he prepared to lead the campaign in person the following year. These preparations in the middle of winter, however, appear to have been too much for his poor health. After a long and difficult illness, Septimius Severus breathed his last on 4 February 211. Those who were hostile towards Antoninus Caracalla claimed that he either speeded up the death or attempted to bribe the doctors to poison his father, and when this failed then executed the doctors because they had not obeyed him. Anne Daguet-Gagey has suggested that Antoninus's actions were actually merciful in intent, wanting to end the sufferings of his father with euthanasia. This is quite possible but cannot be proven.[25] The quotation below (tr. by Banchich) from the so-called *Epitome de Caesaribus*, which is usually considered to be an abbreviated version of Aurelius Victor's books, may actually imply that both Antoninus and Severus were trying to convince the doctors to give Severus a drug to end his suffering. On the other hand, the fact that Severus died after a heavy meal may also suggest that they were ultimately successful in their demand if the drug was placed in the food. However, if Herodian is correct, then the demand put by the son and father to the doctors was ultimately unsuccessful, and it was because of their refusal to put an end to his father's suffering that Antoninus had the doctors killed. I would suggest that the likeliest course of events was that Severus wanted euthanasia and was denied this by his doctors, with the result that Antoninus punished them.

> 'When he was unable to endure the pain of all his limbs, especially upon his feet, in place of a drug, which was being denied him, he too avidly fell upon a meal large

and of very much meat, since he was unable to digest this [suggesting that Severus's health was affected by multiple problems], he was overcome by the indisposition and breathed his last.' (*Epitome* 20.9, tr. by Banchich)

The sources differ on the last words of Severus. Dio claims that his last words to his son were: 'Be harmonious, enrich the soldiers, scorn everybody else.' Then after this, just before his death, he stated: "Come, give it to us, if we have anything to do!", which showed that Severus wanted to work until his very last moment. Aelius Spartianus (*HA Sev.* 23.3ff.), however, writes that Severus's last words (tr. by Hart, pp.254–55, with changes) were: 'When I received the state, I found it disturbed on every side. I leave it in peace, even in Britain. Old and lame, as I am, I leave the Empire firm with my two Antonini, if they are good: But feeble if they are bad.' After which, he gave the last watchword to the tribune: '*Laboramus* (let us toil).' It is impossible to know who is correct, because both versions were clearly meant to convey a message to the readers. It is quite possible that Severus said all of these things during his final moments, and that the difference results from the fact that the last words were reported by different people who had been at Severus's bedside at different times as he neared death.

14.6. Caracalla's Campaign in 211 and the End of the British War

Dio's text indicates that Caracalla had the real power in his hands from the start. This means that despite Caracalla apparently attempting to have himself declared the sole emperor, he simultaneously sought some sort of reconciliation with his brother, presumably in such a manner that Geta would have officially recognized him as his superior. However, when this was not forthcoming, the brothers attempted at least to present a united front by minting coins that celebrated their harmony as rulers, as shown for example by the attached drawing. From the start, Antoninus possessed the means to have his brother killed, but chose not to do so because he attempted a reconciliation with him. Aelius Spartianus's (*HA Car.* 2) words put into the mouth of Antoninus, in which he defended his actions to the Praetorians, sound right. He claimed that he had given his brother every indulgence possible and had even saved him from a conspiracy, but that his brother had repaid this with treachery.[26]

The fact that the Caledonians had revolted created urgency in the situation. Caracalla could not linger in York in an effort to secure his position, with the result that Geta was

Caracalla's Concordia coin with Geta a. 211. Note that the emperor on the left (presumably Caracalla) gives a baton or scroll to the one on the right.
This probably implies a superior position. Drawn after Cohen.

able to gain for himself the support of those who remained behind while his brother campaigned in the north. However, this campaigning enabled Antoninus to endear himself further with the troops, which was later to have great significance. It was presumably during this period that Antoninus abandoned his shaven look and grew a beard to increase his popularity with the soldiers, just as his brother was doing. However, Antoninus never grew a long beard, only a shorter military version, while Geta grew a longer one to endear himself with the conservative senators. Antoninus's two principal goals for the fighting in 211 were to win the commanders (legates, prefects and *duces*) and soldiers over to his side with promises, bribes and booty, and to conduct a successful campaign which would further endear him to them.[27]

Dio relates the following details about events following the demise of Severus:

'After this [the death of his father] Antoninus secured the entire power. Nominally he ruled with his brother, but in reality alone and at once. With the enemy he came to terms [i.e. Antoninus forced them to come to the terms through the success of his campaign], withdrew from their country [i.e. he had advanced to Caledonia], and abandoned the forts [this appears to have been partially true because if there were any forts in Caledonian territory, these were abandoned; but it was not true of the territory held by the Maeatae, where the Romans kept a presence at least until the death of Caracalla]. But his own people he either dismissed (as Papianus the prefect) or else killed (as Euodus, his nurse, Castor, and his wife Plautilla, and the latter's brother Plautius) .... Antoninus had first had the desire to murder his brother while his father was still alive, but had been unable to do so at that time because of Severus, or later, on the road, because of the legions. [This hostile claim by Dio is easy to prove false because he includes material which contradicts this. Caracalla actually sought reconciliation to the last, and even saved his brother once. For this, see my biography of Caracalla.] The men felt very kindly toward the younger son, especially because in appearance he was the very image of his father. [The growing of the beard was a conscious plan by Geta to make his appearance resemble his father's, while it also endeared him with the senatorial party. Caracalla also adopted this same appearance to endear himself with the soldiers. Again, see my biography of Caracalla for further details.] But when Antoninus arrived in Rome, he got rid of this rival also.' (Dio 78.1.1ff., tr. by Forster, p.3, with changes and comments)

Herodian's version is as follows:

'When therefore Antoninus found he could not obtain his ends from the army [to be declared as the sole emperor], he treated with the barbarians, and granted them a peace and having received hostages of their faith, he left their territories and marched back again in haste to his brother and mother. [The fact that Antoninus was no longer with Geta and Julia Domna at the time he negotiated with the barbarians means that he had marched north against them. The fact that the enemies gave hostages to Antoninus means that he had beaten the barbarians in combat because hostages were given only when defeated.]' (Herodian 3.15.6, tr. by Hart, p.159, with changes and comments)

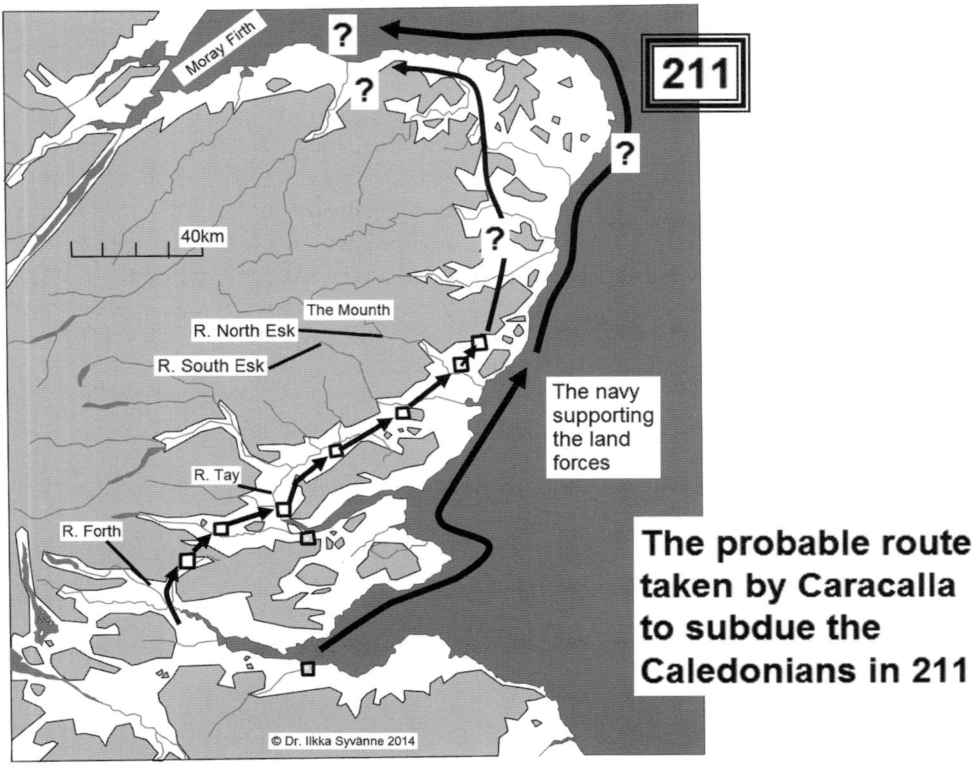

238 Emperor Septimius Severus

The probable route taken by Caracalla to subdue the Caledonians in 211

Coin celebrating the Victoria Britannica of Septimius Severus
Source: Cohen.

The fact that Antoninus marched against the Caledonians in person, defeated them and then forced them to accept his terms of peace means that he ventured further north than previously, his aim having been to subdue the Caledonians. It is therefore likely that his invasion route followed the one adopted in 209. After Antoninus had achieved his goals, he returned to Eburocum. Following this, the brothers began their march to Rome to bury the bones of their father at the Antonine Mausoleum and secure the support of the Senate. The resulting power struggle ended in the death of Geta, for which see my biography of Caracalla.

The campaign had failed to achieve the total subjugation of the island because the sons of Severus lacked the will to continue it to its conclusion, but it had still ended in great success, despite what Dio claims. The Caledonians had recognized the Romans as their masters by handing over hostages and becoming allies of Rome, while the Romans retained a military presence in the north of the province, which is proven by the existence of the garrison at Carpow both under Caracalla and afterwards, as is noted for example by Maxwell (p.36). Maxwell states that Dio's claim that the forts were abandoned immediately is incorrect. Furthermore, the Antonine Wall and the areas just north of it retained their position as the border of the Roman Empire.[28]

Chapter 15

Septimius Severus, 'The Most Glorious of the Emperors'

I have shown that Septimius Severus was very highly esteemed by most of the commentators in his own day and afterwards. A quotation from Dio, included below, shows that even those who were critical of him and his achievements were still forced to admit that he belonged to the category of great Roman emperors. Aelius Spartianus also provides information about the surplus left behind by Severus, but I start with the praise that Herodian (3.15.2) showered on the deceased emperor because it summarises the period view nicely:

> 'At last Severus wasted away but really broken by grief after having acquired greater glory in war than any of the emperors before him. None of the emperors could boast of so many victories won both in civil wars against his rivals and in foreign expeditions against the barbarians.' (Herodian 3.15.2, tr. by Hart, p.156)

Dio is far less positive of his achievements:

> 'He [Severus] was small of stature but strong, though eventually grew very weak from gout: mentally he was very keen and very firm. [As I have already noted above, Severus was one of the great innovators of the Roman Empire. He not only reformed the military and its tactics, but also introduced new civilian institutions to make those function more efficiently.] He wished for more education than he got and for this reason he was sagacious rather than a good speaker. [His great enthusiasm also shows in the good education that he gave his sons. It was thanks to this education and the example that Severus showed that Caracalla become one of the greatest Roman military leaders ever, if not the greatest.] Towards friends not forgetful, to enemies most oppressive, he was capable of everything said about him. Hence he gathered money from every source (save that he killed no one to get it) and met all necessary expenditures quite grudgingly. He restored very many of the ancient buildings and inscribed upon them his own name to signify that he had repaired them so as to be new structures, and from his private funds. Also he spent a great deal uselessly upon renovating and repairing other places [This shows Dio's hostility because periodical renovation is necessary for the upkeep of infrastructure and culture. The renovation of public buildings is confirmed by Aelius Spartianus *HA Sev.* 23. However, Spartianus claims that Severus did not often put his name on these restorations.], erecting, for instance, to Bacchus and Hercules a temple of huge size. Yet, though his expenses were enormous, he left behind not merely a few myriad *denarii*, easily reckoned, but a great many. Again, he rebuked such

persons as were not chaste, even going to the extent of enacting certain laws in regard to adultery, with the result that there were any number of prosecutions for that offence … he too ceased to trouble his head about it.' (Dio 77.16.1f, tr. by Forster, pp.388–89, with changes and comments)

Aelius Spartianus comments on the good shape in which Severus left the Empire:

> 'At his death he left in the public stores corn to serve for seven years to come, enough to be distributed 75,000 modii a day … and oil in such quantity that it was sufficient not only for the city of Rome, but for all Italy for five years if there was need for it.' (Aelius Spartianus, *HA Sev.* 23.2, tr. by Hart, pp.254–55, with changes)

Septimius Severus possessed a brilliant mind, which enabled him to outsmart his enemies in a civil war and to reform the military. He was indeed a Roman Hannibal, a man prepared to fool others with flowery words and promises. reintroducing military trickery as the principal means of defeating enemies. He was also the first emperor who fully understood that his own position depended entirely on the support of the military, and because of this that he bribed its members as much as he could. As noted by Herodian, Severus defeated more enemies than any of his predecessors, including three competing Roman emperors. The first, Julianus, he defeated with his intellect alone, fooling Albinus to back his cause. The second, Niger, he defeated in the first instance by organizing a massive combined and joint operation that was swiftly carried out, and then through the good services of his generals and soldiers. The third of the rivals to the imperial purple, Albinus, he defeated in a truly gargantuan struggle in which although he did not demonstrate any military brilliance, he still won thanks to his vastly superior military forces. It is unlikely to be a coincidence that the soldiers who served under Severus performed so well that Herodian noted that he left behind an invincible military machine. Severus knew how to motivate his soldiers, and it is also probable that he reformed their organization and fighting tactics so that his armies reached the greatest possible combat effectiveness. On top of this, Severus defeated a succession of other enemies, comprising the Oshroeni, Adiabeni, Arabs, Parthians, Samaritans, Jews, Moors and finally the Maeatae and Caledonians. He also crushed or assassinated a succession of domestic enemies who had been plotting against him, meaning that he was able to die peacefully in bed – a rarity for Roman emperors.

Severus made one major mistake in his career, which was to trust Plautianus, a move which came close to costing him his life. Fortunately for Severus, however, the man tasked by Plautianus to perform the murder betrayed the plot. There is of course the possibility that it was Caracalla who had plotted the downfall of Plautianus. but if he did then this certainly saved both Severus and Caracalla from an eventual assassination attempt by Plautianus. Severus also made a serious mistake at the siege of Hatra, but that was not nearly so costly as his blind trust in Plautianus.

Both Aelius Spartianus (*HA Sev.* 18.4ff.) and Aurelius Victor (20.20ff.) shower praise on Severus, stating that he was absolutely implacable to the guilty and to those who failed, while he rewarded ability and efficiency. This assessment appears to be generally accurate, even if one may wonder whether the promotion of Plautianus, Cassius Dio or

Macrinus belong to this category. On the other hand, their major weaknesses appear to have been character rather than performance of duty. Plautianus was certainly very efficient as a spy master, and it is quite possible that both Dio and Macrinus were good legal experts, even if their knowledge of military and other matters was negligible. What is certain is that those appointed by Severus performed their jobs well, because the Roman armed forces he left to his son defeated all the enemies they came across, while there is no definite evidence for the civilian administration performing its functions any more poorly than it did at other times. The fact that Severus appointed equestrians as commanders of his newly created legions is also indicative of his readiness to promote ability. However, it should be remembered that this statement is a generalization. It is clear that Severus did not promote all people of excellence, because many could have posed a threat to the emperor himself. The most notable example of this is the murder of Laetus, who was certainly the most gifted military commander of his day – in fact too successful for his own good. Some of the most gifted commanders during the reign of Severus, however, for example Tiberius Claudius Candidus, had already been promoted to high command under Marcus Aurelius, the cream rising to the top during the Marcomannic War. The same was also true, though, of Severus's wars, the combat performance of the Roman commanders enabling him to promote those who had a gift for fighting.

Septimius Severus's personal life was not a happy one. He lost his first wife, while his second wife, Julia Domna, proved to be an adulteress, on top of which it is probable that she also slept with her son or stepson, Caracalla. As noted by both Aelius Spartianus (*HA Sev.* 18.8ff.) and Aurelius Victor (20.23ff.), the scandalous behaviour of his wife tarnished the otherwise great fame of Severus.[1] Severus was also unable to reconcile his sons with each other, which can probably be counted as his second major mistake. It is very likely that he bears at least part of the responsibility for the death of Geta in the power struggle that followed his death, because he had initially designated only Caracalla as his successor, and when he then also nominated Geta as Augustus to save his life, as it is claimed, this actually sealed his fate. When the two brothers had officially equal powers in a situation in which Caracalla was really the man in charge, it spelled trouble. The only way to save Geta's life would have been to make Geta a commoner, just like Septimius Severus's own brother Geta had been. With Geta able to think of himself as the equal of Caracalla, he was bound to listen to those who urged him to kill his brother, and Caracalla was not a man who would surrender his position.

Aelius Spartianus (*HA Sev.* 20) claims that Severus imitated Antoninus Pius when he nominated both Antoninus Caracalla and Geta as emperors. It is indeed possible that this was his plan. In the case of Marcus Aurelius and Lucius Verus, both were indeed Augusti with officially similar powers, but in practice Verus accepted Aurelius as the senior emperor. One wonders whether this was also Severus's plan, because it is clear that even after the promotion of Geta as Augustus, he trusted military campaigns only to Caracalla. There was thus the implication that Geta was to serve in a lesser capacity as an emperor who controlled taxation and logistics while Caracalla was in charge of the armed forces. If this was Severus's plan, it failed miserably because Geta was not ready to accept Caracalla as his superior, even in a situation in which Dio (78.1) stated in no uncertain terms that after the death of Severus the two brothers were nominally equal but in practice Caracalla assumed all powers. This means that it was Caracalla who was the patient one of the brothers and who followed up the plans of his father, as I have already noted in my biography of him.

Whatever the truth of the above, it is clear that Severus was heartbroken by the situation, and felt that he had not achieved anything with his studies, warfare and imperial rule. Aelius Spartianus (*HA Sev.* 18.11) claims that he was in the habit of saying this quite openly with the words: 'I have been all things, and nothing have I gained.'

Regardless, it is clear that Septimius Severus's legacy for the Roman Empire was a very positive one. The Romans would get their most successful military leader ever in the form of Caracalla, who inherited from his father an invincible military machine and state coffers full of money. Caracalla was a man made in the mould of his father – both were prepared to fool their enemies with promises they did not intend to keep – but with the difference that Caracalla was more violent by nature than his father. If one wants to sum up Septimius Severus as a man and ruler, nothing is better than what the *Epitome* (20.5) stated. This text called Severus the most warlike of all men who had lived up to that moment. It is for that reason little wonder that his successor as emperor, his son Caracalla, was even more warlike and fierce than he was. Consequently, as I have stated in my biography of Caracalla, perhaps the greatest gift that Severus gave for the Romans was the superb upbringing and education that he provided for his son.

A bust of Severus (Louvre) according to Duruy.

Appendix 1

Arrian and Roman Battle Tactics

Aim

The aim of this appendix is to shed light on Roman tactics in the second century. The approach is to use Arrian's *Technê Taktikê* (*Handbook of Tactics*) and *Ektaxis kata Alanôn* (*Expedition against the Alans*) as the basis of this analysis. The reason for this is that Arrian was an experienced military commander who knew the combat methods of his day. I will analyze the contents of both treatises and then compare this information with other evidence that we possess. Both treatises were written during Arrian's tenure as governor of the province of Cappadocia from 130/131 to 137/138. I will also include my own diagrams and those taken from the *Byzantine Interpolation of Aelian* (*Codex Burnley*) to illustrate what Arrian meant.

Background

Arrian's date of birth was at some point between AD 85 and 90. His birthplace was Nicomedia in Bithynia and he belonged to a family of Romanized Greeks, receiving an excellent education. He appears to have idolized and emulated the career of Xenophon the Athenian. Consequently, Arrian became the pupil of the Stoic philosopher Epictetus, joined the Roman military and, just like his idol, wrote a number of technical and philosophical treatises and histories. Arrian appears to have served in Trajan's invasion forces in the Dacian and Parthian wars, after which he was adlected to the Senate by his friend and emperor Hadrian. Arrian then served as a legate of a legion in the Danubian region, and as a governor of Baetica in Spain in about 125. He became a suffect consul in 129 or 130, and then governor of Cappadocia from 130/131 to 137/138. In this capacity, Arrian wrote a report of his circumspection of the Black Sea to the emperor and then stopped an invasion by the Alans in about 135/136 and wrote a report of it (The *Ektaxis kata Alanôn*) to the emperor, thereafter proceeding to Iberia (modern Georgia), which he secured for the Empire. It was at about this time that Arrian also wrote his treatise *Tactics* (*Technê Taktikê*), for Hadrian possibly, with the intention of trying to have his tenure as governor prolonged. Arrian was not successful in his endeavours, however, as towards the end of his life Hadrian had become increasingly hostile towards his old friends. After having completed his time as governor, Arrian retired to Athens, where he became archon in 145/146. He is believed to have died sometime in the 160s.

Analysis of Technê Taktikê

As a well-educated military man, Arrian was eminently qualified to write military reports, military treatises and histories. He knew both Hellenistic tactical theory and contemporary Roman military practices. In order to please his benefactor Hadrian, Arrian mixed both elements together. Arrian knew that Hadrian was very fond of Greek philosophy, which included as a sub-branch military treatises, and he also understood that Hadrian loved being praised for his own innovations and liked to be compared favourably to the ancient Greeks. Consequently, he wrote a treatise which included both ancient and period material. What I aim to do here is to try to separate the two from each other. I will demonstrate, very much contrary to the common belief among the Classicists, that the first portion of Arrian's *Tactics* also includes period material.

Unfortunately, the very beginning of the treatise is lost so we do not know how Arrian intended to present his text to the emperor. Arrian wrote that Pyrrhos, Alexander the son of Pyrrhos, Pausanias, Evangelos, Polybius, Eupolemos, Iphicrates and Poseidonius all wrote military treatises, but claims that none of these were useful because they wrote for those who were already knowledgeable in military matters. Since Aelian used a similar justification for the writing of a tactical treatise, it is clear that both had used the same convention to present their material and possibly also the same source(s)/epitome(s). Arrian's text implies familiarity with the above writers, but it is quite possible that he may have used a later epitome of them which belonged to the same tradition. Just like every extant treatise belonging to the same philosophical tradition, Arrian begins by dividing tactics into land and sea warfare, and then deals only with the former. The reason for this is that the Romans faced no credible naval threat at the turn of the second century AD – hence there was no reason to analyze sea warfare in any detail.

Technê Taktikê (Tactics)

Arrian's *Technê Taktikê* is the most detailed exposé of early second-century Roman tactics that we possess. It is also very useful for us that he includes a comparison between Roman and earlier Greek and Macedonian tactics. As noted, according to Arrian, the earlier Greek military treatises were written only for the knowledgeable. His stated purpose was to write a treatise that would explain tactics in such a manner that everyone would be able to understand them. It is possible that he achieved that in the eyes of the period audience, but as we are so far removed from the realities of that era there exists several different ways to interpret the evidence. What follows is my attempt to do so in a new manner.

Following the traditions of the Greek military treatises, Arrian divided the armed forces into those on land and sea. It is unfortunate that the extant 'Hellenistic' treatises do not give any detailed information regarding naval tactics. For that we have to rely on the sixth-century Syrianos Magister, but it is more than likely that he based his account entirely on the earlier texts referred to above, but which are unfortunately no longer extant. I have included in the following diagram the extant information provided by Aelian and other treatises to complete the missing portions. Men were considered either combatants or non-combatants. Land forces consisted of infantry and mounted units. The infantry comprised the hoplites, light-armed (*psiloi*) and peltasts, while the mounted units consisted of cavalry, elephants and chariots. The basic battle formation was the phalanx and its variants. The size of the army (16,384 heavy infantry, 8,192 light infantry and 4,096 cavalry) in Arrian (9–10, 14, 18) followed the standard theoretical Hellenistic model that was divisible by two down to one soldier (heavy infantry: 16, 32, 64, 128, 256, 512, 1,024, 2,048, 4,096, 8,192, 16,384; light infantry: 8, 16, 32, 64, 128, 256, 512, 1,024, 2,048, 4,096, 8,192; cavalry: 64, 128, 256, 512, 1,024, 2,048, 4,096). As regards the Roman practice, the only relevant figures in these refer to the sizes of the auxiliary and cavalry units, which appear to have been approximately the same. Arrian's referral to 256-man heavy infantry *xenagia* (foreign contingent, i.e. *auxilia*) and 512-strong light infantry *xenagia* may be taken to imply auxiliary infantry units (*auxilia*). One may guess that the same could also have been the case when the Romans collected an army consisting of detachments taken from their parent legions, but obviously there is no definite evidence for this, except perhaps for the later period. It is known that Caracalla recruited a complete Macedonian phalanx in 214. The sixth-century *Strategikon* also refers to a period in the past during which the Roman infantry *tagma* had exactly 256 men. The Roman cavalry had followed Greek practices from the Second Punic War onwards and did not need a similar reform of organization.[1] It consisted of thirty-two-men *turmae* and 512-men *alae*. Arrian (18.3) confirms this by stating that the Romans gave the Greek *hipparchia* of 512 horsemen the name *ala* (*eilê*). Despite the fact that the smallest cavalry unit named by Arrian (18) is the *eilê* of sixty-four horsemen, it is clear that all numbers are divisible with the figure of thirty-two, as in the Greek system. Asclepiodotus (7.4, 7.11) and Aelian (18.5–6, 20.2) also fail to mention the smallest unit, but both still refer to the square array in which there were double the number of men in length than in depth, while the latter even includes the example of eight men in width and four in depth (i.e. thirty-two men). In short, Arrian was just following the system adopted by previous military theorists, who also fail to mention the smallest cavalry unit, which for example the Seleucids called an *oulamos* and the Romans a *turma*.

At the time of Arrian (2, 19), chariots were considered a thing of the past, but there exists evidence for their continued use in Caledonia and Ireland. In addition to this, if we are to believe the *HA*, they were used at least by the Sasanians during the reign of *shahanshah* Ardashir I. The anonymous author of the *De Rebus Bellicis* and Vegetius both included scythed chariots in their discussions. Consequently, it is quite possible that the categories given by Arrian may have had some relevance for his own era and afterwards. Chariots were divided into those with and without scythes. According to Arrian, scythed chariots, like those of the Persians, had either armoured or unarmoured horses and either single, double or many poles. The Britons had used two-horsed chariots that were suitable for driving on all kinds of terrains, while the Persians of old had used two-horsed scythed-chariots with armoured horses. The Cyrenaicans/Marmaridae (*Kyrenaioi*) had also fought from chariots. Most importantly, however, Arrian noted that during his day, chariots were no longer used, but as noted this is slightly inaccurate.

According to Arrian (2, 19), elephants were employed by Indians and Ethiopians and in later times by Macedonians, Carthaginians and Romans. There are several examples of the Romans using elephants in combat, for example against the Macedonians. Julius Caesar is claimed to have used elephants in Britain, while his enemies used elephants in combat in Africa in 46 BC. Elephants may also have been employed during the reign of Claudius I in Britain. The last-known attempt to use elephants in a military function occurred in 193 (Dio 74.16.2, described also in this monograph), but it is possible that Caracalla also intended to use them (Dio 78.7.4). However, on the whole the Romans regarded elephants as useless in war. During the imperial period, Rome usually only used elephants in triumphs and performances, and possibly sometimes in military training. In practice, however, after 46 BC the Romans did not face elephants on the battlefield –

except when fighting in Ethiopia – until the Sasanians reintroduced them. According to Arrian, elephants were divided into two categories: those without turrets and those with them. The tusks of elephants could also be fitted with sharpened iron heads. According to Arrian (19.5), in his times only the Indians and the upper Ethiopians continued to use elephants.

In his *Tactics*, Arrian divided cavalry into two distinct types: those of Hellenistic military theory and those used by contemporary Romans. However, in practice the division was not as straightforward as this implies. For example, the Romans also employed Hellenistic cavalry types as auxiliary units. According to Arrian's classification (*Tactics* 4.1–6), the cavalry proper consisted of fully armoured *katafraktoi* and unarmoured *afraktoi* cavalry. The former wore corslets of scale-armour, linen or horn and thigh guards, and their horses had *parapleuria* and chamfrons. The other name for this type of cavalry was the *thorakitai*. The *parapleuria* is usually translated as side coverings or *flancards*, which presumably were tied together on the horse's chest, but it is also possible that we should interpret this to mean both the *flancard* (*flancois, flanchard*) and *peytral* (chest protection, *poitrel*). In other words, their horses were not as fully armoured as the later *clibanarii*. The unarmoured cavalry comprised the medium cavalry *doratoforoi* (*doru*/spear bearers), *kontoforoi* (*kontos*/pike bearers) and *logchoforoi* (*logche* or *lonche*/lance bearers), and the *akrobolistai* (skirmishers). The *doratoforoi* were those who approached the enemy ranks and fought with the *doré* (*doru*, spears), or charged and drove off the enemy with the *kontoi* in the manner of the Alans and Sarmatians. Those of the *doratoforoi* who carried shields were called *thureoforoi* (*thureos*'shield bearers). The rest of the *doratoforoi* did not carry shields and fought either by using *doru* (*doruforoi*) or *kontos* (*kontoforoi*) spears. After these, as an apparent afterthought, Arrian named the *xystoforoi/xustoforoi* (bearers of the ca. 3.74-metre Macedonian *xyston*/spear) as a subtype of the *doratoforoi*. The skirmishers consisted of those who discharged their weapons from a distance. The first class of the skirmishers was the *Tarentinoi*, which were divided into the *Tarentinoi* proper and the *elafroi* (light troops). They used javelins (*doration*, small spear). The *Tarentinoi* proper skirmished only from a distance by keeping far off or by riding around the enemy in a circle. The *elafroi*, meanwhile, first threw their spears and then advanced to close quarters to fight, either by withholding one spear or by using a *spatha* (double-edged long sword). The second class of skirmishers were the *hippotoxotai* (mounted archers), who were armed with bows like those Armenians and Parthians who were not *kontoforoi*.

Arrian stated in his *Tactics* (4.1–9, esp.4.7–9) that the Roman cavalry consisted of the *kontoforoi* (i.e. *contarii*) who fought in the manner of the Alans and Sarmatians, and of the *logchoforoi/lonchoforoi* (lance bearers). This division, however, is somewhat misleading since all Roman cavalry were taught to be competent as both *kontoforoi* and *logchoforoi*, as well as many other different styles of fighting, including use of the bow and crossbow (e.g. *Tactics* 43.1–44.2), not to mention the fact that the Romans also employed foreign auxiliaries. See also the analysis of the *Ektaxis* below. On the basis of this we can conclude that before combat the Roman commander would decide what type of equipment and tactics his 'native' cavalry would use in battle.

In pitched battles, the *kontoforoi* were used as shock cavalry that charged against the enemy to drive them back with their *kontoi*. The *Interpolation of Aelian* (Devine 38.4–39.4; Dain C4–D4) makes it clear that the Alans and Sarmatians armed with '*megalois*

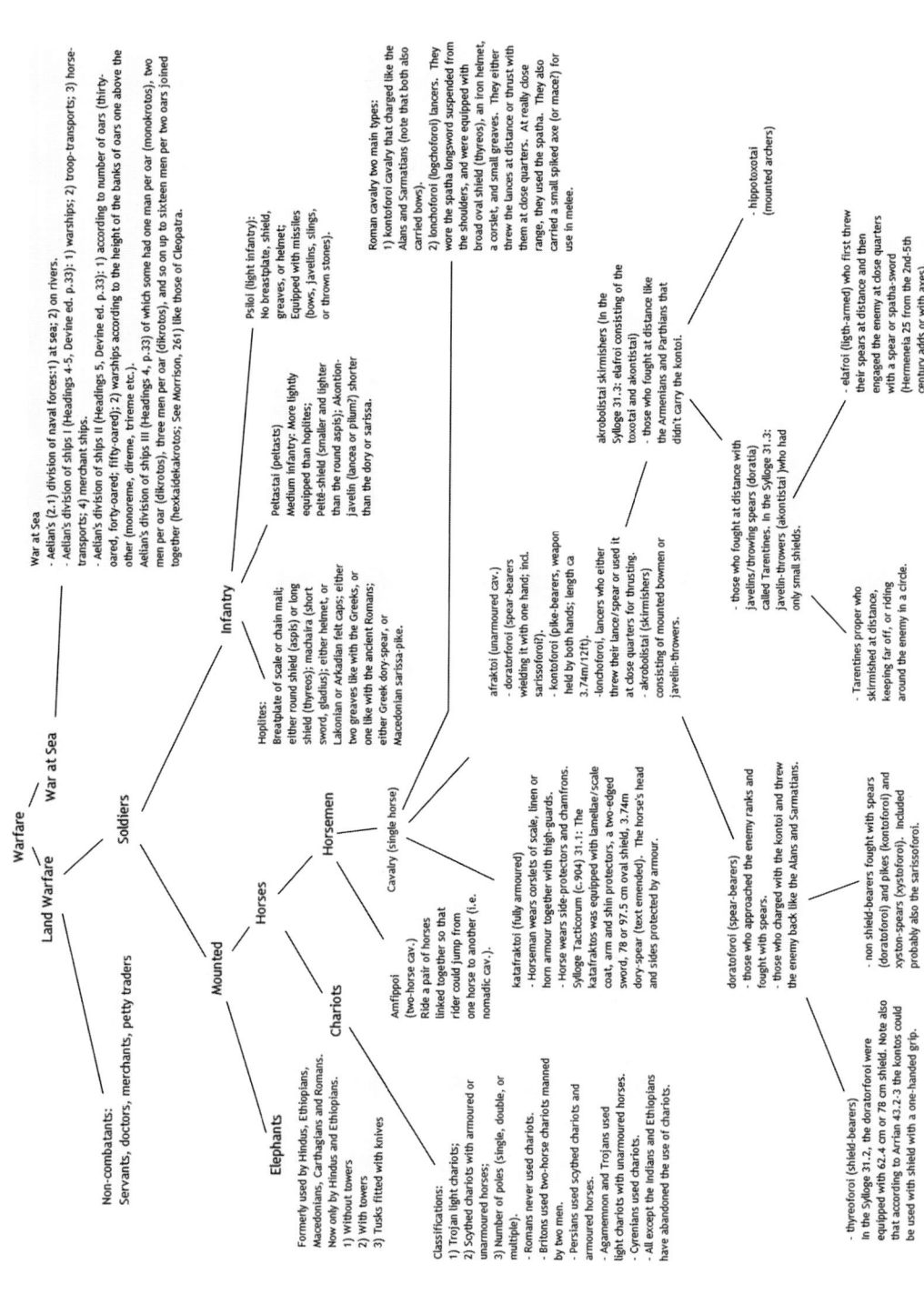

dorasi' (long spears) adopted *heteromekes* (oblong) formations. The information in the sixth-century AD military manual *Strategikon* by Maurice clarifies what sort of formation the Alans and Sarmatians used. They appear to have placed their close order *kontoforoi* (*defensores*/defenders) in alternate order with their skirmishers (*koursores*/runners/ skirmishers). In combat, these skirmishers (i.e. their mounted archers, which also included *kontoforoi* in the front ranks) then advanced first to skirmish, after which they pulled back while the *kontoforoi* charged forward. The Celtic *kontoforoi* shield-bearing cavalry, which seem to have been the principal model for the Romans, were equally adept at using both the runner and defender methods. The Roman *logchoforoi* were equipped with a *spatha* long-sword suspended from the shoulder, broad oval shield (*thureos*), iron helmet, woven *thorax* mail corslet and small greaves. In combat, the horses presumably wore chamfrons and *parapleuria*/sidecoverings (*Tactics* 34.8; *Ektaxis* 31) when needed. In other words, they resembled the *thorakitai* of Polybius (second century BC) and Julian (third century AD). The Roman *kontoforoi* probably wore the same equipment, except that they used the *kontos* instead of the lance. Arrian does not mention the cataphracts, but we know that the Romans had already at least experimented with them during the reign of Trajan or Hadrian, or even before (the Parthian and Armenian auxiliaries certainly included these). The Roman *logchoforoi* carried lances both for throwing and thrusting. At really close quarters they fought with their *spathae*. The horsemen also carried small axes with spikes (like the Greek *elafroi*). Other names for this type of cavalry were probably *thureoforoi* (shield-bearing-troops) or *thorakitai* (when the horse was armoured). The use of these two different types of troops together would have meant that the Romans used the *thureoforoi*/*logchoforoi* as skirmishers and the *kontoforoi* as defenders. Note that their theoretical name changed if their horses wore armour.

As noted above, Arrian divided the Roman infantry into three types. The heaviest type were the hoplites, who were equipped with breastplates, helmets, greaves, round (*aspis*) or oblong (*thureos parameses*, this is the Roman *scutum*) shields, short swords (*machaira*; Roman *gladius*) and spear (*doru*; Roman *hasta* or later *kontarion*) of the type used by the Greeks or Macedonian-type pike (*sarissa*; only used by the Romans when they experimented with the Macedonian phalanx under Nero and Caracalla). According to Arrian, the Greeks and Romans both wore a single greave for the shin and breastplates consisting of scales or chain mail. The lightly armed *psiloi* did not use armour, shields, greaves or helmets, but were equipped with long-range weapons such as bows, light javelins (*akontia*), slings and hand-thrown stones. Note that between a quarter and a third of the legionaries could be used as archers, while some select men (*antesignani, lanciarii*) could be deployed as javelin-armed skirmishers and all could be slingers. The final type of infantry was the peltasts, who had equipment that was lighter than the hoplites but heavier than the *psiloi*. These medium infantry's *pelte* shield was lighter than the *aspis* round shield, and their javelin (*akontion*; light *pilum*/*lancea*?) was shorter than the spear or pike. At least during the late Roman period, heavy infantry legionaries could also be equipped in this manner for difficult terrain,[2] but one suspects that this was also the case earlier with some of the *expediti* troops (those lightly equipped for combat), with the possible exception of their shields, which may have been larger than the *pelte*. In the categorization of Arrian (3.5), the Romans primarily used the hoplite type of infantry, but in practice they also used the *pilum* heavy spear rather than the *hasta* thrusting spear typical for the true hoplites. The archaeological record and works of art prove that the Romans never abandoned the *hasta*, and that it was used by the auxiliaries in particular. The Romans thus employed all of the infantry categories described by Arrian, both among their legions and auxiliaries. It should be noted, however, that in practice there was even greater variety of equipment among the footmen than implied by the Greek categories. In contrast to Arrian's categorization, the light-armed troops could also have armour, helmets and shields. Similarly, the allied troops also employed a greater variety of equipment than this categorization would allow.

In concordance with the demands of the period Arrian lived in, he stressed the importance of military training in units and in conglomerates of units. The different types of units were taught to use their equipment and to operate in various kinds of formations, as well as to employ different kinds of battlefield manoeuvres (doublings, counter-marches, about turn, turning as individuals, wheeling etc.).

The battlefield formation in Arrian's *Tactics* was naturally the infantry phalanx, which consisted of ranks and files, with subunits of different sizes. The difference between the phalanx and cohortal formation was only marginal, as both were deployed in ranks and files. The only fundamental difference was that in the phalanx array the unit files divided themselves in half to form a second combat line, while in the cohortal formation the two (or more lines) always consisted of separate units (cohorts). However, it should be noted that Hannibal's deployment at Zama proves that the phalanx could also be deployed into several lines consisting of separate units if the commander so decided. The Romans used both cohortal and phalanx tactics in the second and third centuries, so it is clear that Arrian's description of the phalanx is also very relevant in the Roman context.

The phalanx was usually divided into four divisions and their subunits for combat. The basic unit was the file (*lochos*), the strength of which varied according to the depth of the formation. According to Arrian (5.4ff.), some made the depth of the *lochos* eight men and others twelve or sixteen. For him, the deepest file was sixteen men and the shallowest four men, the latter of which was called the depthless formation. The double depth of thirty-two men was still considered proportionate and therefore acceptable in the right circumstances. The sixth-century Urbicius and Maurice were to include similar instructions. Depths of ten and twelve men were included as alternatives only because some military theorists preferred these to the traditional options. However, the fact that we find Pompey using a depth of ten ranks at Pharsalus in 48 BC proves that the Romans had enough flexibility to do so when there were extra men available. Another possibility is that these figures included light-armed troops and/or green recruits in the ranks (e.g. eight men plus two archers/recruits, eight men and two archers and two recruits, or eight men and four light-armed). It should be stressed that despite what the theoretical works stated, the basic building block of both Greek and Roman armies was the ten-man group which the Romans called the tent group (*contubernium*). The *contubernium* consisted of a file of eight fighters, one recruit and one servant. Two *contubernia* then made up the sixteen-man file of the phalanx.

Infantry units were deployed either in open, close (*pyknosis*) or locked shields (*synaspismos*) orders. For ease of deployment, the files of the units in the phalanx were divided into first- and second-rank men. Arrian (11.4–12.6) equated the *synaspismos* with the Roman *testudo* formation, which he stated could be a square, circular or oblong in shape. The unfortunate thing about Arrian's description after this (ranks one to four of a phalanx) is that the information was equally true of both the Roman and Macedonian phalanx. My own assumption is that he meant it to be relevant for both, even if it is likely that he referred only to the period Roman array. The file leaders (the first rank) of both Roman and Macedonian phalanxes consisted of the best men, because they were the cutting edge of the phalanx and held the formation together. The next best men were placed in the second rank. In combat, they supported the first rank with their spears (of the *doru* type) and could move forward to take the place of the file leader if they had been killed or wounded. According to Arrian, the enemy could reach and kill the file leader by delivering a blow from above with the short sword (*machaira*), hence the need for the second-rank men to support the front rank with their spears. It is notable that these comments and instructions are relevant only in the context of the Roman or Greek phalanx, and not with the Macedonian phalanx. The ability of the enemy to kill the file leader with a short sword shows that the front-rankers fought at a relatively close distance from their opponents. It also implies that the expectation was that the file leaders would throw their spears and then grasp their swords. The type of spear used by the second-rank men, the *doru*, also proves that Arrian does not describe the Macedonian phalanx, even if the information regarding the quality of the men was relevant to both. Basically, he described the Roman phalanx in the same manner as the sixth-century *Strategikon*, which also required the men in the second rank to use their spears in support of the file leaders, who had thrown their spears and then drawn their swords. Those in the third and fourth ranks were also picked men, like the second-rankers. The four ranks of *doru* bearers in the *synaspismos/testudo* formation is obviously the same array as Arrian (*Ektaxis* 16–17, 26) describes for use against the Alans (see below), and which was also used by the late Romans (see Syvänne, 2004) and Byzantines. In short, there is definite continuity of fighting methods from the first century at least until the thirteenth century.

However, as regards the weapon used by the four ranks in this array, there is a possible discrepancy between Arrian's time and the fifth- to sixth-century practices. In his *Ektaxis*, Arrian states that the four front ranks used a *kontos* spear that had a long slender spearhead which bent on impact, with the implication that this would have been the *pilum*, which would mean that the spears of only the first two ranks could be used for thrusting. The information in *Tactics* may support this, however, because Arrian required that the second rank support the first rank with spears, and was less specific regarding the role of the third and fourth ranks. However, the likening of these four ranks with the Macedonian phalanx with six *sarissae* projecting out of the array, which he described next, suggests the use of the *doru* (*hasta*) and not the *pilum*. Furthermore, the *Ektaxis* makes it very clear that the spearhead of the fourth-ranker reached beyond the front of the formation, with the implication that we are dealing here with a *hasta/doru* type of spear despite the long and slender spearhead.[3]

How long was this Roman and Greek *doru*?[4] The four ranks mean that the length of the hoplite spear had to be at least 2.5 metres, but on the basis of later Byzantine evidence it is probable that it was actually longer (the possible range is from 3.74–5 metres), because the length of the short *kontarion* of Leo the Wise was 8 *pecheis*, which means that one should give each man in the formation at least 46.8cm (short *pechus*) or 62.46cm (long *pechus*) in which to stand. However, the 3.74-metre length is likelier on the basis that it was expected that a soldier wield it with one hand and still somehow throw it if needed. In that case the spear of the fourth man protruded out of the formation about 122.2cm (allowing the rear of the spear to protrude some 65cm behind him), but in my opinion one cannot be too strict about these figures. It is more than likely that the men occupied more space in the array than that, even if one accepts the short *pechus* to be the more likely figure for the length of the short *kontarion*. If each of the men bent his knees and assumed a wider stance of about 65–70cm, as is probable, that would still allow for the spearhead of the last man to reach *ca*. 66cm past the front-ranker, even with the short *pechus*.[5]

After this (12.6ff.), Arrian went on to detail the use and equipment of the Macedonian pike phalanx formation, with six *sarissae* protruding in front of each of the front-rankers. Excluding some probably very short-lived antiquarian experiments by certain Roman emperors like Nero and Caracalla, this had no real importance for the period battlefields – although it is clear that Caracalla's experiment was a success.[6] However, the information regarding the use of the rear guards (12.11) had period relevance. The rear guards were to consist of intelligent and experienced men, whose task it was to control the advance of the phalanx, push the hesitant forwards and tighten the formation when necessary.

The light infantry were deployed here and there as needed (*Tactics* 9, 13–15). This could mean deployment on both sides of the phalanx, in front of the phalanx, on the left and/or right, behind the phalanx, or behind or in front of the wings of the phalanx at an angle. In addition, the files of light-armed troops could be placed between the heavy infantry files. According to Arrian, the most useful tactic was to position the light infantry behind the phalanx. In battle there were many different uses for the archers, javelineers and slingers. They were regarded as useful for opening the engagement, drawing the enemy out of their formation, killing the enemy at a distance, breaking up the enemy phalanx, stopping the enemy cavalry, occupying higher elevations quickly, repelling enemy from these higher areas, scouting, ambush and pursuit. In other words, the light-armed men were regarded as multipurpose troops suitable for battling both in front of the phalanx and with it. Arrian's preference for the various types of auxiliaries was to post them either in front or on the flanks. These instructions were traditional among the Greek military theorists, but still relevant for Arrian's day.

The cavalry was deployed in various different unit formations (square, oblong, rhombus/rhomboid, wedge), each of which had its own advantages, and all are mentioned by Arrian (9, 16ff.). All of these variants appear to have been used by Roman cavalry armies at least until the sixth century. The rhombus, which was invented by the Thessalians, had the advantage that it could be used effectively and quickly to face all four directions, each of which was headed by the best fighters. Arrian (17.1–3) means the smaller non-rank-and-file Thessalian rhombus rather than the 128 horsemen rank-and-file version which was used by the Armenian and Parthian mounted archers (*Byzantine Interpolation of Aelian*, Dain ed. J1–2, Devine ed. 45.1–2; Syvänne, 2010a-b, 2014b, 2017a). On the basis of Arrian's text it is therefore possible that the Romans used both the non-rank-and-file rhombus and the larger 128 men rhombus. The wedge was invented by the Scythians and copied from them by the Thracians and Macedonians. The standard rank-and-file wedge had sixty-four horsemen, but Arrian means the non-rank-and-file version. The principal advantages of this formation were its manoeuvrability and ability to cut through enemy formations – those facing its apex often lost their morale. The wedge continued to be used by nomad barbarian tribesmen as well as by Romans. The square formation was used by the Persians, Sicilians and most of the Greeks (and naturally also by the Romans). Its advantages were manifold. It was the easiest to deploy, because the men were arrayed in ranks and files (rows and columns). It was also easiest to use during both attacks and retreats, and had the advantage that all of the file leaders fell on the foe simultaneously together. The square/oblong array achieved its extreme form, known as *en muraille*, in the eighteenth century. The *en muraille* array did not have intervals between the units.

Unsurprisingly, Arrian paid most attention to the square and oblong formations because these were the most often used arrays. He claimed the best cavalry square formations were those that had double the number in length than depth, for instance twenty long and ten deep. Oddly, Arrian fails to mention the standard formation of the Macedonian era, the square array, which had a width of eight and depth of four. Just like the other treatises, Arrian also mentioned the alternative practice of deploying with a length three times that of the depth (this is also included by Asclepiodotus 7.4 and Aelian 18.6). The deeper cavalry formation did not help in the same manner as deep infantry formations, because the horsemen could not push the horses in front of them in an *othismos* movement (pushing and shoving with shields, like rugby players do with their shoulders in a maul). According to Arrian, the tightening of the formation by placing the horses from the rear between those in front of them did not bring any tangible benefits because it was more likely this would upset the horses. Neither does Arrian include the Greek modification of the standard Persian, Greek and Sicilian array, which consisted of an oblong with a width of sixteen files and depth of eight ranks (Asclepiodotus 7.4) for a total of 128 men – this may have been an oversight or a calculated decision, because it is possible that it was not used by Roman cavalry.

The oblong cavalry formation (*heteromekes taxis*) could be deployed either in width or in depth (*bathos*). In general, the deployment in width was considered the better of the two in combat. The deployment of the oblong formation in depth as column was only thought to be better when the intention was to cut through an enemy formation or when one wanted to conceal a greater numbers of cavalry and thereby lure the enemy into an attack. This latter method found favour in the sixteenth century, when the Reiter cavalry of Central Europe employed it to break an enemy array.

The depthless formation later sometimes favoured by medieval knights consisted of a single front or row (*metōpon*). This was considered useful for raids against unsuspecting enemies or when one wanted to trample opponents or crops underfoot, but unsurprisingly it was thought disadvantageous for long-lasting pitched battles. Even the medieval knights recognized this weakness, deploying their squires behind them as a separate line. Nevertheless, it is still clear that when the intention was a desperate charge straight at the enemy in the manner of medieval knights, there was no better formation than this. On the basis of surviving works of art, Roman cavalry certainly used this method to trample enemy footmen.

The figures given by Arrian suggest the existence of many different ways to form up and combine units. For regular-sized units (of thirty-two, sixty-four, 128, 256 or 512 men), it is easy to understand how the troops were deployed, but for irregular-sized formations it is difficult to see how this was done. For example, when *turmae* were deployed nine wide and three deep (twenty-seven men), ten wide and five deep (fifty men) or twenty wide and ten deep (200 men), it is clear that the corresponding strengths are not divisible with the unit strengths. This means that these formations included the supernumeraries either as part of the array (fifty and 200 men) or outside it (twenty-seven men). It should also be stressed that Arrian considered the ten by five (fifty men) and twenty by ten (200 men) squares to be the best such arrays. These were clearly the precursors of late Roman cavalry tactics, and were apparently already standard methods during Arrian's day. Such arrays could only be achieved by forming the units in such a manner that the squires were sometimes added to the numbers to fill up the ranks or the extra men were given some other tasks.

So how did the Romans combine and form their combat units in a situation where the actual size of the units varied, so that some were well below their paper strength while others were close to it or even had more men? The best clue to this comes in the sixth-century *Strategikon*, which is based on older Roman traditions. It is not without reason that this treatise (12.13) instructed the commanders to deploy their cavalry ten deep when the commander had more than 12,000 horsemen and five deep when he had fewer than that. When the cavalry was deployed separately, the depths varied between five and ten according to the quality of the unit (*Strategikon* Books 1–3 and Syvänne, *The Age of Hippotoxotai*, 2004). How was this achieved when the paper strengths of the units were not suited to it? The answer is by improvising.

In combat, the phalanx tactics required that the soldiers were able to perform several manoeuvres (Arrian 20ff.) with ease so that the various tactical variations could be used as needed, allowing the phalanx formation to be adapted to the circumstances. These movements included the ability to outflank the enemy or its prevention, as well as the cutting through of an enemy formation or its prevention. The soldiers were required to be able to face different directions as individuals, to wheel as units, about-face, perform different kinds of counter-marches (*exelissein*) by file and rank, form up in rows and columns, march in line or column and to double the length or depth. In addition, they needed to be able to use the open order, close order (*pyknosis, ca.* 94cm per man in width) and interlocked shield order (*synaspismos*, shields interlocked rim-to-boss, *ca.* 62–3cm per man).

There were numerous marching and battle formations (Arrian 26ff.): the lateral oblong (*plagia*) phalanx; column (*orthia*) phalanx (the tower formation, called in Greek *pyrgos* and in Latin *turris*);[7] oblique (*loxe*) phalanx; two-fronted (*amfistomos*) phalanx; double phalanx (*amfistomos difalangia*); each other facing (*antistomos*) phalanx; each other facing double phalanx (*antistomos difalangia*); marching column of two phalanxes side by side or behind each other in which the file leaders were on the same side (*homoiostomos difalangia*); marching column in which the leading phalanx and following phalanx had file leaders on different sides (*heterostomos difalangia*); *prostaxis* formation in which the light-armed troops were placed on the flanks; *entaxis* formation, with files of light-armed men placed between heavy infantry files; *hypotaxis* formation in which the light-armed were placed behind the edges of the phalanx in an *epikampios* formation (rear-angled half-square); an interjection of men from the rear to the front (*parembole*); marching formations of one, two, three or four fronts; the wedge (*embolos*); hollow wedge (*koilembolos*); rectangular hollow formation (*plaision*, a hollow oblong in which the light infantry was placed in

Plaision:
The 10 c. AD Byzantine Interpolation of Aelian (Dain M1, M ad fig., Scholium 32, p.106; tr. by A.M. Devine, Aelian's Manual of Hellenistic Military Tactics 48.1, 48.4, Ancient World 19, 1989, p. 65): "This formation [plaision] has a depth much greater than the length or a length much greater than the depth, and is called "an oblong-formation" [plaision] when all its sides consist of heavy infantry, with archers and slingers inside... It is called an "oblong-formation" [plaision] when the deployment takes place on the four sides of a formation not in the shape of a square but in that of an oblong" The diagram is drawn after Codex Burney 108 f.22 ("p.43").

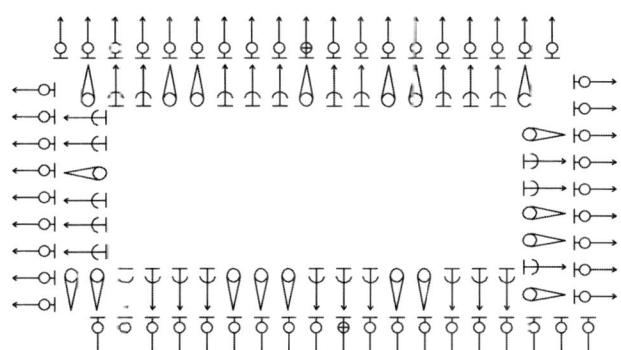

 a file-leader (*lochagos*); a misleading term since in all of the diagrams the *lochagos* is clearly a higher ranking officer (probably a *falangarchês* or in some cases the *kerarchês* or even *strategos/hypostrategos*) usually posted in the front center or in the front right flank of the formation

spear-bearing (*kontos*-bearing) heavy infantryman (*hoplitês kontaratos pezos*); *kontos* was a c. 3.6 m long (cavalry) spear that could be used for both thrusting and throwing.

targeteer or light-armed slinger (*peltastês ê sfendonêtês psilos*); the 10th c. AD infantry peltast seems to have been a javelin thrower.

archer (*psilos toxotês*)

horseman with a spear (*kaballarios kontaratos*)

pezoi meta tzikouriôn êtoi peltastai (infantry armed with battle-axes, in other words peltasts).

 stoma, mouth / front of the array

Antistomos difalangia (fronts against each other facing double phalanx). This array was formed up by opening up a route for the enemy pass through so that its attack would not disrupt the phalanx while also putting the advancing enemy between two phalanxes facing each other. In practice this tactic was not used only against cavalry wedges which is depicted here but also against other cavalry formations meant to break the cohesion of the phalanx and also against elephants and chariots. The *stoma* means the front.

Plinthion (Hollow Square)
10 cent. AD Byzantine Interpolation of Aelian (tr. by A.M. Devine, Aelian's Manual of Hellenistic Military Tactics 42.6, Ancient World 19, 1989, p.62: "It is called a plinthion whenever the formations on the four sides are drawn up identically, so as to be square in shape". The image depicts a hollow square despite its appearance in the Codex Burnley.

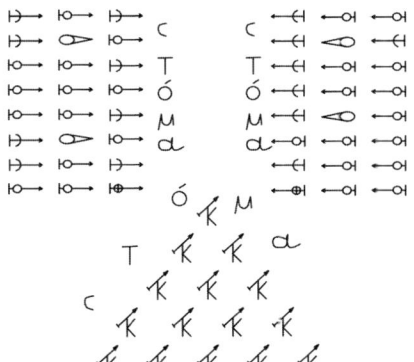

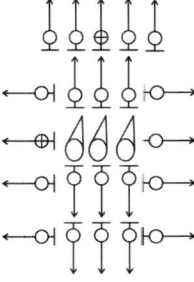

the middle of the heavy); hollow square 'brick' (*plinthion*; square); double outflanking formation (*hyperfalangesis*), and outflanking formation (*hyperkerasis*).

The *kyrte/kurte* (convex) was used against the *epikampios emprosthia* (forward-angled half-square). The text actually has that the *kyrte* was used against *epikampios opisthia* (rearward-angled half-square), but the accompanying diagram in Codex Burnley has the *epikampios emprosthia* so it is clear that there is something amiss either with the text or diagram. My educated guess is that it is with the text because the convex protected the flanks which were threatened if the enemy array was the *epikampios emprosthia* as in the diagram. In grand tactical use the *epikampios emprosthia* was used to subject the enemy to missile fire from the forward pushed wings and also for the outflanking of the enemy formation by crushing its wings. The *kyrte* was used to prevent the outflanking.

The rank-and-file rhombus was opposed by *menoeides* (crescent). This was a unit formation used to subject the attacking rhombus to attacks from the flanks. The counter tactic for the rhombus was to attack the infantry wings with javelins. However, the Macedonians and Romans both also used grand tactical crescent consisting of thousands of men to outflank their enemies.

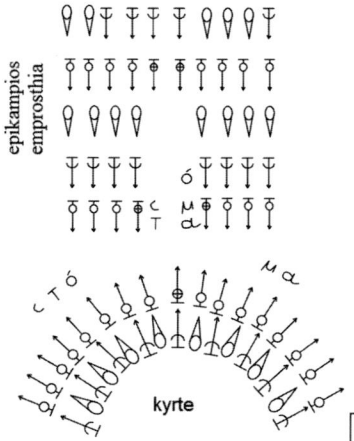

The non-rank-and-file rhombus was opposed by the *epikampios emprosthia* (forward-angled half-square). This is once again unit formation, but the Romans also used a grand tactical version of the *epikampios emprosthia* consisting of thousands of men.

The square cavalry formation used by the Persians, Sicilians and most of the Greeks was opposed by infantry wedge. The Interpolation (Devine 47.3, Dain L3) states that whereas the apex of the cavalry wedge could be formed by one man, the infantry wedge needed more. Note that the Roman infantry wedge used in 193 (see the text) may have only one man at the apex unless we should take the referral to the 200 men wedge only as approximation. The Interpolation (Dain L4-5) continues that Epaminondas had used the wedge at Leuctra and that the wedge was formed up by joined the wings of *amfistomos difalangia* together. This wedge is actually different (see the introduction) from what is depicted in the Codex Burnley shown below. The Burnley version is clearly a unit wedge resembling the one used by the Romans in 193 but with the difference that it has three men in the front rank. This array would have been as a separate wedge in front of the phalanx or as a wedge protruding from it.

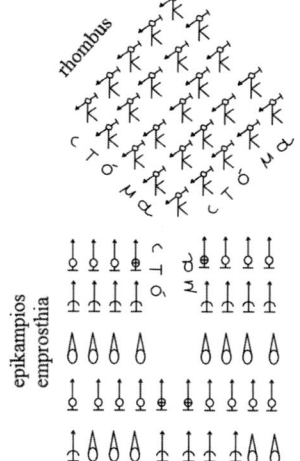

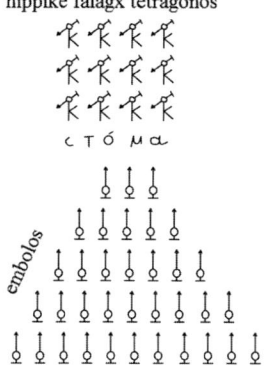

The attached diagrams, taken from the Codex Burnley version of the *Byzantine Interpolation of Aelian*, depict the unit formations mentioned above. The information in the captions has also been taken from the same source.

The baggage train was placed according to the needs of the moment (*Tactics* 30), following the phalanx when the army was invading but being placed in front when the army was marching away from hostile territory. It was placed on the flank when there was the threat from the other side, but was moved inside the phalanx (double phalanx and/or square) when there were potential threats from all directions.

According to Arrian (11), in combat the phalanx was deployed by length whenever the locale made it advantageous. The phalanx was deployed in depth in situations that required a deeper and denser formation. As examples, Arrian gives the battles of Leuctra and Mantinea, where the Thebans used the wedge formation to break up the Spartan phalanx. This was the offensive version of the wedge. Despite the fact that Epaminondas used the wedge on the left, it is likely that during this period the offensive wedge would most often have been used by the centre divisions of the lateral phalanx to cut through the enemy's centre. The counter-manoeuvre against the wedge was to use the hollow wedge to receive it inside its killing zone. The second example in Arrian (11) of the wedge, the defensive deep wedge array, was used against charging Scythians and Sarmatians. We learn from later Byzantine sources that in most cases this would have meant the sending of soldiers in front of the phalanx to break up the impetus of the enemy cavalry charge with a wedge (the front rank kneeling and pointing their spears towards the breasts of the horses), supported by missile fire from the rear ranks. During the period under consideration this would probably have meant the use of either the auxiliaries or the *antesignani/lanciarii*. Despite the fact that Arrian here noted the effectiveness of the wedge against the Sarmatians, on the basis of his *Ektaxis* he himself seems to have favoured the use of the *epikampios emprosthia* against them. However, we cannot exclude the use of the wedge by Arrian, because we do not possess his entire work and the use of the auxiliaries in pursuit behind the pursuing cavalry would have allowed the possibility of deploying them in a wedge formation to break up any possible counter-attacks by the Alans.

The close order formation (*pyknosis*) meant a densification of the phalanx in width and depth. Arrian does not specify its purpose, but from other sources we learn that it was mainly used for offensive purposes. The interlocked shields formation (*synaspismos*) meant the adoption of a very dense phalanx in which there was no longer any freedom of movement. It was generally considered to be a defensive formation. According to Arrian, the Roman equivalent of the *synaspismos* was the tortoise (*chelone* = *testudo*) formation, which could be either square, rounded or oblong in shape. Those standing on the edge of the formation (*plinthion*, little brick) placed their shields in front of themselves, while those behind placed their shields above the heads. According to Arrian, this provided good protection against missiles, and even against stones carried in wagons that on impact simply rolled off. The implication is that the Romans used the *testudo* for both defensive and offensive purposes. The use of circle and square arrays implies a defensive use in battle, while an offensive use of the *testudo* would have occurred during the approach phase of a battle (protecting the troops from missiles) or when the formation approached an enemy wall during a siege (offering protection against missiles and stones). These

Amfistomos falagx (double-fronted phalanx) was used when the enemy had vastly more cavalry. This was a defensive array in which the rear ranks faced backwards. The Roman counterpart was the *orbis*. This Greek version could also become an orbis in practice when the flanks faced outwards to face attacking enemies if these approached from this direction. However, in addition to this the Romans appear to have used a special unit formation with their *testudo* array which was also actually round in shape.

The column version of the *hippikē heteromēkēs ilē* (cavalry oblong wing) had greater depth than width with the aim to break through the enemy array. This formation was opposed by the *plagia falagx* (lateral phalanx). The aim was that if the cavalry managed to pass through, its charge would affect only a small section of the formation.

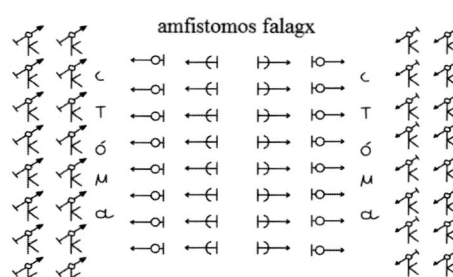

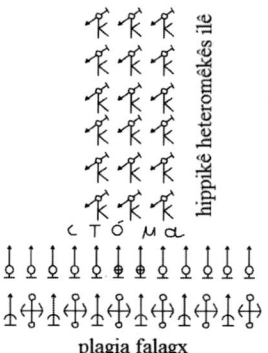

Infantry column (*peri keras, peri orthēs epagōgēs*) was opposed by *koilembolos* (hollow wedge). On the basis of other sources like e.g. Vegetius we know that the hollow wedge was also used against infantry wedge.

hyperfalaggēsis (outflanking phalanx) means outflanking the enemy with both wings.

hyperkerasis means the outflanking of the enemy with one wing.

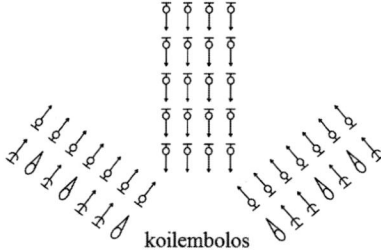

The standard Macedonian phalanx was arrayed as four phalanxes each called *falaggarchia* (4,096 hoplites) each lead by a falangarch. The accompanying diagram shows the locations of these officers in the formation. I have drawn it after *Codex Burnley*, but I have emended eight persons to the two phalanxes on the left which in the diagram have only seven men. In the standard array the light infantry *psiloi* would have been placed behind the heavy infantry, but its place could be varied. The cavalry could be placed either on the wings or behind the infantry.

2nd phalanx

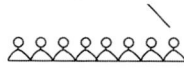

3rd phalanx

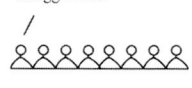

4th phalanx

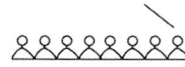

1st phalanx

continued to be standard Roman tactics for centuries to come, and criticism of the use of the hollow square formation and tortoise against the Parthians/Persians by Julius Africanus during the reign of Alexander Severus is simply ill-conceived and incorrect. It was impossible for Roman infantry to catch mobile cavalry in open terrain, hence the use of the hollow square. However, Julius Africanus was correct in criticizing the passive way in which it was used: it should have been used offensively.

The *Tactics* (25ff.) makes clear that the principal means of defeating an enemy were outflanking on one or both flanks, breaking through the enemy formation, missile fire and the successful use of counter-manoeuvres against enemy's initiatives. With overwhelming superiority it was possible to outflank the enemy on both flanks simultaneously. According to Arrian, with equal or slightly smaller forces it was possible to outflank the enemy on one flank with a lengthened line or oblique phalanx. Outflanking with a longer line could be achieved by counter-marching the flank units by rank, by thinning the line or by lengthening the line with light infantry and cavalry. These same manoeuvres could also be used against encircling attempts by the enemy, the two first mentioned being possible only when the enemy was still at a distance. If the enemy had managed to encircle a Roman phalanx, they could respond by forming a two-fronted double phalanx, if there was enough time. In an emergency, the units threatened from the rear could adopt the two-fronted phalanx (*orbis/amfistomos*). As noted, the enemy could be defeated through the use of light infantry missile fire in the right circumstances. It could also be overcome through the adopting of a deep formation or infantry wedge that cut through the enemy infantry. The latter could also be used to counter an enemy cavalry attack. On the other hand, the enemy wedge could be countered through the use of a hollow wedge. From other sources we also know that an infantry phalanx could be opened up if the enemy force consisted of a wedge of cavalry, so men could be posted to engage the cavalry behind the phalanx. For examples, see Syvänne, *MHLR* series.

The cavalry wings could be used either to skirmish with the enemy, to outflank them or to break through with a deep column, wedge or rhombus formation. The cavalry wings could similarly be used to counter such attempts by the enemy. The infantry circle, hollow square and hollow rectangle were undoubtedly used largely as defensive formations against enemies that employed mainly cavalry such as the Sarmatians or Parthians. Arrian does not tell how the double and triple phalanxes were used in battle. However, from the possibly sixth-century Syrianus we learn that the second phalanx was placed behind the first, which besides being a defence against threats from behind could also be employed as a reserve force to outflank the enemy. The triple phalanx has two different varieties: a forward-angled half-square (*epikampios emprosthia*) that was used against cavalry in suitable terrain, as demonstrated by Arrian's *Expedition*; and a rearward-angled half-square (*epikampios opisthia, hypotaxis*) that was used to protect the flanks of the phalanx when it was threatened by cavalry. In Arrian's examples, the wings of the triple phalanxes consisted of auxiliaries (note the *Expedition* and *hypotaxis*), but one may expect that these could also consist of regular units, as they did in the sixth century. However, at this time the auxiliaries could obviously be more easily and speedily deployed in threatened sections than the armour-encumbered heavy legionaries. Additionally, the auxiliaries had greater long-range punching power in missile fire than the legions, while their line infantry were always equipped with spears suited to facing cavalry while the legionaries often used *pilum* javelins.

The most important section of Arrian's *Tactics* describes the period Roman parade ground manoeuvres. These have been studied in detail by Ann Hyland in her brilliant book. Consequently, it suffices here only to summarize those sections that have particular relevance for the battlefields of Arrian's day. According to Arrian, Hadrian had revived the traditional Roman cavalry exercises, which taught the soldiers how to employ their weapons (javelins, spear, pike and swords) effectively in various situations and how to defend themselves. However, even these so-called Roman exercises, which had originally been copied mainly from the Gauls and Spaniards, demonstrate foreign influences too. A good example of this is the use of the dragon standards, which had been copied from the Sarmatians. The soldiers were expected to be able to throw javelins or spears as they rode towards each other or their targets, past each other or their targets and even when they turned about away from the enemy. Likewise, they were required to be able to defend themselves with shields against frontal attacks, attacks from the sides and from the rear. They had to be able to throw a succession of javelins and/or spears in the course of a gallop. They were also expected to be able to employ light javelins, missiles that were fired from a crossbow and stones thrown by sling or hand. Traditional Roman cavalry were thus expected to be able to use javelins, spears, stones and crossbows at a distance, along with the *contus* spear and *spatha* sword in close-quarters fighting.

Arrian's description shows that the *kontos* pike could be used in a great variety of ways, both offensively and defensively. These practices seem to have been copied from the Celts, not the Sarmatians. The Celtic *contus* could be wielded with one hand and was lighter than the Sarmatian version that required a two-handed grip. The Celtic *contus* was used in attack, defence and in pursuit. It was used in fencing manoeuvres for parrying and thrusting, and in quarterstaff-like whirling manoeuvres for strikes against opponents in the front, flank or behind, all this being done while still using the defensive shield. The individual horsemen could use their long swords (*spathae*) by employing a wide variety of strokes, delivering attacks both in pursuit and while riding alongside their enemy. They were even expected to be able to kill with a sword those who had fallen to the ground. The horsemen were also taught how to quickly mount their horses, the climax of the cavalry exercises being a demonstration of the skill of leaping in full armour onto a galloping horse.

The text also shows that the combat helmet of the Roman horsemen usually protected only the head and cheeks, while the parade helmets (used sometimes also in combat) covered the entire face except the eyes. They also carried a shield and wore iron corselets. In combat, the horses were protected by chamfrons, side-coverings and saddle cloths. Even if the horses were not as fully protected as the cataphracts, they were still adequately protected without sacrificing their combat speed and stamina.

As noted above, Arrian's description of the parade ground drill had two parts. The first and most detailed section consisted of the traditional Roman cavalry training drills that had been borrowed from the Celts, while the second part comprised the new training drills introduced by Hadrian. The reader should keep in mind that the drills simulated actual battlefield manoeuvres and therefore indicate how the various types of Roman cavalry forces fought in skirmishes or when charging.

Arrian's parade ground drill began with the charge of the better cavalry units, in which the sections were distinguished by the Roman standards or Scythian dragon standards.[8]

A quarter wheel (*epistrofē*)
Arrian, Tactica 35.6-7:
Arrows show the direction of the movement.
Left diagram/illustration shows the quarter wheeling manoeuvre with a single rank.
Right diagram/illustration shows the quarter wheel with the whole *turma*. Each file simply followed its file leader (and standard in the parade). In order to achieve this, the horsemen/horses used the passage technique. The purpose of this manoeuvre was to try to outflank the enemy or to avoid being outflanked by changing the face of the formation.

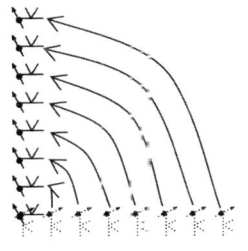

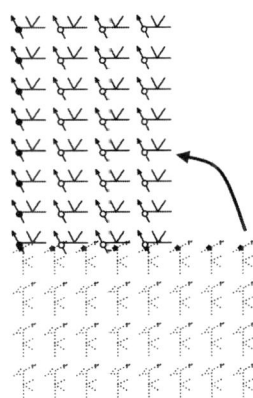

A Quarter Wheel by A Moving Cavalry Unit

This is the manoeuvre that the cavalry units would have usually used while manoeuvring on the battlefield. This is also the type of wheeling that was considered an easy manoeuvre for the cavalry wedge to perform fast. See also the *kontoforoi* outflanking manoeuvre later.

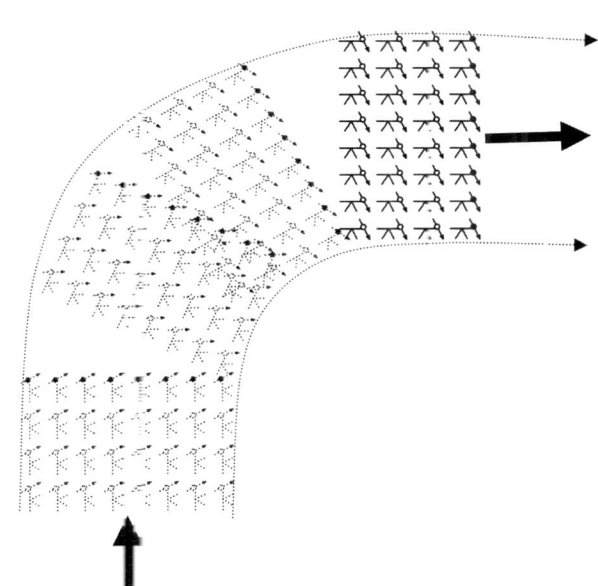

They charged in the widest possible variety of ways, the standards helping to keep the orders/units (*taxeis*) from rushing into each other. The horsemen kept continually counter-marching/folding back (*exeligmoi*), wheeling (*epistrofē*)[9] and attacking while each section (*sêmeia*) followed its standard. As a result, there was no confusion in the *taxeis*/*turmae*.[10] The subsequent details make clear that these *turmae* were deployed four deep and eight wide. The standard wheeling manoeuvres described by the treatises is shown in the first two diagrams. However, in practice the wheeling by units could also be performed while moving. This type of wheeling movement is also shown in the diagrams and would have been the most often used such movement by cavalry units

After this, the horsemen halted in close formation to the left of the tribune, the horses' heads turned backwards, while covering themselves and their mounts with shields in *chelônê*/tortoise formation.[11] The *petrinos* exercise proves that horsemen consisted of two groups (probably of two *turmae*). After the example set by Anne Hyland in her groundbreaking study, I separate the *turmae* into A and B *Turmae* in the accompanying diagrams. Unfortunately, Arrian's description is so inaccurate that it allows several different interpretations. I include here the two most likely. The first of these is mine, whereas the second is a modification based on Hyland's interpretation in which I change her rank of horsemen to mean a file, as stated in the text.

In the first exercise, two horsemen separated from one of the files of *Turma A* to act as targets (36.1–2). The javelins used in the first part of the exercise were of the standard *akontion* type (short and light, presumably *lanceae*), but without iron heads. After the two targets had assumed their position in front of the right wing of the tortoise, the second half of their file charged straight at them, throwing javelins, after which they turned right (36.3). This suggests that the first attackers comprised the rear half of the same file. It also means that the depth of the array was four, with the implication that its width was eight, so that the unit in question was a regular *turma* of thirty-two horsemen. The different files of the *turma* would then have performed the same manoeuvre in succession. I have here made the guess that the attack began with the advance of the right wing. Arrian (37.2–5) follows this by stating that riders (presumably from *Turma B*) suddenly darted forward and galloped in front of their formation to the space between the two target-men and the tortoise (*Turma A*), and threw javelins at the horsemen riding past them. They were to do this towards their unprotected right, which was a difficult combat manoeuvre in itself, but not the most difficult. After passing the line of riders, they were obliged (while turning right) to throw a javelin with a backward movement, which in the Celtic language was called *petrinos* and was considered the most difficult technique of all. Both groups of riders were apparently required to do this, even if the text refers only to the

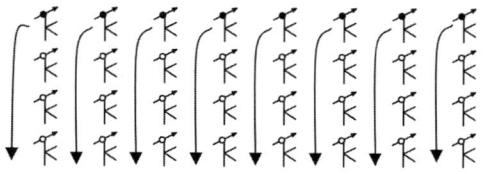

Top: original position with countermarch towards left.

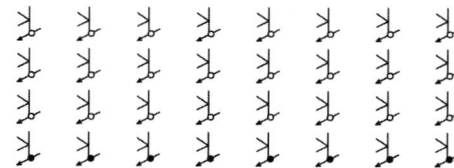

Top: position after manoeuvre

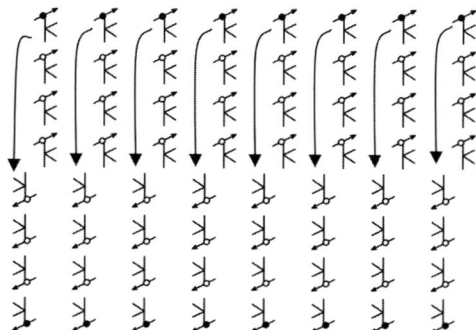

The two different ways to perform a countermarch (doubling back, folding) with cavalry.

Top Left: the file leaders turn either left or right (in the example towards the left) and then lead their files to face the rear.
Top right: the resulting formation when it was done on the spot.
Below Left: The aggressive countermarch in which the files were led forward towards the enemy without any halting in place.

second group. When performing these manoeuvres, the horsemen were required to use their shields for protection, which included the placing of the shield to protect the back (presumably by bringing it over the head to cover the back, with the top portion pointed downwards) when the javelin was thrown backwards. After both *turmae* had performed their manoeuvres, those who had charged first (*Turma A*) were standing again to the right of the tribunal, while the others (*Turma B*) stood on the left (38.1). The soldiers were required to possess adequate numbers of javelins for the entire performance. It is probable that they carried spare javelins in special holders, but Arrian's description makes it clear that while performing the manoeuvres the horsemen held their spare javelins in the left hand, quickly lowering the javelins from their left hand to the right hand, after which the men whirled them above their heads and threw them. This *Petrinos* 1 manoeuvre was to be performed twice by both units, after which it was modified. The illustration *Petrinos Movement* 1 (my interpretation) shows this.

In the modified version of Hyland's interpretation (ranks changed into files in my version), the files of *Turma B* charged at a gallop and threw as many missiles as possible at the shields of the two horsemen, while the files of *Turma A* charged straight at the charging files of *Turma B* and threw javelins at them. After passing the line of *Turma B* riders, the *Turma A* rider was obliged (while turning right) to throw a javelin with a backward movement. The riders of *Turma B* could also target the riders of *Turma A*. As before, the horsemen used their shields as protection.

After the above exercise had been performed twice, the men who had charged from the left (i.e. *Turma B*) no longer veered to the right and rode past the rostra (tribunal), but kept either one or two javelins for a new exercise. Those who kept one rode past the rostra, turned their horse in a circle and threw their javelin as far as they could. Those who had retained two javelins threw them obliquely backwards to their right. I have included here two alternative interpretations based on the above two versions.

According to Hyland's interpretation, when the horsemen had returned to their respective units, they changed roles. In this instance, *Turma B* placed two horsemen in front to act as targets. However, the second *petrinos* manoeuvre was slightly different as can be seen from the following diagrams. Nevertheless, the basic purpose of this exercise was similar to that of the first, namely to teach the horsemen to fight as individual fighters in the files that had charged forward to skirmish. The additional element was the throwing of javelins forward and backward in front of the rostra. This obviously demonstrated similar skills as were required from the horsemen in the Cantabrian gallop or circle that followed this exercise, the only difference between them being that in this exercise the horsemen threw javelins both forward and backward, whereas in the Cantabrian gallop the men used the *xyston/xuston* spear.

The purpose of the *petrinos* exercises was to train the horsemen to skirmish in successive files while protecting themselves against counter-attacks. The sending of files forward from the *turma* was a standard skirmishing tactic that had been used in Persia and Greece and continued to be used as long as there were javelin-armed horsemen. For example, some Roman horsemen engaged the Kutrigur Huns in front of Constantinople in this manner in 559. The typical tactic of the ancient Greeks was to first send files from the flanks and/or centre, and after they had returned either to send the remaining files to skirmish or attack into contact with the entire unit.[12]

264 Emperor Septimius Severus

Petrinos movement 1 (my interpretation)

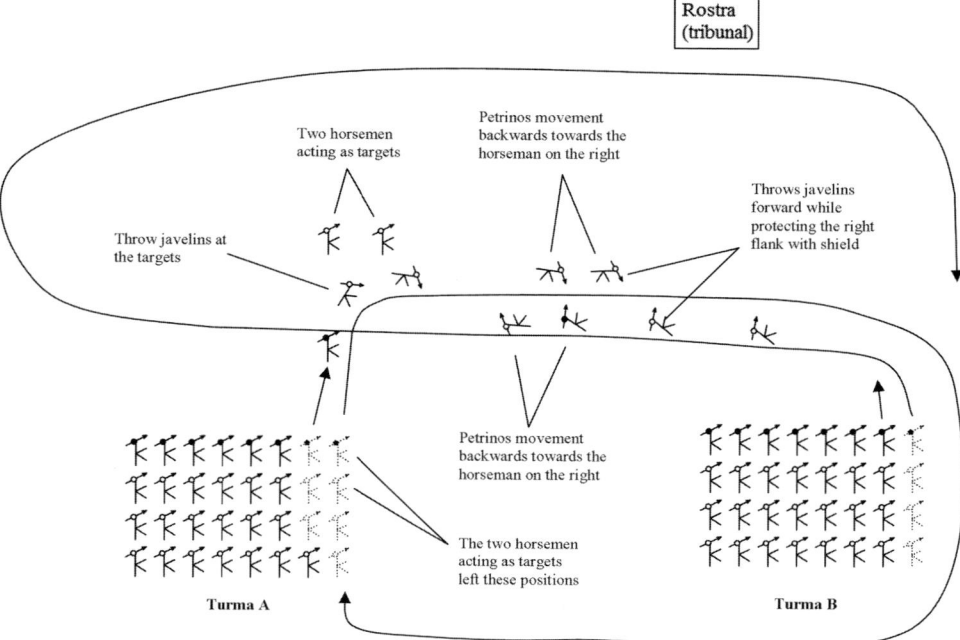

Petrinos movement 1 (adapted from Hyland)

The diagram differs from Hyland's interpretation (1993, 120), but is still heavily indebted to her groundbreaking conclusions. My interpretation differs from hers in that I consider the movement to have been performed successive files of the *turmae*.

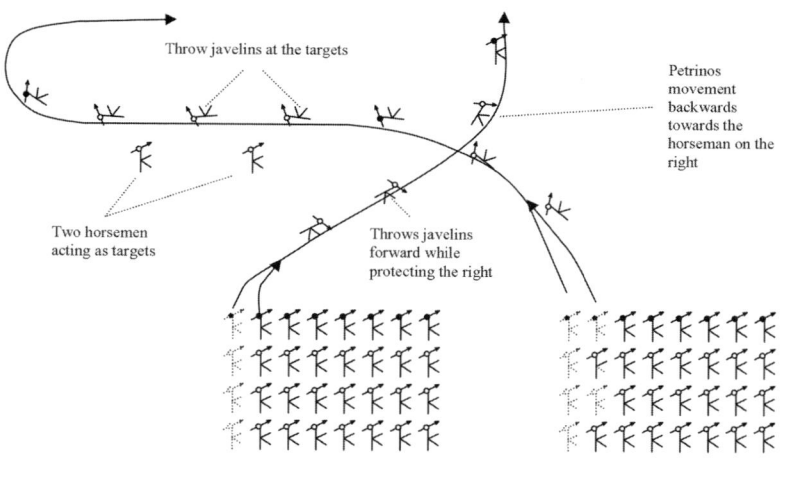

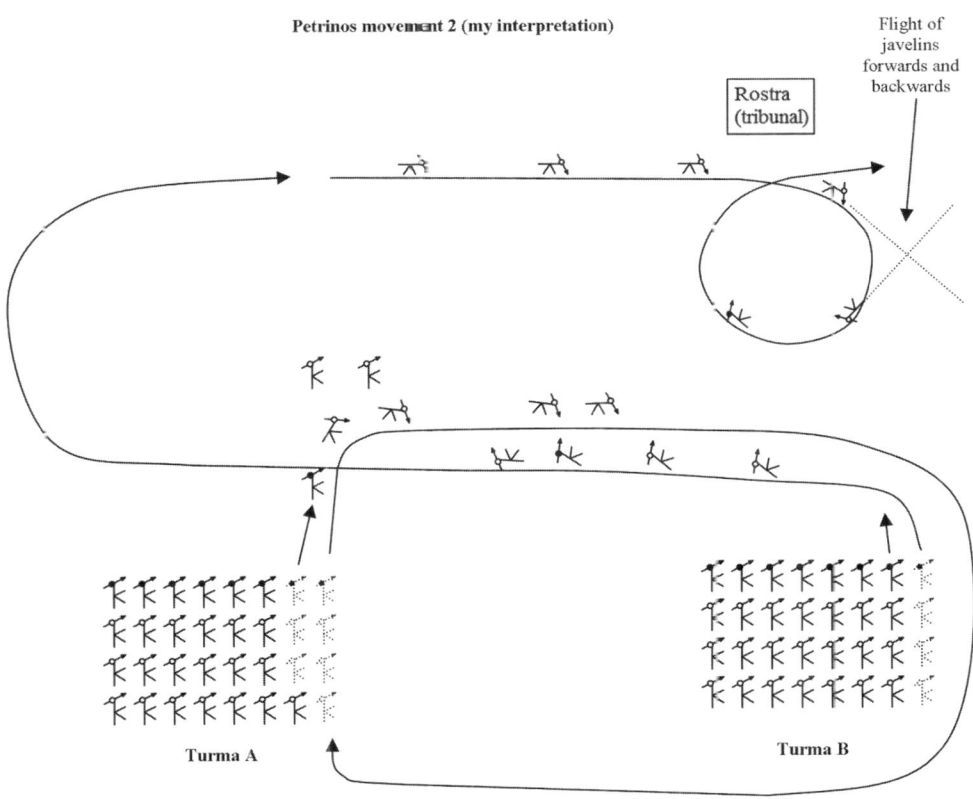

The second part of the exercise consisted of the so-called Cantabrian charge (or gallop, or circle). The manoeuvre got its name from the Iberian tribe of Celtic Cantabrians, from whom the Romans had adopted it. In this exercise, the *akontia* javelins were changed for the *xyston* spears (without iron tips) for training purposes, which on the basis of the use of the verb '*akontizô*' were thrown rather than thrust in this drill. In the Cantabrian gallop, the horsemen of *Turma B* approached as closely as possible their counterparts in the opposing circle. The *xyston* was aimed at the centre of the shield with such power that it could go right through it. Despite the use of the *akontizô*, it was also possible to thrust the *xyston* at the enemy shield when using the Cantabrian gallop, if the timing went awry. The purpose of the Cantabrian gallop was clearly to enable the horsemen in succession to engage their enemies as fast as possible, giving the rider a better chance of avoiding enemy reaction while giving his thrown (or thrust) *xyston* as much striking power as possible. The manoeuvre was equally effective against a static or circling target, or against a skirmishing enemy file. In the latter instance, the aim was to counter-attack the galloping enemy file without passing through it as in the previous *petrinos* exercise. Unfortunately, it is not entirely clear whether the circling movement was continued back to one's own place in the *turma* immediately after encountering the opposing man, or whether the same men continued the same circle until they had no spears left. Considering the length of the *xyston*, it is likely that in practice the soldiers carried only one, making it likely

266 Emperor Septimius Severus

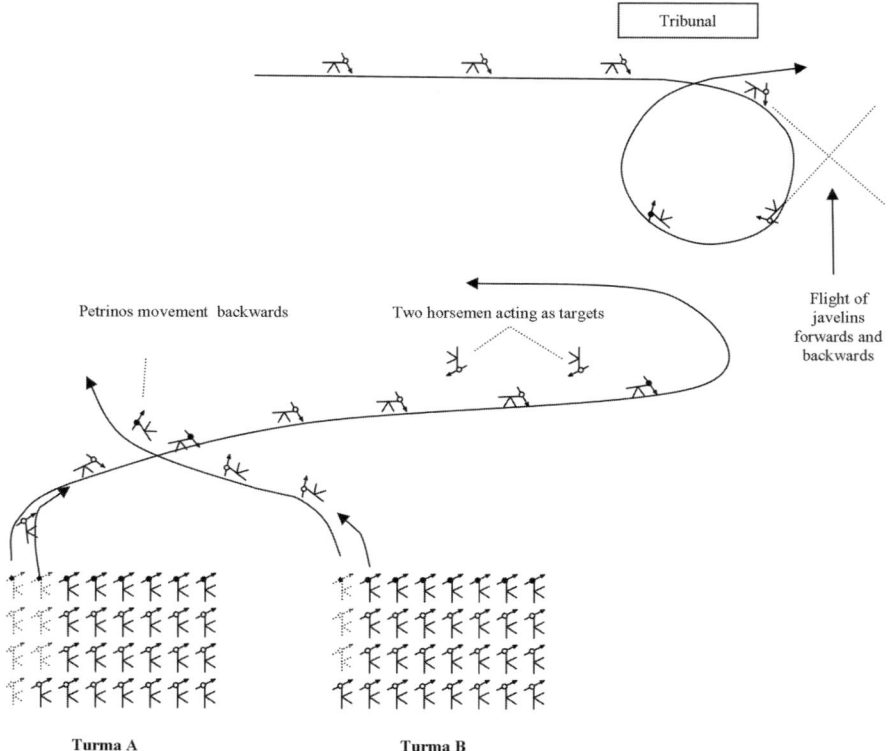

Petrinos movement 2 (modified Hyland)
The diagram differs from Hyland's interpretation (1993, 123), but is still heavily indebted to her groundbreaking conclusions. My interpretation differs from hers in that I consider the movement to have been performed by successive files of the *turmae* and in that the *petrinos* movement was performed by the Turma A horsemen. The second exercise in which the horsemen threw spears in front of the tribunal (emperor and/or high ranking officers judging the performance) follows Hyland's interpretation.

that they continued their gallop right back to their own unit and place. This alternative is shown in the diagram by the broken line. The galloping circle was kept in operation without a break by having each file follow the former. However, if this was true, then the men circled back to the front until all their spears were thrown, while the men of the next file each joined the Cantabrian circle in his turn, one at a time (see below).

Cantabrian Gallop/Circle
Two alternatives shown: 1) The men moved forward in a circular manner and returned right away (broken line) to their place in the array; 2) After throwing one *xyston*, the men circled around in the front until all their spears were thrown, and it was only then that they returned back to their place. The men of the second file would have joined the circle one at a time when they noted that the man in front was returning back.

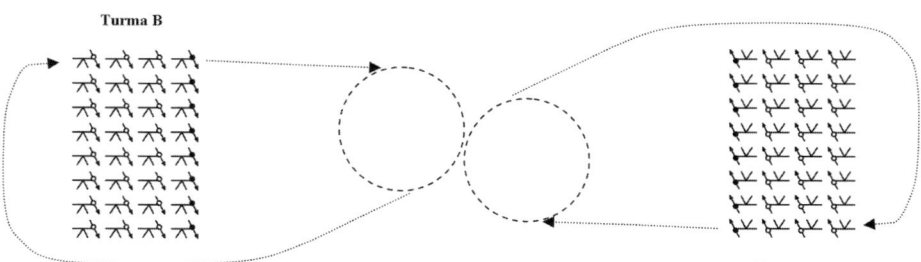

Arrian and Roman Battle Tactics 267

In addition, those horsemen who were expert riders and javelineers gave a display of their proficiency in rapid javelin throwing while galloping the whole length of the parade ground (*ca*. 200 metres). The requirement was to throw as many javelins as possible, as continuously as possible and as far as possible, so that they remained quivering after striking the ground. A good horseman was expected to be able to throw fifteen javelins in the course of his ride (one javelin for every 13 metres), while a real expert could throw as many as twenty (one javelin for every 10 metres). The Roman horsemen carried at least twenty javelins in their 'quiver'. Obviously, most of the javelins were thrown while the horse was still building up speed, since at full gallop the expert horseman would have had to throw almost one javelin per second. If the rider threw more than these he had achieved it by cheating, which was done by throwing two or three while still standing still at the start line. This exercise shows that the best Roman horsemen, namely those posted

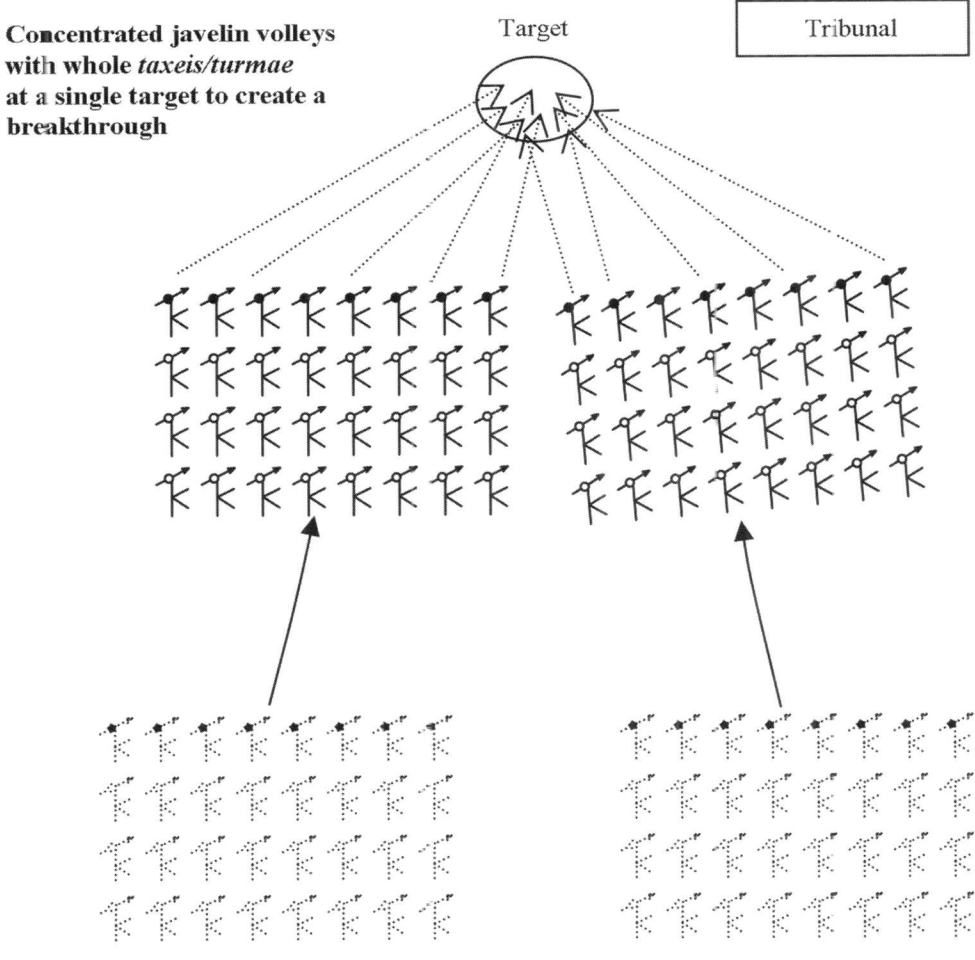

in the front rank, could throw very considerable numbers of short javelins against any enemy attackers who came within range and did not close in immediately. It also shows that the Roman cavalry carried large numbers of weapons with them.

As the above drills were obviously meant for skirmishing, one could easily make the mistake that these methods were dangerous if the Romans faced enemies who charged in unison as a single unit. However, the danger was not as great as one might think at first glance. Firstly, the Roman *turmae* had wide intervals between them, into which the files that had been skirmishing could retreat, while those files that had remained behind could charge at the possibly disordered pursuers; disordered units were always prone to flee when faced with a perfectly aligned formation. The physical closeness of the formation lessened the fear the soldiers felt. The retreating skirmishers could increase this disorder by harassing the attacking enemy with their javelins.

Next, the horsemen were required to arm themselves with strong protective equipment (iron corslets and helmets and heavier shields) and attack in unison. After this the *taxeis* (i.e. in the *turmae*) were to charge swiftly forwards towards the tribune, each man bearing a single *logche* lance, which they were to throw at a target which had been set up to the left of the tribune. This implies that each whole unit threw their spears simultaneously at a single target, which in turn suggests that the rear-rankers threw theirs over the front-rankers in a volley. The tactical intention of this manoeuvre must have been to concentrate the javelin fire of two *turmae* at a single target area simultaneously, with the explicit aim of creating a hole in the enemy line which could then be exploited to create a breakthrough.[13] Despite there being no requirement to do so, the good javelin throwers charged a second time because it gave them pleasure and earned praise from their officers. When they charged a second time, they took two javelins and threw them as accurately as possible while charging forwards in a straight line.

Each horseman then performed an exercise singly in front of the officers. When called upon, each man was to shout 'Present!' and simultaneously gallop forward carrying *logche* lances. He was to throw the first at a target placed on the edge of a dugout area, the second when he was level with the tribune and galloping in a straight line, and the third at a target in front of him while his horse was turning right. The throwing of the lance while making a turn was the most difficult of the throws, and was called a *xynema* in the Celtic language. The purpose of this demonstration was clearly to demonstrate that the horsemen could accurately release their lances at targets while galloping, and especially to show that they could ride straight at the enemy, turn at the last moment and throw a lance accurately while doing this. The best horsemen were able to throw four lances during this exercise: three in the course of gallop and one while turning away. The distinction and praise went to the *turma* that had the largest number of able lance throwers.

It is notable, however, that the very same troops were also taught how to employ crossbows (composite and/or torsion) and to throw stones by hand or by using slings (Arrian 43.1). As was noted by Ann Hyland (1993, p.154), slingers on foot using lead bullets could even outrange some archers, while if horsemen used their slings at a gallop, they could shoot even further than was possible on foot or while stationary. According to Onasander 19.3 (first century AD), the sling was the most deadly weapon in the arsenal of the *psiloi* (light footmen), because the lead slug or bullet appeared to be the 'same colour' as the air and was therefore invisible until it unexpectedly hit an opposing soldier.

It was also very awkward to extract if it hit any unprotected part of the body because it penetrated deep and was difficult to locate. It was also effective against armoured opponents, causing concussion damage when it hit a helmet. Despite its slow rate of fire, the crossbow had the benefit of being able to penetrate most types of armour at long ranges. Despite the fact that crossbows could be used for indirect fire, it is likely that they were most often used at relatively close range through direct fire. The Chinese infantry had used it and its many variants with great success against their nomadic opponents, while the Medieval Europeans were to use it with similar effectiveness against mounted enemies during the eleventh and twelfth centuries.[14]

After showing their ability with missiles, the troopers changed their weapons for the *kontos* pikes (*kontoforoi*) for an exercise that appears to have been performed in *turmae*. The *turmae* again seem to have consisted of two *turmae* and possibly of some separate horsemen who acted as enemy *turmae* on both sides of *Turma A*.[15] Firstly, *Turma A* appears to have charged *Turma B*, which made a defensive counter-charge with their *kontoi* poised forward. *Turma A* then turned and fled while pursued by *Turma B*. Next, as if attacking another enemy, as their horses performed an *epistrofé*[16] (in other words the whole of *Turma B* wheeled), the horsemen raised their shields above their heads, moved them to cover their backs and whirled their *kontoi* over to the other side as if another enemy were charging. In other words, when *Turma B* approached the enemy battle line, they wheeled to outflank their opponents while the enemy wheeled towards them so that that they would not be taken in the flank.[17] In the Celtic language, this pike manoeuvre was called the *toulutegon*, and it was probably performed towards the right because the men whirled their *kontoi* across the neck of the horse (i.e. from left to right). The shields were thrown back to act as a cover against possible enemies (another unit on the enemy line) now behind them. After this, the men drew their *spathae* swords and made a variety of strikes, either reaching their enemies in flight, killing those who had fallen from their horses or striking while riding obliquely alongside. These sword-fighting manoeuvres suggest that the enemy unit had been successfully taken in the flank and that *Turma B* was now pursuing them. Notably, the men had now resorted to the use of swords, which implies that the *toulutegon* meant the lancing of the enemy on the right-hand side while holding the *kontoi* with two hands.[18] The striking of fallen enemies is suggestive that the enemy on the right could not have been more than a few horsemen posing as a whole *turma*, not a *Turma C*, and that there were targets placed on the ground and on posts to act as targets for sword strikes.

After this, the troopers demonstrated all the possible styles and methods of jumping onto their horses, and as a finale they leaped in full armour onto a galloping horse. The last-mentioned drill shows how well trained the horses were. The trooper could whistle or otherwise call his mount to gallop past him so that he could jump onto it in full armour. It required quite a bit of athletic ability on the part of the rider. All of these methods of jumping onto a horse and mounting were also later praised as necessary by Vegetius because it prepared the troopers to real-life situations in which it was necessary to be able to mount their horses quickly. For example, when the enemy was approaching fast or a trooper had fallen from his horse, it was necessary to be able to mount the horse quickly. It should be noted, however, that this high standard was not always reached when the officers were negligent and allowed their troopers too much leisure time. On the basis

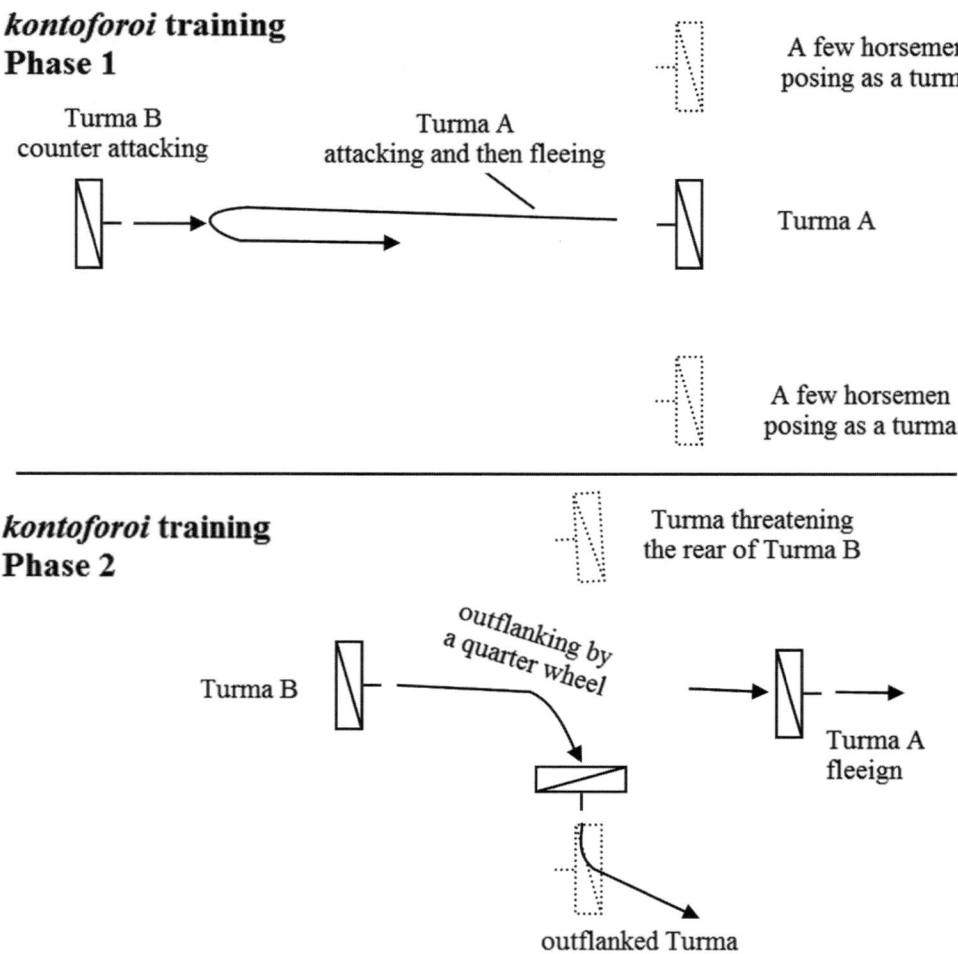

of Fronto's letter to Lucius Verus, Ann Hyland has shown how lax the military discipline had become in Syria during the peaceful reign of Antoninus Pius.

According to Arrian (*Tactics* 44.1), all of the abovementioned training drills were practised by the Roman cavalry since ancient times, but this was not all, as Hadrian had introduced new barbarian cavalry practices. The new training system included manoeuvres used by the Parthian and Armenian horse archers (which implies the use of the cavalry rhombus, see above), along with the turns and feigned retreats of the Sarmatian and Celtic *kontoforoi* (units deployed as oblongs or squares), with the cavalry taking turns to charge and skirmish. This shows that Hadrian expected his cavalry to be a very versatile force that could face any type of enemy in any kind of situation. He even expected them to be proficient in mounted archery. However, it must be noted that it is very unlikely that the regular Roman cavalry achieved the same proficiency with the bow as the Parthians and Armenians. In order to achieve proficiency with the bow while mounted, horsemen needed many years of arduous training. Therefore, it is likely that the best units of mounted archers in Roman service consisted of those from the East.

In addition, Arrian (*Tactics* 44.1) noted that Hadrian required his cavalry to use war cries native to each race, whether Celtic, Getic or Rhaetic cavalry. The Getae were either Thracians or Dacians, but considering the time period the latter is more likely. The Rhaetians were undoubtedly Germans who had settled in Rhaetia. This in turn implies that the Roman cavalry were also trained to use Dacian and Germanic cavalry tactics, the former possibly being based on the use of two horses and the latter on rectangular deep cavalry formations for close-quarters melees with spears and swords. Hadrian (*Tactica* 44.2) had also required that the horses were trained to jump across ditches and leap over walls. He had recognized the need for his cavalry to be able to cross all kinds of obstacles, as they could not know in advance what kinds of obstacles the enemies might devise, for example to protect their camp or battle line.

In summary, the Roman cavalry already received very thorough training in all kinds of manoeuvres before the reign of Hadrian, but after his reforms they can be considered to have been the most versatile cavalry in Europe and the Middle East. Not even the famed Parthian cavalry could have been so versatile. However, we should not be blinded by this. The Parthians and others from the East still had greater quantities of crack mounted archers than did the Romans. Practically all the Parthians were skilled shots with the bow and expert horsemen. In addition, they had first-rate heavy cataphract cavalry, which the Romans could not match in quality or numbers. In pitched battle, the Romans usually had to use their infantry to negate the shock capability of the Parthia cataphracts, because they rarely had enough horsemen, even including foreign auxiliaries, to oppose the tens of thousands of horsemen brought by the enemy.

Ektaxis kata Alanôn (Expedition against the Alans)

Arrian's *Expedition against the Alans* in all probability describes the actual marching and battle formations used by Arrian against the Alans when he was governor of the strategically situated Cappadocia. The marching and battle formations of Arrian demonstrate that there had occurred a major change in the preferred Roman tactical doctrine after the reign of Trajan, and therefore during the reign of Hadrian. The peaceful outlook of Hadrian's foreign policy had clearly allowed him to have a major overhaul of Roman military doctrines. The soldiers had been taught to operate primarily in phalanxes. Hadrian was also a strong advocate of the strategy of preclusive security: he built walls on the borders, most famously Hadrian's Wall in northern Britain, and instituted a very rigorous regime of peacetime military training among the armed forces so that they could learn the new drills thoroughly. It is particularly noteworthy that in the aftermath of the Dacian and Parthian wars, Hadrian paid particular attention to the cavalry, as is attested by Hadrian himself in his speech at Lambaesis and by Arrian. Even though the Romans may have used cataphracts before, it is perhaps no coincidence that the first known cataphract cavalry unit (*Ala I Gallorum et Pannoniorum Catafractata*) dates from the reign of Hadrian. The name suggests a western origin. The most likely source of inspiration would have been the Sarmatian/Alan heavy cavalry of the type shown in the Column of Trajan, but equipped with the Gallic *contus*.

Order of March

Arrian's order of march was as follows. The army was spearheaded by mounted scouts (*kataskopoi*) arrayed in two sections under their own commander. The mounted Petraean Archers (*hippotoxotai*) followed them in two sections under the command of their decurions. After these came the (cavalry) Ala Auriana and the Fourth Raetians commanded by Daphnis the Corinthian. Behind them were the Ala of Colonists and with them the Ituraeans, Cyrenaicans and First Raetians, all under Demetrius. The Celtic cavalry followed them and were deployed in two sections commanded by the centurion in charge of the camp.

The infantry was placed behind and followed four abreast. The implication is that the units mentioned before the infantry were all cavalry.[19] The foot archers marched in front of their heavy infantry. Centurions were arrayed along the marching column to keep the infantry in order. The overall commander, and governor of Cappadocia, Arrian, was usually in front of the infantry column, but rode up and down the whole column regularly to inspect it. First in the infantry marching column were the Italians followed by Cyrenaicans, all under Pulcher, the prefect of the Italians. Behind them were the Bosporan infantry under the command of Lamprocles, and then the Numidians under the prefect Verus. The Numidian cavalry protected the flanks of the marching column. Behind them were the *equites singulares* (governor's bodyguards) and the legionary cavalry (often used as messengers), followed by the artillery train (*katapeltai*).

Next in line was the standard of the Legio XV and its commander Valens, his second-in-command (*hyparchos*), the military tribunes (*chiliarchoi*) and the five centurions (*hekatontarchai*) of the first cohort (*speira*). The javelinmen (*akontistai*) were arrayed in front of the legion's standard. The infantry marched in ranks four abreast. Then followed the standard of the Legio XII, its tribunes and centurions, and after them the infantry in ranks four abreast.

Arrian's text has conflicting information regarding the composition of the next forces in the marching column. In Chapter 7 he states that the hoplites of the allies came after the legions, and in a separate clause that these consisted of the Lesser Armenians and the Trapezuntian hoplites, and of the Colchian and Rhiziarian javelineers/spearmen (*longchoforoi*). In Chapters 12–13 Arrian states that the Armenian commanders commanded both infantry and cavalry, and that all of these included *toxotai* (archers). This mistake is easy to explain because the Lesser Armenians are mentioned separately from the Trapezuntian hoplites and Colchian/Rhizionion *logchoforoi*. In Chapter 14 he actually calls the Trapezuntians *gymnêtikoi* (light-armed). This means that the hoplites of the allies mean only the allied forces in Chapter 7 in general. It should be noted, however, that in military theory the *logchoforoi* signified cavalry javelineers, which may therefore mean that (contrary to common belief) the Trapezuntians, Colchians and Rhizionians were light cavalry, but on balance it seems likelier that these were javelinmen who were deployed behind the heavy infantry (see below). It should also be stressed that Arrian's claim that the Armenian cavalry consisted of archers does not mean that all of them were light cavalry. The Armenian sources prove that the Armenian cavalry consisted of *katafraktoi*, *kontoforoi* and *hippotoxotai*, all of whom were able to use the bow. Behind the allies marched the Apulian infantry. All allies were commanded by Secundinus, the commander of the Apulians. Next came the baggage train that included servants,

Septimius Severus, 'The Most Glorious of the Emperors'   273

Marching Order of Arrian NOT IN SCALE!			Identification of units by Ritterling (1902) and others in the DeVoto ed. pp.105-8	
2 units of scouts		Commander of the scouts	numerus exploratorum	
2 units of Petraean mounted archers		Decurions	equites cohortis III Ulpiae Petraeorum miliariae equitatae sagittariorum	
Ala Auriana Fourth Raetian		Daphnis the Corinthian	ala II Ulpia Auriana equites cohortis III Raetorum equitatae	
Ala of colonists Ituraeans Cyrenaicans First Raetian		Demetrius	ala I Augusta gemina Colonorum equites cohortis cuiusdam Ityraeorum sagittariorum equitatae equites cohortis III Augustae Cyrenaicae sagittariorum equitatae equites cohortis I Raetorum equitatae	
Celtic cavalry		Centurion in charge of the camp	equites cohortis I Germanorum miliariae equitatae	
Light infantry Italians, Cyrenaicans		Pulcher, prefect of Italians	cohors I Italica voluntariorum civium Romanorum vexillatio cohortis III Cyrenaicae	
Light infantry Bosporans		Lamprocles	cohors I Bosporanorum miliaria equitata	
Light infantry Numidians		Prefect Verus	cohors I Numidarum equitata	
Equites singulares Legionary cav.		**ARRIAN**	equites singularis praesidis equites legionarii	Flavius Arrianus, legatus Augusti pro praetore provinciae Cappadociae
artillery				
Javelinmen Standard of Legio XV and officers		Valens praefectus castrorum		legatus legionis M. Vettius Valens praefectus castrorum
Legio XV	equites cohortis I Italicae		legio XV Apollinaris	
Standard of Legio XII and officers		Tribunes		tribuni
Legio XII	ala II Gallorum		legio XII fulminata	
Armenian and Trapezuntian HI. Javelinmen of Colchis and Rhizus Apulian inf.		Secondinus, commander of Apulians	symmachiarii cohors Apuleia civium Romanorum	
baggage train				
Ala of Dacians		commander of Dacians	ala I Ulpia Dacorum	

ala of Gauls and Italian cavalry ride as a single file on both sides of the marching column workmen and other specialists. The rear was brought up by the cavalry *ala* of Dacians. The sides of the marching column were protected by the *ala* of Gauls and the Italian cavalry, which were arrayed on both sides of the marching column in single file. Their prefect was instructed to inspect the flanks regularly.

One notable feature of the composition of Arrian's army is that most of his cavalry consisted of mounted archers (six units plus two Armenian units), and if we designate these according to the units named in the marching order we find that some of those assigned as mounted archers by Arrian contain a mixture of different ethnic troops, suggesting the probability that the Romans already posted more heavily equipped men in the front ranks of such units to make them more suitable for hand-to-hand combat. Another notable thing is that most of the units designated as mounted archers must have come from the Balkans. Consequently, the model for Hadrian's cavalry reforms probably came from the Alans and Sarmatians.

Deployment and Order of Battle

According to Arrian, when the army had reached its intended destination, the cavalry wheeled round in a circular manoeuvre to a square formation and the mounted scouts (*kataskopoi*) were sent ahead to high ground to look out for the enemy. Unfortunately, Arrian does not clarify what he meant by cavalry square formation, but an educated guess would be that the cavalry was arrayed as a square to mark the boundaries of the marching camp or that they deployed in two lines. When given a signal to do so, the men then armed themselves in silence and dressed their ranks, evidently behind the protective screen of cavalry. All this implies the use of spies and scouts ahead of the main column, because it suggests that the general already knew approximately where he wanted to engage the advancing enemy formation. Besides being used for scouting the high ground, the scouts were undoubtedly also used to induce the enemy to approach the chosen battleground. The scouts would have either shown themselves to the enemy to prompt them to come in their direction or they would have skirmished with the enemy and then withdrawn to the battle site.

Each wing of the infantry was to be deployed on the high ground that favoured infantry. In front of the right wing were placed the Italian cohort, as a bulwark to the Armenian infantry and cavalry that were positioned behind as reserves and missile troops. The overall commander of the right wing was Pulcher, the commander of the Italians, while Vasaces and Arbelus commanded the Armenians. In front of the left wing as a phalanx bulwark (*probolē*) were 200 Apulian and 100 Cyrenaican heavy infantry, and behind them the allies (*symmachoi*) from Lesser Armenia (undoubtedly again consisting of both cavalry and light infantry), the light-armed (*gymnetikoi*) men from Trapezus and the Rhizionian 'spearmen' (*logchoforoi*, i.e. javelin/spear-bearers). It is clear that the artillery was positioned behind both wings to provide supporting fire on the approaching enemy at long range (Arrian 19).

Even if not specifically mentioned by Arrian, the arranging of wing units in this manner had several positive battlefield applications and implications. The infantry wings on the higher ground protected the flanks of the army, while the higher elevation allowed the artillery, foot archers and Armenian mounted archers to outrange their opponents, the Alan mounted archers. The artillery engaged the approaching enemy from a distance and channelled the enemy attack towards the centre. When the enemy reached the range of the bowmen, they received further pressure to veer towards the centre. The movement of the Alan wings towards the centre would have created confusion and disorder in their ranks. If the enemy attack was channelled towards the centre, the wing units put them into a crossfire from both sides, but if the enemy persisted in keeping their course the higher ground helped its defenders.

Between the hills was placed an infantry phalanx arrayed eight ranks deep in close order, consisting of Legio XII and XV. The full-strength Legio XV occupied the whole right side and the centre, while the below-strength Legio XII was deployed in the remaining space on the left.

The first four ranks of the legions were equipped with pikes (*kontoi*) that had long iron heads (Arrian, *Ektaxis* 16–17). Unfortunately, Arrian's text allows many different interpretations, as has been noted by numerous scholars. The word '*kontos*' implies long spears or pikes, while the long iron head fits better the heavy *pilum* javelin. However, the structure of the array, with the spears of the first four ranks reaching the front, suggests a longer spear than the *pilum* and the use of the phalanx formation. I thus agree with the well-argued conclusions of Everett Wheeler.[20] The subsequent description of the use of this weapon shows that it was not the *sarissa* pike of the Macedonians, but rather a *hasta*/*kontarion* spear or extra-long version of the *pilum* because these could be used to both thrust and throw. Furthermore, if Arrian had meant the *sarissa*, he would have stated that the spears of the five or six ranks reached the front. It should be noted that regardless of the weapon type (*hasta* or *pilum*), the long iron head would in this case have been necessary for both types of shafted weapons because it prevented the enemy cavalry from cutting off the heads of the weapons when they faced a wall of pointed spears or javelins. This raises the interesting possibility that some of the so-called *pila* heads in archaeological finds could actually have been used on *hastae* spears so that enemy horsemen could not cut them off. It is possible to think that the socketed iron heads were intended for use with the *hastae* while the tanged iron heads were meant for the *pila*. Unfortunately, in Chapter 26 Arrian contradicts himself by stating that the fourth rank used *logche* (i.e. the *lancea pugnatoria*) and not the *kontos* (or *contus*). For further details, see below. When one combines the ability of these *logche* of the fourth rank to reach beyond the first rank with the information that the infantry *logcherofoi* of the Roman general were equipped with *logche* and *aspis*, it becomes possible that their *logche* were at least 3.74 metres long. However, I would suggest that the terminology is in this case inaccurate or that two different types of *logche* were used.

The next four ranks after the foot *kontoforoi* comprised the spearmen/javelin throwers (*logchoforoi*). Considering the fact that both the javelineers and the men of the fourth rank are claimed to have used the *logche*, it is possible that *logche* meant the two different types of *lanceae* spears, namely the *lancea pugnatoria* (long spear) and regular *lancea* (javelin). Behind this phalanx, in the ninth rank, were placed the foot archers (*pezoi toxotai*), consisting of the Numidians, Cyrenaicans, Bosporans and Itureans. It is probable that they were deployed four ranks deep. The battlefield mission of the phalanx was to receive, halt and defeat the frontal charge of the Alan *kontoforoi* lancers. The four front ranks stood their ground, while the rear ranks used missiles to disorder and break up the enemy charge.

The cavalry was drawn up in eight *alae* and *lochoi* (Arrian 20). This statement has proven to be problematic for historians because it is possible to interpret the eight *alae* and *lochoi* as units or as ranks of horsemen. However, in light of the next sentence in the same chapter, it is practically certain that *lochoi* means units and not ranks. Two *lochoi*, consisting of the spearmen/javelin throwers (*logchoforoi*), pike-carrying lancers (*kontoforoi*), swordsmen (*machairoforoi*) and axemen (*pelekoforoi*), were placed on the wings behind the heavy infantry and archers. These two wing *lochoi* were used as wing reserves. The notable thing about these wing *lochoi* is that they are in agreement with the information given by Arrian about the native Roman cavalry in his *Techne Taktikê*. According to Arrian's *Tactics* (4.7–9), the Roman cavalry consisted of the pike-carrying lancers that charged in the manner of the Alans and Sarmatians, and of the javelinmen/spearmen. In combat, the latter either threw or thrust their spears as needed and fought at close range by using *spathae* long swords or small spiked axes.

According to the *Expedition* (31), if the light Alan cavalry was victorious on one wing or the other, the Roman cavalry wings were to attack them in the flank, not with javelins but with swords and axes. In other words, the cavalry charge was to be carried to close quarters, where it was more advantageous to use swords or axes rather than the extra-long *kontos* pike. The notable thing in this context is that Arrian does not separate the *kontoforoi*, *logchoforoi*, *machairoforoi* and *pelekoforoi* into distinct and separate units, implying that the same 512-man *lochos* could possess all of these, possibly so that the *kontoforoi* formed the two front ranks and the *logchoforoi* the next two, or alternatively that there were really two separate classes of units consisting of the *kontoforoi* and *logchoforoi*. In light of the splitting of divisions into wings of *koursores* (runners/chargers/skirmishers) and *defensores* (defenders deployed as close-order soldiers) in the later *Strategikon*, it is possible that the flanks of the *kontoforoi* were protected by *turmae* of *logchoforoi* so that the wings skirmished while the centre charged frontally.

The remaining six *lochoi* were placed in the middle of the phalanxes (i.e. behind the centre consisting of the legions). Many of these were mounted archers (*hippotoxotai*) posted near the legions so that they could shoot over them (20ff.). The problem with this statement is that there is a lacuna between sentences, as a result of which it is possible to interpret the evidence in two different ways. With the reference (27–28) to using only half of the *lochoi* for pursuit, the ones that had been posted (or rather designated to be) in front, while the rest followed them as their defenders, it is possible that three of the *lochoi* consisting of mounted archers were placed just behind the legions and the remaining three further behind. However, there is a serious problem with this, namely the fact that Arrian states (20) that the eight *alae* and *lochoi* were all placed next to infantry (*to de hippikon xumpan kata eilas kai lochous oktô xuntetagmenon efestatô tois pezois*). See the attached diagrams. These reconstructions imply that the Romans would have usually deployed their cavalry combat line just like the Alans, with every other unit as pursuers and defenders, alternatively that the cavalry were in two successive lines of equal strength, or that they used a single long line with two reserve units. Regardless of which alternative one adopts, it is clear that at this time almost all Roman cavalry units could be employed as mounted archers, as required by Hadrian's training doctrine. It is also notable that Arrian's army included all the types of cavalry – even cataphracts (the Armenians) – mentioned in his *Techne Taktikê*, with the armament of the cavalry able to be varied according to the needs of the occasion.

The bodyguard cavalry of the governor, the *equites singulares*, were stationed around Arrian, together with 200 infantrymen chosen from the legions as a personal bodyguard. Centurions (*hekatontarchai*) commanded the infantrymen and bodyguard, while decurions (*dekarchai*) commanded the *equites*. In addition, there were about 100 light-armed *logchoforoi* that were around Arrian so that he could safely inspect the battle line and go wherever needed. The bodyguards of Arrian served as an emergency reserve for the centre. The right-wing infantry and cavalry were commanded by Valens, the legate of the Legio XV, while the tribunes of the Legio XII commanded the infantry and cavalry on the left wing.

As I already noted in *The Age of Hippotoxotai* (p.228, n.1), the battle array of Arrian is essentially the equivalent of the *epikampios emprosthia* formation of the Hellenistic, Late Roman and Byzantine military manuals, with the protruding wings placed on higher ground to subject the approaching enemy cavalry to a crossfire of missiles.

Arrian foresaw several alternative ways in which the battle could progress. In all scenarios the soldiers were expected to keep silent until the enemy approached into firing range. Then they shouted the war-cry as loudly and aggressively as they could to scare the enemy. At the same time the artillery fired bolts and stones, after which the bowmen shot arrows and the javelineers threw their missiles, each at the appropriate range and time. The allies also threw stones at the enemy from the tops of the hills. In the opinion of Arrian, a heavy missile assault from all angles in combination with the war-cry was likely to cause confusion among the enemy horses, with the result that they would not even dare to approach the legions.

Arrian's text provides conflicting information regarding what happened when the Alan cavalry managed to reach the legions. In Chapters 16–18. the first four ranks of legionaries were equipped with the *kontus*, so that the first rank thrust their spears at the chest of the horses and the other three ranks held them like javelins and threw them at the riders or horses. The effectiveness of the *kontos* was said to be based on the fact that when it pierced either shield or armour, it would bend because of the softness of the iron, with the result that the rider would be rendered ineffective. This strongly suggests the use of

Arrian's Battle Order against the Alans

the *pilum*-type heavy javelin, but as noted above it is still possible that the *hastae* were also equipped with the long and slender head at this time. According to the version provided by Chapter 26, the first three ranks were to interlock their shields and stand shoulder-to-shoulder in close order (this implies the use of flat oval shields, but not conclusively so because this was also possible with concave and cylindrical shields) to receive the enemy charge, while the fourth rank threw their *logche*-type spears at the enemy over the heads of the first three ranks. This means that either Arrian or a later copyist has confused the two types of missiles, or the soldiers carried two sorts of spears into combat, or the *logche* and *kontos* are synonymous in this case. The fact that the *lochoforoi* bodyguards of the governor carried *logche* and *aspis* does suggest a probability that the *logche* in question was indeed the same as the Late Roman *kontarion* (a smaller version of the traditional *kontos/contus*) that had a length of 3.74 metres. While this happened, the first rank held their *kontoi* ready, and then at the appropriate moment thrust or threw them at the enemy horses, particularly at their chests.

The facts that the three front ranks interlocked their shields, the front rank was expected to thrust their spears at the chest of the horses and the fourth rank was expected to throw their missiles suggest the use of the defensive *testudo* array, the equivalent of the Late Roman defensive *foulkon* formation. In that array, the front rank either kneeled or crouched very low, the second rank stood a little more upright, the third rank stood almost erect and the fourth rank stood completely straight. The shields were arrayed in a sloping angle that protected the infantry very effectively from missiles and the very long *kontos* pikes/lances. As the enemy horses approached this formation, they first faced a shower of missiles that were bound to disorder their formation, and then an impenetrable obstacle of men and shields bristling with spears. As noted by Arrian, it was very likely that the enemy would be repulsed through the use of this formation and tactic.

If the enemy was forced to flee (27ff.), the infantry was expected to open up their ranks for the cavalry to advance and pursue the defeated enemy. The correct procedure for the pursuit was that only half of the cavalry units chased the enemy while the remainder followed them more deliberately by maintaining ranks and order (27–28). Arrian's instruction (27) that the pursuit was not to be performed by all *lochoi*, but only half of them – those that had been deployed first, or probably rather designated first (?) – has caused confusion among many modern commentators, myself included. Arrian's words unfortunately leave open several possibilities. It is possible that the first half of the *lochoi* pursuing the enemy meant the six *lochoi* of cavalry and probably also the Armenian *symmachoi* (20–21, 27–28), and that their protectors consisted of the legionary cavalry posted behind. This receives support from Arrian's statement (29, see below) that the infantry were to follow the cavalry so that they could protect them in case they were forced to retreat, with the implication that all cavalry had advanced in front of the infantry. However, this is not conclusive because it is possible that Arrian has just omitted some details. Further support comes from the fact that we know from other sources that the Romans used a cavalry formation which had one long first line, with two reserve units (in this case the legionary cavalry) posted behind. The second possibility is that the six *lochoi* had been deployed as a single line next to infantry (as in 20), but only half of these (27, interpreting Arrian's words as those 'designated' to be the first) pursued while the remaining half acted as reserves for the pursuers (28). We may find an answer to the problem from the *Strategikon* (12.1.29ff.) which describes a similar tactical situation. In this example, the infantry *foulkon* brought the enemy to a halt, after which it opened up its formation (infantry units doubling their depth) so that the cavalry pursuers could pass through. The first half of each cavalry *akia/acies* (means both battle line and file) then pursued while the second half of each *akia/acies* followed as their defenders. We can discount the file interpretation, but this still leaves open two other possibilities: 1) The entire front line used as pursuers with the legionary cavalry as its defenders; 2) The deployment of the eight *lochoi* in the front as *koursores* and *defensores* so that every other unit acted as *koursores* in the Alan manner (*Strategikon* 6.2) while the rest followed them as *defensores* and after them the legionary cavalry these as second support line. The second alternative is the likeliest because it reconciles all of the details. It is unlikely to be a coincidence that the *Strategikon* includes both the Alan Drill (6.2, every other unit as pursuers and defenders) and the double cavalry line for a medium sized cavalry force of ca. 5,000–15,000 men (3.8.36–9.5; front line with two reserve divisions) and that this is precisely the same number of horsemen (ca. 5,120) that we find in Arrian's text. Arrian then (28) continued – still in the context of cavalry pursuit – that if the enemy wheeled about, the well-ordered cavalry reserves following after the pursuer would face the disordered enemy with their perfectly aligned formations.

As already noted, Arrian instructed the infantry forces to follow the cavalry (29). The Armenian *toxotai* (archers in this case clearly mean the foot archers on the hills rather

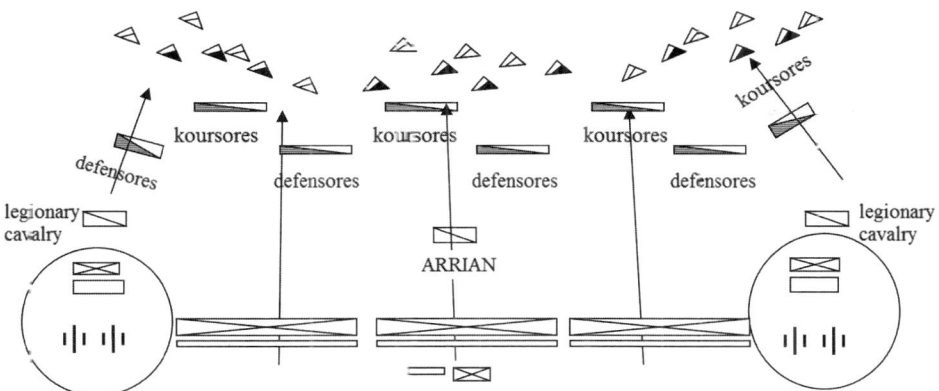

ARRIAN'S CAVALRY FORMATIONS
ABOVE: The guess has been made that Arrian together with his bodyguard cavalry would have followed the pursuing cavalry so as to be able to take command of the army if necessary immediately. The likeliest version of the cavalry array used by Arrian in pursuit implies that the cavalry battle formation consisted of two lines of units and commander's personal bodyguards so that the pursuit of the defeated foe would have been conducted by the Alan Drill formation (every other unit deployed as *koursores* and *defensores*).
BELOW: The array shows how the same cavalry units would have been deployed for cavalry battle. There are several similarities between the *Strategikon* and Arrian: Arrian has *epikampios emprosthia* (infantry front; cavalry behind) with cavalry rear guards (legionary cavalry) while the *Strategikon* has *epikampios opisthia* (infantry front, cavalry behind; which could be transformed into *epikampios emprosthia* by having the wings move forward) similarly with cavalry rear guards.

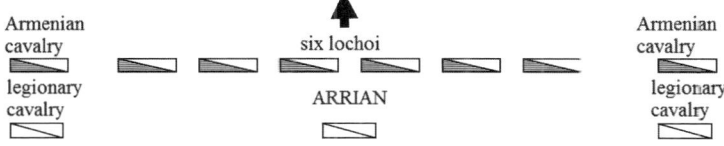

than the cavalry, which are likely to have pursued together with the rest of the cavalry) were also expected to join the pursuit so that the enemy would be unable to regroup. The *logchoforoi* (in this case once again infantry) were to follow the Armenian archers. This means that the pursuing cavalry posted on the flanks were supported first by the light infantry following them and not by the heavier units. The infantry formation (i.e. the legionary phalanx and its archers, and also the heavier infantry units posted on the flanks) also advanced at a quick march and followed the pursuing cavalry so that if the enemy regrouped, they could again provide a protective screen for their cavalry.

The third hypothetical combat situation mentioned by Arrian that has survived (30–31) was that the enemy wheeled about and attempted to outflank the wing. In that case the *psiloi* (i.e. the Armenian archers and the *logchoforoi*) were expected to extend the wings out to the hills. This means that the light infantry on both wings which were closest to the cavalry sought safety from the hills and let the retreating cavalry through, after which they put the pursuing Alans under fire from two sides. Arrian did not consider it likely that the enemy would then be able to force their way through them, but if they somehow managed to fight through one of the wings, the Roman cavalry was then to attack them not with javelins but with swords and axes, because the Scythians – with both men and horses unprotected by armour – were then at disadvantage. The implication is that both the Roman horses and men were protected by armour. This is where Arrian's text unfortunately and abruptly stops.

As regards the battlefield deployment of the Alans, Arrian's text is very interesting. It shows that they deployed their armoured cavalry in the centre of their battle line (17) and the non-armoured cavalry on the extreme flanks (31). Notably, the centre consisted of armoured horsemen and of cavalry carrying shields. It appears probable that the shield was either used by those not employing the *kontos* with two hands or only during the approach, after which it was left hanging on straps on the shoulder or behind the back. On the basis of the Alan drill in the *Strategikon*, the Alan formation consisted of a single line that was divided into three divisions, in which the *moirai* were deployed with wider intervals than usual. The information in the *Strategikon* also implies the use of the oblong cavalry formation by the Alan cavalry, except when the *koursores* were pursuing or skirmishing in front of the line. The real problem with the Alan unit orders is that the sources do not specifically state which order they used in combat and pursuit. However, on the basis of the information in the *Strategikon*, it appears probable that the Alans deployed and used their *defensores* and *koursores* like the Romans did – the only difference being the use of wider intervals between the *moirai*.

Appendix 2

Frontinus and Combat Tactics on Land

It is very unfortunate that we do not possess military treatises which can be pinpointed without any shadow of doubt to the period under analysis. However, we do have them which date from the period before and after this, and also some narrative sources (like the ones which are included in this monograph) that allow the making of some tentative conclusions regarding the combat and military doctrine followed by the Romans at this time. The earlier military treatises of importance are the *Stratagems* of Frontinus and the fragments of his *Tactics* (or *De Officio Militari/ On the Office of General*) in Lydus's treatise of Roman magistracies, and the *Ektaxis kata Alanon* and *Techne Taktike* of Arrian (Arrianos). Both of these date from the early second century. Pseudo-Hygirus's treatise of marching camps may be contemporary to this period, but it does not offer details of period combat tactics. The later treatises include Julius Africanus's *Kestoi*, which dates from *ca*. 231, and the military treatises of Modestus (*ca*. 275?), Vegetius (*ca* 390–450?), the *Peri Strategias* of Syrianus Magister (late sixth century) and the *Strategikon* (late sixth century). I have dealt with the information provided by Arrian in Appendix 1, so I can concentrate here on the text of Frontinus. His *De Officio Militari* (Lydus 3.3) makes clear the standard way to organize higher-ranking officers in the battle array. The supreme commander/emperor (*monarchos, hyparchos/huparchos, Kaisar/Caesar, imperatoros/imperator, autokrator*) was in the centre of the formation and therefore in command of the centre and the army. The commander of the left wing was the cavalry commander (*hipparchos*) or the prefect (*hyparchos/huparchos/praefectus*), while the right wing was commanded by the *praetores* (*praitores*, governors) and *legati* (*legatoi*, legates). The same command structure can be found in Arrian's *Ektaxis kata Alanon* (see Appendix 1) and also in the much later *Strategikon* (see Syvänne, 2004). However, the overall commander was always free to vary this command structure as he deemed fit, so it is not surprising to find that Vegetius (3.18) placed the overall commander on the right side between infantry and cavalry, and the same is implied by Frontinus (*Stratagems* 2.22), who included the famous Battle of Pharsalus among his stratagems. In other words, while the standard tactical doctrine was to place the commander in the centre, in practice he chose his position according to his own plan of battle and the way in which the battle progressed.

The *Stratagems* of Frontinus (esp. 2.3–4) give us a long list of combat formations that he expected the Roman commander to be able to emulate when necessary. This list proves that the Roman armies were trained to fight in scattered manipular order and also in various types of cohortal formation and phalanxes. His list of combat arrays (Greek equivalents given within parentheses) includes the following: a triple line of either maniples or cohorts for the Romans and a triple line of phalanxes for their enemies (*triplex acies*, a variation of the Greek *trifalaggia* but the latter of which could also mean *epikampios*); crescent (*menoeides*); convex (*kurte/kyrte*); *epikampios emprosthia* (forward-angled half-square or rather its variant which was to send wings forward against the enemy's flanks); *epikampios opisthia* (rearward-angled half-square, *trifalaggia*); double line either of legionaries or light-armed (auxiliaries) posted front and legionaries behind (*difalaggia*); cavalry in front and infantry behind; left and right oblique formations (*oblique acie*, a variation of the *loxê falagx*/column); hollow square/oblong (*plinthion*/ square, *plaision*/oblong); phalanx (*plagia falagx*); and a modification of the formations according to the terrain (e.g. an array placed against a river, or in a defile, in which case some of the men could be placed on the heights, e.g. the battles of Cius/Nicaea, Issus and Lugdunum). Modifications of combat tactics include the use of feigned flight (e.g. battles of Issus and Lugdunum), the dismounting of cavalry to fight as infantry, the variation of units from one day to another and the use of field fortifications and hidden traps (e.g. Battle of Lugdunum). The basic tactics were either to break through the enemy formation (e.g. the battles of Issus and Lugdunum) or to outflank it either on one or both flanks (e.g. the Battle of Cius/Nicaea).

Arrian (see Appendix 1) includes a detailed discussion of the Roman version of the phalanx which he used in Cappadocia, so there is no doubt whatsoever that the Romans continued to use phalangial combat arrays throughout their existence, as has been proven by Everett Wheeler in several studies. Nevertheless, Frontinus's text also suggests that the Romans retained their readiness to use manipular and cohortal formations when necessary – the Roman phalanx could be broken up into these smaller units that could be used independently of each other when necessary. The only real difference between the phalangial and cohortal arrays was that in the latter system the reserves consisted of separate units, while in the former the reserve second line (when used) usually comprised one half of each file. However, the Battle of Zama in 202 BC, which is also included in Frontinus's text, demonstrates nicely that the phalanx could also consist of separate units that were posted one after another. Regardless, it is clear from Julius Africanus that the principal Roman combat tactic during this period was based on the phalangial system. He fails to note any difference in combat formation between the Greeks, Macedonians and Romans, except that the principal Roman combat formation was the hollow square while in the case of the former it was the lateral phalanx,[1] although it is possible that this resulted from the reforms of Septimius Severus, who probably organized his new legions as phalanxes.

Frontinus also mentions the tactical unit formations and their use, which include the *globus* (globe, an independently operating unit), *cuneus* (wedge), column or deep formation (a variation of the *loxê falanx*) and *testudo* (tortoise, i.e. *synaspismos*, *foulkon*, *chelone*). We can add to his list of formations in the *Stratagems* the double-front formation (*orbis*, *amfistomos difalaggia*) mentioned later by Vegetius and all Greek-speaking military theorists (Aelian, Arrian, Syrianos, the *Strategikon*), which could be used to face two or all directions simultaneously, the saw (*serra*, Veg. 3.18; probably the same as the *falagga esparmena*/loose phalanx of Asclepiodotus 11.7 and as Frontinus 2.3.20) and also the independently operating irregular *drungus*/*drungos* (throng, *drouggos*). The exact difference if any between the *globus* and *drungus* is not known. Perhaps the former just meant any detached unit operating independently, while the latter was always a unit that was arrayed irregularly.

Notes

Chapter 1
1. This chapter is based on my biography of Caracalla with the addition of some new material. I have tried to articulate my point slightly differently for this book than for other books, but it is possible that there are still similarities despite my best efforts.
2. The national before the *numeri* is meant to separate the ethnic tribal *numeri* from the regular units, which could also be called called *numeri* for a number of reasons. For details of the term *numerus/numeri*, see Southern (1989). I will call the national *numeri* henceforth *numeri*.
3. See Syvänne, 'A Note on the Meaning of Contuberium', available online at academia.edu.
4. See Syvänne (2011), available online at academia.edu.
5. See for example Bohec (1994), 19–67
6. *Aspidoforoi = skoutatoi = scutati = scutum* shield-bearers (large rectangular, round or oblong shields).
7. See Syvänne (2017b), 195.
8. On the basis of the fact that the *hastati, principes* and *triarii* still existed, it is possible to think that these used different types of equipment and weapons so that each of them occupied certain ranks in the formation, but it is also possible to think that these were deployed as separate centuries. It should also be noted that the 300 men *aspidoforoi* cohort of Lydus not only corresponds with the 300 bodyguards of governor, but also with the 300 *scutati* bodyguards of Romulus and the *excubitores* of Tiberius I (Lydus, *De Mag*. 1.9, 1.12), and also with the 300 *speculatores* of the Principate period and the 300 *excubitores* of Leo I (Lydus *De Mag*. 1.16). In short, the 300 men cohort was the typical bodyguard unit of the commanders and emperors throughout the imperial period.
9. For the equipment used during this period, see the conclusions included in this narrative, together with the illustrations and Syvänne (2017b). The other valuable sources consist of D'Amato, Arguin (esp. 159ff.), Bishop & Coulston, Cascarino, Elliot, Feugere, Mattesini and Stephenson. It should be noted that my interpretation of the equipment used during this period is based on these studies, but does not always follow their opinions.
10. This is a useful modern term.
11. Dawson has analyzed the spear lengths in the East Roman sources and notes the problems in interpretation. On the basis of Danish bog finds dated to the second and third centuries, it is very probable that the Romans employed two basic spear lengths: 2.5m and 3.74m. See Syvänne, *Britain in the Age of Arthur*.
12. See Syvänne (2004), with Syvänne, *MHLR*.
13. See Vegetius 1.15–16, 3.14, with Syvänne (2004), Syvänne, *MHLR* and academia.edu articles.
14. Based on Southern's 1989 analysis.
15. See Syvänne, *MHLR Vol. 1* (2017b), Le Bohec (2000, 20ff.; 2009, 24–26); Arguin, 70–85.
16. See for example Dio 55.24.8, 58.2.2–3, with chapter 11.
17. Syvänne (2017b, Index); Arguin, 80–81; Le Bohec (2000, 21–22); Webster, 98–99.
18. This chapter is based on: Fuhrmann (civilian policing esp. 21–87); Isaac (1990); Syvänne, *MHLR* Vol. 1 (2017b). For the role of the *beneficiarius consularis*, see Fuhrmann, Austin and Rankov, and Rankov (1986).

19. For further details, see the indispensable Luttwak with Syvänne (2004, *MHLR*). Some of the generalizations that Luttwak has made do not stand closer scrutiny, but all the same it provides the best overview of the different kinds of strategies adopted. I recommend it highly. For the locations of the legions and other forces, see the maps of legionary dispositions in this monograph, with Farnum and Cascarino.
20. This is once again based on Syvänne (2004), 194ff., with Syvänne (2017b).
21. D'Amato kindly suggested in a personal communication that the Roman military term/ formation *turris* (tower) meant the Greek *pyrgos* in Homer's *Iliad*. I have previously speculated that it would be likely that *turris* meant the column formation. It is thanks to D'Amato that this speculation also finds support from the Greek military terminology. For a good analysis of the Homeric battle descriptions, see Albracht. The idea that the *turris* would mean the column formation is actually an old one, because Justus Lipsius also suggested this in his *Iusti Lipsi De militia Romana*, 1596 (p.280).
22. Based on Syvänne (2004), 202ff.
23. This is based on Syvänne (2004), 203–37.
24. I have discussed this briefly in Syvänne (2004), 206, n.3.
25. Goldsworthy (1998) 180–81, notes the discrepancy in the multiples of three, four and ten deep (Pompey at Pharsalus) and suggests that the depth varied according to the quality of the unit and availability of men, and possibly also from one unit to another. My suggestion is that in most cases there was actually no real discrepancy and that the differences in the numbers usually reflect only the differing numbers of legionary archers assigned for various tasks, and also such situations in which the extra men were just added behind the files to increase the mass, as possibly happened at Pharsalus unless some of the men in the ten-deep formation of Pompey were archers, because it is clear that both Pompey and Caesar employed legionary archers. See Syvänne (2011).
26. See above with Josephus *BJ* 5.52 and Speidel (1978), 4ff. It is likely that the 600-strong unit of bodyguards used by Septimius Severus in 193 was also a unit of provincial *singulares*.
27. See my previous studies (esp. 2004) with e.g. Arrian (Taktike, 30; Appendix 1).
28. *HA Maximini Duo* 2.1–3.6.
29. For an analysis of modern era cavalries, see Nolan with Nosworthy (263–65) and Chauviré (30–53).
30. Aelian and Asclepiodotus mistakenly make this array consist of 113 men, but in truth it consisted of two wedges, as stated by Arrian, who was the only one of the theorists who was actually a soldier. See Appendix 1. However, when there were not enough men for this, the commander could rearrange it according to their availability.
31. See Syvänne, *MHLR Vol. 1*.
32. Presentation on the wars of Germanicus available online at academia.edu.
33. This and the following is based on my earlier studies, especially on Caracalla and *MHLR* series. See also Appendix.
34. For additional information regarding the Roman cataphracts, see Syvänne/Syvanne (2004, *MHLR*); Eadie; Mielczarek; Coulston; and Bishop & Coulston.
35. The Moors were most famous as lightly equipped ferocious mounted javelineers, but they also had mounted archers and infantry javelineers and archers. In general, see Hamdoune together with e.g. Herodian 3.3.4–5, MHLR vols 1–3 and Chapter 13 of this book.
36. Based on Zahariade (2011), D'Amato (2009b), Rankov, Reddé (highly recommended), Pitassi (2009, 2011), Bounegru and Zahariade (Danubian Fleets), Starr, and Syvänne/Syvanne (2004, 2013–2014, *MHLR*, 2017b).
37. This chapter has been adapted from my research paper/presentation held at Norfolk in 2014, which was partially based on my research paper presented at Annapolis in 2013. See also Herodian 2.14.6–7 plus my Caracalla.
38. Bohec (2000), 212.

39. For the Danube fleets, the standard works are Bounegru & Zahariade, together with Zahariede (2011).
40. Based on Reddé; Rankov; D'Amato (2009b); Pitassi; Syvänne (2013–2014, *MLHR*). It should be noted that their views are slightly different from each other and that I have also made my own changes to the list.
41. See Reddé, Syvänne (2013–2014, *MLHR*).
42. I have based my estimate on Reddé's calculations and on the number of scouting boats given for the fleets posted in the area of the former *Classis Moesiaca* (225 *lusoriae*, sixty-eight *judiciariae*, 154 *agrarienses*) in the Theodosian Code (CTh 17 on Jan. 28, 412) but I have interpreted the *lusoriae* as river *liburnae* for this period. I have not included in the estimate the smaller river patrol boats (the equivalents of the *judiciariae*) and inshore patrol boats (the equivalents of the *agrarienses*).
43. Syvänne presentations (2013–2014).
44. This is based on Syvänne (2004) and my presentations (2013–2014).
45. Based on Pitassi; Syvänne (2004); Syvänne (*MHLR Vol. 1*).
46. For a fuller discussion, see Syvänne (2004) and Syvänne (*MHLR Vol.1*).
47. It is because of this that for example Bird (Aur. Vict., 102ff.) claims that the author of the *Historia Augusta* had copied the text of Aurelius Victor, when these show quite distinct similarities. It is actually likely to be the other way around, namely that, unless both Aurelius Victor and Aelius Spartianus (the author in the *HA*) used the same source, that it was actually Aurelius Victor who had used Aelius Spartianus's *Life of Severus*. That would actually explain far better the mistakes that Aurelius Victor makes in his text than if it would be the other way around. Regardless, it is still clear that there are so many similarities between the texts of Aurelius Victor, Aelius Spartianus, Eutropius, Epitome and Orosius that the speculations regarding a common sources, the so-called *Kaisergeschichte*, is quite plausible even if unprovable because it is possible that there were also other sources that shared similar content.

Chapter 2
1. This and the following is primarily based on Spartianus, Birley. 1ff.; Daguet-Gagey, 37ff.; Levick, 23ff. Other sources mentioned where relevant.
2. See also the comments of Levick (23ff., esp. 29–30). She suggests many alternative explanations for the way in which the marriage between the two occurred and also suggests that the story about the horoscope could be *post-eventum* invention. I am going even further than she because in my opinion it is probable that Severus and Julia met already when Severus was in Syria and that she accompanied him to Athens and Gaul as mistress.
3. *HA Pertinax* 4.4–5; Dio 74.1.2; Herodian 2.3.1ff.; Sage, 33–39; Birley, 89; Elliot (2020a), 156.
4. Sage, 35; Elliott (2020a), 150–56.

Chapter 3
1. Dio 74.1.1ff.; *HA Pert.* 4.5ff.; Birley (1988/2000), 88; Hekster, 199, 200–201; Sage, 33–39.
2. Dio 74.1.4ff.; *HA Pert.* 4.5ff.; Birley (1988/2000), 89, Elliott (2020a), 156.
3. *HA Pert.* 4.5ff.; Birley (1988/2000), 89–90; Sage, 37–39.
4. *HA Pert.* 4.7ff.; Birley (1988/2000), 91; Sage, 37–38.
5. Dio 74.7.1ff.; Birley (1988/2000), 93.
6. Dio 74.5.4ff.; *HA Pert.* 4.6.6ff.; Birley (1988/2000), 91; Elliott (2020a), 164–65.
7. Birley (1988/2000), 91–92.
8. Dio 74.6.1ff.; Birley (1988/2000), 93.
9. Dio 74.8.1ff.; Birley (1988/2000), 93–94; Sage, 39.
10. Dio 74.8.1ff.; *HA Pert.* 10.1ff.; Birley (1988/2000), 94; Elliott (2020a), 167–68.
11. Since Tausius was a Tungrian, it has been suspected that he was in truth an *eques singularis Augusti* rather than Praetorian. Speidel (1994, 54–55) refutes this on the basis that there were

Tungrians in the praetorium and Dio states that the killers were Praetorians. This is also confirmed by the fact that Septimius Severus kept Commodus's horse guard, but dismissed the Praetorians because they had murdered Pertinax.
12. *HA Pert.* 10.8ff.; Dio 74.2; Birley (1988/2000), 94–95; Elliott (2020a), 169–76.

Chapter 4
1. Dio 74.11.1ff.; Herod. 2.6.1ff.; Birley (1988/2000), 95.
2. Dio 74.11.1ff.; Herod. 2.6.6 ff.; Birley (1988/2000), 95.
3. Dio 74.12.1ff.; Herod. 2.6.1ff.; Birley (1988/2000), 95–96.
4. Dio 74.13.1ff.; Herod. 2.7.1ff.; Birley (1988/2000), 96.
5. Dio 74.14.3ff.; Herod. 2.7.4ff.
6. Dio 74.14.3ff.; Herod. 2.9.1ff.; Birley (1988/2000), 97–98. For the career of Cilo, see Birley with Handy, 115–16.
7. Dio 74.14.1ff.; Herod. 2.9.1ff.; Birley (1988/2000), 97–98.
8. Dio 74.14.1-2; Herod. 2.9.1ff.
9. The use of the dreams and omens found its way to the military treatises too. For this, see e.g. Frontinus (*Stratagems* 1.9.8ff., 2.4.18). It was also possible to exploit the religious practices of others (see e.g. Frontinus 2.1.16–17). Since it was also known that adverse omens could demoralize the soldiers, the treatises also included methods which could be used to dispel fears inspired by omens (see e.g. Frontinus 1.12). The same type of methods of encouragement were later used e.g. by the emperors Aurelian and Constantine the Great. For these, see my *Aurelian and Probus: The Soldier Emperors Who Saved Rome* with *MHLR vol.1* and Syvänne (2016). The soldiers were superstitious animals, it was for a good reason that such methods were used to manipulate them, and it was because of this that Frontinus (1.9.13) called such methods suitable means of manipulating the simple-minded and those who believed in gods.
10. See my biography of Caracalla for further details.
11. In my opinion, the hegemons should in this case be interpreted to also include the commanders of auxiliary units, hence the inclusion of prefects.
12. Dio 74.15.1ff.; *HA Sev.* 5.1ff.; Whittaker's comments in Herodian, 212–13, 239.
13. Herod. 2.2.7ff. *HA Di. Jul.* 5.1ff., *Sev.* 5.5ff., *Pesc. Nig.* 2.12ff.
14. This and the following chapters are based on: Dio 74.16.1ff., Herod. 2.2.7ff., *HA Di. Jul.* 5.1–8.5, *Sev.* 5.5–6.5., *Pesc. Nig.* 2.12ff.
15. Whittaker (Herodian, 227 n.2) suggests that Crispinus was already killed at Ravenna (*HA Did. Jul.* 8.1, *Sev.* 6.5) and was replaced by Juvenalis, but the fact that the *HA* (*Did. Jul.* 6.3–7.5) states that Crispinus fled to Rome after the fleet of Ravenna changed sides and was then dispatched to Septimius as envoy proves that the killing of Crispinus took place only later when Severus was already closer to the city of Rome.
16. For the career of Iulius Laetus, see Handy, 117–18.
17. Aurelius Victor (19.4), Eutropius (8.7) and Orosius (7.16.6) claim that a battle between Severus and Julianus was fought at the Milvian Bridge, but as is noted by Bird (Aur. Vict. p.101), it is likely that this is some sort of confusion, possibly between the events that took place in 193 and 312. In light of the fact that none of the period sources mention such a battle, it seems quite unlikely that there was one.
18. Whittaker (Herod. 227) with the above-mentioned sources (esp. *HA Sev.* 6.1ff.).
19. Birley, 104–05, with the above-mentioned sources.
20. *HA Sev.* 7.8ff. The simultaneous presence of the army and bribery resembled the so-called 'good cop, bad cop' routine. The bribery and promises in the presence of the army made everyone sigh with relief.
21. The US occupation forces in modern Iraq committed this very same mistake when they sacked the soldiers who had supported them against their master Saddam Hussein, with the very same result.

Notes   287

22. In general for the Praetorians, see: Durry; Bohec (1994/2000 and 2009); Rankov, Cowan (2014); Handy, 174–75; Jallet-Huant.
23. *Chronicle Paschale* (ed. Dindorf, 501–02); Cedrenus (ed. Dindorf, 451); *HA Sev. Alex.* 23.3, *Car.* 5.8, 7.1, *Max. et Balb.* 13.5ff.; Syvänne (2020, Index Aulici).
24. See *HA Pertinax* 8.1, 11.5–6, 13.9, 14.6, with Syvänne (2017b; 2020, Index Aulici).

Chapter 5

1. Herod. 3.1–7, 3.3.4–5; *HA Pesc. Nig.* 5.2ff.
2. Bowersock, 113.
3. Herod. 3.3.4–5; Birley, 117, after Msiha Zkha. Birley makes the claim that Msiha Zkha would indicate that Vologaesus fomented the revolt of the Oshroeni and Adiabeni. Msiha Zkha (98–99; the text is the same word for word as in what is today known as the *Chronicle of Arbela* 6) actually does not contain any such claim. It merely states that Vologaesus IV took many lands from the Romans (this could refer to the towns and cities occupied by the Oshroeni, Adiabeni and Arabs), but then turned against the land of the Persians where he fought against the Persians and Medes in Khorasan. On balance, however, Birley's conclusion does make sense and is probably the likeliest reason for the revolt of the two kingdoms.
4. Dio 75.1–3 (Xiphilinus, Cary ed., 194–96), a quote/translation follows later.
5. Hamza, Hoyland's tr., 58. Hoyland does not attempt to date this information, but in my opinion the years 193–194 would seem to be the best fit.
6. *HA Sev.* 8.6–9.1, *Pesc. Nig.* 5.2.ff.; Herod. 3.1ff.; Dio 75.6.1ff.; PIR L. Fabius Cilo Septimius Catinius Acilianus Lepidus Fulcinianus; Birley, 108.
7. Herod. 2.14.6–7, with Whittaker's comments, 241. For the continued tax requirement to possess triremes, see my 2017b, 64, 77.
8. Birley, 107; Daguet-Gagey, 263–64.
9. Duruy, *Roman History*, vol. 6, 566–67, an English tr. published in the USA; with PIR Arrius Menander and Dio 78.28.
10. All sources admit that Severus possessed some learning even if some of those include some reservations, the most important of which was apparently insufficient pronunciation of Latin: Aur. Vict. 20.21ff.; Eutr. 8.19.1; Epit. 20.8; *HA Sev.* 18.5, *Get.* 2.2; Dio 77.16.1–17.2; Phil. 2.26; Bird (Aur. Vict. 108–09); Syvänne (2017b).
11. It is the inclusion of the *carroballistae* in this context by Vegetius (3.14) that suggests the likelihood that he has understood the *ballistarii* in the late Roman sense as artillerymen and not as crossbowmen, as these were originally.
12. For the career of Tiberius Claudius Candidus, see Handy, 116–17.
13. Marius Maximus was also *legatus legionis primae Italicae* while serving as *dux*.
14. *HA Sev.* 8.6ff. and Herod. 3.1ff.; PIR L. Marius Maximus Perpetuus Aurelianus; PIR Tib. Cl. Candidus; PIR Cn. Marcius Rustius Rufinus; Handy, 116–17.
15. Birley, 114; Daquet-Gagey, 247–49; Grant, 40–42.
16. *HA Sev.* 8.8–9; Birley, 106–08.
17. *HA Sev.* 8.10–9.2; Birley, 109.
18. There is every reason to think that the Cappadocian legions and at least detachments from one or several of the Syrian legions had been sent as reinforcements for Aemilianus because some of the forces under him fled to Armenia and others to the Taurus when they had been defeated. In other words, they fled back to their home bases and homes.
19. For the Battle of Hellespont in 324, see Syvänne, *MHLR vol.1*, 271.
20. PIR Claudius Candidus.
21. PIR Claudius Candidus; Birley 110–12.
22. Birley, 111–12.
23. For the careers of Valerianus and Anullinus, see PIR, and for Valerianus, see Handy, 117.

24. For a full discussion, see my *The Age of Hippotoxotai* and forthcoming *Late Roman Combat Tactics*.
25. This and most of the text in the Cary ed. and Forster tr. is from the epitome of Xiphilinus. A summary of Dio's description of the siege of Byzantium can also be found in Zonaras (Dindorf ed., 1,024).

Chapter 6
1. Birley, 114–15; Bowersock, 112ff.
2. Also in Zonaras (Dindorf ed., 1,024–25) after Dio.
3. See my bio of Caracalla for examples of Dio's repeated lies with which he attempted to blacken the name of Caracalla. We should not forget that Severus was not really in the good books of Dio either, so it is quite easy to see why Dio would have failed to give Septimius any credit for being able to persuade rebel chieftains to desert to the Roman side.
4. I follow here Matti Moosa's translation (137).
5. See Syvänne (2017b), 81.
6. My conclusions are based on the outstanding studies of Goodman (472–87) and Birley (135) and the same sources that they have used, but they do not necessarily draw the same conclusions from the evidence.
7. This is the policy that Vladimir Putin has followed up in Chechnya.
8. Birley, 117. Sage fails to note this Gothic menace.
9. The subjection of these territories under Roman rule is also accepted by Wolski, 189.
10. Birley, 115ff.; PIR Septimius Severus.

Chapter 7
1. Whittaker, Herod. 292–93.
2. Birley (118) notes that a soldier from the Pannonian legion X Gemina died at Ancyra in Galatia on 3 September 195 when returning from Parthia, with the implication that he must have already been dispatched back with Claudius Candidus against Albinus. This is by no means impossible, but strictly speaking does not prove that the entire army was already on its way to the west, even if this is also possible. It is by no means impossible that Septimius would already have sent his Illyrian army well in advance while the war against the Oshroeni, Adiabeni and Arabs was conducted by other forces. The threat of the Gothic invasion would also have made it necessary to dispatch soldiers back to the Balkans. However, it is also possible that this man was on his way to the west for a number of other reasons, which include some logistical task and also the reinforcing of the forces besieging Byzantium. In my opinion, the last-mentioned is actually the likeliest reason because Herodian specifically refers to the sending of reinforcements to the forces besieging Byzantium. In short, the evidence for the redating of the evidence to the year 195 on the basis of this is by no means conclusive.
3. Birley, 117ff.; Bohec (2013), 36; Daguet-Gagey, 262ff.; Christol, 14ff., Levick, 44f.
4. *HA Maximini* 2.1ff.; Jord. Get. 84–86.
5. The evidence which notes the death of the Illyrian soldier at Ancyra should be interpreted to belong to a man who had been sent west in advance, while the problem posed by the inscription of the Aezani can result from the later completion of the inscription.
6. Reference to the title in Birley, 126.
7. Herod. 3.6.10ff.; Bowersock, 112ff.; Daguet-Gagey, 265.
8. Dio 76.5.1ff. Herod. 3.6.10ff., *HA Sev.* 10.7ff.
9. Birley 121ff.; Daguet-Gagey, 265–66; with PIR.
10. Birley, 123.
11. Birley, 122, with PIR.
12. *HA Sev.* 10.7; Herod. 3.7.1ff.; Dio 76.5.1ff.
13. Daguet-Gagey, 266–67; Whittaker, Herod. 295–96; Birley, 123ff., 221.

14. Dio 76.5.1.ff.
15. *HA Sev.*
16. Birley, 123ff.; Whittaker, Herod. 295–99; Daguet-Gagey, 269ff..
17. E.g. Magie, *HA Sev.*, 396, accepts that the battles of Tinurtium and Lyon are one and the same.
18. This view is opposed e.g. by Sage (72–73). He admits that Dio states that both armies consisted of 150,000 men and then goes on to say that there is 'no way of determining the actual size of either army'. This is true only if one rejects the evidence as he does (and like so many other historians like him do) and provides his own guesswork instead. and this in a situation in which he is aware (141) of the fact that in a similar situation both Mark Antony and Octavian had recruited and levied new troops for their civil war. This assumes that similar levying and recruiting would not have taken place now, which flies in the face of the evidence. As we have seen, Septimius Severus specifically ordered Numerianus to levy new soldiers. Simon Elliott (2020b, 28) is non-committal about the numbers, but appears to prefer to think that the two armies consisted of 150,000 men in total. Grant (94, n.12) doubts that either side had 150,000 men. The same is true of MacDowall, who makes his own estimate that Albinus had probably 30,000 men and Severus 40,000. Such estimates are ill-conceived modern hypotheses which do not take into account the very specific period evidence. Both contenders for the throne recruited and conscripted new men into their armies! Their armies were not based solely on the pre-existing forces. In short, there is no need for such scepticism towards the sources and evidence. The Roman Empire could conscript men for short-term service on the spur of the moment – these consisted mostly of the citizen militias and youths. The best slightly later example of this is the massive mobilization of the Italian population by Balbinus and Pupienus against the Emperor Maximinus Thrax in 238. It goes without saying that my reconstruction differs from the reconstructions of those who do not accept period evidence.
19. In other words, I do not accept the location suggested by Maxime Petitjean (presentation available online) or the other suggested locations in Yann Le Bohec. It should also be noted that it is probable that the ravine (i.e. hill) just north of the city of Lyon was steeper during the antiquity than it is today.
20. Dio 75.5.4 (216); Herod. 3.8.2ff. with the comment of Whittaker (305) regarding the timing of the division of Britain; Birley, 125–26; Gonzáles, 65; Syvänne (2017b), 92.
21. Herod. 3.8.2ff.; Birley, 124–27; Spielvogel, 109; PIR.
22. *Chronicle of Arbela* 6. For a different reconstruction of the events and the sequence of events, see Debevoise (258–59) and Sheldon (2010, 165–66). The revolt of the Persians and Medes against the Parthians shows that they were quite dissatisfied with Parthian rule. It is therefore not surprising that we soon find the Persians renewing their revolt under the Sasanian banner.
23. *Chronicle of Arbela* 6.
24. This is slightly inaccurate because Pompey's supporters vowed to follow the example of Sulla in 49 BC. See Syvänne (2011).
25. Herod. 3.8.2ff.; *HA* 12.7ff. with my bio of Caracalla.
26. Herod. 3.8.2ff.; *HA Sev.* 12.7ff.
27. Birley, 128, 221.

Chapter 8
1. *HA Sev.* 14.4, 14.11, 15.1ff.; Birley, 129; Spielvogel, 110. Birley suggests that the forces dispatched in advance to the east would also have included the Parthian legions I and III. This is quite possible if those accompanied Severus to the west, but it is also possible, as I have suggested above, that these had been left in the east already in 196, because the taking of veteran forces from the east against Albinus would have been the better option.
2. Birley, 129.

3. The sequence of events in Herodian might suggest that Severus dealt first with the Armenian problem (i.e. Severus marched against them first by using the Satala road) and marched then south through Adiebene and Mesopotamia to Edessa and it was only then that Abgar submitted and gave Severus auxiliaries for the war against Hatra/Parthia. The problem with this is that Spartianus and Dio both fail to mention any such operation prior to the Parthian campaign. It would be easy to think that these events have been misplaced from the year 195, but I agree with Whittaker (Herod. 316) that there are actually no good reasons to put these events to the year 195 even if the O group of texts omits these events. The reason for this is that Dio describes the events of the year 195 in detail and makes it quite clear that the Armenians remained neutral while Severus attacked the Oshroenians twice. The omission in Dio is easy to explain. We do not possess the original text, just a later summary of it.
4. Whittaker (Herod. 319) needlessly suspects this to be an old campaigner's story. The trick used here can be found from collections of stratagems and also from books of history. It belongs to the same category of stratagems as was used by Hannibal when he shot clay vessels filled up with snakes on enemy ships.
5. See my analysis of Julian's campaign in *MHLR vol. 2*.
6. Sheldon (2010, 166) accepts the existence of this campaign, but her referral to the original source (Dio 75.9) used by Rawlinson (the source she has used) does not contain the information.
7. According to Moses Khorenatsi (210–11), the King of Armenia at this time was Valarsh, but Moses fails to give any information regarding his relationship with Rome. See also my comments regarding this ruler in *Caracalla*.
8. For the former, see my *MHLR vol. 2* and for the latter my *MHLR vol. 5*.
9. For a complete analysis of the Parthian military, see Syvänne (2017a–b, 2018a–b).
10. Another historian who thinks that the Parthians put up feeble resistance is Barnett (23). This view does not take into account the fact that the Parthian cavalry could not really put up any effective resistance against well-ordered infantry such as Severus brought to the scene. Barnett also underestimates the Parthian military capabilities and claims that the King of Kings lacked the means to assemble a large army. As noted, this does not mean that Vologaesus would not have attempted to prevent the siege with the forces that he had. However, there are also those like Sheldon (2010, 167) who believe that there was a pitched battle which ended in Parthian defeat or who like Debevoise (260) think that Ctesiphon put up considerable resistance before it was captured. Spielvogel (113) also notes that the Arch of Severus does include battering rams, with the implication that a real siege took place.
11. According to the version of Dio preserved in Zonaras (Dindorf ed., 1,025 with Latin tr. on 1,026), the killing of Crispus and Laetus took place at the time when Severus was fighting against the Parthians, but this is easy to explain as an overlook by Zonaras. In the fuller version of Xiphilinus, the sequence was Parthian war, the first siege of Hatra, the killing of Crispus and Laetus and the second siege of Hatra, while in the shorter version of Zonaras the first siege of Hatra is left out. This is clearly just an overlook on his part and it is because of this that I have accepted the consensus view. Barrett (14) does not accept that there would have been two separate sieges of Hatra.
12. For this, see my *Aurelian and Probus: The Emperors Who Saved Rome*.
13. I.e. I agree with Sage (99) that the sexual relationship between Severus and Plautianus is doubtful.
14. Sage fails to note this war (84ff.) and only includes it as possibly a fictitious account of banditry in Dio (118–20).
15. Syvänne (2017b), 195–96. However, one could use Aurelius Victor's claims (20.15–16) that Severus reduced the Arabs to a provincial status as soon as he attacked them to support Birley's view, but since Victor connects this with the subdual of the Adiabeni I would suggest that this refers to the year 195. In short, even if one cannot entirely rule out the possibility that the hostile Dio has left out the ultimate success of Severus in this case, it is still more likely that the subdual of Hatra took place under Caracalla.

16. Goodman, 473–75.
17. *HA Sev.* 16.6ff.
18. Bowersock 113–21; Birley, 134–35. Sage (84–85) misplaces this reorganization to have taken place before Severus returned from Ctesiphon. It is clear that he reorganized the provinces only after he had returned from his campaign and was in the area where the changes were made. It is possible that the reorganization was done in stages so that the first portion was done immediately after the first siege of Hatra had ended, and then the rest after the failure of the second campaign.

Chapter 9
1. Sage (88–92) fails to note the strategic purpose of Severus's trip to Egypt and considers it a case of tourism.
2. *HA Sev.* 17.3–4: Rufinus 2.23; Malalas 12.21; Birley, 136–38.
3. Birley, 138–39; Daguet-Gagey, 346–49.
4. *HA Sev.* 17.2ff.; Birley, 135ff.

Chapter 10
1. This interpretation is vehemently opposed by Sage (115). As the following account shows, the innuendo is supported by the sources and circumstantial evidence.
2. Herodian 4.9.3; Aurelius Victor 20 23, 21.2–3; Aelius Spartianus, *HA Sev.* 18.8, 21.7, *Car.* 10; *Epitome* 21.5; Pseudo-Victor, *Epitome De Caesaribus* 21.5; Orosius 7.18. Syvänne (2017b), Index, 'Caracalla, Incest and Sexual Behaviour'. It is clear that Aurelius Victor has either used Aelius Spartianus or rather a common source, probably Marius Maximus. As regards the extant extracts of Dio, which fail to mention this directly, there are two possibilities. Firstly, it is possible that this results from the prudish shortening of the text by Byzantine monks. Secondly, it is possible that Dio (78.16) referred to it indirectly by such statements as that after Caracalla's sexual powers had disappeared he satisfied his lewd desires in a different manner. Thirdly, it is possible that he hid the incest because he was at pains to present Caracalla as being hated by Julia Domna, which was clearly not the case. The problem with Dio's text is that he was constantly at pains to blacken Caracalla's name in every possible way, which included outright lying, with the result that nothing he writes can be accepted without making a thorough analysis of his own text (he has done his job so poorly that he contradicts himself in several places) and other sources.
3. Dio, Cary ed. vol. 2, 330, after Tzetses, *Chil.* 1.798–805; Syvänne (2017b), 183–84.
4. Fitz, 77–79.
5. Herodian, 3.10; Birley, 143–44.
6. Dio 77.1.1ff. (Cary ed., 238ff.); Birley, 144; Syvänne (2017b)/Caracalla, see the Index.
7. Dio 77.1.3ff. (Cary ed., 238ff.), Birley.

Chapter 11
1. This chapter is based on: *HA Sev.* 18.3, Aurelius Victor 20.19; Birley (145–54); Mattingly 82–85; Syvänne, *MHLR vol. 1*, the analysis of the Garamantian military.
2. Bar Hebraeus (55); Jerome (*Chron.* AD 201, ninth persecution); Eusebius (*Ecclesiastical Hist.* 6.1–7, the tenth year in Alexandria, i.e. in 202–203); Birley, 154; Grant, 80.

Chapter 12
1. Syvänne, 2017b, 81ff.
2. Sage (114–17) offers a different analysis.
3. Dio 77.5.1ff.; Herodian. 3.13.2ff.

Chapter 13
1. This chapter is based on my bio of *Caracalla* (2017b), 87ff.
2. This and the following chapters are based on Dio 77.7.1ff.; Herodian 3.13.1ff.; Syvänne (2017b), 87ff. When other sources have been used these are mentioned separately.
3. Syvänne (2006), 79–80.
4. It was this that made Severus's other qualities less offensive to Dio, and it was Caracalla's lack of interest in hearing the opinion of Dio that irritated Dio, on top of the other things that he hated in Caracalla. See my bio of him for further details.
5. Dio 77.16.4–5; Platnaeur, 181–82; Bird, 104.
6. Dio 76.7ff.; Whittaker, Herod. 254–55.
7. Dio 77.8.
8. Sage (117–20) considers it probable that fictional material has entered Dio's account here. I disagree. There is nothing inherently improbable in Dio's account.

Chapter 14
1. This chapter is based on Syvänne (2017b), 92ff.
2. Birley, 170–72 (I do not agree with Birley that the governor's letter would have been pure invention); Daquet-Gagey, 415–18; Syvänne (2017b), 92ff.
3. Birley, 172; Syvänne (2017b), 92ff.
4. A religious cult of twelve priests that worshipped in official capacity the fertility goddess Dea Dia established by Augustus. It included the emperor and members of the imperial family.
5. Syvänne (2017b), 93ff.; Reed, 98–99; Bender, 106; Birley 176. The relevant inscription can easily be found in Campbell (134).
6. The referrals to the building of new granaries and roads in Birley (173), Daquet-Gagey (419) and Syvänne (2017b, 92ff.).
7. A 'general' with a temporary command of units, which clearly suggests that the title of *dux* was already becoming more common than *praepositus*. According to Saxer (122–23), the Romans started to employ the title *dux* for the first time during the Marcomannic War. Before this, the commanders of detachments were *legatus Aug. vex.*, *praefectus vex.*, *praepositus vex.*, *tribunus vex.* During and after the Marcomannic War, the titles were *dux vex.*, *praepositus vex.* and *tribunus vex.*
8. Dio 77.10.1ff.; Birley, 176; Daquet-Gagey, 413–18; Pollard & Berry, 71; Saxer, 48 (includes the actual inscription); Syvänne (2017b), 93–96.
9. Dio77.11ff.; Birley, 174–75.
10. Birley, 173; Daquet-Gagey, 419ff.
11. Birley, 174–75; Daquet-Gagey, 419–24.
12. Maxwell, 38–67; Hanson, 1978; Birley, 170ff.
13. Maxwell, 28. Hanson (1978) camps: Grillone, 480 men per acre; or 380 men per acre; Hanson's average 350 men per acre. Maxwell calculates the size as follows: 40 acre/16 ha = 15,000–20,000 men. Note, however, that some researchers prefer considerably smaller numbers (see e.g. Kamm, 126), but in my opinion this is a mistake.
14. Daquet-Gagey, 425; Elliott (2018), 151ff.
15. Maxwell, 61–63.The presence of detachments from the legions II Augusta and XX Valeria Victrix are attested at Carlisle for the early third century in Pollard & Berry, 89–92, 104. It is probable that the legions would have advanced from there northwards to the western portion of the Antonine Wall.
16. Those interested to read of this theory are advised to read my biography of Caracalla, which includes both my own theory and also that suggested by the archaeologists. Simon Elliott (2018, 150ff.) has further elaborated the favourite theory of the archaeologists by claiming that the Roman army was divided so that Caracalla was in charge of the fast-moving spearhead consisting of two-thirds of the army (the western division) so that it advanced fast along the

north-east Highland Boundary Fault past Kair House, while his father Severus advanced with one-third of the force to Carpow and then across the bridge built there. In the meanwhile, Elliott claims, the British Fleet (he forgets the existence of the other fleets in Britain at this stage) sealed the littoral between Carpow and Kair House so that the Maeatae and Caledonians were trapped within Midland Valley, after which Severus advanced from Carpow northwards to meet his son at Kair House. There are two major problems with this. All of the sources are unanimous that Severus and Caracalla campaigned together during the first campaign because both were present in the same camp and received the surrender of the enemy together. The second major problem with this is that the sources specifically state that the Romans were unable to force the enemy into a battle because they were always able to flee. This means that the barbarians cannot have been trapped. The third major problem is that Dio specifically states that Severus advanced to the extremity of the island, which surely means that he advanced at least as far as Moray Firth, as also stated by Birley. Elliott (2018, 162–63) also goes on to claim that Severus returned to York before the onset of winter, even though Dio specifically states that Severus observed the length of the days and nights specifically in summer and winter, which means that Severus stayed in the north at least until the onset of winter, perhaps until January–February 210, but then returned south because he was certainly at York on 5 May 210. All of the interpretations based on those of archaeology have suffered from one or all of these problems, and it is because of this and because of the fact that I have already dealt with those in my biography of Caracalla that I do not include those here.
17. A military diploma dated to 7 January 210 proves that Geta had been appointed as Augustus while Septimius and Antoninus were still campaigning. For this, see Birley, 274; Daguet-Gagey, 427–28; Levick, 83; Syvänne (2017b), 109–12.
18. Sage (130) considers their accounts patchworks of commonplaces which are not factual or informative. This view fails to take into account the fact that the so-called commonplaces were factual because the tribal warfare in this area retained its characteristics until changed by outside influences. There is once again nothing improbable in these descriptions. On the contrary, those preserve for us a very good overall picture of their fighting methods.
19. Syvänne, research papers (2013–2014).
20. Syvänne (2017b), 108–09.
21. See also the end chapter. Herodian 4.9.3; Aelius Spartianus (*HA Sev.* 18.8ff.; *Car.* 10); Aurelius Victor (20.23ff.); *Epitome* 21.5; Pseudo-Victor, *Epitome De Caesaribus* 21.5; Orosius 7.18; Syvänne (2017b), 110ff.
22. Syvänne (2017b), 112–13.
23. Syvänne (2017b), 113–14.
24. Syvänne (2017b), 113–14.
25. Syvänne (2017b), 115ff.
26. Syvänne (2017b), 115ff.
27. Syvänne (2017b), 115ff.
28. Syvänne (2017b), 117ff. For a completely different analysis, see Sage (131–37), who even fails to note the existence of the last campaign under Caracalla. He claims that it was not Caracalla (139) who pacified Britain for the better part of a century, but Severus. This is completely false. The Britons had revolted after Severus's campaign. It had thereafter required two campaigns by Caracalla to pacify the region. Sage also states (136) that Caracalla 'seems not to have possessed much in the way of strategic or tactical gifts'. Nothing could be further from the truth. Caracalla was one of the most talented military commanders humankind has ever had. For a very thorough rebuttal of all of his claims, see Syvänne (2017b)/Caracalla.

Chapter 15
1. Herodian 4.9.3; Aelius Spartianus (*HA Sev.* 18.8ff.; Car. 10); Aurelius Victor (20.23ff.); *Epitome* 21.5; Pseudo-Victor, *Epitome De Caesaribus* 21.5; Orosius 7.18.

Appendix 1

1. See my Magnesia and Alexander the Great articles on the web (academia.edu) with my *Military History of Late Rome Vol. 1 (MHLR Vol. 1)* (Barnsley, 2015) and *Caracalla* (Barnsley, 2017). Those authors (e.g. Maxime Petitjean, conference paper *Cito parare vistoriam, cito cedere*, available at academia.edu, after Polybius 6.25.1–2, Ps.Hyginus 16) who think that the Romans would have used thirty-horsemen *turma* with three decurions and three *optios* included, or thirty horsemen plus one decurion (for a total of thirty-one horsemen per *turma*), fail to understand that the sources usually used the closest round figure for the unit strengths. Polybius states quite specifically that the Romans copied the Greek practice during the Second Punic War, which means that they discarded the older practice of using thirty-horsemen *turma* at that point in time. However, the referral to the three decurions and three *optios* per thirty-horseman *turma* is accurate in one respect. It is probable that each *turma* consisted of four *contubernia* (tent group) of eight horsemen plus two servants/squires so that each had one decurion in charge of ten men (dekarch of the *Strategikon*), which included one *optio* (pentarch of the *Strategikon*) who acted as commander of five men. In short, there would have been a fourth decurion who acted as commander of the entire *turma* and a fourth *optio* to act as pentarch for the file. When the *turma* was deployed with a width of nine and three deep, the principal decurion and his *optio* (and supernumeraries) stood outside the array to direct its movements, but when the formation was deployed four deep and eight wide they were included in the array. However, on the basis of the information preserved for us by Pseudo-Hyginus and Vegetius, at some point in time the Romans added a supernumerary Decurion for each *turma* so that there were thirty-two horsemen and a Decurion. In practice, this basic organization was adapted to the numbers available and unit formation used so that the *turmae* were divided and united as needed.
2. See referrals to such in all of the volumes of the *MHLR*.
3. See the argumentation in E. Wheeler, 'The Legion as Phalanx in the Late Empire Part 2', *REMA 1* 152ff.
4. Matthew (2012) has estimated that the length of the hoplite spear was about 2.5m. It should be noted that even though this estimate is undoubtedly accurate for the classical period, the length of the spear was increased during the fourth and third centuries BC and could easily have attained the figures suggested by the Byzantine sources.
5. In order for the short eight *pecheis doru/kontarion* to protrude out of the four-rank-formation, each man had to occupy only one *pechus* in the formation, as required by the sixth-century *Peri Strategias/Strategikes*. For a fuller discussion of the figures, see Dawson (2007) who favours the smallest alternative (31.23cm, so that *pechus* = *pous*). However, in my opinion it is difficult to believe that the men could have occupied only 31.23cm in the formation. If one accepts the smallest figure, it would then not be possible for each of the men to have occupied two *pecheis* in depth, because then the spear of the fourth man would not have reached past the front rank (four ranks × two *pecheis* = eight *pecheis*). On paper, Dawson's preferred shorter figures are plausible, but the assumption in the sixth-century *Peri Strategias* that each man occupied only one *pechus* in depth precludes this. The wider stance of 65–70cm per man would be impossible if one equates the *pechus* and *pous* (foot). However, one cannot be too strict about these figures. The 2.5m spear suggested by Dawson is inherently more probable as a throwing weapon than the 3.74m spear, but the evidence still seems to point to the likelihood that the latter figure would be closest to the truth. It is quite possible that the 3.74m spear was a compromise between the conflicting needs of fighting against cavalry and infantry, or that the front rank used shorter spears than the rear rankers (as I have suggested elsewhere).
6. See Syvänne (2017b)/*Caracalla*.
7. I owe the referral to the *purgos/pyrgos* to D'Amato (personal correspondence).
8. For the military manoeuvres performed at Lambaesis for the emperor Hadrian, see Speidel (2006).

9. Hyland (1993), 73, 104–05, has mistakenly on the basis of Walbark's commentary of Polybius interpreted the *epistrofē* as a turning (*klisis*) manoeuvre in which each horseman turned on the spot either left or right, but here the *epistrofē* means undoubtedly a wheeling.
10. Hyland (1993), 73, has mistakenly translated *taxeis* as ranks whereas it most likely means a thirty-two-man *turma*. However, in her commentary she does note that the men consisted of two *turmae*.
11. The text adds that it is the equivalent of the infantry *xynaspismos* (!) formation, which should be emended to *synaspismos*.
12. Syvänne, *MHLR 518–565*, p.355; 2010a-b.
13. For an alternative and different reconstruction, see Hyland (1993), 145–46, 41.2–3.
14. For the Chinese usage, see Cambridge; Selby. For the use of *ballistae* carts by the Romans against the nomads in the manner of the Chinese, see Syvänne (2004). For the effectiveness of the crossbow during the Middle Ages, it suffices to note that the Pope wanted to restrict its use only against the infidels. However, the well-known fate of Richard I should be enough evidence that this instruction was not followed. See also Syvänne, DF 2012. Notably, in the course of history, the use of the crossbow was abandoned in East Rome/Byzantium (Anna Komnena).
15. Ann Hyland (1993), 154, has suggested the possibility that *Turma A* was divided into two groups or that there was also a *Turma C* to act as opponents for *Turma B*. However, on the basis of the subsequent swordplay I consider this to have been unlikely. There could not have been more than a few horsemen acting as enemy units.
16. Incorrectly interpreted by Hyland (1993), 154, as an about turn.
17. For a different interpretation, see Hyland (1993), 154. In my view, the next instruction to use swords in pursuit clearly implies a flank attack, and the placing of the shields on the back was meant as a protection against the enemy unit in the same line on the left of the attacking unit. The *Turma A* that *Turma B* would have been pursuing would in practice have been in flight and not in readiness to attack *Turma B* (unless of course using feigned flight).
18. The other alternative would be that the *toulutegon* meant the throwing of pikes at the enemy at close quarters, but this is less likely.
19. In other words, I do not accept the interpretation that the abovementioned cavalry units would have included infantry, as interpreted by Gilliver (1999), 56. If some of the units in question also included an infantry component, as appears likely, these would have been left behind in garrison duty or they were marching among the infantry.
20. See the argumentation in E. Wheeler, 'The Legion as Phalanx in the Late Empire Part 2', *REMA 1*.

Appendix 2
1. See my analysis of this treatise in *Caracalla* (2017b), Appendix 2.

Select Bibliography

Select Primary Sources Online:
Most of the original sources mentioned below are also available online, either as editions, as translations or as both. The best place to begin seeking these sources is the internet archive. Many university library websites, like that of Heidelberg (highly recommended), offer access to old manuscripts, as well as old and new studies. There is also a plentiful supply of sources on the web for numismatic studies, information regarding auctions and photos of coins – all of this warms the heart of a former coin collector like me. Good places to start searching for numismatic information are *GNC Coins* and George Depeyrot's studies (including those on the web, e.g. on the academia.edu website) and plain simple 'Googling'.

Select Sources:
Albracht, Dr Franz, *Battle and Battle Description in Homer. A Contribution to the History of War*, tr. and ed. by Peter Jones, Malcolm Willcock and Gabriele Wright (London, 2005, orig. 1886, 1895).
D'Amato, R., *Arms and Armour of the Imperial Roman Soldier from Marius to Commodus, 112 BC–AD 192*, illustrations by G. Sumner (Barnsley, 2009a).
D'Amato, R., *Imperial Roman Naval Forces 31 BC–AD 500*, illustrations by G. Sumner (Oxford, 2009b).
Anonymi De rebus bellicis liber, *see* Schneider.
Arguin (Argüín), A.R.M., *El ejército romano en campaña De Septimio Severo a Diocleciano (193–305 D.C.)*, (Sevilla, 2011).
Austin, N.J.E. and Rankov, N.B., *Exploratio* (London and New York, 1995).
Bar Hebraeus, *The Chronography of Gregory Abû'l-Faraj 1225–1286*, tr. by E.A.W. Budge (London, 1932; reprint Amsterdam, 1976).
Barnett, G., 'Father and son invade iraq. The Parthian wars of the first Severi', *Ancient Warfare II.6*, (2009), pp.22–28.
Bede, *see* Giles.
Bertolazzi, Riccardo, 'On the Alleged Treachery of Julia Domna and Septimius Severus' Failed Siege of Hatra', in C. Dunn and E. Carney (eds), *Royal Women and Dynastic Loyalty* (Queenship and Power) (New York, 2018), pp.67–86.
Bird, H.W., *Liber De Caesaribus of Sextus Aurelius Victor* (Liverpool, 1995).
Birley, A.R., *Septimius Severus, the African Emperor* (London and New York, 2000).
Bishop, M.C. and Coulston, J.C.N., *Roman Military Equipment from the Punic Wars to the Fall of Rome* (Oxford, 2nd edn 2006).
Bohec, Yann Le, *The Imperial Roman Army* (London and New York, 1994, 2004).
Bohec, Yann Le, *Histoire le Afrique romaine* (Paris, 2005).
Bohec, Yann Le, *L'armée romaine dans la tourmente* (Paris, 2009).
Bohec, Yann Le, *La bataille de Lyon 197 apr. J.-C.* (Paris, 2013).
Bowersock, G.W., *Roman Arabia* (Harvard, 1983/1994).
Campbell, B., *The Roman Army 31 BC–AD 337: A Sourcebook* (London and New York, 1994).
Cary, E. (ed. and tr.), *Dio's Roman History* (Loeb, 1927).

Cascarino G., *L'esercito romano. Armamento e organizzazione. Vol. II da Augusto ai Severi* (Il Cerchio, 2008).
Chauviré, Frédéric, *The New Knights. The Development of Cavalry in Western Euope, 1562–1700* (Warwick, 2021).
Christol, M., *L'empire romain du IIIe siècle. 192–325 apr.J.-C.* (Paris, 2006).
Chronicle of Arbela, tr. by Peter Kawerau, English tr. by Timothy Kroll. CSCO 468, *Scriptores Syri 200* (Louvain, 1985).
Coulston, J., 'Roman, Parthian and Sassanid tactical developments', in P. Freeman and D.L. Kennedy (eds), *The Defence of the Roman and Byzantine East*, BAR Int. Ser. 297 (Oxford, 1986), pp.59–75.
Cowan, R., *Roman Guardsman 62 BC–AD 324* (Oxford, 2014).
Daquet-Gagey, A., *Septime Sévère* (Paris. 2008).
Dawson, T., '"Fit for the task": equipment sizes and the transmission of military lore, sixth to tenth centuries"' *BMGS* 31.1 (2007), pp.1–12.
Debevoise, N.C., *A Political History of Parthia* (New York, 1938/1968).
Dio, Cassius, *Dio's Roman History*, 9 vols, ed. and tr. by Cary (Loeb).
Durry, M., *Les cohortes prétoriennes* (Paris, 1938).
Eadie, J.W., 'The Development of Roman Mailed Cavalry', *JRS* 37 (1967), pp.161–73.
Elliott, Simon, 'Battle of Lugdunum, AD 197. Clash of the Titans', *AW* 13.3 (2020b), pp.26–35.
Elliott, Simon, *Pertinax: The Son of a Slave Who Became Roman Emperor* (Barnsley, 2020a).
Elliott, Simon, *Septimius Severus in Scotland* (Barnsley, 2018).
Farnum, J.H., *The Positioning of the Roman Imperial Legions*, BAR Int. Ser. 1458. (Oxford, 2005).
Feugere (Feugère), M., tr. by D.G. Smith, *Weapons of the Romans* (Charleston, 1993/2002).
Fitz, J., 'A Military History of Pannonia From the Marcomann Wars to the Death of Alexander Severus (180–235)', *Acta Arcaeologica Tomus* 14 (1962), pp.25–112.
Frontinus, *The Stratagems and the Aqueducts of Rome*, ed. and tr. by Charles Bennett (Cambridge and London, 1925).
Fuhrmann, C.J., *Policing the Roman Empire* (Oxford, 2012).
Geoffrey of Monmouth, *see* Giles.
Giles, J.A., *The Ecclesiastical History of the English Nation translated from the Latin of Venerable Bede* (London, 1845).
Giles, J.A., *History of the Britons by Nennius* (London, 1841).
Giles, J.A., *Old English Chronicles* (includes Geoffrey of Monmouth) (London, 1848).
Goldsworthy, A., *The Roman Army at War 100 BC–AD 200* (Oxford, 1996).
Gonzales (González), J.R., *La dinastía de los Severos. Comienza del declive del Imperio Romano.* (Madrid, 2010).
Goodman, Martin, *Rome and Jerusalem. The Clash of Ancient Civilizations* (New York, 2008).
Grant, M., *The Severans: The changed Roman Empire* (London and New York, 1996).
Hamdoune, C., *Les auxilia externa africains des armées romaines* (Montpellier, 1999).
Hamza, tr. by R.G. Hoyland, in *The 'History of the Kings of the Persians' in Three Arabic Chronicles*, (Liverpoool, 2018), pp.35–78.
Handy, Markus, *Die Severer und das Heer* (Berlin, 2009).
Hanson, W.S., *Agricola and the Conquest of the North* (London, 1987).
Hanson, W.S., 'Roman campaigns north of the Forth-Clyde isthmus: the evidence of the temporary camps', *Proc. Soc. Antiq. Scot.* 109 (1977–1978), pp.140–50.
Hekster, Oliver, *Commodus: An Emperor at the Crossroads*, J.C. Gieben Dutch Monographs on Ancient History and Archaeology Vol 23 (Amsterdam, 2002).
Herodian, *Herodian in Two Volumes*, tr. by C.R. Whittaker (Loeb, 1969).
Historia Augustae, *see* SHA.
Holder, Paul, 'Auxiliary Deployment in the Reign of Hadrian', in *Documenting the Roman Army: Essays in Honour of Margaret Roxan* (ed. J.J. Wilkes) (London, 2003), pp.101–45.

Hoyland, R.G., *Arabia and Arabs from the Bronze Age to the Coming of Islam* (London and New York, 2001).
Hoyland, R.G., *Three Arabic Chronicles* (Liverpoool, 2018), pp.35–78.
Isaac, B.H., *The Limits of Empire: the Roman Army in the East* (Oxford, 1990).
Jallet-Huant M., *La garde prétorienne dans la Rome antique* (Paris, 2009).
Kamm, A., *The Last Frontier: The Roman Invasions of Scotland* (Neil Wilson Publishing, 2009/20012).
Le Bohec, *see* Bohec.
Lenoir, M. (ed.) *Pseudo-Hygin. des fortifications du camp* (Paris, 2002).
Levick, B., *Julia Domna: Syrian Empress* (London and New York, 2007).
Lindenschmit, L., *Tracht und Bewaffnung des römischen Heeres während der Kaiserzeit* (Braunschweig, 1882).
Lydus, Ioannes, *Lydus on Powers of the Magistracies of the Roman Empire*, ed. and tr. by Anastasius C. Bandy (Philadelphia, 1983).
MacDowall, Simon, 'La batalla de Lugdunum', *Desperta Ferro* 35 (2016), pp.31–38.
Magie, *SHA (Scriptores Historiae Augustae)* (1924), English tr. by David Magie (Loeb).
Mattesini, S., *Les Légiones Romaines* (Rome, 2006/8).
Mattingly, D.J., 'Historical Summary', in *The Archaeology of Fazzān. Vol. 1, Synthesis*, ed. by D.J. Mattingly (London, 2003), pp.75–106.
Maxwell, G.S., *The Romans in Scotland* (Edinburgh, 1989).
Michael Syrus, Michael the Syrian and Michael Rabo, *Chronicle*, Armenian version, tr. by Robert Bedrosian (New York, 2013); *The Syriac Chronicle of Michael Rabo (The Great). A Universal History from the Creation*, tr. by Matti Moosa, a publication of the Archdiocese of the Syriac Orthodox Church for the Eastern United States (available online).
Mielczarek, M., *Cataphracti and Clibanarii: Studies on the Heavy Armoured Cavalry of the Ancient World* (Łódź, 1993).
Moses Khorenatsi, *History of the Armenians*, tr. By R.W. Thomson (Cambridge and London, 1978).
Msiha Zkha, in *Sources Syriaques vol.1*, ed. and tr. by A. Mingana (Leipzig, 1908). (The same as the *Chronicle of Arbela*.)
Nennius, *see* Giles.
Nolan, L.E., *Cavalry: Its History and Tactics*, Introduction Jon Coulston (London, 1853; Yardley, 2007).
Nosworthy, Brent, *Battle Tactics of Napoleon and His Enemies* (London, 1995).
Petijean, Maxime, presentation 'Une bataille perdue: Lugdunum 197', available online at academia.edu.
Pollard, N. and Berry, J., *The Complete Roman Legions* (London, 2012).
Rankov, B., *The beneficiarii consularis in the western provinces of the Roman Empire*, unpublished Dissertation (University of Oxford, 1986), available online.
Rankov B., *Guardians of the Roman Empire* (Oxford, 2000).
Reed, N., 'The Scottish campaigns of Septimius Severus', *Proc. Soc. Antiq. Scot.* 108 (1975–1976), pp.92–102.
Ricciardi, R.V., 'Pictorial Graffiti in the City of Hatra', *Electrum 2* (1996), pp.187–203.
Saxer, R., *Epigrapshische Studien 1. Untersuchungen zu den Vexillationen des römisches kaiserheeres von Augustus bis Diokletian* (Köln and Graz, 1967).
Schneider, R. (ed.), *Anonymi De rebus bellicis liber* (Berlin, 1908).
SHA, Scriptores Historiae Augustae, 3 vols, tr. by D. Magie (Loeb, 1921–1932).
Sheldon, R.M., *Rome's Wars in Parthia* (London and Portland, 2010).
Southern, P., 'The Numeri of the Roman Imperial Army', *Britannia* 20 (1989), pp.81–140.
Speidel, M.P., *Guards of the Roman Armies* (Bonn, 1978).
Speidel, M.P., *Riding for Caesar: The Roman Emperors' Horse Guards* (London, 1994).

Speidel, M.P., *Emperor Hadrian's speeches to the African Army – a new Text* (Mainz, 2006)
Spielvogel, Jörg, *Septimius Severus* (Darmstadt, 2006).
Starr, C.G., 'Coastal Defense in the Roman World', *The American Journal of Philology* (1943), pp.56–70.
Starr, C.G., *The Roman Imperial Navy 31 B.C. – A.D. 324* (London, 2nd ed. 1960).
Syvänne (Syvanne/Syvaenne), Ilkka, *Gordian III and Philip the Arab* (Barnsley, 2020).
Syvänne, Ilkka, *MHLR: Military History of Late Rome 361–395* (Barnsley, 2018).
Syvänne, Ilkka, *The Military History of Third Century Iran* (Siedlce, 2018a).
Syvänne, Ilkka, 'Parthian Cataphract vs the Roman Army 53 BC–AD 224', in *Historia i Swiat 2017* (2017a).
Syvänne, Ilkka, *Caracalla: A Military Biography* (Barnsley, 2017b).
Syvänne, Ilkka, *MHLR: A Military History of Late Rome 284–361* (Barnsley, 2015).
Syvänne, Ilkka, research paper 'An Overview of the Late Roman Naval Warfare ad 365–565', *The 10th Maritime Heritage Conference (Norfolk, Virginia, September 17–20, 2014)* (2014a).
Syvänne, Ilkka, research paper 'Rome's Eastern Foreign Policy 324–450', *ASMEA Conference 2014, Oct. 30–Nov. 1, 2014* (2014b).
Syvänne, Ilkka, 'Persia, la caida de un imperio', in *Desperta Ferro* 24 (Julio, 2014b)
Syvänne, Ilkka, 'Arrian/Arrianus', Philosophers of War, 2 vols, eds D. Coetzee and L.W. Eysturlid (Santa Barbara, Denver, Oxford, 2013).
Syvänne, Ilkka, research paper 'An Overview of the Late Roman Naval Warfare 284–395', in *2013 McMullen Naval History Symposium* (2013).
Syvänne, Ilkka, research paper 'Duel for Power. Caesar vs. Pompey 49–48 BC', *Historicon 2011* (2011, available online at academia.edu).
Syvänne, Ilkka, 'The Battle of Magnesia, 189 BC', in *Saga Newsletter 121*, 25–77 (errata in *Saga 122*, 2010a, 49–52).
Syvänne, Ilkka, 'Macedonian Art of War. The Balkans 335 BC, Granicus River 334 BC, and Gaugamela 331 BC', in *Saga Newsletter 123* (2010b, 31–99).
Syvänne, Ilkka, 'Water Supply in the Late Roman Army', in *Environmental History of Water*, eds P.S. Juuti, T.S. Katko and H.S. Vuorinen (IWA Publishing, London, 2006), Chapter 6, pp.69–91.
Syvänne, Ilkka, *The Age of Hippotoxotai, Art of War in Roman Military Revival and Disaster (491–636)*, Acta Universitatis Tamperensis 994 (Tampere University Press, Tampere, 2004).
Webster, G., *The Roman Imperial Army*, 3rd ed., Introduction by Hugh Elton (Oklahoma, 1998).
Wheeler, E.L., 'The Legion as Phalanx'. *Chiron* 9 (1979), pp.303–18.
Wheeler, E.L., 'The Legion as Phalanx in the Late Empire Part 1', in *L'Armée romaine de Dioclétien à Valentinien Ier, Actes du IIIe congrès de Lyon sur l'armée romaine*, eds Y. Le Bohec and C. Wolff (Paris, 2004a), pp.309–58.
Wheeler, E.L., 'The Legion as Phalanx in the Late Empire Part 2', *REMA* 1 (2004b), p.152ff.
Whittaker, C.R., *Herodian*, 2 vols, English tr. (Loeb, 1969).
Wolski, J., *L'Empire des Arsacides* (Louvain, 1993).

Index

Abantus, admiral of Licinius, 103
Abernathy, capital of Picts, 233
Abgar (Abgarus/Abgaros) VIII, King of Osroene/Oshroene (179–211/12), 123, 129, 163, 167, 290
Abyssinia, Abyssinians, *see* Ethiopia
Achaia, 51
Adiabene, Adiabeni, vi, xi, 75, 90, 107–108, 113, 121–5, 127–31, 134, 157–8, 163, 168, 172, 241, 287–8, 290
  Adiabenicus, title, 125, 129
  see also Hatra, Narses, Oshroene, Parthia
Administration (Roman), Administrative, bureaucratic, bureaus, bureaucrats, civil servants, 1–4, 8–9, 25, 35, 52, 60–1, 79, 99, 101, 209–10, 220–1, 224, 226, 232, 242
Adventus coins, 132, 139–40
Aelius Severianus Maximus. P., legate of LG III Cyrenaica, 89, 121
Aemilianus, *see* Asellius
Aemilius Laetus, Quintus. (PP 191–3), 59, 63–4, 66–7, 69, 74, 78, 81
Aemilius Saturninus, Q., (PP 200), 190, 192
Aetius, husband of Septimius Severus's daughter (nothing further is known of him, but on the basis of the marriage a man of some importance), 86
Asclepiodotus, Asklepiodotos, military theorist, 29, 44, 246, 253, 282, 284
Africa (with North Africa), v, vii, xi, 2–3, 47, 50–1, 58, 60–1, 63–4, 74, 78, 91, 102, 108, 137, 156, 161, 183, 185, 194, 197–200, 211, 216, 220, 246, 296–7, 299
  see also Cyrene, Egypt, Ethiopia, Libya, Mauretania, Moors, Tripolitania
Aksum, Aksumites, Axum, *see* Ethiopia
Alamanni, Germanic tribal confederacy, 191, 218
Alans, Ossetes, Sarmatian tribal confederacy, xi, 10, 31, 37, 49, 113, 244, 247, 249, 251, 257, 271, 274–7, 279–81
  see also Sarmatians
Alba Longa/Albanum, city, Latium, Castel Gandolfo, Italy, 88, 161, 209
Alban, St, 232

Albany, Albania (the area north of Hadrian's Wall), 217
Albinus, *see* Clodius Albinus
Alexander Severus, *see* Severus Alexander
Alexander the Great, Macedonian king and tomb/monument of, 101, 110–11, 114, 185–6, 192–3, 201, 294
Alexander ad Issum, 111
  see also Issus
Alexander son of Pyrrhus, Greek military theorist, 245
Alexandria, city and fleet of, Egypt / Alexandrians, 50, 163, 186, 291
Alfenus Senecio, L., governor, 215
Allies Roman, alliance in general, allied, ally (contingents provided by allies also known as *foederati/foideratoi*, Federates or *symmachiarii, symmachoi*), v, xi, 4–5, 19–20, 26, 46, 50, 77, 89, 116, 128, 137–8, 145, 163, 168, 215, 217, 229, 239, 250, 272, 274, 277–8
  see also Auxilia
Almond, river, 223
Ambush, *see* Stratagems
Amici (friends of the emperor), 3, 85, 141
  see also Comes
Ancyra, Galatia city, Ankara, Turkey, 288
Anicius Faustus, Q., (legate, Africa, Upper Moesia), 194, 197
Annona militaris, 25
Antioch, city, xxii, 61, 75, 89, 101, 104, 106–107, 110–12, 114, 116, 123, 161, 163, 166
  see also Issus, Niger
Antoniniana (a title given to a military unit for their loyalty or bravery by Caracalla or Elagabalus), 218–19
Antonine Wall, UK, 156, 216–17, 222–3, 227, 239, 292
Antoninus Magnus, the Great (in official documents Magnus was used to separate Caracalla from Antoninus Pius), *see* Caracalla
Antoninus Pius, emperor (138–61), (Caracalla named after him to join Caracalla with this emperor and Marcus Aurelius), 2, 15, 19, 99, 217, 231, 242, 270

Index   301

Antonine Family/Dynasty (Antoninus Pius, Marcus Aurelius, Commodus and through fake adoption the Severans), 19, 99, 128, 131, 211
Antonius Silo, Roman commander during 1st cent., 40
Antony, Mark (Marcus Antonius), 30, 145, 206, 289
Apamea on the Orontes, Coele Syria, Qalaat al-Mudik, Syria, 123
Apollonius of Tyana, 191
Apuleius Rufinus, consul, 59
Apulia, Apulians, 272, 274
Aquileia, city, Italy, 98
Aquilius, centurion and assassin, 81
Aquilius Felix, M. (possibly to be identified with the above assassin), (career path: *centurio frumentariorum, primus pilus legionis XI Claudiae, praepositus vexillationibus, procurator operum publicorum a. 193, procurator hereditatium patrimonii privati, procurator patrimonii bis, praefectus classis praetoriae Ravennatis*), Severus's henchman, 99
Aquincum, 77
Aquitania (major source of grain), 137
Arabia, Arabs, Saracens, vi, xi, 2, 46, 50, 77, 88–9, 107–108, 113, 121–5, 127–31, 134, 137, 163, 179, 182–5, 241, 287–8, 290, 296–9
Arabicus, title, 125, 129
see also Hatra, Parthia, Yemen
Arbeia (South Shields), 219–20
Arbelus, commander of Armenians, 274
Archers, archery, bow, crossbow, arrow, *arcuballista, manuballista, sagittarii, toxotai*, x, 5–6, 8, 10–12, 15–16, 19–20, 30–1, 37–40, 42, 46, 49, 52, 54, 56, 70, 89–90, 92–3, 105, 107, 112–13, 118, 121–2, 143, 146–7, 163, 167–8, 175, 179, 181, 198, 247, 249–50, 252, 260, 268–72, 274–7, 279–80, 284, 287, 295
  Mounted Archers, multipurpose horsemen, dual purpose horsemen, *hippotoxotai*, 5, 11, 15–16, 19–20, 30–1, 37, 46, 49, 89–90, 107, 112, 121, 143, 146–7, 163, 167–8, 181, 198, 247, 249, 252, 260, 268–72, 274–7, 279, 284
  see also Cavalry
Ardashir I, Artaxerxes I, ruler of Persia, 245
Argarienses, river boat, 285
Argentocoxus Caledonian, 224
Argentorate (Strasbourg), 77, 139
Armenia, Armenians, vi, xi, 89, 101, 104, 106, 109–10, 121, 152, 161, 163, 166, 168, 247, 249, 252, 270, 272, 274, 276, 278–80, 287, 290, 298
Arrabona, 218–19

Arrian, Arrianus, Arrianos Xenophon, historian, military commander and theorist, vii, xi, 10, 29, 31, 33, 36–7, 41–6, 49, 113, 200, 244–82, 284, 299
Arrius Menander, author of *De re militari* and military regulations, 92, 287
Artillery, 7–8, 10, 15, 27, 35, 51–6, 92, 97, 103, 116, 118, 175–7, 179, 272, 274, 277, 287
  see also Ballista, Onager, Siege
Ascania, Lake of, 104–106
  see also Cius, Nicaea
Asellius Aemilianus, Niger's *dux*, 91, 100–102, 104, 106, 287
  wife and children of Aemilianus (hostages of Severus), 91, 100–101
Assassins, assassination, murder, poison, killing, execution, v, 8, 20, 23–4, 29, 56, 62, 64–6, 68–70, 72, 74–5, 80–6, 89–91, 101, 110, 114, 116, 119, 134–5, 137, 142–3, 156, 159–60, 162, 174–7, 186, 190, 203–206, 209, 211–12, 227–9, 233, 235–7, 240–2, 286, 290
Augustus, Augusti, title (Augustus Octavianus included), 3, 23, 78–9, 85, 108, 132, 134–5, 137, 145, 148, 158, 162, 190, 193, 206, 210–11, 214, 220, 227–9, 231–2, 242, 292–3, 297–8
Augustus Octavianus, 1st emperor, 3, 23, 85–6, 145, 148, 158, 193, 206, 211, 214, 227, 292, 297–8
Augusta, title, 191
Aulici (*Corporis in Aula, Protectores, Scholae / Ostensionales*) (imperial bodyguards), 8, 12, 24, 85, 88, 136, 150–1, 204, 210, 221, 287
  see also Bodyguards
Aurelian, emperor (270–5), 286, 290
Aurelius Agaclytus, L., husband of Vibia Sabina, 211
Aurelius Gallus, L., (governor, Lower Moesia), 194
Aurelius Julianus, *evocatus*, 23
Auxilia, Auxiliaries, v, x–xi, 4–5, 8–12, 15, 19–20, 27, 36, 38, 43, 46, 51, 53, 77, 90, 93, 102, 104, 107, 125, 135, 138, 141, 145, 150–1, 157, 163, 167, 221, 223–4, 246–7, 249–50, 252, 257, 259, 271, 282, 286, 290, 297
  see also Allies, *Numeri*

Babylon, city in Babylonia, Parthia, Iraq, 166, 169
Baebius Marcellinus (conspirator), 212
Baetica, *see* Spain
Balbinus, *see* Caelius
Ballista, ballistae, carroballistae, arcuballista, manuballista, arrow-shooters, 8, 12, 15, 27, 31, 53–5, 93, 97, 118, 175–7, 287, 295

Ballistarii, balistarii, 12, 52, 93, 287
  see also Archers, Artillery, Fleets, Siege
Banditry, bandit, brigandage, robber, 24, 86, 89, 124–5, 200, 209, 212–15, 290
  see also Bulla, Claudius
Barsenius, King of Hatra, 89, 163
Bassianus, see Caracalla, Elagabalus, Julius
Bastarnae, Bastarni, mixed tribe, 194
Belgica, 137, 156
Beneficiarii, 25, 283, 298
Berbers, see Moors
Birdoswald (Banna), 219
Bodyguards, Bodyguard (word), 4, 8, 10, 12, 20, 22–4, 26, 36–9, 43, 45, 49, 82–3, 85, 88, 127, 136, 178–9, 184, 190, 194, 197, 204, 213, 221, 272, 277–8, 283–4
  see also *Aulici*, Cavalry (*subentries Equites Mauri, Equites Singulares, Equites Singulares Augusti*), *Evocati, Praetoriani, Stratores, Urbaniciani, Frumentarii, Peregrini, Vigiles*, Intelligence Gathering, *Statores*
Bonnae, 77, 139
Bononia / Boulogne / Gesoriacum, 220
Bosporus, straits of, xi, 116
Bosporan Kingdom/Bosporans, 272, 275
Brigantes, a tribe south of Hadrian's Wall, 156, 215, 217–18
Britain, Britannia, British, vii, xi, 29, 50, 52, 62, 64, 76, 78, 144–5, 149–50, 155–6, 168, 200, 213, 215–39, 246, 271, 283, 289, 293, 297
Bulla, Victor, bandit, 212–15, 220
Byzantium, city, Byzantion, Byzantine, Constantinople, Istanbul, Turkey, vi, xi, 70, 78, 89, 90–1, 98, 100–104, 108, 110, 112, 114, 116–20, 122, 128, 132, 135, 137–8, 244, 251–2, 257, 277, 288, 291, 294–5, 297

Cabillonum, 141
Caelius (Calvinus) Balbinus, D. (councillor of Caracalla and future emperor in 238), 88, 289
Caesar, see Julius Caesar
Caesar, Kaisar, title, 77–8, 108, 132, 134–6, 139, 162–3, 232, 235, 281, 291, 293, 296, 299
Caesarians, imperial freedmen, 213, 228
Caledonia, Caledonians, tribal confederacy in 'Scotland', 51, 145, 150, 156, 198, 215–16, 220–1, 224, 227–8, 233–9, 241, 246, 293
Candidus, see Claudius, Vespronius
Caparcotna (Kfar Otman, Galilee, Israel), 78, 125
Capitol Hill, 85, 159
CARACALLA / CARACALLUS, emperor, [original name: Lucius Septimius Bassianus or Julius Bassianus, renamed Marcus Aurelius Antoninus in 195/6; full name: IMPERATOR CAESAR MARCUS AVRELIVS (SEVERVS) ANTONINVS AVGVSTVS, but is better known with his nickname Caracallus / Caracalla], sole emperor (211–7), vii, ix–x, 14, 19–20, 22, 24, 27, 29, 51, 56–7, 62, 79–80, 82, 85, 88, 92, 112, 119, 125–9, 131–2, 134–6, 139, 141, 143, 145, 148, 157, 159, 161–2, 178–80, 182–3, 185–6, 189–92, 194–5, 197, 200–201, 203–206, 209–12, 214, 216, 218–20, 222–3, 225–9, 231–43, 246, 249, 252, 283–4, 286, 288–95, 299
  see also Syvänne, *Caracalla*
Carlisle (Luguvallum), 232, 292
Carpi, see Dacia
Carroballistae, see Ballistae
Carthage, city, Tunis, Tunisia, 197, 200, 246
Castor, imperial freedman, *cubicularius*, 221, 228–9, 232, 237
Castrum Rauracense, 141
Cavalry, horseman, x–xii, 5–12, 14–16, 19–22, 29, 31, 33–4, 37–49, 83–4, 87, 93–7, 104–105, 107, 112–16, 121–2, 124, 136, 140, 144, 146–57, 165, 168, 173, 179, 181, 198, 213, 221, 228, 245–9, 252–4, 257, 259–82, 290, 294–5, 297–8
  ala, alae, eilê, ilai, 6, 9, 11, 19–20, 149, 246, 271–2, 274–6
Cataphracts, *Cataphractarii (Equites Cataphracti) / katafraktoi*, 11, 19, 46, 95, 121, 146, 168, 247–9, 260, 271–2, 276, 284, 298–9
(cataphract armour used by marines and footmen, 54, 93)
Clibanarii, 12, 247, 298
Contarii, kontoforoi, kontos/contus-bearers, 16, 19, 37, 41, 46, 112, 146, 247–9, 260, 269–72, 275–6, 278, 280
doratoforoi, doruforoi, doryforoi, doru/dory, doration, 10–11, 247–8
doruforoi/doryforoi (bodyguards), 147
equites cohortis, 51
equites itemque pedites iuniores Mauri (a mixed unit of cavalry and infantry with the *iuniores* title proving the existence of *seniores*), 20
Equites Mauri (elite imperial cavalry bodyguards, and mixed infantry and cavalry *numeri*), 20, 45, 88, 107
  see also Bodyguards, Moors
equites singulares (elite cavalry auxiliary or legionary cavalry protecting commanders), 43, 80, 88, 150, 272, 277
  see also *pedites singulares*, Bodyguards
Equites Singulares Augusti (imperial bodyguards of barbarian origin), 4, 22, 24, 43, 46, 69, 150, 221, 285

see also Aulici, Bodyguards, Praetoriani
Turma, turmae, tourmae/tourmai, 6, 8–9, 11,
19–20, 44, 46, 87, 95, 246, 253, 261–7),
294–5
Vexillatio, vexillationes, vexillarii, 6, 9, 11
see also Archers (*subentry* mounted archers),
Aulici, Hatra, Oshroene, Parthia,
Praetoriani,
Channelkirk, 223
Chariot (wagon), war chariot, charioteer, driver, 29, 113, 183, 200, 204, 209, 227, 231, 245–6, 257
see also Supply
Chester (Deva), 78
Chesters (Cilurnum), 219
China, 2, 269, 295
see also Silk Route
Christians, Christianity, Jesus Christ, vii, 25, 63, 125–6, 163, 191, 200, 215–18, 232
see also Religion
Cilicia, Cilician Gates, 106, 108–10, 112, 114, 122, 128, 161
Cilo, see Fabius Cilo
Circus factions (White, Red, Blue, Green), 209
Circus Maximus, 74
Cius, Kios, city and battle of, vi, xi, 90, 100–101, 104–106, 108, 110, 282
City Prefect, see *Praefectus Urbi*
Civilian police, paramilitary forces, police in general including military police, militia, v, 4, 8, 20, 22–6, 51, 173, 200, 213, 283, 289, 297
see also Urbaniciani, Vigiles, Statores, Stationarii, Praetoriani, Bulla, Beneficiarii, Intelligence Gathering
Classis, Classes, see Fleets
Claudius I, emperor (41–54), 246
Claudius, rebel, robber, 124–7, 178, 184
see also Judah haNasi
Claudius Candidus, Tiberius, African senator, Severus's able *dux* (murdered by Severus), 95, 98, 103–106, 108, 123, 127, 137–9, 155, 177, 242, 287–8
Claudius Claudianus, Tiberius, commander of the Dacian army, 138
Claudius Gallus, legate of LG XXII Primigenia, *dux*, 139, 157
Claudius Piso, legate LG V, 218
Claudius Pompeianus, famous Roman general, 66, 82
Claudius Xenophon, procurator, 108, 156
Clodius Albinus (emperor in 193–7), v–vi, ix, 57, 64, 72, 75–8, 80, 84–5, 91, 98, 101, 108, 114, 125, 129, 131–50, 152–60, 168, 205, 215, 217, 241, 288–9

wife and children of Albinus, 91, 142–3, 148, 156
Clodius Balbinus (emperor in 238), 88, 289
Clodius Celsinus, kinsman of Clodius Albinus, 142
Clodius Pupienus Maximus, M. (emperor in 238), 289
Cohortes Urbanae, see Urbaniciani
Colchis, 272
Comes (companion, count, general), *comites*, 3, 95, 135, 220
see also Amici
Comitatenses, Comitatus, 9
Commodus, Marcus Aurelius Commodus Antoninus, emperor (180–93), xii, 20, 24, 57, 59, 61–8, 74, 81, 88, 91, 98, 131, 136, 142, 148, 158, 189, 206, 229, 286, 296–7
Consilium (Emperor's Council), see Council
Constantine I the Great, emperor (306–37), 9, 86, 103, 153, 286
Constantinople (Byzantium), city, see Byzantium
Constans, see Racius
Constantius I, emperor (293–306), 232
Corbridge (Coria), 219
Corn, see Grain
Cornelius Anullinus, P., Severus's *dux, Praefectus Urbi*, 108, 112–15, 128, 161, 287
Cornelius Repentius, son-in-law of Julianus, 72
Cornificia, daughter of M. Aurelius, 211
Corporis in Aula, see Aulici
Council (City), 4, 186
Council (Emperor's private *Consilium*), 2–3, 80, 92
Council (Military), 38, 124
Cramond, 220, 222–3
Crete, 51
Crispinus, see Tullius
Crispus, Constantine the Great's son, 103
see also Julius
Ctesiphon, Parthia city, Iraq, Vologaesus's capital, battles of, xi, 162–6, 169, 173–5, 181, 290–1
Curiales, see Decurions
Customs, see Taxes
Cyprus, 51
Cyrene, Cyrenaica, Cyrenaica, Cyrenaicans, Marmaridae, Garamantes, 198, 200, 246, 272, 274–5, 291
see also Libya, Moors
Cyzicus, city and battle of, vi, xi, 90, 100–105, 110

Dacia, Dacians, army and legions, 75, 77–8, 81, 138, 141, 145, 150–1, 161, 193–4, 244, 271, 274

Danube, river, frontier, vi, 38, 51, 68, 86, 137–8, 193–4, 218–20, 244, 284–5
Dea Dia, fertility goddess, 292
Decanus, decani (infantry leader of ten), 5, 8, 11, 26, 92, 96
Decurions, cavalry leader, 6, 8, 19, 22, 26 (in this case actually infantry *decanus*), 44–5, 95–7, 272, 277, 294
Decurions (class of *curiales* in cities), 1–2, 4
Deira (south of Hadrian's Wall), 217
Dexter, see Domitius
Didius Marinus, L., husband of Cornificia, 211
Diocletian, emperor (284–305), 95, 232, 296, 299
Diplomacy, see Strategy
Domestici, see Aulici
Domitian, Domitianus, emperor (81–96), 191
Domitius Dexter, C., City Prefect, 61, 99, 137
Dover (Dubris), city, 220
Dux, duces, duke (general), 27, 36, 43, 81, 95, 97–8, 101, 103–104, 128–9, 135, 139, 141–2, 145, 220, 229, 237, 287, 292
Dura Europos, Coele Syria city, Syria, 183–4

Eburacum, *see* York
Eclectus, *cubicularius*, conspirator against Commodus, married Marcia after the murder of Commodus (demonstrates that not all *cubicularii* were eunuchs), 64, 66, 70
Edessa, Osroene city, Urfa, Turkey, 123, 129, 167, 290
Egnatius Victor, 218
Egypt, Egyptians, vi, 3, 7, 25, 51, 78, 91, 108, 165, 182, 185–9, 200, 291
see also Alexandria, Arabs, Ethiopia, Libya, Moors, Yemen
Elagabalus, Heliogabalus, emperor, Antoninus Elagabalus, emperor (218–222), ix, 127, 201–202, 218
Elephant, Elephants, War Elephants, 29, 81, 196, 220, 245–7
Eleutherius, Pope, 216–17
Emesa, Homs, Syria, 62, 137
Epaminondas, Theban commander, 257
see also forthcoming Syvänne, *Agesilaos II of Sparta*
Ephesus, Ionia city, Turkey, 220
Epirus, 51
Equestrian Order / Equestrians / Upper Classes, 1–4, 7, 19–20, 51, 91, 136, 138, 156, 211–12, 242
see also Senate
Erucius Clarus, cos. 145/6, 58
Erucius Clarus, informer, 159

Ethiopia, Ethiopians 165, 182, 185–7, 200, 232, 246–7
Ethiopians of Sahara, 200, 232
Ethiopian soldier, Ethiopian *numerus*, 232
Ethnarch, 127, 194
Euodus, Caracalla's teacher, 205, 221, 237
Euphrates, river, 38, 75, 114, 116, 122–3, 166, 168, 183
Eupolemos, military theorists, 245
Evangelos, military theorist, 245
Evocati, evocati Augusti (veterans called back into service and bodyguards of the emperor), 23, 25

Fabius Cilo, L., City Prefect, 77, 81, 91, 102–103, 137, 141, 161, 206, 286–7
Falco, see Sosius
Faustina, wife of Marcus Aurelius, 131
Flavia Titiana (wife of the emperor Pertinax), 72
Flavius Juvenalis (PP 193–199/200), 82, 87, 187, 192, 288
Fleets (navy, naval, ships, galley, *liburna, dromon,* trireme, *trieres,* four, five, six, boat, raft, shipping, maritime, marines, mariners, pontoon bridge, port, harbour, *classis/classes*), iv–v, x–xi, 4, 24, 26, 50–7, 81, 89, 91, 98, 100–106, 110, 112, 116–20, 138, 145, 150, 161–2, 164–6, 168, 192, 196, 212, 217, 220–1, 223–4, 230–1, 235, 245, 284–7, 290, 293, 296, 299
Foederati (Federates), *see* Allies
Fortifications, fortresses, forts, fortified camps, walls (excluding human walls), wagon laager, 4, 12, 27, 31, 34–5, 38, 42–3, 51, 55–6, 74, 81, 89, 100, 107–10, 116, 118–19, 122, 143, 145, 149, 156, 163–4, 167–9, 179–81, 183, 185, 193, 197–8, 200, 215–18, 220, 222–3, 226–7, 232–3, 237, 239, 257, 271, 282, 292, 298
see also Antonine Wall, Byzantium, Hadrian's Wall, Hatra, Siege
Freedmen, 1–3, 51, 69, 203, 211, 213
see also Caesarians
Frumentarii, aggeliaforoi, 4, 23, 25–6, 221
see also Intelligence Gathering, *Peregrini, Speculatores*
FULVIA PIA, mother of Septimius Severus, 58, 61
FULVIA PLAUTILLA, wife of Caracalla and daughter of Plautianus, ix, 189–90, 194, 197, 201, 203, 205–206, 237
FULVIUS PIUS, grandfather of Septimius Severus on his mother's side, 58
FULVIUS PLAUTIANUS, C. (PP 197–Jan. 205), (related to Septimius Severus's mother, possibly a cousin of Septimius?), vi–vii, ix, 68, 77, 82, 91, 137, 140, 160, 162, 177–8, 182, 187,

Index 305

189–92, 194, 196–7, 201, 203–206, 208–209, 241–2, 290
Fulvius Plautius, brother of Plautilla, 206, 237

Gallienus, emperor (253–68), 6–9, 47, 56, 95
Garamantes, Berber tribe, *see* Cyrene
Gaugamela, Alexander the Great vs. Darius III, 110, 299
Gaul, Gauls, Gallia, Gallic, 16, 40–1, 46, 51, 59, 62, 132, 135–44, 149–50, 152, 156, 219–20, 260, 271, 274, 285
Genialis, *see* Titus
Georgia, *see* Iberia, Colchis
German, Germania, Germany Upper (Superior) and Lower (Inferior) and Barbaricum, Fleet of, legions of, Germans, Germanic peoples, x, 15, 22, 50, 59, 64, 75, 77, 79, 137–9, 141, 145–6, 150–1, 156–7, 194, 218, 220–1, 271
  see also Alamanni, Goths, Marcomanni, Quadi, Sciri, Vandals
Germanicus, Roman commander who campaigned in Germania in AD 13–16, 284
Germanicus/Germanicus Maximus, title, 218
Gesoriacum, *see* Bononia
Geta, *see* Septimius, Geta
Getae, *see* Dacians and Goths
Gordian I, emperor in 238, 88
Gordian II, emperor in 238, 88
Gordian III, emperor (238–44), 88, 299
Gold, gold content in coins and medallions, 68, 98, 136, 143, 158–9, 179, 185, 194, 226
Goths, Germanic tribal confederacy (also called Getae and Scythians), vi, 127–8, 138, 145, 150, 152–3, 178, 184, 194, 288
Grain, corn, wheat, barley, rye, 3, 25, 68, 86, 91, 108, 194, 219, 241
Greece, Greeks, Greek, 3, 8, 10, 29, 42, 44–55, 58, 61, 103, 122, 210, 244–6, 249–54, 263, 281–2, 284, 294
Greece, 89, 91, 263
  see also Achaia, Crete, Cyprus, Epirus, Macedonia
Guerrilla, insurgency, skirmishing, skirmishers, vi, 13–16, 19, 45–7, 70, 92, 124, 127, 142–4, 146, 166, 178, 225–6, 230–1, 247, 249, 259–60, 263, 265, 268, 270, 274, 276, 280
  see also Revolt, Stratagems

Hadrian, emperor (117–38), 2, 37, 42, 46, 149, 186, 244–5, 249, 260, 270–1, 274, 276, 294, 297, 299
Hadrian's Wall, UK, 156, 215, 217–18, 220, 222–3, 232

Hadrumentum, 142
Hannibal, great Carthaginian commander idolized by the Punic Septimius Severus, iii, 40, 124, 192–3, 241, 250, 290
Hatra, city, Mesopotamia, Iraq, Hatrans, vi, xi, 55, 89–90, 117, 121–4, 128–30, 161, 163–6, 171–2, 174–82, 241, 290–1, 296, 298
Heliogabalus, *see* Elagabalus
Helios, *see* Sun
Hellespont, Straits of, Battle of, vi, xi, xx, 90, 98, 100–103, 112, 120, 287
Hierapolis, 123, 168
Hispania, *see* Spain
Homosexuals, gays, boy-lover, bisexual, 177–8, 290
Honestiores, 2
Hostages, 67, 77, 91, 100–101, 163, 224, 237, 239
Housesteads (Vercovicium), 219
Humiliores, 2
Huns, 263
Hyginus (Pseudo-Hyginus), military theorist, 6–7, 9–10, 42–4, 51, 281, 294, 298

Iberia (Caucasus), Georgia, 244
Iberia (Spain), 265
Illyria, Illyrikian Drill, Illyrian Army, 47, 51, 75, 79–80, 83, 86, 88–9, 91, 95, 98, 100, 104, 108, 110–11, 122, 137–8, 141, 144, 150–1, 155, 288
  see also Pannonia
India, Indians, Indian Ocean, 2, 50, 185, 196, 246–7
Infantry, footmen, foot, vi, x, xiii, 5–20, 27–43, 45–9, 70, 83, 87, 92–7, 104, 107, 113–15, 122, 144, 146–7, 149–55, 163, 168, 198, 200, 221, 223, 227, 245–6, 249–50, 252–9, 268–9, 271–2, 274–82, 284, 290, 294–5
  see also Allies, Archers, Auxilia, Legions, *Pedites singulares*, Slingers
Intelligence gathering, information gathering, disinformation, informers, couriers, messengers, spying, spies, spy, reconnaissance, reconnoitres, (words), 4–5, 8, 20, 23, 26, 38, 54, 56, 59, 62, 66–7, 69, 74, 79, 81–2, 85, 90, 100, 104, 107, 110, 134, 137, 159, 162, 166, 175, 203–206, 212–13, 242, 272, 274
  see also Frumentarii, *Peregrini*, *Praetoriani*, *Aulici*, *Evocati Speculatores*, *Beneficiarii*, *Urbaniciani*, *Praefectus Urbi*
Ioannes (John) Lydus, 6, 9, 298
Iphicrates, Athenian commander and military theorists, 245
  see also forthcoming Syvänne, *Agesilaos II of Sparta*

Iran, *see* Persia
Irish, Ireland, Irish Sea, Scots, Scotti, 50, 150, 216–17, 246
Isis, Egyptian goddess, 187
Issus, place and site of battles, vi, xi, xxii, 107, 110–16, 128, 282
Iulianus, *see* Julianus
Iuniores unit, 20

Javelin, javelineers, javelinmen, javelin throwers, *pilum, pila, pilarii, doration, doratia, logche, lonche, logchoforoi* (both inf. and cav.), *lancea, lanceae, spiculum, spiculi, akontion, akontia, akontistai*, x, 7, 10, 12, 14–16, 19–20, 29, 32–3, 36–9, 41, 43, 46, 54, 70, 92–3, 101, 105, 107, 112–13, 122, 144, 146, 155, 168, 198, 247–9, 251–2, 259–60, 262–8, 272, 274–8, 280, 284
  see also Auxilia, Cavalry, Infantry, Legions
Jerusalem, Aelia Capitolina, 78, 125, 182–3, 297
Jews, Judaism, Jewish, vi, xi, 26–7, 35, 39–42, 90, 124–7, 163, 165, 178–9, 181–4, 194, 200, 241
  Iudaicus triumphus, Jewish triumph, 125–7, 163, 178–9, 182–3
  see also Samaritans
Josephus, Jewish leader and deserter, historian, 5–6, 9, 26–7, 29, 35–9, 41–4, 46, 284
Judah haNasi, Rabbi and Ethnarch of the Jews, 127, 178
JULIA DOMNA, Augusta, 2nd wife of Septimius Severus, mother or stepmother of Caracalla, ix–x, 59, 61–2, 123–4, 131, 137, 161, 182, 189, 191, 195, 197, 201, 203, 205–206, 224, 231, 237, 242, 285, 291, 296, 298
  mater castrorum in 195, 123, 131
Julia Maesa, sister of Julia Domna, 201
Julia Mamaea (daughter of Julia Maesa, wife of Gessius Marcianus and mother of Alexander Severus), 201–202
Julia Soaemias, also known Sohaemias (daughter of Julia Maesa, wife of Varius Marcellus and mother of Elagabalus), 201–202
Julian Alps, 80
Julian, emperor and usurper (361–3), 166, 168, 173, 249, 290
Julianus, Didius, emperor (193), v, ix, 57–8, 72, 74–6, 78, 80–2, 84, 86, 98, 241, 286
Julianus (Iulius Iulianus?), Severus's informer, 159–60
Julius Africanus, Sex., historian, architect, 259, 281–2
Julius Avitus Alexianus, C., legate, Julia Domna's brother-in-law, 137
Julius Bassianus, father of Julia Domna, 62

Julius Caesar, Roman dictator, 6, 30, 40, 46, 145, 148, 158, 210, 214, 246, 284, 299
Julius Crispus, tribune of the Praetorians, 174, 177, 190, 290
Julius Laetus, Severus's best *dux* (murdered by Severus), 82, 123, 127–8, 130, 142–4, 147–8, 153–4, 156–8, 160, 162, 165, 167–8, 170, 172, 175–7, 242, 286, 290
Julius Pacatianus Caius, governor of Oshroene, *procurator et praeses Alpium Cottiarum*, 91, 123, 129, 135, 138
Julius Septimius Castinus, C. (*legatus, dux* and later councillor of Caracalla), 220
Jupiter, god and temple of, 85, 158–9

Kair House, 293

Laetus, *see* Aemilius, Julius, Maesius
Lateranus, *see* Sextius
Latin, 3, 58, 61, 104, 162, 189, 194, 210, 254, 287, 290, 297
Law, laws, *lex, corpus iuris*, legislation, legal, 1–4, 20, 37, 56, 62, 88, 92, 116, 126, 139–40, 190, 211–12, 241–2
Legate, *legatus, legati*, x, 3, 7–8, 27, 36, 39, 43, 59, 61–2, 75–7, 80–1, 96, 104, 124, 137, 139, 157, 197, 217–18, 220, 237, 244, 277, 281, 287, 292
Legions, legionaries, v, x–xv, 4–20, 24–5, 27, 30, 36–9, 42–3, 46, 51, 54, 59, 61, 64, 68, 75–9, 86–9, 91–7, 99–102, 104, 107, 110, 112, 121, 124–5, 132, 137–9, 141, 145–6, 149–52, 155–7, 161, 194, 197, 209, 217–22, 227, 237, 242, 244, 246, 249–50, 259, 272, 275–80, 282, 284, 287–9, 292, 294–5, 297–9
  legio I Adiutrix, xiv–xv, 75, 77–8, 218
  legio I Italica, xiv–xv, 75, 77, 287
  legio I Minervia, xiv–xv, 77, 139, 220
  legio I Parthica, xv, 6–7, 86–7, 91–7, 138, 152, 221, 289
  legio II Adiutrix, xiv–xv, 75, 77
  legio II Augusta, xiv–xv, 78, 222, 292
  legio II Italica, xiv–xv, 75, 77, 137
  legio II Parthica, x, xv, 6–7, 86–8, 91–7, 138, 152, 161, 209, 221
  legio II Traiana (Egypt), xiv–xv, 78
  legio III Augusta, xiv–xv, 77–8, 194, 197
  legio III Cyrenaica, xiv–xv, 77, 89–90, 121, 125
  legio III Gallica, xiv–xv, 78, 197
  legio III Italica, xiv–xv, 75, 77
  legio III Parthica, xv, 6, 86–7, 91–7, 138, 152, 221, 289
  legio IV Flavia, xiv–xv, 77, 137
  legio IV Parthica, 86, 95, 152

Index 307

legio IV Scythica, xiv–xv, 59, 78, 124
legio V Macedonica, xiv–xv, 77, 138, 218
legio VI Ferrata, xiv–xv, 78, 89, 125
legio VI Victrix, xiv–xv, 78, 222
legio VII Gemina, xiv–xv, 77–8, 137, 156
legio VII Macedonica (Claudia), xiv–xv, 77, 138
legio VIII Augusta, xiv–xv, 77, 139, 151, 220
legio X Fretensis, xiv–xv, 78, 89, 125
legio X Gemina, xiv–xv, 75, 77, 288
legio XI Claudia, xiv–xv, 75, 77
legio XII Fulminata, xiv–xv, 78, 107, 272, 275, 277
legio XIII Gemina, xiv–xv, 77, 138
legio XIV Gemina (Flavia), xiv–xv, 75, 77–8
legio XV Apollinaris, xiv–xv, 78, 107, 272, 275, 277
legio XVI Flavia, xiv–xv, 61, 78, 137
legio XX Valeria Victrix, xiv–xv, 78, 222, 292
legio XXII Primigenia, xiv–xv, 77, 139, 157, 220
legio XXX Ulpia, xiv–xv, 77, 139, 220
naval legions, 51, 54
see also Antoniniani and under the name of the provinces or regions, e.g. Illyria, Moesia, Pannonia, Wales, etc.
Leonards, St, 223
Libya, 38, 79, 91, 177–8, 186, 192, 200
see also Africa, Cyrene, Moors, Punic
Limes, frontier, 4, 194, 218–19
Limitanei, frontier troops, 4, 9
Logistics, see Supply
Lollianus Gentianus, governor of Lugdunensis, 156
Lollianus Titianus, Julianus's supporter, 82
Lucius, king of the Britons, 216–18
Lucius Novius Rufus, governor of Further Spain, supporter of Severus and then of Albinus, 77–8, 137, 156
Lucius Octavius Iulianus (governor, Dacia), 194
Lucius Septimius, killer of Pompey the Great (possible ancestor of Septimius Severus), 186
Lucius Verus, see Verus
Lugdunensis, 59, 61–2, 137, 141, 156
Lugdunum, (mod. Lyon), city and site of battle, vi, x–xi, 62, 93, 137, 140–6, 149–54, 156–7, 160, 215, 282, 289, 296–8
Lupus, see Virius
Lyon, see Lugdunum

Macedonia, Macedonians, Macedonian pike phalanx, 51, 70, 86, 89, 213, 245–7, 249, 251–3, 275, 282, 299
see also Greece

Macrinus, M. Opellius, (Praet. Pref. and councillor of Caracalla, murderer of Caracalla, emperor (217–18), ix, 57, 112, 206, 212, 242
Maesa, see Julia Maesa
Maesius Laetus, Quintus (*Praet. Pref.* 205–214), 192, 204, 208
Maeatae, Maetae, tribal confederacy in 'Scotland', 156, 215–16, 227, 233–4, 237, 241, 293
Main, river, 218
Mamaea, see Julia Mamaea
Marcellus, see Varius
Marcia, Marcia Aurelia Ceionia Demetrias, mistress and murderer of Commodus who married Eclectus, 64–5, 67, 81
Marcius Rustius Rufinus, Cn., Praef. of the Praetorian Fleets, 51, 98, 191–2, 287
Marcomanni, Germanic tribe, Marcomannic wars, 6, 13, 15, 29, 242, 292, 297
see also the forthcoming Syvänne, *Emperor Marcus Aurelius*
Marcus Aurelius, Caesar Marcus Aurelius Antoninus Augustus, emperor (161–80), (Elagabalus and Caracalla both named after him to connect them with his family), 2, 18, 21–2, 34, 58–60, 68–9, 79, 81, 84, 87, 113, 128, 131, 136, 173, 186, 207, 211, 223–4, 231, 242
see also the forthcoming Syvänne, *Emperor Marcus Aurelius*
Marius, famous late Republican era Roman commander, 145, 148, 158, 193, 296
Marius Maximus Perpetuus Aurelianus, historian, commander of the Moesian army, and Urban Pref., 62, 64, 91, 98, 100, 102, 137–8, 156, 162, 287, 291
Marmara, Sea of, see Propontis
Mars, Roman god of war, 218
Martial artist, pugilist, 119
Mauretania, Mauritanians, Fleet of, 50–1, 197–8
see also Africa, Moors
Maurice, Flavius Tiberius Mauricius, emperor (582–602), author of the *Strategikon*, 249–50
see also *Strategikon*, Syvänne, *MHLR 565–602*, forthcoming Syvänne, *Late Roman Combat Tactics*
Maximinus Thrax (C. Julius Verus Maximinus), bodyguard of Septimius Severus (unit: *corporis in aula*, *aulici* probably to be identified with the *protectores* and *scholae*), emperor (235–8), 24, 45, 88, 136, 150, 284, 288–9
Maximus, see Marius Maximus, Clodius Pupienus

Media, Medians, Medes, 129, 157–8, 287, 289
  see also Parthia
Melitene, city, 78, 107–108, 122
Meros (pl. *mere*, military division, roughly the equivalent of legion 6,000–7,000 men), xi, 47, 89–90, 97, 107
Mesopotamia, 119, 128–9, 131–2, 134–7, 163, 165–6, 174, 183, 290
Militia, *see* Civilian Police
Misenum, city, Italia (HQ of the Fleet of Misenum), x, 24, 50–1, 81, 89, 192
  see also Fleets, Praetorian Fleets
Modestus, military theorist (late third cent.), vi, xi, 29, 91–7, 181, 281
  see also Vegetius
Moesia, Upper (Superior) and Lower (Inferior), Army of, Fleet of, 50, 52, 64, 75, 77–8, 91, 97, 100, 102–103, 137–9, 141, 150–1, 194, 221, 285
Mogontiacum, (Mainz), 77, 139
Moira (pl. *moirai*, military division / regiment, later maximum 2,000–3,000), 38, 280
Mons Graupius, battle of, 225
Moors (Mauri, Berbers), people and period views of the people, 19–20, 24, 46, 58, 88–9, 107, 182, 197–8, 200, 221, 241, 284
  see also Africa, Cyrene, Libya
Moray Firth, 228, 293
Mosquito, 164
  see also Vespa

Narses/Narsai/Narseh, king of Adiabene, 157–8
Naval, Navy, *see* Fleets
Nero, emperor, 98, 249, 252
Newstead, Newstead-type, 13, 220, 223
Nicaea, Nikaia, city and battle of, vi, xi, 89–90, 100–101, 104–106, 108, 110, 116, 190–1, 282
  see also Cius
Nicomedia, city, Nicomedians, 101, 104, 244
Niger, *see* Pescennius
Nigrinus, XI Urban Cohort, 23
Nisibis, city, Mesopotamia, Nisibin, Syria, battle of, 122–30, 157–8, 161, 163–71, 174
Noricum, Norici, Noricans, province and inhabitants, 75, 77, 86, 137–41, 150–1, 212–13
North Africa, *see* Africa
Notarii/notarius (secretary/notary), 8
Numeri (*arithmos, arithmoi, katalogoi*), national *numeri, numerus*, v, 4, 19–21, 46, 221, 232, 283, 298
  see also Auxilia
Numerianus, grammarian and self-appointed *dux* of Severus, 140–1, 289
Numerus of *Statores Augusti*, 21

Onager, onagri, catapult, *katapeltai, lithoboloi*, stone thrower, 8, 12, 15, 35, 53–6, 97, 105, 107, 112–13, 116, 118, 164, 175–6, 257, 272, 277
  see also Artillery, Ballista, Priscus
Orient, Oriens, 51
Osroene, Oshroene, Osroenian cavalry, vi, xi, 75, 90–1, 107–108, 113, 121–5, 127–9, 134–5, 158, 163, 167, 241, 287–8, 290
Ostensionales, see Aulici
Ouse, river, 223

Pacatianus, *see* Caius
PACCIA MARCIANA (MARCIA), (Septimius Severus's first wife, the alleged mother of Caracalla in some sources), 59, 62, 189, 195
Palace, Palatine Hill (Palatium), 2–3, 10, 67, 69–70, 74, 82, 85, 145, 159, 203–206, 227
Palmyra, city, Palmyrenes, 175, 183–4
Pannonia (general area) with provinces Pannonia Superior and Inferior, Fleet and Army of, 50, 59, 64, 75, 77, 79, 92, 98, 104, 108, 139, 141–2, 151, 157, 161, 194, 218–19, 221, 271, 288, 297
  see also Illyria
Papinianus, Papinian, Aemilius, jurist (PP in 205–211), 192, 203–204, 208, 213, 221, 229
Paramilitary forces, *see* Civilian Police
Parthia, Parthians, Persia, Persians, Iran, Parthian Military, vi, xi, xvi, 20, 24, 30, 46, 88–91, 108, 112, 121, 125–6, 129, 131, 137, 157–8, 161–75, 177–9, 181–5, 197, 241, 244, 247, 249, 252, 259, 270–1, 288–90, 296–9
Parthicus, Parthicus Maximus, title, Parthian triumph, 125–6, 129, 162, 174, 183
Pathhead, 223
Patruinus, Valerius, (PP ?–212), 192
Pausanias, military theorist, 245
pedites singulares (elite infantry auxiliaries or legionaries protecting commanders), 10, 43, 80
  see also Cavalry (*subentry equites singulares*)
Peregrini, Princeps Peregrinorum, 4, 23, 26, 221
  see also Intelligence gathering, *Frumentarii, Speculatores*
Peri Strategias/Strategikes, 29, 42, 281, 294
  see also Syrianus Magister
Perinthus, city, of, 91, 101–103, 108, 119, 135
Persia, Persis, Fars, xi, 44, 90, 110, 157–8, 168, 173–4, 185, 246, 253, 259, 263, 287, 289, 297, 299
  see also Vologaesus, Arabs, Armenia, Oshroene, Media, Legions (I, II, III Parthica)
Pertinax, P. Helvius, emperor (193), v, ix–x, 29, 43, 57, 61–2, 64, 66–72, 74–5, 78–9, 82, 86, 98, 159, 285–7, 297
  wife and children of Pertinax, 67, 69, 72

Pescennius Niger, rival emperor of Septimius Severus (193–4), v–vi, ix, 4, 57, 61, 72, 74–6, 78–80, 82, 85, 89–91, 97–116, 118, 120–2, 124–6, 128, 134–5, 138, 160, 162–3, 168, 182, 185–7, 197, 241
   wife and children of Niger (hostages of Severus), 91, 101, 135
Philip the Arab, emperor (244–9), 88, 299
Picts, 216–18, 233
Plautianus, *see* Fulvius Plautianus
Plautilla, Publia Fulvia, *see* Fulvia Plautilla
Plautius Quintillus, Marcus Peducaeus (son-in-law of Marcus Aurelius, ally of Severus, murdered by Severus), 81, 211
Poetovio, 141
Pollenius Auspex, A., (uncle of Pollenius Sabennus), 212
Pollenius Sabennus, governor of Noricum, 212
Polybius, historian and military theorist, 245
Pompey the Great, Pompeius Magnus, famous Roman commander, 6, 145, 148, 158, 185–6, 250, 284, 289, 299
   sons of Pompey, 145
Pontus, 51, 116, 119
Popilius Pedo Apronianus (conspirator), 212
Poseidonius, philosopher and military theorist, 245
Praefectus, Prefect, 6–8, 19, 35–6, 39, 79, 187, 237, 272, 274, 281, 286
Praefectus castrorum, 7, 96
Praefectus classis and *Praefectus classium praetoriarum Misenatis et Ravennatis* (Prefect of the Praetorian Fleets Misenum and Ravenna), 51–2, 89, 98, 103, 192
Praefectus fabrorum, 7, 96
Praefectus legionis, 3, 7–8, 79, 91, 96
Praefectus Praetorio (Praetorian Prefect, Prefect of the Guard and acting Prefect), xiii, 1–2, 20, 22, 59, 61, 63, 69, 74, 81–2, 87–8, 140, 150, 177–8, 187, 190–2, 201, 203–205, 208, 213, 221, 229, 237, 281
Praefectus Urbi/ Praefectus Urbis Romae (Urban Prefect of Rome, Prefect of the City), 3, 24, 62, 68, 72, 99, 137, 161, 206
Praefectus vehiculorum, 68, 292
Praefectus vigilum, 24, 137, 161
Praepositus / Praepositi (acting commanders for various purposes), 7, 20, 96, 292
Praetorian Fleets, *see* Fleets, Misenum, *Praetoriani*, *Praefectus Classis*, Ravenna
Praetoriani (Praetorians, Praetorian Guard, Praetorian fleets), x, xiii, 1, 4, 7, 9–11, 20–4, 43, 50–1, 53, 63, 66–7, 69, 72, 74–5, 79–82, 84–9, 91, 97–8, 103–104, 117, 120, 138, 140, 143–4, 147, 150, 155, 160–1, 174, 176–7, 187, 190–2, 194, 197, 208, 210, 213–14, 221, 236, 285–7
   see also Aulici, Bodyguards
Prefect, *see Praefectus*
Princeps Peregrinorum, *see* Peregrini
Priscus, siege engineer, 116, 118, 120, 179
Prisoners, prison, captives, slaves, slavery, 1–3, 69, 82–3, 122, 142, 144, 156, 158, 165–6, 174, 180, 200, 212–13, 218, 297
Probus, husband of Septimius Severus's daughter, prefect of the city in 193 and consul (nothing further is known of him, but on the basis of the marriage a man of some importance; probably to be identified with *dux / praepositus* participating the war in the east in 195 in Dio 76.3.2; and possibly to be identified with the *consul ordinarius* in 220 in *Modesto II Fasti*), 86, 128, 130
Probus, emperor (275–82), 286, 290
Proculus, Torpacion, Christian doctor of Severus, (Caracalla had him executed at York in 211 possibly because as Christian he had refused to kill Severus or refused to commit an act of euthanasia, see pp. 233, 235), 200
Propontis, Sea of Marmara, xi, 98, 100, 103, 116
Propontus, 51
Protector / Protectores / Protectores Domestici, *see Aulici*
Provisions, *see* Supply
Pseudo-Hyginus, *see Hyginus*
Punic, 61, 96, 162, 185, 192, 246, 294, 296
Pupienus, *see* Clodius
Pyrrhus, King of Epirus, military theorist, 245

Quadi, Germanic tribe, 113
Quaestor, 58, 60–1

Racius Constans (governor of Sardinia), 201
Raetia, province, legion, 75, 77, 137–8, 141, 150–1, 215, 218–9, 272
Raphaea, Raphaneae, Rafniye, Syria, 78
Ravenna, city, Italy (HQ of the Fleet of Ravenna), 24, 50–2, 81, 89, 92, 286
   see also Fleets, Praetorian Fleets
Reconnaissance, *see* Intelligence Gathering
Religion, god, gods, 26, 126–7, 139, 179, 182, 187, 190, 200, 217–8, 232–3, 286, 292
   see also Apollo, Christianity, Dea Dia, Isis, Jews, Jupiter, Mars, Samaritans, Sarapis, Sun-god, Virtus
Revolt, rebels, rebellion, mutineers, mutiny, insurrection, 38, 59, 77, 80, 85, 89–90, 99,

101, 107–108, 113, 122, 124–5, 127, 137, 158, 163, 168, 174, 176, 178–82, 197, 215–18, 220, 233–6, 287–9, 293
see also Guerrilla, Usurpation
Rhine, river, 38, 220
Rhizionian, 272, 274
Risingham, 118
Rome, city, Italy, v–vii, 3–4, 20, 24, 51, 58–9, 62–3, 66, 68, 75–85, 87–8, 90–1, 98–9, 108, 132, 134, 136–7, 139–42, 145, 148–9, 151, 157–61, 165, 168, 189–91, 194, 197, 201, 205, 209–10, 212, 217–18, 220, 226, 233, 237–8, 241, 286
see also Capitol, Jupiter, Palace
Rufinus, *see* Marcius

Sagittarii, *see* archers
Salary, salaries, wages, donative, 1–2, 13–14, 51, 66, 68, 85, 98–9, 135–6, 139, 159, 163, 166, 186, 213
 booty, spoils of war, 121–2, 174, 225, 234, 237
 see also Bribery, Prisoners, Taxes, Trade
Samaria, Samaritans, vi, xi, 25, 90, 124–7, 178–9, 182, 241
 see also Jews
Samosata, city, Samsat, Turkey, 78
Samuel, son of Rabbi Isaac, Rabbi, 127
Saracens, *see* Arabs
Sardinia, 51, 58, 201
Sarmatia, Sarmatians, Sarmatian, 15–16, 19, 37, 46, 194, 247, 249, 257, 259–60, 270–1, 274, 276
 see also Alans, Goths, Dacia
Satala, city, 78, 107–108, 290
Saturninus, tribune of the Praetorian Guard, 203
Saturninus, centurion of the Praetorian Guard, 205
 see also Aemilius
Scholae, *see* Aulici
Sciri, Germanic tribe, 194
Scots, Scotti, *see* Irish
Scythia, Scythians, 128, 217–18, 252, 257, 260, 280
 see also Goths
Secondinus, commander of Apulians, 272–3
Sejanus, PP under Tiberius I, 180, 189, 206
Seleuceia/Seleucia Pieria, city, Coele Syria, Maharacik, Turkey, 161
Seleucia, Mesopotamia, close to Ctesiphon, 166, 179
Senate, senators, upper class, nobles, 1–4, 7, 24, 26, 56–8, 61, 66–9, 72, 74, 77–8, 80–3, 85–6, 89, 91, 99, 101, 108, 114, 124–5, 134, 136,

139–40, 142–3, 148, 156–61, 163, 165, 168, 178–9, 183–5, 190–1, 206, 209, 211–12, 217, 237, 239, 244
see also Equestrian Class
Seniores unit, 20
SEPTIMIA OCTAVILLA, Septimius Severus's sister, 61, 162
SEPTIMIUS APER, P. (*cos.* in 153), uncle of Septimius Severus, 58
SEPTIMIUS GETA, father of Septimius Severus, 58, 62
SEPTIMIUS GETA, P., brother of Septimius Severus, 58, 62, 64, 75, 100, 136, 138, 161, 197, 203, 205, 242
SEPTIMIUS GETA, P., emperor (211), son of Septimius Severus, brother of Caracalla, vii, ix–x, 57, 62, 135–6, 161–2, 197, 200, 205, 209, 211, 216–18, 220, 224, 226, 228–9, 231–2, 236–7, 239, 242, 293
SEPTIMIUS MACER, grandfather of Septimius Severus according to the *HA*, but Birley (220) thinks that the name was L. Septimius Severus while Macer was an ancestor, 58
SEPTIMIUS SEVERUS, C., uncle of Septimius Severus, 58, 60
SEPTIMIUS SEVERUS, L. (Lucius Septimius Severus), emperor and father of Caracalla and Geta, v–vii, ix–xi, 6–7, 20, 24, 45, 51, 56, 282, 284–93, 296–9
 Youth and early career in 145/6–193, 58–64
 Under Pertinax in 193, 68
 War against Didius Julianus in 193, 72–88
 War against Pescennius Niger in 193–4, 75–121
 Wars against the Oshroeni, Adiabeni, and Hatrans in 194–5, 121–4, 127–31
 Wars against the Jews and Samaritans in 194–5 or 194–8/9, 124–7
 War against Albinus in 195–7, 132–60
 War against Parthia, Adiebene, Armenia and Hatra in 197–8/9, 161–83
 War against the Jews and Samaritans in 198/9, 124–7, 163, 178–9, 181, 183
 Egypt and the Red Sea in 199–200, 185–8
 Return to Rome in 200–202, 189–96
 African campaign in 202–203, 197–200
 In Italy and Plautianus affair in 203–205, 201–208
 Life in Italy in 205–207, 209–14
 In Britain in 208–211, 215–39
 Daily work routine, 210–11
 Death and reputation, 235–43

Index 311

First wife Paccia Marciana, see Paccia
Daughters with Paccia, 86
  see also Aetius, Probus
Second wife Julia Domna, see Julia Domna
Relationship with Plautianus, see Plautianus
Relationship with sons Caracalla and Geta, see Caracalla, Geta
Relationship with the Goths, see Goths
Legislation and laws, 62, 92, 126, 139–40, 211–12, 241–2
  see also Law
Religion, see Christianity, Religion
Serapis, Sarapis, Egyptian god, Serapeum, 186
Severus, Alexander, emperor, alleged son of Caracalla, 4, 56–7, 88, 95, 127, 202, 258–9, 297
Sextius Lateranus, T., Severus's *dux* (*amicus Septimii Severi*), 123, 127, 130
Ships, see Fleets
Sicca Veneria, 220
Sicily, Sicilians, 44, 51, 59, 62, 206, 253
Siege Warfare, v–vi, xi, 7, 12, 15, 34, 39, 50, 55–6, 90, 96–7, 100, 102, 106–108, 110, 112, 116–20, 122, 124, 127, 132, 135, 137, 139, 151, 157–8, 161–8, 170–1, 173–82, 216–17, 241, 257, 288, 290–1, 296
  see also Artillery, *Ballistae*, Byzantium, Ctesiphon, Hatra, Nisibis, *Onager*, Fleets
Silius Messala, M., (*cos.* 193), 82
Silk Route, 185
Silver / Silver Content in Coins, 68, 98, 143
Singara, 123–4
Singidunum (Belgrade), 77, 137
Slinger, slingers, 10, 12, 15–16, 19, 31, 54, 70, 93, 118, 122, 142–3, 168, 249, 252, 260, 268
Soaemias, see Julia Soaemias
Society (Roman), v, 1–2, 159
Sol, see Sun
Sosius Falco, Pompeius Sosius Falco, Quintus, (*cos.* 193), 67, 69
South Shields, see Arbeia
Spain, Baetica, Hispania, 51, 58–9, 77–8, 86, 137, 143, 156–7, 168, 244
Sparta, Spartans, Spartan phalanx, 257
Speculatores (detached scouts in units and detached service), *Burgus Speculatorius* (Guard Towers), *Speculatores Augusti* (imperial scouts, spies, bodyguards, assassins) in this book the usual meaning is *Speculatores Augusti*, 4, 8, 21, 25, 221, 283
Spying, see Intelligence Gathering
Stationes, station, stationarii, 8, 25
Statores military police, *stator*, *statores Augusti*, Emperor's military police, 8, 21

Stratores (*Stablesiani*), 22
Stratagems, ruses, ambush, surprise, surprise attacks/ assault, night attacks, trickery, fooling, hidden trenches, caltrop, 4, 27, 30, 35, 38, 46, 49, 54, 66–7, 79, 82–3, 85, 89–90, 113, 118, 123–4, 135, 140, 145–7, 149, 154–5, 157, 168, 175, 178, 186, 201–206, 213, 226, 230, 241, 243, 252, 281–2, 286, 290, 297
  see also Assassin, Hostages
Strategikon (military treatise), 5, 29, 31, 33, 40, 42–3, 45–6, 246, 249, 251, 254, 276, 279–82, 294
  see also Maurice, Syvänne *MHLR 565–602* and forthcoming Syvänne, *Late Roman Combat Tactics*
Strategy, diplomacy, envoy, ambassador, embassy, messenger (goals and strategies very broadly conceived), v–vi, xi, 2, 4–5, 20, 25–6, 50, 75–7, 79, 81–2, 88, 100–101, 122, 124, 128–9, 134, 136–7, 140–1, 157, 161, 174, 179, 183, 185, 192, 200, 204, 213, 215, 219, 226, 234, 271–2, 286, 291, 293
  see also Stratagem, Trade
Sulgenius, Fulgenius, Briton leader, 217–18
Sulpicianus, see Titus
Sulla, Cornelius Sulla, L. dictator, 145, 148, 158, 192–3, 289
Sun (Sol, Helios), 179, 182, 190
  see also Elagabalus
Supply, logistics, supply depots/hubs/bases, food, drink, fodder, meat, wine, water, garum, oil, supplying, supplies, provisions, baggage train, wagons, 5, 9, 13, 23, 25, 27, 31, 36, 42–3, 45, 51–2, 56, 68, 77, 80–1, 85–6, 91, 96, 98–9, 101–102, 104, 107–109, 113, 118–20, 123, 136, 138, 157, 161–2, 166, 174, 179, 183, 190–1, 194, 197, 211, 219–20, 223–4, 227, 231, 235–6, 241, 257, 272, 287, 299
  see also Grain, *Frumentarii*, *Praefectus Urbi*, *Annona*, Salary
Sura, city, 123
Symmachiarii, see Allies
Syria, area and fleet and army of, 50, 59, 62, 75, 78, 89, 102, 107, 112, 121, 124–5, 129, 131, 151, 161–3, 168, 178, 180, 182–3, 197, 203, 270, 285, 287, 293
Syrianus Magister, Syrianos Magistros, 245, 259, 281–2
  see also *Peri strategikes*

Tacitus, historian, 40, 46
Tactics, tactic (word), vii, 13–15, 27–9, 41, 45–6, 49, 54, 70–1, 92, 95, 118, 122, 146, 152, 192, 230–1, 234, 240–1, 244–82, 288, 293, 297–8

see also Legions, *Auxilia*, Cavalry, Archers, Macedonia, Bodyguards
Tarracina, 82
Tarraconensis, 137, 156
Taurus Mountains, Range, 89, 101, 104, 107–109, 287
  see also Cilician Gates
Taxes, tax, taxpayers, 1–2, 4, 24–5, 51, 91, 98, 102, 127, 220, 287
  see also Annona, Salary, Trade
Theodosian Code, 285
Thrace, Thracians, 89, 91, 100, 108, 139, 252, 271
Tiberius I, emperor (14–37), 160, 189, 192, 206, 283
Tigris, river, 96, 251–3, 256–7, 261, 266, 293
Tinurtium (Tournus), battle of, vi, 141–3, 160, 289
Titiana, *see* Flavia
Titianus, *see* Lollianus
Titus Cornasidius Sabinus, commander *Alpes Graiae et Poeninae*, 138
Titus Flavius Genialis (PP in 193), 82
Titus Flavius Sulpicianus, father-in-law of Pertinax, 68–9, 72, 74, 159
Titus, emperor (79–81), 39–43
Torpacion/Proculus, Christian physician, 200
Trade, traders, merchants, merchandise, tolls, customs, tariffs, 2, 5, 25–6, 50–1, 62, 68, 91, 98, 118, 183, 185
  see also Taxes
Trajan, emperor (91–117), xi, 22, 27, 34, 40, 43, 46–8, 87, 98, 163–4, 169, 174, 223–4, 244, 249, 271
Trapezus, city, 272, 274
Triarius Maternus, senator, 67
Trier, Treves, 139, 151, 157
Tripolitania, Tripolis, 58, 61, 123, 183, 198, 216
  see also Africa, Cyrene, Libya
Tullius Crispinus, PP in 193, 81–2, 286
Tyana, city, Kemerhisar, Bahçeli, Turkey, 191, 205

Urbaniciani (*Cohortes Urbanae*, Urban Cohorts, sing. *Urbaniacus*), 3–4, 23–4, 62, 82, 86, 88, 150–1, 156, 161, 206, 221
Urban Prefect, *see Praefectus Urbi*
Usurpation, usurper, 5, 8, 26, 64, 75, 79–80, 98, 136, 148–9, 156, 159, 162, 212
  see also Revolt

Valarsh, king of Armenia, 290
  see Syvänne, *Caracalla*
Valens, Roman commander, 272, 277

Valerius, soldier, informer, 175
Valerius Catullinus, Julianus's candidate to replace Severus, 81
Valerius Patruinus (PP ?–212), 192
Valerius Pudens, C., governor of Lower Pannonia, 75, 156, 215
Valerius Valerianus, L., *dux* of Septimius Severus, cavalry commander, 112–15, 129, 287
Vandals, Germanic confederacy, 194
Vasaces, commander of Armenians, 274
Vegetius, military theorist (turn of the fifth cent.), vi, 6, 8–11, 27, 29, 42, 51, 54, 70, 91–7, 155, 181, 246, 269, 281–3, 287, 294
  see also Modestus
Verus, Lucius, co-emperor of Marcus Aurelius (161–9), 69, 211, 216, 231, 242, 270
Verus, Prefect, commander of Numidians, 272
Vesontio, 141
Vespa Orientalis/Oriental hornet, 164
  see also Mosquito
Vespasian, Vespasianus, commander against Jews, emperor (69–79), 38–40, 68
Vespronius Candidus, senator and commander detested by soldiers, 81
Vestal Virgins, 81
Veturius Macrinus, PP (193), 81
Vexillationes (Vexillations), *Vexillarii* (legionary cavalry or any detachment):
  For cavalry *vexillationes*, *see* Cavalry
  Vexillatio as a detachment in general, 298
  vexillarii carrying a *vexillum*, i.e. the *vexillarii* as standard-bearers, 94
Vibia Aurelia Sabina, daughter of Marcus Aurelius, 211
Vibia Perpetua, Christian martyr, 200
Vicar, *vicarius*, 11, 94–5
Vigiles, 4, 23–4, 69, 86, 88, 137, 161
Vindobona, 77
Vindonissa, 141
Virius Lupus, governor of Germania Inferior, 139, 145–6, 156, 215, 217
Virtus, male virtue, 218
Vologaesus / Vologeses III or IV / Valegesos Peroz, King of Parthia (c.145/8–192), 90, 157–8, 162, 164–9, 171, 173–4, 287, 290

Wagon, *see* Chariot, Supply

Yemen, 163
York/Eburacum, city, vii, 78, 216–18, 220–4, 232, 236, 293

Zeugma, city, 78, 123–4